Marxism and Social Movements

Historical Materialism Book Series

The Historical Materialism Book Series is a major publishing initiative of the radical left. The capitalist crisis of the twenty-first century has been met by a resurgence of interest in critical Marxist theory. At the same time, the publishing institutions committed to Marxism have contracted markedly since the high point of the 1970s. The Historical Materialism Book Series is dedicated to addressing this situation by making available important works of Marxist theory. The aim of the series is to publish important theoretical contributions as the basis for vigorous intellectual debate and exchange on the left.

The peer-reviewed series publishes original monographs, translated texts, and reprints of classics across the bounds of academic disciplinary agendas and across the divisions of the left. The series is particularly concerned to encourage the internationalization of Marxist debate and aims to translate significant studies from beyond the English-speaking world.

For a full list of titles in the Historical Materialism Book Series available in paperback from Haymarket Books, visit:
www.haymarketbooks.org/category/hm-series

Marxism and Social Movements

Edited by
Colin Barker, Laurence Cox,
John Krinsky, and Alf Gunvald Nilsen

Haymarket Books
Chicago, IL

First published in 2013 by Brill Academic Publishers, The Netherlands
© 2013 Koninklijke Brill NV, Leiden, The Netherlands

Published in paperback in 2014 by
Haymarket Books
P.O. Box 180165
Chicago, IL 60618
773-583-7884
www.haymarketbooks.org

ISBN: 978-1-60846-372-5

Trade distribution:
In the US, Consortium Book Sales, www.cbsd.com
In Canada, Publishers Group Canada, www.pgcbooks.ca
In the UK, Turnaround Publisher Services, www.turnaround-psl.com
In Australia, Palgrave Macmillan, www.palgravemacmillan.com.au
In all other countries, Publishers Group Worldwide, www.pgw.com

Cover design by Ragina Johnson.

This book was published with the generous support of
Lannan Foundation and the Wallace Global Fund.

Printed in the United States.

10 9 8 7 6 5 4 3 2 1

Library of Congress Cataloging-in-Publication data is available.

Contents

The Politics of Social Movements

Part Three: Seeing the Bigger Picture

Comparative-Historical Perspective

Social Movements Against Neoliberalism

Marxism and Social Movements: An Introduction

Colin Barker, Laurence Cox, John Krinsky and
Alf Gunvald Nilsen

A case for a Marxist revival?

This book starts from a paradox.

On the one hand, Marxism is a body of theory that
developed from and was crafted for social movements.
The work of Marx and Engels represents a distillation
of the experiences, debates, theories and conflicts
faced by the popular movements of the nineteenth
century, that sought in turn to contribute to those
movements' further development. Subsequent developments of Marxist theory in the twentieth century
were intimately linked to the development of oppositional political projects across the globe, ranging from
revolutionary struggles against imperialist wars and
capitalism itself, to anti-colonial movements and the
emergence of new forms of popular assertion in the
post-WWII era.

On the other hand, if the main figures of 'classical
Marxism' all *used* the term 'movement', none seems to
have developed any explicit theorisation of the term.
Moreover, while Marxists have produced groundbreaking studies of specific movements, they have
apparently not produced an explicit 'theory of movements' – that is, a theory which specifically explains
the emergence, character and development of social
movements. Nor have they explored how the concept
of 'movement' might be interwoven with other foundational concepts in Marxist theory like class struggle,
hegemony and revolution or human species being,
alienation and praxis.

There is, in short, a distinct lack of work – scholarly or activist – devoted to thinking through what an integrated Marxist theory of social movements might look like, and what its impact on Marxist theory itself might be. This situation is compounded by the fact that mainstream social movement theory – whether it emerges from American or European academia – consistently avoids debate with Marxist perspectives, although they constitute by some margin the largest alternative body of research on popular movements. Instead, what can only be described as caricatures or straw-man versions of Marxist theory are as widespread in scholarship as in some forms of anti-Marxist activism.

This is, we believe, detrimental for those scholars who are interested in pursuing what Bevington and Dixon have called 'movement-relevant research'[1] – research that is attuned to and addresses the knowledge interests of activists, as opposed to merely scholastic dissections of the character and dynamics of collective action – and especially for activists concerned with the progressive development of their oppositional political projects. The present time is increasingly starting to look like one of those decisive moments in history when 'a chain reaction of insurrections and revolts' give rise to 'new forms of power ... in opposition to the established order, and new visions of the meaning of freedom [are] formulated in the actions of millions of people'.[2]

For the current conjuncture is saturated with protest, with massive demonstrations and sometimes armed conflict erupting across North Africa and the Middle East, Europe and Latin America, with significant echoes elsewhere. It seems appropriate, therefore, to ask whether there are significant connections between these eruptions of popular protest. Large numbers of those actively participating, from Cairo to Athens, from New York to Santiago, think there are. And the connections they draw concern a combination of austerity, rising inequality, dispossession of rights and entitlements and a democratic deficit which enables the imposition of all these by tiny élites, against a background of the world economy's biggest crisis since the 1930s.

There is, in short, 'a system' against which so many of today's protests are pitched, even if they are not articulated solely, or even at all, in the language of 'class'. Yet, there seems to be little recognition of this in contemporary literature on social movements. Indeed, as Gabriel Hetland and Jeff Goodwin document in their contribution to this volume, the very term 'capitalism' has largely disappeared from contemporary social movement theory. Does this mean that social movement scholars must always treat these struggles as discrete and disconnected instances of protest? Or should we, perhaps, try to understand these protests as a 'wave' or an upswing in a 'cycle of contention', and to trace the

---

1. Bevington and Dixon 1995.
2. Katsiaficas 1987, p. 6.

mechanisms of their regional and even global 'contagion'? If we did, it would seem odd, at the very least, not to inquire if the world capitalist system is not somehow responsible for generating them.[3]

Marxism, as an integrating perspective on social relations, does at least have the merit of being able to pose such questions. It also invites us to think about a number of matters of some significance. How are crises linked together? What potentials are there for movements from below to learn and gain strength from each other? How are 'movements from above', as Alf Gunvald Nilsen and Laurence Cox suggest in their chapter, attempting to restore or extend the social power of ruling élites in the face of these crises? If movements from below were to succeed in some sense, what kinds of demands ought they to raise, who should they be seeking to mobilise, and how, and what kinds of organisations should they be trying to develop? Were they to succeed, what would success look like?

Such questions arise fairly naturally from a Marxist perspective, and potentially connect more closely with the concerns of movement participants than does much of contemporary academic social movement theory. However, there still remains the task of developing a specifically *Marxist theory* of social movements. We do not claim to address this task in its entirety in this volume, but we do seek to identify and fill out some of the gaps, and to start the intellectual and political working-through which is clearly called for.

Marxism and mainstream movement theory: never the twain shall meet?

If social movement theorists no longer seem to engage seriously with Marxism, this was not always the case. We can, cautiously, identify two patterns emerging in the 1970s and early 1980s. The story is a fairly familiar one.

In the USA, one outcome of the struggles of the 1960s was that academic theorists sought to construct an alternative to 'collective behaviour' accounts of popular protest. Liberals and leftists, who had participated in or at least sympathised with the Civil Rights movement, the student movement or the opposition to the American war in Vietnam, rejected the predominant 'collective behaviour' case that movements were, bluntly, 'irrational' in their motivations. Marxism was one intellectual resource where some correctives to this dismissal could be found.[4]

---

3. Arrighi, Hopkins and Wallerstein 1989.

4. It was not the only possible resource. Some founders of 'resource mobilisation theory' were so focused on establishing the rationality of protest that, as Perrow 1979, p. 202, quipped in an early critique, they 'removed Freud, but replaced him not with Marx or Lenin but with Milton Friedman'. We note, too, that in this collection of influential essays on resource mobilisation, this is the only reference to Marx or Marxism. Nor

Charles Tilly's work of the late 1970s and early 1980s was crucially informed by and explicitly developed in dialogue with Marxist analysis. In *From Mobilization to Revolution*, for example, the relation he posited between 'groupness' and the capacity to protest closely mirrors discussions within Marxist circles about the ways that urbanisation and workplace concentration enable proletarian organisation. In *The Contentious French*, his insistence that 'repertoires of contention' – namely, routine ways of acting collectively – are linked to the realities of everyday existence would also be familiar to anyone conversant with Marxist cultural analysis, and, more specifically, the work of British and French Marxist historians. Doug McAdam's influential *Political Process and the Development of Black Insurgency, 1930–1970* also sought to incorporate crucial Marxist insights about the potentials for the self-organisation of the powerless. Sidney Tarrow's work in the 1980s discussed a milieu of crisis and tumult in the Italy of the 1960s and 1970s, where Marxisms were being actively debated; his classic *Power in Movement* used Marx, Lenin, and Gramsci in order to frame the key questions facing analysts of social movements (for example, the relationships among large-scale social change, strategy, and symbolic and organisational struggle).[5]

More recently, McAdam, Tarrow and Tilly argued for a reformatting of theory by insisting that movements are but one *form* of 'contentious politics', and seeking to reintegrate revolutions, strikes, and other forms of contention within a more general formal political sociology; one motivating impulse has been a recognition that existing research paradigms have forgotten a key concern at the heart of Marxist theory – that is, the relation of parts to wholes.[6] Social movement theory, it seems, has taken the long way round to arrive at the Marxist commonplace that everyday resistance, popular movements and revolutionary situations are not utterly separate, but that at times one can turn into the other.

In mainland Europe, where Stalinism and dissident Marxisms were still quite dominant on the Left, both engaged writers like André Gorz, Alain Touraine or Rudolf Bahro and academics like Alberto Melucci – who all championed 'new social movements' (NSMs) – took a great deal from the general framework of Marxist analysis, aiming to refashion it for what they understood as the fundamentally changed macro-historical circumstances of developed welfare-state

---

is this unusual: a recent, widely-read reader on social movements by Goodwin and Jasper 2002 contains no references to Marx or Marxism at all, as does a well-regarded work on social movements and culture by Johnston and Klandermans 1995. This is typical of collections by major scholars in the field: any mention of Marxism is often dismissive or cursory.

5. Tilly 1978; 1986; McAdam 1982; Tarrow 1989; 1994.
6. McAdam, Tarrow and Tilly 2001.

capitalism or 'post-industrial' society.[7] In the wake of the events of 1968 and the rise of feminist, ecological and peace movements during the 1970s, a growing chorus of authors came to argue that structural changes in society, politics and economy were displacing 'the working class' as a key actor in social transformation, and that new kinds of issues and actors were emerging to contest the future shape of society. The defeats experienced by 'organised labour' in the late 1970s and 1980s, and the increasingly conservative face of Stalinist and social-democratic parties and their associated trade union hierarchies, contributed to the appeal of such approaches.[8]

Closely related to this trend, in the English-speaking world, was the argument that 'class politics' had been replaced by 'identity politics' – that is, a politics centred on the assertion of subjugated identities and differences based on race and ethnicity, gender and sexuality as opposed to the class-based interest politics of yesteryear.[9] As the 1980s and 1990s proceeded, this argument was increasingly shaped by the institutionalisation of much of the women's movement, along with gay liberation, black and other ethnic minority organisations within the legal system, the Labour and Democratic parties, and radical academia – and by the specifically Anglophone 'culture wars' initiated by the Thatcherite and Reaganite Right, which sought to mobilise against these movement gains.

One result of these various developments has been a narrowing of the understanding of movements and their place in large-scale processes of social change. Playing down the bigger picture of global power relations and the shifting character of socio-economic policy also meant ignoring the role of the grievances generated by these larger-scale changes. Labour movements were, to be sure, rather quiescent, but theorists did not try to explain this historically or to ask how long it would last, given the scale of the onslaught on jobs, wages and conditions. Significant parts of 'the social movement as a whole' were, if not actually written off, certainly sidelined.

Academic and activists' thinking narrowed its interests. The field could be narrowly delimited, such that processes both large and small fell out of view.[10] The result was a historical provincialism in which past struggles from below, and the reshaping of social relations from above, were either denied or assumed to be a feature *only* of the past. The present, it could be assumed, would remain without history.

---

7. Gorz 1973; Touraine 1981; Bahro 1985; Melucci 1989.
8. For a critical review of some of these, see Barker and Dale 1998.
9. Calhoun 1993; Ross 1989; Nicholson and Seidman 1995; Young 1990; Harvey 1996.
10. See Harvey 1996.

This problem is also evident in the analytical severing of links between everyday forms of subaltern self-assertion and 'world-historical movements'[11] capable of effecting systemic transformations. In studies of revolutions, major studies like those by Skocpol, Tilly and Goodwin all showed little interest in the 'social movement' aspect of their development, that is, in the actual and potential role of popular self-activity in shaping their development.[12] However, the kinds of micro-scale cultures and practices of everyday resistance documented by a Paul Willis or a James C. Scott equally fell out of the field of movement studies as 'someone else's problem'.[13] If the 'working class' was largely written off, there was not much point in exploring the nitty-gritty of actual forms of current worker resistance as part of 'social movement' concerns. It could be left to 'labour process' specialists, as could strikes and forms of workplace resistance. This fragmentation was celebrated by Foucauldians and in cultural studies, where everyday resistance was valued but the prospect that it might escalate to something producing substantial structural *change* was anathema. At its worst, social movement studies could become what Touraine called a 'natural sociology of [movement] élites',[14] adequate to understand the routine operations of movement establishments – how NGOs seek to position themselves within the US media or the EU's institutional labyrinth, for example – but with no ability to explain how and why these situations are reshaped and transformed.

The risk, in all this, is of a great impoverishment of sociological and political imaginations, a falling back from the kind of vision that enabled, say, the English historian E.P. Thompson to detect and decode emerging and developing forms of popular struggle in phenomena as varied as eighteenth-century market riots, fence-breaking, poaching or 'rough music'; that enabled Charles Tilly – in an extended dialogue with Thompson's work – to locate a wholesale shift in the repertoires of struggle in the early decades of the nineteenth century; or that enabled Peter Linebaugh and Marcus Rediker to show how the everyday resistance of sailors and slaves could form the ingredients of strikes, rebellions and revolutions that shook the Atlantic world.[15]

The parcelling out of trade unionism and strikes to 'labour studies' or 'industrial relations', of everyday resistance to 'cultural studies', or of revolutions to a specific branch of political science, ignores the crucial role that strikes may play in social movements even today; that social movements draw on resistance ingrained in everyday modes of survival and coping; and that strikes, local

11. Katsiaficas 1987.
12. Barker 2009.
13. Willis 1977; Scott 1990.
14. Touraine 1985.
15. Thompson 1991; Tilly 1986; Linebaugh and Rediker 2000.

cultures of resistance and social movements may, indeed, as David McNally's chapter indicates, play a part in popular revolutions. There is no place in this fragmented theory for the kind of coming together of popular struggles that we have seen across South America in the past decade or which we are currently seeing in many parts of the Arab world.

Politically, what is at risk is the ability to unearth 'how struggles in different socio-spatial arenas and across spatial scales might link with one another'.[16] David Harvey has argued strongly that the postmodern preoccupation with the particularity and singularity of resistance occludes the ways in which 'militant particularisms' are linked to wider social totalities. This preoccupation weakens any analytical and political ability to join the dots between the specific, concrete conflicts that social movements are embroiled in, and to see how they may 'shift gears, transcend particularities, and arrive at some conception of a universal alternative to that social system which is the source of their difficulties'.[17]

Indeed, moving away from Marx has taken modern social movement theory away from the kinds of conversations in which its progenitors had found inspiration, and which still maintain some life within fields such as labour history. Social movement theory risks losing not only a sense of 'the big picture' and especially its economic aspects, but also a sense of 'ordinary' people's potential to make their own history, to form and nurture oppositional cultures, and to contest – and, of course, sometimes to succumb to or support – dominant ideological and organisational ways of interpreting and acting in the world.

Marxism and activists in the new waves of movement struggles

What is to *count* as 'Marxism' is itself a disputed question. Twice, over the past century and more, a dominant interpretation emerged and was institutionalised in a manner that meant abandoning certain ideas of key importance to its founders. These 'official Marxisms' were also subjected to root-and-branch challenges that involved restating the revolutionary core of the tradition. Much of what passes for 'Marxism' in conventional academic discussion, however, has its roots in these institutionalisations.

After Marx and Engels died, European socialism divided over the very meaning of such core ideas as 'class struggle' and 'the state'. What Hal Draper termed 'the two souls of socialism' were fought over within the institutions of the workers' movement.[18]

---

16. Hart 2002, p. 820.
17. Harvey 1996; 2000, p. 241.
18. Draper 1966.

On one side, one powerful trend of 'socialism from above' emerged among the leadership of the parties and unions of the Second International. The struggle for a new society came to be identified with the parliamentary struggle. Here, existing state forms – not excluding colonial empires – were largely accepted, and the winning of votes in elections became the central point of politics. 'Professional' bureaucratic union leaders, heading what were often new mass workers' organisations, became more concerned with negotiating with employers than seeking to expropriate them. If they and the social-democratic party leaders still held to 'Marxism', it was a sanitised, often 'inevitabilitist' and statist version they adopted, disavowing its *revolutionary* and *dialectical* core.[19]

On the Left, representing 'socialism from below', one powerful current adopted one or other version of syndicalism, posing mass working-class insurgency apart from and against 'party' and 'statist' organisations.[20] Specifically Marxist criticism of the 'revisionist' currents within socialism was attempted by Luxemburg, Lenin, Trotsky and others, but not yet with the political heat (or the philosophical depth) that marked such criticism after 1914.

The First World War, and the revolutions it bred, irrevocably divided the forces of socialism, with those who were to become social democrats supporting the mass slaughter of the War. It also sharpened divisions over the very essence of Marxism. The young Gramsci registered part of the issues at stake when he celebrated the 1917 Revolution in Russia as a 'revolution against *Capital*'.[21] The parties of social democracy, henceforth, remained committed to parliamentarism and, in practice, to maintaining the core of capitalist social relations. Some of them retained, for a period, some rhetorical attachment to Marxism, though subsequent development further weakened even this, as first Keynesianism and eventually neoliberal ideas came to dominate their practical thought. These parties, however, retained widespread working-class support, thus posing new strategic dilemmas for those who maintained revolutionary Marxism as the core of their thinking.

The revolutionary wave that ended the First World War and brought down three empires both produced a wave of innovative new forms of struggle and occasioned a major revival and rethinking of Marxist ideas. It enabled – for a period – new conjunctions between syndicalism and Marxism, a developing critique of the 'inevitabilist' strain in 'Second International Marxism' and a reassertion of the 'active side', along with new bonds with struggles against

---

19. Anatomised, for example, in Colletti 1976.
20. For a recent study, see Darlington 2008a.
21. Gramsci 1977a.

colonial and other oppressions.[22] The revolutionary wave manifested itself in a series of important developments in Marxist thinking across a wide range of fields of inquiry, from philosophy, jurisprudence and political economy to linguistics, aesthetics and psychology. Some of the fruits of those developments are still being assimilated and further developed across a broad spectrum of movement-relevant theories even today. (References in this volume to work by Lukács, Gramsci, Vološinov, Bakhtin and Vygotsky offer witness to their continuing influence.)

But impulses towards rediscovery and innovation in Marxism were soon met by counter-impulses towards burying, reversal and silencing. The revolutionary wave fell back. In the one country, Russia, where astonishing advances had been made in 1917, isolation and the pressures of the Civil War all too soon promoted the conditions for what Trotsky and others termed 'degeneration' and 'bureaucratisation'. By the end of the 1920s, Stalin's régime was promoting – in the name of 'Marxism' – a state-driven crash industrialisation drive that demanded the expropriation of the peasantry, complete subordination of labour to 'Communist' managers along with huge cuts in popular living standards, the formation of a vast enslaved workforce in the 'Gulags', medals for motherhood, the silencing of all forms of opposition, mass purges and murders. 'Marxism' was not so much stood on its head as hanged by its heels: Stalinism inverted its anti-state theory of self-emancipation from below into a top-down doctrine of state worship and national accumulation.

The official Communist movement, after the disaster of Hitler's rise to power in Germany, adopted the policy of the 'Popular Front', hoping thereby to ally itself with 'progressive' forces against the fascist threat. That required the active renunciation of working-class revolution, a politics legitimised by reversion to a theory of 'stages' closer to classic 'Menshevism' than to the innovations of Bolshevism. In France and Spain in 1936, and after the War across Western Europe and elsewhere, Communist parties generated a new version of social-democratic practice, pursuing parliamentarist paths and acting as essentially conservative forces in political crises.

The two and a half decades of 'long boom' in world capitalism after the Second World War offered an unfavourable climate for any widespread development of ideas about popular and especially working-class self-emancipation. East, West and South, states took a leading role in economic organisation, whether of a state-socialist, Keynesian or national-developmentalist kind. This situation, and the titanic struggles which had led to the defeat of fascism, welfare-state gains and independence from imperial power in so many states, were also conducive

---

22. One record of this is found in the documents of the early years of the new Communist International: see Riddell (ed.) 1986; 1993; 2002; 2003; 2004; 2011; and forthcoming).

to the identification of popular movements with state power, of socialism with nationalisation, and so on.

If this period saw revolutions aplenty, as the old world empires were broken up by movements of national liberation, once in power they pursued state-led programmes of 'national development', all too soon marked by corruption and authoritarianism. Stalinist 'critical support' for bourgeois nationalism, and geopolitical relations with the Soviet Union and later China, created 'Marxisms' in practice deeply complicit with the new majority world régimes. Eastern Europe was locked in Moscow's imperial embrace. Those who sought to promote a revolutionary socialist politics independent of Washington, Moscow or Beijing were tiny embattled minorities, preserving almost lost traditions – Trotskyist, council-communist, humanist, and so on – and developing only a few new theoretical insights.

Not surprisingly, oppositional movements in Eastern Europe mostly developed anti-Marxist ideas, even if some of the highpoints of their practice – in the Hungarian workers' councils of 1956 or the Polish inter-factory committees of 1970–1 and 1980–1 – seemed to hark back to the structures of the Paris Commune or the soviets of 1917–19. By the time of the new upsurge of movement activity in the 1960s, in France, Italy, Portugal, Chile, Spain and elsewhere, the new emerging Lefts partly defined their politics in radical opposition to both social-democratic and 'official Communist' politics. However, the relative political quiescence of workers' movements in developed capitalism during the postwar period – and Stalinist hostility to independent working-class action in countries like France and Italy – encouraged ideas that the proletariat had been 'incorporated', and that any revolutionary impulses would tend to come from the 'margins', from oppressed communities of colour, from Third World peasants and lumpen-proletarians, from women, or from alienated students in the newly expanded university-sectors. The politics of the New Left of the 1960s and early 1970s were thus often a rather unstable melange of ideas and images drawn from Maoism, Guevarism, Trotskyism, syndicalism, the counter culture and other sources. The same period witnessed a rise in the level of working-class combativity in Europe and North America, opening possibilities for linkages between the New Left and militant trade unionism.

The New Left was associated with an extensive rediscovery of original Marxist themes, signalled by a flourishing of Marxist publications that explored alienation, began to re-read Marx's critique of political economy in new and less 'economistic' ways, rediscovered and developed an emancipatory 'history from below', and began to identify and revive a parallel 'politics from below'. Some impressive beginnings were made in terms of bonds between students and workers. However, actual experiences of popular *revolutions* were limited, even in spite of the important and impressive insurrections in Prague, Paris, and Derry, which were later followed by an actual revolutionary situation in Portugal. The result was an expansion both in the Left's rhetoric of revolution and imagination of its possibilities, as well as in its understanding of who might be 'agents' of revolution.

Furthermore, the great revolt of 1968 'cut across the tripartite division of the world system at the time – the West, the Communist bloc, and the Third World'.[23] These uprisings ranged from successful popular wars for national liberation in parts of sub-Saharan Africa and Vietnam, followed by significant experiments with socialist models of development; the resurgence of popular social movements and guerrilla insurgency in many Latin-American countries and in India; and, towards the close of the decade, the overthrow of the Somoza régime in Nicaragua.[24] Associated with these movements was 'a more radical, a more unambiguously socialist Third Worldism than the first generation Bandung régimes'[25] and a revitalisation of Marxian analyses of the political economy of the capitalist world system.[26]

From the mid-1970s, the wave of working-class militancy in Western countries was first contained (not least by union leaderships) and then increasingly reversed, as the early assaults of neoliberalism were launched against many of the strongest sectors of organised labour. Significant parts of the new left-wing organisations that had mushroomed in the 1960s and early 1970s fell apart; some of their radical support returned to the social-democratic fold, others turned to the identity politics that emerged and rose to temporary dominance in the 1980s. So far as movements were concerned, it seemed that Marxism's second brief flourishing was over.

In the academic world, and especially in the social, historical and cultural fields that had greatest relevance for thinking about movements, postmodernism and poststructuralism seemed triumphant. Often, the 'Marxism' against which they defined themselves was itself a version of the 'Marxisms' against which the best impulses of the new Lefts had themselves struggled: a 'structuralist' rather than humanistic and revolutionary set of impulses, sometimes associated with Althusserian theory.[27] Caricatures of Marxism remained prevalent within academic discourse, and this affected activists to the degree that university settings provided a main source of general ideas. Activists trained in the academy tend to come pre-inoculated against Marxism, albeit a Marxism which is substantially

---

23. Wallerstein 2006, p. 6; see also Arrighi, Hopkins and Wallerstein 1989.
24. Prashad 2008.
25. Berger 2004, p. 19.
26. Seddon 2012; Leys 2009.
27. Althusserianism was a rather limited product of struggle within what was then a still influential French Communist Party, which was belatedly dragging itself out of the embrace of Stalinism and onto a 'Eurocommunist' (avowedly parliamentarist) road. It contributed nothing to Marxism as a theory of emancipation.

imaginary. They also come predisposed to accept powerful 'grand narratives' which explain why power, and explanation, are to be avoided at all costs.

In the real world, however, the neoliberal assault continued, and with ever more force, restructuring global production and with it the world working class, creating new forms of debt dependence and undermining previous welfare systems. Oppositional movements began to cohere around new *anti-capitalist* projects and ideas. Themes of opposition to war *and* to capitalist dispossession took on new force in the new century, and especially as all the classic manifestations of large-scale economic crisis broke across the world from 2007. We are writing this introduction at the end of 2011, against the background of a huge new wave of protests across both the advanced capitalist world and in its peripheries, which call into question both dictatorial and undemocratic régimes (including those imposed by financiers) and the enormously expanded inequality that marks contemporary capitalism.

For Marxists, the situation is paradoxical. On the one hand, we are witnessing an exhilarating new flourishing of movement activity, a slowly resurgent opposition to the onslaughts of neoliberalism in crisis by a globally expanded and recomposed working class, and the expression of widely popular ideological challenges to the fundamental principles of capitalist society. On the other hand, this is, perhaps, the first time since 1848 when specifically Marxist ideas are not the natural *lingua franca* of a rising movement.[28]

The only Marxism that might gain serious purchase in the present period is one that is resolutely committed to popular emancipation 'from below'. It still, we think, has some pressing things to offer, in urgent conversation with today's movements.

That Marxism rests on a proposition and a wager. The proposition is that the core problem facing popular movements in the present epoch is the capitalist system. The wager[29] is that the working class is capable of transforming itself through collective action and organisation to the point where that it can break capitalism apart and lay the foundations of a new cooperative world community. Together, the proposition and the wager provide Marxism with a standard by which to assess the whole panoply of popular forms of resistance to capitalist power in all its oppressive and divisive manifestations, and a reason to participate actively within them.

---

28. Marxism is not, however, absent from the movement: Marxist thinking has been important in the construction of alliances between movements around a shared analysis of, and hostility to, the current economic order as 'neoliberal', in many of the new Latin-American experiments, in explaining the roots of imperial warmongering since 2001 and in opposition to the politics of austerity pursued by governments across the world.
29. Goldmann 1964.

Marxism simultaneously entails a theory of the organisation of power within modern society, a theory of popular agency, and a theory of transformation with strategic consequences. It is an argument *about* movements, and an argument *within* movements.

At the core of capitalism, a specific set of social relations provide an inescapable pattern to the development of social life across the globe, reshaping and subordinating everything to the predominant drive to competitive accumulation, itself fuelled by exploitation. These are the 'social relations of production', a term often misunderstood as defining simply the immediate relations between capitalist and worker 'at the point of production', but actually encompassing the whole world of production, exchange and distribution, of power and culture. If their decoding is the work of the critique of political economy, Marxism views them as a *historical* creation which we can, if we act appropriately, transcend.

Indeed, challenges to their implications are immanent within many kinds of movement practices and demands, whether these touch on the expansion of a variety of rights, access to and control over urban and rural land, claims to respect and opposition to manifold types of discrimination, increased control over decision-making, putting people's needs before property's claims, resistance to imperialist wars, redistribution of income and resources, or the remaking of humanity's practical relationship with nature. It is part of Marxism's work to trace and highlight the interconnections between specific issues and particular repertoires of action, organisation and understanding within movements and the broader social relations of production that – explicitly or implicitly – they confront.

Against the caricatured 'structuralism' so often adopted in academic discourse, Marxism's emphasis falls on agency, on people 'making their own history'. The very social relations of production are themselves the product of ongoing agency, even if in alienating forms, on the part of those who currently suffer their continuation. Individuals acting alone possess little capacity to transform these social relations, but collective activity and organisation contain the potential both to make immediate gains, to roll back some of the most exigent threats to human welfare, but also to lay the foundations of other ways of living and organising society. There is no absolute line of division between movements seeking 'reforms' within existing structures and movements that threaten to surpass their limits. Rather, movements operate on the boundaries between forms of opposition that remain contained within the limits of the system, and those that potentially transgress them. Containment and transgression are tendencies present in most movements, more or less explicitly, and are registered in strategic and tactical arguments within them. The potential for these differences to become significant depend, in part, on scales of involvement, movements' capacity to draw together different particular interests and needs, the generality of demands, the scope and forms of movement-generated organisation, and so forth. Potentials and limits are discovered in practice, through victories and defeats, through confusions and clarifications, through intra-movement dialogues and movement reflexivity.

A key Marxist focus concerns the degree to which, and the organisational forms through which, movement repertoires include the construction of new institutions 'from below', both as means of conducting their struggles and as ways of replacing existing power-setups with alternatives. Against those who argue that movements should *avoid* power, its case is that they can and should *create* radically new and more democratic forms of power as a necessary part of the remaking of social relationships, of reshaping the entire productive and exchange process and – an increasingly urgent question – of reconstructing humanity's relationship with the natural world.

Is there not, however, an unbridgeable gap between such visions and mundane present-day reality? Certainly, the rising and ebbing of Marxism's appeal in different periods rests on experiential feelings about such unbridgeability. Periods of defeat engender defeatist moods and a narrowing of aspiration and imagination, affecting academic as much as popular thought: images of containment and stability predominate, 'grand narratives' evoke mistrust. Small, fragmented reforms and struggles contained within 'proper channels' constitute the horizons of apparent possibility; the spokespeople of narrow 'realism' within movement life – whether in trade unions, political parties, NGOs or in more apparently informal settings – predominate. Yet, within such periods, it is easy to miss the fragility of apparent consensus and everyday conservatism. The most productive Marxist work on questions relating to 'ideology' – whether in Vološinov's 'dialogism' or Gramsci's 'contradictory consciousness' – catches the unsettled, probing and critical quality of all practical social thinking and speech. Seemingly fixed ideas and stances contain subversive and transformative potentials which deterministic accounts of ideology quite miss. Thinking and speech, as Vygotsky and Billig both emphasise,[30] involve a complex dialectic of particularisation and generalisation which is always open to being reformatted in the light of new experiences, of shocks and surprises, of practical blockages and dissonances, which permit and create urgent needs for rethinking and reorganising activity.[31]

---

30. Vygotsky 1986; Billig 1996.
31. We cannot, therefore, agree with Frances Fox Piven and Richard Cloward when they write that the poor 'experience deprivation and oppression within a concrete setting, not as the end product of large and abstract processes, and it is the concrete experience that molds their discontent into specific grievances against specific targets. Workers experience the factory, the speeding rhythm of the assembly line, the foreman, the spies and the guards, the owner and the paycheck. They do not experience monopoly capitalism. People on relief experience the shabby waiting rooms, the overseer or the caseworker, and the dole. They do not experience American social welfare policy... In other

In this view, existing forms of activity and organisation (and of passivity and disorganisation) need to be understood as transitory, inwardly contradictory, and open to large- or small-scale transformation. The real problems for Marxists concern how precisely to grasp this in a given situation, and *what to propose doing about it.* For – as a theory of and for movements – Marxism is only of value as a contribution to the processes of argumentation and transformation within those movements, as an engaged practice that itself develops and learns alongside those with whom it participates in the effort to change the world. It is necessarily 'critical', always looking at the distance between what a movement is doing and whom it is mobilising and for what, and the potential to which it might realistically aspire.

In this sense, and as we think this book demonstrates, Marxism holds a particular strength as a movement theory. While feminist, ecological and anarchist thought all share its movement origins, none holds the same ability to connect the critique of structure with a strategic analysis of social movements both as they are and as they could be – to find within the limitations of the world as it is the potential to create a new world in the teeth of powerful opposition and structural constraints.

Along with this strategic vision, Marxism also contributes an emphasis on the connection between apparently disparate campaigns and issues: struggles over oil and gas, for example, can connect ecological questions with local concerns over health and safety, economic ones over the ownership of natural resources, cultural conflicts over the meaning of place, and, indeed, the politics of policing. It is precisely this mix, well-handled, which can turn an isolated issue into a campaign capable of mobilising large numbers of people in difficult situations over long periods – and which can enable such a campaign to inspire others in the formation of a movement.

Like any practically-oriented theory, Marxism's history shows its proneness to various kinds of pitfalls. Uncritical cheerleading is one risk: the eruption of a new movement, the advent of a novel strategy, a sudden insurgency can renew optimism, but simple celebration is insufficient. Careful measure must be taken not only of new potentials unveiled, but also of the distance still to be travelled, the social forces not yet mobilised, the strategic and organisational problems not yet solved. Marxists, however, can easily fall into an opposite trap, of only seeing

---

words, it is the daily experience of people that shapes their grievances, establishes the measure of their demands, and points out the targets of their anger' (Piven and Cloward 1979, p. 20). That quite ignores the *thinking* and *making sense*, the practical *generalisation*, which is quite as much a part of the experience of the poor or of workers as it is of academics. Gramsci's judgement seems sounder: *everyone is a philosopher*. It is not only Marxists who move between 'levels of analysis' in order to understand and act on the world.

the limits and difficulties, and thus missing the significance of the new, and the way that the class struggle is constantly reconfigured.

An academic or sectarian emphasis on theoretical superiority, an unwillingness to take the risks of direct involvement, and thus an inability to *learn* from a diverse and always contradictory set of movement impulses, have sometimes marked those who, before a shift in circumstances, might have seemed to be the 'vanguard'. Patience and readiness to engage with the unfamiliar have characterised all the interesting Marxists of the past. Passion and a capacity for strategic assessment are not alternatives. At any point in their development, movements – and especially their leading spokespeople – are prone to a degree of self-satisfaction at their achievements. Marxism, intransigently, insists we still have a *world* to win, that the movement still needs to reach and encompass the needs and active involvement of larger majorities, and that a whole totality of social forms still require reconstruction from below. Vital dots remain to be connected, strategic and organisational questions to be argued. Practical and theoretical questions abound for which Marxist thought – as against potential rivals – still offers a valuable arsenal of ideas.

Contesting caricatures of Marxism in scholarship and activism

Defending Marxism's place in social movement theorising is made difficult by the sheer weight of caricatured accounts that have to be overcome. One source of some of these is of course to be found among the defenders of various tyrannical régimes claiming to be 'Marxist', while another can be found among Marxism's own less skilled and more sectarian advocates.

Nevertheless, within social movement studies, it is easier to locate caricatures of Marxist thought than evidence of serious engagement with its substantial critical potential. One such caricature revolves around the claim that Marxism is only capable of addressing the macro-structural aspects of a social movement, and frequently reduces the latter to an epiphenomenon of the former, without sufficient attention to the contingencies of how subjectivities and collective identities are formed. Thus, Alberto Melucci claims that Marxist theory

> focuses on the 'objective' social foundations of collective action. It also derives the meaning of action from its analysis of the social conditions which the actors appear to have in common...Here collective action appears as *actors without action* – while the gap between 'objective conditions' and the empirically observed collective behaviour proves impossible to explain.[32]

32. Melucci 1989, pp. 18, 8.

Elsewhere, he has characterised this 'problem' as follows:

> This is an old Marxist problem, that of the passage from a class in itself to a class for itself, from the material roots of class interests in capitalist relationships to revolutionary action...This immense chasm was inevitably filled by a kind of *deus ex machina* (the party, the intellectuals) that serves as the external supplier of that consciousness which is lacking.[33]

Another well-known caricature is that which criticises Marxism for conceiving of collective action in economically reductionist ways, and for focusing on a narrow range of movement issues to the exclusion of all others (paradoxically, this objection often goes hand in hand with the desire to exclude these same issues as now supposedly dead in the water for all time). Carl Boggs, for example, writes:

> ...it has become increasingly obvious that the new movements have posed important questions concerning bureaucracy, the family, feminism, culture, the ecological crisis, the arms race, and racism that Marxism has failed to confront adequately...Such movements have further called into question the entire productivist framework of Marxism, including its primacy of the industrial working class.[34]

Tarrow relates this problematic to the issue of ideology and consciousness in Marxist theory:

> Concerned with the problem that the workers' movement could not succeed without the participation of a significant proportion of its members, [Marx] developed a theory of 'false' consciousness, by which he meant that if workers failed to act as 'History' dictated, it was because they remained cloaked in a shroud of ignorance woven by their class enemies. The theory was unsatisfactory because no one could say whose consciousness was false and whose was real.[35]

It is, in any case, widely understood that Marxists are only interested in labour movements, that the only 'real' movements are workers' movements, narrowly defined, or those that 'directly address economic and political disenfranchisement'.[36] Indeed, it was for these reasons that Manuel Castells

---

33. Melucci 1992, p. 240.
34. Boggs 1986, p. 9.
35. Tarrow 1998, p. 11. It is not clear where this idea of 'false consciousness' came from. It is not a phrase Marx seems to have used. Lukács, perhaps one of the classic theorists who approached it most closely, explicitly derived his own analysis of the process of class consciousness from Max Weber's notion of ideal types rather than from any Marxist source. Lukács changed his own perspectives in the course of writing *History and Class Consciousness* (Lukács 1971), and the model has found few, if any, Marxist successors.
36. Armstrong and Bernstein 2008, p. 82. These writers criticise political process approaches to social movements as 'neo-Marxist' in inspiration.

From its origins, Marxism has been concerned with the creation of an alternative order of political and social life.

The problem, then, with *not* taking Marxism seriously is that Marxism offers some perspectives that point in promising directions for the kinds of politics that many movement activists – and scholars – say they want. In the chapters that follow, the contributors to this volume take up key areas of Marxist thought that insist on the primacy of *processes* over *things*, on *transformation* over *stasis*, on *praxis* over *theory*, on the *complex relation of parts to wholes* over *structural determinism*, and on *contradiction* over *self-consistency*.

Of course, there is more to Marxism than this, and several chapters expose other key features. But for a body of thought that is alleged to be deterministic, crudely materialist, unchanging, and fixated on a select few features of social and political life, it is important to set the record straight. One *ought not* to think that all organisations act in the same way or that all political parties and trade unions act equally as barriers to political change. One *ought* to be able to contemplate broader social change that endures, rather than being resigned to personally satisfying utopian experiments that leave in place capitalism's broader patterns of capitalist exploitation. One *ought* to be able to think about how modes of representation and political organisation may become transformed in new circumstances, rather than assume they must always tend toward undemocratic rule. Equally, one *ought* to be able to think through the ways that existing political and 'civil society' organisations may simultaneously both challenge and support broader sets of exploitative and repressive social relations – and to fashion strategies for opening up the opportunities that such contradictory forms contain.

And, on the broader scale, one *ought* to be able to think about the ways in which popular movements over the centuries *have* thrown up new modes of self-organisation, forced democratic and welfare concessions and reshaped the political landscape; as William Morris put it, 'I pondered all these things, and how men [sic] fight and lose the battle, and the thing that they fought for comes about in spite of their defeat, and when it comes turns out not to be what they meant, and other men have to fight for what they meant under another name...'[55]

Marxist silences

If we believe that thinking about social movements would be significantly enhanced by serious conversation with the Marxist tradition, the problems do not only concern existing social movement studies and practice. Marxism itself has a fractured and under-developed theory of social movements. Marx and

55. Morris 2001, p. 31.

Marxists have often talked about 'movements' (and even 'social movements'). However, they have rarely stopped to ask what they meant by these terms, and how they might fit into their larger systems of thinking. There has been little explicitly Marxist engagement with the huge flourishing of social movement studies, or inquiry into whether anything might be useful in the battery of arguments, concepts and arguments which those studies have developed.

For Marx and Engels, the term 'social movement', as both Colin Barker and Laurence Cox suggest in their chapters, referred to a whole 'multi-organisational field'.[56] The movement was an amalgam of political parties, trade unions, clubs of various sorts, exile organisations, underground organisations, newspapers, enrolling and representing the serried ranks of the exploited and oppressed. These were by no means all proletarians in the Marxist sense – indeed, it was Marxist historians who explored the multiplicity and diversity of the Parisian *sans culottes* and showed that the working class was not a homogeneous mass but a complex construction. What Marx and Engels *did* argue was that the newly emerging proletariat had a unique significance within 'the social movement', since its expansion, structural power and cultural development offered the prospect of a force capable of leading the complete revolutionary transformation of society. It might, for whole periods, fail to live up to its potential mission, while national and other divisions might divert it from its emancipatory path. Only in the course of huge struggles, and after major defeats as well as advances, might it *learn* to convert its potential into an actual taking and remaking of social power:

> Working-class revolutions...constantly criticise themselves, they continually interrupt their own course, return to what has apparently already been achieved to start it from scratch again. Cruelly and thoroughly they mock the shortcomings, weaknesses and pitiful nature of their first attempts; they seem to throw their opponent down, only for him to draw new strength from the earth and rise up once more against them, yet more gigantic than ever. They shrink back again and again in the face of the undetermined vastness of their own aims, until a situation has been created which makes any turning back impossible, and the conditions themselves cry out: 'Hic Rhodus, hic salta! Here is the rose, dance here!'[57]

The movement itself was the great self-educator, and its tempos and inner developments were the ultimately decisive factor in historical development. Some sense of the complexity of its learning processes can be seen in Marx's letter on Ireland that Barker quotes in his chapter: the English workers, in effect, need

---

56. Klandermans 1992,
57. Marx 1984, pp. 5–6.

to be educated out of anti-Irish prejudice, and this job can only be done by the predominantly peasant-based Irish liberation movement.

'In what relation do the communists stand to the proletarians as a whole?', Marx and Engels asked in the *Communist Manifesto*:

> They do not set up any sectarian principles of their own by which to shape and mould the proletarian movement... The theoretical conclusions of the Communists are in no way based on ideas or principles that have been invented, or discovered, by this or that would-be universal reformer. They merely express, in general terms, actual relations springing from an existing class struggle, from a historical movement going on under our very eyes.[58]

For Marxists, questions about leadership necessarily arose as part of their concerns about the relationship between their party organisations and the movement as a whole. Lenin and Luxemburg engaged in spirited polemics on this issue, with Luxemburg famously declaring that the 'mistakes made by a really revolutionary working-class movement are infinitely, in historical perspective, more fruitful and valuable than the infallibility of the most excellent central committee'.[59] Lenin, who always had a more 'interventionist' view of the Party's ongoing dialogue with the Russian movement, expressed concern that Marxists' enthusiasm for the 'spontaneity' of workers' unrest could blind them to its ideological and organisational contradictions and limitations. The tasks and, indeed, the very membership of the Party could and would alter with changing political conditions: in 1902, Lenin was for strict centralisation, but in 1905 favoured 'opening the gates of the party' to the spontaneously revolutionary workers. Gramsci, whose *Prison Notebooks* partly consist of extended meditations on adapting the politics of Lenin to the different conditions in Western Europe and America, elaborated a distinction between 'traditional' and 'organic' intellectuals and their respective roles in upholding and challenging the dominant modes of organising society, culture, and politics.

In the wake of the Russian Revolution, and later Stalin's purges, doctrinaire ossification of Soviet Marxism, the post-WWII expansion of European welfare states and the tearing down of colonial empires, Marxists could no longer take either 'capitalism' or 'the movement' as steady reference points. Both, separately and together, required theoretical renovation. 'New Lefts' struggled with these questions, with varying degrees of success. Hal Draper's 'Two souls of socialism', expanded theoretically by his *Karl Marx's Theory of Revolution*, represents one

---

58. Marx and Engels 1998, pp. 50–1.
59. Luxemburg cited in Frölich 2010, p. 86.

such attempt, as does Raya Dunayevskaya's *Marxism and Freedom*, among many others.[60]

The problem became acute from the late 1960s onwards. In the West, official labour movements faced militant challenges from within their own ranks, from workforces who were being recomposed by migration and shifting power-balances in workplaces, at the same time as new demands were being voiced, demanding rights and freedoms for people who had been excluded from public political participation and social recognition, such as students, women, racial and ethnic minorities, and sexual minorities. Initially, many of these movements found inspiration and, indeed, key members among Marxists, the best of whom grasped the need to develop their theories of emancipation to catch up with the new forms of movement practice.

From the mid-1970s, however, it was clear that the initiative within Western trade unions was returning to the official leaderships, as workplace militancy declined. The way was prepared for a wave of significant defeats for workers in formerly core industries, as ruling circles – in response to the return of major crises to the world economy after the end of the long postwar boom – began to develop the new strategies and institutional frameworks that we know today as 'neoliberalism'.

Neoliberalism's institutionalisation required the taming and containment of popular resistance, the widening of social inequalities both nationally and internationally, the enlargement of debt financing and the subjection of many developing countries to 'conditionalities' attached to loans from the IMF and World Bank.

In the majority of the world, the decline of national-developmentalism and the country-by-country imposition of IMF rules – against massive popular protest[61] – was in itself a boon to Marxists, as more recent anti-capitalist movements have shown. What undermined the attractiveness of Marxism in this period was, rather, the managing of this neoliberal turn by élites who often (in China and India as in South Africa and Latin America) spoke the language of Marxism, in whole or in part.

In the Soviet bloc, this period saw a decline of the significance of socialist and Marxist ideas for intellectual dissidence and popular culture, as the memory of anti-fascist resistance faded, the identification of Marxism with the régimes gained ground and the intellectual attraction of neoliberal thinking increased.

In the North, the Marxist Left that had grown in scale and self-confidence up to the early 1970s lacked the muscle to organise sufficient resistance to neoliberalism, and was driven back, in some cases being fragmented and dispersed. It

---

60. Draper 1977; 1978; 1986; 1990; Draper and Haberkern 2010; Dunayevskaya 2000.
61. Walton and Seddon 1994.

was in this setting that ideas about 'new social movements' and 'postmodernism' began to gain significant traction in the Western academy. Part of this development involved a questioning of 'class' as an organising category for radical thought, most notably within the field of social history. This was also the period in which several disciplines in the social sciences and humanities underwent a decisive 'linguistic turn'. For social history, this meant a greater suspicion of received categories of 'groupness', in which affiliation could be 'read off' from 'social structure'.

Increasingly, 'postmodern' critiques of (principally Marxist) social history cast doubt on 'class' and 'class struggle'. It was not simply that they discovered that 'grand narratives' were no longer valid; they argued, moreover, that grand narratives were *never* valid to begin with. It turns out that relatively few workers used the 'language of class' in ways commensurate with Marxism in the early decades of the nineteenth century when, according to Thompson, the working class was in the process of its 'making', or later.[62] Defenders of Marxist historical analysis, even while embracing and developing some elements of the linguistic turn, argued that the postmodernists had bent the stick too far: while it was true that one could not read people's political views directly from their social position (actually, few Marxists ever seriously entertained this caricatured idea), it was unrealistic to expect workers of the nineteenth century to sound like Marxist historians, or even like Marx himself.[63] Nevertheless, they did acknowledge that the postmodern turn raised important questions about *how* large collectivities constitute themselves around certain descriptive categories and claim them as their own. That involved a set of questions to which social movement theorisation could have contributed. It did not follow, either, that all claims about 'class' and 'workers' tended toward emancipatory politics. In short, the linguistic and postmodern turns in history and historical social science challenged Marxists to think more generally about the constitution of social subjects and to specify the relations among the relative positions of a variety of social actors in relations of production and reproduction; the different experiences of individuals in those positions, especially as they change and as the structures of these relationships change; organisation, both of daily life and of protest; and the linguistic, cognitive, and emotional ways in and through which these relations and organisations are constituted.

Accordingly, within social history at least, Marxist thinkers did develop a kind of convergence with social movement theory, even if they did not tend to use its formal resources. Both sides were responding to similar sorts of stimuli (namely, the decline of working-class militancy and the 'linguistic' turn in the

---

62. Stedman Jones 1983.
63. Meiksins Wood 1998.

humanities and social sciences), and were landing, by the early 1990s, with a similar set of problems: the relationship between larger-scale social change and particular local events and processes, the nature of organisation and networks, and language and cultural dynamics. While social movement studies developed each of these areas, Marxism and Marxists often steered clear of the increasingly scientistic cast that some of the sociological literature took on, and particularly in the USA.

Of course, there were figures such as Charles Tilly or Marc Steinberg who bridged the two worlds. Both, not coincidentally, became interested – Steinberg explicitly so in his published work – in the work of Mikhail Bakhtin and his collaborators in post-revolutionary Russia, who sought to develop a 'dialogical' approach to language. Dialogical theory offered an alternative to approaches based in 'framing' or the ideas of Foucault. It avoided both the linguistic idealism that resurfaced in postmodern critiques of social history and the crass materialism of Stalinist Marxism (which would become the default model of Marxism in the eyes of its academic critics). Bakhtin and Vološinov developed a grounded, materialist, and relational theory compatible with many aspects of a non-reductionist reading of Marxism, and especially the work of Gramsci.[64] Several contributions to this volume highlight the work of the 'Bakhtin Circle' as a potential resource with two potential strengths. First, it can help to ground a processual conception of class and class formation, and, second, it can offer satisfactory ways of meeting social movement theory's demand for a way of talking about the development of political claims – and hence, too, of the public subjects who make them – as they move from context to context and speaker to speaker.

Discussion originating in Europe about the 'new social movements' also challenged the primacy of class, in ways both similar to and different from the postmodern challenge in social history. Alain Touraine's attention to social movements outside of the 'old' labour movement originated as a *materialist* critique of Marxism. He did not argue that there was no such thing as the working class; on the contrary, he argued that the moment when the working class could realistically provide the motive force in large-scale social change had passed, and that Marxists could not be true radicals unless they recognised this fact. Alberto Melucci argued – like the postmodernists – that the idea that 'social movements' or 'classes' existed was a reification and a poor ontological gamble. To be sure, the problems of aggregating actors' interests into what were clearly movements remained, but he argued for a more processual and culturally charged

---

64. Brandist 1996; Ives 2003.

analysis that would highlight how and why people choose to engage in collective action.

Because the postmodern and NSM critiques are often conflated – a conflation that affected the way the original NSM theories were received, and even elaborated, in the United States and Britain – the charges of ahistoricism and idealism often stuck to both. But like the postmodern challenges in social history, as well as challenges to Marxist conceptions of class among feminist historians, the NSM-oriented critics, diverse as they were, forced similar questions on Marxists concerning the constitution of actors, the making of class, and the role of language and symbolic action in 'experience'.

Rather than being – as some caricatures would have it – a fixed body of doctrine, Marxist thinking has, we think, continued to develop in productive and interesting ways. What no Marxist thinker has seemingly yet succeeded in doing is bringing together the insights gained over the past decades through ongoing *dialogue* with other trends and schools in a distinctively 'Marxist branch of analysis of social movements'. This volume does not aim as high as that, but it does set out to suggest that such an enterprise would be a valuable one, and to demonstrate that the elements of a Marxist analysis of social movements can be shown to exist and be fruitful theoretically, empirically and politically across a wide range of movements, countries and periods.

In a sense, the times are propitious for this challenge. Now, amid global financial collapse and the efflorescence of protest around the world, Marxism has begun to regain some of the credibility it appeared to have lost in the wake of the collapse of the Soviet bloc in the late 1980s and early 1990s. Within the field of political economy, even fairly cursory statements by Marxists are no longer dismissed out of hand. Within human geography, one of whose leading figures is David Harvey, a great deal of important work has had both a Marxist and an activist bent. Studies of community organising and workplace militancy, as well as new global organising strategies joining up such campaigns, have become an important part of the field of urban studies, and has allowed it to link up, though unevenly, with studies of labour organising which have recently come into their own in American sociology. Within the developing field of 'labour and labour movements' – now an official research section of the American Sociological Association – the study of 'class' has undergone a radical expansion. Academics have been catching up with the ongoing practical recomposition of the working class, represented in the activity of women and immigrants, workers excluded from formal bargaining rights under law, and workers in contingent jobs, who have been among those most energetically organising against their bosses, setting up new mutual aid structures, and addressing 'intersectional' or 'co-constitutive' oppressions of race and gender both inside or outside of formal

trade union structures or alliances. More tentatively, 'working-class studies', has brought the lived experience of working-class people to the fore in ways that recall the early years of cultural studies.

As with social history, however, there has been fairly little linkage between current Marxist studies of movements and the body of work that has developed in social movement studies. Both sides could have a lot to learn from each other, if social movement studies were to abandon its general disinterest in the distinctive influence of capitalism on the dynamics of protest, and if labour researchers attended to the important theoretical as well as practical questions involved in critical issues concerning consciousness, organisation, and strategy. It might be premature to say that we all have a world to win, but a more open critical dialogue could be widely beneficial.

Similar arguments can be made, we think, within social movements. The construction of the 'anti-capitalist' (or anti-corporate, alterglobalisation, global justice, and so on) movement has involved the construction and dissemination of extensive popular analyses of neoliberalism and processes of commodification and dispossession. These analyses – present theoretically in the Marxist work of academics ranging from David Harvey to Toni Negri, but also in the strong Marxist influences on more popular figures from Naomi Klein to Michael Moore – did not simply emerge from isolated writers. They are inherent in the production of new kinds of *movement alliances* between indigenous peasants resisting extractive industries, workers struggling against deindustrialisation and capital flight, creative workers trying to make space for non-commodified art, solidarity movements trying to challenge global structures of debt, and so on. Such alliances, sometimes the product of long years of hard work, rely on the development of shared languages of contention – such as 'neoliberalism' or, indeed, 'anti-capitalism' – which enable the messy but practical business of confronting the institutions and cultural power of global élites to be coordinated.

Broadly Marxist analyses of contemporary global capitalism are now current among movement activists in ways that would have been hard to imagine in the early 1990s. With all their divergences, the different movements contesting this régime have learned to work together sufficiently well to constitute a 'movement of movements'. Within this, activists rooted in a plurality of leftist traditions encounter and engage each other in contests for leadership and representation, debates over strategy and tactics, discussions of alliances and issues, and deliberations over the appropriateness of the form of movement institutions (such as the contrast between 'horizontal' and 'vertical' organisation), and the direction that the continual development of collective oppositional action from below is taking. Moreover, and equally importantly, the 'movement of movements' has registered some significant achievements, such as forcing the abandonment of

the Multilateral Agreement on Investment, preventing any successful WTO trade round since 1999, scuppering the proposed Free Trade Area of the Americas and, in most Western countries, substantially undermining any popular legitimacy for the 'War on Terror' announced in 2001.

Indeed, the financial crash of 2008 was itself widely held to confirm the basic analysis of the ills of neoliberalism. Although élites have regained confidence and attempted to define the crash as the fault of excessive state spending rather than of unbridled finance capitalism, popular resistance to austerity measures – from Iceland to Greece and from Spain to the UK – suggests that this is a shallow hegemony indeed. Elsewhere, movements in Latin America have challenged US geopolitical hegemony and the Washington Consensus in a wide range of ways, going far beyond any isolated identity politics or cultural radicalism, combining extensive popular alliances, systematic analyses of the roots of injustice and, in some cases, serious attempts to remake the state. It is too early to tell what direction the popular struggles of the Arab Spring will take, or how European or North-American anti-austerity movements will develop, but all the indications are that Marxism can continue to play a key role in relating the structural causes of popular unrest to strategies to challenge those structures, in practice as well as in theory.

Producing this volume

This effort to fill a gap in the literature began as a set of discussions, over several years, at the annual Alternative Futures and Popular Protest (AFPP) conferences run by Colin Barker and Mike Tyldesley in Manchester. AFPP attracts a wide range of scholars and activists for three days of dialogue on social movements. Typically, the participants are heavily drawn from leftist circles in England, Scotland, Wales, and Ireland, with the regular participation of scholars and scholar-activists from across Europe, Canada, the USA, South Africa, and occasionally also Latin America, Australia and Asia. Trotskyists, autonomists, anarchists, and unaffiliated leftists, people committed to Marxism, people committed to developing questions framed by US-based social movement studies, people committed to poststructuralist theory, as well as resolute defenders of social science and history, thrash out their ideas and differences for three days of presentations, pub visits and group dinners. Over the years, one strand in these debates has been provided by scholars posing serious questions about social movements in a Marxist vein, and putting Marxist resources to innovative and provocative use. After organising a small micro-conference in advance of the 2008 meeting, we resolved to reach beyond even the wide range of scholars who have attended AFPP and to call for contributions to a listserv (online mailing list). The lively

listserv discussion shaped an eventual call for submissions of abstracts for the book. We received more than seventy.

The chapters in this book draw on scholars of anthropology, geography, history, politics, sociology, employment relations, civil society studies and East-Asian studies based in the USA, Britain, Canada, Ireland, Norway, South Africa and India. The book includes theoretical accounts of the relationship between Marxism and social movement studies; analyses of the development and internal tensions of social movements; and historical-comparative and global approaches to social movement studies. Showing the intellectual robustness and empirical purchase of a Marxist approach to movements, it pays attention both to the experience of Northern countries and to that of the global South (China, India, Africa, Latin America and the 'black Atlantic'); ranges historically from the nineteenth to twenty-first centuries; and engages with trade unions, slave and colonial revolts, environmentalism, LGBT movements, peace activism and contemporary anti-capitalist struggles around the world.

With such a diverse set of chapters, there is no question of cooking up, in this volume, *the Marxist theory of social movements.* No such thing exists. Indeed, the reader will find disagreements among our authors, not just in emphases, but in interpretation both of social movement studies *and* of Marxism. Nevertheless, we all agree that it is important to raise the questions of *what a Marxist approach to social movements might look like, and how students of Marxism and social movements can learn from each other.* In answering these questions, the contributors to the volume emphasise different criteria: some are more concerned with faithfulness to the writings of Marx and later authors; others with the empirical and logical strengths offered by a Marxist approach; while still others emphasise Marxism's usefulness for movements. Like the listserv discussion that preceded the proposal stage of this book – and there have been many worthy contributions for which we simply could not find space – this volume is an invitation to what we hope will become a spirited conversation.

In this volume

The book is divided into three sections. The first deals with theoretical frameworks. It explores the possibilities of relating Marxism to social movement theory by asking two sets of questions. What theory of social movements might be said to be implicit within Marxism? And how might a Marxist approach to movements respond to the silences and limitations of conventional social movement theory?

Colin Barker's chapter suggests that the language of 'class struggle' can be translated into a language of 'social movement' – with a Marxist accent. While

contemporary social movement theories rightly stress the networked character of social movements, they pay less attention to their heterogeneity and internal debates. Marx and Engels's writing presents an enormous variety of movements which together encompassed both 'the class struggle' and 'the social movement in general': a perspective on totality characteristic of Marxism. In contemporary capitalism, as the relationship of states and movements has changed, 'the class struggle' now runs not simply between movements but also through them. These developments pose new problems, in areas such as transformations during mass struggles, contradictions in popular consciousness and the relationship of organisations to movements, which this chapter discusses in relation to the work of Luxemburg, Lenin, Trotsky and Gramsci.

Alf Nilsen and Laurence Cox take up the argument that, although Marxism was written 'from and for' social movements, it lacks an explicit theory of social movements. Their chapter sets out to formulate such a theory, outlining a conception of social movements as both 'from below' and (typically, more powerfully) 'from above' and proposing the interaction between these as key in the making and unmaking of social structures. It explores some of the key aspects of this encounter, and proposes a processual analysis in which movements can develop from one level of strength and complexity to another.

Gabriel Hetland and Jeff Goodwin take up the problem from the other side, as it were, in one of two chapters that engages social movement theory more explicitly. They suggest that while 1970s scholarship on social movements often integrated an understanding of capitalist dynamics, more recent work has largely ignored the enabling and constraining effects of capitalism, despite the ever-increasing power of global capitalism. Rather than ascribing this to the shift of attention towards 'new' social movements that have little or nothing to do with capitalism, this chapter shows how the LGBT movement has been powerfully shaped by capitalism, despite neither representing a class nor making primarily economic demands.

John Krinsky takes a different cut at the same issues, but ties together issues within US-dominated social movement theory and the Marxist approaches laid out in Barker's and Cox and Nilsen's earlier chapters. Specifically, the chapter focuses on five areas of Marxist theory – totality, contradiction, immanence, coherence, and praxis – that can more effectively synthesise the disparate parts of contemporary social movement theory and research into a whole that is both more critical and more useful for activists.

The second part of the book explores what a Marxist perspective on social movements has to offer by way of concrete analysis, arguing for a more developmental and dialectical understanding of how movements actually work and in exploring the political questions facing movement activists and thinkers.

It draws on historical and contemporary cases from three continents to bring Marxist theory to bear on questions about organisation, institutionalisation, and engagement with the state. Each chapter probes the immanent potentials in existing forms of popular self-organisation.

Laurence Cox's chapter takes up more explicitly the nineteenth-century usage of 'social movement' as the political self-organisation of the majority of society, a notion which entails a broader sense of possibility and a more interactive sense of social movement development than exists in mainstream social movement theory. It articulates this position theoretically in relation to E.P. Thompson's classic *Making of the English Working Class* – a pivotal book in Marxist thought and in social history – and empirically in relation to the immense variety of working-class self-organisation in contemporary Ireland, which typically eludes more static approaches.

Marc Blecher explores the relationship between the nature of the Chinese working class and the forms of proletarian movements in China from early-twentieth-century industrialisation until now. His chapter argues that the close interconnection of workplace and community in China led to a flourishing of local workplace struggles at the same time as it made it hard to extend working-class power to the regional or national level. Like Cox's piece, it extends the conversation on class formation that was so fertile in the 1980s to social movement theory and contemporary concerns in a way that resituates it at one of the key centres of contemporary capitalist expansion.

Taking aim at both state-centric views of social movements as seeking to restore the developmental state and poststructuralist understandings of movements as rejecting modernisation *tout court*, Alf Gunvald Nilsen's chapter analyses popular opposition to the Narmada dam projects in contemporary India. In showing this opposition's intimate relationship with changing modes of state action as well as its strategic failure in relying on the state as the locus for political action, it contests both state-centric and poststructuralist understandings of the constraints placed on movements by their opponents and by their own stances towards the state. Echoing, in some respects, mainstream social movement scholarship on institutionalisation, 'channeling' of protest, and movement-countermovement dynamics, it nevertheless goes beyond this work by resituating the questions on the broader canvas of global development-politics.

Patrick Bond, Ashwin Desai and Trevor Ngwane analyse the contemporary impasse on the Left in South Africa, made all the more pressing by the extremely high levels of protest there. Drawing on Trotsky's theory of 'combined and uneven development', they explain the development of the problems of neoliberal cooptation of movements – diverted from agitation to 'service delivery' – the strong tendencies toward localism in the widespread protests of the 'poors', and the failures of movement leadership in the context of the neoliberal programme unleashed after Apartheid by the African National Congress and its governing allies, the Congress of South African Trade Unions and the South African Communist Party. They propose a 'combined and uneven Marxism' as a way to investigate the systematic and conjunctural aspects of the current impasse, one that fully recognises the importance of the development of organic intellectuals from within the growing number of different sectors of South-African society that are under neoliberal attack.

Ralph Darlington's chapter looks at debates within industrial relations about bureaucracy and rank-and-file relations within trade unions. It argues, against criticism that the dichotomy is conceptually unsound, that a Marxist approach can give it nuance and multidimensionality. Darlington makes the case that the 'Michelsian dilemma' of inexorable bureaucratisation is not an 'iron law'. Rather, bureaucratisation is a process that occurs in particular cases, and to greater or lesser degrees, through a set of determinations both internal and external to an organisation. The chapter suggests a broader applicability of this approach to social movement organisations beyond labour.

A context of extreme repression, the uprooting of an annual encampment of protesting teachers, led to the 2006 uprising in Oaxaca (Mexico), which Chris Hesketh examines in his chapter. Drawing on the Marxist geography of figures such as Henri Lefebvre and David Harvey, Hesketh compares the Oaxaca uprising to the Zapatista uprising in 1994 in terms of the 'spatial projects' that each expressed. The central idea is that capital requires the conquest of space, and that the APPO movement in Oaxaca and the Zapatista movement in Chiapas, in different ways and with varying degrees of success, extended new social relations over spaces that Mexican and international capital sought for its own. Hesketh acknowledges that these spatial projects are incomplete, and raises the question of whether these insurrectionary projects are at all compatible with parliamentary strategies or other engagements with the state that risk the 'reinscription' of the movements into the 'normal' politics of 'coerced marginalisation' of Mexico's poor and indigenous communities.

The third section of the book is largely comparative-historical, drawing on a variety of historical cases to develop ideas about how to understand contemporary movement formations. It builds on the previous sections in that it probes areas of activity that social movement studies often leave aside, such as the development of localised oppositional cultures, contradictory consciousness, and the importance of the *longue durée* in political analysis.

The section begins with Paul Blackledge's observation that social movement theory has largely sidestepped the investigation of the 'cultures of resistance' that generate all manner of challenges to the 'rule of law,' including social movements. Blackledge draws on the British Marxist historians of the mid-twentieth century, arguing that Bakhtinian views of language can underwrite their ideas of class consciousness and identity, and offer a response to postmodernist challenges. He invites us to recognise that even other movements that make claims for specific identities, and that pursue direct action rather than radical reformism – namely, 'new social movements' – are best seen as different aspects of a reaction to capitalist alienation. He asks, in other words, that we see apparently different sorts of movements as related facets of a whole, but whose mediations through language differ and diverge.

Neil Davidson also considers different sorts of social movements, but here trains his focus on right-wing movements, such as Catholic Absolutism in nineteenth-century Naples, the Ku Klux Klan in the postbellum American South, and the Irish Protestant Ascendancy in the early 1920s. Davidson cuts against the grain of Nilsen and Cox's argument about social movements from above, as he insists that right-wing movements can also be 'from below' both in terms of their class origins, and in terms of their challenge to the hegemony of ruling élites. Davidson then applies lessons from these cases to the current surge of 'Tea Party' politics in the United States. He takes issue with Lenin's suggestion that even when masses' revolt is motivated by their most 'reactionary fantasies' they are '*objectively* attacking capital'. Instead, Davidson argues – this time *with* Lenin – that socialists have to remain committed not just to following movements, but to offering direction to them.

Hira Singh offers a historical defence of class analysis when applied to nineteenth-century India, both the part under British rule and that under Indian jurisdiction. He shifts the ground in this section somewhat away from questions of consciousness, but complements Høgsbjerg's argument for what critical race-theorists call 'intersectionality', or the mutual reinforcement and mutual alteration of various 'types' of oppression and resistance. Seeing the division of India into separate jurisdictional areas as the outcome of resistance to colonialism over the long period of British involvement, Singh takes equal aim at Marx's own writings on India (which saw the Revolt of 1857 as an anomalous outburst) and at writers in the subaltern studies tradition for not fully appreciating the dynamics of colonial class formation in India.

Questions about 'reactionary fantasies' and much else resurface in Christian Høgsbjerg's chapter on C.L.R. James's *History of Negro Revolt*. James's classic work on the Haitian Revolution, *The Black Jacobins*, was situated within a larger perspective on the importance of black movements in the making of the modern world.[65] His analysis took in the USA from the Civil War to Marcus Garvey, anti-colonial rebellions and millennial religion in Africa, and contemporary struggles in the Caribbean. Importantly, far from discounting protest that was

---

65. James 2001.

not explicitly – or even 'objectively' – class-based, James argued eloquently for the importance of autonomous black protest, even when it took such forms as Garveyism or the otherworldly Jehovah's Witnesses. James probed what Gramsci called 'contradictory consciousness', namely, the mismatch between how people live and how they talk about their lives and form belief systems about them. James saw in these contradictions potentials that could be developed in directions different from those of nationalism and religious fervour, holding up the 'San Domingo' – Haitian – Revolution as a comparative yardstick. Further, the chapter uses James's work to think about the dialectical relationship both between the political economy of global capitalism and racialised hierarchies of domination, and between processes of class and racialised struggle as an important corrective to analyses that place 'race' and 'class' as essentially opposed identities.

The last four chapters of the book focus on contemporary social movements against neoliberal capitalism and the difficulty of confronting a mode of governing that explicitly attacks collectivities.

Chik Collins uses a Marxist approach to cognition, developed through the work of Lev Vygotsky, and broadly compatible with the 'dialogical' theories of language propounded by Bakhtin and Vološinov. He explores how the Scottish state's relegitimation of the 'political voice' of the poor gave working-class organisers early warning of a new twist in the neoliberal agenda, which sought to pit the poor against their own organisations. The chapter gives a twist on the organisational studies in the second part of the book by showing how state actors can seek to insert themselves into class formation, by claiming for themselves the right to speak for the poor. The chapter also offers an example of a direct involvement of research with community organising.

Elizabeth Humphrys develops Gramsci's concept of the organic intellectual to distinguish between movement campaigners, who focus on a single sector of the movement, and movement dialoguers, who aim to give expression to a wider process of social change. Reflecting on the absence of a structure for such dialoguers in the Australian Global Justice Movement, she argues that this was an important cause of its rapid collapse after 11 September 2001. Humphrys's chapter dovetails well with work in social movement studies that investigate the strategic importance of people occupying various positions in movement networks. That she derives a similar perspective from Gramsci's work is another indication of the fruitfulness of greater interchange.

Heike Schaumberg, by contrast, asks a fundamental question about the self-organisation of the working class. In contrast to Humphrys's shared interest with Gramsci in identifying leadership positions and potentials within movements, Schaumberg draws on a study of the 2001 uprising in Argentina to argue that

that inherited notions of what organisation looks like block us from understanding new or alternative forms of working-class self-organisation. This is important both because the destruction of working-class communities' organisational infrastructure by neoliberal policies generates new organisation, which may be more or less conducive to political action and more or less likely to attract official repression.

David McNally analyses the dialectics of working-class reformation in the neoliberal period. He discusses the convergence of *campesino* and indigenous resistance with rural and urban wage-labourer resistance in Bolivia (2000–7) and Oaxaca (2006) into new kinds of class movements, and suggests that there is a common dynamic between them and the uprisings in Tunisia and Egypt, where radical labour unions played key coordinating and instigating roles in the protests in early 2011. McNally shows that these are processes of class formation and of generalising a new class consciousness. Citing E.P. Thompson, he argues that in these struggles, 'class manifests itself in and through key dynamics of modern society'; it describes *'the way the machine works* once it is set in motion – not this interest or that interest, but the *friction* of interests – the movement itself, the heat, the thundering noise'.

We feel that between them the various chapters and perspectives collected in this volume show the 'reality and power, the 'this-worldliness' of Marxist thinking on social movements, and demonstrate its relevance to movement-activists and researchers alike. In reflecting on, distilling and articulating the development of movement practice and theory across so many movements, periods and regions of the world, they also continue the deeper Marxist project of a theory which is not simply 'applied from above' to the popular movements that shake states and transform economic relations, but remains open to learning and dialogue in both directions.

Part One

Theoretical Frameworks

Marxism and Social Movements

Class Struggle and Social Movements
Colin Barker

For almost forty years we have stressed the class
struggle as the immediate driving power of history, and in particular the class struggle between
the bourgeoisie and proletariat as the great lever
of the modern social revolution... We expressly
formulated the battle-cry: The emancipation of
the working class is conquered by the working
classes themselves.[1]

1

Marxism's approach to social movements is framed by
a theory of 'class struggle'. Marx denied that he discovered the 'class struggle', attributing this to the historians of the French Revolution. He did, however, make a
fundamental claim about his own approach:

What I did that was new was to prove: 1) that the
existence of classes is only bound up with particular historical phases in the development of
production, 2) that the class struggle necessarily
leads to the dictatorship of the proletariat, 3) that
this dictatorship itself only constitutes the transition to the abolition of all classes and to a classless society.[2]

For Marx and Engels, 'class struggle' did not simply
describe a core characteristic of historical forms of

1. Marx and Engels 1975a, pp. 374–5.
2. Marx 1965a.

society, but was the means by which capitalism could be revolutionised and classes themselves could be eradicated. Since their time, of course, the word 'dictatorship' has taken on terrifying associations, which were not part of their meaning.[3] They sought a radical democratisation of political, social and economic life, carried through by working people. In 1871, they found a model of this 'dictatorship of the proletariat' in the ultra-democratic organisation of the Paris Commune.[4]

This transformation demanded a *social revolution*, for two reasons. First, no other method could separate the ruling class from their property and power. Second, only active participation in a revolutionary movement could enable the oppressed to get rid of 'the muck of ages' and transform themselves into subjects capable of remaking the world.[5] Here, goal and means, social and personal transformation, were indissolubly connected.

Thus, questions about revolution and social movements did not form two distinct literatures, as is common on most contemporary social science. They were parts of a single story.

But a big question remains: how to get from present-day capitalist reality to this goal? In *The Poverty of Philosophy*, Marx offered a metaphorical answer: the working class as a 'class *vis-à-vis* capital' must become a 'class for itself'. But that gnomic phrase tells us nothing about what political processes might be involved. David Lockwood suggested that Marxists tend to imagine a 'proletarian end-shift', in which, one fine day, the entire working class will finally agree together that it is time to end capitalism.[6] Such a scenario is deeply implausible. The whole experience of workers' movements over two centuries suggests that things never become so simplified. In any case, Marx and Marxists supported and participated in a host of movements that make no sense if they are simply reduced to a notion of 'class against class' – resistance, for example, to slavery, to national oppression, to skill-privilege, to racism, to sexism, to homophobia, to religious discrimination, to oppression of peasants and students, to imperialist wars and environmental degradation, and so on. What have these matters to do with a 'class for itself'?

What, then, is the theoretical status of 'class struggle', and how might it be sensibly related to discussion of 'social movements'?

3. Draper 1987.
4. Marx 1974b; Engels 1971, p. 34.
5. Marx and Engels 1965a, p. 86.
6. Lockwood 1992.

2

Conceptually and historically, 'class struggle' precedes any 'formation' of classes as potential actors, or any necessary 'consciousness' of class. Exploring eighteenth-century England, Edward Thompson pointed to a set of processes and relationships which he termed 'class struggle without class'. The customary practices of the eighteenth-century poor included forms of everyday resistance, which the poor did not conceptualise in 'class' terms, although these arose from the antagonisms inherent in developing capitalism. Further, Thompson's study of the early-nineteenth-century working class explored how English workers did, indeed, develop a 'class sense' of the conflict between themselves and the British bourgeoisie and its state. The practice of class struggle, one might say, led workers to form themselves into a consciously developing 'class', and it was in this sense that 'the working class was present at its own making'.[7]

Indeed, Thompson gives very good expression to much of the 'relational' quality of the term class:

> When, in discussing class, one finds oneself too frequently commencing sentences with 'it', it is time to place oneself under some historical control, or one is in danger of becoming the slave of one's own categories. Sociologists who have stopped the time-machine and, with a good deal of conceptual huffing and puffing, have gone down to the engine-room to look, tell us that nowhere at all have they been able to locate and classify a class. They can only find a multitude of people with different occupations, incomes, status-hierarchies, and the rest. Of course they are right, for class is not this or that part of the machine, but *the way the machine works* once it is set in motion – not this interest and that interest, but the *friction* of interests – the movement itself, the heat, the thundering noise. Class is a social and cultural formation (often finding institutional expression) which cannot be defined abstractly, or in isolation, but only in terms of relationship with other classes; and, ultimately, the definition can only be made in the medium of *time* – that is, action and reaction, change and conflict...[8]

'Class struggle' is inherently a process involving (at least) two sides. One side involves multifarious forms of resistance to exploitation and oppression; the other includes the equally varied means by which ruling groups work to maintain their positions and to contain such resistance. Studying class struggle requires as much attention to the activities of ruling classes and their allies as to those who may, potentially, oppose them.

---

7. Thompson 1963; 1978a.
8. Thompson 1965, p. 357.

3

Historically, class struggle has taken many forms. Behind these variations lie what Marx called 'the mode of production' – or sometimes 'mode of intercourse' or 'mode of cooperation'. These terms summarise the characteristic ways in which, over whole epochs, people organise the reproduction of their necessities and their social relations. We can distinguish modes of production by the ways that surplus labour is 'pumped' out of direct producers. This

> determines the relationship of domination and servitude, as this grows directly out of production itself and reacts back on it as a determinant. On this is based the entire configuration of the economic community rising from the actual relations of production, and hence also its specific political form. It is in each case the direct relationship of the owners of the conditions of production to the immediate producers ... in which we find the innermost secret, the hidden basis of the entire social edifice, and hence also the political form of the relationship of sovereignty and servitude, in short, the specific form of state in each case.[9]

Within capitalism, the 'specific economic form' of surplus labour is *surplus-value*, surplus in the money-form, circulated in commodity markets and accumulated by the bearers of capital. A number of core contradictions mark this form of social productive cooperation, conditioning the forms of class struggle.

First, capitalist appropriation rests on its seeming opposite. Marx's analysis of *value, money* and *exchange* initially accepts a crucial claim within liberal political economy: namely, that these core economic relationships involve a form of *human freedom and equality*. Expanding capitalist commodity relations have proved compatible with the development of 'rights': to equality before the law, to freedoms of contract and expression, to universal adult suffrage. Generalised market exchange has built 'a very Eden of the innate rights of man ... the exclusive realm of Freedom, Equality, Property and Bentham'.[10] Capitalism does not require the directly coercive and unfree relations of ancient despotisms, slaveries and feudalisms. Indeed, much of the politics of class struggle over the past two centuries has involved a contested but real expansion of rights. If the human rights project is still uncompleted, its proponents also have much to celebrate.

Second, however, an exclusive focus on the 'surface' of market exchanges fails to account for capitalism's all-too-apparent inequalities of wealth and power. To understand these, we must explore the netherworld of production, outside and beneath the market, where economic necessity compels workers owning only their labour power to seek employment. Inside the workplace, equal rights are

9. Marx 1981, p. 927.
10. Marx 1976a, p. 280.

dramatically transformed into a world of 'despotism' where some are bosses and others are 'hands', where the employment contract demands 'a promise to obey'. Market freedom disappears: workers are subjected to the will of others, and labour to enrich the property-controlling minority. Capitalism's socio-politics combine antagonistic principles: freedom and unfreedom, equality and inequality, property and propertylessness.

Third, capitalism is dominated by not only exploitation but also competition. Competition between capitals provides the system's core compulsion, 'accumulation for the sake of accumulation'. Each capital, in order to survive, must endlessly innovate in ways of extracting surplus value from labour, giving capitalism its dynamic expansionism. This unprecedented system has generated vast increases in human productivity, forcibly drawing the entire globe into a single interacting world economy. It is also a system beyond anyone's power to control. Capitalism simultaneously generates untold riches alongside grinding poverty, ferocious expansions and convulsive collapses, immense growth in both human creativity and destructiveness.

The 'pumping' of surplus value sets up systematic conflicts across the whole face of society. Capital's endless drive for surplus value directly opposes wage labour's needs, making 'class struggle' an inherent property of this system of social relations. Yet, even considered at its most abstract level, class struggle is interwoven with competitive impulses. If those who play the part of capital form a working fraternity *vis-à-vis* labour, they are also, at the same time, a band of 'enemy brothers'.[11] And if the bearers of wage labour may represent a unity *vis-à-vis* capital, competition also divides them into potentially 'enemy brothers and sisters'.

This suggests that translating 'class interests' into political action must always be a difficult process within capitalism, for the social forces at its heart are characterised by competitive rivalries and mutual conflicts. To add to the problems, Marx identifies two other reasons why the proletariat might find its 'grave-digging' work difficult. First, subjected to 'the dull compulsion of economic relations', the worker 'by education, tradition, habit, looks upon the conditions of that mode of production as self-evident laws of Nature'.[12] Second, ideologies supportive of the dominant class(es) have their impact: 'The ruling ideas of every age have ever been the ideas of its ruling class'.[13] Marxism's posited goal and means, it seems, will be difficult to achieve, and certainly not 'automatic'.

There is a further complication. Historically, capitalism has expanded not only by 'economic' means. Its history includes colonial subjugation of whole

11. Marx 1981, p. 362.
12. Marx 1976a, p. 899.
13. Marx and Engels 1973, p. 85.

peoples, slavery and forced labour, coerced breaking up of older systems of social reproduction, immensely destructive wars, along with the promotion of racist, sexual, religious and other oppressions. Both capitalism's development and the resistance against it have always entailed more than a simple economic opposition between capital and labour.

4

Marxists thus face a series of theoretical and practical-strategic problems. Part of capitalism's complexity rests on its multi-layered quality, whose representation requires different degrees of generality. Opposition to capitalism must handle multiple manifestations, which are, while interlinked, not all of the same order. Marx himself was explicit about the distinction between different levels of abstraction and concreteness.[14]

Marx's master work, *Capital*, mostly explores the capitalist system at a high level of abstraction. Its landscape is populated by 'bearers of economic relations': the capitalist, the labourer, the financier, the landowner, and so on. These appear as 'cartoon' characters lacking all but the most general history. They speak no definite language and draw on no particular cultural traditions. These abstractions are required to identify capitalism's underlying processes, relationships and tendencies of development. They are not, however, the end of the process of portraying the whole system. The whole theoretical movement in Marx's presentation involves an expanding spiral, from the 'core' of capitalism towards its variegated 'surface'. At each step, new 'determinations' and complexities are introduced, and Marx's 'cartoon characters' both take on additional features, and face new strategic problems.

Thinking about 'class struggle' in these terms, it is apparent that it, too, is a concept involving a high level of abstraction, generalising from a multitude of forms of both domination and resistance across whole historical epochs. Much greater historical concreteness is required, however, to explore how people, as Marx puts it, 'fight it out'. *Classes* are not themselves coherent political actors, capable of acting as single entities: they are inwardly divided by particular interests, subject to conflicting impulses. 'Class issues', meaning problems arising from capitalism's underlying character, do, certainly, confront political actors, but how these actors respond is 'mediated' by a host of concrete particulars.

Marxism is sometimes described as a 'structuralist' theory – with no real room for social movements, or, indeed, for human agency. This seems mistaken. Rather, Marx construes agency and structure as dialectical poles of an ongoing

---

14. Marx 1904; 1973; Ilyenkov 1982; Ollman 2003.

and developing unity. Human beings actively create their own history, though not under conditions of their own choosing. On one hand, they necessarily enter into social relations that are the product of previous activity and independent of their will.[15] Such social relations possess their own 'emergent properties' independent of the individuals who compose them: for instance, divisions of labour, rules, patterns of rights and responsibilities. They co-exist at a whole number of levels, all the way from epochal 'modes of production' to the immediate and local relations of family, neighbourhood, or workplace. On the other hand, the people who, as active, reflective beings, compose these various systems of activity also actively remake them as they 'live' them. They regularly run up against features of these systems that impede them in the pursuit of their (self-developing) needs and goals. As they seek to resolve these engendered problems, they act in ways that are liable to disrupt existing patterns, generating conflicts that potentially reconfigure both their social relations and themselves as actors. Such a general conception underlies a Marxist approach to social movements.

Only at a level more immediate than that explored in Marx's *Capital* can we locate definite people, speaking in particular tongues and with their own histories and traditions, struggling to understand and achieve control of their material and social conditions. It is at this more immediate level, of more 'concrete' socio-cultural formations, that 'social movements' emerge, as specific forms of social and political activity. Movements are *mediated* expressions of class struggle.

5

How might Marxists approach the question of 'social movements' or 'movements'? Here, we come up against a difficulty: Marx, Engels and their successors regularly used these terms, but seem never to have defined them. We shall first need some work of interpretation and reconstruction. There is some kinship between Marxist usages and those in contemporary academic scholarship, but also some significant differentiation. Most academic scholarship does not attempt to link 'movements' to 'class struggle' or, indeed, to 'revolution'.

Defining social movements, it has been suggested, is a 'theoretical nightmare'.[16] Difficult as the enterprise is, given the enormous variety of movement phenomena, some points of outline do seem possible.

First, movements are *collective achievements*. Some forms of resistance to oppression and exploitation remain largely *individual*. Thus, in the decades before the Civil Rights movement, black resistance to Jim Crow in the American

---

15. Marx 1904.
16. Marwell and Oliver 1984.

South included extensive *migration* to the North and West. Class struggle under 'Communism' took individual forms, as absenteeism, job-changing and 'lack of enthusiasm'.[17] A brilliant ethnography of environmental suffering in an Argentinian shantytown describes how social and political agencies contribute to a 'confusion' that inhibits effective collective organisation.[18] By contrast, a *movement* entails some kind of organisation, implying not just collective identities but collective *projects*, and mutual sharing of ideas. A movement's emergence transcends atomised ways of coping with problems engendered by capitalism's workings. This is one reason for Marxism's interest in social movements: collective organisation contains immanent possibilities of alternative ways of organising human cooperation.

Second, movements have a characteristic organisational shape. They are 'reticulate' – network-like – entities.[19] It is perhaps easier to define a movement by what it is *not*: 'organisations' – parties, unions, churches, NGOs, militias, and so on – are distinct from but may be part of movements. A movement's 'network' pattern is immensely variable, and capable of being reshaped and extended, depending on its connecting 'nodes', or broadly the ways that its various 'activists' relate to each other. Being 'reticulate', it permits actors with varied perspectives, interests and associations to mobilise themselves in their own fashion and determine their own contributions to its overall development.

Third – a feature less developed in the academic literature[20] – movements are also simultaneously fields of argument. What is the movement's meaning and purpose? What is it seeking to defend or change? How are its boundaries defined? Who are its opponents? How should it define and how pursue its objectives? What strategies, tactics, repertoires of collective activity should it deploy? How should it respond to specific events and crises? All these and other matters are open to ongoing contestation among a movement's varied adherents.

Fourth, participation in such arguments is not restricted to a movement's adherents. A movement's *opponents* have good reasons to try to influence how it interprets and seeks to change the world. Their means of exerting such influence vary considerably, but if they are powerful they include the deployment of state-force and law, the mass media, or the cooptation of movement 'leaders'. The 'class struggle' occurs not only *between* movements and their antagonists, but also *within* them: their ideas, forms of organisation and repertoires of contention are all within their opponents' 'strategic sights'.[21]

---

17. Cliff 1974; Hankiss 1989.
18. Auyero and Swistun 2009.
19. Gerlach and Hine 1970; Diani 1992.
20. But see Zirakzadeh 2006.
21. Shandro 1995.

Fifth, movements are neither necessarily 'bottom-up' nor 'progressive' phenomena. Alf Nilsen and Laurence Cox suggest the category of 'movements from above'.[22] Capitalism's characteristic dynamics demand periodic restructuring of social relationships, sometimes in quite fundamental ways. Ruling-class initiatives sometimes involve many of the features of 'movement' organisation: campaigning, mobilising, seeking allies, publicising arguments, and so on. Nor are movements the property only of the Left. The 'Jim Crow' system in the US South was first installed by an organised racist movement, with élite backing, directed at the subjugation of the former slaves. That racism also contributed to the defeat of American populism and to major defeats for labour in the 1920s. Movements of the Left have regularly had to contend with not only employers and states, but also opposing movements that included members of 'lower classes'. From 'Church and King' mobs to the Black Hundreds, from Mussolini's *fascisti* and Hitler's black and brown shirts to the contemporary regrowth of European fascism, the Right has adopted movement forms as its own, along with many elements of the 'repertoire' of the Left.

Even 'movements from below' can combine 'progressive' and 'regressive' features in one and the same struggle. Marc Steinberg explores how early-nineteenth-century silk weavers developed forms of organisation and demands that simultaneously defended their trade against capital's depredations and lowered the status of women.[23] Those who campaign to defend jobs and community resources within decaying industries and towns often summon up, among those they mobilise, voices blaming migrant workers, 'cheap labour' in other countries, and targets other than capital and the state.

6

Marxist thinking on social movements is shaped by its characteristic focus on capitalism as a system, or *totality*. Marx and Engels, like other nineteenth-century thinkers, wrote of 'the social movement' to describe the upsurge in popular organisation in their own period. The term encompassed revolutions, trade unionism, suffrage movements, nascent feminism, emerging socialist and utopian ideas, demands for national independence and unification, and peasant-pressure for land. All these, taken together, constituted a single reality: 'the social movement', a notion with a loose *class* reference, indexing political and social organisation by 'the poor', 'the plebs', 'the working classes', all those contesting 'the social question'.

22. Nilsen and Cox 2006; see also Nilsen and Cox in this volume.
23. Steinberg 1994.

The emergence of 'the social movement' announced transformations in the activities and resources of the dispossessed similar to those explored by Charles Tilly: the shift from *local* and often 'customary' forms and repertoires of popular resistance-activity to *national* and *political* forms,[24] and also to transnational forms. 'The social movement' denoted a whole field of emerging political and social struggles, seen as mutually interacting, sometimes underground and sometimes overt, and together embodying a challenge to both inherited and new forms of class privilege and domination. For Marx and Engels, the social movement was a whole with many parts, moving – at variable speed and with differential success – towards a condition where it might engage in capitalism's total overthrow.

This usage is rather unfamiliar today, although 1960s radicals saw no difficulty in talking about 'the movement' as a single differentiated whole. Nowadays, however, most students of 'social movements' work with a background assumption: that social movements are many, disconnected from each other, and thus capable of being studied in isolation from each other. That assumption has become a kind of taken-for-granted common sense, which structures much important work.

Consider, for example, Doug McAdam's classic study, *Political Process and the Development of Black Insurgency*.[25] McAdam's work, clearly influenced by aspects of Marxism, argues that neither pluralist nor élite theory adequately captures the reality of political power relations. He shows how the Civil Rights movement, in its heyday, made use of the internal dynamics of US politics to both isolate the Southern supremacists and compel a reluctant federal government to intervene on its side. He explores the decline of black insurgency in the later 1960s: the 'Southern question' had been largely settled by granting essential civil rights, and when the movement attempted to take up wider issues about racism and inequality in US society, it was beaten back. There is, though, a question McAdam does not address, which greatly exercised the minds of movement participants in the period. *Could things have turned out differently?* That question touches on more than just 'black insurgency' for – though following their own slightly different timetables – *other* movements born in the 1960s also experienced 'heyday' and 'decline'.

McAdam focuses only on the question of *black* insurgency. However, as the Civil Rights movement developed, black insurgency became enmeshed with other issues and conflicts, expanding its strategic dilemmas. Should Civil Rights organisations take positions on the Vietnam War? Was there any place in such organisations for whites, or for alliances with 'white' organisations and movements? If the 'black power' slogan were adopted, which of a range of its possible

---

24. Tilly 1986; 1993.
25. McAdam 1982.

meanings should be stressed? Different groupings – SCLC, SNCC, CORE, cultural nationalists, the Black Panthers, DRUM and others – developed answers to these questions with greater and lesser degrees of promise. Further complexity was injected by the growth, *within and against* existing and developing movement organisations, of second-wave feminism, whose first impulses were felt within black and student radical organisations.[26] Besides all that, moreover, there was a small but real increase in trade-union combativity, notably in 'wildcat' strikes involving both white and black workers, though not on the scale of the 1930s;[27] while extensive resistance movements developed within and around the US military.[28]

The growing variety of movement participants also expanded the range of contested issues. Questions about class power and the nature of the whole social system forced themselves onto movement agendas. The same fragmentation that marked the decline in black insurgency also occurred among students: Students for a Democratic Society, faced with a strategic impasse, fell apart after 1968, splitting into 'a system of sects'.[29] No relatively hegemonic party of the Left emerged within North America: that failure made its own contribution to the decline of black insurgency, and was replicated in interconnected movements across the world in the 1960s and early 1970s.[30]

McAdam's narrow focus on a single movement, separate from its larger context and its own interconnections with other movements, leaves part of the story untold. The apparently abstract question of 'totality' (or 'the social movement') suggests relevant questions to be posed about and within movements. It implies critical probing of the limits of existing forms of movement activity, organisation and ideas, and of the kinds of *interventions* that Marxists might make with respect to existing movement practice and ideology. It also implies a very *broad* reading of 'class struggle'.

7

Some accounts assume that 'class struggle' refers only to immediate conflicts between capitalists and workers over matters like wages, hours or working conditions, and that such struggles enjoy some kind of 'primacy' over all other questions. There is little warrant for this in Marx.

---

26. Freeman 1975.
27. Fantasia and Stepan-Norris 2004, p. 568.
28. Neale 2001.
29. Friedman 1984–5.
30. Harman 1998a.

Certainly, Marx, Engels, and their successors paid great attention to the 'labour movement' aspect. They treated labour movements – trade unions, socialist parties, cooperatives, and such like – as embodying a *combination* of struggle against the rule of capital with submission to its dictates. Marx adopted a critical stance towards existing working-class practices and institutions. They did not – unlike many nineteenth-century socialists – *reject* unions and strikers, but rather urged that their demands (such as 'a fair day's work for a fair day's pay') and their forms of organisation were *insufficient*. Trade unionism limited itself to 'guerrilla war against the effects of the existing system' instead of using its organised power to end the wages system itself. The workers' movement needed to go beyond *economic* struggles to a *political* movement, 'a movement of the *class*, with the object of enforcing its interests in a general form, in a form possessing general, socially coercive force'.[31] However, Marx also celebrated the Ten Hours campaigns, and the cooperative workshops, not so much for their immediate achievements as for outlining the beginnings of a 'political economy of labour'.[32] The argument is characteristic of Marx's *revolutionary* theory: he looks within existing movement practice for *intimations* of future possibilities, for what is potentially *immanent* within it, and draws its significance to the movement's attention.

Trade-union struggles certainly do have a particular significance for Marxism. Workers engaging in strikes, the most characteristic form of union action, do – even if limited measure – challenge capital's power. Further, collective action itself changes its participants, partly transforming their views of their own potentials and their relations with fellow workers. In this sense, Lenin described unions as 'schools of communism'. However, the *limitations and contradictions* of trade unionism remain significant. As the 'labour movement' has emerged as a recognised and licensed agency of working-class representation, it has also commonly *narrowed* its ideological agenda. Trade unions appear as agencies of both struggle for and containment of workers' demands. They are, Gramsci commented, 'in a sense an integral part of capitalist society, and have a function that is inherent in a regime of private property ... The trade union has an essentially competitive, not communist, character. It cannot be the instrument for a radical renovation of society'.[33] That said, 'trade unionism' is not a fixed quality.[34] Like all movement questions, unions' forms and activities are highly *contestable*, and their history is one of great variation. 'Unofficial' and 'wildcat' strikes have been quite as numerous as 'official' strikes. In the USA, for example, the Knights

---

31. Marx 1965b, p. 271.
32. Marx 1974a, pp. 79–80.
33. Gramsci 1977b, p. 99.
34. Cliff and Gluckstein 1986.

of Labour and the IWW were very different from the AFL, while the rise of the CIO in the 1930s added yet more diversity to the mix. Distinct forms contain very different *developmental potentials*, from moderate bargaining over wages to revolutionary insurgency.

Moreover, 'labour movements' must be judged not simply by how they engage with employers, but how they relate to *other* forms of oppression and exploitation within capitalism. Marx, a strong supporter of Irish independence, explored how anti-Irish prejudice divided and held back the English workers' movement. In 1869, he changed his mind about how this problem might be solved:

> it is in the direct and absolute interest of the English working class to get rid of their present connection with Ireland... For a long time I believed that it would be possible to overthrow the Irish regime by English working class ascendancy... Deeper study has now convinced me of the opposite. The English working class will *never accomplish anything* before it has got rid of Ireland. The lever must be applied in Ireland. That is why the Irish question is so important for the social movement in general.[35]

Here, Marx takes the 'social movement in general' as his standpoint. He does not idealise the English workers' movement – indeed, his correspondence is full of rueful remarks about its general backwardness after Chartism's 1848 defeat. His opponents, like Proudhon and Bakunin, were prone to reduce the struggle for a dictatorship of the proletariat to a simplistic struggle of 'class against class', resisting his support for both Polish and Irish emancipation.[36] Marx, rather, treats the struggle against *national oppression*, in still-agrarian nations, as a condition for advance by 'the social movement in general'. Marx likewise supported the nascent anti-colonial movement in India. On anti-slavery, he was explicit about its inter-connection with the workers' movement: 'In the United States of North America, every independent movement of the workers was paralysed so long as slavery disfigured a part of the Republic. Labour cannot emancipate itself in the white skin where in the black it is branded'.[37] The centrality of 'class struggle' does not make 'economic' questions somehow 'more important'. Struggles against oppression – whether based on nationality, ethnicity, religion, gender, skill, or sexuality – are not *distinct* from or *opposed* to class struggle, but are mutually interdependent parts of the social movement against capitalism as a totality.

---

35. Marx 1965c, p. 232.
36. Anderson 2010, pp. 146–7.
37. Marx 1976a, p. 414.

8

After Marx and Engels died, their successors had to deal with a series of inter-related issues. The next century and a quarter saw capitalism expand across the globe, generate immensely convulsive wars and crises, and take on new political, economic and cultural forms. Its development transformed the character of its subordinate classes, reshaping both the environment and the inner character of 'the social movement'. Twentieth and twenty-first century Marxists were compelled to re-examine their theory and practice.

The first challenge was 'revisionism', developing within the new mass socialist parties and declaring both that capitalism had outgrown Marx's vision of a crisis-ridden system and that insurrectionary politics were outmoded. Socialism could advance by peaceful, parliamentary means.[38] In a trenchant critique, Rosa Luxemburg attacked the revisionists' theoretical premises, suggesting that they pointed not to a different road to socialism but to a *different* goal: 'Instead of taking a stand for the establishment of a new society they take a stand for surface modifications of the old society'.[39]

Revisionism – otherwise labelled 'reformism' or 'opportunism' – had only weakly developed in the world of Marx and Engels. When they met its manifestations, they opposed them, but it was not a pressing issue for their generation. They tended to *explain* it as an outgrowth of the continuing influence in the workers' movement of a petty bourgeoisie whose significance capitalist development would itself tend to diminish.[40] For their heirs, however, reformism became far a more critical problem, especially from 1914, when almost all the parties of the Second International backed their respective governments in the mutual slaughter of the First World War, opposing strikes and mutinies, and accepting worsened living conditions for the workers they claimed to represent. In the mass insurgencies that accompanied and accomplished the end of the War, Social-Democratic party and union leaders repeatedly demonstrated their strictly *counter*-revolutionary stances.

Better and worse accounts of the roots of reformism were produced. Lenin and Zinoviev, struggling to understand Social Democracy's great betrayal in 1914, attributed it to the influence of a 'labour aristocracy' of skilled workers, bought off with super-profits generated by imperialism. Here, one difficulty was that, if workers' standards of living in advanced capitalist nations did rise, the rise was *general* and not restricted to a small minority; also, the link to imperialism did not explain why similar tendencies appeared within movements in former

---

38. Bernstein 1961.
39. Luxemburg 1970, p. 78.
40. Johnson 1980.

colonies and 'backward countries'. Attempts to explain political phenomena as unmediated responses to economic relations are always liable to fail. Reformism's roots lie deeper.[41]

When Marx and Engels wrote the *Communist Manifesto*, the working class was a tiny minority of the world's productive population. Expanding capitalism enlarged it enormously over the next century and a half. In the process, capital and its states system altered their organisational forms, continuously reshaping the forces of labour and their potential for resistance. Movements, developing in both antagonistic and cooperative interaction with capitals and states, made significant if partial gains, notably in the whole field of 'rights', thereby altering capitalism's political structures. However, these transformations also brought new problems within movements.

Unevenly, often after severe struggles, more and more states conceded universal adult suffrage, expanded state 'welfare', licensed such forms of popular contestation as strikes, street demonstrations or public rallies, and loosened censorship, promoting the conditions for social movement expansion. In the same process, however, they sought to delimit and channel movements within paths conducive to continuing capitalist reproduction. Legalised movement organisations created new career-paths and statuses for officials and representatives in unions, parties, associations, NGOs and other bodies. Labour bureaucracies offer the very model of this emergent layer, mediating between movements and their opponents. Their growth as institutionalised parts of the 'earthworks of civil society' and the 'integral state'[42] set up new forms of differentiation within movements.

Reformism, an active and pervasive ingredient in movement-life, is a contradictory phenomenon. Functioning, on one side, as a protean mechanism of movement containment and limitation, it also embodies and expresses impulses to resistance and popular struggle – the very condition for its widespread influence. Reformism, deeply implanted within popular movements in upturns as well as downturns, set up significant strategic dilemmas for Marxists, committed to a vision of revolution in which real popular majorities become the conscious agents of transformation.

9

Practical questions about how Marxists might actively *intervene* in everyday movement life, and thus about *party* formation, were inextricably linked to issues regarding the forms and possibilities of popular consciousness, psychology,

---

41. Cliff 2003; Post 2010.
42. Gramsci 1971.

language and ideology. For Marx and Engels, these matters lacked the centrality they developed for their successors.

Revolution, Marx suggested, resembles a mole: it seems quite absent, and then suddenly surfaces. Long periods pass when nothing significant seems to change, when images of social stability and predictability predominate. They are unexpectedly interrupted by what Teodor Shanin calls 'axial' stages:

> The locks of rigidly patterned behaviours, self-censored imaginations, and self-evident stereotypes of common sense are broken, and the sky seems the limit, or all hell seems let loose. The 'alternativity' of history, the significance of consciousness, and particularly the scope for originality and choice, increase dramatically. The 'turning' taken then by a society establishes its pattern of development for decades or centuries...[43]

In such 'axial' stages, ideas and aspirations alter with great speed. Some of the key inner processes in what Sidney Tarrow would later term 'cycles of protest'[44] were first delineated by Rosa Luxemburg in a brilliant booklet on Russia's mass strikes in 1905.[45] These strikes revealed a revolutionary alternative to the piecemeal forms of struggle in Germany. There, 'political' issues were the business only of the parliamentary party, while trade-unions stuck to strictly 'economic' questions; on both sides, leadership apparatuses monopolised direction. Mass strikes involved struggles, simultaneously economic and political, in which the masses *directed themselves*, and in so doing advanced their own cultural and organisational capacities. These movements drew in previously unorganised layers as they spread out from the traditional militant centres, with a rapidity quite distinct from the measured timetables of electoral politics. Mass strikes generated new and old organisational forms: unions, political clubs, and the like. Most importantly, workers' very participation in collective struggle raised their intellectual and spiritual level. These phenomena occurred with a high degree of 'spontaneity', that is, independently of any leadership from a party or union.

There is enduring value in Luxemburg's account of how, in mass movements, workers transcend the 'normal' distinctions between politics and economics, draw in new layers, develop new organisational capacities and make large cultural and intellectual leaps. Indeed, if we recognise such phenomena in a host of movements over the century since *The Mass Strike*, it was Luxemburg who taught us to see them. Also, scaled down, they have also appeared in innumerable local

43. Shanin 1986, p. 312.
44. Tarrow 1989a; 1989b; 1994.
45. Luxemburg 1986.

struggles, as 'consciousness-raising during episodes of collective action'.[46] And yet, there is a difficulty.

Luxemburg suggested that the forces unleashed by such movements were unstoppable: 'once the ball is set rolling then social democracy, whether it wills it or not, can never again bring it to a standstill'. In 1918–19, she was proved tragically wrong. Germany's war was abruptly ended by a mass movement on an even larger scale than Luxemburg had described, with military mutinies, mass strikes, and the formation of workers' and soldiers' councils. The SPD and trade-union leaders, initially opposing the insurgency, nonetheless sprang to its head and sought to contain it within parliamentarist limits, allying themselves with right-wing army officers in the *Freikorps*. When, in January 1919, the newly formed Communist Party, against Luxemburg's advice, launched a premature insurrection of the minority (the 'Spartakus Uprising'), the *Freikorps* was deployed. Luxemburg, Liebknecht and other communist leaders were murdered, and the movement was thrown back.

Luxemburg's brilliant insights in *The Mass Strike* lacked a sense of their opposites. In absolutist Russia, the phenomena Luxemburg describes could appear in relatively pure form, for all parties and unions were illegal. Elsewhere, however, popular insurgency regularly appeared in combination with forces seeking to derail it, producing a *struggle of tendencies inside the movement*. This crucial feature is missing from Luxemburg's account. It was later central to the development of other Marxists' theory and practice with respect to social movements.

Luxemburg's term 'spontaneity' is problematical. It refers, positively, to self-generated tendencies for workers in struggle to surpass previous limits to their organisation, activity and consciousness. But this is one-sided. *Not only* are workers capable of immense leaps in consciousness and organisation, and of moving towards socialist ideas independently of parties, but *also*, 'spontaneously', whole sections of the working class regularly manifest conservative tendencies as well, giving electoral and other support to their rulers. Some become strike breakers, racists, wife beaters and homophobes. There is, in Lenin's careful phrase, 'spontaneity and spontaneity': 'The working class spontaneously gravitates towards socialism; but the most widespread (and continuously and diversely revived) bourgeois ideology none the less spontaneously imposes itself upon the worker to a still greater degree'.[47]

---

46. Klandermans 1992.
47. Lenin 1961, p. 386. There is, Gramsci adds, no such thing as 'pure' spontaneity: in the 'most spontaneous' movement, the elements of conscious leadership are there, but leave no record of themselves (Gramsci 1971, p. 196). Francesca Polletta 2006 notes that 'spontaneity' can provide a 'mobilising myth' that conceals the role of conscious organisation.

Other Marxist accounts – such as those of Lenin, Trotsky or Gramsci – offer a strong sense of popular consciousness as *contradictory*, and *uneven*. It is contradictory in including both 'advanced' and 'backward' ideas, ideas close to socialism and others that remain trapped within the circuits of capitalist reproduction. It is uneven in that, within popular movements, different layers develop at different speeds and with varying outcomes. Movements, moreover, are not just inwardly differentiated: their overall development occurs *dialogically* through the social interactions between different individuals, groups, tendencies and parties within them – but also between them and their opponents.[48] Movements struggle with their opponents, but they also struggle among themselves about how to struggle. The inner life of movements consists in ongoing practical conversations, proposals and responses, provisional agreements, divisions and arguments that shift and refocus in response to events and situations. Temporary and unstable majorities and minorities emerge and disperse.

Such a view of movement 'consciousness' emerges within the better Marxist accounts of strategy and tactics. The early Communist International's intense debates on these matters, where newly formed parties struggled to master the political storms of the postwar years, reveal some of the issues at stake.

One temptation was 'ultra-leftism'. Essentially sectarian, ultra-leftism assumed that only the views and desires of the existing Left counted, forgetting that the socialist project required the active participation of the majority of the working class. Impatiently 'writing off' the majority meant abandoning them to reformist or conservative leaderships. Rejecting parliamentarism as a means of achieving socialism could be confused with rejecting the need to defend parliamentary democracy against fascism. Ultra-leftism contributed to disasters for the workers' movement in Germany (in 1919, 1921, and 1933), as well as in Italy and Bulgaria.[49]

It took time, and hard-won experience, before an outline alternative to ultra-left voluntarism emerged, in the shape of the 'united front'.[50] This assumed separate communist organisation, but sought to combine it with close engagement with social-democratic and other 'moderate' forces. Communists should regularly be proposing common forms of collective action on mutually agreed aims, from defence of trade-union organisation to anti-fascist activity and even, where appropriate, to the formation of soviets. The stress on *common action* assumes that collective action is the crucible in which new ideas and forms of organisation develop, and that communists, working alongside wider forces, can win them to more directly revolutionary perspectives.

---

48. Steinberg 1999b.
49. Claudín 1975; Hallas 1985.
50. Riddell 2011a.

Gramsci, much of whose *Prison Notebooks* involve an extended meditation on these issues, distinguished between 'common sense' (the normal admixture of contradictory elements in popular consciousness) and 'good sense' (those elements within common sense whose roots in popular experience are open to socialist development). The Marxist aim is to actively promote good sense, not by imposing some new principle of action or thought from outside a movement, but rather by working to 'renovate' and 'make critical' an already existing form of practice.[51] Movements have themselves already accumulated repertoires of activity, organisation and ideas, with whose development communists should engage, in ongoing practical dialogue.

10

Another risk was the very 'workerism' that critics often assume to be emblematic of Marxism. One aspect of the problem was signaled in Lenin's remarks about the 1916 Easter Rising in Dublin:

> To imagine that social revolution is *conceivable* without revolts by small nations in the colonies and in Europe, without revolutionary outbursts by a section of the petty bourgeoisie *with all its prejudices*, without a movement of the politically non-conscious proletarian and semi-proletarian masses against oppression by the landowners, the church, and the monarchy, against national oppression, etc. – to imagine all this is to *repudiate social revolution.* So one army lines up in one place and says, 'We are for socialism', and another, somewhere else and says, 'We are for imperialism', and that will be a social revolution! Only those who hold such a ridiculously pedantic view could vilify the Irish rebellion by calling it a 'putsch'.
>
> Whoever expects a 'pure' social revolution will *never* live to see it. Such a person pays lip-service to revolution without understanding what revolution is.[52]

Popular insurgencies involve all manner of social forces, not just employed workers. Unemployed and economically marginal groups, but also for example peasants, are likely to participate, each with their own demands and their own developmental tempos. In particular circumstances, issues relating to the rights of nationalities, religious and other oppressed groups will erupt forcefully. Indeed, the readiness of workers' parties to ally themselves with such forces can shape movements' fate. Such issues exploded in Russia with full force in 1917, and again in Hungary and Italy in 1919 – with sharply different outcomes. In

---

51. Gramsci 1971, pp. 330–1.
52. Lenin 1964, pp. 355–6.

Russia, Bolshevik support for peasants' land-demands was a key to the success of the October Revolution, while in Hungary and Italy, where the Left effectively ignored peasant and farm-labourer struggles, movements suffered crushing defeats. At play was the same principle that Marx had identified in his support for Irish independence: a movement that did not struggle for *general emancipation*, against *all* forms of oppression, would be neutered. Pure 'workerism' was a recipe for defeat. Revolutionaries should be, in Lenin's phrase, 'tribunes of the oppressed', actively seeking workers' organisations' support for struggles by other oppressed groups. Those oppressed groups were, furthermore, themselves active makers of their own history, often fighting their own way into 'the social movement as a whole' to challenge and transform it.

The experience of the following century suggests that the shaking up of social-movement life by something 'from without' is a recurring theme. Developing capitalism enlarges and empowers new layers, providing resources to pose new demands and thus to enrich the social movement with new perspectives and new layers of activists. Successive waves of colonised and enslaved peoples, migrants, working women, white-collar employees, indigenous peoples, college and school students, gays and lesbians have all, in different ways and times, fought their way into 'the social movement in general'. In the process, they have reshaped 'class struggle' and enriched the notion of human emancipation.

11

From the early 1920s, Marxist practical and theoretical development was stunted and diminished. The immensely influential Russian Revolution of 1917 was isolated and rapidly 'degenerated'. Stalin, though claiming a Marxist heritage, in practice perverted and reversed the entire tradition. 'Communism' in Russia came to mean the opposite of everything Marx had stood for: subordination of labour to accumulation; extensive forced labour; dispossession of the peasantry; national oppression; worship of the state; oppression of women, gays and Jews; imperialist expansion into Eastern Europe; and the brutal silencing of dissent. Outside Russia, Communist Parties in advanced capitalism first reverted to an ultra-left lunacy (its worst manifestation being the division of the German workers' movement in the face of Hitler), and then proceeded to develop a second wave of organised reformism, containing militant insurgencies. In 'Third World' countries, they promoted state-led industrialisation.

The Marxist Left – those who adhered to the original emancipatory and revolutionary vision – were isolated, confused and battered. The revival of a 'New Left' in the aftermath of Russia's crushing of the 1956 Hungarian Revolution provided some space for development, with new opportunities emerging with the 'cycle of revolt' of the 1960s and early 1970s. But if the Left grew, it struggled to make sense of its own history and suffered multiple internal splits. The Left could not prevent the containment and decline of the movement as a whole, or halt the large-scale defeats that working people suffered as the neoliberal 'movement from above' gained strength. The three decades from the mid-1970s witnessed a major enlargement and reshaping of the working class across the globe, as movement life both diversified and fragmented, with Marxist ideas receding in influence.

Capitalism, however, has a habit of hammering itself back into the consciousness of those who have forgotten its reality. Drafting this in the summer of 2011, with more financial crises erupting daily, with revolutionary uprisings continuing across the Arab world, and with a rising tide of revolt against the impositions of neoliberal 'structural adjustments' now reaching into core cities of the advanced industrial powers, it seems appropriate to ask whether Marx's vision of 'the social movement' challenging capitalism may yet have legs. It is a tradition of criticism and of activism with a very plausible case for rediscovery.

What Would a Marxist Theory of Social Movements Look Like?

Alf Gunvald Nilsen and Laurence Cox

A Marxist theory of social movements?[1]

Theory is a tool that activists use when their movements are not moving: when, despite their best efforts, they find that decisions are being made at levels they cannot affect, that the institutions they try to use are not on their side, or that their mobilisations are contained and constrained, theory offers the hope of understanding, and challenging, this situation. But not all tools are equally fit for the job.

In some cases, movements are offered the worldly wisdom of accepting the limitations of a social order that is often willing to accept their presence in return for political cooptation. In other cases, they are met by a celebration of their current situation and thinking which is initially welcome but leaves no space for learning, development or change. Both approaches in effect ratify the status quo – the one celebrating

---

1. This chapter draws heavily on our joint work in this area, now stretching across over a decade. An initial outline of a Marxist theory of social movements can be found in Cox 1999a; see also Cox 1999b; and, in a somewhat different form, in Cox in this volume. This approach is reworked and elaborated in Cox and Nilsen 2005a; 2005b; Nilsen 2007a; Nilsen and Cox 2006; and Cox 2005 – between them representing a single joint project summarised in Nilsen 2009a, which this chapter develops. Empirically, we have applied this approach in greatest depth to India – in Nilsen 2006; 2007b; 2008; 2010; 2011; and in this volume – and to Ireland, in Mullan and Cox 2000; Cox 2006; 2007b; Cox and Curry 2010; and Cox and Ní Dhorchaigh 2011. Some of its political implications are expressed in Nilsen 2007b; Cox 2007a; 2010a; and 2010b. Finally, Geoghegan and Cox 2001; Barker and Cox 2002; Cox and Nilsen 2007; and Cox and Fominaya 2009, are related approaches, challenging mainstream social movements literature from the standpoint of activist knowledge production.

normality and acceptance, the other celebrating resistance but uninterested in the practicalities of change.

Part of the problem, we suggest, is that many of the theories on offer (including in movement contexts) are thoroughly academic *in origin*; their purpose is not to change the world but to explain, celebrate or condemn.[2] Because they are not geared to action, defeats follow – as leaderships focus on carving out a niche in the status quo, or the celebration of radical otherness runs into non-discursive forms of power. It is our own experience of these weaknesses which has led us to ask more from theory than a badge of academic identity or political status – to demand, in fact, that it help us think about what to do.[3]

In this chapter, we set out to illustrate how Marxism – born out of the experiences, debates, theories and conflicts of popular movements – can respond to this demand. We work towards a coherent theory of collective action that is (a) consistent with central Marxist propositions, (b) practically useful for movement practitioners and (c) does not start by assuming *a priori* that local, geographical or historical realities are fixed and untouched by human action – in other words, a theory that takes movements seriously as social forces that continue to change our world.

We propose a framework geared towards the open ended analysis of movement-processes in specific places. Its universalising assumptions are restricted to the most abstract micro-analyses of human action and to the most general macro-perspectives on social order. The framework we propose is processual: it encompasses everyday struggles as well as counter-hegemonic projects, and tries to make sense of the way in which activists can move from one towards the other through collective learning. Crucially, we do not see this expansion and development as a foregone conclusion, but as a potential: activist aspirations to transform society can *sometimes* be realised, and have contributed to major social changes. Finally, we broaden the definition of 'social movement' to include the collective action of dominant social groups: the structures that subaltern groups mobilise around are the contestable outcomes of human practice, rather than absolute givens.

Theoretical starting points

Marxism sees the social world as a constant making and unmaking of social structures of human needs and capacities – structures that are constructed through

---

2. Barker and Cox 2002.

3. Other chapters in this book develop a critique of that brand of academic social movement theory which does not even attempt to be 'movement relevant' or engage in real dialogue with practitioners (see also Flacks 2004; Bevington and Dixon 2005).

the conflictual encounter between what we call social movements from above and social movements from below.

More abstractly, human beings articulate and seek to meet their needs by deploying their practical, bodily, semiotic, and intellectual capacities within historically evolving social formations: 'the satisfaction of the first need... leads to new needs; and this production of new needs is the first historical act'.[4] Because human beings must cooperate in order to satisfy their needs, this throws up social formations within which they can do so – but which also exert pressures on and set limits to the ways in which they do this. The outcome of this is a dominant structure of entrenched needs and capacities – a way of doing society – which privileges certain needs and capacities over others in ways that represent a relatively stable relationship of power between dominant and subaltern groups within that society.

Structures like this are not static, however. Contention between dominant and subaltern social groups leads to constant processes of change. At times, the overarching social framework can remain intact even while the dominant structure of entrenched needs and capacities is modified. At other times, all elements of an arrangement can be contested without the 'frontlines' changing substantially for decades. At still other times, systemic convulsions bring about a complete rupture of such structures and the social formation that has crystallised around them, giving rise to something new and altogether different. Social movements play a central role in these processes: by mobilising to defend or carve out a space to meet their specific needs within an existing social formation (for instance, liberal feminism); by developing new meanings, values, practices and relationships around emergent structures of radical needs and capacities that cannot be fully realised within existing structures (for instance, radical feminism); or by attempting to ally with other agents in the hope of creating new kinds of society (for instance, socialist feminism).

Social movements: a definition

Social movements are often thought of in field-specific terms, as a particular form of extra-parliamentary political activity, characterised by certain specific institutional and organisational features.[5] In contrast, we propose a wider definition of social movements as a process in which a specific social group develops a collective project of skilled activities centred on a rationality – a particular way

---

4. Marx and Engels 1975b, p. 42.
5. See Tilly 2004.

of making sense of and relating to the social world – that tries to change or maintain a dominant structure of entrenched needs and capacities, in part or whole.

The starting point is everyday practices developed in response to specific needs, problems and places, materially grounded in concrete situations, and hence a specific group; but to become a movement, participants need to connect with other such practices by articulating something more abstract, a 'local rationality' that can be recognised by potential allies. Significantly, such processes unfold in conflict with the collective projects of other groups within a given social formation.

This kind of praxis is both the subject and the object of social movements. It is their subject, in that movement activity is nothing more or less than the conscious deployment of human capacities to meet human needs – albeit in complex ways, as when we reflect on what alliances will make it possible for us to resist attempts to privatise basic services. It is also their object, in that movements try to change or maintain the structures that organise human activity and/or the direction in which those structures develop. This, in turn, means that we see social structures and social formations as the sediment of movement struggles, and as a kind of truce line continually probed for weaknesses and repudiated as soon as this seems worthwhile – by social movements from above and social movements from below.

Social movements from above

'From castles and palaces and churches to prisons and workhouses and schools; from weapons of war to a controlled press' wrote Raymond Williams, 'any ruling class, in variable ways though always materially, produces a social and political order'.[6] This productive activity is the essence of the 'social movement from above', which we define as the development of a collective project by dominant groups, consisting of skilled activities centred on a rationality that seek to maintain or modify a dominant structure of entrenched needs and capacities, in ways that aim to reproduce and/or extend the hegemonic position of dominant groups within a given social formation.

The skilled activities that make up such projects span a wide spectrum, from industrial organisation models to counterinsurgency operations and neoliberal crisis management.[7] The projects of social movements from above involve rationalities expressed in ideological offensives – such as moral campaigns against 'sloth and indolence' in the era of primitive accumulation, or Thatcher's

---

6. Williams 1977, p. 93.
7. See Hoogvelt 2001; Pilger 2003; Klein 2007.

anti-collectivist populism – for which élites seek to gain popular consent.[8] The organisations involved are immensely varied – ranging from Freemasonry in the eighteenth century, via New Right parties and conservative think tanks in the 1980s, to transnational institutions such as the WTO and the World Bank/IMF in the present.[9] The aim of these organisations is essentially to construct unity between dominant social groups – a unity that cannot be taken for granted, and which sometimes unravels.

From both activist and analytical points of view, there are two advantages of reading politics in this way. Firstly, showing the coherence and purposive direction of such projects is important to activists, who otherwise have to learn painfully and in the first person the limits of élite tolerance for needs that contradict such projects. This explains an important dimension of movement-variability, in terms of how far particular movement goals can easily be accommodated within these terms. Secondly, showing the socially constructed nature of these projects is important, politically and intellectually, in understanding that they can be challenged and, on occasion, defeated. Without this, we are left facing social structure as an unchangeable Thing and universalising power relations that are, in fact, specific to a given place at a given time.

Social movements from above create and pursue their projects for the construction, reproduction, and extension of hegemony on the basis of the superior access of dominant social groups to economic, political and cultural power-resources. This makes such movements qualitatively different from movements from below. Therefore, we shall discuss each element in more detail.

A directive role in economic organisation

Movements from above draw upon and try to maintain or expand the directive role of dominant groups in economic organisation. Exploitation is not a self-perpetuating feature of society; it 'will tend to evoke resistance, if only in such molecular forms as sabotage and ca' canny'.[10] For accumulation to proceed smoothly, and for the power relations that are the foundation of accumulation to be sustained, such resistance must be repressed or accommodated in some way.[11]

While even routine exploitation must be actively and consciously reproduced, new forms of exploitation particularly need to be actively created through projects seeking to advance a new 'mode in which surplus labour [can be] extracted

---

8. See Perelman 2000; Hall 1983.
9. See Van der Pijl 1995; Robinson 2004.
10. Callinicos 1988, p. 51.
11. See Braverman 1974; Burawoy 1982.

from the actual producer'[12] – whether this takes the form of a transition from feudal serfdom and commoning to capitalist wage-labour, or a shift from Fordist factory production to precarious service sector employment. Behind what looks like 'the silent compulsion of economic relations'[13] lies conscious collective agency and the organisation of alliances around particular projects to impose, maintain, extend or restore particular economic rationalities in the form of what Jessop calls 'accumulation strategies'.[14]

Thus, rather than conceiving of agency as a sort of froth on the surface of capital, it can be argued, for example, that the churning of struggles between movements from above and movements from below during the 'long nineteenth century'[15] had, by the end of the Second World War, created favourable conditions for accumulation strategies that centred on 're-embedding' the economy in a régime of state regulation and intervention. In the global North, this took the form of Keynesian welfare state compromises; in the South, it assumed the form of national-developmental alliances.[16] The specific manifestations of these accumulation strategies varied greatly, in large part due to the specific struggles that characterised specific locales.[17]

When the alliances which underpinned these accumulation strategies unravelled, this was, in turn, intrinsically related to popular struggles to advance excluded needs and capacities, prompting an offensive from key members of the dominant alliance who no longer found their interests best served by continued loyalty to the previous strategies.[18] This conflictual unravelling and the subsequent turn to neoliberalism occurred in different ways and degrees, and with different – not always successful – outcomes in different parts of the world, depending on popular resistance.[19]

Differential access to the state

Under normal circumstances, dominant social groups enjoy privileged access to 'the political power that is pre-eminently ascribed to the state'.[20] This expresses the fact that the formation of the state as a system of political control and domination went hand-in-hand with the division of society into a contradictory and

---

12. Marx, cited in De Ste. Croix 1981, p. 51.
13. Marx 1976a, p. 899.
14. Jessop 1990.
15. Hobsbawm 1988a; 1988b; 1989.
16. See Lash and Urry 1987; Harvey 1990; Kiely 2009; Silver and Slater 1999; Motta and Nilsen 2011.
17. See Esping-Andersen 1990; Kohli 2004.
18. See Wainwright 1994; Lash and Urry 1987.
19. Harvey 2005.
20. Poulantzas 1978, p. 147.

conflictual relation between 'the class which performs the sum of social labour and the class or classes which perform no labour but nonetheless appropriate the social surplus'.[21] The state is geared towards administering the functioning and reproduction of fundamental structures of class power, and – as activists tend to discover – it is, therefore, also inherently constituted in such a way as to have 'unequal and asymmetrical effects on the ability of social groups to realize their interests through political action'.[22]

In capitalist societies, performing this task entails guaranteeing the right to private property in the means of production and labour power, underwriting the enforcement of contracts, providing protection for the mechanisms of accumulation, eliminating barriers to the mobility of capital and labour, and stabilising monetary régimes. This is done by intervening in the accumulation process, by providing necessary public goods and infrastructures, by mediating in conflicts between capital and labour, and – as witnessed in the recent spate of bailouts after the 2008 financial collapse – by managing crises in the capitalist economy.[23] Beyond this, the capitalist state is also central to reproducing those social and cultural institutions that are important in shaping and sustaining accumulation – notably gendered divisions of labour, the patriarchal family, and racial hierarchies.[24]

However, like the matrix of power that it regulates and reproduces, the state and the form that it assumes in a specific place and time is a 'condensation of a relationship of forces defined precisely by struggle'.[25] The structures of political representation and state intervention are subject to change as an outcome of movement struggles, not least because of the importance of alliance, consent, and legitimacy in the construction of hegemony. For example, in the global North, the removals of qualifications on the right to vote based on property, gender and race were key achievements of the workers' movement, the women's movement, and the Civil Rights movement. In the global South, national sovereignty and the national-developmentalist state were the outcomes of protracted struggles for national liberation from colonial rule. In Western countries, the transition from the 'night watchman state' of the nineteenth and early twentieth century to the post-war Keynesian welfare state was the result of labour struggles from the 1890s to the 1940s.[26]

These changes were, in large part, the result of widespread collective agency from below; but they also stopped short of revolutionary transformation, in that

---

21. Smith 1990, p. 41.
22. Jessop 1982, p. 224.
23. D. Harvey 2001, pp. 274–5.
24. Kotz, McDonough and Reich 1994.
25. Poulantzas 1978, p. 147.
26. Cox 1987.

most were concessions granted by dominant groups seeking to negotiate new truce lines in the face of popular movements. The state remains, therefore, a congealment of a wider matrix of power-laden social relations, which 'can never be equally accessible to all forces and equally available for all purposes'.[27] This becomes particularly evident when social movements from above take the political initiative; not for nothing are the supposedly anti-state neoliberal projects of the 1980s identified with Margaret Thatcher and Ronald Reagan's terms in office.[28]

Moulding everyday routines and common sense

The supremacy of a social group, Gramsci noted, will manifest itself in two ways: 'the function of hegemony which the dominant group exercises throughout society and ... that of "direct domination" or command exercised through the State'.[29] When social movements from above mobilise to mould everyday routines and common sense, they are operating on the former terrain, seeking to secure '[t]he "spontaneous" consent given by the great masses of the population to the general direction imposed on social life by the dominant fundamental group'.[30]

Gaining the consent of subaltern groups comes in part from winning acceptance for ideologies of dominance in which the hegemonic projects of social movements from above 'are conceived of, and presented, as being the motor force of a universal expansion, of a development of all the "national" energies', and underpinned by 'the belief about everything that exists, that it is "natural", that it should exist'.[31] As such, national-developmental states portray mega-projects that dispossess marginal peasants of their land and livelihoods as serving the universal progress of the nation towards modernity, while neoliberal states portray union busting, wage freezes, and cutbacks in public spending as necessary means by which to attract global capital, which is, in turn, in the interest of all.

However, at a more fundamental level, hegemony entails 'in effect a saturation of the whole process of living ... of the whole substance of lived identities and relationships'.[32] This is Gramsci's 'directive' intellectual activity: social movements from above shape everyday routines and common sense in a way that enables them to manage the task of providing effective directions and orientations to the life-activity of different social groups, meet *some* of their diverse needs and provide a language with which they can express their thoughts.

---

27. Jessop 1990, p. 250.
28. Harvey 2005.
29. Gramsci 1998, p. 57.
30. Gramsci 1998, p. 12.
31. Gramsci 1998, pp. 182, 157.
32. Williams 1977, p. 110.

However, hegemony 'does not just passively exist as a form of dominance'.[33] Gramsci pointed out that the 'common sense' that guides the life-activity of subaltern groups is a form of 'contradictory consciousness', fusing ideologies of dominance and hegemonic ways of being in the world with the practical and often tacit subaltern experience of the existent state of affairs as problematic, and the subaltern skills and responses developed in response to this experience.[34]

Thus, hegemony is vulnerable to resistance, and resistance often draws on subaltern appropriations and inversions of ideologies of dominance. Social movements opposing large dams in India portray dispossession as evidence of the state's betrayal of the postcolonial development project; anti-austerity protests point out the contradiction between neoliberal market ideology and state bailouts of the banking sector. When we study how movements from above use their leading position to mould everyday routines and common sense, we see this 'not as a finished and monolithic ideological formation but as a problematic, contested, political process of struggle'.[35]

Strategies of social movements from above: defensive/offensive

If movements from above can mobilise these economic, political and cultural resources when they try to expand or maintain the position of dominant groups, they do so in interaction movements from below, and this 'field of force'[36] has consequences for their strategies, which we broadly categorise as defensive or offensive strategies.

Defensive strategies tend to be deployed in the context of substantial challenges from blow, and can involve either accommodation or repression. A defensive strategy focused on accommodation typically revolves around granting concessions to the claims and demands of movements from below with the aim of appeasing and defusing a force that might otherwise threaten the existing social formation. A key example would be the mid-twentieth-century reforms implemented in much of Western Europe in response to workers' movements. As this example suggests, such strategies often involve playing on existing differences within movements from below: alliances with social democrats against more radical Left actors, or coopting leaderships into positions of relative power while demobilising the movement.

Defensive strategies centred on repression involve violent coercion and the suspension of civil rights, such as the state-terrorism unleashed by authoritarian

---

33. Williams 1977, p. 112.
34. Gramsci 1998, p. 333.
35. Roseberry 1995, p. 77.
36. Thompson 1978a, p. 151.

régimes in Latin America against radical popular movements in the 1970s and 1980s as part of the implementation of neoliberal economic policies, 'anti-terrorist' legislation allowing for the generalised surveillance of everyday life, or the criminalisation of counter-cultures seen as potential sources of large-scale protest, as in the UK's 1994 Criminal Justice Act.[37]

Hegemony is, of course, always 'consent armoured by coercion'.[38] Thus the defensive strategies of movements from above always involve *some* accommodation and *some* repression, while varying in emphasis. Successful repressive strategies rely on a substantial coalition willing to support them, established by offering concessions to more moderate movements from below. Conversely, accommodative strategies are often accompanied by the criminalisation of more radical movements. Thus in constructing the historic bloc that underpinned Western Europe's postwar class compromise, more moderate unions and skilled workers were typically incorporated into corporatist arrangements with the state and capital, while more militant unions and unskilled workers were often excluded and subject to repression.[39]

Offensive strategies from above typically involve attacks on the truce lines left by movement struggles of the past, undermining and reversing the victories and concessions won by movements from below. Thus they are aimed either at attaining hegemony for newly dominant social groups, or at restoring the power of already-dominant groups, and are typically deployed at times of crisis and breakdown of all or part of a social formation.

An example of the former would be the bourgeois revolutions involved in the rise of capitalism in England, France and the USA. These revolutions, and the movements from above which formed themselves in these processes, represented 'the development of a group in society with an independent economic base, which attacks obstacles to a democratic version of capitalism that have been inherited from the past'.[40] Neoliberalism is, of course, the most recent example of an offensive movement from above seeking to restore and extend the hegemony of already-dominant social groups. Its prime achievement has been restoring the class power of capital by fundamentally undermining the social restrictions and regulations imposed on capitalist accumulation as a result of working-class struggles in the first half of the twentieth century.[41]

In yet other cases, social movements from above may show the dynamics of a 'passive revolution', where an alliance between existing and new dominant

---

37. See Klein 2007; Mattelart 2010; McKay 1996.
38. Gramsci 1998, p. 276.
39. Cox 1987.
40. Moore 1991, p. xxi.
41. Harvey 2005.

groups via the state enables the introduction of a new form of capitalism without directly dislodging existing dominant groups and the social relations on which their hegemony has been constructed.[42] Such dynamics were characteristic, for example, of the articulation of India's postcolonial development project, and of neoliberal restructuring in Mexico and Chile.[43]

It should be clear from the complexity and scope of these examples that we are suggesting categories which are useful for empirical research and practical strategy, rather than watertight conceptual compartments. Such categories help us see neoliberalism as process and project rather than eternal reality; to contrast the very different possibilities and limits of resistance in different places; and to think about how and where we can extend our alliances, raise the costs of the neoliberal assault and detach its allies. This is where mobilisation to transcend and construct something more valuable than 'the house that neoliberalism built' begins. This brings us to social movements from below.

Social movements from below

Social movements from below can be defined as collective projects developed and pursued by subaltern groups, organising a range of locally-generated skilled activities around a rationality that seeks to either challenge the constraints that a dominant structure of needs and capacities imposes upon the development of new needs and capacities, or to defend aspects of an existing, negotiated structure which accommodate their specific needs and capacities.

We start from Piven and Cloward's simple but incisive observation that subaltern groups 'experience deprivation and oppression within a concrete setting, not as the end result of large and abstract processes ... it is the daily experience of people that shapes their grievances, establishes the measure of their demands, and points out the targets of their anger'.[44] However, these experiences are not simply isolated instances of wrongdoing or frustration. Rather, they are 'clues to underlying structures and relationships which are not observable other than through the particular phenomena or events that they produce'.[45]

These structures and relationships can be made explicit when movement participants combine and extend their 'fragmented knowledge' in ways that enable them to develop 'a better understanding of the social mechanisms at work, so as to direct their efforts in order that their intentions might be more

---

42. Gramsci 1998.
43. Kaviraj 1997; Morton 2007a; Motta 2008.
44. Piven and Cloward 1977, pp. 20–1.
45. Wainwright 1994, p. 7.

efficiently fulfilled'.[46] This, in turn, means that the grievances, demands and targets may expand: from oppositional collective action bound by scope, aims and cultural 'language' to a specific, situated and local experience, towards mutual recognition across difference in wider-ranging and more radical projects for change.

We shall refer to the realisation of this potential as a movement-process, and propose the concepts of local rationality, militant particularism, campaigns and social movement projects as tools to make sense of different aspects of movement processes. The idea of a process centred on widening and deepening the scope of collective action from below is often criticised, in academic contexts, as being linear or teleological in nature. This is not our thinking: the unfolding of movement-processes is not a predetermined necessity. However, over the past two centuries, social movements from below have repeatedly proven themselves capable of developing in such a way. We are trying, therefore, to develop concepts that can grasp this contingent potential for subaltern groups to develop their skilled activity collectively, and that can help activists think what to do, in the sense of being aware of what may be possible and what it might look like.

Local rationalities and militant particularisms

The 'common sense' that underpins people's everyday activity, Gramsci suggested, is an amalgamation of elements originating in the hegemonic projects of social movements from above and the contradictory logic of 'good sense' – those aspects of subaltern consciousness that indicate that 'the social group in question may indeed have its own conception of the world'.[47] We term this second form of practical consciousness a *local rationality*, the articulation of this conception in ways that can be generalised beyond their starting point; in movement contexts, this means the ways of being, doing and thinking that people develop as attempts to oppose the everyday routines and received wisdoms that define the hegemonic elements of common sense.

Local rationalities are not an essential characteristic of the social being of subaltern groups, or a form of insurrectionary otherness hermetically sealed off from the hegemonic projects of social movements from above. Rather, local rationalities are forged in and through historically constituted relations between social groups which are differentially endowed in terms of 'the extent of their control of social relations and ... the scope of their transformative powers'.[48] Embedded in unequal power relations, people do their best to develop their needs and

46. Wainwright 1994, p. 108; Kilgore 1999; Barker and Cox 2002.
47. Gramsci 1998, pp. 327–8, 333.
48. Sewell 1992, p. 20.

capacities. In so doing, some of their activities may fall into line with the proposals and propositions of the established orders; others do not.

In some cases, they articulate local rationalities to defend previously negotiated spaces which accommodate subaltern needs and capacities within a dominant structure of entrenched needs and capacities. In other cases, local rationalities are articulated as attempts to transgress constraints imposed on the development of new needs and capacities among subaltern groups. In the first case, local rationalities are typically shaped in defensive ways, opposing attempts from above at reordering extant structures in order to extend the power base of dominant groups. For example, eighteenth-century food riots were famously mediated through local rationalities centred on the idea of a 'moral economy' regulating relations between dominant and subaltern groups.[49]

In the second case, local rationalities typically take a more offensive form, as subaltern groups try to carve out greater space for the satisfaction, deployment and development of emergent radical needs and capacities. For example, the urban counter-cultural movement-networks analysed by Cox sought to develop spaces for autonomous self development against the constraints of labour market and family structures.[50]

Moreover, local rationalities can be more or less developed and articulated in the collective skilled activity of subaltern social groups as against those forms of rationality that characterise the hegemonic projects of movements from above. In highly repressive contexts, local rationalities may exist for long periods as what Scott calls 'hidden transcripts' – a 'critique of power spoken behind the back of the dominant' and concealed under a veil of feigned compliance and deference.[51] In other cases, such rationalities may exist much more openly and thoroughly as a cultural fabric saturating the outlook and activity of subaltern groups in overt and entrenched 'cultures of resistance'.[52]

If local rationalities are increasingly articulated, this can lead to direct confrontations with and defiance of social movements from above. For example, Fantasia has analysed one such process animating collective action among iron-foundry workers in New Jersey. In this case, intra-group affinities between workers energised a series of direct confrontations with plant management over specific workplace grievances. Eventually, this took the form of an informal network among those workers oriented towards radical union activism, which in turn enabled workers to carry out militant wildcat strikes that gained important

49. Thompson 1991.
50. See Cox 1999a.
51. Scott 1990, p. xii.
52. Peluso 1992.

concessions from the factory owners.[53] Such moments are, of course, the starting point of most struggles. As participants come to discover that those above them are not on their side, they start to voice publicly what has previously been said only in private or not at all, and act in their own name and on their own behalf. Feminist consciousness raising is another well-known example of this process.

Drawing on Williams[54] and Harvey,[55] we term such struggles *militant particularisms*. This refers to forms of struggle that emerge when a subaltern group deploys specific skills and knowledges in open confrontation with a dominant group in a particular place at a particular time, in a particular conflict over a particular issue. The term highlights the way in which 'politics is always embedded in "ways of life" and "structures of feeling" peculiar to places and communities'.[56] This embeddedness is reflected in the issues that are struggled over and the practices, skills, idioms and imaginaries deployed in such confrontations.

This is local rationality with the emphasis very much still on the local; but articulated so as to form a clear and identifiable 'us' in opposition to 'them', and – more importantly – 'their' attempts to make 'us' act as they would like and think in ways that suit them. It is spoken and acted publicly, and in ways that enable the bridging of (some of) the million and one different potential internal conflicts and tensions within the struggle. Of course this process may not be sustained, and militant particularisms are often major achievements, subject to disintegration or attacks from above using clientelistic relationships, 'divide and conquer' or the cooptation of leaders.

From militant particularisms to campaigns

When they survive all this, however, the practices, skills, idioms and imaginaries of which militant particularisms are made up can be generalised further – a further articulation of local rationality – and, in this way, they can transcend the particular place and time of their emergence and be used across a spectrum of specific situations and singular struggles.

This happens when activists involved in a militant particularist struggle in one given location make connections with other activists engaged in similar struggles elsewhere. Through making such connections, activists typically discover and create common ground: common denominators are discovered in the apparently disparate conflicts in which they are engaged; common enemies are named; common strategies and collective identities are developed across social and spatial boundaries.

---

53. Fantasia 1988.
54. Williams 1989.
55. Harvey 1996; 2000.
56. Harvey 2000, p. 55.

These practical activities of mutual learning and development of self-understanding, communication, cooperation and organisation between militant particularisms bring about a widening and deepening of the scope of collective action; as such, they constitute another stage of the process in which movements from below 'shift gears' and 'transcend particularities'. This act of '"translation" from the concrete to the abstract' is already present, of course, as individuals hitherto divided by family, neighbourhood, loyalty, gender, and so on come to work together in a single militant particularism; the formation of campaigns takes this a stage further, beyond the internal radicalisation of the lifeworld to the connection, and further radicalisation, of multiple lifeworlds.[57]

The organisation of militant particularisms across social and spatial boundaries involves something more than putting potatoes in a sack. It entails the creation of a form of movement activity that we shall refer to as *campaigns*, defined as the organisation of a range of local responses to specific situations in ways that connect people across those situations, around a generalised challenge to the dominant forces which construct those situations.

For example, the massive popular campaign against dam-building in the Narmada Valley in central India emerged as grassroots groups in peasant communities across the states of Gujarat, Maharashtra, and Madhya Pradesh started to coordinate their efforts to secure compensation for the loss of land that these communities would suffer as a result of the submergence caused by the dam-projects. Faced with recalcitrant state authorities, their demands were radicalised towards opposition to the Narmada dams at a pan-state level, spearheaded by the *Narmada Bachao Andolan*. In turn, the campaign was embedded in national and transnational movement networks that articulated a generic politics of opposition to large dams, and championed the exploration of alternative methods of water-management.[58]

Towards social-movement projects

If the development of campaigns involves transcending the boundaries of militant particularisms through translation between local struggles, the construction of collective identities that cut across socio-spatial divides, and the widening of activist perceptions of the limits of the possible, they are still a limited form of collective action in that they do not take aim at the social totality as an object to be transformed; and, of course, many campaigns do stop here.

However, if activists pursue the activity of connecting different localised struggles and, indeed, seemingly different struggles; if they ask critical questions

---

57. Harvey 2000, p. 242.
58. Nilsen 2010.

about the structures that create the problems they address and frustrate their campaigns – and if the movement's goals or actors are not ones that can easily be accommodated or repressed – they can come to an understanding of the systemic dimensions of the specific field they are working in. From this awareness, activists can start to move beyond the field-specific nature of the campaign, towards a form of movement activity that sees the social whole as the object of challenge or transformation.

This has powerful effects on a movement-process, is hard to achieve and is often bitterly contested – both internally, and by more powerful, wealthier and culturally dominant opponents. Attempting to argue that a process of industrial struggle can and should go further, and become a socialist movement or demand a welfare state; pushing a women's movement beyond the demand for legislative equality towards the attempt to restructure society on a non-patriarchal basis; turning a movement against nuclear power plants into a movement for a different kind of economy; turning a student movement into a revolutionary movement – even where the organisation remains nominally the same, its structures and practices, ideas and strategies, allies and repertoires will have to change dramatically.

We propose the term *social movement project* for these forms of collective agency, defined as (a) challenges to the social totality which that (b) aim to control the self-production of society and (c) have or are developing the potential for the kind of hegemony – leading the skilled activity of different social groups – that would make (b) and hence (a) possible. At the heart of these challenges, there lie emergent structures of radical needs and capacities, and the transformative potential of a movement project lies in the goal of realising these structures.

The anti-capitalist movement is a good example of a social movement project. Erupting with full force in the late 1990s, generating a dramatic anti-war movement in the early 2000s, finding new life in anti-austerity struggles from Iceland to Greece in the late 2000s and now underpinning much of the Occupy! movement, it is the outcome of a long process of collaboration and communication between campaigns and the militant particularist struggles organised through these campaigns, going back to the early 1990s.[59] In this process, 'particular struggles came to be understood in terms of a more general set of interconnections between problems and movements worldwide'.[60] Slogans such as 'Another World is Possible', 'Peoples of Europe rise up' or 'We are the 99 percent' highlight this sense of a shared (if complex) 'we' and insist that ways of socially organising needs and capacities outside the logics of neoliberal capitalism are within reach.

59. See Wilkin 2000; Broad and Heckscher 2003.
60. Gill 2000, p. 138.

This marks a clear rupture *vis-à-vis* the initial forms of protest against neoliberal restructuring, which were essentially defensive in character: strike waves in the global North that sought to restore Keynesian rights and entitlements and IMF riots in the global South that sought to restore the social wage guaranteed in the developmentalist pact between the state and the popular classes.[61] It also marks a rupture *vis-à-vis* many of the single-issue campaigns of the 1990s, which primarily sought to curtail the scope of the project of neoliberal restructuring.[62]

As activists in the anti-capitalist movement can testify, the trajectories of social movement projects are open-ended. They depend on contingencies such as the forging of more and stronger connections with localised struggles – and thus the capacity for hegemony – as well as its capacity for resilience in the face of opposition from movements from above. However, a social movement project that has developed significant momentum can reasonably be expected to result in the development of a *potentially* revolutionary situation.

Social movements and struggles over historicity

Movements from above and below struggle over historicity[63] – that is, they engage and encounter each other in struggles over the direction and form of the development of the social organisation of human needs and capacities. Such struggles occur when movements from below have returned 'up' the sequence, from opposing hegemonic routines in localised struggles to opposing the structures from which those routines emerge, and, ultimately, to opposing the movements from above that installed those structures or led the construction of the truce lines within which those structures are entrenched. This process of movement development gives rise to what Gramsci called an 'organic crisis':

> In every country the process is different, although the content is the same. And the content is the crisis of the ruling class's hegemony, which occurs either because the ruling class has failed in some major political undertaking for which it has requested, or forcibly extracted, the consent of the broad masses...or because huge masses...have passed suddenly from a state of political passivity to a certain activity, and put forward demands which taken together, albeit not organically formulated, add up to a revolution. A 'crisis of authority' is spoken of: this is precisely the crisis of hegemony, or general crisis of the state.[64]

---

61. Walton and Seddon 1994.
62. Broad and Hecksher 2003.
63. Touraine 1981.
64. Gramsci 1998, p. 210.

It is not – or rarely – the case that revolutionary movements from below independently launch a war of manoeuvre against a beleaguered, passive, decaying order which is capable of little more than a defensive response to the challenge from below (although there are moments, such as 1789 and 1917, when a ruling order is just this feeble). As Hall[65] notes, such defensive responses from dominant groups are insufficient in an organic crisis, where ' "the lower classes" *do not want* to live in the old way and the "upper classes" *cannot carry on in the old way*'.[66] In this context, the restoration of hegemony requires a 'formative' effort – in the terms suggested above, an offensive movement strategy from above. Thatcherism represented one such response in the context of the collapse of Keynesianism, to the double pressure of movements from below and economic crisis.[67]

Thus, organic crises and their trajectory are typically shaped not simply by movements from below, but also by offensive movements from above, led by fractions of dominant groups taking aim at social structures marked by the past victories of movements from below and which constrain dominant groups. They typically seek to disaggregate movements from below and construct new alliances around a distinct movement-project of their own.

At the heart of such a scenario lies the suspension of those 'truce lines' handed down from past rounds of movement struggles, and thus also the eruption of the antagonisms and contradictions that they held in check. New terrains of struggle open up, in which movements from above and below vie for command over the direction of imminent systemic changes, or seek to prevent these changes from happening in the first place.

To give two examples, as briefly as possible: if, as Lash and Urry and Wainwright propose,[68] Keynesianism was undermined not simply by a generalised financial and legitimation crisis,[69] but also by the rise of labour struggles, movements against private patriarchy and the uprising of oppressed ethnic groups from Alabama to Belfast – then the crisis was ultimately resolved by the previously marginal New Right welding together élite defectors from the old alliance around the economic project of neoliberalism and popular groups willing to be organised in terms of a new kind of right-wing populism.[70]

While organic crises are, by definition, radically contingent, it is clear that, as particular movements come to gain hegemony through partial or total victories, the space of contention will be narrowed down through a dynamic of

65. Hall 1983.
66. Lenin 1920, p. 54.
67. Hall 1983.
68. Lash and Urry 1987; Wainwright 1994.
69. Offe 1985a.
70. Harvey 2005; Overbeek 1990.

'path-dependency', where developing social changes take a direction that closes off or crowds out other possibilities.

As a provisional guideline, we might suggest that movement projects from below that reach some kind of provisional hegemony are able to produce a revolutionary situation (naturally, the outcome is contingent); movement projects from below that are 'disarmed' through accommodative responses from above tend to lead to significant reformist change, while the basic structures of the society 'return to normalcy', at least for a time; and a successful offensive social movement from above leads to significant modifications in favour of dominant social groups, reversing restraints on their power.

What factors make it likely that a situation of organic crisis will have an outcome in line with the ambitions and aspirations of social movements from below? The first and foremost factor is that subaltern struggles need to be *developed* from militant particularism to campaigns, and from campaigns to movement project – and in ways that are in line with local rationalities from below. Constructing a movement in this way entails continuing the project of articulating local rationalities from the specific and local to the specific and national or transnational, and, ultimately, to target the system as a whole in the name of an alternative way of 'doing society'. It is clear that, short of revolutionary situations, such 'counter-hegemony' can only be limited, incipient, and partial.

Nevertheless, in situations where (as at present) the old order is unable to come up with a plan B, despite its manifest incapacity to fulfil the promises on which the consent of its allies and passive supporters lie – in relation to economic crisis, geopolitical rule or, indeed, rising tides – it is in the development of popular consensus around a radically different approach that societies can change direction. In some ways, the only real question is whether this consensus will be shaped from below, or from above by some horrendous new populism or fascism whose contours are not yet visible.

If we want to remain true to the local rationalities that motivate our particular and general struggles against the social order we are in, our job is thus to find ways of agreeing a direction more consistent with these rationalities – a 'social movement project' that can gain sufficient consent to win out when it matters. In this situation, what Marxism brings is the sedimented learning of earlier periods when militant particularisms developed into movement projects that shook the Earth, dethroned kings, sent empires packing and forced the construction of welfare states – and the awareness that the present order is not written in stone, but is a precarious truce line, capable not only of neoliberal restoration but also of the creation of a new kind of world.

Social Movement Studies and Its Discontents

The Strange Disappearance of Capitalism from Social Movement Studies

Gabriel Hetland and Jeff Goodwin[1]

Introduction

Over the last several decades, a perplexing development has occurred within the field of social movement studies. While capitalism has spread to nearly every corner of the globe, scholars who specialise in the study of social movements, especially in the United States, have increasingly ignored the ways in which capitalism shapes social movements. The first part of this paper analyses this strange disappearance of capitalism from social movement studies during the past few decades. We suggest that analyses of social movements have suffered from this theoretical neglect in a number of identifiable ways. In the second part of the paper, we support this claim by examining a 'hard' case for our thesis, namely, the gay and lesbian (or LGBT) movement. The dynamics of capitalism are presumably *least* relevant for 'new social movements,' including the LGBT movement, which are not centrally concerned with economic, labour, workplace or other 'materialist' issues. If this is so, then perhaps the disappearance of capitalism from social movement studies is a relatively benign development. We show, however, that the dynamics of capitalism have, in fact, mattered significantly, and in a variety of ways, to the LGBT movement. We conclude that movement scholars, including scholars of new social movements,

---

1. Both authors contributed equally to this chapter, and are listed in reverse alphabetical order.

need to pay – or, more accurately, *repay* – greater attention to the dynamics of capitalism. It is time to bring capitalism back into social movement studies.

The rise and fall of capitalism in social movement studies

Although it is now largely forgotten, the dynamics of capitalism played an extremely important role in many, if not most, of the seminal North-American studies of social movements written by social scientists during the 1970s. A series of important studies of movements and revolutions appeared in the United States in the late 1970s and early 1980s, which had the effect of radically reorienting the academic study of movements and political conflict. The field moved away from primarily psychological and social-psychological treatments of political protest – studies that often cast a very negative light on protest – to more sympathetic analyses that emphasised the importance of resources, power, solidarities, and opportunities for movements. Movements were no longer viewed as irrational outbursts, but as eminently rational forms of politics by other means. But all this is now common wisdom among movement scholars. What has been forgotten is that these same studies tended to emphasise quite strongly the effects of capitalism on movements.

Among the more important such studies were Jeffery Paige's *Agrarian Revolution*,[2] Michael Schwartz's *Radical Protest and Social Structure*,[3] Francis Fox Piven and Richard Cloward's *Poor People's Movements*,[4] Charles Tilly's 'resolutely pro-Marxian' *From Mobilization to Revolution*,[5] Theda Skocpol's *States and Social Revolutions*,[6] and Doug McAdam's *Political Process and the Development of Black Insurgency*.[7] The dynamics of capitalism figure prominently in all of these studies, sometimes constraining and sometimes inciting or enabling collective action. By capitalism, these authors generally mean a mode of production in which a class that owns the means of production (capitalists) employs a class that must sell its labour power in exchange for a wage or salary (workers), and in which market competition among capitalists leads to a constant reinvestment of part of the surplus (or profits) in the production process (that is, capital accumulation). The dynamics of capitalism that these authors emphasise include processes directly linked to capital accumulation, especially the proletarianisation

---

2. Paige 1975.
3. Schwartz 1988.
4. Piven and Cloward 1977.
5. Tilly 1978, p. 48. See also many of Tilly's other writings from this period, such as Tilly, Tilly and Tilly 1975; Tilly 1982.
6. Skocpol 1979. See also Skocpol and Trimberger 1994.
7. McAdam 1999. See also Anderson-Sherman and McAdam 1982.

(or commodification) of labour, the comodification of productive forces generally, and the concentration and centralisation of capital.

The authors of these groundbreaking works believed that capitalism was
crucial for understanding movements because of a variety of important causal
mechanisms. Capitalist institutions (factories, railroads, banks, and so on) or
institutions that capitalists may come to control (such as legislatures, courts
and police) are often the source or target of popular grievances, especially (but
not only) during times of economic crisis; these institutions, moreover, shape
collective identities and solidarities – and not just *class* solidarities – in particular ways; they also distribute power and resources unevenly to different social
classes and fractions of classes; they both facilitate and inhibit specific group-
alliances based on common or divergent interests; class divisions, furthermore,
often penetrate and fracture particular movements; and ideologies and cultural
assumptions linked to capitalism powerfully shape movement strategies and
demands. The effects of capitalism on collective action, for these authors, are
both direct and indirect (that is, mediated by other processes) and are the result
of both short- and long-term processes.

In McAdam's influential study of the US Civil Rights movement, to take one
well-known example, the disintegration of the Southern cotton sharecropping
economy, which was based on 'extra-economic' coercion, and the concomitant
movement of African Americans into urban-based waged jobs, is portrayed as a
necessary precondition for the emergence of that movement. McAdam writes,
'If one had to identify the factor most responsible for undermining the political
conditions that, at the turn of the [twentieth] century, had relegated blacks to
a position of political impotence, it would have to be the gradual collapse of
cotton as the backbone of the southern economy'.[8] The collapse of the South's
cotton economy, in McAdam's account, facilitated the emergence of the Civil
Rights movement mainly indirectly, through its effects on politics and on
the 'indigenous organisation' and beliefs of African Americans. Note, moreover,
that this economic process was crucially important for the very possibility of
the Civil Rights movement, even though this movement was not itself a *class*-
based insurgency making primarily economic demands; rather, the movement
was a cross-class coalition – linking working- and middle-class African Americans as well as sympathetic whites – whose primary demands (at least until the
movement fractured in the late 1960s) were desegregation and voting rights.
(McAdam explicitly noted, incidentally, that his 'political-process' perspective
on movements 'combines aspects of both the élite and Marxist models of power
in America'.)[9]

---

8. McAdam 1999, p. 73.
9. McAdam 1999, p. 38.

The groundbreaking movement scholarship of the 1970s, we should note, not only emphasised the causal importance of capitalism for collective action but also tended to view capitalism, ultimately, as a major – and perhaps *the* major – constraint on human freedom. A number of these studies have an unmistakably anti-capitalist tone, a normative quality that is quite rare in contemporary scholarship on movements. To take just two examples, Piven and Cloward begin their study of 'poor people's movements' with a critique of the 'mystifying' quality of capitalist democracy:

> Power is rooted in the control of coercive force and in control of the means of production. However, in capitalist societies this reality is not legitimated by rendering the powerful divine, but by obscuring their existence... [through] electoral-representative institutions [that] proclaim the franchise, not force and wealth, as the basis for the accumulation of power.[10]

And Skocpol concludes her important comparative study of revolutions by suggesting that 'Marx's call for working-class-based socialism remains valid for advanced societies; nothing in the last hundred years of world history has undercut the compelling potential, indeed necessity, of that call'.[11]

More recent studies of social movements have not only lacked this anti-capitalist spirit, but also largely ignored, with very few exceptions,[12] the enabling and constraining effects of capitalism. We concur, in particular, with Richard Flacks's observation that 'One of Marx's central analytic strategies... is missing from contemporary theories [of social movements] – namely, his effort to embed power relations in an analysis of the political economy as a whole'.[13] Recent scholarship tends to overlook not only the direct and proximate effects of capitalist institutions on collective action, but also the ways in which capitalist dynamics indirectly influence the possibilities for protest, sometimes over many years or even decades, by, for example, shaping political institutions, political alliances, social ties, and cultural idioms. Instead, recent scholarship tends to focus on *short-term* shifts in 'cultural framings,' social networks, and especially 'political opportunities,' rarely examining the deeper causes of such shifts; in fact, most movement scholars now treat this last set of factors as independent variables, neglecting the ways in which they may be powerfully shaped by capitalism.

We find evidence for these claims by examining (1) the leading journals in the field of social movement studies, (2) recent award-winning books and articles

---

10. Piven and Cloward 1977, p. 2.
11. Skocpol 1979, p. 292.
12. Such as Sklair 1995; Buechler 2000; Clawson 2003; and Schurman and Munro 2009.
13. Flacks 2004, p. 139.

in the field, and (3) current textbooks and handbooks on social movements. Let us begin by considering the content of the two main English-language journals dedicated to the analysis of social movements, namely, *Mobilization* (which is based in the USA) and *Social Movement Studies* (based in the UK). *Mobilization* began publication in 1996 and *Social Movement Studies* in 2002. By the 1990s, the evidence indicates, a concern with capitalism had virtually disappeared from the field. Indeed, the reader of these journals is struck by the almost complete absence of economic analysis in their pages.

This conclusion is based on our content analysis of both the titles and abstracts of all articles published in *Mobilization* from its founding in 1996 up to 2007 (a period of 12 years) and in *Social Movement Studies* from its founding in 2002 up to 2007 (a period of six years). The results of this analysis are striking. For *Mobilization*, in a total of 183 article titles and abstracts, the word 'capitalism' appears exactly once – in an abstract – and even the more neutral word 'economy' appears in only one title and two abstracts. The words 'class conflict' and 'class struggle' do not appear in a single article title or abstract. By contrast, the concept of 'political opportunities' appears in 11 titles and 42 abstracts, and the concept of 'frame' or 'framing' appears in nine titles and 24 abstracts.

The results are quite similar for *Social Movement Studies*. In a total of 71 article titles and abstracts, the word 'capitalism' appears in one article title and three abstracts, and the word 'economy' appears in one title and one abstract. Again, the words 'class conflict' and 'class struggle' do not appear in a single title or abstract. By contrast, the concept of 'political opportunities' appears in three titles and six abstracts, and the concept of 'frame' or 'framing' appears in three titles and 10 abstracts. Our impression is that the articles in *Social Movement Studies* are somewhat more theoretically diverse than those in *Mobilization* (there is less conventional 'political opportunity' and 'frame' analysis in the former), but this theoretical diversity does not include political economy perspectives.

These results are all the more striking given that the publishing histories of *Mobilization* and *Social Movement Studies* largely coincide with the history of the so-called global justice movement (also called the anti- or alter-globalisation movement), a movement with strong anti-capitalist, or at least anti-corporate, demands. This movement has not been overlooked by these journals, but the treatment of it in their pages, oddly, does not reflect a strong interest in linking it with the dynamics of global capitalism. Thirteen articles on the global justice movement were published in *Mobilization* between 1996 and 2007 (7 percent of all articles published in the journal), but only three can be said to evince a political economy perspective. Nine articles on the global justice movement were published in *Social Movement Studies* between 2002 and 2007 (nearly 13 percent of all articles published in that journal), but only two reflect a substantial concern with capitalism or political economy. (Other recent studies of anti-corporate activism that is not linked to the global-justice movement also pay scant attention to the dynamics of capitalism.)[14]

Of course, this type of content analysis is a rather crude method for measuring the substantive content of a journal, but we believe it quite accurately reflects the marked inattention to the dynamics of capitalism – whether at the local, national, or global (or 'world-systemic') level – among English-speaking and especially US scholars in the field of social movement studies. A concern with political economy is also only barely evident in the books and articles that have been honoured recently by the American Sociological Association's section on 'Collective Behavior and Social Movements' (CBSM). The section's website[15] lists 19 books that received the section's book prize from 1988 to 2010 (a prize was not awarded every year) and 11 articles that received the section's best-article prize from 2002 to 2009 (there were co-winners for some of these years). In our review of this literature, we found that only two of the prize-winning books and none of the articles treated the dynamics of capitalism as particularly important for purposes of explanation. The two books are Charles Tilly's *Popular Contention in Great Britain, 1754–1837*,[16] which looks at class-based (and other) forms of mobilisation during the period under study, and Rick Fantasia's *Cultures of Solidarity: Consciousness, Action and Contemporary American Workers*,[17] a study of working-class consciousness in the contemporary United States. In the rest of this literature, capitalism is, at best, a minor theme, if it is mentioned at all.

Finally, capitalism is also scarcely evident in current textbooks and handbooks on social movements. Here, we will focus on just three examples, albeit prominent ones: Donatella della Porta and Mario Diani's *Social Movements: An Introduction*;[18] *The Blackwell Companion to Social Movements*, edited by David A. Snow, Sarah A. Soule, and Hanspeter Kriesi;[19] and Charles Tilly and Sidney Tarrow's *Contentious Politics*.[20]

Della Porta and Diani's textbook is least problematic, from our point of view.[21] (We wonder if this is not related to the fact that the authors are from Italy, whose academic and political cultures are rather different than those in the Anglo-American world.) Their volume includes an interesting chapter entitled 'Social Changes and Social Movements', in which economic factors and processes are shown to be important for movements. The authors do not discuss the dynamics

14. For example Raeburn 2004; Soule 2009.
15. See http://www2.asanet.org/sectioncbsm/awards.html.
16. Tilly 1995.
17. Fantasia 1988.
18. Della Porta and Diani 2006.
19. Snow, Soule and Kriesi 2004.
20. Tilly and Tarrow 2007.
21. Della Porta and Diani 2006.

of 'capitalism' *as such* (a word they very seldom use), but they do note how class conflicts – including strikes, protests by the unemployed, and so on – as well as movements of the 'new middle class' are rooted in the changing 'social structure' of 'industrial societies'. The authors also note how 'economic globalisation' has catalysed protest in recent years. However, their concern with socio-economic structures, social change, and class cleavages is almost entirely confined to this single chapter. Indeed, they justify this with the claim that 'collective action does not spring automatically from structural tensions', and so the bulk of their book is 'dedicated to the mechanisms which contribute to an explanation of the shift from structure to action' – mechanisms having to do with 'the availability of organizational resources, the ability of movement leaders to produce appropriate ideological representations, and the presence of a favorable political context'.[22] But this assumes that such resources, ideologies, and contexts are substantially if not wholly detached from the dynamic structure and practices of capitalism, a view that we would, of course, challenge.

Like the Della Porta and Diani volume, only one chapter in *The Blackwell Companion to Social Movements* emphasises capitalist dynamics,[23] namely a chapter on the US labour movement by Rick Fantasia and Judith Stepan-Norris. The other 28 chapters of this large volume barely mention capitalism or economic processes at all. (A partial exception is the chapter on transnational movements by Jackie Smith, which briefly discusses the 'world capitalist economy'.) The index reveals only a handful of references in the volume's seven hundred pages to capitalism, 'economics', or corporations. 'Class struggle' and 'class conflict' are referenced exactly once. And Gary Marx is referenced more frequently than Karl Marx.

However, the apotheosis of the disappearance of capitalism from social movement studies may well be Charles Tilly and Sidney Tarrow's *Contentious Politics*,[24] a textbook based on ideas first developed in McAdam, Tarrow, and Tilly's *Dynamics of Contention*.[25] As mentioned, the earlier work of Tilly and McAdam did emphasise – indeed, often *strongly* emphasised – capitalist dynamics, including the collapse of agricultural production based on extra-economic coercion (McAdam) and the more general process of proletarianisation (Tilly). In *Contentious Politics*, however, capitalism has disappeared completely. The book makes no mention whatsoever of capitalism, proletarianisation, class conflict, or political economy generally. This is remarkable for a book explicitly designed to provide undergraduate and graduate students with the analytical tools and procedures they will need to understand social movements, revolutions, nationalist movements,

22. Della Porta and Diani 2006, p. 63.
23. Snow, Soule and Kriesi 2004.
24. Tilly and Tarrow 2007.
25. McAdam, Tarrow and Tilly 2001.

transnational struggles, and 'contentious politics' generally. Instead of situating these conflicts against the historical backdrop of capitalism and state building, as Tilly once prescribed, *Contentious Politics* discusses (and formally defines) a number of very general 'mechanisms' and 'processes' that allegedly illuminate a wide range of concrete episodes of political conflict. The authors make some effort to link these mechanisms and processes to state structures and 'routine' politics, but they say nothing about how these mechanisms and processes might relate to the dynamics of the capitalist economy. One can only infer that either no such relations exist or they are not worthy of attention, and that students today need not bother to learn about the institutions and trajectories of capitalist economies in order to understand social movements, revolutions, or political conflict more generally. By contrast, in *From Mobilization to Revolution*, published in 1978, Tilly wrote: 'Over the long run, the reorganization of production creates the chief historical actors, the major constellations of interests, the basic threats to those interests, and principal conditions for transfers of power [that is, revolutions]'.[26] But the 'reorganization of production' is not to be found among the mechanisms and processes emphasised by Tilly and Tarrow thirty years later.

What happened? What might account for this strange disappearance of capitalism from social movement studies? Here, we can only speculate, but we would argue that this transformation is the result of several linked factors, including the waning of Marxism in the social sciences after the 1970s, the so-called 'cultural turn' in academia, and a growing emphasis on micro- and meso-level analysis – including framing and network analysis – in social movement studies proper. (It is also possible that some scholars in the USA have avoided the conceptual vocabulary, if not the concerns, of Marxist political economy for fear of not being published or tenured.) Our aim, here, is not to criticise cultural, framing, or network analysis, but simply to point out that these have effectively – and *unnecessarily* – 'crowded out' a concern with political economy in the field. As a result, a number of promising causal mechanisms linked to the dynamics of capitalism are no longer even considered worthy of attention by movement-scholars.

These claims about the factors behind the disappearance of capitalism from movement studies are speculative, based on observations of changing academic tendencies over the past few decades. It is, in fact, very difficult to determine precisely why academic fashions and styles change over time, sometimes quite dramatically over just a few years. But the results are clear and ironic: During an era in which global capitalism became ever more powerful – an era when capitalism triumphed over Soviet-style Communism – it also became increasingly

---

26. Tilly 1978, p. 194.

invisible to scholars of popular movements, especially in the United States. Even a recent volume on the 'silences' in social movement theorising is silent about capitalism and political economy.[27] For us, however, the key question is not *why* capitalism has disappeared from movement studies, but whether the analysis of movements has suffered as a result. We believe that it has.

How does capitalism matter?

We have already suggested some of the ways in which capitalism might shape social movements, including non-class-based movements. We thus believe that the common justification for the neglect of political economy by movement-scholars – namely, that most social movements (perhaps *all* of them, other than the labour movement) are not about class or 'materialist' concerns and thus have no discernible connection to capitalism – is empirically and analytically untenable. McAdam's study of the US Civil Rights movement,[28] quoted above, clearly demonstrates that ethnic (or 'racial') and other non-class-based movements may be powerfully shaped by political-economic factors. To support this claim further, we examine below a movement that seemingly has nothing, or very little, to do with issues of class, work, or political economy, namely, the gay and lesbian (or LGBT) movement. Our reading of the literature on this and other movements suggests that the dynamics of capitalism and political-economic factors potentially matter for *all* movements in at least four specific ways:

1. Capitalist dynamics alternately inhibit or facilitate the formation of new *collective identities and solidarities*, including both class- and non-class identities. In this way, capitalism shapes the very conditions of existence of many social movements.
2. The balance of class forces in a society powerfully shapes the way movements evolve over time and *what they can win* for their constituents.
3. Class divisions generated by capitalism may unevenly penetrate and fracture movements. The balance of class forces *within* movements – sometimes more and sometimes less organised and self-conscious – may powerfully shape *movement goals and strategies.*
4. Finally, ideologies and cultural idioms closely linked to capitalist institutions and practices may also strongly influence movement strategies and goals.

---

27. Aminzade et al. 2001.
28. McAdam 1999.

A 'hard' case study: the LGBT movement

The rise of 'new social movements' over the last several decades may explain the declining attention given to capitalism and political economy within contemporary social movement studies. (Although during the 1980s, several European scholars sought to explain 'new social movements' precisely in terms of the changing configuration of capitalism.)[29] Unlike 'old' social movements – pre-eminently the labour movement – in which issues of material deprivation and inequality are considered central, new social movements are typically seen as revolving around 'non-material' or 'post-materialist' issues, including lifestyles, identities, and 'recognition'.[30]

As Taylor and Van Dyke note, 'The core thesis of [New Social Movement theory] is that that new social movements, such as the women's, peace, gay and lesbian, environmental, animal rights, disability rights, mental health, antiglobalization movements, and even the New Christian Right and contemporary hate movements, are unique in that they are less concerned with economic redistribution and policy changes than with issues of the quality of life, personal growth and autonomy, and identity and self-affirmation'.[31] The LGBT movement, which we use as a shorthand expression for the family of movements focused on issues of sexual orientation, is thus a paradigmatic example of a new social movement. As such, the LGBT movement is a particularly 'hard' test case for our claim that the dynamics of capitalism should be brought back into social movement scholarship.

Not surprisingly, most recent scholarship on the LGBT movement in the field of social movement studies pays little attention to issues of political economy and class, instead focusing on issues of individual and collective identity-construction and emotion.[32] Between 1996 and 2007, the journal *Mobilization* published four articles that focused centrally on LGBT movements (2 percent of all articles published in the journal); not surprisingly, none evinced an economic or political economy perspective. The journal *Social Movement Studies* published two articles on LGBT movements between 2002 and 2007 (about 3 percent of all articles published in that journal); again, neither of these articles was substantially concerned with the dynamics of capitalism. Nor were the two articles on the LGBT movement that have been recognised by the ASA's CBSM section.[33] (No study of the LGBT movement has yet won the section's book prize.)

---

29. See Steinmetz 1994 for an overview.
30. For example Inglehard 1990; Fraser 1997. Fraser, to be sure, emphasises the need to combine a focus on recognition with one on redistribution. Her work thus attempts to bridge the divide between 'old' and 'new' social movements.
31. Taylor and Van Dyke 2004, p. 273.
32. Such as Armstrong 2002; Rimmerman 2008; and Gould 2009.
33. Armstrong and Crage 2006; Taylor et al. 2009.

As suggested above, however, we believe that the dynamics of the capitalist economy have profoundly shaped the LGBT movement – although to sustain this claim, we must necessarily turn to scholarship that either predates or falls outside the contemporary field of movement studies. To begin with, capitalist development was a necessary condition for the initial emergence and subsequent elaboration of LGBT identities and solidarities. Although it may defy current wisdom, the idea that there is an important – indeed, fundamental – relationship between capitalist development and the emergence of LGBT identities is hardly original. This idea was, in fact, one of the starting points for John D'Emilio's pioneering book on gay and lesbian history, *Sexual Politics, Sexual Communities*, as well as an influential paper, 'Capitalism and Gay Identity', published the same year.[34] The fact that D'Emilio wrote during a period in which political economy and class analysis still occupied a relatively important, if declining, place within social movement studies and social science generally is probably not coincidental. D'Emilio's book and paper appeared just a year after the publication of McAdam's influential study of the Civil Rights movement.

According to D'Emilio, the initial emergence of a collective and publicly visible gay and lesbian identity in the United States was dependent – just as for the African-American Civil Rights movement – upon the expansion of wage labour. This process of 'proletarianisation' diminished the economic importance of the family unit, thereby undermining the material basis for 'traditional' heteronormative sexual relations and creating at least the possibility for more fluid sexual practices and identities.[35] Moreover, the urbanisation that resulted from capitalist industrialisation facilitated the formation of communities based on sexualities and lifestyles. The large, anonymous cities created by capitalist industrialisation made possible the emergence of hidden, 'underground' gay and lesbian subcultures, typically centered around commercial bars, clubs, and other establishments. In a recent interview, D'Emilio summarises his argument in 'Capitalism and Gay Identity':

> The thrust of the argument...was that the shift from kinship forms of production to individual wage labor opened a social and economic space that allowed individuals to live, to survive, outside a reproductive household. Same-sex desire could congeal into a personal identity and a way of life. The opportunity for that to happen was distributed differently depending on one's relation to capitalist modes of production. In the U.S., that meant men more than women, whites more than Blacks, the native-born more than immigrants, and the middle class more than the working class. But the heart of it

---

34. D'Emilio 1983a; 1983b; see also Adam 1987.
35. See also Therborn 2004.

is individuals able to make a living rather than livelihoods being dependent on family groupings.[36]

Capitalist development was central not only to the initial emergence of gay and lesbian solidarities in the late nineteenth and early twentieth centuries, but also to the subsequent development of such identities over the course of the twentieth century. As D'Emilio notes, the economic and demographic changes brought about by the Second World War played an especially important role in the expansion of a postwar gay identity in the 1940s and the subsequent rise of the so-called 'homophile' movement in the 1950s. The initial leaders of the Mattachine Society, the central organisation of the early homophile movement, were former Communist Party militants, whose organising skills had been honed in their fight against capitalism and who utilised their understanding of class consciousness and organisation as a model for the homophile movement.[37] Steve Valocchi[38] is equally emphatic about the connections between the dynamics of capitalist development and the consolidation of a 'class-inflected' gay and lesbian identity in the middle of the twentieth century (a point we elaborate in our discussion of how class divisions have shaped the LGBT movement).

The reconfiguration of a new lesbian collective identity in the 1970s is also connected to capitalism. This is because the 'objective possibility'[39] of lesbianism as a historically and sociologically significant phenomenon, like the rise of 'second-wave' feminism (with which it is closely connected), was predicated upon long-term shifts in the capitalist economy, especially women's increasing participation in the labour force. As Virginia Woolf noted in an earlier era,[40] the ability of women to achieve their full intellectual – and, we might add, sexual – development is dependent upon their ability to achieve economic independence from men.[41] The expansion of 'free' wage labour, in short, was a necessary precondition for the development of powerful movements for civil rights and political influence not only by African Americans (and women), but also by gay men and lesbians. In a sense, these movements thereby completed earlier democratic or 'bourgeois' revolutions of the eighteenth and nineteenth centuries that only partially extended the civil, political, and social rights that we associate with full citizenship.

A second way in which capitalism has been of significance for the LGBT movement concerns the impact of the balance of class forces in society on the

---

36. Quoted in Wolf 2009.
37. D'Emilio 1983a; Adam 1987; Armstrong 2002.
38. Valocchi 1999.
39. Weber 1949.
40. Woolf 2005.
41. See also Klein 1984.

movement's efficacy at any given point in time. As the contributors to Gerald Hunt's volume *Laboring for Rights* demonstrate,[42] the strength of the organised labour movement – especially what Hunt terms 'the extent of [its] historical commitment to "social unionism" '[43] – has been of crucial importance for LGBT movements both over time and across a variety of national contexts (and at the sub- and transnational levels). The relative strength of organised labour movements has also indirectly affected LGBT movements due to the histori- cal role labour movements have played in the development of welfare states in different national contexts.[44] As our discussion of the debate over same-sex marriage in the USA demonstrates (see below), the national characteristics of welfare states have had an important influence on LGBT movements. (Hunt's volume points to an opportunity, as yet unexplored, to link LGBT politics to the 'varieties-of-capitalism' literature,[45] which emphasises cross-national variations in capitalist institutions and their consequences.)

David Rayside's[46] contribution to Hunt's volume examines the contrasting trajectories of LGBT movements and labour relations in four European nations (France, Germany, the Netherlands, and Britain) as well as the influence of LGBT movements on several transnational institutions (the Council of Europe, the European Community, and the European Union). Rayside finds that the rights of LGBT populations have advanced furthest in northern-European nations, such as the Netherlands, Norway, and Denmark, which are also, not coincidentally, the countries where social democratic parties have been strongest. Indeed, Ray- side draws an explicit connection between political economy and LGBT rights, arguing that 'Those countries in which most progress has been made toward equality for gays and lesbians (in northern Europe) are also countries with the most advanced labor-relations systems'.[47]

A glance at the countries in which same-sex marriage was first legalised (see Table 1) provides further evidence of a link between social democracy and LGBT rights. Of the seven countries in which same-sex marriage was legal as of 2009, four are strongly social democratic (the Netherlands, Belgium, Norway, and Sweden) and the other three all have at least fairly strong labour movements (Spain,[48] Canada, and South Africa).

All this raises the question of what might account for the evident connection between social democracy and LGBT rights. While it is beyond the scope of this

42. Hunt 1999a.
43. Hunt 1999b, p. 7.
44. Such as Esping-Andersen 1990.
45. See Hall and Soskice 2001.
46. Rayside 1999.
47. Rayside 1999, p. 230.
48. Spain's law recognising gay marriage was enacted by a Socialist government.

Table 1. *Countries in which same-sex marriage was first legalised*

Netherlands (2001)
Belgium (2003)
Spain (2005)
Canada (2005)
South Africa (2006)
Norway (2009)
Sweden (2009)

paper to provide a complete answer to this question, it seems likely the support for LGBT rights in strongly social-democratic countries may have something to do with the levels of social solidarity in these countries. Göran Therborn[49] suggests as much, in citing the 'secular pluralism' prevalent in northern Europe as a chief factor favoring the greater acceptance of same-sex marriage in the region. A second factor worth considering is the inclusive nature of the state in social-democratic nations. This possibility is supported by Rayside's analysis of the way in which the Dutch state – which, he argues, 'reflects a general pattern of interest-group inclusion in elaborate consultative exercises designed to arrive at consensus'[50] – helped to promote LGBT rights, by (eventually) incorporating rather than repressing the country's main gay and lesbian organisation, the *Cultuur en Ontspannings Centrum* (COC).

A final factor worth examining relates to the transition from industrial to post-industrial politics. According to Therborn,[51] this shift – from a class-based politics focused on *necessity* to a post-class-based politics focused on *choice* – accounts for the emergence of sexuality and other 'choice'-based issues in Swedish politics from the 1980s onwards. Rayside's examination of how 'shifts in the balance of union membership away from the industrial working class have opened up unions to social causes',[52] prompting a greater willingness on the part of Dutch unions to embrace LGBT issues, provides further support for this view. Rayside finds that individual union support for LGBT issues is usually greatest when unions 1) have a historically weak relationship with the state and 2) are confronted with significant membership losses and demographic shifts. This demonstrates the importance of paying close attention to the specific ways in which issues of class and sexuality intersect in particular countries at particular times.

---

49. Therborn 2004, p. 223.
50. Rayside 1999, p. 212.
51. Therborn 1992, p. 104.
52. Rayside 1999, p. 213.

The fight over same-sex marriage in the USA provides a nice illustration of this point. Although the issue is complex and, certainly, not reducible to political-economic factors, there is an important sense in which material considerations are central to the struggle for same-sex marriage in the United States. Especially important, in this regard, is the relative weakness of the US welfare state as compared to more social-democratic states in Europe and elsewhere.[53] This weakness – as is well known – is, in turn, closely tied to the weakness of the labour movement in the United States, a result of the absence of a labour party and comparatively low union density. Accordingly, in the United States, many of the social benefits provided by the state in other national contexts are, instead, directly tied to employment – of oneself or of one's spouse.[54] One of the most important benefits tied to employment is, of course, healthcare, and as Rimmerman points out in his discussion of same-sex marriage, 'Health insurance is a major issue for everyone in a country that provides health care as a privilege rather than as a right'.[55]

While there are, of course, many non-economic factors to consider, here, including the stigma and psychological costs of exclusion from a central cultural rite, the economic benefits attached to marriage in the United States should not be underestimated. One recent study found that the price of being a gay couple in the United States can amount, across one's lifetime, to over $467,000, mainly due to exclusion from one's partner's health-insurance, Social Security, and spousal Individual Retirement Account benefits.[56] This has undoubtedly provided a powerful impetus for the LGBT movement to take up the demand for marriage rights. Indeed, this point is also not lost upon *opponents* of marriage rights for gays and lesbians, who argue that 'by embracing same-sex marriage, lesbian and gay movements are endorsing the real economic privileges associated with marriage as an institution in the United States, such as healthcare coverage, inheritance rights, Social Security survivors' benefits, and tax breaks'.[57] In short, the salience of LGBT campaigns for same-sex marriage is shaped, in significant part, by specific political-economic contexts that reflect something of the balance of class forces in a given society.

Capitalism has also been of significance for LGBT movements insofar as class relations have unevenly penetrated and fractured these movements. Surprisingly, however, this process has been almost totally ignored in recent accounts of the LGBT movement in the United States. Elizabeth Armstrong's important and

---

53. For example Esping-Andersen 1990.
54. Fantasia and Voss 2004.
55. Rimmerman 2008, p. 119.
56. Bernard and Lieber 2009.
57. Rimmerman 2008, p. 126.

well-received study, *Forging Gay Identities*,[58] is illustrative. In fact, among recent scholars of the LGBT movement, Armstrong stands out for at least acknowledging the importance of class for the movement, titling one of her chapters, 'Exclusions: Gender, Race, and Class in the Gay Identity Movement, 1981–1994'. It is, therefore, quite telling (and more than a little ironic) that Armstrong's own analysis, in this chapter, ends up reproducing one of the very 'exclusions' she set out to highlight, namely, that of class. The lack of substantive attention to class stands in marked contrast to the chapter's detailed treatment of gender and race. While race and gender are each discussed in separate sections of the chapter, the importance of class for the movement is never independently examined.

The question of class has received much more attention in scholarship addressing the often contentious relationship between the LGBT and labour movements[59] – a scholarship that has developed outside and independently of the field of social movement studies.[60] The contributors to Krupat and McCreery's edited volume, *Out at Work: Building a Gay-Labor Alliance*,[61] examined the ups and downs of this relationship in the United States moving from 'labor's dark age'[62] to the historic 1997 founding of 'Pride at Work,' the AFL-CIO's first official constituency group devoted to LGBT members.[63] Krupat and McCreery rightly wondered whether it is possible 'to conceive of a gay doctor and a lesbian police officer bound by a common class interest'.[64] Their initial response to this question was in the affirmative, based on the fact that in 'the thirty-nine states where employers may legally fire workers simply because they are known or thought to be gay, these workers would be equally vulnerable, despite traditional class distinctions such as disparities in income and education'.[65] But other contributors to the same volume point to the continuing fact of class divisions within the LGBT movement.

For instance, Amber Hollibaugh, in conversation with Nikhil Pal Singh, argues that 'social movements that are advocacy movements – the queer movements, the sexuality movements, the HIV movements – have come to reflect more and more fundamentally the class of the people who dominate them'.[66] Hollibaugh

---

58. Armstrong 2002.
59. Hunt 1999a, Krupat and McCreery 2001a.
60. We can only note in passing that social movement studies and labour studies have developed separately in the United States. The ASA has separate sections on 'Collective Behavior and Social Movements' and 'Labor and Labor Movements'.
61. Krupat and McCreery 2001a.
62. Krupat 2001.
63. Sweeney 2001.
64. Krupat and McCreery 2001b, p. xvii.
65. Ibid.
66. Hollibaugh and Singh 2001, p. 73.

cites the example of how LGBT organisations dealt with President Clinton's so-called 'Don't ask, don't tell' policy toward gays in the armed forces:

> The queer organizations in conflict with Clinton's 'Don't ask, don't tell' policy said the policy discriminated against guys at West Point. They didn't ask, 'Who are the majority of gay people in the military?' The majority are poor women and men of color who joined the army or navy or air force because they had no job options where they were. Policy on gays in the military is most felt by the foot soldier, by the guy who is a faggot who flies a helicopter or a dyke who drives an army supply truck. Not having those people represented as the driving force behind an agenda for gay rights in the military reflected the class politics of these movements and the economics that fueled those campaigns.[67]

As Hollibaugh points out, this is but one example of the many ways in which class divides the LGBT movement: 'Much of the gay movement, in my experience, has been willing to forego substantive discussion about anything of concern to anyone but a privileged and small part of homosexuality in this culture. The politics of these gay movements are determined by the economic position of those who own the movement'.[68]

Valocchi[69] is also centrally concerned with class divisions within the LGBT movement. He seeks to understand how a multiplicity of sexual practices and identities – varying by class, race, and gender – were reduced to a singular definition of homosexuality, one based solely on same-sex object choice. According to Valocchi, there are two reasons why this occurred – both of which have to do with class. First, defining homo- and heterosexuality as based exclusively upon sexual object choice helped middle-class gays *and* straights to alleviate their 'gender-related anxieties about work and family',[70] which stemmed from the changing meanings of 'masculine' and 'feminine' roles in the world of non-manual, white-collar work. Valocchi emphasises, however, that far from being 'natural' or universal, this middle-class definition of homosexuality as same-sex object-choice initially 'coexisted with a variety of alternative definitions in working class and African-American urban communities'.[71] In order to understand how the middle-class definition of homosexuality came to prevail over alternative definitions, it is necessary to examine the actions of a second group of actors: 'progressive' middle-class reformers.

According to Valocchi, the actions of these reformers, along with the 'reform-minded capitalists' with whom they collaborated, must be understood within

---

67. Hollibaugh and Singh 2001, pp. 73–4.
68. Hollibaugh and Singh 2001, p. 74.
69. Valocchi 1999.
70. Valocchi 1999, p. 212.
71. Valocchi 1999, p. 210.

the context of the shift from 'competitive' to 'reform' capitalism in the early decades of the twentieth century – reinforcing the importance of situating the LGBT movement within its larger political-economic context. Valocchi writes: 'As market relations drastically altered the landscape of virtually every social institution, they created a host of social problems; at least that is how a reform-minded middle-class came to see issues of immigration, race, crime, labor conflict, and sexual difference'.[72]

These 'social problems' – along with the pressing need to 'maintain ... conditions of profitable capital accumulation in an increasingly unstable economic world' – gave rise to the project of 'building a more secure capitalism in the United States'.[73] As Valocchi notes, 'This was a project that involved interventions not only in the economic realm but in the social and cultural realms as well ... In the arena of sexuality, it was a project whereby a professional middle class harnessed the economic power of capitalists to the political power of the state to create a collective gay identity that stressed same-sex desire and the hetero/homo binary'.[74]

Valocchi explains that there was a two-step process involved in this. First, middle-class men in white-collar positions experienced growing anxieties about their participation in 'feminine' (that is, non-manual) work. Policing the boundary between hetero- and homosexuality was a way for these anxiety-ridden men to reassert their masculinity. This led to a more rigid definition of homosexuality in terms of same-sex object choice. This definition was then enforced in order to unify a range of 'deviant' sexual practices, subsuming different groups under the rubric of 'homosexuals'. While Velocchi suggests that this new definition may not have sat comfortably with certain groups, it was increasingly embraced by middle-class 'homosexual' activists who were seeking acceptance as a non-threatening 'minority' group.

As these examples makes clear, the politics of the LGBT movement – including its goals, strategies, and discourse – cannot be understood without attention to the class composition – and class ideologies – of its members and leaders.

We turn, finally, to a brief discussion of the pervasive and, for us, insidious role of capitalist ideology in the LGBT 'workplace' movement in the United States. (The fact that a workplace movement *exists* within the larger LGBT movement suggests that 'new social movements', despite some definitions of that term, may, in fact, have important 'materialist' concerns.) In her excellent analysis of the LGBT workplace movement in the United States, entitled *Changing Corporate*

---

72. Valocchi 1999, p. 209.
73. Ibid.
74. Ibid.

America from Inside Out: Lesbian and Gay Workplace Rights,[75] Nicole Raeburn highlights several factors that make it more likely for large Fortune 500 corporations to adopt LGBT workplace benefits, including non-discrimination policies and health insurance for domestic partners. These factors include changes in the external political environment, isomorphic pressure from competing companies, and internal pressure from LGBT activist networks operating within a given firm. Raeburn sees this last factor as the most important of all (although she notes that isomorphic pressure within a given industry may increase in importance over time).

Despite the crucial importance of social movement activism in the struggle for LGBT workplace rights, Raeburn also finds that in public accounts of the extension of workplace rights to LGBT employees – accounts by corporate executives, the media, and *even by LGBT employee-activists themselves* – the importance of employee activism tends to be downplayed, if not completely ignored. Instead, the extension of benefits and workplace rights to LGBT employees is most often explained through what Raeburn calls an 'ideology of profits'.[76] In this 'profit-centered account,' the explanation for why corporations extend benefits to LGBT employees rests on the 'bottom line' – that is, corporations adopt LGBT-friendly policies not because of social movements, but because it is profitable to do so.

The 'ideology of profits' has become a powerful tool, consciously used by LGBT activists in their struggle to win workplace rights. The problem with this profit-centric story is not simply that it is empirically wrong, but that it may, in fact, make the *future* conquest of LGBT workplace rights more difficult by convincing LGBT employees that social movement activism is not (or is no longer) important. As Raeburn notes:

> profit-centered explanations of equitable-benefits adoption treat the process of policy change too narrowly... In such tellings of the story, there appear to be no 'live and in the flesh' change agents at all, just the amorphous market and its competitive pressures spurring companies to play follow-the-leader.

The problem is that, 'Left with this impression, many gay and lesbian workers in yet-to-adopt companies may decide that mobilizing for equitable benefits is unnecessary'.[77]

The significance of this finding goes beyond the LGBT workplace movement, touching on the relationship between capitalist ideology – including ideas associated with 'market fundamentalism'[78] – and social movements generally. As

---

75. Raeburn 2004.
76. Raeburn 2004, p. 250.
77. Raeburn 2004, p. 252.
78. For example, Soros 1998.

Raeburn demonstrates, in contexts like the contemporary United States, where market ideology is pervasive, the efficacy of social movement activists can come to depend upon their ability to successfully frame movement success in market-friendly terms. In such contexts, movement efficacy is thus dependent upon a denial of the very existence of movements. This process, in turn, further strengthens the perverse power of market ideology, while simultaneously decreasing the likelihood of future social movement mobilisation.

Conclusion

The preceding analysis of the LGBT movement suggests that even 'new social movements' that are neither class-based nor centrally concerned with economic or 'materialist' issues may be powerfully shaped by capitalism in a number of distinct ways. Our more general conclusion is that the academic field of social movement studies has paid a heavy *and unnecessary* theoretical price for its recent neglect of capitalism and political economy. We have identified a number of very important causal processes – direct and indirect, short- and long-term – which are now routinely ignored by movement scholars, who have tended, in recent years, to focus exclusively on the short-term and proximate causes of collective action, especially changing political opportunities and strategic framing by movement leaders. Greater attention to causal mechanisms associated with the dynamics of global capitalism will undoubtedly improve the quality of much current social movement analysis – including the analysis of changing political opportunities and strategic framing. In sum, it is time to bring capitalism back into social movement studies.

Marxism and the Politics of Possibility: Beyond Academic Boundaries
John Krinsky

Introduction

February 2011, City Hall Park, New York City. Ten thousand people mass together on a clear morning to proclaim their solidarity with public sector workers in the state of Wisconsin. With their supporters, public sector workers have been protesting for more than two weeks at the capitol in Madison, and have occupied the building. There, Governor Scott Walker has just proposed a law ending union rights for public sector workers. We stand on the sidewalk, penned into areas separated by metal police barriers, holding placards, shouting slogans and appreciation to passing, honking motorists, and listening to a stream of union bigwigs and politicians from the Democratic Party denounce Governor Walker, Republican legislators, and policies that have caused epochal inequality in the United States. The crowd at City Hall has gathered on three days' notice, contacted by friends, unions, and other organisations, most often through email lists, such as those maintained by MoveOn.org, an online, centre-left advocacy broker.

A visitor from Wisconsin reads out a statement of solidarity from her daughter's friend, an Egyptian student who has joined the Revolution with hundreds of thousands of others demonstrating in Tahrir Square, in Cairo. During these weeks, images of solidarity signs from Madison, Wisconsin to Cairo and back circulate on the Internet.

Vast gulfs separate the demonstrations at City Hall Park, the state capitol in Madison, and in Tahrir Square and before that in Tunisia, as well as the revolutionary situations in the Middle East and the often militant demonstrations and strikes in Greece, Britain, and so on which preceded them. Nevertheless, the important element of mutual public statements of solidarity between Madison and Cairo is that far-flung protesters are drawing inspiration from each other and beginning to see their struggles as connected. This opens up a set of questions that is at once analytical and political:

- How *are* contemporary struggles of people from Egypt to Wisconsin, and from Greece to India connected?
- Given the connection among struggles, how can people best conduct local action while building solidarity with others in ways that advance a larger project of freedom?
- How do activists and others make sense of these struggles, why do they do so as they do, and what can be done to promote alternatives to dominant ways of understanding contemporary social relations?
- How do the legacies of previous struggles prepare us for – or impede us from – fulfilling these tasks?

These are not *precisely* the questions that scholars of social movements have been asking for the last thirty years or so, but they do bear some family resemblance to their more scholarly cousins. The academic versions most often lead to answers that aspire to a generality that the more activist-analytical ones do not. Academic social movement scholarship asks questions that then get sorted into 'theories', or 'approaches' whose tenets are supposed to apply across cases and generate testable hypotheses in a predictable way.

This chapter will begin by briefly reviewing these theories according to what kinds of questions they ask and answers they offer. I will argue that each of them *does* have something to offer an activist understanding of social movements, but that each is also one-sided. They all suggest facets of movement dynamics, but do so as if they were unconnected to each other, or imply that their collisions are contingent rather than systematic. I then offer a different, Marxist approach, drawn largely from the work of Antonio Gramsci, and highlighting five key aspects of Marxism, namely: *dialectical totality, contradiction, immanence, coherence*, and *praxis*. What I mean by these will become apparent, but for now it will suffice to say that these aspects shift the analytical and political ground of academic theories towards the initial set of questions, making them both more useful for activism and more comprehensive.

Academic social movement theories

Contemporary social movement theories have formed loosely bounded 'schools' identifiable by their main concerns. The 'Collective Behaviour' tradition dating from the early 1960s is interested in the social-psychological question of why people surrender their individual autonomy to collective action.[1] The 'Resource Mobilisation' school argues that while grievances are omnipresent and ongoing, actual protest occurs when divisions among élites raise the costs of repression and push non-élite groups into alliances with fractions of élites.[2]

The 'Political Process' approach, which has dominated social movement theory in the United States for thirty years, extends and alters Resource Mobilisation by arguing that: 1) indigenous organisation is critical to sustained protest mobilisation; 2) activists must mobilise on the basis of alternative understandings of prevailing power relations and must see them as changeable, and, therefore, look for ways to 'frame' public debates symbolically so as to build broader and stronger organisations and coalitions; 3) political opportunities can be more or less institutionalised in a given régime, so that mobilisation can itself become a more or less regular feature of political systems; and 4) forms of protest, organisation, and claim making are cultural and historical, in that, through repetition, they congeal, over time, into 'repertoires' of associated performances that shape our very understandings of what counts as political protest.[3] Accordingly, the Political Process approach has spawned research on the relationships between types of régime and protest dynamics; diffusion of protest performances and the formation of repertoires; activists' efforts to 'frame' new understandings of protest; and the relationship between types of organisation or organisational roles and the conduct of protest activities.

The 'Dynamics of Contention' or DOC approach, developed by some of the same scholars responsible for Political Process theory, finds that amidst all the 'process' in Political Process, there is little theorisation of action. To grasp this, DOC proposes that political contention (including but not limited to social movements) be broken down into micro-processes or 'mechanisms' that unfold between or among actors (though actors could be individuals or collectives). This approach allows scholars to investigate how local protest, involving few people, grows or 'shifts scale', and how new politicised identities form. Smaller processes such as symbolic boundary formation, brokerage among two or more actors, and certification – or

---

1. Smelser 1962.
2. McCarthy and Zald 1977.
3. McAdam 1982; McAdam, McCarthy and Zald (eds.) 1996; Tarrow 1998.

acceptance of an outsider by established, powerful actors – could be put together in different sequences to understand movement dynamics.[4]

New Social movement theory (NSM) is another response to Political Process and Resource Mobilisation theories. NSM developed mainly in Western Europe in the 1980s, in response both to the rationalist assumptions of the Resource Mobilisation approach and to the reductive ways in which some Marxists conceived of social movements and class. Though a diverse group, NSM theorists argue that we should see 'identity' as supplanting 'interest' at the heart of social movements, and that 'interest' is too static a category, without a sense of how identities are composed. Further, drawing on social movements since the 1960s, many NSM theorists focus on personal authenticity and self-determination.[5] In the 1980s, it appeared that state-administered welfare capitalism had met many of the demands of organised labour and that labour-movements (identified with 'the working class') had become rigid and demobilised. At the same time, women, people of colour, and gays, lesbians, and bisexuals, were claiming citizenship rights, other movements warned that consumer capitalism was producing a profoundly alienating culture and destroying the environment, while the Cold War powers threatened everyone with nuclear annihilation. NSM theorists, accordingly, often found the Political Process and Resource Mobilisation approaches' focus on challengers' efforts to be included in or to enlarge the polity, rather than on efforts to transform it, too focused on the state, and too accepting of the materialist biases of dominant culture.

In Europe, NSM theory's inquiry into identity was linked to scholars' attempts to envisage a new revolutionary subject from the movements that blossomed in the 1960s. In the United States, NSM theorists put subjectivity at the heart their inquiries into identity. What people think and feel is the key to understanding new movements. Further, the focus on subjectivity informs other critiques of Political Process theory and DOC that claim that they are bloodless; and, in being bloodless, are unable to understand their own central processes, such as 'attributions of opportunity and threat'.

Others, such as James Jasper,[6] argue that the lack of subjectivity in social movement theories demands a radical move *away* from considering how larger organisations like states or systems like capitalism prompt and limit protest and *towards* looking for 'micro-foundations', in which people's understandings of their situations and, crucially, strategic choices in the face of common dilemmas take centre stage. Here, as in a 'multi-institutional approach', such as that recently

---

4. See, for instance, Melucci 1996a; see also McAdam, Tarrow and Tilly 2001.
5. See, for instance, Cohen 1985; Melucci 1989; Offe 1985b; Touraine 1981; also see Buechler 1995.
6. Jasper 2004.

put forward by Elisabeth Armstrong and Mary Bernstein,[7] action unfolds as people whose action and thoughts are shot through with larger cultural frameworks move among institutional settings or 'arenas', along the way developing and reformulating a range of alliances and new interpretations of events.

In all these approaches, there are echoes of the more activist questions suggested earlier, but they are posed differently; Political Process, Resource Mobilisation, and DOC approaches seem more abstract, and focus, ultimately, on establishing a kind of value-neutral social-scientific understanding of movement dynamics. They are concerned about getting the object of the study 'right'. NSM theory, which at least implicitly entails a radical democratic project, by contrast systematically overstates the novelty of NSMs, often treats identities as clearly bounded (repeating the mistake of the 'interest'-based theories it criticises), and tends to prefer generalisations about culture and cultural change to more grounded criticism of socio-cultural dynamics. Nevertheless, all can point us to important ideas: for questions of international connections among movements, Political Process and Resource Mobilisation theories would direct us to studying transnational networks of activists, on the one hand, and the structure of global élites, on the other, while NSM theory would point to a broader shift in collective identities with the spread of a global culture. The DOC approach might build on the Political Process and Resource Mobilisation theories to focus on the ways in which Internet-mediated communication changes the requirements for identity formation. A multi-institutional approach and a micro-foundational approach might highlight the ways in which international, national, and local arenas or institutions relate to – and often conflict with – each other. Similarly, questions about how activists understand their actions and connections with others will be less central to DOC and Resource Mobilisation, but might be investigated by means of theories of framing or studies of repertoire formation in Political Process theory.

Taken as broader approaches to the movements, however, existing social movement studies remain one-sided and largely incapable of furnishing movements with useful theory. By one-sided, I mean that theories of movements take aspects that scholars find neglected in existing research, such as movements' organisational capacities and élite-allies (Resource Mobilisation), participants' collective identities (NSM theory), and even diverse, situated actions and dilemmas (DOC and 'strategic' approaches), and raise them to the status of *the most important* thing to explain or *most important explanation* of social movement action. Despite the requisite disclaimers that accompany social-science writing, this is generally the case and recognisable to anyone who regularly reads in the

---

7. Armstrong and Bernstein 2008.

field. As a result, social movement scholars rarely take positions with respect to larger debates about power, the economy and the state, and only uneasily – and, sometimes, guiltily – acknowledge their own political projects in their work. They tend, in other words, to understand politics as being somehow *outside* of their own analyses. It is, therefore, difficult for people more actively involved in efforts at social change, in all their variability and complexity, to learn even from the useful aspects of social movement theories.

Marxism and social analysis

Most academic studies of movements cleave to an ideal of value-free social science. This ideal, dating from the late nineteenth and early twentieth centuries, was generated both by the business-led backlash against party politics, which sought a public administration freed from the prejudices of politics (and from the democratic pressures to which it was subject), and by centre-right figures in academia, such as Max Weber.[8] Marxism departs from this conception in favour of an *engaged* view of social theory. I will present this alternative first with reference to five of its major features: *totality, contradiction, immanence, coherence, and praxis.*

Totality

Marxism begins by seeing the world as a *dialectical totality*. Marxists, that is, understand the social world as in a state of constant change, and thus as composing and composed by the many relationships among people, the natural world, and the products of human labour. These are not just 'parts' that can be summed together; rather, they are elements always defined by their *internal relations to the whole*.[9] Nevertheless, this totality cannot be comprehended all at once; rather, it must be understood by a process of careful abstraction, by identifying key relationships, and understanding the relation of parts to wholes. If we consider, for example, the uprising in Egypt in early 2011, we could understand it as part of a yearning for democracy in the Arab world, as it and other revolutions throughout the Middle East suggest. This would be one-sided. As Adam Hanieh argues,[10] there is no clear separation between the 'political' and 'economic' aspects of the revolts, and the Mubarak régime's embrace of neoliberalism, prompted by loan agreements with international financial institutions such as the IMF and the World Bank, resulted in declining living standards for

---

8. See, for instance, Kaufmann 1956.
9. Ollman 2003.
10. Hanieh 2011.

most Egyptians amid economic growth and the massive concentration of wealth. This is not to say that the uprisings in Egypt were *economically determined*, in the sense of being *predestined*. The question is, rather, how we understand the relationship between neoliberal policies, mass impoverishment, the way in which the régime lost even the veneer of popular legitimacy over the course of a decade of protest, and why the protest coalesced as it did when it did. This means, furthermore, that our understanding of the Egyptian Revolution must take into view the economic importance of the military, its cultural importance (greeted initially as guardians of the people by many Tahrir Square protesters), as well as its efforts to ban strikes, given the decade or more of independent labour protest leading up to the 2011 Revolution against the Mubarak régime. We need to understand the reasons that the Egyptian judiciary resisted impunity for the Mubarak régime and its allies and continually challenged its legitimacy, while also understanding the basis of the Muslim Brothers' strength and internal divisions. Moreover, we have to understand the US government's relationship with the Egyptian military, so that efforts at solidarity with the Egyptian Revolution directed towards our own governments are consonant with revolutionary, rather than reactionary tendencies there. The idea, again, is to resist the academic temptation to treat each facet of political action that presents itself as complete and bounded in itself. Instead, we should specify the ways in which we can look at protest dynamics, government restrictions, internal movement splits, foreign entanglements, and financial conditions as necessarily bound up with each other.

Contradiction

A second aspect of Marxist dialectics is *contradiction*. Contradiction is a central principle of dialectics, and one of its distinguishing features as an approach to knowledge: in a dialectical approach, something can be X and *not* X. How? Because dialectics is fundamentally about studying change and relationships, and the 'thingness' of anything is an abstraction from a spatial and temporal set of changing relationships, and so already contains within it a state beyond itself. This is centrally related to totality, since contradictions become evident at different levels of analysis and abstraction.

Let us take an example in the study of social movements: social movements often have more 'reformist' and more 'radical' wings, networks of activists that are joined together, but who often disagree, not just about tactics, but also about goals, about the extent of the relevant group being politically represented, and about who best represents this group. Reformist activists often take dominant categories of social groups for granted and seek political equality, social inclusion, or economic benefits for that group, while more radical activists seek to change the entire outlines of the social institutions and categories on which existing exclusions are based. Gamson notes this tension in his work on gay activism's encounter with queer activism in the early 1990s, arguing that this is a fundamental contradiction in identity movements.[11] The contradiction goes further, however, and affects political representation in movements *as such*, because movements always *at least raise the question* of how to represent a subordinate group in order to abolish the conditions of their subordination (and thus, a key element in their 'groupness'). This is as fundamental to queer movements and anti-racism as it is to revolutionary socialism. Movements operate, therefore, on the seams of social contradictions between what *is* and what *could be*; but as such, they develop their own internal contradictions between reformist and radical tendencies. Reformers will experience contradictions between their strategies and the intransigence of oppression; radicals will experience contradictions as they face internal struggles over whether it is necessary to 'prefigure' new social arrangements, or whether one can 'dismantle the Master's house with the Master's tools', to use the poet Audre Lorde's terms.[12] Nevertheless, radicals' commitment to the self-activation of subordinated groups – rather than their being represented by élites, either from outside or from within the group – tends to cast the conditions of subordination to the forefront, as reformist measures tend to reinforce larger systems of subordination even while benefiting some members of previously subordinated groups.

Similarly, Marxists are perfectly capable of understanding the state as a multi-sited institutional amalgam of often-conflicting groups, in which institutional rules form that may be at odds with each other, and thus form, in Armstrong and Bernstein's terms, 'contradictions'.[13] The difference is that, at a higher level of analysis, Marxists also identify contradictions at the heart of the state, taken in aggregate, according to its governing function. For states – whatever their forms – depend on the taxation of economic surplus in order to fund their operations. Because of this, they require some level of legitimacy among the population that generates this surplus. This requires some combination of force and consent, and consent is usually at least partly 'bought' by the state's provisions for people's material needs and well-being. At the same time, however, to the extent that the state provides for popular needs, it needs to tax accumulated wealth, and since this is concentrated among owners of capital who can often invest their capital elsewhere, states can be caught in the contradiction between accumulation and legitimisation.[14] States develop various solutions for dealing with this contradiction, both through internal institutional design – for instance,

11. Gamson 1995.
12. Lorde 1984.
13. Armstrong and Bernstein 2008, p. 86.
14. See, for example, O'Connor 1973.

privatisation of public services, recognition of corporate rights, and the promotion of civic service and volunteering – and external relations with transnational financial institutions such as the World Bank and International Monetary Fund. These solutions set important parameters around the institutional contradictions that occur at the 'meso' level of analysis favoured by institutional analysts like Armstrong and Bernstein.

Immanence

Marx describes his method as 'regard[ing] every historically developed form as being in a fluid state, in motion, and therefore grasps its transient aspect as well'.[15] The principle of contradiction – whether at the level of a movement, disaggregated social institutions or states – is critical to understanding this. If, as Marx writes, 'men make their own history, but not in circumstances they choose freely',[16] the constant is that people are socially engaged in working upon their social and material worlds, and thus *have* to deal with contradictions at every level and in every aspect of social life. Nevertheless, as pragmatists would also point out, in doing so, they unite past-, present-, and future-oriented action in ways that either reinforce their inability to overcome particular contradictions, or indicate at least the *potential* to do so.

'Immanence' is another way of speaking about this potential to change the world. Derived from religious language denoting a god that is manifest in everything, immanence, here, suggests that change itself is an aspect of everything, though not everything is constantly changing, still less in anything like the same ways or speed. The *potential* for human action to effect significant changes on its environments and its protagonists, however, is revealed even where it *fails* to overcome the contradictions to which it is directed. The task of political analysis is to identify important parts of the totality of human relations, the contradictions to which they are subject, and the potentials for change that are revealed when these contradictions erupt. For example, in instances of mass upheaval, such as the demonstrations in early 2011 in Tahrir Square, we find potentials for self-organisation – such as in the provision of healthcare, sanitation and food – critical for developing alternatives to a reliance on state provision, even though the demonstrations ultimately gave way to a considerable increase in the power of military officials, who also control significant portions of Egypt's wealth. They also revealed new ways in which communication-technologies and on-the-ground organising can be combined to keep officials on their back foot during the initial stages of a mobilisation. Meanwhile, for those paying attention

---

15. Marx 1976b, p. 103.
16. Marx 1963a, p. 1.

to the development of protest in Egypt over the previous decade, earlier protests among judges and workers revealed the potential for a powerful anti-governmental coalition to form between professionals, labourers, and the unemployed. Equally, we also find activists fighting against an authoritarian régime in the Middle East making connections to struggles against a democratically elected governor in the Midwestern United States.

Three things follow from the centrality of identifying potentials for change to Marxist dialectics. First is the danger of falling into mere speculation. One cannot predict a revolution based on a small demonstration of very committed activists. There may be a political temptation to do so, on occasion, but what Gramsci called a 'realist' or 'historicist' conception of immanence must identify potentials to be developed rather than predict certainties.[17] To be sure, Marxist writing sometimes does do the latter, as in the stirring prose of the *Communist Manifesto*. This leads to the second point about realist immanence, namely, that it is inextricably tied to practice and to larger elements of Marxist theory. The *Communist Manifesto*'s strength lies in its forceful, rhetorical positing of the immanent potential of the working class to change the totality of human relations in favour of a more emancipatory and democratic future. At times, this seems like a certainty; at others, a more contingent outcome of struggle. To the extent that it appears as a certainty, it must be understood as hortatory rhetoric, located in the particular time and place of its production, and as an intervention in it.

More generally, Gramsci argues:

> Anybody who makes a prediction has in fact a 'programme' for whose victory he is working, and his prediction is precisely an element contributing to that victory. This does not mean that prediction need always be arbitrary and gratuitous, or simply tendentious. Indeed one might say that only to the extent to which the objective aspect of prediction is linked to a programme does it acquire its objectivity.[18]

Third, precisely because discovering and developing potentials for action is central to Marxism, learning and consciousness are at the heart of Marxist dialectics.[19] Marxism is concerned especially in identifying those movements and moments of collective action that develop people's consciousness of our broader interconnections, and allow people not just to 'internalise' new ideas, repertoires of action and organisation, and political vocabularies, but also to

---

17. Gramsci 1971, p. 399.
18. Gramsci 1971, p. 171.
19. This is a feature of dialectical thinking in general. See, for example, Dewey 1938 for a Pragmatist understanding of education that is close to Marxism's view.

'externalise' their actions as to transform the world around them in increasingly significant ways.

Coherence

The work of the Italian Marxist Antonio Gramsci offers perhaps the clearest distinction between realist and speculative immanence, and a form of analysis that places the analyst within, rather than above social relations. Gramsci's role as a leader of the Communist Party of Italy in the 1920s (he spent the late 1920s and 1930s in jail, nearly until his death in 1937) also put him at the centre of life-and-death strategic discussions about the direction of the Party and of the world communist movement. Gramsci viewed strategy through the lens of *coherence*, or the ways in which, amid an ever-changing world, stability is created in ways that produce inequalities of power. His analyses all focus on the ways in which organisational, linguistic, ideological, economic and coercive relations can be woven together so that a particular configuration of them seems natural and stable. His studies of different sorts of intellectuals (organic and traditional) and their role in producing knowledge; of language policy and political participation; of socialist strategy; of Italian Fascism; and of new relations of production in the United States; are all geared toward understanding their connections to political-intellectual-ethical projects that cohere and 'make sense'. Gramsci indicates something other than logical coherence; he is interested in coherence not as a formal property, but as historical and political connections that have only to be *more stable* than competing attempts to form alternatives. Accordingly, coherence *implies* its own contradiction: if coherence implies domination and an 'integration of practical and theoretical elements that increase not only logical consistency, but also the capacity to act', those subject to dominance find that their practices are characterised by *incoherence*.[20] The disorganisation of subordinate groups is often experienced as powerlessness. Because, for Gramsci, coherence implies the ability to articulate sustained sets of actions, organisations, and languages, the obstacles facing subordinate groups are formidable. Even when these groups *are* able to participate politically, they often do so in ways that may advance some aspect of their interests, but reinforce the larger, systematic relationships that result in their powerlessness in the first place.

Socio-historical coherence enters social movement theory as 'repertoires of action' and related concepts concerning organisation and discourse.[21] Embedded in the material routines of daily life, repertoires are relatively stable ways in which actors interact with others (such as protesters and police, radicals and

---

20. Thomas 2009, p. 370.
21. See, for instance, Tilly 1995; see also Clemens 1997; Steinberg 1994; 1999b.

moderates) that form the basis for improvisation. Tilly notes, for example, that in a premodern 'repertoire of contention', characterised more by actions like grain-seizures than by mass marches, there had to be regularly scheduled markets near which grain-silos were built, and there had to be an agricultural system that created a surplus while also generating hunger. Repertoires cohere not because of any intrinsic or logical necessity, but because the performances that compose them accrete over time, growing out of historically available resources. They are not static, however. Tilly describes repertoires as *interactive* in that they describe ways of interacting among allies, opponents, and other audience-actor configurations; as such, they are subject to their own contingency.

Repertoires are marked not just by everyday routines, but by the political projects that compose them. They are not neutral. The more nationally focused 'social movement' repertoire of the nineteenth and twentieth centuries, for example, featured indirect protest and demands instead of direct action seeking immediate satisfaction. This was in recognition, however, of the concentration of power in national governments, itself a project of élites' accumulation strategies.[22] Similarly, the fact that City Hall protesters in February 2011 acceded to being penned in by metal police barricades speaks to a repertoire shift in which protester-police relations have become ever more controlled.

Marc Steinberg and others have drawn on the work of V.N. Vološinov and Mikhail Bakhtin, early Soviet theorists of language and socio-linguistics, deepening Tilly's understanding of repertoires and extending it to speech and communication.[23] For Vološinov and Bakhtin, speech is irreducibly social, historical, and interactive, or 'dialogic'. People fashion their own speech in anticipation of a response (whether or not they get the response they anticipate!), and are able to do so, in large measure, because ways of speaking are structured by genres, which, like repertoires, accrete over time, linked to the specific times and places of their generation and use. Accordingly, meaning is always created through social interaction, and through the interaction of signs with other signs through their use (rather than through their opposition to other signs in a larger, structural system in which agency plays little evident role).

Work that focuses on the coherence of ways of acting and talking (and also, by extension, of organising) raises the question of the relationship between relatively coherent genres and repertoires and the hegemonic *projects* of actors, as well as the conditions that make these projects possible, but which are also changed by them. To understand this as a question of the relationship of a 'superstructure' to a 'base', is only useful in the most impressionistic, metaphorical sense. The

22. Tilly 1995.
23. For example, Barker 2006a; Krinsky 2007; Blackledge, this volume; also see Vološinov 1973; Bakhtin 1981.

Marxism of Gramsci and of Vološinov, no less than the sociological and historical insights they have inspired in contemporary work, show the impossibility of
treating language, organisation, and action as mere froth on the great waves of
history. In fact, they open actual practice to critique, since a key task of Marxist
analysis is in discerning how our current ways of being and acting are historically grounded, and how they may sustain or subvert the governing projects of
dominant social groups.

Praxis

Ultimately, of course, Marxism is geared towards praxis, towards a theoretically
infused acting upon the world. In fact, Marxism does not even make sense without praxis. Remember Gramsci's point about people making a prediction having
a project that they are trying to accomplish: not only are people always engaged
politically when they intervene in social processes, but the truth-value of any
prediction lies in its accomplishment. It has the potential to be true only to the
extent that people are working, or have shown themselves to be capable of working, towards this accomplishment.

Incorporating praxis into a theory has several important consequences. First,
orienting theory to practice means trying to understand what practice or agency
is and how it works. Recall that practice itself is one *aspect* of a totality: as such,
it entails past, present and the potentials of the future, and unfolds at multiple
levels of analysis, in sometimes contradictory ways. Drawing on the Pragmatist
tradition, Emirbayer and Mische capture at least some of this view in their conception of agency as being a 'chordal triad' combining past-, present-, and future-
oriented interactions among social actors.[24] As in a chord, the notes of memory,
tradition, and habit; problem solving; and long-term projects; are always struck
together, but receive different emphasis or prominence. It is clear that when
actual praxis is robbed of significant *projective* elements – that is, an orientation to the future – the real potentials of their agency to realise transformative
social change are deeply compromised. It is partly for this reason that when
Marx speaks about the 'silent compulsion of economic relations set[ting] the
seal on the domination of the capitalist over the worker',[25] it is to indicate that
the present-oriented concern with existence keeps workers within the confines
of their 'education, tradition, and habit', and very nearly completely shuts down
projective elements of praxis.

---

24. Emirbayer and Mische 1998.
25. Marx 1976a, p. 899.

A second consequence of incorporating praxis into a theory of movements is a real shift in the kinds of questions that you ask. Recall that academic social movement theories typically ask variants of the following sets of questions:

- Why do movements arise when they do?
- What is the relationship of movements to more 'formal' political formations?
- How do movement activists spur others into action?
- Why do movement organisations organise as they do?

These are, without doubt, important questions. Moreover, movement scholars have imparted to them a great deal of nuance, even to the extent that they regularly call into question whether social movements are 'things' worth studying, distinct from other political formations, and whether their analysis crowds out analysis of these other formations.[26] Ever since the beginnings of contemporary movement-theories in the late 1960s, scholars have searched for metaphors, such as social movement *organisations* in social movement *industries* or social movement *communities*, in order to try to distinguish different levels of analysis. Others attempt to delimit the meaning of 'social movement' to a historically specific *form* of 'contentious politics', a more inclusive category encompassing strikes, revolutions, shaming rituals, and other public forms of expressing grievances.

However many insights answers to these questions have generated, they have tended to do so by throwing together, rather than reconciling, theoretically disparate approaches. Thus, for the purposes of explaining the macrodynamics of the appearance of protest, analysts can use theories that focus on anonymous forces of economic or political history, while in order to explain how activists spur others into action, they can use theories that privilege the interpretive frameworks or emotional states of mind of the mobilised. The theories do not have to have anything to do with each other.

The task of Marxist theory is to generate insights across levels of analysis and lead us to directly confront the relations *between* the questions posed by existing movement theories. To break the boundaries separating the subdisciplinary inquiries in the social movements field implies a shift toward praxis, and the questions that flow from it. Recall that these questions are, *at the same time*, pitched at higher and lower levels of generality: If we are to ask questions like 'what kind of organisation is required to make a coherent challenge to neoliberal capitalist policies?', we cannot answer them without reference to actual contemporary or historical examples that demonstrate at least some group's capability to make such a challenge, to formulate alternative politics, generate strategies that block

---

26. See, for instance, Burstein 1998; Walder 2009.

neoliberal dominance, and so on. What this means is that it is difficult to have a Marxist theory of social movements generalisable outside of actual instances of movement. Praxis generates specific kinds of questions that the standpoint of totality reminds us are not 'cases', but facets of an interrelated whole. As a facet of Marxist analysis, then, praxis is inseparable from totality, contradiction, immanence, and coherence. In spite of the apparent 'grand theory' of Marxism, praxis has a way of disciplining and making theory more reflexive and modest even than the apparently less ambitious 'middle-range' theories popular among academic theorists.

Marxist analysis is tethered to praxis and its development. This makes it centrally concerned with learning and consciousness. Here, too, connections with Pragmatism are significant, as suggested earlier. A more specifically Marxist-inspired view of learning grew up around Lev Vygotsky, a psychologist in the Soviet Union active in the 1920s and early 1930s, and was taken in several directions by his students after his death. The important aspect of Vygotsky's heritage, in terms of our current discussion, is that *even at the level of learning*, it shows that 'mind' is a *social relation* rather than an individual property stored in the head.[27] While this has since become a well-understood idea in several branches of psychology, pedagogy, artificial intelligence, and studies of human-computer interaction, the 'cultural-historical' school of psychology focuses on the ways in which people learn through acting in concrete, historically determinate situations in attempts to craft coherence amid social contradictions.[28] Learning – the development of consciousness – thus depends on actively changing the world around you, and can, equally, be stymied by the intractability of certain contradictions. However, the cultural-historical approach to learning has a more comprehensive approach to the weight of the world we have already created than does Pragmatism. If, like Pragmatism, the cultural-historical approach focuses on the ways that people solve problems together and in so doing develop a larger concept of their world, the difference is that, as Gramsci indicates, this process of generalisation can be blocked by the inequalities in the civil society institutions that the Pragmatists celebrate.[29] Put differently, the Pragmatists' wish for democratic self-discovery fails to recognise that the institutions in which they hope this might take place are themselves subject to more general contradictory tendencies, not least of which is capitalist exploitation.

27. Vygotsky 1978.
28. Krinsky and Barker 2009; Collins, this volume.
29. Gramsci 1971, p. 373.

Towards a new synthesis

Dialectics and complexity in the study of social movements

A Marxist approach to social movements asks similar questions to those of academic theory, but not precisely the *same* questions. Marxist analysis of social movements can, certainly, learn valuable lessons from academic analyses, since academic theories express *some* element of truth, however one-sidedly. Similarly, though economics is a critical aspect of Marxist analysis, a focus on relations of production can be just as one-sided as a focus on the state, symbolic interaction, and repertoires of protest, if treated in isolation from everything else.

Does this mean that a Marxist approach to movements has to do absolutely everything at the same time? Do the demands of a contradictory totality mean that we get paralysed by complexity? No.

Dialectical thought does not, of course, have a corner on complexity: Surely Gamson and Meyer were right to insist both on the variability in the stability of institutional and non-institutional determinants of 'political opportunities' along with 1) their propensity to spill over national boundaries; and 2) the element of interpretation implicit in their being viewed *as* opportunities. This immensely clarified the analytical dimensions of a term that they, rightly, said had become 'a sponge that soaks up every aspect of the social movement environment'.[30] Similarly, McAdam, Tarrow, and Tilly were correct to argue that the *causal stories* underpinning models of social movement emergence, conduct, and outcomes bore only passing relation to the more static, categorical models of opportunity, framing, and organisation that they themselves had set in motion.[31] Indeed, their argument for mechanisms struck many as being too-complex, or, more precisely, insufficiently parsimonious.

The demand for parsimony in scientific theories may also explain why Gamson and Meyer's insights were never fully taken up by Political Process scholars. Perhaps these and other promising directions in social movement theory never caught on because academic theory demands consistent reduction of complexity and does not furnish *a reason* for why complexity might be important. If, however, as with Marxism, its demand instead grows out of *praxis*, complexity does not appear as a property to be liked or disliked for its own sake, nor for the sake of a better *analysis*. Instead, the demand to know what can be made of shows of international solidarity with very different protests half a world away; the demand to know what needs to happen in order to change dominant terms of debate about public sector employees or about the military; the demand to

---

30. Gamson and Meyer 1996, p. 275.
31. McAdam, Tarrow and Tilly 2001, p. 18.

know how to avoid repeating the mistakes of previous activists, but also not to write off older tactics that failed, if they might be more successfully applied in new circumstances; all these will inevitably generate complex answers. They may or may not be helped along by academic work in social movement theory, but questions of praxis will force the analyst not only to make informed gambles on one course of action or another, but also to do so in ways that identify the kinds of contradictions and potentials for action that are integral to Marxist method.

The economic moment and others

Beyond method, Marxist theory has always insisted that a key part of any explanation of social phenomena, and a key area for the strategic application of activism, lies in what is often too reductively understood as the 'economic' sphere. At the level of analysis of the human species, Marx understood that a key element of our existence and our history is the basic fact that we *have* a history by which we make our own world according to plans, that we materialise our thought in and through social relations, and that we think within the broad limits set by our material and social relations. Marx's general observation forces us to think about the ways in which we organise the production of our world. This larger fact about the human species means that the 'economic' is always present in our analyses of social situations, though reducing the production of our world to economic relations does it a disservice. Not every effort to organise political and social life from below – or from above – has an *immediate* economic referent, nor are all particular dilemmas or contradictions caused by economic tensions.[32] This would be a laughable proposition. But *neglecting* the economic moment in the ways we produce our world and the inequities that consign the majority of humanity to poverty, precariousness, and powerless is *not* a laughing matter.

The economic moment in analysis has, therefore, a further corollary, namely that the working class has the immanent capacity to change the world in a more democratic direction. This 'working class', however, is constituted through a shifting set of relations, expanding and contracting, more and less coherent at different times and places. In spite of the clearly revolutionary role played by the bourgeoisie – one fully recognised by Marx and Engels in the *Manifesto*, and one that is still massively transforming the globe – Marxism gambles on the working class because of the fundamental incapacity of capitalism, which is built on exploitation, to deliver on its emancipatory promises of self-determination. Does this mean that the only or most important movements are always labour movements or 'class movements'? Of course not. But it does mean that Marxists are concerned to see the potentials for broader change within more self-limited ones

---

32. See Gramsci 1971, p. 407.

and to criticise those self-limiting tendencies within movements, including those of the working class, and to constantly push for the analysis of real relationships and their potential for expansion instead of static, self-enclosed categories.[33]

Models for Marxist movement analysis

Throughout this chapter, I have referred to elements of an analysis of social movements that I think hold considerable promise, but which, as tendencies hanging along the edges of mainstream, syncretic academic social movement theories, have not fully gained their due, either in academic circles or, frankly, in activist ones. I want, to suggest, here, that they can be usefully brought together by understanding them to speak to somewhat different levels of abstraction, albeit always implicated in one another.

The study of social movements has focused chiefly on social movement formation (including political opportunities and the creation of new identities), efforts to spur people to action (including framing and other forms of movement 'talk'), and organisation (including such issues as tendencies to oligarchy, the channelling of protest into institutionally acceptable means, and the opposition of instrumental and prefigurative organisation). It has, however, treated these questions as self-contained. Marxism, by contrast, treats these problems as interwoven, by beginning not from rational, individual motivations, but from social interaction. Even if we begin from the microfoundations of individual consciousness, we are not immediately caught up in general assumptions about this consciousness and motivations, but can begin with concrete, historical, and observable interactions. If we are working within the cultural-historical tradition, and see such issues as identity-formation and even strategy as learning processes shaped in interaction, then we are confronted with the inadequacy of confining our inquiry to the immediate and present world of the people interacting. We need, in other words, to scale up our analysis to encompass genres and repertoires of interaction, along with their material preconditions. Otherwise, we would be bound to deterministic explanations of interaction relying on initial resources and game-theoretic algorithms that rob interaction of its specific content. If, however, we accept that interactions are contingent, that how they turn out is not the only way they *could have* turned out, or that their effects might spill over the boundaries of people obviously interacting, we need a way to understand the real potential of interactions. Further, the space of interactions is itself shaped by larger, historical institutional developments, which cannot, in turn, be understood without reference to political projects and attempts to form hegemonic coherence. To be

---

33. See Flacks 2004; Goodwin and Hetland, this volume; also see Buechler 2000 for an attempt to theorise the economic moment across social movement theories.

sure, these are questions of organisation, but they arise from a consideration of consciousness and meaning. Unless, again, we are forced into narrowly rationalistic assumptions, we cannot understand these projects without a sense of the larger stakes involved: to what extent do these projects, if realised, alter our ways of living, and of creating and recreating our world? Ultimately, this is the critical question facing both scholars of social movements and activists.

Conclusion

In contrast to academic social movement theory, which treats issues of organisation, larger political dynamics, and cultural work as separate problems, Marxism's view of social relations as a totality – albeit one structured by contradictions – is better suited to answering the kinds of questions movement participants ask about the possibilities for common struggles for self-determination. By focusing on the ways in which activists and others make sense of their movements, learn in interaction with each other, and fashion relatively coherent genres and repertoires, the Marxist tradition provides the means of critically assessing the ways in which movements challenge and support hegemonic projects. By taking the historical legacies of previous movements seriously; by trying to understand the ways in which institutions that shape contentious interactions form; and by attending to the unevenness, the contradictions, and conflicts facing those who try to change their circumstances 'from the bottom up', Marxism offers a view of social movements that helps identify the ways in which previous struggles constrain, enable, and indicate possible ways forward for future action. Activists in Egypt and Wisconsin recognised, in February 2011, that their struggles were, at least in some ways, linked by their resistance to neoliberal capitalism, and that fighting a kleptocratic military dictatorship and fighting a democratically elected group of extremists opposed to even the most basic workers' rights and social redistribution were, in some ways, of a piece. Perhaps analysts of social movements should entertain their insight as serious enough to bear critical inquiry and action.

Part Two

How Social Movements Work

Developmental Perspectives on Social Movements

Eppur Si Muove: Thinking 'the Social Movement'[1]
Laurence Cox

2011 was a good year for social movement researchers. The extraordinary events of the 'Arab Spring' and the anti-austerity protests in Europe were widely covered in the mass media, noticed by students and even our colleagues. Of course, the visibility or otherwise of social movements is historically conditioned, in academia as in popular awareness or in the media; within academia, the decades since 1968 have seen an increasingly institutionalised and systematic representation of collective action, and an increasingly established body of teachers, researchers, experts and otherwise 'official' commentators on this pre-eminently unofficial activity.

In this process, social movement studies have become a minor, but familiar, field of academia, routinely included in general textbooks. As students' first encounter is, increasingly, in the classroom rather than as participants, the *academic* field has become increasingly self-sufficient. New researchers read official (and remarkably uncritical) histories of its origins, and they are presented with an increasingly closed canonical literature. Dialogue with the outside world can come to seem irrelevant;[2] the outside world, whether movement participants or researchers in related fields, returns this lack of interest.[3]

1. This paper owes a great debt to Colin Barker, whose comradeship has been inspirational, and to long years of writing with the immensely rigorous Alf Nilsen. Neither, of course, are responsible for its weaknesses. Thanks are due to both them and John Krinsky for comments on an earlier draft.
2. Geoghegan and Cox 2001.
3. Bevington and Dixon 2005.

This paper steps back from this situation to explore a wider history of ideas and an alternative, and older, usage of the phrase 'social movement', grounded in a broader awareness of historical possibility and a more dialectical sense of social development than contemporary 'social movement studies' usage. It then explores one way this figure of thought has been developed, in E.P. Thompson's *Making of the English Working Class*. Here, the alternative understanding is deployed to great effect, covering a wide range of historical phenomena, their interconnections and transformations. Enormously influential on 'history from below', studies of popular culture, and discussions of social class, Thompson's work shows a different way of thinking 'social movement'. Lastly, the paper uses this alternative understanding to think aspects of contemporary working-class self-organisation in Ireland, which – because they do not behave as proper social movements ought to are hard to understand within mainstream approaches.

This is quite an ambitious programme, and I am not a specialist on nineteenth-century intellectual history, or the British Marxist historians.[4] I hope to be able, at least, to sketch out the area and, perhaps, provoke some discussion of whether – as researchers or participants – it is wise to allow the routine academic processes of field construction to define the limits of our own understanding.

Thinking 'the social movement'

The phrase 'social movement' is sometimes ascribed to the German political economist Lorenz von Stein in the title of his *Geschichte der socialen Bewegung in Frankreich: von 1789 bis auf unsere Tage* ['History of the Social Movement in France from 1789 until the Present'].[5] In fact, the term had already been used in the 1840s; Von Stein is, nevertheless, a good point to start the discussion.

His book is a study of revolutionary France, in the period which saw the Great Revolution of 1789–1815, the July Revolution of 1830 and the 1848 Revolution. Its three volumes are: 1) *Der begriff der Gesellschaft und die sociale Geschichte der französischen Revolution bis zum Jahre 1830* ['The Concept of Society and the Social History of the French Revolution up to 1830']; 2) *Die industrielle Gesellschaft. Der socialismus und communismus Frankreichs von 1830 bis 1848* ['Industrial Society: French Socialism and Communism from 1830 to 1848']; and 3) *Das Königthum, die Republik, und die Souveränetät der französischen Gesellschaft seit*

---

4. The late great Dorothy Thompson was kind enough to indicate that she felt an earlier version of this paper had substantially captured her husband's thinking on this matter (personal communication).

5. Von Stein 1850–5.

der Februarrevolution 1848 ['The Monarchy, the Republic, and the Sovereignty of French Society since the February Revolution of 1848'].[6]

At first glance, this might not seem very surprising; the French Revolution is a defining moment of the modernity which social movements are said to characterise, seeing classic developments in citizenship, the standardising of a particular repertoire of protest, and so on. But the study of revolutions and that of social movements are now routinely separated off as separate fields.[7]

Indeed, conventionally, 'social movements' are praised for *not* being revolutionary; for operating in 'civil society' rather than in the state, or for being non-violent, as against the violence assumed to be defining of revolutions. They are often seen as taking the social order for granted: structured by the shifting alliance patterns of élites rather than creating their own, seeking the attention of the mainstream media rather than developing autonomous means of communication, governed by the availability of resources rather than trying to challenge their distribution, and so on.

An alternative understanding

Underlying Von Stein's title is a rather different way of understanding 'social movement', one which this liberal university professor shared with political refugees and revolutionaries such as Marx and Engels. This was the common property of the European nineteenth century, a mode in which its intellectuals reflected on their shared experience. That experience was different in important ways from what underlies 'social movement studies'.

Firstly, it was an experience of frequently contested, and rapidly changing, 'fields' within society (as against the remarkable stability of the basic institutional structures of Western Europe and North America in the post-1968 period). This experience did not encourage seeing a particular institutional order as everlasting, or understanding movements as restricted to a particular location within that order. Intellectuals saw movements not only as challenging the given

---

6. Von Stein's interests were very wide-ranging. He also wrote on Schleswig-Holstein (*Denkschrift über die Zollverhältnisse der Herzogthümer Schleswig und Holstein, mit besonderer Berücksichtigung eines Anschlusses derselben an den Zollverein*, 1848); political science (*System der Staatswissenschaft*, 1852); public administration (*Handbuch der Verwaltungslehre mit Vergleichung der Literatur und Gesetzgebung von Frankreich, England und Deutschland*, 1870); the politics of the military (*Die Lehre vom Heerwesen. Als Theil der Staatswissenschaft*, 1872); women and political economy (*Die Frau auf dem Gebiete der Nationalökonomie*, 1875; legal studies (*Gegenwart und Zukunft der Rechts- und Staatswissenschaft Deutschlands*, 1876); and landed property (*Die drei Fragen des Grundbesitzes und ihre Zukunft: die irische, die continentale und die transatlantische Frage*, 1881).

7. The formalistic 'dynamics of contention' approach (McAdam, Tilly and Tarrow 2001) includes both along with wars, nationalism and many other kinds of conflict, although not seeing them as intrinsically related.

institutional order, but as transforming it; this was, after all, the legacy of the French Revolution. (It might be said that in some ways, social movement studies embodies the legacy of the Cold War.)

Secondly, the basic nature of the state was constantly challenged and remade by society in the most dramatic ways – not only through democratic and social-ist revolutions, but also through the nationalist movements which increasingly threatened the dynastic states of the time. As such, the neat separation between 'social movements' and 'revolutions' was made neither by observers, nor by many participants, nor (come to that) by states and police forces. (After 1968, by contrast, many participants stressed their non-revolutionary aspirations as a source of self-defence in the years of Nixon and Brezhnev, the *strategia della tensione* and witch hunts against 'fellow travellers'; contemporary writing still often includes ritual condemnation of Marxism and revolutions.)

Thirdly, it was a period in which, partly for these reasons, social movements did not sustain the continuous institutional presence that has characterised Western societies since the defeat of fascism and even more so since the 1960s.[8] Instead, their situation alternated between periods of savage repression and rev-olutionary 'waves'. Although the conspiracy theory propagated by Abbé Barruel and reworked by Jules Michelet, in which all revolutions were the product of a hidden tradition of illuminist groups,[9] encouraged political fantasies in which secret movements were ever-present,[10] it was not until the end of the nineteenth century that actually-existing movements became a stable field with a constant 'above ground' existence and could be theorised using static concepts, in a hand-ful of countries. For most of the world, this situation has arrived within recent memory, even where it can be said to have arrived at all.

The social movement and the social question

One key to understanding the nineteenth-century usage of 'social movement' lies in the shifting meanings of the word 'social'. As Williams notes, earlier usage was restricted in meaning, either to friendship in general, as in 'socialising', or to the small circles of friends and acquaintances who *counted* in the world, a usage preserved in 'high society' or 'socialite'.[11]

---

8. The 'social movement society' concept (Meyer and Tarrow 1998) illustrates this by contrast.
9. The general theory is outlined in the title of John Robison's 1798 book, *Proofs of a Conspiracy Against All the Religions and Governments of Europe, Carried on in the Secret Meetings of Free Masons, Illuminati, and Reading Societies, Collected from Good Authorities.*
10. Hutton 1999.
11. Williams 1983.

In the late eighteenth and the nineteenth century, this élite society – the world of the Court, the aristocracy and the bourgeois novel – found itself increasingly under threat from the world of those who did *not* count. The 'plebs', the *menu peuple* – tradesmen, artisans, workers, radicalised intellectuals and peasants – started to become actors upon the world stage, and the primary meaning of 'society' shifted to entail this sense of the vast world *beyond* high society.

Although members of the élite were, of course, closely familiar with the wider world individually – their own servants, hired hands, villagers, and so on – this shift in usage marked an encounter with *collective* agency and a new kind of uncertainty: a sense that localised, specific forms of domination are no longer enough, a lesson underlined by the revolutions marked out by Von Stein's dates. There was a need to *understand* that wider society in more abstract and general terms; this concern over the threat to social order from the social effects of capitalism is a foundational theme in sociology, from Tönnies and Durkheim to the Chicago school.

All this created a need to *control*, to take appropriate action, outside the customary means of social control and traditionalised routines which were breaking down. Society could be controlled through the increasing development of institutions of coercion – modern police forces, the political police and the standing army; through disciplinary methods, from Foucault's prison and asylum to modern medicine and psychiatry, or Thompson's work discipline and religious sanctification of obedience; or through the (liberal, later Fabian) attempt to resolve underlying grievances and sources of tension.

'Social', in this sense, is the referent of 'the social question': the source of threats to 'the social order' identified by those who looked at 'society' from a bird's eye perspective and were in a position to propose and, occasionally, to take action. It refers, in particular, to the unruly towns and cities of industrialising Europe; and, within them, to the uncontrolled and, perhaps, uncontrollable energies of social groups whose own internal life was seen as the source of the threat. That key word of the period, the 'mob', is an abbreviation of the Latin *mobile vulgus*, 'the mobile crowd' – or, as it might also be translated, 'the social movement'.[12]

The group that seemed most alien, with least to lose, and most threatening was the developing industrial working class; next to this, the 'many-headed hydra'[13] of soldiers, sailors, slaves and traditional forms of manual labour; and Thompson's 'demotic' groups – the craftspeople and small traders, journeymen

---

12. Thompson 1963, pp. 78–9, notes that Radicals and Chartists used the term 'Mobility' for their demonstrations.
13. Linebaugh 2001.

and semi-proletarian peasants who filled out the complex 'social' of nineteenth-century Europe.

As such, 'the social question' – and, with it, 'the social movement – had a *class* referent from the outset. Although this was not, by later standards, an unambiguous referent, it clearly referred to the *lower* classes, and to those whose deference was not ensured by traditional methods of rural social control. Sherlock Holmes' spectacular forays[14] into the 'criminal classes' of deepest, darkest London and beyond – beggars and opium users, gangs and race-touts, trade unions and secret societies – represent a fantastical means of engagement with these same anxieties.[15]

New kinds of movement

So much for 'the social'. But what is 'the social movement'? Raschke writes of the 'age of revolutions':

> Movement became used as a metaphor for social change. The concept of movement also served for the deciphering of the inner connections of social development ('laws of movement')...
>
> [E]arly liberals from the 1830s spoke of themselves as movement in the sense of the only political direction which opposed the forces of inertia: of the 'party of movement' or the movement party...[16]
>
> The 'social movement' is first discovered as the workers' movement: the concepts of social movement and workers' movement become accepted in the course of the 1840s. The concept is thus first applied to a movement with 'social' goals, that is, to a collective with socialist answers to the 'social question'. The chronologically preceding liberal, national and democratic movement was not yet grasped with the concept of *social* movement; this only becomes possible with growing neutralisation of the term social movement.[17]

While Raschke, following 1980s usage, often defines movements in terms of issues and goals – 'peace movement', 'green movement' – as von Stein and the discussion above suggests, 'social' referred as much or more to the *agent*: 'workers' movement', 'women's movement'. This is important not just analytically, but

---

14. Doyle 1981.

15. Thomas 1998.

16. The *Oxford English Dictionary* illustrates this meaning with quotes from the 1830s and 1840s, ranging from the more élitist ('The new doctrines of Radical Reformers, and of that section amongst political men denominated the Movement party' – De Quincey in 1835) to the more social ('The popular side in the great questions of English history, the side, in later language, of the movement' – Arnold in 1842). It derives the usage from the French *le parti du mouvement*.

17. Raschke 1988, p. 23, my translation.

also politically: the 'social movement' of the 1840s was not middle-class reformers seeking to soften the troubles of the poor, but the movement that included the poor themselves, a movement (as the first chapter of *The Making of the English Working Class* has it) of 'Members unlimited'.

This social movement was the self-activity of the 'lower classes', or that part of their activity *not* controlled by élites, whether in fantasies of manipulation by outside agitators, or real versions from 'Church and King' mobs to Methodism. For most of the nineteenth century and, indeed, later, this self activity was illegal in most of Europe, and subject to more or less violent repression, whether it consisted of open public meetings, political societies, an uncensored political press, trade unions, or demonstrations.[18] The monarchies and limited parliamentary régimes that dominated European politics did not take kindly to such activity.[19] This conflict structured themes shared by many movements of the time: 'The rights to which reformers laid claim in 1819 were those of political organisation, the freedom of the press, and the freedom of public meeting; beyond these three, there was the right to vote'.[20] These were freedoms which, Thompson argues, working-class ideology continued to value in the longer term.[21] Revolutionary periods saw such liberties widely taken, both as expressions of pressure from below and as concessions from above. They were periods in which this self-activity could be seen to have a visible effect on the world of wealth and power. Conservatives such as Weber, no less than radicals like Marx, expected that this self-activity would prevail eventually.

'The social movement', then, took place over a long timescale, with bursts of activity and visibility in revolutionary periods, but otherwise present in that abstract and general sense of 'society' outside such moments, whether as grievance and need, as potential and tradition, or as organisation and 'subversion'.

This is the process whereby a 'class in itself' becomes a 'class for itself'.[22] Here, in the lead-up to the revolutions of 1848, are Marx and Engels[23] discussing the process:

---

18. The more deferential and less autonomous structures of the petition or the *cahiers de doléances*, along with more ritualised expressions of popular feeling such as the funeral, were often more accessible for precisely this reason.

19. Von Stein and Marx both experienced this personally – Marx being exiled from Germany and France; less dramatically, Von Stein's support for the independence of Schleswig-Holstein cost him his job at the University of Kiel.

20. Thompson 1963, p. 738.

21. Thompson 1963, p. 805.

22. Marx himself never seems to have used the latter phrase, but I think later Marxist usage is right to include the distinction. In *Poverty of Philosophy*, he uses the phrase 'class vis-à-vis capital', highlighting the constitutive role of conflict in arriving at conscious collective agency. My thanks to Colin Barker for pointing this out.

23. In Marx and Engels, the word 'movement', unqualified, is used with various kinds of referent. It is used in a relatively trivial sense, as in 'the anti-Church movement' (Marx in the *Neue Oder-Zeitung*, 28 June 1855), or 'the Young-Hegelian movement' (in

> The proletariat goes through various stages of development. With its birth begins its struggle with the bourgeoisie ... At this stage, the labourers still form an incoherent mass scattered over the whole country, and broken up by their mutual competition ... But with the development of industry, the proletariat not only increases in number; it becomes concentrated in greater masses, its strength grows, and it feels that strength more ... Thereupon, the workers begin to form combinations (trade unions) against the bourgeois; they club together in order to keep up the rate of wages; they found permanent associations in order to make provision beforehand for these occasional revolts ... Now and then the workers are victorious, but only for a time. The real fruit of their battles lie not in the immediate result, but in the ever expanding union of the workers.

Another phrase for 'the social movement', in other words, is *class* in the active sense. It is not that class is something *other* than, and explaining, the social movement: 'Let us not say that the social movement excludes a political movement. There is no political movement which is not at the same time social'.[24] Class, in an analysis such as this, is an active term, developing from a situation of *practical* passivity (though even at the earliest stages, there is struggle and competition) to where action is organised, conscious and coordinated. This theme lies at the heart of Thompson's *Making of the English Working Class*.

Class and 'the social movement'

This section draws on the work of E.P. Thompson to illustrate how this understanding of 'the social movement' is used by skilled hands to show how a class makes itself, the complex and changing structures of social movement, and social movement as development-in-struggle. Thompson deploys this understanding in a range of ways: leaving aside his more practically-directed works from the New Left and the peace movement, his historical work explores explicit political opposition,[25] barely articulate resistance,[26] underlying normative aspects of

---

the *German Ideology*). It is used of 'social movement organisations', as of 'labour movements' (in the *Condition of the Working Class in England*), or in the case of the Chartists (Engels in *La Reforme*, 10 January 1848). It is used for revolutionary and pre-revolutionary situations, as in 'the revolutionary movement in Germany' (Marx in *Neue Rheinische Zeitung*, 184, January 1849) or 'the reform movement in France' (Engels in the *Northern Star*, 20 November 1847), and so on. It is also used in more general formulations – 'the proletarian movement' (in *The Bakuninists at Work*), 'the modern working-class movement' (*On the history of early Christianity*), or 'the historical movement' (*On the Jewish Question*) – that approach the sense indicated above.

24. Marx 1963b, p. 244.
25. Thompson 1963.
26. Thompson 1990.

popular culture,[27] the biographies of a leading activist[28] and a radical mystic,[29] as well as theoretical polemic.[30]

Thompson and other Marxist historians were used by social movement authors like Tilly,[31] but have not been recognised as significant theorists – perhaps because they work with a very different kind of theory.[32] Thompson is occasionally cited as an 'add-on' to conventional social movement theory, for example by Mueller,[33] Jasper[34] and della Porta and Diani,[35] but without being allowed to disturb its basic conceptualisations.[36] Conversely, movement *participants* often read and respond to his work in ways that most social movement authors are denied.

This section sketches out Thompson's usage in *The Making of the English Working Class*, his most influential work and the one which shows best the range of his usage. I am, therefore, privileging his practical understanding over the explicit theoretical analysis in his *Poverty of Theory*: since my argument is that 'class', here, refers to a particular understanding of 'the social movement', the point is best made by showing that understanding at work. I start with an analysis of the structure of Thompson's book.

How does a class make itself?

The Making of the English Working Class has three main sections. The first discusses the inheritance of ideas, organisational practice and individuals from the eighteenth century that the nineteenth-century social movement drew upon in its self-formation as the working class. That inheritance included the organising tradition of Corresponding Societies, the language of radical Dissent, the moral economy and forms of popular resistance of the less articulate majority,

---

27. Thompson 199.
28. Thompson 1976.
29. E.P. Thompson 1993.
30. Thompson 1978b. Note that I am not, here, considering the broader debate on Thompson's influence and arguments (such as MARHO 1983; H. Kaye 1984; 1990; Stedman Jones 1983; Joyce 1993; Palmer 1994; McNally 1993). There are, of course, many questions to be asked about a work now fifty years old, and I would not accept every point of Thompson's arguments. Here, my purpose, is, rather, to show how Thompson articulates the alternative understanding of 'social movement', and to argue for its fruitfulness as a mode of enquiry, both academically and politically.
31. For example Tilly 1995, p. 35.
32. Thompson 1978b.
33. Mueller 1992.
34. Jasper 1997.
35. Della Porta and Diani 1999.
36. An earlier version of this chapter was prepared for a 2002 conference on the British Marxist historians and social movements.

developing political ideologies from the 'Norman yoke' to the language of human rights, and the history of the proto-revolutionary wave of the 1790s.

These are presented, not as unquestioned 'frames' within which subsequent organisers had to locate themselves, but as tools that people used in their attempts to reshape their world, constraints on how they could express what they needed to say, and models that they struggled to change. As Vester puts it, this is a sense of social movement as a learning process – not a top-down 'banking model' of education, but one of practical learning and creativity.[37] Another way of putting this is to say that participants were 'present at [their] own making':[38] they did not start out as isolated rational individuals, but as people who already had particular ways of understanding their situation and acting upon it.

'Movement', then, consists both of the *development* of rationality, in the sense of developing more accurate forms of self-understanding and more effective means of expressing and struggling to realise one's own needs – and of the blind alleys, the mistakes which Thompson discusses so eloquently, and which necessarily form part of the whole. In the 1960s, the language of triumphal progress was still powerful on the Left; half a century later, we might be more inclined to explore 'causes which were lost' at earlier points: 'After all, we are not at the end of social evolution ourselves'.[39]

The second section discusses what might be called 'movements from above', the processes of exploitation, of domination and of the creation of hegemony – not primarily as seen from above, but as experienced by the participants of the social movement, their own changing experience of their working lives, their 'standard of living', and the communities they lived in. Thus Thompson discusses the economic movement of proletarianisation in all its complexity; the political and juridical movement of repression, in its various forms; and the cultural movement of Methodism and industrial labour discipline.

By contrast with social movement theory's normal assumption of a more or less static, neutral state against which social movements act, this model sees the actors of 'the social movement' as affected from the outset by (logically, more powerful) movements from above – by the people and institutions who (outside of revolutionary periods) drive the commodification of human beings as labour power, attempt to ensure their containment within the given political order, and labour for their incorporation into appropriately subordinate ideologies.

Because the social movement is a threat, in other words, and a powerful one, the dominant order cannot exist without continually responding to it, and

---

37. Vester 1975.
38. Thompson 1963, p. 9.
39. Thompson 1963, p. 13.

modifying its responses as and when they prove ineffective. Or, as Thompson put it: 'The notion of class entails the notion of historical relationship'.[40]

As in other dialectical works of social movement research, such as those of Fantasia[41] or Piven and Cloward,[42] an adequate account of social movements has to be an account of this continuous conflict, whose previous truce lines mark the borders from which new movements start: 'this question of the *limits* beyond which the Englishman was not prepared to be "pushed around", and the limits beyond which authority did not dare to go, is crucial to an understanding of the period'.[43]

The third section discusses the 'new' working-class presence, as it shaped itself with this inheritance and in this struggle that it was born into. It focuses on the London crowd, the processes of unionising and direct action, the political movements and the class consciousness that resulted from all this. The question of 'outcomes', occasionally flagged up in social movement research, acquires a different implication, in these situations. Outcomes do include, certainly, the victories gained or lost in the external conflict. But they also include, as the *Manifesto* stresses, the *internal* victories and defeats – the development or decline of participants' self-confidence, of their self-understanding, of the toolbox of organising skills and political language they can draw on, and their alliances or isolation.

This is a point that Hal Draper famously made in his *Two Souls of Socialism*:[44] that there is a fundamental difference between organising strategies that seek only to achieve redistribution, and those that seek to change the balance of power, between movements *for* the poor and movements *of* the poor – paralleling Thompson's discussion of the 'tension between authoritarian and democratic tendencies' in Methodism.[45]

'The social movement' carries a different *kind* of assumption of rationality. Rather than assuming (along with resource mobilisation theorists) that all individuals are equally rational (in the same egoistic and rather short-sighted way), or implying (as the 'straw man' account of Marxism has it) that working-class

---

40. Thompson 1963, p. 9.
41. Fantasia 1988.
42. Piven and Cloward 1977.
43. Thompson 1963, p. 87.
44. Draper 1966.
45. Thompson 1963, p. 50. It is, perhaps, also possible to locate here the rational kernel lost in the noise of caricatures of the 'new social movements' argument: that there is a fundamental difference between the 'New Left' inheritance of 1956 and 1968, for which what is crucial is to change the structures of *power*, and the 'Old Left', Stalinist or Social-Democratic one, for which the goal was the achievement of state power by a different *élite*. This argument was fought out at earlier points within the socialist movement – by Luxemburg and Gramsci, for example – and today reappears between the technocratic 'realists' of the established Left and advocates of grassroots organising.

movements necessarily approximate rationality, this understanding sets out to *ask* how far and to what extent movement actors succeed in developing understandings and ways of acting that enable them to articulate their tacit knowledge, struggle effectively to meet their needs and remake the world on their terms.[46] It does not assume that they always succeed in doing so; but it does assume that it is worth asking the question.[47]

Excursus: writing the contemporary social movement

It might be worth pausing, briefly, to imagine how this same structure might be used in an account of the contemporary social movement. Firstly, we might explore the various legacies of '1968' – on the inherited traditions of the Old Left and the fragile formations of the New Left, in the various histories of cadre-groups and urban initiatives, counter culture and institutionalisation processes.[48] Then, we might look at the impact of the 'class struggle from above' represented by disorganised capitalism and neoliberal globalisation, linking these to the Thatcherite development of a right-wing 'common sense', the formation of individualist strands within the 'New Age', and so on.[49] Thirdly, we might examine the 'new social movements' in the 1970s and 1980s and their radicalisation in the 1990s,[50] alongside the history of the defeat of organised labour in the earlier period and the revival of grassroots struggle in the worldwide 'anti-capitalist movement' – from Chiapas and Caracas to Genova and the anti-war protests of February 2003 – and finish with an attempt to understand the fragmentation of US hegemony in Latin America and the Arab world and struggles around neoliberal austerity in Europe.

This would not be a history of a single 'movement', in the sense of the labour movement, the peace movement or the women's movement. It would be a history of shifting popular attempts to develop effective organisation and theory, identities and everyday routines in the face of a powerful ruling-class offensive. It would place the *interconnections* between 'movements' at the centre of the analysis, as against the fragmented discussion of single movements[51]. Most

---

46. Wainwright 1994.

47. Marxists expect the capacity for rationality to *differ* between different social classes; this explains the consistent failure of medieval peasant movements, despite massive superiority of (potential) numbers, by contrast with twentieth-century peasant movements allied to workers and led by urban intellectuals (Rudé 1980) and working-class movements. This analysis may or may not be accurate, but it is reasonable to explore the issue, rather than presuming or denying rationality by theoretical *fiat*.

48. Cox 2001.

49. Wainwright 1994.

50. Epstein 1993.

51. Colin Barker rightly points out that we can usefully ask how some of the 'fragments' (Rowbotham, Segal and Wainwright 1981) made significant steps forward which

crucially, the story would not hold 'class', 'gender', or 'ethnicity', outside the analysis, as 'independent variables' relating to 'structure', any more than it would treat 'globalisation' or 'the Cold War' as outside factors.

Thinking 'the social movement'

Thus far, I have proposed an alternative tradition of theorising 'the social movement', deriving from the nineteenth century and continuing to the present day in some forms of Marxism. This approach theorises the self-creation of class, focusing on the development of practical rationality and the impact of *other* movements from above. If this active meaning of 'class' embodies the sense of 'the social movement', it is an interesting experiment to substitute 'movement' for 'class' in some of Thompson's famous formulations: 'Movement happens when some people, as a result of common experiences (inherited or shared), feel and articulate the identity of their interests as between themselves, and as against other people whose interests are different from (and usually opposed to) theirs...' Definitions such as Diani's[52] include these elements but lose the centrality of *relationship*. Or again: '[This book] is a study in an active process, which owes as much to agency as to conditioning. The social movement did not rise like the sun at an appointed time. It was present at its own making'. So much, one might say, for positivist attempts to 'explain' or 'predict' movements: explanation lies in people's own attempts to make sense of and transform their own situation – and in how other people have constructed that situation.

The structures of social movement

These are broad-brush statements. How does the analysis work at a finer level? Here is Thompson discussing the varying relationship between community structures, political organisation, and ideology:

> 'Radical London' has always been more heterogeneous and fluid in its social and occupational definition than the Midlands or Northern centres grouped around two or three staple industries. Popular movements in London have often lacked the coherence and stamina which results from the involvement of an entire community in common occupational and social tensions. On the other hand, they have generally been more subject to intellectual and 'ideal'

---

other parts of the wider 'movement' adopted, fully or in part, such as 'the understanding of women's liberation, or ecological questions, or anti-racism, or LGBT issues, and indeed religious oppression. In all of this and more, underlying images of 'the working class' also broadened and altered' (personal communication).

52. Diani 1992.

motivations...London Radicalism early acquired a greater sophistication
from the need to knit diverse agitations into a common movement.[53]

Far from the one-to-one relationship between occupational class and social
movement imagined by naïve sociological critiques of Marxism, Thompson
shows how forms of active self-expression have different relationships to occupational situations. This same kind of 'layered' thinking appears throughout:
'If we are concerned with historical change we must attend to the articulate
minorities [such as the English Jacobins]. But these minorities arise from a less
articulate majority whose consciousness may be described as being, at this time,
"sub-political"...'[54]

This introduces a discussion of individual breaking of despised laws, popular
riots and insurrections, and so on, as expressions of this consciousness. Such an
approach runs radically counter to the kind of social movement writing in which
'movement' is defined as a particular type of organisation, and what falls 'below'
this (such as popular culture and rioting), 'above' it (such as political parties and
revolutions) or, come to that, 'beside' it (such as popular religion) are ruled as
falling on the territory of some other sub-discipline; the inter-relationships are
central to understanding.

Social movement as development

This 'layered' approach is also a *developmental* model: time and again, Thompson
makes comments such as 'behind every form of popular direct action some legitimising notion of right is to be found' or '[such riots] required more preparation
and organisation than is at first apparent'.[55] The relationship, between the articulate minorities and less articulate majority is not one between structure and
agency, or between objective class and class consciousness. It is between different *degrees* of awareness and self-activity, between a broader, shared culture, in
which past gains are sedimented as popular traditions, and a more conscious and
political sphere, from which new traditions are, at times, successfully developed:
'[P]opular revolutionary crises...arise from exactly this kind of conjunction
between the grievances of the majority and the aspiration articulated by the
politically conscious minority'.[56]

These 'conjunctions' are not between fixed categories, but between situations
which movements struggle to change: '[The London mob] was a transitional

53. Thompson 1963, p. 23; compare pp. 513–14.
54. Thompson 1963, p. 59.
55. Thompson 1963, pp. 73 and 70.
56. Thompson 1963: 184.

mob, on its way to becoming a self-conscious Radical crowd; the leaven of Dissent and of political education was at work, giving to the people a predisposition to turn out in defence of popular liberties, in defiance of authority...'[57]

Similar analyses, of the tensions and developments within popular attempts at self-activity, recur in the discussion of popular Methodism[58] and of the Westminster election committee.[59] This sense of movement as change is one of the greatest strengths of the *Making*: '[Between 1815 and 1850] [t]he reformers ceased to fear 'the mob', while the authorities were forced to build barracks and take precautions against the "revolutionary crowd". This is one of those facts of history so big that it is easily overlooked, or assumed without question; and yet it indicates a major shift in emphasis in the inarticulate, "sub-political" attitudes of the masses'.[60]

Thompson repeatedly draws our attention to the development of crucial qualities such as autonomy, organisation, and self-awareness: 'Luddism [is] a manifestation of a working-class culture of greater independence and complexity than any known to the eighteenth century. The twenty years of the illegal tradition before 1811 are years of a richness at which we can only guess; in particular in the trade union movement, new experiments, growing experience and literacy, greater political awareness, are evident on every side...'[61]

'Movement' is no bad metaphor for this; and movement can go in both directions, undermining these achievements: 'The persecution [of 1798] tore the last Jacobin intellectuals apart from the artisans and labourers...At the other pole, we have the disorganised and persecuted working men, without national leadership, struggling to maintain some kind of illegal organisation'.[62]

If movements are learning processes, learning takes time and is sedimented in ideas, people and organisations which are fragile and subject to all sorts of reversals.

Movement in struggle

This development spans multiple 'movements', in the language of contemporary social movement theory. One of Thompson's great strengths is his ability to *integrate* the history of separate developments, to find links between the Painites of the 1790s and the Luddites of the 1810s, or between Luddites and

---

57. Thompson 1963, p. 75.
58. See Thompson 1963, Chapter 11.
59. See Thompson 1963, Chapter 13.
60. Thompson 1963, p. 85.
61. Thompson 1963, p. 658.
62. Thompson 1963, pp. 193–4.

later trade unionists; but also the coming together of different traditions within a single movement: '. . . when Luddism came to Lancashire it did not move into any vacuum. There were already, in Manchester and the larger centres, artisan unions, secret committees of the weavers, and some old and new groups of Painite Radicals, with an ebullient Irish fringe'.[63]

Like orthodox social movement theory, Thompson explores the means of organising available, but marks these down as *classed*: 'Working men were not, after all, strangers to these forms of activity; couriers passed regularly, on illicit trade union business, between all parts of Britain'.[64]

On the other side, the development of the popular movement stimulates fear in the ruling classes: 'Here is something unusual – pitmen, keelmen, cloth-dressers, cutlers . . . working men in villages and towns over the whole country claiming general rights for themselves. It was this – and not the French Terror – that threw the propertied classes into panic'.[65]

Conversely: '. . . at each point where [the worker] sought to resist exploitation, he was met by the forces of employer or State, and commonly both'.[66]

There is a dialectic between two movements, from above and below, not an interaction between multiple, discrete movements and a neutral state. The 'movement from above', in the 1790s, included state repression, the encouragement of 'Church-and-King' mob violence, publications, and organisations.[67]

Indeed, at times – in the struggle for hegemony in Methodism, and the ambiguous relationship of middle-class nonconformity and radicalism to plebeian rebellion – these are struggles happening *within* a single organisational context: 'the working-class community injected into the chapels its own values of mutual aid, neighbourliness and solidarity',[68] or else within different organisations of the same movement: 'In [the Primitive Methodists] and other sects, the local preachers made the Church their own; and for this reason these sects contributed far more directly to the later history of trade unionism and political Radicalism than the orthodox Connexion'.[69]

Ultimately, Thompson's history shows the development of a *single* movement (struggling against a more powerful and opposing movement). That movement is embodied in different themes (industrial, political, religious, ritual) at different times and places, sometimes formed into complex alliances, sometimes fragmented and isolated, but developing and changing. It is not a single network,

63. Thompson 1963, p. 651.
64. Thompson 1963, p. 183.
65. Thompson 1963, p. 114.
66. Thompson 1963, p. 218.
67. Thompson 1963, p. 123.
68. Thompson 1963, p. 431.
69. Thompson 1963, p. 436.

with a common shared identity, as in Diani's definition.[70] Rather, such networks and identities are themselves occasional *achievements* in the developing self-consciousness and self-activity of the social movement:[71]

> ... the outstanding fact of the period between 1790 and 1830 is the formation of 'the working class'. This is revealed, first, in the growth of class-consciousness: the consciousness of an identity of interests as between all those diverse groups of working people and as against the interests of other classes. And, second, in the growth of corresponding forms of political and industrial organisation. By 1832 there were strongly based and self-conscious working-class institutions – trade unions, friendly societies, educational and religious movements, political organisations, periodicals – working-class intellectual traditions, working-class community-patterns, and a working-class structure of feeling.[72]

To make this kind of analysis – and explain why some 'constructions of identity' *work* – Thompson has to look behind identity to interests: while, by the end of the period, these interests were part of the movement's shared identity, this was not so at the outset. His account could not be written without that judgement, which rests on a broader analysis as to the the situations from which people take action.

The 'straw man' version of Marxism – first there are classes, and then they do social movements – is correct to recognise that the Marxist account of 'social movement' is not a sub-discipline able to bracket questions about the wider society. It fails to understand, however, that the Marxist account is one of movements *as* class struggle: not something that pre-existing classes go out and do, but the conflict where classes are formed: '... class is a relationship, and not a thing'.[73]

Researchers often write of past movements as though the existence of a self-conscious and organised working class was somehow a natural feature of late nineteenth- or early twentieth-century society; a careful reading of *The Making of the English Working Class* shows, rather, to what extent this existence as organised subject was a historical achievement.

---

70. Diani 1992.

71. This recognition of the processual nature of identity has made its way into constructivist studies from Marxism, via Touraine (see, for instance, Touraine 1981) and Melucci (for instance, Melucci 1989). What is usually lost (other than acknowledgement of its origin) is a recognition that *this is what good organisers always tried to do*: to build a broader sense of 'we', not for its own sake, but as a way of creating broader and more radical coalitions capable of challenging powerfully-supported structural inequalities. For precisely these reasons, late nineteenth-century socialists engaged with trade union organisation, international solidarity, resistance to oppression, support for suffragettes, and, come to that, radical movements in art and literature.

72. Thompson 1963, pp. 212–13.

73. Thompson 1963, p. 11.

The social movement in contemporary Ireland

'Scientific socialism' was only used in opposition to utopian socialism, which wants to attach the people to new delusions, instead of limiting its science to the knowledge of the social movement made by the people itself [*Erkenntnis der vom Volk selbst gemachten sozialen Bewegung*][74]

Finally, I want to discuss the contemporary self-organisation of working-class communities in the Republic of Ireland. This is a large and complex process, and was, until recently, the single largest part of the social movement in Ireland, in terms of *active* participants. This movement includes community development, in the sense of a codified and self-aware model of bottom-up practice applied to a range of different campaigns and organisations; a more varied sphere of community politics, in the sense of locally-based forms of formal action expressing working-class needs; an underlying community culture and identity; and specialised activities such as community education (participatory adult-education serving popular needs) and community media (press-, radio- and video-groups). All of these are characterised by their twofold grounding in local working-class communities: as the expression of the identity and needs of these communities, but also as movements *of* these communities, in the sense of a shared culture of radical-democratic organisation.[75]

The branches of a single tree

This is an eminently Thompsonian development, and cannot be understood in separation from *other* aspects of working-class self-organisation in Ireland. These are many and varied. They include economic forms of organisation, notably trade union, credit union, and some degree of cooperativist traditions. So, too, political organisation on the contested territory of socialist, nationalist and labour parties,[76] with its constant battles for hegemony between autonomous and coopted modes of politics. Another aspect is the churches and other forms of voluntary association, where working-class contents conflict with forms created from above.

---

74. Marx 1974a, p. 337.

75. This movement is now starting to attract substantial attention from participant-researchers, as in the cases of Bridgeman 2010; Geoghegan 2000; Geoghegan and Cox 2001; Powell and Geoghegan 2004; Gillan 2010a; 2010b; Lyder 2009; Mullan and Cox 2000; Punch 2009; as well as my own work in the area (Cox 2001b; 2007; 2010). See also Boyle 2005. I have been fortunate enough to work with some truly remarkable activists in movement and academic contexts over the last fifteen years, and this section draws on these experiences and discussions.

76. Hanley and Millar 2009.

They also include other popularly-based campaigns, with some degree of environmental justice campaigns,[77] peace activism (especially around the sensitive issue of Irish 'neutrality'), feminist organisation (notably community women's groups),[78] grassroots urban republicanism and international solidarity activism. At times, these stand separately; at others, powerfully, they come together,[79] as was partly the case in the struggle over Shell's gas pipeline at Rossport.

Rather than see these, as would orthodox 'social movement studies', as so many *different* movements, it makes more sense to start from their interconnections, in terms of participants, political traditions, organising skills and shared culture. In this perspective, we have so many different aspects of the *same* social movement, whose linkages, mergers and separations can be understood in a historical perspective: not that this movement died, and this movement was born, but that the one movement changed its shape.[80]

Implicit within either perspective is a political analysis. The one I am arguing for sees the broader sense of unity and direction as something that may be inarticulate or contested at a certain given time, but widely shared and explicitly stated at other times. It assumes that there are, ultimately, common concerns and needs, and while participants may not always be able to realise those fully, they will continue to take action around them.

Resisting the ahistorical assumption – in Europe, where most states have been created or remade within living memory and with the substantial participation of popular movements – that the framework of state and society is fundamentally given, this perspective allows movements to come together to challenge the wider picture, as when Irish peasants won the land and a nationalist movement achieved partial independence, and to move from what are conventionally separated off as 'social movement studies' into revolutions.

Common sense and good sense

While such moments are rare, movements themselves refuse to remain neatly boxed up. General concepts of class, revolutionary rhetoric, international connections and an awareness of this shared heritage are widely, if unevenly, felt. And individual activists make these connections practically, in the course of their lives, but also in the course of their week. This has to be taken seriously: not only how movements present themselves within the system when lobbying or seeking funding, but also how they see themselves.

77. Allen 2004.
78. Coulter 1993.
79. Cox 2007b.
80. Cox 2001b; 2006; 2010.

As Geoghegan shows, working-class community activists routinely think and speak in two ways: within the limited terms and language set by state funding agencies and their own boards of management, and in the more politicised and class-oriented understandings underpinning their own practice.[81] In situations where even most paid participants were on short-term and low-waged contracts and were deeply cynical about official processes, their involvement 'in and against the state' was best understood as *one* aspect of their practice, rather than the whole:[82] the bigger picture is in struggle with the organisational forms, and not only in Ireland.[83]

With Gramsci, we can say that there is often a tension between the hegemonic 'common sense' expressed by particular organisations, and the grassroots 'good sense' which the movement as a whole seeks to articulate. This relationship – and the tension between a narrowly organisational perspective and the broader goal of transformation of state and society – is a constitutive one, and not only for this movement. We miss something important when we separate the two off into different fields of thought.

In Ireland, community movements were instrumental in the 1980s in pushing for 'partnership' with the state, in an attempt to force it to live up to its claims to be an agent of developmental modernisation. But amidst the crisis of Irish neoliberalism, partnership is being abandoned from above. Participants who had fully experienced its limitations but accepted them on a day-to-day basis now have less and less to defend; many are returning to a larger sense of purpose and loyalty, even as they struggle to find better organisational forms for their own struggles.[84]

The legacy of clientelist partnership is not a trivial one: it was a costly mistake, and, after two decades, many more experienced participants will not be willing or able to return 'outside'. The weakness of popular responses to cuts and IMF bailouts to date has shown the depth of the *organisational* failure of the Irish movement; an adequate response will come not from the organisations, but from the wider good sense articulated by the movement, which is now able to come to the fore.[85] Over the past few years, my experience of activists I have met is that they are angry and have taken defeats, but not defeated; there is a

81. Geoghegan 2000.
82. London-Edinburgh Weekend Return Group 1980.
83. Wainwright 2009.
84. Cox 2010a.
85. Tellingly, for example, Community Media Network decided already in 2008 to pull back from the organisation-building mode of developing community-television in favour of a return to grassroots 'capacity building' work with working class communities (Gillan 2010). See also Cox 2011.

willingness to fight, and an energy for new approaches, even where it is not clear what shape the movement will take.

The perspective of participants themselves

As all this implies, these are articulate, literate and highly reflective movements, with a number of institutions of self-education: the training grounds of the Left and republican parties, the trade and credit unions, the structures of community education and the training programmes of community workers, the written and broadcast expression of community media and the traditions of oral history within specific communities.

These movements are not only objects of theory: they are also *creators* of theory. The relationship between Thompson and the adult education movement is well-known; but his writing was also informed by his participation in the Communist and New Left movements, his involvement with Eastern European dissidence and Western European anti-nuclear organising, and (indirectly, but not irrelevantly) by his familiarity with movement thought from earlier generations, from the Muggletonians and the English Jacobins to Blake and Morris. As O'Connor wrote of Raymond Williams: '... he writes this but these political intentions and movements write him'.[86]

Social movement studies, with its scholastic isolation of 'theorists' for study, has little place for this kind of perspective, and – at best – grants movements the right to propose new matter for scholarly consideration. But movements consist of conscious, reflective people, who are inevitably thinking *beyond* taken-for-granted routines, both in the direction of the unorganised and in the direction of the future.

This is what enables us to call them *movements*: they are not simply the reproduction of unreflected activity, but creative processes which – in order to mobilise the unmobilised and change the world – have to keep on reaching beyond themselves. They are constantly in debate over 'what should we do?', contesting given assumptions as to how the world is. They continually generate 'how-to-do-it' theory, whether in cultural traditions, informal apprenticeship and 'mentoring' situations, or formal training programmes and manuals.[87] 'Thus working men [sic] formed a picture of the organisation of society, out of their own experience and with the help of their hard-won and erratic education...'[88]

---

86. O'Connor 1989, pp. 125–6.
87. Barker and Cox 2002; Cox 1998.
88. Thompson 1963, p. 782.

Such pictures, we might add, contributed massively to the understandings which figures like Marx, Durkheim or Weber would later draw on, formalise and elaborate.

In conclusion

In this chapter, I have attempted, as far as possible, to avoid 'theoretical imperialism', and to allow nineteenth-century language, E.P. Thompson's mid-twentieth-century writing and the struggles of contemporary working-class community activists to inhabit their own worlds, rather than attempting to squeeze them all into tightly formalised concepts. These different languages express much hard-won learning; and we easily lose information if we standardise too quickly on our own terms, rather than first listening closely to what is said.[89]

This chapter has argued that a broader conception of social movement sees it as encompassing the full scale of collective human agency, from 'everyday resistance' and 'hidden transcripts' to revolutions and struggles over hegemony; that we should see the forms or categories that this takes as historically conditioned, including their internal differentiation, the relationships between different parts of the movement, and struggles with more powerful opponents; and that this is grounded in material reality, needs and interests.

This approach, perhaps, has the merit of highlighting not just what social movements do, but what they do it *for* – and of recalling the important fact that they sometimes win by transforming the structures and categories by which they are supposed to be constrained and defined. As researchers, one of our tasks is to theorise in ways adequate to this reality – and to do so in dialogue with participants and their own modes of thought.

---

89. With Alf Nilsen (and in our joint chapter in this volume) I have attempted a more formal statement of what I think are the common features of the alternative conception.

Class Formation and the Labour Movement in Revolutionary China
Marc Blecher

During the first fifty years after its birth, at the turn of the twentieth century, the Chinese working class responded to the shocks of early industrialisation with impressive organisational virtuosity and political ferocity. In the factories and the cities, it mounted a fairly steady drumbeat of resistance to capital and its political allies – a somewhat surprising development for a class short on some of the key prerequisites highlighted by Marxist theory, such as social homogeneity, developed class consciousness, and short-term economic crisis. Yet it could organise on the regional or national scale only in the early and mid-1920s and the late 1940s, when the Communist Party was able to provide organisation, coordination and leadership for working class revolutionary politics. As such, it never achieved hegemony within China's Revolution. Both the local strength and wider weakness of China's proletariat stem from its complex pattern of class-formation.

Ira Katznelson has argued that class and class-formation have four distinct aspects, which can be denoted, in shorthand, as economic, social, cultural and political. The economic is the strictly material aspect, rooted in the structures and processes of capitalism: the commodification of labour and capital, the labour market, the wage relation, and the exploitation of labour through the extraction of surplus value. Next comes 'the social organization of society lived by actual people in real social formations', including workers' origins, workplace social traditions, norms and relations, and the specific social, cultural and micro-political aspects of the labour market.[1] The cultural aspects of class and class formation refer to shared dispositions – 'the ways [workers] construct meaning to make their way through the experienced world', the 'plausible and meaningful responses to the circumstances workers find themselves in'.[2] Included, here, are questions about the kinds of social and political affinities that workers conceive as most important or salient. Finally, for Katznelson, the political aspects of class refer to organisation and collective action. Here, I would add the question of politicisation: the extent to which the working class organises and acts *vis-à-vis* not just employers, but also the state. Do they focus on forming unions or parties (or both)? Do they strike or hold political demonstrations?

Katznelson's conceptualisation is grounded in Marxism's holistic and dialectical approach. His overarching theoretical points are that class involves economic, social, cultural and political moments, and that there is no simple or straightforward theoretical relationship among them. Indeed, that relationship is conceived not in causal terms – even complex, contingent ones – but rather in dialectical ones that, in Harvey's words, 'take account of the unfolding and dynamic relations...so as to capture fluidity and motion'.[3] As such, he is at pains to combat any mechanistic materialism according to which the economic aspects of class shape social structures, in turn producing cultural understandings (such as 'consciousness') that influence politics. Rather, class formation is 'the conditional (but not random) process of connection' among the four aspects of class.[4]

This chapter deploys Katznelson's conceptualisation of class formation in order to explain the puzzle of the somewhat surprising strengths of China's working-class movement, alongside its limitations in driving the Revolution more broadly. It argues that both the proletarian movement's political robustness as well as its inability to achieve hegemony are best explained by the complex structures and processes of working-class formation. What the Chinese proletariat did was shaped most profoundly by the kind of class it was and the ways it developed – by its class formation, as noun and verb.

---

1. Katznelson 1986, p. 16.
2. Katznelson 1986, pp. 18–19.
3. Harvey 2010, pp. 11–12.
4. Katznelson 1986, p. 21.

Economic aspects of class formation

With the advent of modern industrialisation starting at the turn of the twentieth century, China's newly forming working class was subjected to particularly harsh capitalist exploitation. In the 1920s, workers were so famished that they defied Engel's Law by spending any additional income that might come their way on food. Housing was no better. In one survey, more than half of working-class families did not even have a single room to themselves. Many rural migrants were too poor to keep their families in the city, so they lived in dormitories, twelve or fifteen to a room. Yet significant proportions of workers – often over half – could not even afford such substandard food and housing, as indicated by their high rates of debt (for which they paid usurious levels of interest, sometimes over a hundred percent per year).[5]

While China lacked anything that could be called a 'labour aristocracy' of well-off workers, there were significant wage differentials within the working class. Large discrepancies prevailed across sectors and even within the same firm. For example, skilled silk reelers received over seven times the hourly wage of cocoon cleaners. In Japanese-owned firms, Chinese workers were often paid only half as much as their Japanese counterparts. The gap between male and female workers was of a similar proportion, and it widened over time.[6]

Wage labour developed quickly, despite the fact that precapitalist forms such as guilds and apprentice systems, though in steady decline, remained in place for a considerable period of time, even in parts of the modern industrial sector.[7] Moreover, the new capitalist wage labour remained embedded in a number of traditional, precapitalist social and political institutions, as we shall explain. Meagre wages were reduced further by fines, fees and 'gifts' to foremen and gang-bosses, as well as insurance schemes. Worse yet, bosses often subjected their workers to lengthy wage arrears. Bonuses – a not-so-hidden form of wage arrears – were commonly used to enforce discipline. Workers were often subjected to forced overtime, in many cases with no pay increment. Sometimes, they were even paid in kind rather than in cash, which increased workers' dependence on their employers.

Job guarantees and services such as free housing and food were sometimes offered to skilled workers, who were valuable and in short supply. For unskilled workers, however, such benefits were virtually unheard of.[8] In many cases, even

---

5. Chesneaux 1968, pp. 97–105.
6. Honig 1986, p. 55.
7. Chesneaux 1968, p. 118.
8. Howard 1998, Chapter 4.

bathrooms and first aid were not provided.[9] Turnover was high, partly for this reason, but mostly because managers were free to fire workers at will.[10] China had a huge reserve army of the unemployed, which kept wages low and conditions of work miserable. Unemployment was often astronomical, reaching up to half the labour force at some junctures. In Chongqing, over two-thirds of labour disputes in 1945–6 were over firings.[11]

Finally, proletarianisation involved a relentless process of deskilling. In the Chongqing arsenals, for example, in 1934, skilled workers outnumbered the semi-skilled and unskilled by two-to-one; by 1945, the proportions were roughly equal.[12] There, and in many other sectors, managers increased extraction of relative surplus value through mechanisation, standardisation, and Taylorisation of the labour process. And, of course, on the labour market unskilled workers could be paid much less than skilled ones.

In conclusion, the Chinese working class that formed in the first half of the twentieth century suffered profoundly and in multifarious ways from the material effects of capitalist industrialisation. They were exploited, in the strict Marxist sense of providing a fount for the production and extraction of a great deal of surplus value. They toiled long hours in horrific conditions for minuscule and irregular compensation. They lacked even a modicum of employment security and benefits. They were deprived of their existing skills, not to mention the opportunity to learn new ones. This was a class whose material circumstances provided a great deal against which to inveigh. Whether, when and how they would do so, however, depended on far more than their miserable material milieu.

Social aspects of class formation

How China's workers reacted to all this turned, in part, on who they were. Most were first-generation rural emigrants.[13] Less than one-quarter of Shanghai's population in 1930 had been born in the city, or, indeed, any city.[14] In the Tianjin textile sector, the figure was more like five percent.[15] As outsiders to the city with little or no education, sophistication or familiarity with urban life, these villagers needed, and were readily attracted to, formal and informal institutions

9. Chesneaux 1968, p. 375.
10. Cheaneaux 1968, pp. 90ff.
11. Howard 1998, Chapter 7.
12. Howard 1998, p. 170.
13. Howard 1998, p. 180.
14. S.A. Smith 2002, p. 15.
15. Hershatter 1986, p. 49.

that introduced and acclimatised them to the metropole. One was the labour boss, who generally recruited farmers from a specific locality in which he had contacts. As such, workers usually came to the city as part of a group of fellow *landsleute*. Of course, such wholesaling exerted downward pressure on wages – a case of the social shaping the economic. Moreover, since the contracting unit was generally such a group, workers tended to be assigned to workshops alongside people of similar origin. This produced a pattern of regional and even local segmentation on the shopfloor. It also promoted the elaboration of a set of particularistic institutions – native-place groups, sisterhoods and brotherhoods, and secret societies. As we shall see, such origins and institutions complicated, but did not undermine, solidarity and contentious collective action. They also focused workers' cultural and political horizons on the enterprise rather than their class or the state, a matter to which we shall return.

Both women and men were significantly represented in China's working class. They tended to be segregated by sector, with women predominating in the textile industry and other sweatshop sectors, and men in other lines of modern factory production, such as armaments, as well as in artisanal and handicraft fields and in non-factory work such as construction, transportation and the docks. Therefore, while the working class as a whole was more male than female, women actually outnumbered men by large margins in the Shanghai factory proletariat, both at the turn of the century and still in 1928.[16] Within factories, a gender-based division of labour prevailed, though as the decades rolled on, women came to be employed in lines of work that had previously been male preserves, largely as a result of male workers' resistance[17] – a clear instance of the political reshaping the social.

Chinese and foreign capitalists, particularly those in the textile sector, employed child labour as well, though the practice declined over time.[18] Children aside, most workers were young, at least when they were first recruited, since it was easier for the callow unmarried to leave the village, and because labour bosses preferred the heartier and unencumbered. In late 1920s Tianjin, for example, 85 percent of cotton mill workers were under 30 years old. Most were poorly educated and unskilled.[19]

Chinese workers were often recruited into the proletariat through non-market processes that trapped them in patron-client relationships. Sometimes there were even intermediaries between the proletarian recruits and the

---

16. S.A. Smith 2002, p. 18.
17. Honig 1986, p. 50.
18. Chesneaux 1968, p. 65; Hershatter 1986, p. 53.
19. Hershatter 1986, p. 54.

factory bosses. Secret societies and criminal gangs were involved as well. In Chongqing, the Green Gang and the Society of Elders and Brothers were active in channeling workers into industrial employment.[20] Shanghai's powerful, fearsome Green Gang controlled labour recruitment in the city's cotton mills. It did not so much contract female labour to factories as virtually come to own the young women, often selling them as maids or prostitutes and, of course, using them to satisfy their own sexual appetites. From the women's point of view, these criminal 'contractors' were an even bigger problem than the factory managers, even though the latter were also known to harass female employees sexually.[21]

In this context, workplace social relations were, predictably, despotic and often downright abusive. Visits to the toilet were regimented and timed. Employers had workers searched at factory gates and required them to carry identification cards. They treated rule breakers with public shaming, beatings and incarceration in the plant for a week or more.[22] Indeed, many plants were militarised, replete with private goons or even local police[23] – an instance of the state directly enforcing economic exploitation and social oppression on the shopfloor. In the Shanghai cotton mills, overseers prowled the aisles, rapping the knuckles of women whom they judged to be underperforming.[24] Incidents in which workers suffered some particularly egregious abuse were often the causes of strikes.

Work was dirty and dangerous. There were virtually no protections against pollution. Workers generally lived and worked in the same clothes. Showers or baths were sometimes provided, but often used communal water, and were generally filthy.[25] Many factories lacked the simplest first aid facilities; when they had them, workers were sometimes afraid to visit, for fear of being sent home or fired. Morbidity rates were far higher for factory workers than for their demographic equivalents in other sectors.[26]

In short, in the first half of the twentieth century, Chinese workers found themselves in a social milieu that was a radical break from their previous experience. Born villagers, most found the city unfamiliar, difficult to navigate and frightening. They thus became dependent on abusive intermediaries. For so many women to be working outside their homes must surely have been experienced by both sexes as an extraordinary break with the past. The multiple radical novelties of social life in early proletarian China gave rise to a variety of adaptive

---

20. Howard 1998, p. 178.
21. Honig 1968, pp. 12–31, 144, 247; Hershatter 1968, pp. 160–1.
22. Hershatter 1968, p. 160; Howard 1998, pp. 275–6.
23. Hershatter 1986, p. 161.
24. Honig 1986, p. 144.
25. Hershatter 1986, p. 154.
26. Howard 1998, pp. 227ff.

institutions – clientelistic labour markets and formal and informal social organisations – that subordinated and segmented the working class.

Cultural aspects of class formation

How did workers in these material conditions and social milieux apprehend their world? The universe of elements comprising working class culture included understandings and dispositions relating to class, gender, nation, and particularistic relationships such as those based on workers' native place, clientelism, or affiliation with formal or informal organisations.

The modern Chinese term for 'class' (*jieji*) actually has a long history dating back to the Chinese classics.[27] As early as 1905, striking workers protested their 'exploitation' (*boxue*). From the earliest days of industrialisation, then, Chinese workers were clearly disposed to see themselves as sharing work-related interests and identities with fellow workers. But workers expressed such interests in various ways. Without any apparent influence from Marx (much less Hegel!), and in a surprising rejection of Confucian hegemony, they spoke of enlightenment to the potentiality of freely chosen human will and self-improvement, and liberation from fatalistic, slavish subservience to traditional norms. Education became a major theme in workers' movements, both as a resource that leaders and donors would supply, but also something of which enthusiastic proletarians seeking self-betterment would avail themselves. The achievement of human dignity and a respected place in society – of no longer being beasts of burden 'like cattle and horses' – was an oft-repeated goal, to be achieved through concerted action. In this connection, labour itself was portrayed as moral, noble and even sacred. Moreover, it could contribute to national development. Solidarity with fellow workers in constructing this new world was a value in itself.[28]

Even as workers developed this sense of their class's project, they often identified their interests as consistent – or at least not inconsistent – with those of other classes. They appealed to employers by reminding them of their duty to treat workers fairly and to care for their well-being.[29] A common term for class was *jie*, which can be translated as 'level', 'rank' or 'stratum' – that is, a component part of a unified whole.[30] The boundaries of the 'working class' could take in anyone who did physical work, including employers.

The tenacious cultural perceptions and bonds linking workers with other classes were more than a holdover of Confucian cosmology emphasising harmony.

27. S.A. Smith 2002, p. 129.
28. S.A. Smith 2002, Chapter 6.
29. S.A. Smith 2002, p. 59.
30. S.A. Smith 2002, p. 52.

They were also propelled by the novel and active principle of nationalism. Workers often conceptualised themselves and their class as 'creators of the nation's wealth, as the key to its economic modernization' that was necessary to triumph over the foreigners, and as 'selfless fighters against imperialism'. Both conservative political leaderships like the post-1927 Nationalist Party as well as radical intellectuals 'interpellated them as members of the Chinese nation rather than of a working class, urging them to organize in order to make their distinctive contribution to nation-building'.[31] This message resonated with many workers. Through the fatal year of 1927, when, in the infamous 'White Terror', Chiang Kai-shek made a rightward move and crushed Shanghai's radical labour movement, workers were much more inclined to struggle against foreign than Chinese employers.[32] Yet consciousness of class and nation were not opposed, but complementary. Workers understood that they were exploited and oppressed as workers, but that their main enemy was foreign: both individual foreign capitalists for whom they may have worked, but also imperialism more generally, which kept China weak, dependent and impoverished.

Gender was another necessary and potent part of working-class self-understanding. Even before the collapse of the Qing dynasty, during the earliest days of China's industrialisation, most strikers were women. They called themselves not workers (gongren) so much as 'women workers' (nügong), a term that fuses gender and class. They organised their own unions and strikes, though this was at least as much – if not more – a function of the division of labour by gender as of any specifically feminist consciousness. And when they did do so, they often singled out specifically feminist issues such as sexual harassment or childcare. Yet women understood the indignities inflicted on them as a particularly egregious effect of imperialism and capitalism, more than of patriarchy as such.[33]

Likewise, and grounded in the processes of labour recruitment, regional and particularistic ties were prominent in workers' thinking. As we shall see, workers were often organised and mobilised into contentious collective action through such localistic or clientelist loyalties. Yet, as with gender, there is little evidence that workers enmeshed in such networks and organisations understood their interests as profoundly tied up with these specific social affinities. They rarely took action in terms of their interests as workers from a given locality or secret society. While such particularistic cleavages did bring the occasional strike or protest to grief by undermining workers' class and nationalist solidarity,

---

31. S.A. Smith 2002, p. 261.
32. S.A. Smith 2002, p. 209.
33. S.A. Smith 2002, pp. 206–7.

more often than not workers demonstrated the capacity to overcome these differences.[34]

In conclusion, class and nation were the dominant features of Chinese workers' cognitive map of their world and their understandings of their place in it. Moreover, these two affinities were closely intertwined and complementary, rather than contradictory. Workers' *Weltanschauungen* were also infused with gender and various particularistic sensibilities, though these did not appear to conflict with their class-based and nationalistic forms of consciousness or predispositions to organise and act upon them.

Political aspects of class formation

Organisation

The Chinese working class came together in a dizzying array of organisations, formal and informal: particularistic ones such as secret societies, gangs, brotherhoods and sisterhoods, and native-place networks and groups; philanthropic and self-help outfits; unions; militias; and parties.

Workers' overwhelmingly rural origins contributed to the elaboration of a panoply of particularistic organisations. One type was the regionally-based, informal but organisationally complex gangs (*bang*). They had resonances with secret societies: workers actually 'joined' (rather than simply belonging to them by virtue of their origin), and the process required recommendation by an existing member. They functioned like guilds, cultivating, protecting and monopolising particular trades. They were, however, less formally organised, often clandestine, and they tended to operate in less skilled trades, such as coolie transport, or semi-skilled or unskilled labour in particular sectors such as tanning, construction, shipfitting and the docks. Internal social and micro-political relations were structured around patron-client norms. Externally, gangs often fought each other, sometimes literally, to secure labour market niches – a clear instance of the political 'superstructure' reshaping the economic 'base'. Brotherhoods and sisterhoods formed another sort of particularistic institution. They were minuscule groupings – generally numbering up to ten – of men or women who took simple, *ad hoc* oaths to protect and provide for each other in the event of misfortune. They vicariated familial bonds in the alienating urban milieu: members addressed each other as sister or auntie, or brother or uncle. Secret societies were yet another such organisation. They were the largest, most formally and

---

34. S.A. Smith 2002, pp. 83, 263, 269; Perry 1993.

organisationally developed such group, characterised by elaborate rules and strict hierarchy. They often dominated the labour market in particular sectors, such as the Green Gang's legendary monopoly of the Shanghai docks. All told, the Green Gang could probably count a constituency of one-fifth of the city's proletariat.[35]

Liberal and developmental reformers, including some foreigners, established organisations to promote industrial modernisation and help workers subsist or advance in the labour market. The patriotic and modernising fervour of the 4 May (1919) Movement spawned a panoply of political, social improvement, and academic organisations. Some included employers as well as workers; they were modernising versions of guilds. As part of their efforts to promote Chinese industrial growth in order to challenge the economic offensives of foreigners, these outfits developed education and training programmes for workers and labour movement activists.[36]

Labour unions proliferated throughout the period under study. Many were *ad hoc* outfits that developed out of the heat of a wildcat strike and disappeared once it was settled. Others grew up, especially in the radicalising atmosphere of the 4 May period, as specifically working class alternatives to the cross-class industrial organisations. Most were rooted in particular trades and in localities and/or native place groups. Their regional character was a natural effect of the country's geographic and political fragmentation. Trade union federations were established in key industrial provinces and cities, where they became involved not just in organising drives but also, and often mainly, in political movements. By 1927, the All-China General Union proved capable of organising a one-hour general strike joined by two million workers across seven provinces.[37]

Unions ran the gamut in terms of their militancy and political complexion. Many were aggressive in promoting workers' interests, especially in the heady political atmosphere that prevailed from the 1910s up to the White Terror of 1927. Their pugnacity did not always serve the working class or the labour movement as a whole, however. Rivalry among competing unions undermined important strikes.[38] After their rightward turn in 1927, the Nationalists established 'yellow' unions and labour federations to control the working class and promote its collaboration with capital. Yet even some of these proved capable of becoming genuine labour organisations once the political atmosphere changed. The Chinese

---

35. S.A. Smith 2002, p. 31.
36. Chesneaux 1968, pp. 158–61; Honig 1986, pp. 217–22.
37. Chesneaux 1968, pp. 345–7.
38. Tsin 1999, pp. 131–39.

Association of Labour, established in 1935 as a state corporatist outfit, became 'an outspoken representative for labor's independent interests' a decade later.[39]

Chinese workers also formed militias. Years before the Chinese Communist Party (CCP) was founded, striking workers formed their own 'workers' patrols' in several cities to prevent scabbing. Over the years, proletarian militias continued to form and re-form, sometimes organised spontaneously by workers, but more often by the Nationalists, their merchant allies, the Communists, warlords and secret societies. Even when workers joined militias established by others, though, they were not always loyal followers. The Communist Party often had trouble reining in their radicalism – in 1945, militias turned criticism sessions into bloodbaths – or preventing them from turning into gangs of self-serving thugs.[40]

Finally, there were political parties. In the flush of the 1911 Revolution, the Labour Party put in a brief appearance; it was part society for promoting industrialisation, part provider of social services for workers, part strike organiser and supporter, part political advocate, and part vanguard for the national revolution. Meanwhile, a number of anarchist parties gained working-class support throughout the 1910s. By the mid-1920s, they had succumbed both to warlord repression as well as to the exertions of the CCP, formed in 1921. Until 1927, the Communists were allied in a 'United Front' with the still-progressive Nationalists, who were content to leave labour organising to the Communists. However, they lost their capacity to lead the labour movement after Chiang Kai-shek turned on them in 1927. The Communists returned to that role after they patched up their differences with the Nationalists in the 'Second United Front' of 1937.

While the Communists played a very significant role in mobilising and leading the labour movement in the early and mid-1920s, and again in the late 1940s, the working class also evinced its own capacity for spontaneous organisational virtuosity independent of the Party. The Guangzhou proletariat was organised and militant well in advance of any Communist mobilisation.[41] As noted above, workers frequently created unions on the fly out of spontaneous strike- and protest initiatives. In the 1940s they elaborated what Joshua Howard terms a 'subculture of opposition', including publications, mutual-aid societies, reading groups, and night schools.[42] These were connected to Communist Party cells, but were not their creatures or subjects.

Overall, then, the Chinese working class elaborated a broad and complex set of organisations during the first half of the twentieth century, reflecting the full complexity of this rapidly forming class. Some of them, such as the clientelist

39. Howard 1998, pp. 467ff.
40. Perry 2006, Chapters 1–3.
41. Shaffer 1982, p. 212.
42. Howard 1998, pp. 447ff.

and particularistic institutions of the labour market and social life, embodied the working class's newness, its continuing roots in pre-industrial society, and thus its weaknesses. Yet even these organisations did not impede the rapid development of more modern forms of working-class organisation. Moreover, these organisational achievements cannot be chalked up solely to the initiatives of skilled and committed political entrepreneurs and leaders. For as we have seen, the Chinese working class also showed its capacity for a great deal of self-organisation.

Contentious collective action

During the first half of the twentieth century, Chinese workers engaged in a great deal of contentious collective action, which took many forms. They struck, sometimes in a spontaneous, unorganised, wildcat manner, and sometimes in planned walkouts that were even concerted across enterprises or localities. They participated in broad popular campaigns such as the 4 May (1919) or 30 May (1925) Movements. They undertook slowdowns and campaigns of industrial sabotage and theft. They joined boycotts. They beat up managers. They worked with the Chinese Communist Party for revolution. They did all this against a wide range of targets: individual supervisors and managers, both Chinese and foreign; foreign governments operating in China; and Chinese politicians. The issues that propelled them were just as numerous: wages, bonuses, profit sharing, apprenticeships, internal labour markets, hours, vacations, arrears, sick pay and benefits, working conditions, shopfloor management, welfare (including factory meals, maternity leave, and daycare), death benefits, job security, severance pay, reinstatement of fired workers, physical abuse by managers, insurance, social recognition and respect, national humiliation, union recognition, the right to political expression (such as permission to wear Sun Yat-sen jackets or to celebrate May Day), political and economic corruption, and simple human dignity. Finally, the participants in contentious collective action ran the full gamut of the working class: more and less skilled, female and male, old and young, inland and coastal, employees of foreign and Chinese firms, members and non-members of secret societies and gangs, and from sectors and industrial branches of all kinds. In short, working-class contentious collective action at the micro level – in particular in factories and the localities – percolated over much of the first half of the twentieth century, grounded in the variegated economic, social, cultural and political aspects of working-class formation.

Yet it crested in macro-level regional and national movements only in the early and mid-1920s and the late 1940s. In early 1922, the Hong Kong Seaman's Strike eventually spread to other ports, both in China and abroad, while also provoking a sympathy strike of other workers in the colony, bringing the local economy to a halt. That autumn, a series of four major strikes broke out in Hunan. The workers won each strike, though by the end of the year their unions had been destroyed by warlord authorities. After going into decline in 1923 and 1924, the labour movement peaked again after 1925 with the 30 May Movement, named for an incident in which British troops in Shanghai fired at a crowd of demonstrators – killing ten – themselves protesting the killing of a striking worker at a Japanese cotton plant a few days earlier. A massive wave of nationwide strikes and demonstrations followed, lasting three months. 1926 and 1927 saw the Three Armed Uprisings in Shanghai, the last of which set the stage for the Nationalist- and Communist-led Northern Expedition's arrival in China's major industrial centre. This two-year burst of proletarian activism came to a bloody end in the White Terror of 1927. Contentious working-class collective action on the national canvas peaked again in the second half of the 1940s, when strikes became more common in a number of cities, including Shanghai and Chongqing.

What can explain the puzzle of a more persistent labour movement at the micro level, but a spasmodic one at the national level? In terms of the economic aspects of class formation, it could be argued that the efflorescence of the 1940s was related to specific economic factors such as the spike in inflation and the declining demand for labour with the end of wartime production. Yet other economic dynamics of capitalism, such as the Great Depression, which struck China hard, did not coincide with any upsurge in contentious collective action beyond the local level. Likewise, it is difficult to relate the ebb and flow of regional and national proletarian protest to shifts in the social aspects of class formation. Neither life on the shopfloor nor the other social structures in which the working class was immersed underwent significant changes corresponding to anything like the macro-level rhythms of contentious collective action. Nor, it is safe to say, did workers' underlying cultural predispositions and cognitive maps of the world.

What did move in beat to regional or national labour activism were certain aspects of the country's politics. In the mid-1920s, the Nationalist Party was a vibrant, progressive, populistic and young movement-based organisation that had acquired a strong political base in Guangzhou, a military force capable of advancing its aspirations to unify the country under its reformist programme, and an alliance with the energetic, up-and-coming Communist Party. Starting in 1926, its Northern Expedition liberated city after city, and region after region, from rule by the gentry and warlord satraps. In the late 1940s, the country was again in a time of political flux. The Nationalists were trying to re-establish political control after the defeat of Japan, but lacked the capacity or legitimacy to do so. The CCP, by contrast, was on the move, ramping up its political and military struggles with the Nationalists.

At the macro level, then, what was the precise relationship of these political openings to the development of labour contention? It is tempting to see the peak periods of contentious working-class collective action as openings in China's political opportunity structure.[43] After all, from 1919 to 1927, and again in the latter half of the 1940s, China lacked a coherent, capable national government, and was starting to generate credible revolutionary movements. On closer inspection, however, many aspects of the political opportunity structure were also decidedly unfavourable to working-class contentious collective action across much of these periods. China may have undergone a great deal of development of new political ideas, organisation and general ferment starting in May 1919, but the costs and risks to political movements remained formidable in subsequent years. Striking Hunan workers and their leaders learned as much, to their deadly cost, when provincial warlords suppressed their movement, killing 35 strikers in the infamous 7 February (1923) incident, and with the subsequent destruction, in December of that year, of the Shuikoushan Workers' Club, which had led the last of the major strikes. The 30 May Movement occurred not at a moment of political opening, but precisely in response to a violent fusillade against the labour movement. It and the Three Armed Uprisings were not so much results of a political opening, as attempts to create the conditions for the Northern Expedition to establish one – and they were, ultimately, betrayed in the White Terror, the bloodiest suppression ever encountered by China's working class. In the years following the end of the Second World War, workers mobilised in cities that were once again under the control of the proto-fascist Republic run by the Nationalist Party, a state that could reasonably have been thought to be set to gain in capacity now that the Japanese had been defeated and the United States, increasingly concerned about the emerging Cold War, was supporting it, however half-heartedly.

What the early and mid-1920s and the late 1940s shared, however, was a rising level of activism and boldness by radical leadership associated with the Communist Party. Young, energetic, committed party activists were involved in all of the Hunan strikes of 1922, providing crucial leadership and coordination. They were conspicuous in organising the 30 May Movement. They played the key role in mobilising workers for the Three Armed Uprisings. From 1945–9, the CCP, now liberated from its preoccupation with the Anti-Japanese War and from the constraints imposed by its 'United Front' with the Nationalists, began to divert some of its energies into urban revolutionary struggles. It was behind the resurgence of the labour movement in Shanghai, Chongqing and other cities.

---

43. Tarrow 1994, pp. 19–20.

It is not hard to see why the Party was necessary for a macro-level labour-movement. China's political institutions did not offer particularly favourable conditions for the development of the labour movement. Political fragmentation, warlord repression, imperialism, and civil war threw up serious obstacles to regional and national organisation and mobilisation. The Party possessed informational, organisational and communicational capabilities and a strategic view that local activists lacked. Its effects on working-class contentious collective action were both direct but also structural and indirect. For example, in explaining the 1946 Chongqing strike wave, Howard writes that 'ongoing negotiations between the Nationalists and Communists opened up political space for social movements, since the government did not want to appear too heavy handed'.[44]

Yet the CCP did not produce the Chinese labour movement or its most contentious moments of collective action. As we have seen, Chinese workers had formed a class capable of undertaking meaningful contentious collective action long before the formation of the Party. And even afterwards, workers often organised strikes and demonstrations without its help. Their political self-mobilisation was fostered by the economic, social and cultural aspects of working-class formation. The Chinese proletariat suffered terrible economic exploitation. Socially, workers were knitted together in all manner of networks and institutions. Far from undermining their capacity for contentious collective action, the particularistic relationships within the Chinese working class actually promoted it.[45] Secret societies, gangs, and even labour bosses and foremen often helped to organise strikes. Moreover, workers were emboldened by rural roots that provided a ready escape route in the event that protest went badly. Culturally, the Chinese proletariat's world-view, complicated as it was by a concept of class that was not always confrontational and jostled together with non-class concepts, was, nonetheless, sufficiently potent to drive a persistent labour movement. Politically, moreover, Chinese workers demonstrated ongoing organisational and mobilisational virtuosity even in the absence of the Party's leadership.

Politicisation

What, then, was the political character of all this working-class contentious collective action? Was it oriented mainly to economic, social, cultural or political demands? Was it directed against employers or political authorities? Did it connect them, and if so how? Did it result in integration or incorporation of the

---

44. Howard 1998, p. 486.
45. Perry 1993.

working class into the country's major political institutions? What were its consequences for political change?

Katznelson has shown how, in the United States, class-based organisation – primarily in unions – and political organisation – primarily in parties and urban political machines – were relatively autonomous, which undermined class politics.[46] In China, by contrast, class-based organisations and movements were linked closely with political organisations and ideologies. Anarchist outfits worked closely with the labour-movement in the 1910s and early 1920s. The Communist Party – and, until 1927, also the Nationalist Party – cultivated the labour movement. They not only purposively created the political conditions for working-class resistance, but they actively encouraged the development of unions as well as slowdowns, strikes, boycotts and demonstrations. Nationalism, the dominant political force of the day, sunk deep roots in the working class.

When all was said and done, however, Chinese workers were not incorporated in a significant way into either the Republic or the Communist Party's movement against it. These disjunctures had institutional roots on each side. The Nationalist Party, focused on putting together a broad, cross-class nationalist coalition, did not focus on binding the working class to itself. Until 1927, it left labour organising and mobilisation to the CCP. After 1927, any efforts to link itself in a fascistic way to the working class were superficial and ineffective, due to the Republic's low capacity, high autonomy, its need to suppress the working class in the interests of the bourgeoisie and the war effort, and its distraction by its military conflicts with Japan and the Communists. The CCP, in rural exile, lost the capacity to engage effectively with the working class from 1927 to 1945 (with only a few exceptions, such as in Shanghai in the late 1930s). And despite its many efforts at mass work, the CCP was a Leninist party admitting only a tiny minority and operating in secret. In sharp contrast with the United States, where the universal male franchise and the activity and proximity of urban political machines made for close ties between workers – as citizens in their neighbourhoods, not as proletarians in their factories – and urban political machines, in China, workers experienced both the Nationalists and the CCP as more remote.[47]

Most Chinese working-class politics focused on workplaces and economic issues. As we have seen, the major issues provoking slowdowns and strikes had to do with workers' livelihoods. Union recognition – a political issue – was also often a prominent concern, but it is significant that workers pursued it mainly through strikes rather than legislative campaigns or other political avenues. Even workers' predisposition to nationalism played out in their contentious collective action as attacks on their foreign bosses. This localistic focus, of course, reflects

46. Katznelson 1986, p. 26.
47. Katznelson 1981.

the social aspects of working-class formation, which were, primarily, geographically specific and enterprise-based. The propinquitous horizon of those structures was itself a product of the economic, social and macro-political aspects of class formation. China's modern industrial sector was geographically fragmented by the splintered pattern of imperialism as well as the historically strong localism of Chinese artisanal manufacturing. The localistic nature of labour recruitment and the division of labour reinforced this centrifugality. Moreover, at the national level, there were no coherent, robust institutions (such as a powerful legislature or established corporatist peak associations and arrangements) to attract the interest and energy of the working class or its organisations.

Yet none of this precluded the participation of workers in political movements, whether local or even regional and national. It just means that when they did do so at the macro level – for instance, during the 4 May or 30 May Movements or in the late 1940s – they were responding to mobilisation by political leadership, to which they proved available and amenable. Willingness to join or abjure from political activity when encouraged is, however, fundamentally different from structural integration or incorporation into political institutions on an ongoing basis. And without that, the proletariat was not a significant force in the politics of the Chinese Revolution.

In the longer term, the exclusion of the Chinese working class from national politics prefigured a pattern of working-class politics in the Maoist and structural reform periods more determined by the impulses and interpellation of the state than by the working class's own sense of its political place. Ultimately, working-class formation in China left the proletariat without significant experience or expectations of national political self-determination. This explains, at least in part, why Chinese workers responded vigorously to radical Maoist mobilisation in the Cultural Revolution, but then largely acquiesced to the post-1978 structural reforms that knocked the working class from its Maoist-era pedestal.

Conclusion

During the first half of the twentieth century, a large, variegated and active working class formed in China. Like many of its fellow 'Third World' proletariats, in economic terms it experienced profound immiseration stemming from intense exploitation and oppression within China's late, rapidly developing, and, in part, imperially driven capitalism. It underwent a profound shock to its social life, as rural people found themselves adrift in a brave new urban world, thrown together in radically unfamiliar ways with members of the opposite sex and with people from far-flung localities. It sought the protection of a range of particularistic associations to cushion the blow. Culturally, the proletariat developed strong senses of class and nation, also novel and unfamiliar ideas, while retaining older ones of gender, locality and fellowship. Politically, it spawned a breathless pattern of organisation and local collective action, much of it spontaneous, without leadership from leftist intellectuals and parties. It did all this despite being shot through with all manner of internal cleavages and carrying within itself significant non-class ideologies. And its movement generally politicised the bread-and-butter issues that stimulated it, linking them to questions of state and nation, while also raising the most profound ontological questions of human dignity.

However, in the end, the proletariat did not achieve hegemony within China's revolutionary movement. The country was too fragmented and fissiparous to permit the working class consistently to extend its social and political movement across a wider canvas without leadership capable of operating at this level. When the Communist Party began to make this a possibility in the mid-1920s and latter 1940s, workers rose to the occasion, without relinquishing local initiative or allowing their social and political movement to become a mere appendage of the CCP. Moreover, even when the working-class movement metastasised, it tended to keep its focus local and economic more than politically revolutionary. Thus it was unable to establish a secure political foothold in the new institutions of power, to which it remained subordinate in the Maoist period even despite its occasional radicalism, not to mention under the structural reforms that followed.

Marxism's contribution to explaining politics lies in its insistence on grounding analysis in a holistic approach to the dynamics of class, which it understands as both a noun and a verb. Classes are structures in motion, tension, and ongoing (re-)formation. This approach can incorporate insights from more segmented, causally-oriented social science, while always seeking a more powerful analysis by placing them within a larger and more complex and dialectical frame. Political opportunity theory may, indeed, help explain the uneven rhythms of regional and national labour mobilisation in China, even despite the ambiguities of ascertaining just how much opportunity there really was at particular moments. Moreover, political resource theories allied to opportunity theory are also well attuned to analysing the capacity of the working class to take advantage of opportunity. But wider questions remain as to the ways in which it would do so and the built-in contradictions it would encounter along the way. Analysis of working-class formation as a whole points, for example, to the variegated, interrelated roots of the Chinese working class's local strength and regional and national weakness and, going further, the dialectical relationship between them.

In both the United States and China, the working class, while achieving significant levels of mobilisation that produced real gains, nonetheless failed to achieve political hegemony. Katznelson deploys a Marxist analysis to show how, in the US example, this was a result of crucial social, cultural and political aspects of class formation: the physical separation of workplaces, where unions were strong, from residential communities set within a Gramscian 'trench system' of well institutionalised government, oriented almost exclusively to neighbourhoods rather than factories, and open enough to incorporate workers through powerful urban political machines and the universal franchise.[48] China provides something of a mirror image. There was no such physical separation of work and community; on the contrary, they were fused. Workers were, therefore, incorporated into a panoply of particularistic social and cultural relationships, both vertical ones that generally discouraged activism and horizontal ones that often encouraged it. Weak political institutionalisation and endemic political instability often encouraged spontaneous working-class protest locally, even while posing obstacles to extending proletarian power regionally or nationally. What both explanations have in common, however, is their reliance on broad configurations of class formation that highlight the overarching contours of their profoundly different labour movements, even as both failed to achieve hegemony.

---

48. Ibid.

Contesting the Postcolonial Development Project: A Marxist Perspective on Popular Resistance in the Narmada Valley[1]

Alf Gunvald Nilsen

Introduction

As evidenced by the ongoing wave of popular uprisings in North Africa and the Middle East, it is arguably in the global South that the most intense and advanced popular struggles against neoliberal globalisation are taking place. This is true across the regions of Latin America, Asia, and Africa, which, during the past three decades, have witnessed the emergence of a wide array of movements challenging the dispossession, exclusion, and poverty that have followed in the wake of the neoliberal counter-revolution.[2]

The lineage of these movements reaches back to the worldwide revolt of 1968, which manifested itself in the global South as an attack on 'the nationalism and institutionalized elite politics...of the first generation of independent Third World states' in the form of new social movements and radicalised struggles for national liberation.[3] When neoliberal policy régimes were imposed through structural adjustment in the 1980s, a new round of popular protest erupted, in which popular classes sought to reclaim the social wage from

---

1. This chapter presents arguments and empirical data that I have developed and presented previously in Nilsen 2007b, 2008, 2010, and 2011. The chapter draws heavily on these previous publications. My analysis of the *Narmada Bachao Andolan* owes a great deal to my joint work with Laurence Cox, who has taught me most of what I know about how to think about social movements with and through Marxist theory.
2. Motta and Nilsen 2011; McMichael 2009.
3. Watts 2001, p. 172; see also Berger 2004; Prashad 2008.

which they had benefited during the heyday of the developmental state.[4] The current praxis of social movements in the global South seems to have developed beyond this defensive register towards a more offensive prefiguration of alternatives to processes of popular disenfranchisement and deprivation. The praxis of social movements in the global South constitutes a reinvention of the direction and meaning of development, at a time when the cracks and fissures of neoliberal hegemony are widening rapidly.[5] It is precisely for this reason that we need to develop conceptually adequate and politically enabling analyses of the character and dynamics of subaltern resistance in the global South. In this chapter, I seek to contribute to this task by developing a Marxist analysis of popular resistance to dam-building on the Narmada River in India.

From the late 1960s onwards, India witnessed the emergence of new social movements (NSMs) that mobilised subaltern communities who had remained peripheral to the workings of the developmental state, and had fallen outside the political ambit of mainstream left-wing parties. These NSMs challenged the centralised developmentalism of the Nehru era, and fought for alternatives based on democratic participation, community control over natural resources, and the recognition of oppressed identities.[6]

From the mid-1980s onwards, as Adivasi[7] subsistence peasants and caste-Hindu farming communities started to mobilise against displacement by large dams, the Narmada Valley became an increasingly central arena for these struggles. The target of their mobilisation was the Narmada Valley Development-Project (NVDP), which envisages the construction of more than three thousand dams of varying sizes on the Narmada river, which runs from the Maikal ranges in Amarkantak in the Shahol district of Northern Madhya Pradesh to the Arabian Sea at Bharuch, Gujarat.[8] Initially organised as social action groups across the three

---

4. Walton and Seddon 1994.
5. Motta and Nilsen 2011.
6. Omvedt 1993; Vanaik 1990.
7. The term 'Adivasi' literally means 'first inhabitant', and was coined by tribal rights activists early in the twentieth century to express their claim to being the indigenous people of India. The Indian government does not recognise Adivasis as being indigenous people, but defines Adivasi communities as belonging to the category of Scheduled Tribes as per the Fifth and Sixth Schedules of the Indian Constitution. The Fifth and Sixth Schedules – Schedules are basically lists in the Constitution that categorise and tabulate the bureaucratic activity and policy of the Government – provide an array of protective legislation, special entitlements and reservations for Adivasis. As such, they are expressive of the historical subordination and marginalisation of Adivasis in Indian society.
8. Several dams in the scheme – the Tawa dam (1973), Bargi (1989), the Barna, Sukta and Kolar dams, and, most recently, the Indira Sagar Project – have been completed. The concrete work on the SSP was brought to completion on 32 December 2006; the dam currently stands at 120 metres. The MHP was at a standstill from 2000 to 2006 due to a lack of funding, but construction work – and protest – resumed in 2006 as funds were

riparian states of Maharashtra, Gujarat and Madhya Pradesh, the affected communities eventually coalesced into the pan-state organisation *Narmada Bachao Andolan* (NBA; 'Save the Narmada Movement') in the late 1980s. At the centre of the NBA's activism was a campaign to cancel the Sardar Sarovar Project (SSP). The SSP is the kingpin of the overall scheme for harnessing the Narmada River. Built in eastern Gujarat, it will affect as many as one million people across the three riparian states, with the brunt of the displacement taking place in western Madhya Pradesh. Furthermore, the anti-dam campaign, which also targeted other parts of the NVDP, has been embedded in a trenchant critique of India's postcolonial development project.[9]

The struggle against large dams on the Narmada River unfolded over more than a decade, until it eventually foundered as the result of a Supreme Court verdict in October 2000, which approved the completion of the SSP. Despite its eventual defeat, an engagement with the trajectory of the Narmada movement and its politics of resistance can be immensely valuable, both theoretically and politically, for efforts to develop a Marxist approach to social movements in the global South.

Theoretical orientations

Conceptualisations of social movements in the global South tend to be dominated by one of two perspectives, either a poststructuralist approach, or a state-centric approach, both of which are theoretically and politically fallacious.

Poststructuralist approaches typically posit social movements in the global South as collective agents that articulate a politics of difference in opposition to a discourse of development that, as one key exponent of this approach has put it, dictates 'the marginalization and disqualification of non-Western knowledge systems'.[10] For example, in his analysis of NSMs in India, Parajuli has argued that the key contribution of these struggles is the renewal and reassertion of 'subjugated traditions of knowledge' in opposition to 'the whole edifice of modern resource management and development'.[11] Escobar has asserted that social movements in the global South represent 'alternatives to development, that is, the rejection of the entire paradigm altogether'.[12] These movements, then, become harbingers of a 'post-development era', which can generate 'more radical

---

made available through various financial institutions. At the time of writing, construction of the MHP is almost complete.
9. Baviskar 1995; Nilsen 2010.
10. Escobar 1995, p. 13.
11. Parajuli 1996, pp. 32–3.
12. Escobar 1995, p. 215.

transformations of the modern capitalist order and the search for alternative ways of organizing societies and economies, of satisfying needs, of healing and living'.[13]

State-centric approaches typically posit social movements as collective agents that claim 'their rights to greater access to a more generous idea of development'.[14] These perspectives tend to put the state at the centre of their analyses, and assert that 'it is misleading to assume that people are always empowered in opposition to the state, or that they fail to seek power from within state structures'.[15] The role of social movements, then, is that of enabling subaltern claim making on the state and pushing states to implement policy régimes that favour subaltern groups and poor people.[16] As such, the discussion of subaltern empowerment in India in the work of Corbridge, Williams, Srivastava, and Véron concludes that political strategy should be focused on widening 'those spaces of empowerment that can be found in a world of the second-best' rather than pursuing 'a Jacobin conception of politics which depends upon the idea of perfectibility, or an "ideal outside"'.[17]

In different ways, both perspectives fail to develop a differentiated conception of strategy that accurately gauges the limits and possibilities that social movements face in their conflicts with the institutions, practices, and discourses of the postcolonial development project.

Poststructuralist approaches fail to grasp the way in which subaltern resistance emerges from within a totality that is structured in crucial ways by the hegemony of dominant social groups. Thus, in their insistence that social movements in the global South operate in and from 'an authentic site of autonomous insurrection beyond development',[18] they fail to adequately conceptualise how social movements from below tend to construct their resistance through oppositional articulations and appropriations of the postcolonial development project – and, therefore, also the specific political enablements and constraints that subaltern groups are faced with in this process.[19] The postcolonial development project, in turn, becomes exclusively 'a discourse of control', rather than a set of multivalent idioms that can be put at the centre of 'a discourse of entitlement'.[20]

State-centric perspectives fail to recognise that subaltern resistance may become a counter-hegemonic social force capable of transcending and transforming a given totality and the hegemonic position of dominant social groups

13. Escobar 1992, p. 48.
14. Rangan 2000, p. 222.
15. Corbridge and Harriss 2000, p. 208.
16. See Sandbrook et al. 2007; Heller 2000.
17. Corbridge et al. 2005, p. 186.
18. Moore 2000, p. 171.
19. Sinha 2003; Moore 1998; 2000.
20. Cooper and Packard 1997, p. 4.

within this totality. The political scope of social movements from below is, therefore, circumscribed to claim-making on the state. At best, social movements are
conceived as forces advancing a rejuvenated social democracy for the global
South.[21] This fallacy is further compounded by the fact that state-centric perspectives fail to acknowledge how the modal role of the state in the reproduction
of fundamental power structures entails its institutions, practices, and discourses
having 'unequal and asymmetrical effects on the ability of social groups to realize their interests through political action'.[22]

As a result of these shortcomings, both perspectives fail to develop an adequately differentiated conception of strategy. What is needed is a perspective
that steers clear of the Scylla of positing social movements from below as the
inhabitants of an autonomous subaltern domain and the Charybdis of locking
subaltern resistance into a capitalist present without any potential for decisively
rupturing extant power relations.

A fruitful point of departure for developing such a perspective can arguably be
found in Gramsci's insistence that subalternity, and the struggle to challenge and
rupture it, is a relational and developmental process. 'Subaltern groups', Gramsci
wrote, 'are always subject to the activity of ruling groups, even when they rebel
and rise up: only "permanent" victory breaks their subordination, and that not
immediately'.[23] What this crucial passage brings out, of course, is the simple
fact that subordination shapes the life-worlds of the subaltern in a multiplicity
of ways, and that even their opposition and their repertoires of contention are
shaped by the power of dominant social groups. Autonomy, then, is not a given
or essential feature of subalternity, as it is often made out to be in poststructuralist approaches.[24]

Yet, at the same time, Gramsci does not posit subalternity and extant power
relations as immutable. Relations of power and dominance can be ruptured by
the self-activity of the popular classes, but this self-activity is developmental: it
moves through phases, from limited attempts at collective assertion through the
extant institutions of dominant social groups to – potentially – the creation of
political formations that assert the 'integral autonomy' of subaltern groups outside of extant structures and institutions.[25]

---

21. See Sandbrook et. al. 2007.
22. Jessop 1982, p. 224; see also Nilsen 2011.
23. Gramsci 1998, pp. 54–5.
24. The question of subaltern autonomy is, of course, a central one in the debate over
the subaltern studies project and its approach to popular resistance in colonial India. See
Nilsen 2009b for a critical discussion.
25. Gramsci 1998, p. 52; see also Green, 2002.

It is precisely 'the line of development towards integral autonomy'[26] that should be at the centre of our analytical attention. In a genuinely dialectical approach, the collective articulation of oppositional rationalities and projects that animates the development of subaltern resistance will, then, be thought of as a conflictual process that unfolds within a field of force[27] simultaneously constituted by and constitutive of past, present, and future struggles between social movements from above and social movements from below.[28] On this basis, it is possible to explore the concrete ways in which movements from below develop, with a focus on how oppositional skills, practices, and imaginaries are crafted by appropriating and contesting the material and semiotic structures through which dominant social groups exercise hegemony. Fundamental to this exploration is an interest in unearthing patterns of enablement and constraint that movements from below encounter in these contestations and appropriations. In discovering such patterns, we are likely to approach something along the lines of 'useable knowledge for those seeking social change'.[29]

The Narmada dams and India's postcolonial development project

Overall, the Narmada dam-projects have effected a dual transformation that amounts to a process of 'accumulation by dispossession'.[30] As a result of the construction of large dams, property rights in water and electricity, as well as profitable investment opportunities, are concentrated in the hands of regional, national and global propertied élites, while the displacement of peasant producers from their land without adequate resettlement and rehabilitation generates pressures towards proletarianisation.[31] In terms of the SSP – the central target of the NBA's anti-dam campaign and a publicly funded project – accumulation by dispossession occurs through the expropriation of Adivasi communities who engage in subsistence production in Gujarat, Maharashtra and Madhya Pradesh, the concurrent pressure towards their proletarianisation, as well as the expropriation of caste-Hindu farming communities who engage in petty commodity production in western Madhya Pradesh. Simultaneously, it will

---

26. Gramsci 1998, p. 52.
27. I draw the concept 'field of force' from Thompson's initial formulation in his 1978 discussion of the relationship between dominant and subaltern social groups in eighteenth-century England and Roseberry 1994's subsequent discussion of the complexities of the relations that criss-cross such fields.
28. Cox and Nilsen, this volume; Cox 1999a; Nilsen 2009a.
29. Flacks, cited in Bevington and Dixon 2005, p. 189.
30. Harvey 2003; 2005.
31. Nilsen 2010; Whitehead 2010.

transform property rights in water in favour of dominant proprietary classes in industry and agriculture in Central Gujarat.[32]

The Narmada dams are exemplary of a consistent distributional bias in river-valley development projects in postcolonial India. Dubbed by Nehru the as 'modern temples' of the newborn nation, the actual track record of the 1,300 or so large dams that have been constructed since Independence in 1947 suggests that these projects have not made an unambiguous contribution towards national progress.

In terms of the impact of dams on irrigation, the *India Case Study Report* for the World Commission on Dams argues that this has been 'almost entirely distributional'. Actual increases in irrigation and agricultural yields have been systematically overestimated. Powerful groups in the command areas of the dams have cornered the benefits actually generated, all at the expense of the public and those affected by the project. Moreover, in terms of financial costs and benefits, the scenario has been one of both rising capital outlays and rising financial losses.[33] As dams are largely funded with public money, the operational losses amount to 'implicit subsidies which the state governments provide to beneficiary farmers'.[34]

An exact calculation of the number of people displaced by large dams since Independence is difficult to provide, but ranges somewhere between 21 and 33 million people. India's record on resettlement and rehabilitation is a dismal one. In spite of the extensive powers of expropriation bestowed upon the state, there is, as of yet, no national legal framework protecting the rights of project-affected persons or laying down uniform national guidelines for the conduct of resettlement and rehabilitation.[35] Thus, most of the people who are displaced by large dams in India have been confronted with 'the option of starving to death or walking several kilometres to the nearest town, sitting in the marketplace ... offering themselves as wage labour, like goods on sale'.[36] Crucially, marginal and subsistence-oriented populations face this situation more often than other groups. As Whitehead points out, 'the marginality of the scheduled tribes in India stands in contrast to their predominance in the populations displaced by dams and other development projects'.[37] Whereas Adivasis constitute only eight percent of India's population, they make up as much as forty to fifty percent of those who have been displaced by dams in the postcolonial era. An additional ten percent of those displaced are Dalits.[38] Resorting to migration in search of waged

---

32. Nilsen 2010; Dwivedi 2006.
33. Rangachari et al. 2000, pp. 56–7, 60–5; see also Singh 1997; Klingensmith 2007.
34. Rangachari et al. 2000, p. 65.
35. Parasuraman 1999.
36. Roy 2002, p. 103.
37. Whitehead 2003, p. 3.
38. See also Singh 1997.

work, those who are displaced by large dams have come to swell the ranks of India's 'footloose proletariat'[39] – that is, the migrant workers who survive on the extreme margins of the country's vast informal economy.

This consistent distributional bias points to how the central outcome of the construction of large dams has been to concentrate *de facto* property rights in irrigation and electricity in the hands of an emergent class of capitalist farmers – key segments of what Bardhan has referred to as India's 'dominant proprietary classes'[40] – whilst disproportionately dispossessing subaltern social groups of their social means of subsistence and production.[41]

This dynamic, in turn, is not unique to dam-building. Rather, it is linked to a fundamental and overarching aspect of the 'passive revolution' that has moulded the political economy of capitalism in postcolonial India.[42] In this process, state-led development strategies have resulted in the transfer and concentration of productive resources in such a way as to 'enhance the power of those who were the most important holders of property rights – in the first place, the industrial and commercial bourgeoisie and the rich peasantry – and of the bureaucratic office holders whose discretionary powers were increased with the greatly expanded role of the bureaucracy as a whole'.[43]

India's passive revolution was, in turn, the result of a crucial dialectic of mobilisation from above and below that unfolded during the closing decades of the struggle for independence. Of course, the Indian National Congress shaped India's freedom struggle in crucial ways. An élite-controlled organisation from the outset, the Congress moved towards mass mobilisation as a key strategy under Gandhi's tutelage in the 1920s. However, radical pressures from below, whether from peasant masses demanding radical land reform or militant labour movements seeking to push Congress to the left, were quickly defused and demobilised.[44] This meant, in turn, that the basis for the implementation of radical reform at the coming of independence was decisively weakened.[45] In contrast, élite groups mobilised effectively and successfully to mould the coming of independence according to their interests. The domestic industrial bourgeoisie shaped industrial policy in such a way as to curtail the capacity of the postcolonial state to secure that public funds were deployed in socially useful ways.[46] Dominant agrarian groups were effective in undermining ambitions of radical

39. Breman 1996.
40. Bardhan 1998.
41. See Whitehead 2003.
42. Chatterjee 1993; Kaviraj 1997.
43. Corbridge and Harriss 2000, p. 65.
44. Sarkar 1983; Guha 1997.
45. Chibber 2003; Frankel 2005.
46. Chibber 2003.

land reform and other forms of state intervention in the agrarian economy.[47] After 1947, the Congress came to dominate national politics and, therefore, also the postcolonial state. Within this 'dominant party system', subaltern groups were consistently denied unmediated access to the state apparatus. Congress hegemony by and large left local power structures intact and poor social majorities thus remained dependent upon local notables in accessing the state. The result was the failure to convert 'the superior numbers of the poor into a powerful political resource'.[48]

Thus, India's postcolonial development project was crucially shaped by a social movement from above, anchored in the capacity of the country's dominant proprietary classes to set limits to and exert pressures on the articulation and implementation of state development strategies in ways that served their interests in warding off challenges to their dominant status and in expanding and entrenching the preconditions for a deepening of capitalist relations. Since the early 1990s, developmentalism has given way to neoliberalism in India.[49] This move has, however, been fiercely contested by subaltern groups who find their livelihoods and life-worlds endangered by this turn to the market at the behest of bullish élites who seek to integrate into the orbits of the global capitalist economy. In the current conjuncture, then, it is more crucial than ever to draw strategic lessons from and for popular struggles, and, on this note, I turn to investigate the character and dynamics of the *Narmada Bachao Andolan*.

The Narmada movement and the relational dynamics of resistance

'Far too often', writes Donald Moore, 'contemporary analyses eclipse the micropolitics through which global development discourses are refracted, reworked, and sometimes subverted in particular localities'.[50] This is also true of scholarly representations of the Narmada movement. For example, Pablo Kala has argued, with regard to the *Narmada Bachao Andolan*'s politics of resistance to large dams, that it opposes 'the lived space of the adivasi and peasant' to 'the abstract space of the state and of transnational corporations'.[51] Although suggestive, Kala's dichotomic conception fails to note the relational poetics of the NBA's discourse of resistance; that is, it is a discourse of resistance that has been crafted by appropriating elements of the state's developmental ideology and inflecting it with subversive and oppositional meanings that indict the actual direction

---

47. Byres 1981; Frankel 2005.
48. Frankel 2005, p. 25.
49. Chatterjee 2008.
50. Moore 2000, p. 655.
51. Kala 2001, p. 14.

of development in India and the way in which it has exploited, excluded, and marginalised subaltern social groups.

In conjunction with the monsoon *Satyagraha* of 2000, the NBA staged a celebration of India's Independence Day on 15 August.[52] In the Adivasi village of Nimgavhan, on the Maharashtra side of the Narmada River, Independence Day began with the hoisting of both the Indian flag and the NBA's banner by a veteran Gandhian and respected freedom fighter, Siddharaj Dhadda. Following the flag hoisting, a confrontation broke out. Two teachers were present at the ceremony. These teachers were employed at local state-run schools, but most of the time they were absent from the schools they were supposed to be running. Agitated villagers and activists confronted the teachers, and argued that their vocation amounted to little more than picking up their pay cheques. This dismal state of affairs was then thrown into sharp relief with the following point on the programme: the congratulation of young Adivasis who had fared well in official schools after first having completed basic schooling in the *Andolan*'s *Jeevan Shalas* – literally 'schools for life' built and run by the *Andolan* with a curriculum adapted to Adivasi realities.

The celebrations continued in the nearby village of Domkhedi with the inauguration of a microhydel project. A check dam had been constructed on a small stream adjacent to Domkhedi, which, when combined with a pedal-powered generator, provided electricity to the village for the first time ever. Whereas the SSP threatened to displace the villagers from their lands and produce costly electricity that would only be available to affluent and predominantly urban consumers, here was a project controlled and executed at village level that actually had the potential of delivering a tangible improvement in people's lives.

Thus, on 15 August 2000, Independence Day, a social practice of commemoration was appropriated by a social movement for insurgent purposes and transformed into an idiom of resistance. Through this practice of commemoration, the NBA effectively put the collective memories of the nation's past to use to serve the needs of the present, and they did this by creating and conveying a narrative with a definite moral message. Crucially, it was a narrative that recognised the freedom struggle and the attainment of Independence through that struggle

---

52. In the NBA's repertoire of contention, the term '*Satyagraha*' is associated the annual protest events that took place during the monsoon months (June, July, August and September) every year from 1991 until 2002. Basically, what the *Satyagraha* revolved around was a braving of the rising of the waters of the Narmada which set in with the monsoon rains and the closing of the floodgates of the SSP. The *Satyagrahas* are centred on one or two villages in the tribal areas of Maharashtra and Madhya Pradesh, where the resident families, NBA activists, and domestic and international supporters of the movement stand their ground as the waters rise. The braving of the waters thus signals a defiance of the displacement wrought by the project, and constitutes an emotive image of the opposition to dam-building on the Narmada.

as fundamental events and achievements – the presence of freedom fighters, the unfolding and hoisting of the Indian flag, indeed, the very celebration of Independence Day testify to this.

However, at the same time, it was a narrative that portrayed the postcolonial development project as profoundly out of kilter. India's 'tryst with destiny' had gone awry; the promises of freedom and development had been hijacked by élite interests and betrayed, leaving large sections of the population by the wayside as outcasts. This betrayal was efficiently brought out by the contrasts evoked in the celebrations: the putrid condition of state schooling versus the vivacity of the *jeevan shalas*; the destruction wrought by the SSP versus the benefits brought to local communities by the micro-hydroelectric project. What they articulated through the celebrations was not a particularistic and insular politics of place, turning their backs on freedom and development. The focus on the NBA's constructive activities was expressive of an alternative political project of development, which resonated far beyond the Narmada Valley. The movement thus projected itself as an agent on a mission to reinvent the ideals of freedom and development. A subsequent press release issued by the movement stated: 'Independence Day is so often a celebration of a country's victory over oppression, but in Nimgavhan, it had an additional meaning of the people's continued resistance against the injustice and exploitation within a nation'.[53]

Now, I do not, of course, labour under the misconception that a closely orchestrated protest event such as this and the discourse of resistance that it conveys constitutes a perfect reflection of a uniform and collective consciousness that stretches out into every nook and cranny of the Narmada movement. However, it nonetheless testifies to and underscores the essentially *immanent* character of movements such as the NBA, in that it is expressive of a social movement project that is an immanent rather than external challenge to the postcolonial development project.

This is the case in two ways: first, it is a social movement project that emerges from the internal contradictions of a determinate historical trajectory of postcolonial capitalist development; secondly, it seeks to challenge these contradictions through a critique that appropriates and inverts the central idioms through which legitimacy for the postcolonial development project was sought. On the first point, rather than articulating a discourse of resistance as a response to modernist encroachments upon otherness, the NBA has arguably given voice to an emergent structure of radical needs and capacities – that is, a structure of needs and capacities that has emerged but cannot be satisfied within the parameters of the dominant trajectory of development. In terms of the latter point, rather than

---

53. NBA 2000.

rejecting development as such, the NBA posits itself as an agent on a mission to reclaim and reinvent development. When the NBA uses Independence Day to call attention to the wide discrepancies between the lofty promises of better-ment for all and the reality of the systematic marginalisation of large sections of the population, it effectively destabilises the 'supra-class, eternal character' that dominant social groups in India have sought to impart to development as an 'ideological sign'.[54] Conversely, by displaying alternative approaches to develop-ment, such as the *Jeevan Shalas* and the micro-hydel project, the NBA intimates an alternative meaning of development that expresses the social experiences and aspirations of subaltern social groups and seeks to establish social tenure for these meanings.[55]

Indeed, it is a general feature of the development of social movements from below that the local rationalities from which the collective skilled activity of subaltern social groups flow are forged in relation to the hegemonic projects of social movements from above, which seek to create and consolidate structures that give direction and meaning to the routines and experiences of everyday life. Now, this engagement with extant material and semiotic structures will, inevi-tably, be an experience partly of enablement and partly of constraint. This is a central concern in the following section, which focuses on the NBA's encounters with state power in their campaign against the Narmada dams.

Subaltern encounters with the state

A virtue of the state-centric approach to social movements in the South is that it is predicated on an understanding of how the resistance of subaltern groups tends to proceed via appropriations of institutions, practices, and discourses that constitute the pillars of hegemony, and put these to use in ways that reflect their interests, experiences and ambitions. Nevertheless, they fail to interrogate the structural limits to subaltern emancipation inherent to the state and the politi-cal ramifications that flow from this. A comparison of different phases of the movement-process in the Narmada Valley will help to clarify this point.

Fighting everyday tyranny

Social action groups working among the dam-affected communities in the Narmada Valley spawned the struggle against the Narmada dam projects. In the Adivasi communities of the sub-district of Alirajpur in Western Madhya Pradesh,

---

54. Vološinov 1973, p. 23.
55. Barker 2002; Steinberg 1999a.

it was the *Khedut Mazdoor Chetna Sangath* (KMCS) trade union that played this role.[56]

The KMCS emerged through a process in which urban educated activists joined hands with village communities in challenging a condition which can be referred to as everyday tyranny – that is, a range of violent, coercive, and extortive practices meted out against the Adivasis by the local representatives of the state.[57] Everyday tyranny essentially revolved around forest rangers, police, and revenue officials exacting bribes – both in cash and in kind – from Adivasis in exchange for turning a blind eye to their use of state-owned forests for cultivation, timber and fuel collection, and other related activities necessary for their livelihoods. Demands for bribes were, in turn, underpinned by a very real threat of violence; as one KMCS activist explained, if local police officers discovered a villager walking along the road carrying an axe or a sickle, they would often bring the person to the police outpost, where he would be beaten up and then made to pay a bribe in order to avoid criminal charges.[58]

Everyday tyranny, then, was a local state-society relationship far removed from the liberal-democratic ideals of citizenship enshrined in the Indian Constitution. Indeed, one could say that the local state in Alirajpur was not encountered as a set of agencies and functionaries providing services for, and accountable to, the citizens of a political community; on the contrary, Adivasi 'sightings of the state'[59] were centred on seemingly all-powerful tyrants who imposed a cruel, heavy-handed régime of extortion upon their subjects, and who responded to defiance with violence.

Everyday tyranny, however, was challenged when urban, educated activists came into contact with the Adivasi communities in the early 1980s. In a series of confrontations with local state officials, activists and villagers pointed out the illegality of coercion and extortion. Whereas the initial response was one of violence – several of the activists were severely beaten – the mobilisation-process gathered pace when activists and villagers staged a *dharna* in protest against the violent practices of the local representatives of the state, a demonstration that took place outside the administrative headquarters in the town of Alirajpur. The media picked up on the protest, and it quickly became news. As a response, the Chief Minister intervened and suspended several forest guards who were responsible for the beating of one of the activists. High-ranking officials of the Madhya Pradesh Forest-Department was sent to Alirajpur to discuss the problems that villagers faced in their encounters with local forest rangers. In the meeting, it was stressed that forest rangers were not entitled to demand

56. See Baviskar 1995; Nilsen 2010.
57. Nilsen 2007b; 2008; 2011.
58. See Nilsen 2010; 2011.
59. Corbridge et al. 2005, p. 5.

bribes, and that any further malpractice should be reported directly to the Forest Conservator. In the context of the widespread repression that reigned in Alirajpur, this, of course, constituted a major victory, and it became the basis for further mobilisation in the region.

Through the eventual formation of the KMCS as a trade union, activists proceeded to create an awareness in the Adivasi communities of constitutional rights and entitlements, as well as defending the communities' customary rights to the forest.[60] The result of this process was a profound transformation in the character of subaltern 'sightings of the state' in Alirajpur. Where Adivasis had once seen state officials as all-powerful figures, they now came to see public servants whose powers were defined and circumscribed by law and who were accountable to them as citizens; where the villagers had once seen a state apparatus whose activities centred on the forceful exaction of tribute payments, they came to see an institution that was supposed to provide services and safeguard rights, an institution upon which they could make rights-based claims and demands, and in whose running they could participate. It was, then, a process through which subjugated communities emerged as agents capable of engaging 'with the state as citizens, or as members of populations with legally defined or politically inspired expectations';[61] and they did so with a great deal of success.

The anti-dam campaign

However, if we turn to the trajectory of the NBA's campaign against the SSP, we encounter a very different scenario. The NBA put forward its demand for a review of the SSP in 1990, hoping to create a situation in which the project would be found to be technically unfeasible or in violation of social and environmental regulations, such that it would have to be abandoned. This strategy eventually proved to be a cul de sac.[62]

The trajectory of the demand for a review exhibited a clear pattern: at the state level, promises to implement a review were first made and then reneged upon due to internal differences in the state government, or simply not followed up at all; similarly, at the federal level, promises were made and reneged upon, but here as a direct consequence of the pressure exerted by the Government of Gujarat. Indeed, even Prime Minister V.P. Singh, who nurtured close relations with India's new social movements, shied away from implementing a review in the face of the counter-mobilisation staged by Chimanbhai Patel, Chief Minister

60. Baviskar 1995, p. 195.
61. Corbridge et al. 2005, p. 13.
62. See Nilsen 2010.

of Gujarat and a leading representative of the dominant Patidar landowning classes in the southern and central parts of the state.

The process culminated in one of the NBA's most spectacular and dramatic protest actions: the *Jan Vikas Sangharsh Yatra* ['March of Struggle for People's Development']. In December 1990 and January 1991, six thousand people marched from the town of Badwani in Madhya Pradesh towards the SSP dam-site in Gujarat. The march was stopped at the border to Gujarat, and a protracted stand-off unfolded, with several activists going on a 21-day hunger strike. The central government announced that a review would be carried out, and in 1993, following further dramatic actions by the NBA, a Five Member Group (FMG) was assigned the task of reviewing the project. Its efforts were effectively undermined both by central politicians and the Government of Gujarat. The FMG's report, which was made public in 1994 and lent credence to the NBA's case, was largely inconsequential. This occurred even in a context of élite fragmentation: in Gujarat, Chief Minister and ardent SSP-advocate Chimanbhai Patel had passed away; in Madhya Pradesh, the Congress and Digvijay Singh, brandishing a pro-civil society agenda and arguing for a reduction of the height of the SSP, had won the state elections. It is quite possible to tease out cracks and fissures that appeared in the state system throughout this process, but the central dynamic was that of the dominant proprietary classes and their representatives closing ranks whenever they were truly tested.

A similar pattern can be found in the NBA's engagement with the Supreme Court. In May 1994, the NBA submitted a case of public-interest litigation against the SSP to the Supreme Court, claiming that the execution of the project constituted a violation of people's basic right to life and livelihood. An important part of the rationale for doing so was the fact that India's Supreme Court had obtained a reputation for its pro-activist leanings. The initial experience with the NBA's case seemed to confirm this reputation. The Supreme Court imposed a stay on the SSP in 1995, and when senior Members of Parliament expressed their dismay over the Supreme Court's meddling in inter-state affairs during hearings in 1997, the Court staunchly refused to lift the stay on the dam. Once again, then, a chasm can be identified within the state system. However, this chasm was effectively brushed aside with the Supreme Court's October 2000 verdict stating that the SSP should be completed as quickly as possible, and the clear statement accompanying the verdict insisting that the Court was not to serve as an arena for contesting state development strategies. Once again, the ranks of the state system – ironically enough, by means of a clear reference to the separation of state powers – were closed, and the closure was in favour of dominant social groups.

Encountering enablements, encountering constraints

In addressing these two encounters with the state, we have to grapple with two very different outcomes. The case of the KMCS certainly does illustrate the potential for empowerment that resides in subaltern appropriations of what Abrams calls the 'state idea'[63] – namely, the representation of the state as a coherent body external to society, which neutrally arbitrates in conflicts between equals. It also demonstrates that the 'state system' – that is, the 'palpable nexus of practice and institutional structure centred in government'[64] – is not a tightly sutured Leviathan, and that it may well be 'made to do the bidding of India's lower orders'.[65] In the case of the *Andolan*'s struggle for review of the SSP and its turn to the Supreme Court, however, the state system appears more as 'a committee for managing the common affairs of the bourgeoisie', and the state idea as an ideological veil which 'contrives to deny the existence of connections which would if recognised be incompatible with the claimed autonomy and integration of the state'.[66]

The explanation for these different outcomes must be sought, I believe, in the different character of the oppositional projects pursued by the KMCS and the NBA, and the way in which the latter levelled a challenge against the capitalist nature of the Indian state and the way in which it had authored and executed a passive revolution. The KMCS offensive against the everyday tyranny of the local state – significant though it was for the communities involved – was centred on a claim to which the higher echelons of the state system could concede without undermining their own authority and without going against the interests of extra-local proprietary élites. The NBA's campaign against dam building, however, was pitted directly against the vested interests of the proprietary élites of southern and central Gujarat, whose capacity to influence the workings of the state outshone that of the Adivasis and petty-commodity producers mobilised by the NBA in Madhya Pradesh and Maharashtra.

This can, of course, be read as testimony to Corbridge and Harriss's argument that the extent to which subaltern groups can make claims on the state is subject to conjunctural fluctuations related to regional and state-specific balances of class power. However, I would argue that in the case of the NBA's anti-dam campaign, it is also possible to detect constraints to subaltern claim making on the state that are of a more structural character. This is so because the campaign was

---

63. Abrams 1988, p. 82.
64. Ibid.
65. Corbridge and Harriss 2000, p. 239.
66. Abrams 1988, p. 77.

not only directed against one particular dam project. It was deeply embedded in a general opposition to dam building as a development strategy, as well as a critique of India's postcolonial development project. Moreover, the NBA was a driving force in the formation of a social movement project for alternative development in the form of the National Alliance of People's Movements. As such, the NBA challenged one of the chief modalities through which the state – despite its liberal-democratic pretensions to neutrality – has secured the constitution and reproduction of accumulation in the passive revolution that has expanded and entrenched capitalist relations in postcolonial India.

The virtue of these examples is that they push us to think about questions of power and politics that we can ill afford to displace from our analytical gaze if we are concerned with subaltern empowerment. Accordingly, whilst, on the one hand, it is necessary to acknowledge 'the possibilities for empowerment that might exist within India's polity',[67] it is, on the other hand, equally imperative to give serious thought to the limits that might exist to those possibilities, as well as what this entails, in practical and strategic terms, for new social movements in contemporary India. Whereas the state – at least in its liberal-democratic incarnation – is not 'a fixed sum of resources which can be appropriated by one social force to the exclusion of others',[68] it is also the case that it 'can never be equally accessible to all forces and equally available for all purposes.[69]

The limits to what subaltern groups can achieve via the state reflects, in turn, the historically specific unity imposed upon the state – as an 'institutional ensemble' – by social movements from above, by means of their hegemonic projects. State power, then, must ultimately be understood in terms of 'the power of the social forces acting in and through it'[70] and their greater control of structures and relations. Hence, when social movements like the NBA encounter these limits, it should compel us to think about how these limits can be transcended. I address this task in the concluding remarks.

Concluding remarks

A theory of social movements that is truly relevant to the needs and knowledge-interests of activists will, above all, seek to contribute to what Marx referred to (in a letter he wrote to Arnold Ruge in 1843) as 'the self-clarification ... of the struggles and wishes of the age'. In this chapter, I have tried to take some

---

67. Corbridge and Harriss 2000, p. 238.
68. Jessop 1982, p. 225.
69. Jessop 1990, p. 250.
70. Jessop 1990, p. 256.

initial steps towards crafting a perspective that may be of some use in the self-clarification of the struggles of social movements in the global South, via a Marxist interrogation of the trajectory and dynamics of popular resistance to large dams in India's Narmada Valley.

The Narmada movement, I have argued, emerged from within India's post-colonial development project – essentially, a passive revolution by capital – and has crafted its oppositional project through an appropriation of some of the central idioms of this project. I have also argued that in engaging the post-colonial state, the Narmada movement has arguably encountered the limits of what social movements can expect to achieve within the parameters of the Indian polity.

The element of self-clarification in this kind of approach lies in the way in which it traces lines of development from subalternity to integral autonomy and the patterns of enablement and constraint that movements encounter as they move along this line by crafting oppositional practices and imaginaries, and prompts us to think about how to distill generic strategic lessons from this. In this case, the central question revolves around the dynamics of subaltern encounters with state power: how can social movements from below strategically balance 'conjunctural opportunities' for and 'structural constraints'[71] to subaltern emancipation in and through the state?

My response to this question would be to steer a course between the abrogated view of politics that characterises state centrism and 'the simplistic notions of anti-institutional purity'[72] that often characterise poststructuralist approaches. An awareness of the limits to the changes that can be achieved via the institutions, procedures and discourses of the state does not translate into an on-principle rejection of any engagement with the state. Given the relational nature of state power, such recourse might also bear fruits. This, however, does not imply positing interaction and negotiation with the state as 'the be-all and end-all of movement activity'.[73] Rather, it means advocating a position that explicitly seeks to take account of both the potential and the limits of political action within the state system. In other words, what is advocated, here, is an instrumental rather than a committed engagement[74] with the state – that is, an approach to interaction with the state based on limited expectations of what can be gained and a clear perception of what is risked in pursuing this avenue. It also entails an awareness that a challenge to the structures of power on which the state

---

71. Jessop 1982, p. 253.
72. Poulantzas 1978, p. 153.
73. Geoghegan and Cox 2001, p. 7.
74. I owe this distinction to Laurence Cox.

rests and which it is instrumental in reproducing is best done through the construction of a counter-hegemonic project, one that seeks to develop the mobilisational capacity and oppositional practices of subaltern groups to the point where they can successfully challenge extant power structures and their entrenched institutional manifestations.

The Politics of Social Movements

The Marxist Rank-and-File/Bureaucracy Analysis of Trade Unionism: Some Implications for the Study of Social Movement Organisations*

Ralph Darlington

Introduction

While Michels drew attention to the way in which social democratic political parties and trade unions are characterised by their bureaucratic forms of organisation and leadership – with a hierarchy of officers, concentrated decision-making and command flowing down – it seems clear that contemporary social movement organisations have not been immune from the emergence of similar bureaucratic features.[1] Indeed, some commentators have even gone so far as to argue that the so-called Michelsian dilemma – that if you organise mass organisations in order to gain power, they inevitably become bureaucratised and less democratic over time – applies to most social movement organisations.[2]

This chapter attempts to explore the issue of bureaucracy by re-evaluating the classic Marxist analysis of the rank-and-file/bureaucracy model of trade unionism; and, in the process, making some generalisations that may be of relevance to social movement organisations more broadly. Such a round about route can be viewed as a useful exercise not only on the basis that there has been a much longer and more extensive reflection on

* I would like to thank Sage for permission to reproduce parts of the article 'A Reappraisal of the Rank-and-File Versus Bureaucracy Debate' by Ralph Darlington and Martin Upchurch that appeared in the journal *Capital & Class*, vol. 36, no. 1, 2012.

1. Michels 1962.
2. Meyer 2007; Piven and Cloward 1979.

the problem of bureaucracy within the world of trade unionism (and academic industrial relations), but also because there are important common dilemmas facing trade unions and broader social movements that highlight certain analogies across the different contexts. The fact that some unions have been intimately involved in social movements, and that union organising initiatives have, in certain instances, served as a model for social movement organisations, makes the exercise even more pertinent.

Of course, it has long been acknowledged that a hierarchy of bureaucratic and conservative full-time officials acquire interests, perspectives and resources that tend to channel trade union policies towards accommodation with employers and/or governments, the avoidance of strikes and an overall commitment to the existing social and political order.[3] Yet, as a number of commentators have pointed out, Michels's alleged 'iron law of oligarchy' – despite becoming accepted as 'orthodoxy' in the academic fields of political science and industrial relations over the postwar years – presented an over-determined model of bureaucracy that neglected important countervailing democratic pressures originating from membership organisation and struggle.[4] Indeed, in contrast to Michels's pessimistic assumptions, the early-twentieth-century British revolutionary-syndicalist tradition highlighted the potential for militant 'direct action' and independent rank-and-file organisation that bypassed the 'class collaboration' of union officials.[5] Likewise, during the early 1970s upsurge in industrial militancy in Britain, shop stewards' organisation proved highly responsive to the spontaneous demands of the rank-and-file, often leading strike activity independently (and even in defiance) of official union leaders.[6]

However, with the dramatic decline in industrial struggle that occurred in Britain from the late 1970s onwards, there was an enhanced tendency towards what was termed a 'bureaucratisation of the rank-and-file' within shop stewards' organisation, with the growing influence of a 'semi-bureaucracy' of full-time workplace union reps who increasingly acted in ways that restrained rather than encouraged their members' militancy.[7] For Hyman, this development underlined the extent to which the 'problem of bureaucracy' could not be viewed as being primarily rooted in the interests of a specific layer of full-time officials (FTOs), but rather as a set of social relationships that permeated the whole practice of trade unionism at *every level* of the representative structure.[8] As a result, it

3. See for example, Luxemburg 1986; Michels 1962; Murphy 1972; Webb 1920; Mills 1948.
4. See for example, Hyman 1971; Barker 2001.
5. Darlington 2008a; 2008b.
6. Darlington and Lyddon 2001.
7. Hyman 1979b.
8. Hyman 1979b, p. 61.

was suggested, intra-union relations could no longer be reduced to a cleavage between a 'trade union bureaucracy' (signified by a distinct stratum of full-time union officials) and a 'rank-and-file' (workplace union members and their lay reps/shop stewards) along the lines of the classic Marxist analytical model.

Similarly, a number of other commentators have criticised the so-called 'rank-and-filist' perspective, suggesting that there is no clear demarcation line between 'officialdom' and the 'rank-and-file'; that FTOs are often responsive to their members and there is no differentiation of interests between them; that left-wing union officials have more in common with left-wing shop stewards than their right-wing counterparts; and that FTOs do not necessarily tend towards conservatism and their members towards militancy.[9] What has united all of these different specific forms of critique is the view that the rank-and-file/bureaucracy model is insufficiently coherent or empirically grounded to be of any use, either for theoretical endeavour or practical application.[10] Even some Marxist-influenced writers such as Kelly, McIlroy and Campbell and Gall have accepted the broad contours of this analysis of bureaucracy within trade unionism.[11] Certainly, there has been little attempt, over the last thirty years, to provide any systematic defence of the rank-and-file/bureaucracy model.

This chapter attempts to fill the gap, providing a much more developed, nuanced and multidimensional revolutionary Marxist conception than has gone before; one which, in the process, explores the limits and potential of the Michelsian dilemma and its implications for the study of broader social movement organisations.

The trade union bureaucracy

Its social role

First, the existence of a distinct stratum of full-time professional trade union officials is inherent in the very nature of trade unionism within capitalist society, in which union struggles tend to be concerned with improving the terms on which workers are exploited, not with ending that exploitation. By confining the class struggle to the search for reforms within the limits of capitalism, there is an in-built presumption that the antagonistic interests of capital and labour can, somehow, be accommodated, with the consequence that workers' struggles, however

9. See Gore 1982; Kelly 1988; McIlroy 1988; Heery and Fosh 1990; Heery and Kelly 1990; Kelly and Heery 1994; Zeitlin 1987; 1989a; 1989b.
10. Zeitlin 1989a, p. 60.
11. Kelly 1988; McIlroy 1999; Campbell 2003.

militant, must ultimately result in a compromise. It is this situation that generates a permanent apparatus of FTOs whose job is to mediate between capital and labour and to specialise in negotiating the terms of such compromises.[12]

Such officials occupy a unique social position, one different from the bulk of the rank-and-file union members they represent. They are neither *employers* nor *workers*. While they might employ secretaries and research assistants to work on their behalf in union headquarters, unlike a capitalist enterprise, this is clearly not where they gain their economic or social status. But conversely, the full-time union official is not merely an ordinary worker either. Rank-and-file workers are obligated to sell their labour power to an employer, and their immediate material interest is bound up with ensuring they get the maximum possible return for that sale. Everyday subordination and exploitation – inherent in the experience of wage-labour – periodically leads them to rebel collectively against managerial authority (and, sometimes, even against the official trade union structures and bargaining procedures that can become fetters on their self-activity and objectives). In the course of their struggles to build up the strength of union organisation, many workers (notwithstanding the fact that they themselves are subject to conservative pressures and their struggles can often be highly fragmented in character) can come up against the limits of the capitalist system. Out of that conflict, workers (only a small minority in 'normal' periods, but potentially *en masse* during periods of acute economic and political crisis) can be encouraged to understand the need to overthrow capitalist social relations of production.

By contrast, while trade union officials also depend on a money-wage, this is something gained from a *union*, not from an employer. In fact, not only is the possibility of pay rises bound up with the continuation of the union as an employer, but the officials' very existence – in terms of the source of their security, power and status – is indissolubly connected with the existence of the unions.[13] As a consequence, they come under strong pressure to view themselves as having a vested interest in the continuation of the wage-labour and capitalist order from which trade unions derive their function. In turn, this can lead to the establishment of inherently socially accommodating relationships with employers and the state. As such, the limits of trade union officialdom are determined by their social situation.

The sharp contrast between rank-and-file workers' social position and FTOs can become particularly evident during strike activity. The most basic necessities of workers' lives can often depend on the outcome of such struggles with employers, whereas union officials' lives tend to go on much the same, whether

---

12. Callinicos 1995, p. 17.
13. J. Kaye 1984, p. 10.

those struggles are won or lost. If workers begin to take on the employers themselves through militant forms of strike action, then the union officials' function
of attempting to resolve conflict by negotiating compromises can be called into
question. Obviously, the more militant and broader the struggle, the more dramatic such a divide between officials and the rank-and-file can become. While for
workers, a mass strike driven from below (for example, against both an employer
and government policies) can potentially raise the prospect of the revolutionary
transformation of society, for the official, it can seem to represent a threat to
their *raison d'être*. Indeed, officials have traditionally been as afraid of a *successful* confrontation with the government as an unsuccessful one, with numerous
historical examples of the way in which, at times of crisis and class-confrontation,
they have demonstrated their ultimate loyalty to the existing system.

One of the most famous examples of this took place in Britain in 1919, when
Prime Minister Lloyd George told the leaders of the miners', railwaymen's and
transport workers' unions that they were essentially approaching a dual-power
situation, and that if they called a strike, the Government would be defeated, and
it would be up to them to run the country. Confronted with the possibility of
actually overthrowing the system, the union leaders recoiled – in the immortal
words of railway workers' leader Jimmy Thomas: 'I have never disguised that in
a challenge to the Constitution, God help us unless the Government won'.[14]

Its bargaining function

Second, there is the bargaining function of union officials. Despite the fact that
trade unions have arisen as an expression and vehicle of the class struggle to
advance workers' interests against those of capital, FTOs are subject to powerful
moderating pressures to accept the parameters of a set of bargaining institutions
dominated by capital. As Luxemburg argued, the preservation of the union's
machine – its headquarters, finance and organisation – effectively becomes an
'end in itself' rather than a means to achieve improved terms and conditions of
employment for workers.[15] Institutional pressures towards an 'accommodation
with external power' lead to resistance to objectives and action (such as militant
strike activity) which push 'too far' and unduly antagonise employers and the
state and potentially risk a full-blown confrontation that threatens the unions'
organisational security and financial assets.[16] In the process, even though union
officials often express their members' consciousness of grievances, they can also
often tend to view strikes as an unnecessary disruption and a potential threat to

14. Miliband 1972, p. 134.
15. Luxemburg 1986, pp. 87–8.
16. Hyman 1975a, pp. 89–90.

the maintenance of a stable bargaining relationship. There is a natural tendency to define the conduct and outcome of collective bargaining as being dependent on their own 'professional' competence and expertise, acting *on behalf* of their members, rather than encouraging the members to secure the full fruits of their labour *for themselves* through collective mobilisation.

Thus, the central paradox that although the process of collective bargaining can win significant material improvements for rank-and-file workers, as well as impose limits on the arbitrary power of employers, it also institutionalises industrial conflict. It subordinates the relatively autonomous, informal and oppositional activity that workers can mount to limit managerial autonomy by channelling workers' grievances into relatively innocuous forms, defining bargaining issues within a narrow focus so as to render the task of achieving compromise with employers more tractable.[17] As a consequence, union officials can sometimes act, in Mills's famous phrase, as 'manager[s] of discontent'.[18]

Similarly, Gramsci drew attention to the exercise of control *over* workers by union officials through the very process by which unions seek to win improvements *for* them.[19] While it is, undoubtedly, a vital achievement that union officials (utilising the threat/use of rank-and-file industrial strength) can win material improvements for their members and impose limits on the arbitrary power of employers through the process of collective bargaining, they are subject to powerful influences to conceive the form of 'industrial legality' thus established – one that reflects the continuing preponderance of employer power over that of workers and their union organisation – as a permanent state of affairs.

While the ordinary worker, perpetually subject to economic exploitation and deprivation of control, is always liable to overturn some aspect of this 'industrial legality', the union official, by contrast, is under intense pressure to 'keep faith' with their negotiating partners, to regard each conflict as a 'problem' to be resolved within a framework defined by the prevailing system. It is for this reason that they often tend to limit workers' struggles and to end strikes on 'compromise' terms in ways that can be detrimental to rank-and-file interests and aspirations.

Its social position

Third, there are the material benefits that FTOs enjoy. To begin with, they are the recipients of substantial salaries and other financial rewards. Indeed, the

---

17. Hyman 1975b, p. xxv; 1984, p. 141.
18. Mills 1948, p. 9.
19. Gramsci 1969, p. 15.

general secretaries of Britain's 15 biggest unions currently earn between £84,000 and £112,000 in basic salary,[20] compared with the median gross annual earnings for full-time employees of £25,123.[21] For example, in 2009, Derek Simpson, joint general secretary of Unite, received a salary of £97,027 as well £89,599 in benefits including pension, housing and car benefits, totalling £186,626; Dave Prentis, general secretary of Unison, received a salary of £94,953 plus £24,311 pension-contributions and £10,845 in expenses and car benefits, totalling £130,109. Below the level of general secretaries, other national officials, as well as regional and local-area officials, are also well-rewarded, with high salaries as compared to their members.

While such financial benefits do not, in themselves, necessarily lead to conservativism, when combined with other material factors, they do conspire to place FTOs in a different social environment from the bulk of their members. Even though many officials may work long hours in stressful, demanding jobs, and spend periods away from home, in general, their relatively secure jobs and salaries contrast starkly with the much lower pay, hazardous and dissatisfying work and precarious living standards of the members they represent. Certainly, union officials are not usually subject to management bullying, attacks on pay, having their workload increased, being victimised, laid-off or habitually enduring the threat of job loss or redundancy from employers. A degree of social isolation arises from the inevitable change in job context, with officials spending a good proportion of their time involved in a steady succession of union meetings and negotiations with employers, often isolated from the bulk of the members they represent.[22]

The cumulative effect of such changed social conditions is that they are under enormous pressure to absorb some of the employers' outlook, to have 'a greater understanding of, and sympathy for, their erstwhile opponents' and, ultimately, to become power-brokers in search of compromise and moderation.[23]

Its link to social democracy

Fourth, there is the link between full-time union officialdom and social democracy, with the union bureaucracy finding its political expression in labour and socialist parties that seek to reform capitalism while leaving its exploitative social relations intact, corresponding closely to the pursuit of compromise between

---

20. As of 2010, according to the Certification Officer's website, <www.certoffice.org>.
21. According to the Government's 2009 Annual Survey of Hours and Earnings.
22. Pannekoek 1936; Callinicos 1982.
23. Kelly 1988, p. 151.

labour and capital that is the trade union officials' own *raison d'être*. Sometimes, the link between union officialdom and social-democratic parties takes a formal, institutional shape, as in the case of Britain through union funding and union representation at every level of the Labour Party, and sometimes an informal one, although the alliance between union officials and reformist parliamentarians is no less real in countries like Germany.[24]

As Upchurch *et al.* have explained, social democracy is a historical phenomenon marked by the *de facto* integration of the labour movement into parliamentary democracy[25] – a process in Britain that Miliband termed 'Labourism'.[26] This integration was achieved through a historic 'settlement' in which trade union officialdom recognised the legitimacy of private property and the market in return for 'concessions' based on the delivery of state-welfare and state-support for collective bargaining. The ability of labour movements to extract concessions was based on the close institutional connections between trade unions and a 'dominant party of labour' with an ideological commitment to social justice, political liberalism and the welfare state. Social-democratic trade unionism was the product of this 'specific social structuration' marked by a contingent relationship between a growing industrial working class, trade unions, reformist labour and socialist parties and the nation state.[27] The principal objective of social-democratic trade unions *vis-à-vis* the party was the winning of elections in order to facilitate the development of electoral programmes that would augment the industrial power and influence of the trade unions.

While social democracy was progressive in that it based itself upon working-class solidarity that went beyond the business or craft interests common to many early trade unions, the interests of class solidarity were always contained by party and union officials, who fought consistently against workers' power over capital whenever rights of ownership and control were challenged from below. As a result of this 'specific social structuration', social-democratic trade union leaders (both right and left-wing) carried out their position as mediators between capital and labour through a process of 'bureaucratic consolidation'[28]

In the case of Britain's Labour Party, from its inception it institutionalised the divorce between 'economic' and 'political' activity characteristic of capitalist parliamentary democracy, and thereby reinforced the process by which workers' struggles have been confined within strict limits. Thus, the idea that the unions

---

24. Callinicos 1995, p. 23.
25. Upchurch, Taylor and Mathers 2009.
26. Miliband 1972.
27. Moschonas 2002, p. 17.
28. Upchurch, Taylor and Mathers 2009.

might attempt to utilise industrial militancy for *political* ends – to seriously challenge or bring down the government – has always been rejected by national union leaders. Loyalty to the Labour Party, especially when Labour is in office, has encouraged ministers to repeatedly put pressure on officials not to under-mine 'their' government, with the result that they have often blocked and/or defused workers' militancy. Because of their position in society, union leaders have been far more susceptible to this kind of influence than rank-and-file union-members. But even when out of office, the Labour Party has been able to pres-surise them into dampening down strike action and dropping left-wing policies, on the basis that strikes and radicalism would make Labour appear 'irrespon-sible' and harm the Party's electoral prospects.[29] Such pressures have even been apparent within those unions not formally affiliated to the Labour Party, but nonetheless still politically influenced by Labourism.

It is true that there have often been strains and tensions between the unions and the Labour Party: for example, the increasingly critical stance being taken by some union leaders towards the Labour government's 'Social Contract' in the late 1970s and the New Labour government's neoliberal policies during the early 2000s. Yet union officialdom's overall ideological and political loyalty to Labourism has proved to be one of the clearest manifestations of the limitations of trade unionism and of the tendency to confine workers' struggles within the framework of capitalist society.

Its centralised power

Fifth, there is the highly centralised form of administration and power wielded by FTOs. Like all other large-scale organisations within capitalist society, trade unions tend to develop a hierarchical and bureaucratic structure with their own specialised personnel. While such an elaborate system of organisation is partly inherent in the requirement that unions are administratively efficient, it is also reinforced by the self-limiting nature of their relationship with employ-ers and/or the state, and the membership's consequent reliance on officials to act on their behalf, as an intermediary between capital and labour. In turn, this structure invariably gives the small centralised stratum of union officials who exercise control over the organisational machinery enormous authority, power and advantage over the rank-and-file. It is true that this power 'rarely derives from crude coercion and manipulation but rather from some form of accom-modation between the leading officials and other key "lay" participants in the

---

29. Miliband 1972; Coates 1975; 1980; 1989; Taylor 1989; 1993.

decision-making process'.[30] Nonetheless, such power manifests itself in many different ways, including financial resources, specialist knowledge, control of internal formal channels of communication, political skills of leadership, and in defining the choices available to the organisation and its members.[31] While such features exist, to some extent, within *all* labour-movement organisations, their manifestation is particularly acute in trade unions, notwithstanding important counter-tendencies towards democracy and accountability.

Clearly, the degree of internal democracy is likely to vary across different unions and be affected by (amongst other things) whether officials are elected or appointed, the overall number of officials and the ratio of officials to members, the degree of autonomy of union branches and workplace union organisation, the homogeneity of members, the extent of voluntary participation and activity, and the number of independent channels of communication available to opposition groups. But the relative passivity that generally characterises the majority of ordinary union-members, as opposed to a minority of reps and/or activists, in day-to-day internal organisational and political process – apart from during those periods of heightened industrial militancy and collective mobilisation when the participatory and democratic impulse from below can be considerably enhanced – means that a good deal of permanent power tends to rest with those who hold the highest official positions.[32] Hence the officials' ability, for example, to override important policy decisions taken at (formally speaking) highly democratic annual national conferences of membership representatives.

Historically, there has been a tendency for most FTOs (beyond the position of general secretary) to be appointed, rather than elected, to office; but even when elected and subject to formal institutions of accountability (in Britain, it is a requirement of employment legislation that all senior officials are elected), they are still liable to exercise disproportionate decision-making authority, influence and control over policy within the unions.[33] Likewise, their intervention within the collective bargaining arena and around strike activity can also often be crucial, if not decisive.

Qualifications and counter-tendencies

Hyman has argued that the characterisation of *all* union officials as 'villains' who consistently '[sell] out their valiant members' is too one-dimensional.[34] Likewise,

30. Hyman 1980, p. 73.
31. Michels 1962.
32. See Goldstein 1952; Allen 1954; Lipset, Trow and Coleman 1962; Moran 1974.
33. See Undy and Martin 1984; Kelly and Heery 1994; Daniels and McIlroy 2009.
34. Hyman 2003, p. 189.

Kelly has complained that the term 'trade union bureaucrat' has often been misconceived 'as a fixed and invariant type, always and everywhere subject to same eternal laws of bureaucratic conduct and impervious to historical change'.[35] In fact, some revolutionary Marxist writers have long recognised that there are important qualifications and counter-tendencies that also need to be taken into account in any fully-rounded analysis.[36]

Its dual social function

Just as there are limits to the aggressive potential of trade unions, preventing them from acting as revolutionary agents, so, too, are there limits to their ability to collaborate with the employers and the state – since ultimately, their survival is dependent on their ability to represent members' interests against those of their adversaries. Therefore, unions represent both an accommodation to capitalism and *also* a challenge to its priorities; and it is because unions are not simply organisations serving to incorporate the working class, that FTOs are not simply 'fire-extinguishers of the revolution'. Rather, 'they perform a dual role, both shackling their members to the system and bringing home limited benefits within it', with the balance between these contradictory roles varying between different historical periods, contexts, and even individual officials, depending on the relative pressures placed upon them and the actual course of workers' struggles.[37]

On the one hand, if FTOs entirely failed to articulate their members' grievances and, at least on occasion, to sanction or even lead strike action that delivered at least some improvements in pay and conditions, there would be the danger they would lose support in the union. The rank-and-file might bypass them by acting unofficially, mounting an internal challenge to their position, or even relinquishing their membership of the union. This, in turn, could result in organisational disintegration and a reduction in the political power of the officials in negotiations with employers and/or the state. As a consequence, FTOs cannot ignore their members' interests and aspirations completely. On the other hand, if they collaborated too closely with employers and/or the state, the union officials' power would be totally undermined, because the only reason that they are taken seriously is that they represent social forces that pose the potential for resistance to capital. As such, they may sometimes feel obliged – particularly when severe constraints are placed on the unions and its members, or when they find themselves completely ignored at the negotiating table – to threaten

---

35. Kelly 1988, p. 160.
36. Anderson 1967; Cliff 1969; 1970; 1971; Draper 1970.
37. Anderson 1967, pp. 272–7.

or even organise strike action. Thus, the need to preserve the security of union organisation does not always necessarily result in officials attempting to scale down members' aspirations, but can also be served, occasionally and in certain contexts, by the mobilisation of the rank-and-file and a challenge to employer prerogatives.[38]

In other words, the role of trade union officialdom is more complex than the simple caricature of 'officials always playing Brutus' often ascribed to Marxists.[39] Certainly, in Britain there have been periods when union officials have opposed practically all strikes, as from 1940 to the mid-1950s; furthermore, since the defeat of the 1984–5 miners' strike, many union officials have tended to assume that strikes are outmoded, counter-productive and unlikely to be successful. But there have also been periods when (even right-wing) union officials have actually led a good many official and national strikes, as during the 1970s and early 1980s; moreover, despite the massive decline in the level of strike activity over the last thirty years, there has been a number of officially-led strikes. Sometimes, officials have even been prepared to lead strike action against Labour governments, as with the 1978–9 'Winter of Discontent' or in opposition to aspects of New Labour policy in the early 2000s. Nor are officials always forced into calling action by a so-called insurgent rank-and-file, straining at the leash for all-out action. On occasions, they have taken the initiative in attempting to mobilise workers for strike action even when there has been little pressure from below, and/or have called for strikes under the pressure of a militant minority but been rebuffed by a majority of the members in a national ballot (that said, sometimes their own inadequate agitation and preparation to win support for action has contributed to such an outcome).

At the very least, officials are, in general, conscientious, committed and hard-working individuals, motivated by the genuine desire to defend and improve their members' pay and conditions, and supportive of shop stewards and union reps' efforts to organise workers and recruit new members. All of this is important in terms of officials' overall attitude and behaviour towards employers and/or the government and their susceptibility to rank-and-file pressure. This means that the role of FTOs in galvanising workers' militancy alongside shop-floor union activists can, on occasion, be crucial to the instigation, nature and outcome of strike-activity.

Yet the fact that the conservatism of FTOs is 'contingent and historically determined' by the relative strength of the internal and external forces bearing upon them does not mean they are 'merely ciphers who carry out the members'

---

38. Cliff and Gluckstein 1986, pp. 27–8.
39. McIlroy 1988, p. 145.

wishes in a direct and uncomplicated manner'.[40] Recognising that attempts to suppress rank-and-file militancy may prove unsuccessful and merely discredit their position in the eyes of members and employers alike, a degree of endorsement of militant action or even taking the lead in recommending a strike might well appear to be the most prudent course of action. But this can, sometimes, effectively be part of an exercise in 'controlled militancy', whereby the officials lead the struggle at least in part as a means of keeping control over its main direction.[41] Notwithstanding occasional militant rhetoric, they are, in general, motivated by the desire to restrict the action to a merely demonstrative or tokenistic form, and to bring it to an end at the earliest opportunity, irrespective of the merits of the issue, thereby ensuring the members 'let off steam' in a relatively harmless fashion.

Its internal differentiation

Another criticism levelled at the notion of the 'trade union bureaucracy' is that there is considerable internal differentiation within the ranks of full-time officialdom, and that such divisions may be just as significant as those between officials and members.[42] Certainly, officials in different industries with different occupational groups and different particular union traditions will find themselves under varying pressures from below and above, resulting in a range of leadership styles, also shaped by officials' own personalities and aspirations. The existence of hierarchical levels within union officialdom can mean there are differences, for example, between the general secretary and other national officials, between national and local officials, and between officials with responsibilities for collective bargaining and a cadre of dedicated 'organisers' focused on union recruitment. Likewise, there can be differences in terms of gender and ethnicity, with potential implications for the behaviour of officials and their relationship with members.[43]

In addition, union-officials are not the same ideologically and politically, with the differences between *left-* and *right*-wing officials sometimes of considerable significance. A long and enduring tradition inside the British trade union movement (notably associated with the Communist Party) has insisted – on the basis that the main division within the unions is a political one between left and right – upon the need to concentrate on getting left-wing officials elected via 'Broad Left' coalitions such that the unions can be won to more militant policies.[44]

---

40. Bramble 1993, p. 24.
41. Hyman 1973, p. 109.
42. Heery and Fosh 1990.
43. Heery and Kelly 1988.
44. Roberts 1976.

The growth of such Broad Lefts in many unions has been a symptom of growing impatience with the union bureaucracy and a sign that activists have attempted to find an organisational and political solution to perceived problems.

Arguably, the weakness of the Broad Left strategy is that it puts the emphasis on winning left-wing control of the *official union machine* rather than the building of strong *rank-and-file organisation*. Ironically, the British miners won their greatest victories in the national strikes of 1972 and 1974 despite the leadership of a right-wing president (Joe Gormley), essentially because the independent initiative and momentum from below (combined with the active solidarity received from other workers) was so powerful. By contrast, the miners suffered their greatest defeat in 1984–5 under a left-wing president (Arthur Scargill), arising from the relative weakness of rank-and-file organisation within the NUM and among other trade unionists in general.[45]

But in any case, the *differences* between left- and right-wing union officials are, ultimately, less important than what *unites* them at the most primary level and at decisive moments. This is because even though left-wing officials are more likely to encourage workers' struggles, they are still part of the same social group as their right-wing counterparts and, therefore, subject to the same bureaucratic and conservative pressures that affect *all* union officials. As the 1926 General Strike in Britain confirmed, the in-built structural pressures to which they are subject mean that, at the end of the day, left-wing officials are just as capable of holding back workers' struggles as their right-wing counterparts.[46] Even Arthur Scargill, easily one of the most high-profile left-wing union officials there has ever been in Britain, became a 'prisoner' of the bureaucratic apparatus within the miners' union during the 1984–5 miners' strike, with his refusal to appeal over the heads of union officials for rank-and-file solidarity action.[47]

In other words, while the political differences between left- and right-wing officials are potentially important in influencing their behaviour, they are *secondary* to the common material role, position and interests that bind *all* officials together as a distinct social group and, therefore, *subordinate* to the much more fundamental antagonism of interests that exists within the trade union movement, namely that between the union bureaucracy *as a whole* and their rank-and-file members. The fact that left-wing officials might be elected into office does not do away with the need for rank-and-file pressure, democratic accountability and independent organisation. As the Clyde Workers' Committee declared in November 1915: 'We will support the officials just so long as they

45. Callinicos and Simons 1985; Darlington 2005.
46. Hinton and Hyman 1975, pp. 59–60.
47. Callinicos and Simons 1985, pp. 242–7; Darlington 2005, pp. 84–6.

represent the workers, but we will act independently immediately they misrepresent them'.[48]

The rank-and-file

Clearly, the term 'rank-and-file' provides only a broad categorisation of the layers of union membership that exist below the level of FTOs, which includes full-time workplace convenors, senior stewards, section reps, union branch activists and the mass of ordinary union members. It would be wrong to exaggerate the homogeneity and militancy of this broadly defined grouping, given that the membership of unions is fractured along a number of lines, with divisions based on industry, occupation, skill, gender and ethnicity. These divisions embrace but also extend beyond the workplace, and can, at times, become quite pronounced.

Moreover, rank-and-file members do, clearly, vary in terms of their level of commitment to trade unionism. For example, there are stewards and reps – or what the Webbs called the 'non-commissioned officers' of the union movement[49] – who work alongside members and yet are also distinct by virtue of their activism, knowledge and experience in union matters. With a significant layer of stewards now on full-time release from work, or sitting on the regional committees and national executives of their unions, there can also be an important element of differentiation. Likewise, we cannot assume a complete identity of interest between the minority of *militant activists* that operate inside the unions and the mass of members.[50] For example, the revolutionary syndicalists of the early twentieth century often regarded themselves as the authentic voice of the rank-and-file, insofar as their arguments chimed with the often ill-articulated discontent of the mass of workers, and they attempted to constitute an alternative leadership to that of full-time union officialdom.[51] However, they only gained the allegiance of a minority of the working-class movement as a whole, and they were not the only influential political forces. In other words, at any one time, the 'rank-and-file' effectively consists of several different rank-and-files, each subject to internal division, with a provisional and not unproblematic relationship to the majority of union members.

Finally, we should recognise that conflict within trade unions over policy and strategy can also give rise to factional struggles for power between different

48. Clyde Workers' Committee leaflet, Beveridge Collection, British Library of Political and Economic Science, Section 3, Item 5.
49. Webb and Webb 1920, p. 577.
50. Gore 1982, p. 69.
51. Holton 1976; Darlington 2008a; 2008b.

groups of leaders, activists and members that can *cut across hierarchical levels*. This can bring together a broad, overlapping layer of FTOs, regional and local officials, union branch officers, stewards, activists and members, into loose left-wing (or organised Broad Left) caucuses. Within such caucuses, the simple dividing line between 'officials' and 'rank-and-file' can become blurred, with the precise interaction between them varying according to unions' different internal structure.[52] Indeed, one of the key aspects of recent developments in public-sector trade unionism in Britain has been the way in which strikes have been orchestrated by a combination of rank-and-file activists and lay national executive committee members working with sections of full-time union officialdom.[53]

Notwithstanding such differentiation, it is the exploitative social relations at the heart of capitalist society to which the mass of rank-and-file union members are subject, that provide the material basis for collective workers' struggles with inherently (albeit usually not explicit) revolutionary anti-capitalist objectives, and which, therefore, distinguish them from FTOs. It is this that means that the idea of the 'rank-and-file' is not devoid of analytical use, even if it encompasses an internally differentiated layer of members.[54]

Workplace union reps' organisation

The centralised structure of trade union officialdom, its isolation from the members and often-perceived 'betrayal' of workers' struggles has historically led to the growth of structures able to react more immediately to the everyday conflicts in the workplace and which can potentially be mobilised in defiance of (or even opposition to) union officialdom.[55] Thus, in Britain since the late nineteenth century, shop stewards' and other forms of lay workplace union representation has provided a classic example of such rank-and-file organisation. In the 1960s, the willingness of stewards to mobilise their members for strike activity, often independently of FTOs, bred a degree of self-reliance and self-assertiveness termed the 'challenge from below'.[56] It was this that provided the springboard for the generalised industrial and political militancy that followed during the early 1970s. In the process, the Communist Party's self-proclaimed 'official unofficial' body, the Liaison Committee for the Defence of Trade Unions, played a central role in

---

52. Cronin 1989, p. 82; Price 1989, pp. 69–70; Zeitlin 1989b, p. 95.
53. Upchurch, Flynn and Croucher 2008.
54. Bramble 1993, pp. 17–19.
55. Callinicos 1982, p. 6.
56. Flanders 1970.

linking together a layer of militant stewards across different unions, maintaining pressure on union officials and stimulating militant strike action.[57]

From a revolutionary Marxist point of view, shop stewards' organisation has always been of immense significance, as became evident with the experience of the Shop Stewards' and Workers' Committee Movement in Britain during the First World War. During what was another period of mass industrial struggle, political radicalisation and the development of self-confident workplace union organisation, it became possible for a network of shop stewards, operating both within and outside official union structures, to transform fragmented forms of *organisation* in different workplaces into a national rank-and-file *movement*, linking together hundreds of thousands of workers such as to provide an alternative leadership independent of union officialdom. J.T. Murphy and other stewards' leaders began to recognise that this rank-and-file movement could supersede the trade unions and challenge the economic and political power of the capitalist class as a whole, effectively becoming organs of workers' power or embryonic workers' councils – the institutional form through which the working class could take control of society and establish its own state power, as had occurred in Bolshevik Russia.[58]

However, if rank-and-file organisations have the potential to become organs of workers' power, there is nothing inevitable about this happening. In Britain, the strength and militancy of shop stewards' organisation has varied considerably, depending on the shifting balance between labour and capital. In the wake of the defeats and retreat of the trade-union movement in the 1980s and 1990s, stewards' organisation became a faint echo of that of the early 1970s, let alone the First World War, with the 'challenge from below' probably at its lowest ebb since the early 1930s. Moreover, as Hyman – drawing on the work of other contemporaneous commentators[59] – justifiably pointed out: 'workplace trade unionism has always displayed contradictory tendencies, involving certain parallels with the role of full-time officialdom'.[60] This is because stewards' dependence on 'management's goodwill' to preserve stable workplace union organisation, together with the quest for incremental concessions, can draw them (as it does FTOs) into an 'orderly' bargaining relationship, in which they sometimes exercise a restraining and disciplinary role over their members.[61] As such, although often stewards

---

57. McIlroy and Campbell 1999; Darlington and Lyddon 2001.
58. Murphy 1941; Pribicevic 1959; Hinton 1973; Darlington 1998.
59. Turner, Clack and Roberts 1967; McCarthy 1967; McCarthy and Parker 1968; Royal Commission 1968; Cliff and Barker 1966; Cliff 1970; Beynon 1973; Lane 1974.
60. Hyman 1980, p. 74.
61. Hyman 1975a, p. 168.

express rank-and-file members' grievances through collective action, they can also, sometimes, be an important moderating influence.

By the late 1970s and early 1980s, amidst a collapse in the level of industrial struggle, there was, undoubtedly, a qualitative accentuation of the trend towards bureaucratisation and a partial incorporation of previously independent and disruptive steward organisations within the body of official unionism.[62] According to Hyman, the result was that 'shop stewards too [became] "managers of discontent": sustaining job control within the boundaries of negotiation with management authority and capitalist priorities, rather than (apart from the most exceptional circumstances) pursuing frontal opposition'.[63] Arguably, such an interpretation overstated the tendencies towards hierarchy, centralisation and bureaucracy that operated within stewards' organisations *as a whole* at the time, and downplayed some of the important counter-tendencies.[64] Nonetheless, the problem of stewards' bureaucratisation has, undoubtedly, remained of enduring relevance over the last three decades. Restructuring and job losses in the areas of employment that were once bastions of workplace union strength, the unrelenting neoliberal offensive under successive governments, and successive series of workers' defeats combined to inflict an enormous toll on stewards' organisation, the legacy of which has become graphically evident in the decline in the numbers of stewards and reps from some three hundred thousand in 1980 to approximately half that figure today.[65]

While stewards' organisation has remained central in important arenas of employment, the problem of bureaucratisation has remained pervasive in a number of areas, with senior full-time stewards (particularly those representing large union branches) continuing to be remote from their members and, sometimes, even a barrier to union organising initiatives.[66] Even though stewards have, in general, often displayed an extraordinary level of commitment in holding together workplace union organisation for many years, some of them (often feeling beleaguered and defensive in relation to employers) have also displayed characteristics similar to FTOs in terms of their disinclination towards militant resistance and strike activity. This bureaucratising and conservative process has been reinforced by the decline in workers' collective struggles, lack of rank-and-file confidence *vis-à-vis* management, decline in the number of on-site stewards (with some reps effectively covering a number of different geographical

---

62. Lyddon 1977; Terry 1978; 1983; Cliff 1979; Hyman 1979a; 1979b; 1980; Beecham 1984; Beynon 1984.
63. Hyman 1979b, p. 42.
64. Darlington 1994, pp. 26–39.
65. Charlwood and Forth 2008; WERS 2004; Nowak 2009; BERR 2009.
66. Waddington and Kerr 2009; Darlington 2010.

work-locations), increase in the ratio of members to stewards, longer average tenure of office than previously, and an ageing of union representation.

Yet despite the considerable weakening of workplace unionism over the last thirty years, and the bureaucratic tendencies to which stewards and reps' organisation has been subject, they still remain, to a large extent, the backbone of the trade union movement in dealing with workers' grievances, standing up to management and attempting to preserve pay and conditions, and they retain the latent ability to provide a significant counterweight to union-officialdom. Moreover, despite their sometimes full-time status inside the workplace, stewards generally remain *qualitatively different* from FTOs in their potential responsiveness to rank-and-file pressure, with a number of counter-pressures and informal workplace sanctions to those acting solely to bureaucratise stewards' organisation.

While it is true that both face similar contradictory pressures – in terms of their role as a bargaining agent in union-employer relations – as we have seen, as a wage labourer, the steward or rep's position is dependant on capitalist exploitation and the class struggle in a way that the position of the FTO is not. In addition, they are subject to election or re-election and directly responsive to a 'constituency' whose day-to-day problems they often share. Most (although not all) stewards do not move away geographically and organisationally to carry out their representational duties in separation from the experience of their members. Instead they spend most of their time working alongside those whom they represent. Because they can be removed by the members on the basis of their performance, they provide an instrument than can be subordinated to the rank-and-file in a much more direct fashion than any FTO could ever be, however left-wing (and whether elected or appointed). While the bureaucratisation of workplace unionism *has*, to some extent, potentially blurred the distinction between the 'union bureaucracy' and the 'rank-and-file', it has not removed the *underlying fundamental cleavage of interests* within trade unionism *overall*.

The relationship between the rank-and-file and the trade union bureaucracy

If the relationship between shop stewards and FTOs can be characterised as a tension between *independence* and *dependence*, clearly the relationship is, not a fixed phenomenon, but rather is largely dependent on the ebbs and flows of the class struggle.[67] Indeed, the history of stewards' organisation has been a history of the shifting balance between independence and dependence in relation to

---

67. Boraston, Clegg and Rimmer 1975; Hyman and Fryer 1975; Darlington 1994.

full-time trade union officialdom.[68] Thus, in Britain during the early 1970s, the high level of workers' struggle and the victories of key sections of workers encouraged the development of strong, self-reliant stewards' organisation relatively combative in its relationship to employers and the government, which, in turn, encouraged stewards to act relatively independently of the officials and sometimes in open defiance of their wishes. By contrast, in the thirty-year period since, with stewards' confidence in mounting an effective fightback against employers and the government very much on the defensive (a process reinforced by the reluctance of FTOs to rally the forces of organised labour and the resulting series of unnecessary defeats of workers' struggles) there has been a considerable weakening of rank-and-file organisation, with stewards increasingly becoming more dependent on officials.[69] Most strikes, even those of a national character, have been quite limited and short-lived (usually only one or two days of action), and officials have tended to remain firmly in control, in the absence of a sufficiently strong grassroots organisation.

Nonetheless, there have been some important exceptions to this general picture in recent years: for instance, the unlawful strike activity that flared up in 2009, launched by thousands of construction workers at sites across the country, based on a combative shop stewards' activist network that was able to take the initiative semi-independently of union officials. Likewise, there have been a number of disputes in other areas of employment over recent years that have underlined the centrality of workplace union reps' organisation to the process of collective mobilisation, for example those by rail, Tube, postal, local-government and civil service workers.[70]

At the very least, the historical record suggests there is no justification for assuming that the present weaknesses of shop stewards' organisation will necessarily be either permanent or irreversible. Not only could the balance of class forces be reversed at some stage in the future (with the revival of mass workers' struggle and an upsurge of union membership and activism), but even the most bureaucratised stewards' organisation could be forced into leading action itself or be bypassed by an influx of a new generation of activists and reps. In the process, the balance struck between the general, contradictory tendencies within stewards' relationship to FTOs could also be radically altered.[71]

---

68. Darlington 1994, p. 40.
69. Cliff 1979; Darlington 1994; 2002; Cohen 2006.
70. Darlington 2009a; 2009b; 2009c; 2010; Kimber 2009; M. Smith 2002; 2003.
71. For consideration of whether the union bureaucracy could somehow be removed, or the official machinery wrested from their control *this side* of a socialist revolution that completely transformed social relations, see Darlington 1998, pp. 60–3; 2009a, pp. 219–32.

Some conclusions

In attempting to defend and refine the classical revolutionary Marxist analytical framework, it has been argued that the dichotomy within trade unions between the 'rank-and-file' and the 'union bureaucracy' is a meaningful generalisation of a real contradiction, notwithstanding the fact that it is, inevitably, a simplification of a rather more complex reality. Unless the *fundamental* and *primary* dynamic of such relations are at the centre of analysis, the significance of the secondary, more complicated sub-features can easily be misunderstood. Of course, it is true that theoretical and analytical concepts 'should reflect, organise and inform empirical evidence, rather than compress it into neatly labelled boxes at the cost of distortion'.[72] But so long as we draw out and specify variation and nuance and remain alert to reductionism, then the most useful way of understanding intra-union relations is through the rank-and-file/bureaucracy lens.

What are the broader implications of such a Marxist analysis for the study of social movement organisations? First, unlike standard social science, uncomfortable as it is with the notion of *contradiction*, there is the relevance of a conceptual and analytical framework that maintains the tension in the dialectic, rather than throwing it out. Second, also apparent is the necessity of an approach that operates at multiple *levels of analysis* if it is to adequately take into account the complex webs of association between officials, reps, activists and members. Third, there is the *openness of developmental possibilities*, which recognises that the so-called Michelsian dilemma of an 'iron law of oligarchy' is not a lock but merely a law of tendency, and one that is simultaneously subject to important countervailing democratic tendencies.

Fourth – and, perhaps, most crucially – in a similar way to that by which which the directness of the *labour-capital relation is mediated* through official trade unionism, many different types of social movement organisation also tend to confront capital in a mediated fashion (for example, through state services and regulatory agencies that interact with capital and the state), and are, therefore, likewise propelled onto the horns of a similarly complex, problematic and contradictory set of relations. If union officialdom's bureaucratic conservatism is caused less by the unintended consequences of an *internal* logic of development (in the way Michels suggested) than as a product of pressures from *external* agencies, combined with the unions' own reformist political practice and acceptance of the broad framework of capitalist society and the state, then such pressures also confront social movement organisations.

---

72. Daniels and McIlroy 2009, pp. 3–5.

Defending Place, Remaking Space: Social Movements in Oaxaca and Chiapas
Chris Hesketh

Whilst Henri Lefebvre's magisterial work *The Production of Space* inspired a number of Marxist-oriented thinkers to take seriously the relationship between capitalism and the distinct geographies associated with this form of accumulation, relatively less attention has been focused on how social movements have sought to contest and remake space in a radically different image.[1] This chapter seeks to address this lacuna with a focus on the novel forms of resistance that have been articulated in the southern Mexican states of Oaxaca and Chiapas. In recent years, this area has become a 'spatial target' for a new round of investment and transformation, most notably with mega-projects such as the *Plan Puebla Panama* (now renamed *Plan Mesoamerica*) but also through everyday initiatives to transform property relations so as to make them more amenable to capital accumulation. However, this has been rigorously contested by – largely indigenous – social movements. Refusing to accept the model of 'accumulation by dispossession' that has increasingly come to characterise the neoliberal phase of capitalism, these movements have, instead, sought to defend place and produce alternative forms of spatial transformation, whilst advancing novel forms of political participation. In doing so, these movements have

---

1. The work of David Harvey 1990; 2006; 2010; and Neil Smith 2008 is frequently (if not exclusively) 'capitalocentric', (Gibson-Graham 2006, p. 6). Some notable efforts have been made, however, to expand their work to engage with social movement activism: see, for example, Nilsen 2010.

posed important questions about agency, the locus for political contestation, and the meaning of democratic participation.

Politicising space

On 1 January 1994, in the southern-Mexican state of Chiapas, an indigenous rebel-group calling itself the *Ejército Zapatista de Liberación Nacional* [EZLN, 'Zapatista Army of National Liberation'] rose up in response to the Government's new economic orientation, most visibly signalled with the signing of the North American Free Trade Agreement (NAFTA) that was due to come into effect on that very day. Since then, the Zapatistas have vigorously contested state control, as well as attempts to draw them into official channels of political participation. Instead, on the land that they have taken over (or 'recuperated', as they put it) they have sought to construct an autonomous form of governance based on the will of their communities, not recognising state law.

Meanwhile, in the summer of 2006, in Oaxaca, another southern-Mexican state, the violent dislodgement of the annual teacher's *plantón* [encampment] led to the creation of a broad collection of social movements, trade unions and civil-society organisations coming together under the banner of the *Asamblea Popular de los Pueblos de Oaxaca* [APPO, 'Popular Assembly of the Peoples of Oaxaca']. Barricades were set up throughout the city and public buildings and symbols of power were taken over, as a state of 'ingovernability' was declared. The Oaxaca Commune (as it came to be known) was subsequently defeated after a protracted period of struggle, and their main demand (getting rid of the Governor) was not achieved. Nevertheless, since this time, social movement activism in the state has proliferated, centred on opposition to neoliberal development projects and localised authoritarianism. Instead, drawing on the region's indigenous cultural practices, there have been attempts to reinvent community and reorient development towards more socially just and ecologically sustainable ends.

What both of these cases represent is an effort to craft new geographical relations of power. They call into question the legitimacy of the state as the cornerstone of political praxis as well as the efficacy and desirability of representative democracy, and its associated form of citizenship.[2] In this way, they pose a challenge to the viability of capitalist social relations, as they have placed issues of who has the right to produce space firmly at the forefront of the political agenda.

---

2. See Yashar 2005.

Why, then, have issues of space, and, in particular, control over the production of space, been raised to such prominence? In order to answer this question, the chapter will be set out as follows. First, it is necessary to begin with a theoretical discussion of the dynamics of capitalism as a mode of production. Capitalism, after all, is the hegemonic socio-economic model of development of our time, and has become even more so in the last twenty years. It is imperative, therefore, that we understand its relationship to space, if we are to 'decolonise development' and explore alternatives.[3] Second, we will explore the antinomies of Mexico's capitalist development trajectory, which directly presaged the current politicisation of space by social movements. Third, the concrete actions of two social movements in Oaxaca and Chiapas will be examined in terms of alternative spatial projects. Lastly, we shall make some concluding comments on the relationship between space, social movements and democracy.

Spaces of capital

Grappling with the question of why, contrary to the predictions of some of Marxism's prophets, capitalism had failed to collapse, Lefebvre argued that whilst its internal contradictions had not been resolved, they had been attenuated somewhat: 'We cannot calculate at what price, but we do know the means: *by occupying space, by producing a space*'.[4] Whereas previous modes of production had an essentially conservative basis to their spatio-temporal matrix – seeking to hold down transformation where possible, and relying on an essential fixity of space for political control – capitalism, by contrast, is a revolutionary mode of production that actively needs to transform space for its own survival.[5] In its search for profit, capital is, therefore, forced to create 'new objective social definitions of time and space'.[6] This can be achieved through an intensive enlargement of capital (the deepening process of commodification) or the extensive enlargement of capital (involving its geographical expansion to new areas).[7] This is, however, not a process free from contradiction and tension. For example, the manner in which space and spatial relations are altered can profoundly affect the character of particular places, creating opportunities for some whilst dispossessing others (as will be demonstrated later). Spatial transformations frequently, therefore, become the object of intense struggle (against de-industrialisation, highway or

---

3. Wainwright 2008, pp. 2, 7.
4. Lefebvre 1976, p. 21.
5. Poulantzas 1978, pp. 102–3.
6. Harvey 1996, p. 240.
7. Robinson 2004, p. 7. Contrary to Warren Magnuson 1996, p. 47, therefore, the search for political space is not something solely confined to the Left.

airport construction, the closure of mines, and so on).[8] Therefore, as Lefebvre puts it: 'If space as a whole has become the place where the reproduction of the relations of production is located, it has also become the terrain for a vast confrontation which creates its centre now here, now there, and therefore which cannot be localised or diffused'.[9]

It is, in other words, the object of class struggle to decide who has the right to participate in the production of space. This is, therefore, a fundamentally democratic issue, but one that falls outside of the limits of liberal democracy, with its focus on the individual and private property. It is thus here that a Marxist analysis of social movements can have purchase. But how, then, does this abstract discussion relate to the specificities of Mexico? The argument that will now be made is that, owing to the manner of capitalist development that has taken place within Mexico, many indigenous movements increasingly see the state as illegitimate, since the spatial project that it is pursuing threatens their means of survival. This has been accelerated by neoliberal restructuring programmes that have integrated the country into global networks of production and undercut formerly prevalent subsistence activities.[10] Mexico is, therefore, witnessing a clashing of spatial projects that are antithetical to one another.

To understand the relationship between space and social movements in Mexico at this current juncture, it is important to provide a brief explanation regarding the historical sociology of the modern Mexican state, as this will allow us to see what it is that has changed in recent years that has provoked this challenge. It is necessary, therefore, to go back to the Mexican Revolution, when the modern state was effectively founded. As has been argued elsewhere, this can be usefully analysed in terms of Gramsci's notion of 'passive revolution'.[11] This involves the state-led reorganisation of social relations, leading to the restoration/extension of class-power and the diffusion of subaltern pressures, through key material concessions. As Alex Callinicos elegantly clarifies in relation to this process, 'revolutionary strains are at once displaced and partially fulfilled'.[12]

Lefebvre makes the point that all social relations are, at the same time, spatial relations.[13] As passive revolutionary activity involves the restructuring of social relations, it follows that it also involves the restructuring of space. Indeed, following the Mexican Revolution, the production of space was essential in placating

8. Harvey 1993, pp. 6–8.
9. Lefebvre 1976, p. 85.
10. Hesketh 2010, pp. 399–402, Nash 1994, pp. 10–12.
11. Hesketh 2010; Morton 2010. The term 'passive revolution' refers to the *outcome* of a particular period of upheaval, and does not in any way imply that the subaltern classes were literally passive.
12. Callinicos 2010, p. 498.
13. Lefebvre 1991, p. 129.

widespread discontent. A principle cause of anger and key source of continuing peasant unrest was the prevailing system of land tenure and its increasing concentration in a few hands, rendering the majority of the population landless. Reform of the agricultural sector thus became a central pillar of the 1934–40 Cárdenas administration. Under Cárdenas, the *ejido* was created, which was to stabilise the Mexican countryside for almost thirty years.[14] The process of land reform profoundly altered the geography of the Mexican countryside. Whilst *ejidal* land only accounted for 13 percent of cropland in 1930, by 1940 this figure was 47 percent.[15] Through the breakup of large *haciendas*, not only were peasants pacified and the state's legitimacy enhanced, but, furthermore, the land reform process helped destroy a key barrier to capital accumulation, that of the status-based *latifundia*, with its associated idle means of production. Labour was 'freed' from bondage (facilitating the urbanisation of Mexico as mass migration resulted), the countryside was opened up to capitalisation, and resources transferred toward industrial production. Land reform thus served to 'entrench capitalism in Mexico'.[16] Often, the land granted in the form of *ejidos* was insufficient alone for the reproduction of a community. Seasonal work was, therefore, essential, but it was often poorly compensated, as reproduction of labour power also took place within newly created communal spaces. The *ejido*, in other words, became the geographical realisation *par excellence* of passive revolution; offering limited (but important) concessions, whilst offsetting more radical demands. However, although the discussion thus far has focused on tactics from above, it must not be forgotten that we are dealing with the constant process of contestation of these meanings from below. The process of land reform had a dual aspect. On the one hand, it did, indeed, enhance the legitimacy of the state, extend its means of corporatist control and serve as means of extending capitalist social relations. However, at the same time, it also provided the 'physical and social base for development and institutionalisation of indigenous territorial claims'.[17] Space was, in other words, the object of struggle, and non-capitalist sites remained an essential component of the Mexican landscape, constituting part of a complex economy and influencing in turn the specificity of capitalist development.[18] However, whilst indigenous peasants and the state could be allies at this specific juncture, their spatial projects would grow to become irreconcilably hostile as both developed over time.

---

14. McCaughan 1993, p. 20. *Ejidos* were government-created communal lands, reminiscent of the pre-Hispanic form of land tenure.
15. Hansen 1971, p. 32.
16. Otero 1999, p. 33; Morton 2012, pp. 83–6.
17. Bobrow-Strain 2005, p. 752.
18. On this issue, see Gibson-Graham 2006, p. 13.

There is not space for a full discussion of ISI in this chapter, other than to say that it would inscribe its own contradictions as a spatial project.[19] In the 1960s and 1970s, it went into decline both as a hegemonic project and as an accumulation strategy. This was visible with a slower rate of growth, and a falling rate of profit, alongside a rise in urban and rural guerrilla movements (especially after the infamous 1968 massacre of students in Tlatelolco). Independent peasant unions also began to emerge outside of the state's traditional corporatist networks. Mexico, in short, was experiencing an 'incorporation crisis', in the sense that ISI was not economically or politically able to create the conditions to include all groups in society.[20] The production of nationally protected space – vital to fostering the conditions whereby capitalist class processes could be safely incubated – now became the barrier to further accumulation, as corporations sought integration into the world-market in order to widen their sales base. Historically, when a state's configuration of space and scale show themselves to be incapable of ensuring the profitability of capital, restructuring takes place 'in significant, if always highly contested ways'.[21] This would prove to be the case here, and was given extra impetus by the debt crisis that hit Mexico (and the rest of Latin America) in 1982. The crisis came to be used as an opportunity to fundamentally restructure the Mexican economy along neoliberal lines. The significance of this process has been to transform previous spatial arrangements into ones more commensurable with capital accumulation. Making space an attractive destination for foreign investment thus became a vital policy priority. In order to accomplish this task, the state has become an agent of 'primitive accumulation' in Mexico.

Alongside a decline in real wages, reductions in social expenditure, and the privatisation of state-owned enterprises, came an attempt to transform land-tenure. Factors such as *ejido* land – essential to the stability of ISI – now became spaces through which the capital relation could be extended as the state sought to reorient production to the export market. Article 27 of the Constitution – the cornerstone of the Mexican state's covenant with the peasantry in the aftermath of the Revolution, guaranteeing its responsibility to provided land to those without it – was repealed by Carlos Salinas in 1992, demonstrating the new policy priorities of the Mexican state. As well as ending the Government's responsibility to redistribute land, the revision to Article 27 also made provisions for formerly inalienable *ejido* land to be rented or sold. Whilst maintaining a limit on the maximum an individual could hold (100 hectares), corporations could now own

19. See Hesketh 2010.
20. Luna and Figuiera 2009.
21. Brenner 1998, p. 472.

up to 2,500 hectares, as long as 25 individuals were associate members.[22] Despite the Government's rhetoric of support for autonomous *ejidal* organisations, these communities lacked the resources to compete successfully in the transition to a fully capitalist market. The emerging discourse of individual rights, or what Neil Harvey refers to as 'market citizenship', was thus insensitive to people's highly differentiated capacities to enjoy these rights.[23]

The proposed change in spatial arrangements can be expected to have the most important implications for the southern states of Mexico, where the largest proportion of communal and *ejidal* land is held. Organisations such as the World Bank have argued that the opaqueness of property rights in the southern states is an impediment to investment and increased prosperity.[24] The Mexican government has sought to rectify this through the *Programa de Certificación de Derecho Ejidales y Titulación de Solares Urbanos* [PROCEDE, 'Programme for the Certification of Agrarian Rights']. This is a supposedly voluntary programme into which communities could enter to officially have their lands demarcated and a title granted.[25] Certification of *ejidal* land is a precondition for the decision to then privatise or rent out the land. In planning terms, the southern states have become 'spatial targets' for a new round of capital accumulation.[26]. Key to this is the *Plan Puebla Panama* (later renamed the *Plan Mesoamerica*), which seeks to integrate the south of Mexico and Central America into a free-trade zone, in the same manner as other trading blocs that have created economies of scale. Key features of this plan are: agricultural plantations controlled by multinational corporations, transnational road networks, interoceanic canals and the development of new port capacities linked with commercial corridors.[27] New sites of *maquiladora* production are also planned. State planners have recognised that, since the passage of NAFTA, although the northern parts of the country have been able to take advantage of free trade with the US, the south has had neither help from the state nor access to markets, leaving it unable to increase its competitiveness in the global economy.[28] Furthermore, there has been a realisation among some élites that the old economic models of development, based on extensive cattle rearing, petroleum, extraction and agricultural colonisation, has both brought about environmental problems and contributed to political agitation. This had led to the development of a new 'ecological' model of capitalism

---

22. Otero 1999, p. 47.
23. N. Harvey 2001.
24. Hall and Humphrey 2003.
25. Just how voluntary it was has been questioned by, for instance, Ita 2006, p. 152; and Pisa 1994, p. 290, who highlight the necessity of entering into the programme in order to receive government credit.
26. Brenner 1997, p. 280.
27. Coronado and Mora 2006, p. 26.
28. Davíla et al. 2002; N. Harvey 2006, p. 212.

for the southern Mexican states that promotes practices such as eco-tourism and bio-prospecting.[29] This is a reimagining of space that is frequently silent with regard to the practice of democracy. Despite the fact that thousands of people could be affected by such proposals, they have rarely been consulted or included in the design of the plan, except for the assumption they will serve as a cheap source of labour. Instead, southern Mexico is presented as a place without people, a place without history, but a place (somehow) with a future.[30] The right to a different sort of space is thereby denied. All this very much fits the model of 'accumulation by dispossession' characteristic of the neoliberal phase of capitalist development. This involves the 'appropriation and cooptation of pre-existing cultural and social achievements as well as confrontation and supersession'. It happens to 'any social formation or territory that is brought or inserts itself into the logic of capitalist development'.[31]

However, this is only half the story. One must be careful not to elide the fact that this is a far from uncontested process. Capital cannot simply be said to produce a world after its own image.[32] Non-capitalist spaces interpenetrate and influence the trajectory of capitalism, and resistance in the form of counter-spaces also thwarts capital's attempts to transform the world in the realisation of its own concept. In the context of Mexico, faced with the shift from 'controlled inclusion' to 'coerced marginalisation' from the national state's new orientation, and the closure of opportunity in terms of employment opportunities or possibilities for land redistribution, social movements have fought to construct alternative spaces for political contestation and alternative forms of citizenship.[33] This must be viewed as a process of class struggle between those who seek to transform space such that it is ever more functional for capital accumulation (abstract space), and those who seek to construct another way of life through the creation of genuinely 'differential space', asserting another kind of cultural being.[34] It is for this reason that a Marxist analysis of social movements must be concerned with issues of space. Let us now explore these issues in more empirical detail in order to unpack this argument, beginning with the state of Oaxaca.

29. N. Harvey 2001; 2006.
30. N. Harvey 2006, p. 211.
31. Harvey 2003, pp. 145–6, 153.
32. As Smith 2008, pp. 7, 186 suggests.
33. Oxhorn 1995; N. Harvey 2001. The 'war on drugs' is, perhaps, the most visible manifestation of this coerced marginalisation. It has aptly been described by one US diplomat as 'armouring NAFTA' (Carlson 2008, p. 17).
34. Lefebvre 1991, pp. 53–7; 2003, p. 98; see also Harvey 2000, pp. 83, 251.

Oaxaca

Oaxaca has a long and successful history of resistance to colonial and neocolonial policies of dispossession. The ferocity of native resistance and their determination to hold on to their communal land was fundamental to the property regime that evolved in the region, with Spanish landholdings not developing nearly as extensively here as in other areas of Mexico.[35] A further testament to this is the fact that, despite having just 3.4 percent of the national population, it contains over 20 percent of all the nation's 2438 municipalities (numbering 570 in total).[36] Since 1995, 412 have governed themselves according to their own 'usos y costumbres' [practices and customs].[37] This arrangement did not fall from the sky, nor were they created by chance. Rather, they are the result of a long struggle for autonomy.[38] Further evidence for Oaxaca's strong communal traditions is the fact that it is the state with the lowest rate of adoption of the PROCEDE, with only 20.5 percent of the surface area being certified.[39] Demographically, Oaxaca contains the highest proportion of indigenous inhabitants in Mexico. It is also one of the poorest states in Mexico. According to the *Programa de las Naciones Unidad para el Desarollo* [PNUD, United Nations Development Programme] Oaxaca ranks 31st out of Mexico's 32 states for its Human Development Index.[40]

Attempted neoliberal modernising developments have taken place in Oaxaca under the auspices of highly authoritarian governors.[41] The apogee of this authoritarianism was reached under the governorship of Ulises Ruiz Ortiz. From the outset, his time in office was characterised by the systematic violation of human rights, corruption and the heavy use of repression against social protest. According to a study by the *Centro de Investigación y Docencia Económica* [CIDE, 'Centre for Research and Teaching in Economics'] Oaxaca came in last place nationally for the management of funds, and was ranked extremely low both in transparency and access to information.[42] Adding to public anger was the

---

35. Murphy and Stepick 1991, p. 18; Taylor 1972.
36. The intention of the Spanish crown being to divide and rule the population more effectively.
37. This involves a grounding of politics in the community assembly, from which members are elected to serve *cargos* (burdens) of a period usually up to three years. These are seen less as positions of prestige and more of a community service that people have an obligation to take part in.
38. Esteva 2001, p. 258.
39. Ita 2006, p. 155.
40. PNUD 2009, p. 6.
41. This includes the expansion of tourism, natural resources extraction by TNCs and the targeting of the Isthmus of Tehuantepec as an alternative to the over-capacitated Panama Canal.
42. Martínez Vásquez 2007, p. 19.

remodelling of the historical symbols of the city, described as the systematic destruction of the state's natural and historical patrimony.[43] Significantly, this included moving a key site of authority – the *Palacio de Gobierno* – from the Zócolo (the historic centre of social protest) to a suburb on the outskirts of the town in a bid to 'cleanse' public space of undesirable elements.[44] Cultural diversity came to be promoted in Oaxaca as a commodity, and packaged within a framework of individualised rights in a bid to promote the image of the state as a 'traditional' indigenous tourist mecca. Furthermore, in 2004, Ruiz Ortiz introduced the 'Pact of Oaxaca', which sought to prohibit public protests, which were thought to represent a danger to foreign investment.[45] The clash between Oaxaca's deepening authoritarianism with neoliberal features, and increased societal demands was most visibly manifested with the formation of the APPO in the summer of 2006.

On 22 May, for the twenty-sixth year in a row, the teachers' union (Section 22) began their annual strike demanding better terms for teachers (and students), as well as improvements to classroom infrastructure. A series of megamarches were also coordinated in order to protest against the repression in the state. However, in an atmosphere where social protest had effectively been criminalised, rather than listening to the demands of the teachers, the Government made an extraordinary attempt to dislodge the *plantón* by force on June 14. This act of public repression has been described by one observer as signifying 'not only a crisis of the government but of the political regime' in Oaxaca.[46] The struggle that followed goes to the heart of the question: who has a right to public space? Following these events (and seeking to galvanise a wider movement), the teachers convened an assembly on 20 June, to which they invited various official groups that they hoped to mobilise in support of their struggle. However, rather than the twenty or so organisations that had been invited to attend, over three hundred civil-society organisations arrived, armed with a plethora of social grievances.[47] What had begun as a trade-union struggle was thus converted into a wider movement of discontent.[48] The authoritarian governorship of Ruiz Ortiz acted as a centripetal force for all of the state's oppositional social forces. Organised political groups that had suffered repression all came together under the APPO banner.[49]

---

43. Esteva 2007, p. 84.
44. Poole 2009, p. 197. In a similar fashion, indigenous stallholders saw their market pushed from the centre to the periphery in the 1960s when local merchants demanded this for reasons of public hygiene (Clark 1996, p. 273).
45. Poole 2007a, pp. 10–11.
46. Martínez Vásquez 2007, p. 9.
47. Esteva 2008, personal interview, Oaxaca.
48. Esteva 2007, p. 80.
49. For a list of these political groups as well as civil-society organisations, see Martínez Vásquez 2007, p. 70.

The APPO thus 'became a symbol of popular cohesion and a trigger for political change'.[50] Thousands of barricades were erected throughout the city, in a spontaneous rejection of governmental authority. All official government-activities were suspended for five months, as a state of 'ingovernability' was declared. From simply having the *plantón* taking over public space in the Zócolo, new encampments were set up around the headquarters of the legislature, the municipal palace and the judicial buildings, as well as the official house to which the Governor had been despatched in Santa María Coyotepec.[51] Human circles were formed around all of the symbols of state power, and public space became forcefully reclaimed in an assertion of what Henri Lefebvre refers to as the 'right to the city'.[52] Recalling these events, one participant of the barricades describes them as 'the moment when the people from below took their lives in their own hands'.[53] These barricades raised in defence public space also became, for many, sites where political consciousness and practical collective action began to be developed. Radio- and television-stations were also taken over, to be used in the propaganda war which the Government had quickly launched. These became autonomous spaces through which a genuine 'people's news' was broadcast. One of these stations, *Radio Universidad*, became the most listened to in the city and the Central Valley.[54] Many of the demands that began to be formulated had a long history in Oaxaca, such as those regarding teachers' and women's struggles, indigenous rights and demands for increased autonomy. Therefore, although the APPO was novel in its organisational form, this was made possible 'by its grounding in a familiar language of popular democracy, dissent and *rebeldía*'.[55]

The emergence of the APPO points us towards the failure of social inclusion in Oaxaca, and the breakdown of representative democracy as the public were shut out from participation in civic life.[56] The widespread support that the teachers received and the authoritarian response that it provoked thus have to be placed in the context of the increasing inability of the local government to attend to the demands of society. The rise of the APPO movement can be interpreted as the absence of hegemony and the increasing turn towards repression.[57] One of its chief accomplishments was to directly politicise the everyday control of social space in an urban context.[58] Nevertheless, in many respects, the

---

50. Stout 2010, p. 37.
51. Martínez Vásquez 2007, pp. 80, 89.
52. Lefebvre 1986.
53. Venegas 2009, personal interview, Oaxaca.
54. Martínez Vásquez 2007, p. 93.
55. Poole 2007b.
56. Poole 2009, p. 201.
57. Martínez Vásquez 2007, p. 79. For an analysis of this trend throughout Latin America, see Robinson 2008, p. 37.
58. Gibler 2009, p. 185.

APPO as a social movement proved to be ephemeral, and this should give us pause for thought. The principal demand articulated by the APPO (and, indeed, the one point of commonality among the diverse objectives advanced), namely that Ulises Ruiz Ortiz step down, was unsuccessful. He finally left office when his term expired in November 2010. This can be viewed as a classic example of what has been termed 'boundary control', whereby a conflict remains localised rather than shifting onto a wider national or transnational arena.[59] Vicente Fox (President of Mexico, 2000–6) was a member of the *Partido Acción Nacional* [PAN, 'National-Action Party']; as such, the unpopularity of a member of a rival political party was not necessarily a bad thing, as long as this conflict could be contained.[60]

This confirms the point that social struggles restricted to one 'theatre of action' are always liable to being rolled back, for want of advances in other areas.[61] Another problem that the movement in Oaxaca faced concerned ideological division. The APPO was always a heterogeneous collection of different movements (it was a genuine movement of movements), yet a fundamental faultline emerged between those who wanted to organise as a more traditional political organisation, and those that remained wedded to grassroots activism outside of electoral politics. Lastly, despite its diverse membership, the APPO was heavily reliant upon the teachers' union for their political strength, with Section 22 constituting the closest thing to an organised, oppositional class-force in Oaxaca. When the teachers finally did decide to return to work, following limited concessions, the multiple social movements drifted apart.[62] Obviously, one cannot omit from the problem the role of state repression, with many activists either beaten or jailed and a number of people killed in clashes with police, reminding us that the 'the visible fist of the state must complete the invisible hand of the market'.[63] Nevertheless, in spite of these setbacks, it should be noted that insubordination can leave important residual effects.[64] This reappropriation of space could possibly serve a prefigurative or pedagogical function, demonstrating possibilities for the future.[65]

---

59. Gibson 2005. Gustavo Esteva (2009, personal interview, Oaxaca) recounts, in relation to this point, that the lack of wider networks of solidarity was the APPO's greatest weakness, stating: 'We were so powerful in Oaxaca, we forgot that we were living in Mexico'.
60. Ulises Ruiz Ortiz was a member of the *Partido Revolucionario Institucional* [PRI, 'Insitutional Revolutionary Party'].
61. Harvey 2000, p. 234.
62. Waterbury 2007.
63. Amin 2011, p. 15.
64. Holloway 2002a, p. 159.
65. Lefebvre 1991, pp. 167–8.

Since the summer of 2006, social struggle in Oaxaca has broadened and evolved. It is no longer about the exit of a Governor, but about wider changes to the political system. Efforts to recuperate public spaces also remain strong. As one activist recounted: 'In almost the entire city there are alternative projects of the people. People are looking for options that they didn't look for before 2006'.[66] The APPO has retained a presence among various *colonias*, as well as in numerous rural towns. In some cases, former PRI-dominated urban areas have been taken over by autonomous committees. These committees collectively decide on what public resources they need and try to organise to provide public services for the community, in the manner of the indigenous tradition. Additionally, there has been the development of various civil-society groups who have been energised by the struggle of the APPO. One such group is *Voces Oaxaqueñas Construyendo Autonomia y Libertad* [VOCAL, 'Oaxacan Voices Building Autonomy and Liberty']. This group has been active in campaigns for food sovereignty and alternative energy production, and have also been actively engaged in key struggles within the state, such as the fate of the autonomous community of San Juan Copola. Overall, then, the APPO has become the inspiration for the formation of an anti-authoritarian, socially inclusive and collective model of social movement organisation (in spite of the ambiguous nature of the APPO itself).[67]

It is clear that the historical defence of place and the long struggle against exploitation have provided the collective form of social organisation through which capitalism can be resisted in Oaxaca. It is by virtue of democratic control of their own communities that many indigenous communities have proven able to deny capital the right to expand. In this respect, the spatial structure of the assembly is both a political tool and an end in itself.[68] One prominent example of this is the opposition to *Libramiento Sur*, a super-highway project costing 548 million *pesos*, officially announced by the *Secretaría de Obras Públicas* [SOP, 'Secretary of Public Works'] and *Caminos y Aeropistasde Oaxaca* [CAO, 'Roads and Airstrips of Oaxaca'] in October 2009.[69] This highway is meant to dramatically reduce the time it takes to get to the coastal beach resorts of the state (such as Puerto Escondido and Huatulco).[70] It would also facilitate quicker transportation of natural resources extracted in the state. As should be obvious, a development like this can only take place through a transformation of existing space. The PROCEDE sets the conditions whereby this can be made possible, through the alienation or renting of communal lands. However, Zaachila, one community

---

66. Valencia Nuñez 2009, personal interview, Oaxaca.
67. Martínez Vásquez 2007, p. 72.
68. Esteva 2009, personal interview, Oaxaca.
69. Noticias 2010a.
70. Hautulco is one of five 'integrally planned resorts' created by the *Fondo Nacional de Formento Al Turismo* [FONATUR, National Fund for Developing Tourism].

that risks being directly affected by this highway, has already begun the process of organising against it. While it was previously a PRI stronghold, a large section of this municipality have since 2006 allied themselves with the APPO, in a bid to widen their struggle. The authority of the community assembly has been invoked in order to challenge any potential threats to their lands. The *ejidatarios* of the community have claimed that the community assembly has no knowledge of the project, nor does it have the approval of the municipal president.[71] At the same time as the project was finally officially announced, the community assembly voted unanimously to reject it, arguing that not only would it cause irreparable damage to the agriculture, ecology and water systems of the area, but also that it would lead the community to stop producing certain things of cultural value.[72] As one *ejidatario* argued: 'It is something more than just a field, it is a feeling we carry inside of us. It is a love of our land'.[73] Following consultations with their community assemblies, a further six communities from the Central Valleys have joined them in opposing the passage of the highway (San Pedro Ixtalahuaca, Tiracoz, Cuilapam, San José Atzompa, and Santa María Atzompa).

This view of land is widely shared among the indigenous population of Oaxaca and, indeed, throughout Mexico. This process of resistance is an example of the 'recuperation of the power of the assembly and the fortification of community life'.[74] In other words communities are able to draw upon traditions of resistance and collective power that have been developed over centuries of struggle, which are now used to inform present struggles against dispossession. An indigenous community member from the Sierra Norte claims that these conflicts are intensifying, as laws are closing down ways to officially gain land, and little is left to redistribute.[75] He argues, therefore, that in the context of an expansionary capitalist system, communities defending their land and territory have the potential to form powerful social movements against dispossession. Indeed, it is this commonality of experience that gives highly place-specific movements that ability to 'jump scales' and link to other groups suffering similar experiences.[76] In this case, not only was the community of Zaachila able to link with other groups in the state of Oaxaca facing dispossession, but an alliance also was formed with the *Frente del Pueblo en Defensa de La Tierra* [FPDT, 'People's Front in Defence of the Land'] in Atenco. Atenco has been an adherent of the Zapatistas 'Other Campaign', and came to national attention when residents successfully blocked plans to construct an airport on their lands, subsequently declaring themselves

71. Noticias 2009.
72. Noticias 2010b.
73. Noticias 2010b.
74. Maldonado 2009, personal interview, Oaxaca.
75. Cruz 2009, personal interview, Oaxaca.
76. Smith 1993, p. 97.

an autonomous municipality. The defence of place does not, therefore, preclude wider links being formed. Rather, movements can be Janus-faced, being simultaneously both introverted and extroverted.[77] This is an example of what David Harvey calls 'militant particularism', whereby '[i]deals forged out of the affirmative experience of solidarities in one place get generalized and universalized as a working model of a new form of society'.[78] It is vital, therefore, that cultural struggles such as these, fighting to retain access to land, remain linked to a wider analysis of political economy, allowing them to move beyond their everyday life and connect to other movements.[79]

Oaxaca is, after all, clearly an example of a highly global struggle inserted into particularly local conditions. Mexico has, in recent years, become a prime site for transnational capital investment in extractive industries. This trend has rekindled mining activity in Oaxaca, as it is an area rich in carbon, silver and gold. There are currently over 22 large mining projects in the state, and – as one CODEP activist outlined – each month, more and more concessions are being granted by the Government.[80] We can thus note clearly the connections between the arrival of transnational capital and agrarian reform (as private companies were previously banned from such associations).

One such spatial target for resource extraction has been the municipality of San José del Progreso. The recent experiences of this community perhaps represent what some in Oaxaca are calling an attempted 'economic reconquest'. Here, the Government, in conjunction with the municipal president and 10 individuals from the *ejido*, sold thousands of hectares of concessions to the company *Minerales de Oaxaca*, who, in turn, sold the land to Cuzcatlán, a local affiliate of Canadian TNC Fortuna Silver. According to an official report by Fortuna Silver, they have 23 mineral concessions totalling 43,520 hectares in the region.[81] This has aroused fierce opposition from the community, who have protested that the mining project will contaminate water sources and threaten the agricultural basis of community life. As one resident said, 'We can live without gold and silver in our community. We cannot live without land'.[82] Some members of the community took the decision to blockade the mine, and have declared that they will never consent to it reopening. In response to this, over seven hundred troops were sent in to smash the blockade. Currently, the entrance to the mine is under armed guard, and, at the time of writing, violent struggle continues, with

---

77. Castree 2004, p. 150.
78. Harvey 1996, p. 32.
79. Harvey 2000, p. 74.
80. López 2009, personal interview, Oaxaca.
81. A report in Mexican daily *La Jornada* estimates that, state-wide, there are roughly six hundred thousand hectares of mining concessions (Ríos 2009).
82. Resident of San José del Progreso, 2009, personal interview, Oaxaca.

the mine officially due to reopen in August of 2011.[83] One resident is under no illusions as to the root of the conflict, declaring it to be 'about the ambition of capitalism'.[84] The community are refusing to recognise the authority of the president, and are forming alliances with the teachers' movement in order to defend their land. Both the APPO and Section 22 have, thus far, been highly active in defending the community, and have promised to come to their aid should the Government seek to reopen the mine. This strategy of defending place is an important aspect of class struggle, since it represents the refusal of the extension of commodification. This stands in stark contrast to the view of resistance that has recently been popularised, defined in terms of an evacuation of place, or even vaguer notions of 'exile' or 'flight'.[85] As Harvey has argued, struggles of this sort become class projects when they involve 'a direct challenge to the circulation and accumulation of capital which currently dictates what environmental transformations occur'.[86]

Understanding the manner in which property relations evolved in Mexico, with the state acting as the arbiter of agrarian conflict and the agent of redistribution, is crucial to understanding the nature of modern resistance movements, as it is now the state acting as the intermediary in granting concessions to TNCs. Whilst the state may have been an ally of some communities in Oaxaca following the Revolution,[87] it is now more and more identified as the principal enemy of indigenous communities. Historically, and continuing to this day, Oaxaca's communities remain fragmented, and conflict has been pervasive owing to territorial boundary disputes. This has resulted in individual communities fiercely defending their right to land and territory, but often without links to a wider movement. However, with the increasing threat of displacement, communities are more and more learning to share their experiences with one another in a bid to build alliances and collective forms of struggle. The APPO itself, however, remains more of an idea, or ideal to be striven for, rather than a coherent organisation. According to Oaxacan activist and intellectual Gustavo Esteva, 'the APPO has never existed. The APPO is a possibility. It is something being constructed today'.[88] Much effort still has to be made in finding a way to coordinate the disparate interests involved, as well as mediating between urban and rural demands in the efforts to create a viable alternative geographical project. Furthermore, links will have to be built with other movements, both nationally and

---

83. Two people have died in 2011 as a result of this dispute and the local priest Padre Martin was badly beaten for speaking out against the mine.
84. Resident of San José del Progreso, 2009, personal interview, Oaxaca.
85. Deleuze and Guattari 1998; Hardt and Negri 2000, p. 206.
86. Harvey 1996, p. 401.
87. Stephen 1998, p. 22.
88. Esteva, personal interview 2009, Oaxaca.

internationally. The Zapatista movement in the neighbouring state of Chiapas has, perhaps, done the most to inspire thinking about how this might be possible. They have managed to transcend inter-ethnic division and, instead, built an alternative development trajectory based around shared aspirations. Although some serious issues remain with regards to their politics, they have, nevertheless, proven to be a crucial reference point for the global anti-capitalist movement. Let us now turn to their struggle.

Chiapas

As noted in the introduction, on 1 January 1994, the day that the North American Free Trade Agreement (NAFTA) was due to come into effect, the Zapatistas began a territorial response to the Mexican state's policy of dispossession. As well as being one of Mexico's poorest states, Chiapas also had the most unresolved land disputes in the country.[89] Revisions to Article 27 had rendered these claims obsolete, however, while Mexico's entry into NAFTA threatened the ability of indigenous farmers to survive, as it phased out price supports and import restrictions, exposing them to (massively state-subsidised) US-produced corn. Again, this shows how the spaces of capital have encroached upon the subsistence-activities of the indigenous, and have, in the process, often mobilised them in response as an oppositional class force.[90] The Zapatistas called NAFTA a 'death-sentence for the indigenous people', and their spokesperson Subcomandante Marcos, declared that the Mexican peasantry were to be 'the sacrificial lambs of NAFTA'.[91]

In response to this challenge, the Zapatistas have put into practice Lefebvre's message stressing that to change life, 'we must first change space'.[92] Following the uprising, over 250,000 hectares of land were recuperated from private hands.[93] Land-invasions multiplied in the wake of the rebellion, as peasants from a whole spectrum of political positions took over private property. Thus, 'contrary to both the plans of the neoliberal policy makers and the fears of critics on the Left, land tenure in Chiapas underwent a rapid repeasantisation and reindigenisation rather than privatisation and concentration'.[94] The significance of the Zapatista uprising has been to move from using the space of the community as a purely defensive means, to one which is also used for transformative purposes. As Neil

---

89. Van der Haar 2005, p. 504.
90. Indeed, this has been a growing trend throughout Latin America in recent decades.
91. Benjamin 1995, p. 67.
92. Lefebvre 1991, p. 190.
93. Vilafuerte Solís 2005, p. 467.
94. Bobrow-Strain 2007, p. 3.

Harvey puts it: 'Against the effect of economic, ecological and political crisis, the community has been converted into a strategic resource for the reconstruction of the bonds of solidarity and the defence of natural resources'.[95] The former director of *Desarrollo Económico y Social de los Mexicanos Indígenas* [DESMI, 'Indigenous Mexican Social and Economic Development'], a San Cristóbal based NGO that has worked in Chiapas with indigenous groups for over thirty years, argues that the Zapatista communities have been involved in a profound process of change. Although collective work has a long history in Chiapas, the idea of collective ownership of property, in terms of the means of production, has been something new that the Zapatistas have contributed to.[96] This reclaiming of space has also been developed into a new territorial form of politics. In December of 1995, 38 'autonomous municipalities' were declared. These counter-spaces were to be governed by the people's own political will, beyond the purview of the state. Indeed upon entering into their territory one is greeted with a sign that reads '*Aquí, manda el Pueblo y el gobierno obedece*' ['here, the people command and the government obeys'].

The Zapatistas draw on specific indigenous traditions, built up in Chiapas and other areas of Mexico. The community assembly, for example, is utilised as a tool to discuss problems through until consensus is reached.[97] Various principles that began to be developed amongst the indigenous communities during the 1970s in dialogue with liberation theology, such as *mandar obedeciendo* [to command obeying], have been continued and converted into part of the guiding philosophy underpinning the movement.[98] Furthermore, they draw upon and develop the pluri-ethnic conceptions of autonomy that were developed in the eastern parts of the state, owing to its history of migratory communities.[99] The Zapatista uprising has also illuminated important dynamics of contemporary class struggles, namely, that they are increasingly 'inscribed in space'.[100] Like the APPO uprising in Oaxaca, the Zapatista rebellion can, similarly, be interpreted as a refusal of the model of 'accumulation by dispossession' that capitalism is increasingly reliant upon. In a more thoroughgoing sense than the APPO, however, the Zapatistas have done this by a reclaiming of social space in which the logic of capital does not operate and alternative forms of production are propagated. The formation of the autonomous municipalities in the wake of the rebellion represents a clear counter-hegemonic challenge to the geographical sites of state-power in

---

95. N. Harvey 2006, p. 215.
96. Santiago 2008, personal interview, San Cristóbal.
97. See Barmeyer 2009 for a discussion of how this form of democracy functions, plus a critique of the reality as compared to rhetoric.
98. Leyva Solano 2001, pp. 23–6.
99. Castillo 2003, pp. 74–7; N. Harvey 2001.
100. Lefebvre 1991, p. 55.

Chiapas, and the subsequent creation of the *Juntas de Buen Gobierno* in 2003 was an attempt to further consolidate this. By 2000, the EZLN had a presence in over a third of all the municipalities of Chiapas.[101] As such, they directly challenge the ability of the state and capital to produce spaces through which new rounds of accumulation can occur. This demonstrates how multiculturalism can have an important class content when expressed in terms of a distributional right to space.[102] As Robinson argues in relation to this point: 'The fundamental indigenous notion of "mother earth", as something that cannot be "owned" much less privatized, and which must be respected and sustained, is diametrically opposed to global capitalism's drive to commodify and plunder nature'.[103] The Zapatista project is one that is based on collective action for collective need (expressed in the guiding maxim *'Para todos todo, nada para nosotros'* ['for everyone everything, nothing for ourselves']. Luis Lorenzano insists that 'Zapatismo cannot be understood except as an experience of communal/popular power'.[104] This point is important, as it recognises the contemporary spatiality of the class struggles that have been increasingly prominent in Latin America during recent decades in efforts to retain access to basic services.[105] This spatialising of class struggles moves us away from a dogmatic and exclusionary conception of class that views only workplace-struggles at the point of production as relevant. Instead, once we open up class struggle to the terrain of the lived space of the community, it also encompasses concerns such as gender and environmental issues.[106] Their struggle is also not merely one of resistance, but also one of active transformation. As Subcomandante Marcos declared with regard to this point, the current system 'is based upon our weakness. To our lack of alternative proposals, they offer the continuation of the nightmare. We must go beyond lamentations and propose new possibilities'.[107]

By taking on functions normally associated with the state, the Zapatistas have challenged its hegemony on an everyday basis, whether in schools, *ejidos*, churches, or other sites.[108] As Van der Haar argues, the EZLN 'sought to displace the state and deny the Mexican government legitimacy because the latter had betrayed the revolutionary project'.[109] Rather than seeking to capture state power and use it instrumentally to achieve their objectives, the Zapatista model of organisation is prefigurative, organically constructing a new type of social

---

101. Barmeyer 2009, pp. 231, 60.
102. See Gibson-Graham 2006, p. 179.
103. Robinson 2008, pp. 302–3.
104. Lorenzano 1998, p. 133.
105. Portes 1985, p. 31.
106. Harvey 2003, pp. 170–1.
107. Marcos 2001, p. 92.
108. Barmeyer 2009, p. 2; Harvey 1999, p. 260.
109. Van der Haar 2005, p. 489.

relations as a lived experience of creative experimentation. The Zapatistas have thus learnt from the failures of previous social movements in Chiapas who were coopted by the state and rendered powerless.

In practice, this has involved the production of counter-spaces (or non-alienated spaces), whereby the users of space have retaken control of their own lives and political activity is no longer solely associated with fleeting, privileged moments.[110]

What, then, have been the Zapatistas' key proposals? Politically, one can identify the production of three spatial levels at which Zapatista politics now functions, within their territorial zone of influence. These are the community level; the municipal level; and the level of the *caracoles*, which operate on a regional scale. These spatial scales are linked together as networks of resistance.[111] The *caracoles* (which house the five *Juntas de Buen Gobierno*, JBG) were formed when the Government refused to ratify the original San Andrés Accords agreed at peace talks in 1996, instead finally passing a watered-down version of the bill in 2001, which failed to recognise the Zapatistas' fundamental demands for cultural rights to autonomy and the use and benefit of their territory.[112] Following this, the Zapatistas decided to put the accords into effect unilaterally. They are an example of urban experimentation in which the Zapatistas have been involved, housing as they do key economic foundations of Zapatismo, as well as schools, health clinics, and meeting centres. The premise of creating this level of government was to coordinate better the efforts of the autonomous municipalities, to counter the unevenness of development that had taken place between areas under Zapatista influence, and provide a focal point for people wishing to engage with the movement.[113] Meaning 'snail' or 'shell' in Spanish, the idea of the *caracoles* was for knowledge to spiral outwards among their communities.

Drawing on the indigenous tradition of the *cargo*, members of the community assembly are elected to the municipal government, where they generally serve a term of around two to three years. The municipal government contains the general command, the agrarian council and the honour and justice commissions. Members work for one or two days a week, and then return to their communities. Members of the municipal government are further divided in three teams of seven or eight people to occupy positions on the JBG. These teams rotate every

---

110. Lefebvre 2008, p. 92; 2009, pp. 147–50.
111. González Cassanova 2005.
112. Mora 2007, p. 71; for further details, see People's Global Action 2007.
113. For example, a ten percent tax is made on all solidarity contributions from NGOs working in Zapatista territory. A ten percent tax is also levied on any government project that wants to pass through their zone of influence (JBG, La Realidad, personal interview, 2009).

ten days or so. The principle of rotation is important for a number of reasons, both economic and political. Economically, it is vital to allow members to return to their communities to be able to plant seeds and tend crops (as work on the *Junta* is an unpaid responsibility, rather than a position of prestige). However, in rotating in this manner, an important political mechanism is also put into effect, as it ensures that representatives are constantly in contact with their social base. It is a new way of doing politics 'so that the task of governing is not exclusive to one group, so that there are no "professional" leaders, so that learning is for the greatest number of people, and so that the idea that government can only be carried out by "special people" is rejected'.[114] A member of the JBG at La Realidad described the *Juntas* as a space in which they learned to construct autonomy. Therefore, 'the *Junta* is like a school where we learn to govern'.[115]

Education itself is, perhaps, the most advanced aspect of Zapatismo, not only in the sense that it is the most active and pervasive, with each community now having a school, but also in the sense that it is seeking to ground education within the people's own reality, in terms of history and social environment. Education promoters are now sent to each village where maths, history and language tuition are taught in whatever language the children speak.[116] A system has been created whereby those who gain literacy can then serve the community, either through working on the *Juntas* or themselves becoming education promoters and thus collectively raising the community's education level. The Zapatistas have also developed an autonomous form of health-provision. Each autonomous municipality now has its own health clinic, with prominent hospitals such as the 'Commandata Ramona' clinic located in La Garrucha and the 'Guadalupana' clinic at Oventik. These clinics conduct health consultations and minor surgeries within Zapatista territory, and are free for Zapatista members, whilst those from non-Zapatista communities are only asked to pay a small fee. This is not to say that the Zapatistas' communities represent some idealised utopia or that their political strategies have been totally unproblematic. Their refusal to accept any form of government help has, according to one anthropologist, led to increased material hardships, inter-communal strife and caused higher illiteracy rates as teachers were forced to leave the communities. It has also caused many to leave the movement altogether, as they are unable to cope with the required austerity.[117] Some have also criticised their project of autonomy, claiming that their unwillingness to engage with the issue of state power at the national level ultimately

---

114. Marcos 2004.
115. JBG La Realidad, personal interview, 2009.
116. Education promoter, personal interview, La Realidad 2009.
117. Barmeyer 2009, pp. 112–13.

fails to provide a viable political alternative and will end up being self-defeating.[118] Others point out that the Zapatistas have failed to affect the deepening of neoliberalism within Mexico as a whole, whilst within Chiapas, agriculture has continued to decline and emigration to the United States has continued apace.[119] Such criticisms were amplified in the wake of the 2006 presidential election, with many questioning the Zapatistas' intransigent stance towards electoral participation.[120] Marcos fiercely denounced the leftist candidate Andrés Manuel López Obrador, who had promised to revise NAFTA and concentrate state resources on the poor and marginalised and ended up losing the election by just 0.6 percent to the conservative Felipe Calderón, whose programme has furthered the capital-restructuring carried out by Vicente Fox, while militarising Mexican society. At the same time, this criticism must be tempered with the fact the Zapatistas have also proved to be a vital force for democratisation in Mexico, helping to end the 71-year rule of the PRI.[121] They have also helped to redefine strategies of resistance in an age of global capital. This stems from their consolidation of local power, but with a supranational projection that poses a critique of neoliberal capitalism. This has proved influential to resistance to megaprojects such as *Plan Puebla Panama*, where over a hundred social movements have created a network of resistance basing themselves within their everyday social reality but also looking for alternative means of integration.[122]

Conclusion

It is clear that in the south of Mexico, there is a growing clash between spatial projects that are inimical to one another. On the one hand, capital must continue expand, and search out new areas for accumulation if it is not to perish. However, the conditions of this expansion would consign an alternative way of life to history. Social movements in this region have, therefore, increasingly sought to defend their rights to land and territory through the creation of a differential form of space. This politicisation of space by subaltern actors and the demand to have the right to control and shape one's lived environment is a profoundly democratic issue, but at the same time, one that goes beyond its common understanding. The remaking of space by social movements is, therefore, at the same time a remaking of democracy, as it calls for the permanent

---

118. Brass 2005, p. 667; Callinicos 2003, p. 94. It could be argued, however, that it is precisely in the formation of these counter-spaces that state sovereignty is challenged.
119. Collier and Collier 2005, p. 458; Villafurte Solis 2005, p. 463.
120. Castillo 2006.
121. Collier and Collier 2005, p. 450.
122. Coronado and Mora 2006, p. 36.

participation of people in civic life. As has been pointed out, 'the greatest challenge to capitalism would be an extension of democracy beyond its narrowly
circumscribed limits'.[123] It is clear that these 'counter-spaces' or 'spaces of resistance' face many challenges. Foremost among these is the need to 'scale up' their
activism and link with wider movements. There are also practical difficulties
of avoiding becoming reinscribed into the state apparatus through a mixture
of coercion and inducements, which may blunt the struggles through passive-
revolutionary strategies. Social movements must, therefore, remain vigilant of
the danger of a triple trap, which involves *substituting* authority in place of the
movements; the *transfer* of responsibility from activists to 'leaders'; and, finally,
the *displacement* of social movement objectives to ones set by the established
order.[124] This is no easy challenge, yet as the spaces of capital have sought to
shut down alternative spaces of existence, it has become an ever more vital task.
Social movements in southern Mexico are demonstrating that alternatives still
remain, and that other worlds are, indeed, possible.

---

123. Meiksins Wood 1995, p. 15.
124. Lefebvre 2003, p. 99.

Uneven and Combined Marxism within South Africa's Urban Social Movements[1]

Patrick Bond, Ashwin Desai and Trevor Ngwane

Introduction

The political dynamics of contemporary South Africa are rife with contradiction. On the one hand, it is among the most consistently contentious places on Earth, with insurgent communities capable of mounting disruptive protest on a nearly constant basis, rooted in the poor areas of the half-dozen major cities as well as neglected and multiply-oppressed black residential areas of declining towns. On the other hand, even the best-known contemporary South-African social movements, for all their sound, lack a certain measure of fury.

In the face of the Government's embrace of neoliberal social policies since shortly after the fall of Apartheid, what are often called 'service delivery protests' occurring many thousands of times a year, according to police statistics,[2] are at once the site of poor people's demands for greater responsiveness to human needs in general, but also intensely localised and self-limited in their politics. The upsurge of protest since the late 1990s invariably invokes images of the anti-Apartheid

1. The authors thank John Krinsky for fusing the authors' three disparate arguments, originally made at a Harold Wolpe Lecture in Durban in mid-2010. His care and sophistication in identifying solutions to our own conceptual problems remind us of the merits of internationalist collaboration and comparative Marxist praxis. The subsequent events at Marikana where a massacre of 34 striking workers was followed by an unprecedented wildcat strike wave are not covered in this chapter, but the lack of contagion from workplace to community underscores our arguments about shortcomings of the society's uneven and combined resistance scene.
2. Mottiar and Bond 2011; Duncan and Vally 2008.

struggle and thus focuses analysis on continuities and breaks between the old anti-Apartheid mass action and the new mass action in post-Apartheid society.[3] And yet, the majority of community protesters operate in close interconnection with parts of the Tripartite Alliance, composed of the African National Congress (ANC), the trade-union movement represented by the Congress of South African Trades Unions (COSATU) and the South African Communist Party (SACP), and so the line between insurgencies and governing organisations is not always clear. Yet their geographic and political isolation from each other has contributed to their having little leverage over the Alliance, which, notwithstanding some resistance by unions and communists, embraced neoliberal policies in the transition from anti-Apartheid resistance to class-apartheid government in 1994.

But beyond the community protests, the problems that have faced more traditional radical social movements in South Africa are, in many respects, familiar to students of social movements elsewhere: of moving from movement to governing; of cooptation and shifting roles *vis-à-vis* the state; of the limits of localism; and of the joining of community and workplace-based organising to forge a strong working-class politics. These are all the subject of considerable scholarship, both within and outside of the Marxist tradition, and within and outside of South Africa.[4] We argue here, however, that in the South-African context, these can be more clearly seen as symptomatic questions of a larger problematic, what we term, following Trotsky, the problem of 'uneven and combined Marxism'.

For Trotsky, 'uneven and combined development' was a fundamentally dialectical framework through which he sought first to theorise the relations between Russia's nascent industrial base (and hence, also, Russia's urban proletariat), and its backward, semi-feudal rural relations, and second, following this, the revolutionary potentials for Russia at the time of the Revolution. For Trotsky, this implied understanding the relationship between forms of capital both within Russia and across borders. Uneven development means that extremely different relations of production coexist within and across territory, while combined development suggests that the 'less developed' are not simply archaic and ultimately bound to 'catch up' at some point with the more advanced, perhaps going through the same 'stages' of development. (The South-African modernisation narrative since the early 2000s, shared by former president Thabo Mbeki and current president Jacob Zuma, is that the 'two economies' are 'structurally disconnected'.)[5]

---

3. For a sample of the debates on the independent Left, see Alexander 2010; Ballard et al. 2006; Bond 2006; Desai 2002; Duncan and Vally 2008; Maharaj, Desai and Bond 2011; Runciman 2011; Sinwell 2011; Williams 2006.

4. For example DeFilippis, Fisher and Schragge 2010; Piven and Cloward 1979; Katznelson 1981.

5. Bond and Desai 2006; Maharaj, Desai and Bond 2011.

Instead, it means that in order to understand the revolutionary possibilities of a given moment, it is important to understand how more and less advanced relations of production are related, how they often reinforce each other, and how their contradictions may lead to revolutionary advances in developmentally 'less advanced' contexts. 'Uneven and combined *Marxism*' implies a way of considering the difficulties of constructing independent-left politics in the conjuncture of a long-term capitalist stagnation in a twenty-first century South Africa in which some sectors of the economy – construction, finance and commerce – have been booming while many other former labour-intensive sectors of manufacturing have been deindustrialised (or shifted from general production for a local mass market to niche production for a global upper-class market, such as luxury cars and garments), and in which large sections of society are still peripheral – aside from serving as a reserve army of unneeded surplus labour – to the interests of capital, domestic and global. The unevenness is also geographical, with small areas of South Africa operating within a circuit of luxury consumption and new technologies, but others such as ex-bantustan rural areas continuing their decline. The unevenness of sector and space is no surprise, of course, since capital has always flowed to sites of higher profitability, not serving to bring about tendencies towards equilibrium, but rather to exacerbate differentials and enhance inequalities. The word 'combined' is important in South Africa because of the ways in which capital interacts the non-capitalist sectors and spaces, including women's reproductive sites and mutual-aid systems, spaces of community commons, state services, and nature.

Unevenness is obvious across the cities and townships (and towns and dorpies or villages) where battles rage, among the sectors of capital, and across scales of struggle. The 'combined' part of anti-capitalism is an area that we are yet to see fully invoked (in the spirit of, for example, the Latin-American mobilisations foregrounding indigenous movements' struggles), because of the complexities of organising the unorganised – especially women – in shack settlements and rural areas where the act of daily survival in the interstices of capitalist/non-capitalist articulations generates far more collisions of political self-interest than standard Marxist urban theory has so far elucidated.

To speak of uneven and combined Marxism is, therefore, to invoke a political project on the South-African Left that *cannot but* begin with the contradictory totality of the country's social relations, both internal and external, at multiple geographic scales and at vastly different levels of development. And yet, the beginning cannot also be the end; the challenge for South-African Left politics is to create a hegemonic formation from this unevenness that is capable of moving towards fulfilling the global Left's hopes in the anti-Apartheid struggle, which was, at the same time, in many respects, also an anti-capitalist struggle.

But to articulate a Left politics on this uneven ground is also to enrich the typically imported Marxist analysis, in the sense that the South-African experience heightens and encapsulates several otherwise familiar tensions – urban/rural; worker/poor; local/national/global; society/nature; gender; and so on – and can show, therefore, perhaps more clearly than can other contexts, the essential relations among them.

In what follows, we begin by describing the contemporary contours of protest in South Africa, and then return to the problem of the hegemony of the Tripartite Alliance and its embrace of neoliberal policies, even if this has itself been somewhat uneven and the source of some tension among Alliance members. We then discuss the development of a strategic impasse among South-African social movements, and present and subject to critique several theoretically informed alternative routes out of or around the apparent cul de sac. We conclude by rearticulating more precisely the stakes in proposing an uneven and combined Marxism; and rather than proposing solutions, we draw upon it to pose more sharply the strategic questions for an agency-centred South-African Left.

Contemporary South-African protest

Writing five years after the end of Apartheid, Andrew Nash observed:

> The struggle against Apartheid became at times a focus of the hopes of the revolutionary left around the world. It represents a missed opportunity for the left not only in the more obvious sense that it did not result in a real challenge to the power of global capitalism. It was also an opportunity to transform the historical relationship of Marxist theory and working class politics, and overcome the division which allows a dialectical Marxism to flourish in the universities and journals, while working-class politics are dominated by the managerialism of Soviet Marxism or social-democracy.[6]

This sense of a lost opportunity persists in South-African politics today. It is found in the widespread discontent in townships and shack-dweller communities on the urban periphery over the rising cost of living and of previously state-provided services such as water and electricity; it is found in the militant protests among the poor demanding the reorganisation of districts, such that poor and rich areas are not administratively separated, thereby hampering the poor's ability to gain access to resources and public services (as in the towns of Khutsong and Balfour); it is seen in the divisions within the ANC, SACP and COSATU; and it is seen in the Treatment Action Campaign's successful and well-known

---

6. Nash 1999, p. 79.

battle against Thabo Mbeki's AIDS denialism and against Big Pharma's price-gouging of anti-retroviral medicines. And yet, in many of the successful instances of protest – for example, the reconnection of water and electricity,[7] the rolling-back of privatisation schemes,[8] and the reduction in the price of anti-retrovirals from \$15,000 per person to zero[9] – revolutionary Marxists played important leadership roles, suggesting, perhaps, that Nash bends the stick a bit too far.

Nevertheless, the question of how far to bend the stick remains. There is no question that opposition to racial apartheid also had within it the seeds of opposition to class apartheid. This can be seen in the Treatment Action Campaign's successful attack, not just on price gouging by Big Pharma, but also on *intellectual property rights*, which were curtailed by the 2001 Doha exemption for medical emergencies. It can be seen in the Soweto Electricity Crisis Committee's work since 2000, not only to fight against the privatisation of the electricity-company, rate-hikes, and electricity cut-offs, but also to teach people how to illegally reconnect themselves to the grid. These are only part of what Peter Alexander calls a 'rebellion of the poor'. In the wake of the introduction of the 'Growth, Employment and Redistribution' strategy (or 'GEAR') that marked the Alliance's definitive turn toward neoliberal macroeconomic policy, the most militant communities that took to the streets in protest and that formed the new urban social movements were relatively privileged. They already had houses, but were now fighting a defensive battle just to stay on in the urban ghettoes. Those who clung on to spaces in the city in shacks appeared to be more patient. The Alliance's promises to the poor included gaining access to the formal ghetto, while at the same time, its municipal officials were evicting others for non-payment as employment became increasingly precarious and unemployment increased to more than forty percent of the workforce. For a while, the enormous legitimacy of the ANC explained this patience.

But from the late 1990s, ongoing waves of protests broke out across the country's formal townships and shack settlements, with 'new urban social movements' formed in Durban, Johannesburg and Cape Town from 1999 onwards. Though the first waves ebbed after a national protest at the World Summit on Sustainable Development in 2002, more surges were noticed from mid-2004 in Zevenfontein, north of Johannesburg; in Harrismith in the Free State (where repression was marked by shootings and a death); and in Durban's Kennedy Road, beginning in early 2005, where shack-dweller protest coalesced into the *Abahlali baseMjondolo* (shack-dwellers' movement).

---

7. Bond 2011.
8. Bond 2006.
9. Geffen 2010.

However, in many cases, what started out as insurgencies outside the control of the Alliance were siphoned off into calls for participation, legal challenges, and 'voice'. Furthermore, one of the striking elements of South-African protest is its failure to 'scale up,' or join together either geographically or politically. With a few exceptions, the recent upsurge of service delivery protests have taken the form of 'popcorn protests', that is, movements that fly high, move according to where the wind blows – even in xenophobic directions, at times – and then fall to rest quite quickly.[10] There have been several attempts at coordination since the mid-2000s: Johannesburg's Anti-Privatisation Forum, bringing together service-delivery protest-groups, students, left-wing political activists (including, at first, some in the municipal workers' union and the SACP), and independent-left trade unions; the Social Movements Indaba, which from 2002–8 brought together community-struggles; and, since 2011, the Democratic Left Front, which has taken a similar initiative. Despite these efforts, and in part because of continual splintering of independent Left forces and a failure to make common cause with the left wing of the labour movement, no common programmes or bridge-building organisational strategies able to challenge neoliberalism on a national level have been developed. Three elements of this failure – reflecting the uneven and combined nature of anti-capitalism in South Africa today – are worth noting, here: the importance of access, localism, and leadership.

Access

Social movements often organise around sets of demands on the state that are, at least in principle, winnable. Service delivery protests targeting the privatisation of water supply or high charges for water use by the local water-authority, the regressive kilowatt-per-hour charge on electricity, or the eviction of shack-dwellers from squatted land, all imply the possibility of success. In Durban's rebellious Chatsworth community,[11] for example, in order to achieve *de facto* recognition and, therefore, the delivery of services that would keep the movement constituency close to its leadership, movement activists increasingly joined with the city council in various committees to administer and monitor the movement's success. A decade after the initial 1999 uprising, political work mainly involved technical issues and oversight over upgrading, liaison with welfare departments and a range of other interventions, which were less a matter of pressing for radical policy change than focusing on merely getting existing policy implemented.[12] This also inevitably brought the movement into close working

---

10. Petras and Morley 1990, p. 53.
11. Desai 2002.
12. Hinely 2009.

relationships with ANC local councilors and limited the autonomy of the movement, and ultimately led to enormous disappointments in Chatsworth when official promises were broken and municipal contractors engaged in fraud.

Likewise, in Durban's shack lands, in order to get recognition from the local council, shack-dweller activists had to ensure that no more shacks were built. Activists had to also ward off competitors. This was especially so if an organisation defined its role as ensuring delivery. It was paradoxical but increasingly common for movements to take political positions sharply critical of neoliberal policies, on the one hand, while negotiating for better delivery within these policy frameworks, on the other.

Of course, this is a common feature of social movements, and of poor people's movements beyond the South-African context. There is a recurring question of how to consolidate a movement's 'victories' without demobilising it, and how to move beyond the initial 'winnable' demands to more radical ones that cannot be so easily administered. In the South-African context, however, this problem is deepened by the sheer weight and presence of the ANC. Though there is a significant variety of political positions taken by local ANC branches and officials, larger matters of policy and financing are settled at the centre, while implementation – and enforcement – depend greatly on the local level. Reaching the centre is, therefore, fundamentally difficult, given the fact that the service delivery protests tend to limit their demands to locally constituted authorities, with the possible exception of Eskom, the utility providing ninety-five percent of South Africa's electricity (Eskom sells energy both to municipalities as well as to four million individual households – mainly in black townships and rural areas – who were retail customers dating back to the Apartheid era). Access problems thus imply a need for protesters to 'jump scale' from local to national, and sometimes also to global, for the World Bank has been known to give what it once termed 'instrumental' advice on matters such as water pricing.[13]

Localism and the geographic scales of protest-organisation

Marxist urban theorists, following the geographer Henri Lefebvre, speak of social relations unfolding on multiple geographic scales. Scales combine aspects of people's own construction of the extent of their social relations, and boundaries of the arenas in which they exist. They thus also depend on historically accreted understandings of the spatial limitations exerted on these relations, and on the physical properties that may inscribe them. As Marston writes, they 'are the outcome of, both everyday life and macro-level social structures'.[14] Finally,

---

13. Bond 2000; 2002.
14. Marston 2000, p. 221.

the framings of scale – framings that can have both rhetorical and material consequences – are often contradictory and contested and are not necessarily enduring. To say, therefore, that contemporary South-African protest is charac-teristically *local* in orientation – with several exceptions, such as the Treatment Action Campaign and, for a time, the Jubilee SA network, as well as some of the more innovative community groups in the major cities –is to make an observa-tion about the scale of the protests.

There is nothing inherently wrong with the localist orientation of protest. To the extent that participants stop evictions that affect them; to the extent that they force local authorities to increase the free allowance of electricity and water and lower fees for anything above the survival allowance; to the extent that a 'resi-due' of protest emerges as a local institutional safeguard against further abuse; to this extent, they are better off for having protested. From a Marxist perspective, however, limiting protest to the local scale both narrows the immediate trans-formative potential of social movements and, in the longer term, disadvantages both the movements and the people who compose them. The same can be said about sectoral narrowness, in which struggles concerning the 'water sector', the advocacy of economic reform, gender, energy justice, climate activism, access to education, healthcare advocacy and myriad other specific struggles, fail to join the dots between each other, both in South Africa and across the world (notwithstanding the existence of a World Social Forum movement meant – but apparently unable – to solve this problem).[15]

What does going beyond localism mean? To ask the question begs, first of all, a more precise definition of what constitutes the 'local' in the present case. Here, we propose that in South-African protest, 'local' denotes a focus on administra-tive and jurisdictional boundaries, on the one hand, and on the site of social reproduction, on the other. The extremely vigorous protest movements in the country focus most of their attention on the failings of local councils and govern-ments, which are themselves both the local enforcers of ANC policies formulated on the national scale – often influenced by the demands of global brokers of capital (the South-African treasury places great stock in its international credit-ratings) – and often political machines in which allegiance to the present ANC line is paramount for gaining access to decision-making processes. They are also focused on the circumstances of life in communities in which many people share abysmal living conditions.

As people active in these struggles, we can confirm that these were not origi-nally meant to be narrow and localised. We initially shared the hope that strug-gles at the community level – at what could, provisionally, be called the point

15. Bond 2005.

of reproduction – would have a quality and depth to them that would enable radical social antagonisms to flourish in ways unthinkable in the world of regular wage work, at the 'point of production'. As an idea, it makes sense. People live in communities 24 hours a day. With a huge mass of unemployed people stuck in these ghettos, many with experience in previous struggles, including that against Apartheid, it would be easy for demands made from these sites to be backed up with the force of mass organisations. All that was needed was a focus on bread-and-butter township- or shack dwellers' issues, and then an ideological extrapolation to broader political questions. Or so our thinking went, along with that of various segments of the independent – non-ANC, non-SACP – Left.

Focusing on the site of reproduction made sense in another way. In fact, the townships, shack-dweller communities, flat-dweller communities, and dorpies of South Africa contain a vast amount of economic activity, and the unemployed are, as often as not, also the marginally employed, the unofficially employed, and the precariously employed, which also means that they play no role in the country's pre-eminent labour organisation, COSATU, which has its base in the country's heavy and extractive industries and the public sector. Only the narrowest view of the working class would ignore this group.

And yet, the local community as a site of post-Apartheid resistance to neoliberalism has been much more difficult to sustain. Partly it is because of an assumption, seldom made by those actually living in townships, that there exist substantial grounds for unity flowing simply from the fact of living under the same conditions. One version of this assumption, as articulated with regard to Latin-American cities by James Petras and Morris Morley, is that:

> The power of these new social movements comes from the fact that they draw on the vast heterogeneous labour force that populates the main thoroughfares and the alleyways; the marketplaces and street corners; the interstices of the economy and the nerve centres of production; the exchange and finance centres; the university plazas, railway stations and the wharves – all are brought together in complex localized structures which feed into tumultuous homogenizing national movements.[16]

But in the South-African context, while localism produced militancy, it did not necessarily produce solidarity with any regularity. Indeed, shack-dwellers often face the ire of those with a tighter, but still tenuous, hold on stable tenure in the townships. Township residents can be mobilised for violence against shack-dwellers and immigrants as much as they can be mobilised for solidarity.

Another source of optimism for the fusing of proletarian and precariat identities is alluded to by John Saul, recalling arguments made nearly four

---

16. Petras and Morley 1990, p. 53.

decades ago: 'In a capitalism in crisis the "classic strengths of the urban working class" could become "more evident", with 'the upper stratum of the workers [then] most likely to identify downward [to become] a leading force within a revolutionary alliance of exploited elements in the society'.[17]

In the South-African context, therefore, the mobilisation of communities could, in theory, join up with the existing organisation of workers through COSATU, provided the latter could peel itself away from allegiance to the ANC and the Alliance's embrace of neoliberalism, especially in the light of clearly deteriorating conditions.

But beyond the disappointments generated by a COSATU much changed by its entry into the Alliance and the decline of the shop-steward leadership that provided much of its strength during the anti-Apartheid struggle, local communities were themselves difficult to coalesce around consistent analyses of the problems that led to their oppression, while abstraction from the local to *multiple* scales proved difficult once the problems of evictions, electricity, sewerage, and drinking water were addressed.

Finally, it must be said that from a strategic point of view, there is some value in being able to organise at a scale commensurate with that of one's adversary's organisation. The ANC is organised at the national level, and it staffs its organisation by positioning cadre in local areas. This means that it centralises power and is able to exert significant – though far from total – control over local cadre. Thus, although some local councilors, for example, are more 'trigger happy' when it comes to repressing service delivery and shack-dweller protests (and there have been more than a dozen deaths of protesters at the hands of police and non-official enforcers), the ANC's centralised organisation, which is extremely averse to criticism, has set a policy of repression while also trying to channel protest into the least threatening, least direct forms, such as marches, as opposed to land-occupations. The ANC's factional violence against its own cadres is notorious, such as in Durban, where, in mid-2011, the party's leader was assassinated. But by December 2011, the ANC city manager and political élites were sufficiently united to unleash thugs on Democratic Left Front activists, who had staged a march of more than 5,000 against the United Nations' climate summit and a few days later held up signs in City Hall during a visit by Zuma.

Leadership

Another set of problems arising from contemporary South-African protest also familiar to students of social movements and revolutionary politics is the problem of leadership, and particularly the role of intellectuals in the movement.

---

17. Saul 1975, p. 306.

Antonio Gramsci's analysis of intellectuals is apposite, here. Gramsci argues, in essence, that intellectuals are those who give shape, through mental labour, to specific sets and sites of social relations. Those whom he calls 'traditional' intellectuals are those whose roles as intellectuals were formed in earlier periods, and thus appear as separate from, and above, contemporary class relations and antagonisms, such as clergy and professional scholars and teachers. 'Organic' intellectuals, by contrast, are those whose intellectual labours shape the projects of entire groups of people, such as industrialists and union militants. Traditional intellectuals can, by virtue of their social position, make claims about universals, whereas organic intellectuals allegedly articulate particularities. However, as Gramsci makes clear, traditional intellectuals are just as moored to class as are organic ones; in fact, newly dominant groups work not only through their own organic intellectuals, such as managers and consultants, but also through traditional intellectuals.[18] In South Africa, many organic intellectuals arose out of the anti-Apartheid struggle. Many were linked to the trade-union movement, others to the ANC, still others to the SACP, and others to the Trotskyist and other independent left-wing formations. Even since the Apartheid-period, the boundary between organisations of traditional intellectuals – for instance, the universities and NGOs – and the organisations that produced and were produced by organic intellectuals in and of social movements has been a porous one. Student militants were enormously important to the anti-Apartheid struggle, and post-Apartheid South-African universities have been home to some academics who have aligned themselves closely with, and worked within, the social movements. The question this has raised within social movements, however, is the issue of vanguardism.

In some social movement efforts, significant participation by university-based and foundation-funded scholar activists and NGOs seemed, to other participants, to reproduce inequalities. Accusations of 'ventriloquism' and 'substitutionism' by academics within movements have been traded.[19] Some university-based intellectuals have argued that since 'the poor are the embodiment of the truth', the role of traditional intellectuals is to reflect their positions to the world and simply act in concert with the poor.[20] This kind of analysis sometimes results in the romanticisation of urban social movements, and also denies the complex articulations of movements and the education of their leaders. There is no doubt about the dangers of vanguardism. The question is

---

18. See Gramsci 1971, pp. 4–23.
19. See, for example, debates initiated by Bohmke 2009a; 2009b; 2010a; and 2010b; and the reactions in *PoliticsWeb* and *Pambazuka*.
20. See critical discussion initiated by Walsh 2008.

244 • Patrick Bond, Ashwin Desai and Trevor Ngwane

whether a populism that homogenises 'the poor' is capable of building the necessary coalitions to bring protest up to a regularly coordinated, non-local scale.

The question of leadership has also led to the involution of protest, especially
divisions within social movements and their networks including the Anti-
Privatisation Forum, Soweto Electricity Crisis Committee, Western Cape Anti-
Evictions Campaign, Landless People's Movement, Jubilee South Africa and
Social Movements Indaba. These divisions are, however, more a symptom than
a cause of the strategic impasse faced by South-African urban movements today.
Scholars of movements have noted that internal tensions often come to the fore
when there is no clear way forward for externally oriented action.[21]

Together, the contradictory tendencies of access, localism, and leadership
have produced a movement sector that is at once extraordinarily militant in its
actions and profoundly moderate in its politics. The increasing turn away from
electoral politics in poor areas in favour of protest politics signals a strong disen-
chantment with the apparatus of representative government and with the actual
governance by (mostly) ANC officials. On the other hand, in spite of this dis-
enchantment, South-African movements are nowhere near articulating alternatives, and doing so would require movement leaders to engage in the sustained
dialogue necessary to abstract from local concerns to national, and even international ones. The potential is there: the Treatment Action Campaign's successful demand for decommodified and locally-made (generic) AIDS medicines, and
the Campaign against Water Privatisation's fight against Johannesburg Water's
management being outsourced to Suez, took activism in these sectors out of
tired social policy or NGO-delivery debates, and set them at the cutting edge of
the world's anti-neoliberal backlash.

Tripartite Alliance hegemony

Another inescapable feature of South Africa's contemporary politics is the continued – though increasingly fragile – hegemony of the ANC. The ANC enjoys
an enormous amount of legitimacy and ongoing prestige, in spite of the fact that
nearly twenty years of ANC rule has resulted in deepening poverty and inequality, and in spite of the visible divisions within the ANC, as, for example, in the
clashes between President Jacob Zuma and his predecessor, Thabo Mbeki, and
between Zuma and the ANC Youth-League leader, Julius Malema. The ANC was
the main organisation of the international anti-Apartheid struggle, and even
though it was banned within South Africa from 1963 to 1990, quickly reasserted
itself as the largest, best-organised group capable of taking the reins of power

---

21. See Polletta 2005.

during the early-1990s transition. In establishing its hegemony at the local level, it supplanted already-existing organisations with its own (for instance, women's organisations and youth groups), and has dominated electoral politics since the first post-Apartheid elections in 1994.

The Tripartite Alliance is dominated by the ANC, which, under Mandela, began to separate the ideological strands that had underpinned the most militant elements of the anti-Apartheid movement, both in South Africa and abroad. Capital flight increased after the democratic elections of 1994, and in reaction, in early 1995 the ANC government relaxed exchange controls to prove its new loyalty to the Washington Consensus. By the mid-1990s, indeed, ANC leaders had distanced the party from the interventionist currents in the movement. In his first interview after winning the presidency in 1994, Mandela stated: 'In our economic policies ... there is not a single reference to nationalisation, and this is not accidental. There is not a single slogan that will connect us with any Marxist ideology'. Although he inexplicably missed the nationalisation mandate he was given in the 1994 *Reconstruction and Development Programme*,[22] Mandela's specific reference to Marxist ideology in many senses reflects the strong strand of anti-capitalist thinking that linked into resurgent struggles against Apartheid from the early 1970s. Through its policy and slogan of Black Economic Empowerment (BEE), moreover, the ANC deracialised capitalism – albeit for a very few billionaires – and separated the profitability dynamic of South-African capitalism from racial domination. The latter has remained strong, of course, but more notable is the rise of class apartheid techniques.[23]

Mandela's avowed anti-Marxism did not, however, so alienate the SACP and COSATU that they abandoned the coalition. On the contrary, the initial redistributive promises in the ANC platform – eclipsed by GEAR in 1996, as well as by numerous White Papers starting in mid-1994 – gave the SACP and COSATU power in administering what might, in other circumstances, have been the development of a managerialist, social-democratic welfare state. The SACP chairman, after all, was Joe Slovo (prior to his death in early 1995), and his 1994 U-turn towards a fully neoliberal housing policy,[24] as the World Bank explicitly recommended, was the main signal that the *Reconstruction and Development Programme* was finished before it had even begun. Slovo reversed nearly every major mandate with which he had been provided.

Though centralised, corporatist bargaining was not part even of the initial coalition deal, COSATU had a prominent place at the table in order to represent the concerns of the organised working class. It did so with enough friction with

---

22. ANC 1994, p. 80.
23. Bond 2005.
24. Bond 2000; Republic of South Africa 1994.

the ANC that it could boast of putting up a fight, even while lauding the (not really corporatist) arrangements of the Alliance *as* corporatist, suggesting that it in fact had codetermination-powers (in sites like the National Economic Development and Labour Council), and that the working class was more institutionally powerful than it patently was. After all, in the post-Apartheid era, the share of profits relative to wages shifted in favour of capital by nine percentage points. And the SACP gained some power over the state's redistributionist functions, with the Mandela era witnessing its Central Committee members in positions including the ministers or deputy ministers of trade and industry, public works, housing, transport, public services and even defence. At the same time, this meant that the SACP had something to lose from challenging the ANC within the coalition too strongly, and it was consistent with the Party's longstanding line that racial democracy had to precede the larger economic project of socialism. It also meant that the Party would be at the frontlines of managing a rapidly changing urban landscape, as the lifting of Apartheid-era residency laws resulted in the vast growth of shack-communities, both on the urban periphery and in already urbanised township areas. That the Party endorsed GEAR and the neoliberal Africa strategy (the New Partnership for Africa's Development) and supported a platform that put private investment at the centre of its housing strategy – in a period characterised by capital flight – suggests that it was a comfortable member of the publicly anti-Marxist ANC-led Coalition, and that its constant support for the Coalition's neoliberal macroeconomic initiatives at multiple levels in 1996, 2001 and 2010 should not surprise.[25]

Nevertheless, the Alliance's cohesion and hegemony has not been rock-solid. There have, from the start, been tensions both between COSATU and the ANC and within COSATU *about* the ANC and the union federation's role in the Alliance and what it gets out of it. These tensions extend back in time to before COSATU's founding in 1985, and speak both to the shopfloor-militancy of 1970s unionism in South Africa and to the tensions around the integration of the union movement into the nationalist project. But these tensions were raised with GEAR's introduction by the ruling party's neoliberal bloc, and ultimately resulted in COSATU's support for Jacob Zuma's successful bid for the ANC leadership against Thabo Mbeki in the 2007 ANC National Conference, and Mbeki's humiliating firing from the presidency by the ANC in September 2008.

And yet Zuma's government has done little better than Mbeki's, and has not changed the country's neoliberal macroeconomic course.[26] A three-week strike of public sector workers in 2010, most of whom were members of COSATU, and

---

25. Bond 2000.
26. Maharaj, Desai and Bond 2011.

which both imposed real hardship and threatened to spread to other sectors of the economy, signalled the ripening of the contradictions of COSATU's continued alliance with the ANC. COSATU's membership has become older and more skilled as neoliberalism has resulted in segmented labour-markets and the proliferation of informal work, and a growing proportion of its members are employees of the state. COSATU depends on the ANC-dominated state both for this and for access to a different lifestyle for leaders who move into government positions. On the other hand, continued austerity and attempts to squeeze public sector workers – visible from Johannesburg to Wisconsin, from Durban to Athens – in the face of already desperately inadequate services and a massive and visible gap between rich and poor (even among Africans), has led at least one COSATU leader to criticise Zuma's government as becoming a 'predator state'.[27]

The fraying hegemony of the ANC with respect to its Alliance partners, and the simple refusal of many township- and shack-dweller communities to engage any more in the formal political process, signify South Africa's deep crisis. Nevertheless, the protests raise the questions of whether dissent is solely about the delivery of services, or whether it signifies a bigger dissatisfaction with the social order as such? Do protesters see continuity between the anti-Apartheid struggle and the struggle today? Even in extreme cases of struggle (such as the disputes over district boundaries in Khutsong), the leading activists retained connections to the Alliance, which, given its legitimacy from the anti-Apartheid struggle and its patronage networks, were more durable than the centrifugal pressure to disconnect. And if a crisis consists in the fact that 'the old is dying, but the new cannot yet be born',[28] it begs the question of what 'the new' is and what its birthing process could look like.

Theorising the strategic impasse

The question of how to move out of the crisis to a renewed revolutionary politics that separates the nationalist project from the politics of neoliberal development has garnered several answers. Each is partial, and each, as we will argue, is inadequate to the task. In this section of the chapter, we will examine three that have particular currency: the expansion of rights through litigation; the claim for 'the right to the city', which is distinct from juridical rights talk; and the creation of spaces for 'participation'. In the following section, we will revisit the question of the impasse with reference to a reformulated Marxist account of uneven and combined development.

27. Vavi 2011.
28. Gramsci 1971, p. 276.

Rights

Community-based social movements have repeatedly gone to court to enforce their rights. Actual 'victories' in court are beyond our quibbling, and, indeed, some offensive victories (nevirapine to halt HIV transmission during birth) and defensive successes (halting evictions) are occasionally recorded. Nevertheless, we consider insidious the constitutionalist discourse that envelops individual cases in an overall strategy: the idea that 'the turn to law' is a good or beneficial thing to do with the energies, affinities, possibilities and power of a movement.

The 'turn-to-law' discourse bears the unmistakable scent of reform without a strategic sense of how to make more fundamental demands that bring into question barriers as large as property relations. The result is the kind of 'reformist reform' (as Gorz put it)[29] that entrenches the *status quo*. (In contrast, non-reformist reforms work *against* the internal logic of the dominant system, and strengthen rather than coopt the counterhegemonic challengers.) In this sense, the illegal occupation of land is far more powerful than a court's ultimate granting of tenure to the occupiers. The turn to constitutionalism also has consequences for movement leadership; it is based on the conception that a certain professional legal caste among us can secure meaningful precedents in the constitutional court (and consequent compliance by the executive) that advance the struggle of the poor in a fundamental way.

To be clear, we are not opposed to going to court. This may be useful, from time to time. But as a strategy – rather than as a tactic – it is limited, and unable to compensate for weaknesses in protest organisation and militancy. For example, the Treatment Action Campaign's victory against Mbeki in late 2003 was spurred, to some extent, by a mid-2001 Constitutional Court ruling that compelled his government to provide nevirapine to HIV-positive pregnant women, in order to prevent mother-to-child transmission. In general, it is fair to say that the rights narrative was important to reducing stigmatisation and providing 'dignity' to those claiming their health-rights. Also successful in the Constitutional Court was Durban's *Abahlali baseMjondolo* shack dwellers' movement, which in 2009 won a major victory against a provincial housing ordinance justifying forced removals. Such removals continue unhindered, unfortunately, and at nearly the same moment that *Abahlali baseMjondolo* won the court victory, they were violently uprooted from their base in Kennedy Road.

Thus, as Rosenberg indicates, writing in the critical legal studies tradition, rights depend on their enforcement, and courts cannot compel this.[30] Further, court judgments can be reversed: a crucial rights narrative test came in the

29. Gorz 1967.
30. Rosenberg 1993.

struggle to expand water provision to low-income Sowetans. The Anti-Privatisation Forum claimed a victory in 2006, since, following community struggles, water in Johannesburg is now produced and distributed by public agencies (the multinational firm involved in Soweto's water contract, Suez, was sent back to Paris after its controversial 2001–6 protest-ridden management of municipal water). In April 2008, a major constitutional lawsuit in the High Court resulted in a doubling of free water to 50 litres per person per day and the prohibition of pre-payment water meters.[31] But the Constitutional Court reversed this decision in October 2009, on the grounds that judges should not make such detailed policy, and that the prevailing amounts of water and the self-disconnection delivery system were perfectly reasonable within the ambit of the South African Bill of Rights. Once again, this meant that activists were thrown back to understanding the limits of constitutionalism: they recommitted to illegal reconnections, if required.[32]

We object, therefore, simply to the subordination of a political discourse to a legal discourse – even if superficially an empowering one, in terms of 'rights' narratives – and thus to the subordination of a radical discourse to a liberal one. As Alan Hunt and Gary Wickham argue, discourse 'structures the possibility of what gets included and excluded and what gets done and what remains undone. Discourses authorize some to speak, some views to be taken seriously, while others are marginalized, derided, excluded and even prohibited'.[33] By flirting with legalism and the rights discourse, movements have seen their demands watered down into court pleadings. Heartfelt pleas are offered, but for the observance of the purely procedural: consult us before you evict us. Demands for housing that could be generalised and spread, become demands for '*in situ* upgrading' and 'reasonable government action' and hence feed the politics of local solutions, to the exclusion of demands that can be 'scaled up'.

Right to the city

An alternative formulation of 'rights' is given by Henri Lefebvre and David Harvey's 'right-to-the-city' argument. Harvey is clear that the 'right to the city' is a *collective* right, rather than a liberal-individualist one, and is based on the idea that 'the freedom to make and remake our cities and ourselves is...the most precious yet most neglected of our human rights'. Because Harvey links urbanisation and, therefore, the way of life of an increasing majority of humanity, to the absorption of capitalist surplus, the 'right to the city' implies empowering the

31. Bond and Dugard 2008.
32. Bond 2011a.
33. Hunt and Wickam 1994, pp. 8–9.

mass of people to take from capitalists the power to produce their way of life and learn to wield it themselves. The current crisis of global capital has led to some of the uneven developments to which we have already referred in South Africa. The explosion in the price of real estate (a nearly four-hundred percent increase from 1997 through to the 2007 peak) was facilitated not only by local overaccumulation, but also by the influxes of surplus global capital, thus contributing to the boom-bust dynamic in the construction-trades even as the rest of the economy stagnated or worse. 'The results', Harvey writes, 'are indelibly etched on the spatial forms of our cities, which increasingly consist of fortified fragments, gated communities, and privatized public spaces kept under constant surveillance'. He continues, quoting Marcello Balbo:

> [The city] is splitting into different separated parts, with the apparent forma-
> tion of many 'microstates'. Wealthy neighbourhoods provided with all kinds
> of services, such as exclusive schools, golf courses, tennis courts and private
> police patrolling the area around the clock intertwine with illegal settlements
> where water is available only at public fountains, no sanitation system exists,
> electricity is pirated by a privileged few, the roads become mud streams when-
> ever it rains, and where house-sharing is the norm...

Harvey sees the 'right to the city' as a 'both a working slogan and political ideal' to democratise the 'necessary connection between urbanization and surplus production and use'.[34] However, in the South African context, the slogan has been taken up both by proponents of legalistic means of struggle and by the more autonomist-oriented shack dweller campaigns, and so the 'right to the city' can be seen as a kind of ambiguous hinge that joins quite different political orientations. For example, Marie Huchzermeyer argues that the South-African Constitution mandates 'an equal right to the city' and that this requires movements to pursue marginal gains through the courts: 'Urban Reform in this sense is a pragmatic commitment to gradual but radical change towards grassroots autonomy as a basis for equal rights'. After all, she argues, 'three components of the right to the city – equal participation in decision making, equal access to and use of the city and equal access to basic services – have all been brought before the Constitutional Court through a coalition between grassroots social movements and a sympathetic middle-class network'. Nevertheless, she also argues that human rights 'language is fast being usurped by the mainstream within the UN, UN-Habitat, NGOs, think tanks, consultants etc., in something of an empty buzz word, where the concept of grassroots autonomy and meaningful convergence is completely forgotten'.[35]

---

34. Harvey 2008.
35. Huchzermeyer 2009, pp. 3–4.

Unfortunately, given the power imbalances that exist, Huchzermeyer and others who make the 'right-to-the-city' claim run the risk of merely extending a slogan, rather than a strategic vision, to the question of the current impasse in South-African social movements. The danger, here, is particularly felt in the ways in which 'the city' can be taken to mean 'particular cities' (which, on one level, they must) and, therefore, to privilege local politics and local solutions, without a larger-scale analysis that could provide a kind of standard by which locally generated choices and strategies could be subjected to criticism. One result is that like groups often accept each other's political stances, while discounting the possibilities of coalition across types of community: hence, for example, 'Abahlalism' – 'shack dwellerism' – arises as a kind of autonomistic-populist practice in which the deep suspicion of *non*-shack dwellers, even if sometimes deserved, finds its mirror image in the idea that political ideas are invalidated or validated simply by virtue of their issuing from 'the poor'.[36]

'Participation'

A clause in the Constitution, as well as various laws, compels municipalities to involve residents in 'community participation' processes as to enable people to directly influence the decisions that affect them. John Williams, reporting on research in the Western Cape, finds that 'Most community participation exercises in post-Apartheid South Africa are largely spectator politics, where ordinary people have mostly become endorsees of pre-designed planning programmes, [and] are often the objects of administrative manipulation'. As a result, formal municipal governance processes are 'a limited form of democracy [that] give[s] rise to an administered society rather than a democratic society' since there is no real debate of policy or of social programmes by the working-class electorate and government officials.[37] A study of community participation in local economic development processes in Durban by Richard Ballard and his colleagues reveals that such processes allow ordinary people 'to demand accountability' from 'elected representatives and sometimes quite senior officials'. However, they are 'consultative rather than participatory' and 'invariably become conspicuous for the issues they leave out, and for the voices they did not hear'.[38]

This was particularly apparent in the way that the Durban 'Citizen's Voice' process was handled by the city and the main water NGO (Mvula Trust), invoking participation by what might be termed 'civilised society' as a way of encouraging

---

36. Desai 2006.
37. Williams 2006.
38. Ballard et al. 2006, p. 4.

poor communities *to consume less water* just after the municipal prices had doubled, in real terms, over a period of six years.[39]

In a different vein, David Hemson concludes that 'community participation in South Africa is informed by the memory of community struggle – a radical form of participation – against the racist Apartheid State' and that this must be harnessed. 'It is precisely this repertoire of radical strategies that can and should be revisited and adapted, to advance the interests of the materially marginalized communities at the local level'.[40] Luke Sinwell applies a theoretical approach first developed in the South-African context by Faranak Miraftab,[41] based on a distinction between 'invited' versus 'invented' spaces of popular participation. The ward committees, *imbizos* [government-initiated public forums] and integrated development-plans of invited participation contrast with invented spaces through 'self-activity' such as community self-organisation, direct action and other non-official mechanisms of exerting pressure. Based on extensive research conducted in Alexandra, one of the country's oldest and poorest black working-class townships, he concludes that progressive change is more likely to emanate from the use of invented rather than invited spaces. However, Sinwell laments that community activism in the invented spaces also fails to question power-relations and social structures in a fundamental way. Community organisations tend to work within budgetary constraints set by the state and, as a result, community groups end up competing among themselves for limited resources rather than questioning the neoliberal framework and its ideological underpinnings.[42]

Combined and uneven development; combined and uneven Marxism

The importance of Marxist criticism is to uncover, in particular situations, what is 'systematic' and what is 'conjunctural', as Gramsci put it.[43] This, in turn, helps to distinguish – and, therefore, to both facilitate and structure discussion about – short- and longer-term demands. The 'pure militancy' of an immediate politics of the poor does not do this easily. It is, rather, through dialogue – not just among 'the poor', but among the several sectors of society caught at various points in the contradictions of neoliberalism – that a larger political formation capable of a sustained revolt against capital, and the creation of a new order, can be built.

---

39. Bond 2011b.
40. Hemson 2004.
41. Sinwell 2009, p. 31.
42. Miraftab 2004.
43. Gramsci 1971, p. 177.

Here, Trotsky's understanding of 'combined and uneven development' is useful. Though it can be read somewhat more broadly, most interpretations of Trotsky understand him to have meant 'combined' development to refer to the relations among different levels of development *within* a given national context.[44] In South Africa, the logical corollary is to 'articulations of modes of production,' a concept promoted by Harold Wolpe to explain race-class politics linking sites of surplus value extraction to bantustans (where impoverished women provided the reproduction of cheap labour at a vast distance), but which is even more relevant in post-Apartheid South Africa, given enhanced migrancy, xenophobia and adverse gender power relations.[45] Geographers such as David Harvey and Neil Smith have emphasised that even within nations, the combined unevenness of development is given spatial expression. Apartheid was, in its nature, both a racial order and a spatial one, and it enforced uneven *and* combined development in almost caricatured forms. The systematic separation of racial groups, the profound underdevelopment of black areas, and the racial segmentation of labour markets, suggested to many on the Left (including us), as we noted earlier, that the fight against Apartheid was coterminous with the fight against capitalism. Though we were correct that capitalism and racism were mutually reinforcing during the twentieth century, the conventional mistake by radicals was in thinking that the defeat of one durable but ultimately conjunctural manifestation of racism, Apartheid, would bring the capitalist system to its knees.

Accordingly, we found that Apartheid was conjunctural, but uneven and combined development is systematic.[46] The particular spatial manifestations of uneven and combined development are also conjunctural, though, again, they can be extremely durable. Hence, fights against eviction or for clean and affordable water, even while encountering the severe power of state coercion, and sometimes taking years to resolve, do little to change the systematic dynamics of uneven and combined development, deepened in new ways in neoliberal South Africa.

Trotsky also marshalled the theory of uneven and combined development to argue against 'stageism' or the idea that revolutionary politics depended on a given country going through the specific, drawn-out processes of capitalist development found in other countries. What this meant, however, was that coalitions among workers across space *and* across situations in the process of capital accumulation (such as industrial workers and peasants) were central to revolutionary potentials, but, moreover, that these potentials were *realisable*, even if with difficulty. The contemporary conjuncture in South Africa, beset by the

---

44. Barker 2006b; Trotsky 1962.
45. Wolpe 1980.
46. Maharaj, Desai and Bond 2011; Bond 2005.

entrenched neoliberalism imposed by a weakening but still-present ruling Alliance dominated by the ANC, has seen the accumulation of protests by township-residents over services, shack dwellers over evictions and services, and by relatively 'privileged' public sector workers over pay and the quality of services they provide. Though the public sector workers' strike was suspended without winning the union's key demands, it came close to bringing out private sector workers – all in the formal sector – as well.

The question for an 'uneven, combined Marxism' is how to *take advantage* of the unevenness and particular conjunctural combinations of social relations in South Africa and beyond. The present period in South Africa exemplifies the dynamics of uneven and combined development and its spatial and social consequences. Within South Africa, it is important to think about how, for example, shack-dwellers' struggles and public sector workers' struggles could be linked up, even as the latter's relative privilege and operation in the formal labour market may make them wary of such an alliance, and as the former's distrust of cooptation creates an equal hesitancy. The Durban climate summit – the Conference of the Parties 17 – illustrated how very difficult it is to conjoin labour, community and environmental considerations (especially in the context of a set-piece 'Global-Day-of-Action' march on 3 December 2011), when distances between constituencies, political traditions and issue areas remain debilitating.[47]

How could a joined-up movement respond to the conjunctural pressures upon it, such as the apparent *advantages* to the unemployed of labour market flexibilisation schemes or to the quality of life of township residents of evicting shack-dweller settlements? What kind of ways can – or should – Marxists talk about taking on the systemic problems of uneven and combined development with people who are located in different, and even sometimes opposed, areas of this combination? What organisational forms might be applied to start this conversation, and yet keep it focused on the systematic elements of the present? How do we move beyond the concern for access, the localism, the constitutionalism, and the anti-political populism of contemporary protest – even as these sometimes yield concrete results – while also moving beyond the ambiguity of a simple slogan? To us, the protests represent a profound critique of neoliberalism by working-class communities. But are protesters aware of the greater significance of their protests? And to what extent do protesters' demands require solutions that challenge neoliberal policy, and even entail a challenge to the capitalist mode of production? Or is it the case that the overarching neoliberal economic framework constrains the realisation of not only the people's aspirations, but their ability to think beyond capitalism?

---

47. Bond 2011c.

We agree with Andrew Nash that the answers to these questions will not come through the elaboration of a new, 'proper' Marxist line by mainly university-based, white intellectuals, and that the great task of a renewal of South-African Marxism will depend on the elaboration of a new stratum of organic intellectuals from the movements (though not necessarily bypassing the universities) who can, perhaps, move among them in ways that enable them to abstract from the local without abandoning its reality. Being able to do this partly depends on the ability of South-African movements to look beyond themselves, to a world increasingly resistant to neoliberalism and to contribute to, and take from, a growing global movement. The successes of the Treatment Action Campaign were one such contribution, although this movement also teaches the dangers of self-liquidation into state-conjoined service delivery and narrow sectoral politics, as well as a seeming overreliance on foreign funding.

In encountering similar-but-different movements and contexts, movement intellectuals gain new perspectives on the possibilities of coalitions and on the similar-but-different permutations of combined and uneven development elsewhere; these can enhance their capacity to reinterpret local conditions by denaturalising existing political categories and divisions. Indeed, in calling for a 'combined and uneven Marxism', we intend to suggest that the way forward cannot lie in the search for the pure revolutionary subject, whether the worker, the township 'poors', the shack dweller, the organic feminist, the red-green social environmentalist, or anyone else; and it cannot lie in the search for the perfect location, whether the household, community, farm, benefits office, oil refinery or factory. Combined and uneven development makes clear that if the Marxist view that people are a 'nexus of social relations' holds, a combined and uneven Marxism must draw on the interdependence of locations in these relations in order to reinforce our interdependence, rather than accepting the capitalist combination of unevenness and mutual social antagonisms among those from whom capital is extracted. Of course, this is to state a problem rather than to proclaim a new strategy. However, consistent with the argument above, it is only through the development of organic intellectuals from within the movements, and their discussions and alliances with one another as well as with 'traditional' Marxist intellectuals, that a way forward will be found.

Part Three
Seeing the Bigger Picture

Comparative-Historical Perspectives

Thinking About (New) Social Movements: Some Insights from the British Marxist Historians
Paul Blackledge

Introduction

Over the last few decades, Marxism has fallen out of favour with European students of social movements. Typically, it has been suggested that the rise of 'new social movements' (NSM) illuminates the transition from an industrial to a post-industrial or postmodern society and that this new world undermines old left-ist assumptions not only about the working class, but also about the nature of the political itself. Concretely, NSM theory emerged in the late 1970s as an attempt to make sense of those feminist, environmental, peace and other social movements that waxed as the workers' movement waned. And whereas old social(ist) move-ments were widely perceived to be class-based and orientated to the seizure of state power, NSM theorists argued that these new movements are best understood in terms of identity-based struggles against 'the grip of power'.[1]

Nonetheless, despite their rejection of class-based politics, NSM theorists such as Alain Touraine and Alberto Melucci have not not simply dismissed Marx-ism. Instead, they criticise Marx's supposed economic determinism from the point of view of his famous claim that men make history but not under circum-stances of their own choosing. Touraine and Melucci independently built upon this aspect of Marx's work to

---

1. Touraine, quoted in Tilly and Wood 2009, p. 71.

criticise what they took to be the structural functionalism found elsewhere in his *oeuvre*. They argue that in the *Eighteenth Brumaire*, Marx points beyond his own materialism to a model of social change that is alive to the normative dimension of action, and thus able to comprehend the ways in which social solidarities and conflicts are made and remade through cultural struggles over discursive representations of experience.[2]

Touraine and Melucci are right to suggest that Marx's famous aphorism from the *Eighteenth Brumaire* implies an engagement with the normative dimension of agency. However, their claim that this approach contradicts Marx's broader theory of history is much more problematic.[3] The most powerful interpretations of historical materialism have consistently sought to relate human agency to social structure without reducing one to the other, and attempts to reduce Marxism to a crudely deterministic variant of structural functionalism are wont to miss its potential to enrich the study of social movements. As we shall see, Marx points towards a non-reductive theory of social change that stresses the importance of language and culture in social life without losing sight of the way material interests are rooted in social relations. By contrast, many NSM theorists have, through the influence of the 'linguistic turn', tended to invert the errors of crude materialism by effectively unhinging language from the material world. Associated with poststructuralist theory, this approach replaced the traditional methods of social theory, according to which language was a window onto reality, with a model that, most radically, insisted 'there is nothing outside the text'.[4] This shift lent itself to descriptive and superficial accounts of social life which one-sidedly emphasized difference over time at the expense of a more dialectical assessment of change and continuity.

In this essay, I explore ways in which Marxism might contribute to the study of social movements through an engagement with some of the work of the British Marxist historians.[5] In their work, this group – whose number includes such titans in the field as Edward Thompson, Eric Hobsbawm, and Christopher Hill – evidence Marxism's ability to deal with issues of intentionality and ethics in

2. Touraine 2007, p. 50; compare Touraine 1981; Melucci 1996b; Nash 2000, pp. 132, 137.
3. Blackledge 2006, pp. 153–91; 2012.
4. Palmer 1990, p. 5.
5. By the 'British Marxist historians', I refer to what Harvey Kaye has called a loosely constituted 'theoretical tradition' that had at its core a number of key activists who had been schooled in the anti-fascist movements of the 1930s and the Communist Party Historians' Group (CPHG) thereafter (Kaye 1995, p. 3). Launched in the wake of the Second World War to inform the production of a new edition of Leslie Morton's *A People's History of England*, the CPHG lasted (in its original form) until the New Left's break with Stalinism in 1956. Several of the relatively small number of the historians who were brought together in this group became towering figures in their respective fields, and, to differing degrees, each of them engaged with what might be called, following Craig Calhoun, 'old' new social movements: see Blackledge 2008; Calhoun 1995.

human agency without losing sight of the structural coordinates of action. I argue that their work is best understood not as a variant of either economic determinism or structural functionalism, but rather through the lens of Vološinov's sophisticated dialogical approach to the study of language. Conceived thus, their *oeuvre* can be mined for insights into a model of historical materialism which not only challenges the reduction of Marxism to a crude materialism, but also suggests continuities between so-called 'old' and 'new' social movements. By taking seriously issues of human agency as purposeful activity, the British Marxist historians' 'worm's eye view' of the past[6] informed numerous engagements with social movements that grasped the specificity of these movements while showing how they illuminate the social essence. And once detached from some weak methodological formulations, the insights of this tradition imply a theory that is able both to historicise and politically criticise NSM theory.

In his critique of overly simplistic attempts to contrast old and new social movements, Craig Calhoun refers to the continuity between research into NSMs and Thompson's analysis of social movements in his classic *The Making of the English Working Class*.[7] My essay effectively extends this insight to explore a living tradition of Marxist historiography that breaks down the dichotomy between old and new movements. My argument coheres with the work of those Marxist students of social movements who have suggested that the seeming decline of working-class radicalism and the rise of identity politics need not confound a sophisticated, humanist and, consequently, ethical interpretation of Marxism.[8]

The problem of language and experience within British Marxist historiography

In his *Marxism and Linguistics*, Stalin notoriously insisted that society's ideological, political and legal superstructure merely 'reflected' changes in the social base (relations of production) which in turn reflected changes in 'the productive forces'. Consequently, or so he claimed, 'the sphere of action of the superstructure is narrow and restricted'.[9] If these lines summed up Stalin's reductionist and fatalistic caricature of Marxism, Louis Althusser's claim that 'history is a ... *process without a subject*' informed Edward Thompson's argument that, despite differences about the conception of the primacy of the productive forces, Althusser

---

6. Hill 1975, p. 14.
7. Calhoun 1995, p. 174.
8. Barker and Dale 1998; see Harman 1998a.
9. Stalin quoted in Thompson 1978b, p. 79.

shared with Stalin a reified and, therefore, grossly inadequate conception of historical agency.[10]

Two decades earlier, Thompson framed his own break with Stalinism in terms of a re-engagement with the problem of human agency. In 'Socialist Humanism: An Epistle to the Philistines', he criticised what he called vulgar Marxism for its tendency 'to derive all analysis of political manifestations directly and in an oversimplified manner from economic causations'.[11] Moreover, he suggested that this mistake could not simply be laid at Stalin's door, for Marx and Engels, too, in their cruder moments, had explained revolutions mechanically in terms of the clash between forces and relations of production rather than as products of the agency of real men and women. Furthermore, he argued that this weakness in their *oeuvre* was most apparent in their deployment of the base-superstructure metaphor. Thompson insisted that this was a 'bad and dangerous model, since Stalin used it not as an image of men changing in society, but as a mechanical model, operating semi-automatically and independently of human agency'.[12] It was thus against the background of Stalin's crude economic determinism that Thompson stressed the vital role of human agency in history.

Two decades later, he extended his analysis of the concrete mediation between social being and social consciousness through the concept of human 'experience'. Experience, he argued, 'arises spontaneously within social being' and acts to exert 'pressure' which sets 'limits' to consciousness.[13] Though powerfully deployed by Thompson in his historical writings, the theoretical weaknesses of this concept have been forcefully drawn out by Perry Anderson. Anderson suggests that Thompson's conception of 'experience' elided at least two distinct denotations of this term: one of which situated it squarely within consciousness, while the other placed it in a mediating role between being and consciousness. This ambiguity reflected ordinary usage, in which 'experience' refers both to the lived occurrence and to 'a subsequent process of learning from such occurrences'. Anderson insists that this elision meant that Thompson too-swiftly skirted over the problematic ways in which experiences are interpreted.[14]

A similar argument marked the point of departure for Gareth Stedman Jones's influential break with Marxism.[15] He effectively criticises Thompson and Thompsonian Marxists for their refusal to extend Thompson's criticisms of Marx's base-superstructure metaphor to a more general repudiation of materialism. Stedman

---

10. Althusser 1976, p. 83; Thompson 1978b, p. 79.
11. Thompson 1957, pp. 106–8.
12. Thompson 1957, p. 113.
13. Thompson 1978b, pp. 7–9.
14. Anderson 1980, pp. 25–9.
15. Dworkin 2007, p. 107.

Jones argues that, despite Thompson's deployment of the concepts of experience and culture in *The Making of the English Working Class*, he was unable to extricate himself from the materialist errors of Marxism because he failed to recognise that, far from mediating between consciousness and some underlying reality, these concepts were themselves inherently linguistic: 'experiences' were interpreted through language, which could not be reduced to a superstructural reflection of economic relations.[16]

If the thrust of Stedman Jones's argument broadly coheres with the general implications of the linguistic turn and the more specific claims of NSM theory, it is interesting to note that none of the Marxists who challenged the substantive reinterpretation of Chartism that followed Stedman Jones's methodological critique of Thompsonian Marxism denied what is, in many ways, a defining characteristic of NSM theory: the importance of language to the production of solidarities and conflicts within the 'cultural realm'.

What these Marxists did challenge was Stedman Jones's 'particular version of linguistic analysis'.[17] Thus Neville Kirk, for instance, insisted that by 'effectively dissolv[ing] reality back into language' Stedman Jones precluded 'any real engagement between language, politics and the "social"'.[18] Developing a similar point, Raphael Samuel insisted, 'the historical record cannot be read only as a system of signs', for historians must look beyond language if they are to measure 'words against deeds'.[19] More substantively, Dorothy Thompson argued that she found it 'difficult to believe that anyone who has worked in the archives and has studied the published and unpublished language of the Chartists can fail to see that the idea that above all united them into a nation-wide movement was the belief that there was a profound unity of interest between working people of all kinds'.[20] Likewise, John Saville found that he could make sense of Chartism only by going beyond interpretations that focused on its formally moderate political demands. Saville argued that it was precisely because the demands for the People's Charter were rooted in an underlying class struggle at the point of production that Chartism was able not only to win a mass working-class base, but also generated such a popular and reactionary middle-class response.[21]

More generally, Marc Steinberg convincingly argues that Stedman Jones and other similar critics of Thompson deployed a reified methodology that blinded them to the reality of class struggle. Put simply, Steinberg suggests that these critics

---

16. Stedman Jones 1983, pp. 6–8, 12.
17. Eley and Nield 2007, p. 101.
18. Kirk 1997, p. 333; 1996; Foster 1985; Callinicos 2004, pp. 143ff.
19. Samuel 1992, pp. 245–6.
20. D. Thompson 1993, p. 36.
21. Saville 1987, pp. 224–7.

of Thompson worked with caricatured conception of class consciousness – as a distinct discourse within society – that acted to obscure real languages of class. Class consciousness, he insists, is best understood not as a fully fledged discourse in and of itself, but rather emerges 'through the friction of discourses produced in struggle'.[22]

By relating language to social relations without mechanical reductionism, these British Marxist historians and others writing in their wake suggested a conception of language that was very different to the caricatured interpretation of Marxism drawn from Stalin and commonly encountered in NSM literature. This is evident in Christopher Hill's criticism of John Pocock's claim that 'men cannot do what they have no means of saying they have done'. Hill argues that this claim involves a profound misunderstanding of the historical record. Indeed, the truth is that 'things precede words ... new words were needed because new things happened'.[23] Concretely, Hill discusses how the meaning of the word 'revolution' changed in seventeenth-century England. He suggests that seventeenth-century thinkers picked up an old term with a technical meaning, revolving, and imbued it with a new political connotation: 'men groped for new words to describe what they were experiencing'.[24]

According to Hill, to adequately understand seventeenth-century politics, the historian must analyse language and changing social practice in their dynamic inter-relationship; for to analyse only one side of this process would be to commit the sin of reductionism. Interestingly, a similar point was made by Thompson in a reply to critics of his essay 'The Moral Economy of the Crowd'. He suggested that those critics of his work influenced by the linguistic turn tended to mirror rather than overcome the weaknesses of opposite criticisms made by more traditional, economistic, social historians. Whereas the latter tended to a reductive materialism, the former merely inverted this position in a tendency to an 'imperialistic' reduction of the cultural to the linguistic.[25]

Though Thompson's negative criticisms of linguistic and economistic reductionism hit their mark, his own more positive *theoretical* attempt to navigate a course between the Scylla of crude materialism and the Charybdis of linguistic idealism was, as I suggested in my discussion of the concept of experience, somewhat less successful. To escape these twin errors demanded, at the very least, a stronger conceptualisation of experience. Something along these lines has been separately suggested by Chris Harman and Marc Steinberg.

---

22. Steinberg 1999b, p. 230.
23. Hill 1990, pp. 97–8.
24. Hill 1990, p. 100.
25. Thompson 1991, pp. 262, 273–5.

In a Gramscian development of the exchange between Thompson and Anderson, Harman argues that 'when people are engaged in material practice they have an immediate awareness of their action and of the part of the world it impinges on which is unlikely to be false'. Nevertheless, alongside this understanding of their immediate position, there tends to be 'a more general consciousness', which, because it is less constrained by immediate practice, is more open to false interpretation.[26] If this situation, which seems to be an intrinsic potential of social life, opens up the possibility of a gap or even a contradiction between general and specific aspects of consciousness, Harman suggests that in societies characterised by class divisions, there is a material basis for false generalisations: ruling groups have a stake in portraying their narrow concerns as the general interest. Nonetheless, any attempt systematically to distort consciousness in this direction will tend to come into conflict with the immediate experiences of many outside the ruling group.

This tension between the consciousness of these experiences and the more general world-views of the ruling groups can perhaps be understood in terms of Bakhtin's distinction between primary (simple) and secondary (more complex) speech-genres. According to Bakhtin, primary speech genres have an 'immediate relation to actual reality and to the real utterances of others', while more complex (secondary) speech genres emerge out of these utterances. Concretely, he suggests that the gap between primary and secondary speech-genres could be understood as a tension between unmediated communication and mediated 'ideology', and this tension opens the door to struggles over the interpretation of experience. Language, from this perspective, far from being a mere superstructural reflection of reality, becomes the medium through which conflicts over meaning are fought.[27]

According to Steinberg, conflicts of this type will tend to be most marked in periods of struggle. He suggests that 'Thompson's focus on experience directs analysis to the dynamics of struggle within concrete communities'.[28] Moreover, he insists that it is an easy enough process to reinterpret Thompson's insights in terms of a sophisticated, Bakhtinian, model of language that escapes the idealism characteristic of poststructuralist variants of the linguistic turn. From this perspective, linguistic contestation is best understood as operating within a language-genre, rather than between distinct discourses. Moreover, because Bakhtin and Vološinov highlight the inseparability of the discursive and the

---

26. Harman 1998b, p. 35.
27. Bakhtin 1986, p. 62; 1985, p. 7.
28. Steinberg 1999b, p. 5.

material, this process of contestation highlights deeper class relations that are not readily perceptible on a superficial analysis.[29]

Though Steinberg interprets his conception of language in opposition to Marx's base-superstructure metaphor, Harman situates competing interpretations of experience in relation to this metaphor through the claim that competing generalisations have roots in class divisions.[30] His argument is influenced by Gramsci's comments on contradictory consciousness. According to Gramsci 'the active man of the masses works practically, but he does not have a clear, theoretical consciousness of his actions, which is also a knowledge of the world insofar as he changes it'. It is this general consciousness that can 'bind him to a certain social group, influence his moral behaviour and the direction of his will in a more or less powerful way'.[31] This model is suggestive of a non-reductive relationship between social being and consciousness through experience, in which class conflicts are fought, in part, as conflicts over meaning within language.

Whatever the limitations of Thompson's model of experience, something like this conception of the mediating role of experience and the contested nature of language (especially in struggle) has been a commonplace within the historical work of the British Marxist historians. Indeed, little else can explain the powerful fruits of their focus on language and ideas. Typical, in this respect, is the method suggested by Victor Kiernan in one of his studies on Shakespeare. He argues that an adequate understanding of the emergence and reception of literary and cultural works must begin by placing them within broader material relations: cultural analyses must proceed from an examination of society's 'fundamental basis' in 'the way in which mankind earns its livelihood' because 'ideas can only take effect after men and women have been prepared by experience to open their minds'.[32] That other British Marxist historians took special note of the active role of ideas in history is clear from George Rudé's comments on his and Eric Hobsbawm's analysis of the Captain Swing Revolt of 1830. He suggests that they (and, he adds, Christopher Hill), 'have been concerned with the ideology of the common people' and, in particular, with the way in which ideas might, as Marx claimed, 'grip the masses'.[33] Interestingly, Rudé suggests that the Captain Swing social movement, alongside a number of other such movements, helped bring to the surface an 'underlying sense of "justice"' and played a part in constituting a tradition of struggles for justice within the British and international labour movements.[34] Hobsbawm recognises a similarly general craving for

---

29. Steinberg 1996, pp. 207–8.
30. Harman 1998b, p. 37.
31. Gramsci quoted in Harman 1998b, pp. 45–6.
32. Kiernan 1996, pp. 4, 14.
33. Rudé 1983, p. 53.
34. Rudé 1983, p. 54.

justice within peasant societies, through his analysis of the myth of social banditry. Whether or not actual social bandits lived up to the ideals ascribed to
Robin Hood, the fact that peasants chose to believe they did is indicative, Hobsbawm claims, of a universal desire for justice.[35]

This is not to suggest that the British Marxist historians were wont to reduce
concrete movements into false universals. Rather, as Rodney Hilton points out
in his discussion of medieval peasant revolts, while freedom might be a universal
demand of movements from below, its concrete form 'acquired significance only
in specific contexts'.[36] Indeed, it was precisely to capture the specific concrete
content of individual social movements that Hilton argues against reductionism
and for 'reclaim[ing] historical materialism for the historian'.[37]

Despite the potentially academic (in the worse sense of the word) implications of this demand, the British Marxist historians resisted the pull towards
narrow specialisation that might be inferred from such a claim. One reason
for this, as Hobsbawm notes, follows from the structure of Marx's concept of
class. Because this is a relational concept, it informs a methodology that leads
from Hill's 'worm's eye view' towards analyses of society as a totality.[38] Far from
reducing myriad forms of oppression to aspects of class exploitation, the great
strength of this method is that by illuminating the sociological totality, it is able
to inform a strategy that relates these various movements to a broader struggle
for freedom against alienation. Moreover, as Terry Eagleton suggests, though it
would be a mistake to conflate Marx's base-superstructure metaphor with his
claim that being determines consciousness, 'since what has been historically
preponderant in "social being" has in fact been exploitative economic production, it is plausible to believe that it is this which must have been the most significant influence on human consciousness'.[39] There is, of course, a large gap
between the claim that exploitative relations are the essence of the social totality
and attempts to mechanically reduce non-economic relations to this essence.
Indeed, it is for this reason that Marx's base-superstructure metaphor is not, as
Thompson would have it, irredeemably reductionist. Rather, as Hobsbawm and
similarly Miller argue, though it could be applied mechanically, it need not be,
and certainly was not applied in such a way by Marx and his 'most insightful
followers'.[40]

Interestingly, it is not difficult to integrate Thompson's approach to the
study of social movements into Marx's base-superstructure model, once we

---

35. Hobsbawm 2001, p. 61.
36. Hilton 1973, p. 73; 1976, p. 174ff.
37. Hilton 1990, p. 10.
38. Hobsbawm 1997, p. 87.
39. Eagleton 1989, p. 173.
40. Hobsbawm 1997, pp. 145–6; Miller 1984, p. 271.

look beyond caricatured readings of the latter. In this respect, Bryan Palmer's claim that 'Thompson's force as an historian' derives, in part, from 'his grasp of a Vološinovian sense of the multi-accentuality of language',[41] is suggestive of an alternative to the approach that too easily reduces the British Marxist historians to an attempt to 'transcend the base-superstructure model'.[42]

According to Vološinov, because Saussure, in his fundamental work on language, prioritised the study of *langue* over *parole*, he tended to reify language by effectively ridding it of its human content.[43] As against this method, Vološinov wrote that signs are not simply arbitrary elements of a linguistic structure, but rather are sites 'of a process of signification', and signification itself 'emerges in the course of social interaction'. As Sayers comments: 'we make reference through the play of differences among signs, but equally the development of such networks of signs depends on reference (including references to other discourses) and practical involvement in the world'.[44] Consequently, signs can be 'multi-accentuated': different people can use them in a variety of context dependent ways.[45] Lecercle points out that because Vološinov insists that signs cannot adequately be understood except in relation to their use by concrete actors in concrete contexts, he securely roots language within society's material base. Moreover, he avoided the trap, suggested by Stedman Jones, of believing that language unproblematically refers back to some anterior reality. Rather, Vološinov insisted that social being is 'refracted', not 'reflected', within language, while deploying the concept of refraction in a way that underpinned the idea of the relative autonomy of politics without losing sense of its materiality.[46] Indeed, he provided a positive counter to Laclau and Mouffe's famous claim that the use of the base-superstructure metaphor within the classical-Marxist tradition 'prevented any conception of the autonomy of the political',[47] through his suggestion that language is best understood via a sophisticated rendering of just this metaphor: words are the 'transitional link between the socio-political order and ideology in the narrow sense'. He argued:

> Every sign ... is a construct between socially organised persons in the process of their interaction. Therefore, the forms of signs are conditioned above all by the social organisation of the participants involved and also by the immediate conditions of their interaction. When these forms change, so does sign. And it should be one of the tasks of the study of ideologies to trace this social life

---

41. Palmer 1990, p. 69; Steinberg 1996; 1999b; Passmore 2003, p. 137.
42. Kaye 1995, p. 221.
43. McNally 2001a, p. 111.
44. Sayers 2000, p. 38.
45. Lecercle 2006, pp. 106–7.
46. Lecercle 2006, pp. 109–10; Bennett 1979, p. 81; Brandist 2002, p. 76.
47. Laclau and Mouffe 1985, p. 31.

of the verbal sign. Only so approached can the problem of the relationship between sign and existence find its concrete expression; only then will the process of the causal shaping of the sign by existence stand out as a process of genuine existence-to-sign transit, of genuine refraction of existence in the sign.[48]

As against Saussure's one-sided prioritisation of *langue* over *parole*, Vološinov emphasised the importance of living speech to the study of language, whilst aiming to avoid the subjectivist inversion of Saussure's 'abstract objectivism'.[49] He argued that 'words are always filled with content and meaning drawn from behaviour or ideology'; or, more simply, 'the utterance is a social phenomenon'.[50] In consequence, whereas Saussure's approach lent itself to abstract formalism, since it divorced the study of language from its concrete expression in dialogue, Vološinov's focus on speech as a concrete activity allowed him to conceptualise language in all its richness, as a part of social being. In this respect, as McNally argues, 'the importance of the base-superstructure metaphor' for Vološinov 'resides in its insistence that ideological conflicts are significantly determined by the practical activities of people organised in a mode of production, social-productive relations and class struggles'. Moreover, because Vološinov rejected the reified caricature of Marx's concepts, he understood society's economic base not as a thing, but as a unified collection of more or less antagonistic human practices.[51] It is in the context of these conflictual practices that the meanings of words are generated and fought over.

From a similar perspective, Terry Eagleton argues that the base-superstructure metaphor is best understood not as a model of the reflection of real practices in unreal ideas, but rather as an articulation of the way in which language refracts social relations in consciousness. Language *per se* is not superstructural; rather, '[a]n institution or practice is "superstructural" when, and only when, it acts in some way as a support to the exploitative or oppressive nature of social relations'.[52] From this perspective, Bakhtinian secondary speech-genres become superstructural when and only when they act to fix the base by legitimising existing social relations. By illuminating the way that language relates to underlying relations, this approach has the merit of underpinning the possibility of *Ideologiekritik*: the project of distinguishing between the way 'society presents itself in the discourse that seeks to legitimise it and its real structures constituted by

48. Vološinov 1973, pp. 19, 21.
49. McNally 2001a, p. 112.
50. Vološinov 1973, pp. 70, 82.
51. McNally 2001a, p. 113.
52. Eagleton 1989, p. 174.

exploitation and class antagonism'.[53] By suggesting that there is nothing outside the text, poststructuralist theories of language and, similarly, aspects of NSM theory, undermine any attempt to examine the essence beneath appearance. This approach lends itself to the reproduction of the superficial, descriptive, method of analysis characteristic of traditional history.[54] Conversely, the claim that Marxism involves a reductive conception of politics is best understood as a caricatured misunderstanding of the attempt to ensure that politics is materially grounded.

Politics

Although NSM theory rejected Marx's supposed economic determinism or structural functionalism, in favour of a culturalist conception of politics in which politics is conceived as a process of making and remaking solidarities and alliances between culturally constituted groups, this standpoint paralleled, though in a less materialist register, certain formulations of the method of leading figures amongst the British Marxist historians. For instance, Eric Hobsbawm writes of the parallels between the work of the British Marxist historians and Gramsci's sophisticated interpretation of Marxism.[55] This parallel between Gramsci's thought and the work of the British Marxist historians has been highlighted on numerous occasions.[56] Harvey Kaye, for instance, suggests that insofar as Gramsci's ideas were developed by the British Marxist historians, they are best understood in terms of Marx's critique of abstractly moralistic approaches to politics. Because Gramsci, like Marx before him, conceived the ideals of the socialist movement in terms of social practices rooted within social relations, he conceived socialism, in the words of the American Marxist historian David Montgomery, as growing 'from the work and living patterns of working people'.[57]

Though formulations such as this can be read in a mechanically materialistic fashion, they need not be, and insofar as the British Marxist historians analysed social movements along these lines they certainly were not conceptualised in such a way. Rather, as Hobsbawm writes, Marxism is 'not just about "what history shows us will happen", but also about "what must be done"'.[58] Amongst the British Marxist historians, perhaps the most sophisticated attempt to deploy a non-reductionist reading of the base-superstructure metaphor is to be found in

53. Jarvis 1998, p. 67; Callinicos 2006, p. 70.
54. Jarvis 1998, p. 67.
55. Hobsbawm 2011, pp. 321, 341.
56. Kaye 1995, p. 245.
57. Kaye 1995, p. 246.
58. Hobsbawm 1998, p. 28.

Geoffrey de Ste. Croix's *The Class Struggle in the Ancient Greek World*. At one level, the subject matter of this magnificent book is far removed from the world of new social movements. Nevertheless, De Ste. Croix's work is interesting both for his magisterial articulation and defence of Marx's conception of class struggle, and for his critical engagement with the work of other better-known British Marxist historians. De Ste. Croix's book combines fulsome praise for the work of Rudé, Hobsbawm, Hill, Thompson and Hilton with criticisms of their tendency to conflate class with class consciousness, which, he argues, opened their work up to criticisms from the standpoint of the linguistic turn. Commenting, for instance, on claims made by Thompson and Hobsbawm that, in Hobsbawm's words, 'class and class consciousness are inseparable', De Ste. Croix argues that this position involves a one-sided misreading of Marx's method. For De Ste. Croix, the key to Marx's success as a social theorist lay in his recognition that exploitation is the key hallmark of class, and that this is an objective social relationship underpinning the emergence of class '"struggles", "conflicts", "antagonisms", "oppositions" or "tensions"'.[59] De Ste. Croix suggests that while the British Marxist historians wrote of class and class-conflicts in terms that implicitly recognise the prior existence of contradictory social relations before people become conscious of these relations, there was a tendency amongst them, especially marked in Thompson's theoretical writings, to deny this, or to so mediate it as make it analytically worthless.

The great strength of De Ste. Croix's view, by contrast, as Scott Meikle insists, is that by grasping the 'essence' of any mode of production to consist, in Marx's words, in 'the specific economic form in which unpaid labour is pumped out of the direct producers', he was able to 'illuminate the historical process' in a way that escapes the limitations of the crass empiricism into which so much historical writing falls.[60]

Unfortunately, the strengths of this method are lost on those modern writers who equate essentialism with reductionism. And, to the extent that Marx's method was caricatured first by Kautsky and then by Stalin, it is understandable that it has been thus rejected. Nonetheless, as De Ste. Croix insists, Marx's method does not 'in any way exclude an understanding of the role of ideas, which (as Marx well knew) can often become autonomous and acquire a life of their own'. Marx's key innovation is not to reduce everything to economics or class, but to grasp the determining role of 'the social relations into which men enter in the course of the productive process'.[61] Rather than reject this method in a knee-jerk fashion, it is better to ask what exactly Marx meant by determination.

59. De Ste. Croix 1981, pp. 50, 57, 62–3.
60. Meikle 1983, p. 150.
61. De Ste. Croix 1981, p. 26.

272 • Paul Blackledge

On this issue, it is instructive to return to the exchange on method opened by Thompson's 'Socialist Humanism'. Alastair MacIntyre, in a contribution to this debate which Thompson described as being 'of the first importance...to the historian',[62] articulates a sophisticated reworking of the base-superstructure metaphor that escapes the common criticism that it involved a mechanically causal relationship from the economy to politics. In 'Notes from the Moral Wilderness', MacIntyre argues that Stalin's insistence that history's general course was predictable rested on a misconception of the role of the base-superstructure metaphor in Marxist theory. What Marx suggested, when he deployed this metaphor, was not a mechanically causal relationship. Rather, he is best understood through Hegelian lenses, as pointing to a process in which society's economic base provides 'a framework within which superstructures arise, a set of relations around which the human relations can entwine themselves, a kernel of human relationships from which all else grows'. From this perspective, MacIntyre argues that creating the base and superstructure 'are not two activities but one'. Stalin's account of historical progress noted above could not be further from Marx's model.[63] As to the place of language in this model, MacIntyre argues that 'to understand a concept, to grasp the meaning of the words which express it, is always...to grasp the role of the concept in language and social life...Different forms of social life will provide different roles for concepts to play'.[64] If these arguments read very much like a text written under the influence of the linguistic turn, the fact that MacIntyre considered himself a Marxist when he wrote them should remind us that Marxists were taking the problem of language seriously long before the implosion of Althusserianism.

From a broadly similar perspective, Hobsbawm argues that Marxism is best understood as positing a layered conception of reality, in which purposeful human agency is framed by, but not mechanically reducible to, 'social relations of production'.[65] If the proof of the pudding is in the eating, evidence of the power of this general approach is in the quality of the writing of Marxist historians generally and the British Marxist historians more specifically.

It is clear, for instance, that Hobsbawm places purposeful human agency at the core of his understanding of Marxism. Thus, in *Captain Swing*, he and Rudé wrote not merely of the causes of the movement, but also of the 'reasons' informing the decisions made by craftsmen to join the labourers' cause.[66] Kaye similarly comments on Rudé's *Wilkes and Liberty*, that whilst Rudé 'grants that there

---

62. Thompson 1978b, p. 401.
63. MacIntyre 2008, p. 55.
64. MacIntyre 1967, pp. 2, 8.
65. Hobsbawm 1997, p. 152.
66. Hobsbawm and Rudé 1969, p. 246.

was a significant relationship between the "material" motivation of the "inferior sort"...and the Wilkite movements...he says the former does not sufficiently explain the latter'.[67] Analyses such as these point to the truth of the distinction, too-often lost in the literature on NSMs, between what Hobsbawm calls 'Marxist' and 'vulgar-Marxist' approaches to the study of history.[68]

More generally, although Hobsbawm shows that the actions of particular individuals could adequately be understood only through a detailed reconstruction of their intentions and desires, he argues that patterns could be discerned from these actions that illuminated the broader social context experienced by these actors. Thus, for instance, in his classic study of social bandits, alongside a discussion of the 'strength, bravery, cunning and determination' of bandits, he shows how these characteristics came to the fore in the context of poverty and injustice: banditry was 'a cry of lost people against a cruel and atomised society'.[69] And, perhaps just as significantly, these stories continue to resonate in the modern world, particularly amongst poorer groups, because 'everyone has personal experience of being unjustly treated by individuals and institutions, and the poor, weak and helpless have it a lot of the time'.[70] Hobsbawm thus tacitly posits a non-mechanical but no less real link between experience and consciousness.

Extending a similar perspective in his *Liberty against the Law*, Christopher Hill illuminates the historically contested nature of the concept of freedom over the period of transition to modernity in the seventeenth century. By asking of the English ideology of freedom, 'liberty for whom?', Hill engages with literature on a wide variety of movements and ideas to explore conflicts over the meaning of freedom.[71] Like Hobsbawm, he uses the example of the continued resonance of the Robin Hood myth over the period when we saw monarchical power give way to the 'rule of law' to illuminate the continuing class biases of the modern system – biases that were illuminated both by numerous social movements for freedom and by the way that some forms of criminality were celebrated within popular culture. Thus, through examinations of pirates, highwaymen, gypsies, and such like, Hill deconstructs the self-image of capitalism as the realisation of freedom to illuminate its real essence as a system of unfreedoms and injustices supported by the rule of law.

If Hill traces contestations over the meaning of freedom through the seventeenth century, Peter Linebaugh develops similar themes in his magisterial analysis of the use of the death penalty as a means of social control over London's

---

67. Kaye 1988, p. 21.
68. Hobsbawm 1997, p. 145.
69. Hobsbawm 2001, pp. 95, 192.
70. Hobsbawm 2001, p. 189.
71. Hill 1996, p. 19.

poor in the eighteenth century. Linebaugh shows that the hanged 'belonged to the poor' and that not only did novel, capitalist, forms of exploitation cause or modify 'forms of criminal activity' but also that these forms of criminality 'caused major changes in capitalism'.[72] Through this dialectical approach to the study of crime and punishment, and, in particular, to the developing forms of social conflict at Tyburn, Linebaugh is able to show how over the eighteenth century, public executions increasingly lost their ability to 'awe and terrorize the London multitude'.[73] If individual agents created this change, it was, nonetheless, made against the backdrop of 'a transition period of class relations, during which older forms of conflict were replaced by new ones'.[74] This approach to understanding change over the eighteenth century effectively extends Thompson's critique of mechanical materialism, without embracing the new idealism of Thompson's post-Marxist critics. Linebaugh conceives the relationship between class and consciousness in a manner alive to the fact that relations of production were in a process of change throughout this period. His successful attempt to relate class and consciousness is thus realised without committing the vulgar error of assuming a simple model of class consciousness 'waxing or waning' in relationship to a 'fixed' conception of class structure.[75]

Linebaugh develops this argument further in a work co-written with Marcus Rediker. In their history of the social conflicts in the Atlantic economy in the late seventeenth and early eighteenth centuries, *The Many-Headed Hydra*, they argue that the ships at the core of this economy 'became both an engine of capitalism in the wake of the bourgeois revolution in England and a setting of resistance'.[76] While Rediker, in his magnificent extension of this argument *The Slave Ship*, situates the social movements of slaves against the backdrop of 'common experiences of expropriation and enslavement', he refuses to reduce the former to the latter. And, because the social movements of slaves involve purposeful action, this means that the outcomes of these movements were open-ended.[77]

Conclusion

Whereas NSM theorists have welcomed the shift from old to new social movements as a move from instrumental, statist to ethical, anti-statist politics,[78] Eric Hobsbawm famously criticised the ineffectiveness of 'primitive' anti-statist

72. Linebaugh 1991, p. xxi.
73. Linebaugh 1991, p. 280.
74. Linebaugh 1991, p. 286.
75. Thompson, quoted in Dworkin 2007, p. 52.
76. Linebaugh and Rediker 2000, p. 144.
77. Rediker 2007, pp. 284, 292, 298.
78. Cohen 1985; Bookchin 1989.

(anarchistic) direct action movements by contrast with more effective statist forms of socialism.[79] Unfortunately, social democracy and Stalinism proved to be infinitely less effective than Hobsbawm imagined. And this ineffectiveness opens the door to new forms of direct action. As Victor Kiernan argues, though direct action has always existed as a practice, as a principle 'it could only emerge in a society long familiar with other, more 'constitutional' methods, and as an expression of dissatisfaction with them'.[80] In part, at least, this is precisely the turn taken by social movements in the 1970s and 1980s.

Unfortunately, NSM theory has tended to reify this shift as a profound historical break. If this approach is the flipside to Hobsbawm's earlier and somewhat teleological account of the move away from primitive rebellion, elsewhere the work of the British Marxist historians tends to support Calhoun's contention regarding the continuity between older and newer social movements. Moreover, by contextualising various distinct social movements against the backdrop of capitalist relations of production without reducing them to these relations, the British Marxist historians and other similar writers were able to provide a rich account of these movements that informed a strategic orientation: related by their varied struggles against diverse aspects of alienation, these movements could potentially be drawn together as parts of a broader socialist movement against alienation.

If Stalin's economic determinism was blind to the rich variety of these movements, NSM theory tends towards the opposite error of recognising no common material interest across them. At their best, by contrast, the British Marxist historians point to a method by which we might overcome the limitations of both of these approaches through a model of language and culture that is alive to the specificity of distinct movements while relating these movements to overarching relations that mediate against reifying the differences between them. Whatever weaknesses there are with the work of the British Marxist historians, because they point beyond differences between various movements without dissolving these differences their work retains its relevance to anti-capitalists aiming at building alliances that are rooted in a deep, shared interest in overcoming capitalism.

79. Hobsbawm 1971, p. vii; 1973, p. 83.
80. Kiernan 1989, p. 18.

Right-Wing Social Movements: The Political Indeterminacy of Mass Mobilisation
Neil Davidson

1

When the term 'social movement' re-entered wide-spread use during the 1970s, it was generally in connection with what were termed the 'new social movements' – those attempts to end various forms of oppression or to achieve other goals not specific to a single social group, such as banning nuclear weapons or defending the environment. Some of these, the most important of which was the movement for black Civil Rights in the United States, had actually emerged as early as the 1940s, but most were products of the following two decades. Nevertheless, the adjective 'new' was always something of a misnomer: any surviving Suffragettes would have been surprised to learn that the women's liberation movement had begun in the 1960s. In practice, however, the supposed novelty of these movements was not based on the historical absence of mobilisation over these issues, but on three contemporary characteristics distinguishing them from their predecessors. First, these new formations were not based on the working class or its organisations and tended, instead, to be led by individuals from the middle classes – specifically from the new middle-class – although they all had working-class members and often sought trade-union affiliations.[1] Second, they distinguished between their methods of organisation and those of both the trade-union movement and the

---

1. Byrne 1997, pp. 18–19, 64–74.

political Left, which 'new movement' figures accused of being hierarchical and authoritarian.[2] Third, insofar as they recognised predecessors, their methods of campaigning had shifted from an earlier emphasis on lobbying to one on direct action.[3]

In retrospect, it can be seen that by the time the various movements were classified as 'new', a shift from resisting oppression to merely asserting identity was underway as part of the general retreat of the Left from the mid-1970s in the face of the neoliberal ascendancy: the shortening of 'women's liberation movement' to 'women's movement' had more significance than the dropping of one word might suggest.

Although social movements are one of those phenomena that are easier to identify than to define, some generalisations about their nature are possible. Social movements tend to be broader than a specific campaign. Thus, campaigns for equal pay or the legalisation of abortion were components of the women's liberation movement, but did not in themselves constitute distinct social movements. In the British context, a handful of campaigns have some of the quality of social movements because of their deep and lasting impact on public life, above all those associated with the Campaign for Nuclear Disarmament, the Vietnam Solidarity Campaign, the Anti-Nazi League, the Anti-Poll Tax Federation and the Stop the War Coalition. At the same time, social movements tend to be more diffuse than political parties – partly because of the relative permanence of 'political' as opposed to 'movement' organisation, and partly because political parties have to take positions on the entire range of issues that concern their supporters. A social movement concerned with, say, opposing racism need not have a position on global warming – indeed, it would not survive very long if it insisted that its members adhere to one – while a party can scarcely avoid doing so. In practice, social movements can involve a range of different parties, in the way that 'the socialist movement' in Britain before the First World War included, among others, the British Socialist Party, the Independent Labour Party, the Socialist Labour Party and the Socialist Party of Great Britain.

However, if there is one dominant assumption concerning the politics of social movements, it is that expressed by Byrne: 'Social movement supporters are clearly located on the left of the political spectrum'.[4] Indeed, it is not unusual for the terms 'popular movement' and 'social movement' to be treated as virtually synonymous. Since the majority of people, by definition, do not belong to the ruling class, social movements will tend to be composed of members of the oppressed groups and exploited classes that do constitute that majority, and

2. Wainwright 1979, pp. 6–18.
3. Aronowitz 2003, pp. 147–8.
4. Byrne 1997, p. 74.

they will also tend to be directed towards goals which are in the interest of these groups and classes.

We cannot, however, equate all social movements with what the Stalinist tradition used to call 'progressive' politics. Attempts to do so depend rely either on a self-confirming definition by which only left-wing movements are designated as social, or on the indefensible assumption that popular movements cannot be oppressive or act against their own long-term interests. The historical record does not support such definitions or assumptions. The new social movements have both 'right'- as well as 'left'-wing predecessors. Consideration of these earlier examples may help us to understand, in general terms, why the former types are also possible today.

2

During the Napoleonic Wars, the French occupying armies attempted to impose bourgeois revolution 'from above and outside' on the absolutist régimes of Western and Southern Europe, in alliance with local liberals. Yet in at least two important cases, those of Spain and Naples, the republics established by Napoleon were resisted, not merely by representatives of the feudal ruling class, using conscripts and mercenaries, but by popular uprisings dedicated to restoring Church and King, often operating completely outwith the command or control of the élites. It is meaningless to describe these revolts as nationalist in inspiration, since the kingdoms of Spain and Naples which the insurgents sought to defend were, in their different ways, the antithesis of modern nation states. Indeed, in both cases, modern nation states were precisely what the hated liberals were attempting to construct. Yet the mass of the population, who might have benefited from the overthrow of feudalism, were isolated from the liberals by the latter's bourgeois status and relative wealth – 'a liberal is a man in a carriage', as the Spanish saying went. The liberals heightened their social distance from the masses by relying on a foreign power and by offering no positive reforms to the peasantry. Presented with a mere change in the mechanism of exploitation, but one which would, nevertheless, destroy the only aspects of society that offered stability and consolation, the masses rejected the new order arms-in-hand.[5]

In Spain, the deep contradictions within a popular resistance dedicated to restoring one of the most reactionary régimes in Europe were captured by Goya in *The Disasters of War*, expressing both his awareness of the tragedy and his ambivalence towards the forces involved. Yet if the meaning of the movement was ambiguous, the outcome – the restoration of Church and King – was not in

---

5. Torras 1977, pp. 74, 75.

doubt.[6] Naples, where the French-established Republic failed to abolish feudal relations on the land but, instead, raised taxes on the peasants and urban poor, was retaken by Calabrian forces and the British, involving a slaughter lasting for two weeks in which Republicans were massacred by the urban poor and the lumpen proletariat.[7]

The Spanish peasants and Neapolitan urban masses, facing a choice of two evils, actively embraced the one that was familiar to them and, at least, preserved their existing life world. Nevertheless, these struggles, the Spanish in particular, involved self-sacrifice and collective organisation linked to overt forms of class-hostility, albeit one focused almost entirely on the external foreign enemy and its internal supporters, who were seen as both betraying the kingdom and seeking to impose new forms of exploitation. The liberal revolutionaries could offer the masses nothing, and the resulting absence of popular opposition to the old régimes was one reason why bourgeois revolutions in both Spain and what would eventually become Italy were delayed for so long after these initial top-down attempts.

There were other circumstances, too, where a combination of independent small producers and workers could be mobilised for entirely reactionary ends. Unlike the Spanish or Neapolitan events, the American Civil War was a successful bourgeois revolution, in that it removed from the Federal capitalist republic the threat posed by an expansionist Confederate slave society. The Northern triumph was made possible by the abolition of slavery, but the victors' attempts to democratise the South, above all by supporting the black population's claims to political equality, were inconsistent and uneven. They ceased entirely in 1877, when Federal troops were withdrawn from the former Confederate states. Long before that point – indeed, almost from the end of the Civil War – the former slaveowners had unleashed a movement to impose new forms of labour discipline and social control over the now-free blacks, above all through the Ku Klux Klan. This was, certainly, initiated and led by members of the Southern élite, rather than reflecting a spontaneous movement from below of poor whites.[8] The former Southern slaveowners were scarcely numerous enough to carry out the levels of repression exercised against the black population after 1865, and had, therefore, to rely on support from white yeoman-farmers and the petty bourgeoisie. Why did these two groups align themselves with their ruling class?

The majority of Southerners had not been slaveowners and there were major class differences between them and the yeoman farmers, who, nevertheless, aspired to the position of the former.[9] The problem for the ruling class was not

---

6. Fraser 2008, p. 480.
7. Duggan 2007, pp. 121, 123.
8. Foner 1990, pp. 186–7.
9. Fox-Genovese and Genovese 1983, p. 263.

so much with the yeomen, however, as with the whites below them in the social structure, those who did not own slaves and who had little or no chance of ever owning them. It was in order to prevent the emergence of solidarity between this group and black slaves that the condition of racialised slavery had to be absolute.[10] The decisive issue was whether, once slavery had been abolished, the former slaves could form an alliance with the majority of non-ruling class whites, with both groups then allying with the organised working class in the North. Obviously, the Southern ruling class did everything they could to prevent such an outcome and were largely successful in doing so. The question is whether this was preordained by the strength of a racism that was impossible to dislodge in the decade following Lee's surrender, or whether a different strategy – either on the part of the Radical Republicans or through the intervention of the Northern trade-union movement – could have overcome it.

In the event, the actual outcome after 1877 was a social structure in which, across large areas of the South, the petty bourgeoisie and white workers were complicit in an institutionalised régime of terror against the black population, which led, between 1890 and 1930, to three thousand black Americans being tortured and killed, often as part of a public spectacle.[11] Yet none of this actually improved the conditions of the white population in the South below the level of ruling plantocracy and the social layers immediately surrounding it. A careful paper by Szymanski published a hundred years after the end of Reconstruction showed that 'the more intense racial discrimination is, the lower are white earnings *because* of the effect of the intermediate variable of working class solidarity' and concluded: 'No matter how measured, whites do not benefit economically by economic discrimination [against non-whites]'.[12] Why, then, did they not ally with the blacks?

In his pioneering study of reconstruction, Du Bois demonstrated how structural racism prevented poor whites from uniting with blacks to the benefit of their rulers by providing them with 'psychic compensation' for their own poverty.[13] The white Southern petty bourgeoisie and working class had marginally superior material conditions to their black neighbours, but significantly inferior material conditions to other whites in areas where blacks were not subject to the same degree of systematic oppression. This marginal material superiority acquired a quite disproportionate social significance compared to its economic value, allied as it was to the non-economic psycho-social compensation whites received from occupying a position of absolute ascendancy over the blacks. The majority of Southern whites, most of the time, appear not to have considered

10. Allen 1997, p. 249.
11. Tolnay and Beck 1992, p. 28.
12. Szymanski 1976, pp. 412, 413.
13. Du Bois 1969, pp. 700–1.

282 • Neil Davidson

what conditions existed elsewhere or how their own might be raised to that level.

My final example, Ulster prior to the partition of Ireland in 1922, in many respects resembles the situation in the Southern states of the US. The protagonists were almost entirely members of the Protestant industrial working class and their families. Protestant industrial workers enjoyed a higher standard of living than Catholics, since the former had access to more skilled, better-paying jobs and marginally better housing. The relative differences were probably no greater than the differences between poor whites and blacks in the South post-1865, while both communities were better off than either of those in Southern Ireland. Although the Orange Lodges embedded the ideology of Ulster Loyalism in a strong organisational base, material self-interest played a stronger role. The comparison that Protestant workers made was not primarily with their Catholic co-workers, but with the peasant Catholic population of the rest of Ireland, whose fate they would supposedly have to share following Irish independence; this provided the element of rationality in the decision of most Protestants to remain Unionists.[14]

Each of the cases discussed involves subordinate classes and groups willingly participating in and sometimes providing the main social basis for movements in support of Catholic absolutism, white supremacy or the Protestant Ascendancy. In the American and Irish cases, at least, left-wing alternatives did emerge, seeking to address the concerns of those sections of the oppressed who had been harnessed behind reaction: in the South during the era of labour-populism during the 1890s, and in Ulster immediately before the First World War and again during the Great Depression of the 1930s. These alternatives failed to produce lasting unity; but if their lack of success was not inevitable, it does testify to the ideological strength of the movements they opposed. Are these examples peculiar to their own times and circumstances, or can they also illuminate the nature of contemporary right-wing social movements under neoliberal capitalism?

3

The capitalist ruling class does not generally require social movements to achieve its objectives, least of all in the developed West. Unlike most previous ruling classes, it does not tend to directly control states, but can usually rely on them to act in its collective interest, though not always the interest of individual firms or sectors. Where social movements apparently supportive of business objectives do emerge, it usually transpires that they are, in fact, modern examples of

---

14. McCann 1972, pp. 10, 11.

the type of public-relations offensive familiar since the beginning of the twentieth century: they are 'astroturf', rather than genuine grassroots mobilisations. Astroturf campaigns usually involve PR agencies hired by industry-wide corporate coalitions to argue that, in the title of one exposé, 'toxic sludge is good for you' – as apparently are cigarette-smoking, deforestation and abolishing the minimum wage.[15] Front organisations staffed by agency employees create the illusion of a movement by bombarding politicians with telephone calls, letters and emails, usually to prevent regulatory legislation from being enacted or to exert pressure for its repeal. The expansion of electronic media has taken astroturfing into the blogosphere, enabling more general campaigns to alter public perception, often – as in the case of climate change – by creating an atmosphere of doubt or controversy that does not exist within the scientific community, but that makes it easier for politicians to succumb to corporate pressure while claiming to be responsive to public opinion.

Similar pseudo-mobilisations, in defence of political régimes rather than corporate interests, can appear more plausible as social movements, if only because they involve the physical presence of demonstrators on the streets rather than in the virtual sphere. No less fraudulent, they take a wider range of forms and are usually found in the Global South, especially where representative democracy is weakly embedded. One variant, seen most recently across the Middle East and North Africa during the revolutions of 2011, simply involves state employees and hired criminal elements being organised by the police to attack opposition forces, as occurred, for example, in Yemen.[16]

The people taking part in these operations, even if they lack autonomy, do share a material interest in their actions, since they rely on the state for their living. Members of the security forces, in particular, are concerned to preserve whatever dictatorship they happen to serve, since any serious revolution would threaten a purging of the state apparatus, an end to their relatively privileged position, and possible retribution for their many crimes and violations. Their slogans do not, of course, focus on these vulgar personal concerns, but on the indispensability of the Great Leader and the need to repel traitorous foreign-funded attempts to undermine the unity of the people. Such forces do not constitute genuine counter-movements, since they are not merely dependent on the state, but are mobilised by the state and have no independent organisational life outside it.

Even the most dictatorial régimes have a class basis of support beyond paid officials – the petty-bourgeois trader deploring the breakdown of order and stability is the characteristic figure here. But these are not the forces that régimes

15. Stauber and Rampton 1995.
16. Rosen 2011, p. 34.

rely on for their salvation *in extremis*. They tend to be activated only in two ways. One is through one-off events, like the pro-De Gaulle demonstration that marked the end of the events of May 1968 in France. The other is through short bursts of protest, like those directed against the Allende government in Chile during the early 1970s or the Chávez government in Venezuela. These manifestations lack the organisational structures and long-term objectives of social movements. Is it possible, then, for there to be genuine right-wing social movements, whose members have not simply been hired to promote or defend the interests of corporations and régimes?

4

There are, certainly, fewer right-wing than left-wing social movements, although there have certainly been mobilisations against left-wing governments.[17] Examples of right-wing mobilisation, in this sense, are most commonly found where reformist governments in the Global South have faced opposition from middle-class opponents hostile to redistributive policies to the advantage the poor or the working class. These have involved elements of self-organisation, as with the Thai People's Alliance for Democracy ('the yellow shirts') who forced the resignation of Prime Minister Thaksin Shinawatra in 2006 – although the key factor in achieving this result was that their demonstrations allowed the army to intervene to 'restore order'.

However, 'right-wing' should not be understood in too-narrow a party-political sense. The very notion of 'the social' means that mobilising issues will tend to be not particular government-policies, or even particular governments, but longer-term developments that may have been supported by governments of different political persuasions and that the movement wants to stop or restrict, like abortion, immigration or welfare-spending.

We should probably distinguish between the common objectives of the global ruling class as pursued by the various components of the state-system, on the one hand, and of 'right-wing' or 'conservative' social movements, on the other. For all practical purposes, members of the ruling class in the West are united in accepting neoliberalism as the only viable way of organising capitalism as an *economic* system; but the same class is divided in relation to how capitalism should be organised as a *social* system. They may all be neoliberals now, but they are not all neoconservatives. In the United States, both Democrats and Republicans are openly committed to capitalism, but there are also real divisions

---

17. Della Porta and Diani 2006, p. 217.

of opinion between them concerning, for example, gay rights or environmental protection.

What, for the sake of simplicity, we might call 'the needs of capital' – however problematic the term – are not always aligned with the issues that concern groups who, in most other respects, are supporters of the system. Right-wing social movements can relate to the accumulation strategies of capital in three ways:

1. They are directly supportive
2. They are compatible with and/or indirectly supportive through strengthening ideological positions associated with capitalist rule, but that may not be essential to it.
3. They are indirectly and possibly unintentionally destabilising.

Until recently at any rate, examples of type 1 have been very rare indeed, since, for reasons set out in the previous section, capitalists prefer to use corporate pressure rather than popular support to achieve their political goals. Examples of type 2 are the most frequent but, as I will argue below, we are likely to see more examples of type 3. The first question we have to ask, however, concerns the social composition of right-wing social movements, regardless of the ultimate compatibility of their activities with capital.

The role of the middle classes is crucial, here. Wacquant has outlined the general shift in attitude that accompanied the imposition of neoliberalism, where their frustrations can be directed against the state, on the one hand, and the 'undeserving' poor, on the other – both being regarded as parasitic.[18] Whether these antagonistic feelings are directed more towards the former or the latter depends on where exactly one is situated within the middle classes. Berlet and Lyons observe that, in the context of the United States, there are 'two versions of secular right-wing populism', each drawing on a different class base: 'one centred around "get the government off my back" economic libertarianism coupled with a rejection of mainstream political parties (more attractive to the upper middle class and small entrepreneurs); the other based on xenophobia and ethnocentric nationalism (more attractive to the lower middle class and wage workers)'.[19] The next two sections will look more closely at these two loci and the groups associated with them.

---

18. Wacquant 2009, p. 57.
19. Berlet and Lyons 2000, pp. 347–8.

5

The middle class consists of three broad groupings, two of which are historically of very long standing: the traditional petty bourgeoisie and the professions. Both of these consist, in different ways, of the self-employed, although there are, of course, enormous differences in income and social status between representative figures of the first group, like a shopkeeper, and that of the second, like a doctor. The third group, emerging almost entirely within the twentieth century, is 'the new middle class', itself comprising two components: members with a managerial and supervisory role, and those who function as semi-autonomous employees. Both occupy what Wright calls 'contradictory' class locations.[20]

In addition to the objective occupational divide within the new middle class, there is also a subjective political divide across it. Members tend to align themselves politically on the basis of whether they work in the public or private sectors, with the former orientating along social-democratic or (in the United States) liberal-democratic politics, and the latter conservatism.[21] It is not, however, the occupation that produces the political allegiance, but the allegiance that tends to make certain occupations attractive.

What is the significance, for our discussion, of the growth of the new middle class and the nature of its occupational and political divisions? The middle classes are often portrayed as incapable of independent action, forced to vacillate politically until forced to choose between, or divide between, the bourgeoisie and the proletariat. The classic presentation of this case is in Trotsky's writings on Germany from the last days of the Weimar Republic; but this analysis, for all its brilliance, was intended to explain an extreme and atypical situation.[22] In normal circumstances, where civil war is not on the agenda, the room for manoeuvre of the middle classes is greater than Trotsky and those who have uncritically followed him suggest. Indeed, the leadership and much of the rank-and-file of the new 'left-wing' social movements came from professional and new middle-class fractions, particularly in the welfare and 'creative' occupations.[23] But new middle-class activists can be both liberal ('left-wing') on social issues and neoliberal on economic ones.[24]

Since neoliberalism emerged as the dominant form of capitalist organisation in the mid-1970s, what we might call the 'right-wing', private-sector orientated wing of the new middle class has begun to assert itself as an independent social

20. Wright 1978, pp. 61–3, 74–87.
21. Bagguley 1995, p. 304; Heath and Savage 1995, pp. 291–2; Lasch and Urry 1987, p. 195; Adonis and Pollard 1998, pp. 106, 112–13.
22. Trotsky 1975, pp. 271–3.
23. Bagguley 1995, pp. 308–9.
24. Savage et al. 1992, pp. 204, 206, 207.

force. In the mid-1980s, Davis noted the rise of what he called 'overconsumption-ism', by which he meant not the expenditure habits of the very rich, but rather, 'an increasing political subsidization of a mass layer of managers, professionals, new entrepreneurs and rentiers who, faced with rapidly declining organisation among the working poor and minorities during the 1970s, have been overwhelmingly successful in profiting from both inflation and expanded state expenditure'. These groups (to whom Davis also added 'credentialed technicians') constituted nearly a quarter of the US labour force by the late 1970s, and have continued growing since. The political basis for the transition from Fordism to overconsumptionism in the USA was 'neither militant labour nor reactionary capital, but insurgent middle strata', which during the 1970s began to mobilise against the social gains of the previous decade, above all against integration and bussing.[25] Galbraith observed that the beneficiaries of neoliberalism were the majority – not of the population or even the electorate, of course, 'but of those who actually vote', 'the Contented Electoral Majority': 'They rule under the rich cloak of democracy, a democracy in which the less fortunate do not participate'. And, as he correctly notes, this minority-majority are 'very angry and very articulate about what seems to invade their state of self satisfaction'.[26] What kind of issues might provoke their anger and stimulate their articulacy? According to Davis: 'The most powerful "social movement" in contemporary Southern California is that of affluent homeowners, organized by notional community designations or tract names, engaged in the defence of home values and neighbourhood exclusivity'.[27]

Galbraith identified three possible factors that might overturn the culture of contentment among the beneficiaries of neoliberalism: of these, 'military misadventure' has been followed by 'deep recession', while 'growing unrest' is unlikely to be far behind.[28] The problem is that the direction into which this combination of catastrophes will push the professional and new middle classes is underdetermined. It makes more effective use of public services than the working class, but this also means that it can also be seriously affected by cuts in state provision.[29] Although the neoliberal boom after 1982 enabled the issue to be avoided, the return of recession since 2008 has made it inescapable. One response would simply be for the professional and new middle classes to appropriate part of the state for themselves. In Britain, for example, responsibility for implementing neoliberal anti-reforms is being spread beyond governing parties and central

25. Davis 1986, pp. 211, 221–2.
26. Galbraith 1992, p. 15.
27. Davis 1990, p. 153.
28. Galbraith 1992, pp. 172–3.
29. Hughley 1995, pp. 330–1.

state apparatuses to elected bodies whose policy options are severely restricted both by statute and reliance on the Treasury for most of their funding. Neoliberal attitudes towards the mass of the population involve an uneasy combination of private suspicion over what they might do without state surveillance and repression, and public disquisitions on the need to listen to The People, provided, of course, that politicians are being asked to listen to the right sort of people with the right sort of demands – in other words, longer prison sentences and more restricted immigration, rather than higher taxation for the rich or military withdrawal from Afghanistan. In the case of devolution, the assumption is that the people most likely to participate in local decision making will be members of the middle classes, who can be expected to behave, *en masse*, in ways that will impose restrictions on local taxation and public spending, and thus maintain the neoliberal order with a supposedly popular mandate.

A model for 'returning power to the people' along these lines was built early on in the neoliberal experiment, in the United States. One feature of 'the New Federalism' of the early 1990s was 'shifting control of social programs back to state and local levels' which 'would also entail a shift in accountability for the administration of these programs'.[30] The most fully developed version can be found in California. Since the mid-1970s, politics in the world's eighth biggest economy has been characterised by a combination of falling voter participation among working-class and minority groups, and a targeted use of local referendums on 'propositions'. The latter have been designed to defend property values by blocking integrated schooling and urban development, and by preventing progressive taxation.[31] Proposition 13 was passed in 1978 and signalled the commencement of the neoliberal era in the United States, capping taxes on property, even though house values were rising. As a result, the burden of taxation fell disproportionately on income tax, even though, for most workers, salaries and wages were stagnant or falling – and even increasing income tax requires a two-thirds majority in both Houses of the State Legislature. It is the self-interested behaviour of a mobilised middle class that has brought California to its current fiscal crisis, where the usual remedies of cutting public services, including child healthcare, are now being offered as a solution to the structural inability of the state to raise the necessary levels of taxation.

Another aspect is the emergence of gated communities with inhabitants below the level of the bourgeoisie. In these, residents have to sign an agreement where the developer stipulates what types of activity are permissible and expected. Ironically, these can be quite as complex, prescriptive and designed to control the behaviour of inhabitants as those that local councils used to impose

---

30. Hughley 1995, p. 327.
31. Davis 1986, pp. 221–30; Davis 1990, Chapter 3.

on their tenants. In return, occupants are provided with private services such as rubbish disposal. The obvious development, which has already become a reality in parts of the United States, including – naturally – California, but also Florida and Minnesota, is that the occupants will withdraw from local taxation on the grounds that it involves them in paying for services that they do not receive while simultaneously paying separately for those that they do: the rules and charges imposed in gated communities are, effectively, laws and taxes.[32] Yet only the very upper echelons of the middle class can afford this level of social withdrawal. We are likely to see, therefore, increased struggles for access to resources at local levels in which sections of the middle class attempt to monopolise these for themselves. In Britain, this will occur most blatantly in the field of education, as middle-class parents move from targeting schools as the most suitable for their children to establishing their own on the basis of government-funding that would otherwise have been invested in the state sector. How large a proportion of the professional and new middle classes will pursue this path, rather than one of defending the welfare state and public provision more generally, will depend on the strength of a working-class movement advocating the latter as an alternative.

6

Unfortunately, the reactionary role of sections of the professional and new middle class does not exhaust the social basis of right-wing social movements. Since the majority of the population are exploited and oppressed, such movements must draw support from their ranks. There is nothing inherently implausible about this, since members of these classes are not always fully aware of their own interests. It is a Marxist truism dating back to the very formation of historical materialism that the ideas of the ruling class tend to be the ruling ideas.[33] Marx and Engels subsequently revised this potentially élitist proposition in more dialectical terms, both elsewhere in the *German Ideology* and in other works.[34] Later Marxists, above all Gramsci, showed that most members of the subordinate classes have highly contradictory forms of consciousness.[35] Nevertheless, the capitalist system could not survive unless it was accepted at some level, most of the time, by the majority of the people who live under it. The implications of this are darker than is sometimes supposed.

---

32. Minton 2009, p. 77.
33. Marx and Engels 1975b, p. 59.
34. Marx 1975a, p. 7, thesis 3; Marx and Engels 1975b, pp. 52–3.
35. Gramsci 1971, pp. 333–4.

The consciousness of the subaltern classes is, as Gramsci says, typically contradictory. A characteristic form involves a reformist inability to conceive of
anything beyond capitalism, while opposing specific effects of the system. But
the alternatives are not restricted to active rejection, at one extreme, and passive acceptance, at the other. There can also be *active* support, the internalisa-
tion of capitalist values associated with the system to the point where they can
lead to action. Marxists and other anti-capitalist radicals frequently point out
that, rather than men benefiting from the oppression of women, whites from the
oppression of blacks, or straights from the oppression of gays, it is capitalism or
the bourgeoisie who do so. This is a useful corrective to the argument, common
in many left-wing movements, that each form of oppression is separate from
the others and that none has any necessary connection to the capitalist system.
Nevertheless, it fails to take seriously the distinction made by Lukács between
'what men *in fact* thought, felt and wanted at any point in the class structure'
and 'the thoughts and feelings which men would have in a particular situation if
they were *able* to assess both it and the interests arising from it in their impact
on immediate action and on the whole structure of society'.[36] For we cannot
assume that members of the working class are not only capable of having, but
actually *have* the thoughts and feelings 'appropriate to their objective situation'.
What if workers do not attain this level of consciousness?

Socialism became possible on a world scale at some point in the early decades
of the twentieth century, but several generations have lived and died since then.
Many of those people have either been unaware of 'the standpoint of the working class' or have simply refused to adopt it. Instead, a significant minority have
taken positions supportive of, for example, racial oppression, which may not
have benefited them compared with the benefits they would have received by
struggling for racial equality, let alone full social equality. Without some degree
of class consciousness, however, they need not ever consider this alternative: in
the immediate context of their situation, a stance detrimental to working-class
interests as a whole may make sense to particular individual members of the
working class. Lukács once wrote of revisionism – which, in this context, can be
taken to mean reformism more generally – that: '*It always sacrifices the genuine interests of the class as a whole ... so as to represent the immediate interests
of specific groups*'.[37] Working-class people who participate in right-wing social
movements have, in effect, taken this a stage further, by sacrificing even the
interests of specific groups in favour of their immediate individual interests, usually equated with a supra-class national interest.[38]

---

36. Lukács 1971, p. 51.
37. Lukács 1970, p. 56.
38. Ibid.

It is, nevertheless, extremely unlikely that a right-wing social movement could be entirely composed of working-class members. Those that are not simply social movements of the professional and new middle class aimed at essentially economic ends will tend to combine workers in unstable alliances with sections of the traditional petty bourgeoisie. In these cases, inter-class tensions are temporarily overridden by the mobilising issue, a process made easier by the fact that, in relatively superficial cultural terms – in other words, everything that does not immediately relate to the workplace – the traditional petty bourgeoisie and the working class can often be indistinguishable in terms of language, dress and leisure activities. A self-employed electrician and a council refuse collector will drink in the same bars; a lawyer and a postman will not. But the working-class presence will also tend to produce expressions of misdirected hostility towards perceived ruling-class interests.[39] Unfortunately, the spectacle of the working class or the oppressed more generally mobilising against their own interests alongside members of other social classes has produced a number of inadequate responses from socialists.

One is the claim that working-class demands or actions that might appear reactionary actually contain a rational core which renders them defensible by the Left. There was a more than a flavour of this during the Lindsey oil-refinery strike during 2009 in which the slogan 'British jobs for British workers' was raised, with clear xenophobic if not actually racist intent, against Eastern European migrant-labourers. It is true that non-British nationals are hired by businesses on lower wages and worse conditions, with the effect of these being extended across industry as a whole; but the solution is to unionise migrant workers, not blame them for their employers' cost-cutting. Similar exculpatory attitudes have been displayed in relation to vigilante violence against, for example, suspected drug dealers and paedophiles, on the grounds that this represents 'people's justice', autonomous actions of self-policing outwith the parameters of the bourgeois state. Of course, there are situations where workers effectively impose their own 'legality', most obviously in relation to strike breakers during industrial disputes; but these are quite different from members of a community turning on each other at the behest of media-inspired moral panics.

The other inadequate response is the argument that, even if working-class people participate in them, right-wing movements are illegitimate because they are funded or led by wealthy corporation or individuals. This argument inverts the classic conservative theme that popular unrest against the established order is never, as it were, natural, but always orchestrated by external forces ('outside agitators'), inventing or, at most, manipulating grievances in order to further

---

39. Berlet and Lyons 2000, p. 349.

their own ends.[40] Glenn Beck, the Fox News ideologue, was heavily involved in launching the Tea Party movement in the United States and oil-magnates, the Koch brothers, supplied the funding. For commentators like Monbiot, these facts are decisive.[41] It is not clear why this disqualifies the Tea Party from consideration as a social movement. According to Della Porta and Diani, members of social movements in general display three characteristics: they are 'involved in conflictual relations with clearly identified opponents', 'linked by dense informal networks' and 'share a distinct collective identity'.[42] Members of the Tea Party and those of earlier right-wing insurgencies in the US display all of these characteristics.[43] The people organised by these movements may well be morally wrong and politically misguided, but it is patronising – and, above all, politically useless – to pretend that they are simply being manipulated by élite puppet-masters. Indeed, to do so is simply to adopt the conservative position that sees all mass mobilisations as externally inspired while reversing the direction of the political inspiration. In fact, as Bageant writes: 'The New Conservatism arose in the same way left-wing movements do, by approximately the same process, and for the same reasons: widespread but unacknowledged dissatisfaction, in this case with the erosion of "traditional" life and values in America as working people perceive them'.[44]

The real question is, surely, why working-class people in particular would be predisposed to respond positively to right-wing arguments. Dismissing them on grounds of irrationality is simply an evasion. As Berlet and Lyons write: 'Right-wing populist claims are no more and no less irrational than conventional claims that presidential elections express the will of the people, that economic health can be measured by the profits of multimillion dollar corporations, or that US military interventions in Haiti or Somalia or Kosovo or wherever are designed to promote democracy and human rights'.[45] Yet these beliefs, which are accepted by many more people than those who believe in, say, the literal truth of the Book of Genesis, are not treated as signs of insanity. The issue, as Berlet argued elsewhere, is not 'personal pathology' but collective 'desperation'.[46] It is more illuminating to ask how such movements come into existence and how far they offer false solutions to genuine problems.

The roots of the US militia movement, for example, lay in the crisis of farming communities during the 1980s. During the previous decade, the Nixon administration had encouraged farmers to take out loans, on floating interest-rates, in

---

40. Harris 1971, pp. 115–16.
41. Monbiot 2010.
42. Della Porta and Diani 2006, p. 20.
43. Frank 2004, pp. 175, 247.
44. Bageant 2007, pp. 81–2; see also Davis 2007, p. 57.
45. Berlet and Lyons 2000, p. 348.
46. Berlet 1995, p. 285.

order to expand agricultural production. The loans were arranged through one state-body (or as militias would say, 'the Government'), namely the Farm Home Administration; but from 1979, the now heavily-indebted farmers were quickly subjected to several interest-rate rises in succession at the hands of another state (or 'government') body, the Federal Reserve, as Chairman Paul Volker instituted the famous economic 'shock' associated with his name. Foreclosures by the banks and consolidations at the hands of agricultural corporations inevitably followed. In this case, a particular explanation for the farmers' economic griev-ances became an entry-point more generally for the right-wing politics of the Republican Party and beyond them, for those of the militias, the Klan and neo-Nazis.[47]

Less apparently explicable is the way in which working-class people in the United States have apparently moved in the opposite direction, from right-wing social positions to economic ones. As against those, like Frank, who find this incomprehensible, Davis argues that, in fact, the capture of working-class con-sciousness by social conservatism is more apparent than real: 'the real Achil-les' Heel' of the Democrats in 2004 was 'the economy, not morality'. While 'Kulturkampf may have played an important role at the margin', Davis points out that there are real class-issues involved: 'visceral blue-collar contempt for the urban knowledge-industry elites...is, after all, grounded in real historic defeat and class humiliation.... With union halls shut down and the indepen-dent press extinct, it is not surprising that many poor white people search for answers in their churches or from demagogues like Limbaugh and Dobbs on the radio'.[48] Davis is, undoubtedly, right that a majority of the people involved in right-wing social movements do so because of underlying economic concerns; the more relevant point is, perhaps, whether – in the absence of any left-wing solution to those concerns – they continue to demand the implementation of their social programme as a condition of support for politicians who claim to represent them.

7

Diamond is thus correct that leftist critics of the US Christian Right are wrong to adopt what she calls 'a view of conspiracies by small right-wing cliques to stage-manage what was truly a mass movement'. She is also right to emphasise the complexity of right-wing populism towards 'existing power structures', being 'partially *oppositional* and partially...*system supportive*'.[49] What is, perhaps,

---

47. Gallaher 2004, p. 186.
48. Davis 2007, p. 50.
49. Diamond 1995, p. 6.

more interesting, here, is less the consciously oppositional elements of their ideology, which tend to be directed against the socio-cultural views of one wing of the ruling class, and more what I referred to earlier as outcomes that might be unintentionally 'detrimental' to capital.

Since the late 1960s, Republicans in the USA have been increasingly reliant on communities of fundamentalist-Christian believers, whose activism allows them to be mobilised for voting purposes. Phillips, himself a one-time Republican strategist, has argued that this had benefits, not only for his erstwhile party, but for the broader ruling class whose interests it represents.[50] But this religious core vote – or, at any rate, their leadership – naturally also demand the implementation of policies in return for their support. Writers like Frank argue that the demands of popular conservatism are precisely those that are never met, while those of the élites always are. He describes 'the backlash' as being, 'like a French Revolution in reverse – one in which the sans-culottes pour down the street demanding more power for the aristocracy'.[51] Frank underestimates the way in which fundamentalist demands have, in fact, been implemented in relation, for example, to sex education or reproduction rights. Ruling classes can cope with this, since their children will always be educated and they will always have access to abortion. But, as Lilla points out, because the Tea Party is not a wholly-owned subsidiary of the Republicans, it is 'transforming American conservatism . . . the more it tries to exploit the energy of the Tea Party rebellion, the cruder the conservative movement becomes in its thinking and its rhetoric. . . . Today's conservatives prefer the company of anti-intellectuals who know how to exploit nonintellectuals, as Sarah Palin does so masterfully'.[52]

There are two potential problems, here, for the Republicans and the conservative wing of the US ruling class more generally. On the one hand, the extremism of fundamentalist Christianity may alienate the electoral 'middle ground' on which the results of American elections increasingly depend. On the other, and more importantly, politicians may be constrained from undertaking policies that may be necessary for American capitalism, or be forced into taking decisions that may harm it. The constraints imposed by the need to placate a religious base also affect the United States' position in relation to other advanced states: 'Realistically, these events and circumstances hardly encourage foreign central bankers, diplomats, or political leaders to buy and hold U.S. Treasury Bonds, support American energy profligacy, join U.S. ventures in the Middle East, or believe that young people unskilled in mathematics, addled by credit cards, and weaned on so-called intelligent design instead of evolution will somehow retool

---

50. Phillips 2006, pp. 393–4.
51. Frank 2004, pp. 8, 109.
52. Lilla 2010.

American science for another generation of world industrial leadership'.[53] This is not merely speculative. In Britain before 1997, the Conservatives unleashed an imperial nationalism in relation to 'Europe', not because the European Union was in any sense hostile to neoliberalism, but as an ideological diversion from the failure of neoliberalism to transform the fortunes of British capital. The nationalism invoked for this purpose has now created a major obstacle for British politicians and state managers who want to pursue a strategy of greater European integration, however rational that may be from their perspective.[54]

As such, there can be situations where there is a genuine 'non-identity of interest' between capitalists and what are – from their point of view – the irrational demands made by the social base of the political party that they prefer to have custody of the state. The most extreme case, that of the German Nazi régime, offers several examples of policies that were irrational, not only from the capitalist perspective, but also from that of the state as a war-making machine. As Mason noted, 'the racial-ethical utopia ... was taken so seriously by the political leadership, in particular by Hitler and by the SS, that in decisive questions even the urgent material needs of the system were sacrificed to it'.[55] For example, despite a desperate shortage of labour, Hitler resisted female conscription until after German defeat at Stalingrad, apparently out of ideological concern over a potential decline in the birth rate (and hence to the strength of the 'Aryan' race) and the threat to female morals. Even then, it was applied half-heartedly and widely evaded.[56] But the unavoidable example, and one of the most difficult of all historical problems, is the motivation behind the Holocaust.

In an outstanding discussion, Callinicos rightly points out that, in general terms, 'the extermination of the Jews cannot be explained in economic terms'. He clearly sees the connection between the Holocaust and German capitalism as an example of an interpenetration of interests, in this case between 'German big business' and 'a movement whose racist and pseudo-revolutionary ideology drove it towards the Holocaust'. Callinicos sums up his position by quoting Kreiger: 'German capitalism didn't need the Holocaust. But it needed the Nazis, and *they* needed the Holocaust'.[57] But where did the Nazis' 'racist and pseudo-revolutionary ideology' come from in the first place? Callinicos only sees a connection with capitalism as arising from the immediate needs of the economy at a time of crisis, which could seem reductionist. However, the ideological formation of the Nazi worldview took place over a much longer period, combining

53. Phillips 2006, p. 394.
54. Gowan 1996, pp. 99–103.
55. Mason 1995, p. 74.
56. Kershaw 2000, pp. 563, 567–8, 713.
57. Callinicos 2001, pp. 403, 406, 413, Note 95.

a series of determinations arising from the contradictions of German and European capitalism, including extreme right-wing nationalism, racism in its anti-Semitic form, disappointed imperialism, a taste for violence acquired in the trenches, and so on.[58] In other words, adapting Kreiger, we might say that German capitalism did not need the Holocaust, but the long-term development of German capitalism produced, through a series of mediations, the ideology of Nazism, which did contain the possibility of a Holocaust. When German capitalists turned to the Nazis in their moment of crisis, they gave them the opportunity to realise that possibility, however irrelevant and outright damaging it was to German capital's more overarching imperial project.

8

The preceding discussion suggests three conclusions.

1) Although less frequent than those of the Left, right-wing social movements have existed since the later stages of the transition to capitalism. Their incidence is likely to increase under current neoliberal conditions, as the withdrawal of state-provision will lead groups to defend their access to increasingly scarce resources using methods hitherto associated mainly with the Left.

2) The last real possibilities of socialist revolution in the West appeared during the years between 1968 and 1975, and, even then, nowhere progressed beyond the preliminary stages. Consequently, today's Left has – beyond very general if formally correct observations – little conception of what revolution might take. In particular, there is a problem with the idea that revolution will simply involve revolutionary masses on the one side and the capitalist state on the other, and with vacillating reformists occupying the space between. In other words, workers and their class allies will only confront each other on opposite sides of the barricades if parts of their forces are directly employed within the apparatus of repression. There is a famous discussion by Lenin, part of which reads as follows:

> The socialist revolution in Europe cannot be anything other than an outburst of mass struggle on the part of all and sundry oppressed and discontented elements. Inevitably, sections of the petty bourgeoisie and of the backward workers will participate in it – without such participation, mass struggle is impossible, without it no revolution is possible – and just as inevitably will they bring into the movement their prejudices, their reactionary fantasies, their weaknesses and errors. But objectively they will attack capital...[59]

58. Evans 2003, pp. 22–76; Kershaw 2007, pp. 438–44.
59. Lenin 1964, p. 356.

The last clause in this passage is open to doubt. Why should forces mobilised by 'their prejudices [and] their reactionary fantasies' necessarily be 'objectively' opposed to capital? If the preceding arguments are correct, we should just as easily expect movements to arise that will attempt to defend the existing order, or their members' place in an idealised version of it, independently or in parallel with the state. The ruling classes would, surely, overlook any longer-term difficulties these movements might cause for capital, so long as they contributed to the immediate goal of suppressing revolutionary possibilities.

3) In terms of seeking alliances, the working-class movement is unlikely to find them in those sections of the professional and new middle-classes that have a material interest in preserving the capitalist system. There are, however, far greater possibilities among the petty bourgeoisie and 'public sector' new middle class – and, in this respect, the ability of some of their members to mobilise, even in right-wing social movements, should be seen in a potentially positive light, since the focus of their frustration or discontent need not be decided in advance. Here, Lenin's argument retains its relevance, when he writes that 'the class-conscious vanguard of the revolution, the advanced proletariat, expressing this objective truth of a variegated and discordant, motley and outwardly fragmented, mass struggle, will he able to unite and direct it, capture power, seize the banks, expropriate the trusts which all hate'.[60] After all, given the disappointments of the century since these words were written, we might want to render the argument in more conditional terms. Nevertheless, the central point remains valid: the indeterminacy of social movements means that their ultimate direction will always depend on the availability of a persuasive socialist politics.

---

60. Lenin 1964, p. 356.

Class, Caste, Colonial Rule and Resistance: The Revolt of 1857 in India
Hira Singh

Precolonial Indian society and social movements in colonial India

The recognition and understanding of precolonial class – and *caste* structure in India is essential to an understanding of not only the social movements, but of the entire colonial socio-economic formation. Social movements in colonial India, including the Revolt of 1857, were products of the internal dynamics of the existing class – and *caste* relations.

Marx, nineteenth-century Indian society, and British colonial rule

Marx's assessment of British colonial rule in India was based on his understanding of nineteeth-century Indian society. India, for Marx, was part of the Orient, different in essential ways from the West. One important area of difference between the West and the Orient, according to him, was in the functions of the Government. Governments in Asia, he wrote in 1853, were concerned mainly with three departments: the Department of Finance (the plunder of the interior), the Department of War (the plunder of the exterior), and that of Public Works, especially artificial irrigation by canals and waterworks, the basis of Oriental agriculture. In the West, the provision of irrigation was met by voluntary associations and private enterprise. Not so in the Orient. A combination of a low level of 'civilisation' and the vastness of the territory forced the Oriental governments to undertake the economic function of providing public works (irrigation).[1]

The distinguishing feature of nineteenth-century Indian society, according to Marx, was the domestic union of agriculture and industry. These two features – central government taking care of public works, and the domestic union of agriculture and industry – brought about a certain social system in India, the so-called *village system* (italics original) endowed with a 'peculiar character', that remained unchanged until the inception of British colonial rule. In spite of all political and dynastic changes, the internal economy of the village system remained unchanged. He arrived at this understanding of Indian society based on the evidence presented in an old official report of the British House of Commons on Indian affairs.[2]

Indian society and the Indian people had no history. Notwithstanding the succession of empires, India was a static, unresisting, changeless society. Marx saw India's colonisation almost as a historical inevitability. India was conquered by other foreign powers prior to the British, but the British conquest and colonisation was historically the most progressive. This was so since all previous conquerors of India, being relatively less civilised, were absorbed into Indian civilisation. Most notably, they were not capable of altering the basis of Indian society and culture. All their destruction was confined to the surface.

England, on the other hand, being a superior civilisation, having conquered and colonised India, was destined to fulfil its double mission of the destruction of the old, stagnant village structure of the Asiatic mode and to lay down the material foundation of 'Western society in Asia'. All over India, British steam and science uprooted the union between agriculture and manufacturing industry – the foundation of the Asiatic mode of production and its political form, oriental despotism. This is what distinguished British colonial rule from India's past history.[3]

According to Marx, British colonial rule, in spite of all its limitations, did create conditions of regeneration. Marx counts among the conditions of regeneration resulting from British colonial rule the political unity of India (far more extensive than that during Mughal rule), modern military organisation, the free press, and a new class of Indians with modern education under English supervision. Finally, the two most important innovations of colonial rule, first the introduction of private property in land (*zemindari* and *ryotwari*) and, second, the development of communication and transport, especially the steam engine, which would annex India to the West. One can, in fact, see a similarity between Marx's understanding

1. Marx 1978, p. 15.
2. Marx 1978, pp. 16–17.
3. Marx 1978, pp. 14–16, 29–30.

of the peasantry in the *Eighteenth Brumaire*, its lack of social intercourse and of class consciousness due to bad communication, and the isolated village communities in India. He thought that the development of railways would break that isolation. Modern industry, resulting from the railway system, he thought, would dissolve the hereditary division of labour of the traditional Indian caste system, that 'decisive impediment to Indian progress and Indian power'.[4]

Marx criticised the inhumanity and brutality of colonial rule. He empathised with the sufferings of individual manufacturers and their families in the colony. However, at the same time, he approved of the destructive role of British colonial rule. The peculiar village community, divided by caste and characterised by a general 'slavery', he argued, fettered the growth of human beings, who, rather than rising to their potential to becoming the 'sovereign of circumstances', were 'brutalised' by the worship of nature, cows, and monkeys, a degradation of humanity. British colonial rule would free Indian society from its stagnant economy, caste division, and religious superstitions.[5]

Thus, even though English intervention was motivated by the 'vilest' self interest, it was revolutionary in nature – an 'unconscious tool of history' – hence, emancipatory in effect. But for this, mankind in Asia could not fulfil its destiny.[6] Whatever the sufferings of India and the Indians, British colonial rule was, in the last analysis, good for humanity.[7]

The Revolt of 1857

On May 10 1857, the soldiers of the British Indian Army in Meerut rose in revolt against their European officers. The Revolt very soon took on the form of a popular rebellion against British colonial rule in India, then represented by the East India Company. In the course of ten days, English administration in the Province of Oudh, the main centre of the rebellion, 'vanished like a dream and not left a wrack behind'.[8] The most important aspect of the Revolt that concerns us, here, was that the landlords and the peasants of Oudh joined the soldiers' rebellion, turning it into a popular insurgency.[9]

---

4. Marx 1978, pp. 30–2.
5. Marx 1978, pp. 31–2.
6. Marx and Engels 1978, p. 18.
7. Marx 1978, pp. 18–19.
8. Khaldun 1957, p. 1.
9. For a Marxist account of the Revolt, see, in particular, Joshi 1957; Singh and Awasthi 2008.

Quarrel over a name

The Revolt of 1857 has been named differently by different parties, depending on their social location and ideological orientation. The controversy over the name was first raised inside the British ruling class itself. The defenders of the East India Company called it the 'Sepoy Mutiny'! The opponents of the Company, the representatives of the British industrial bourgeoisie, called it a national rebellion. Marx (who wrote extensively about the Revolt) and Engels called it the 'Indian War of Independence', Lord Canning first called it 'mutiny', then 'rebellion', then finally, a 'revolt'. Subsequently, he characterised it as 'a rebellion fomented by the Brahmins on religious pretences'. Charles Ball called it 'the rebellion of a whole people incited to outrage by resentment for imaginary wrongs and sustained in their delusions by hatred and fanaticism'.[10] The controversy over naming the Revolt is a reflection of the more serious question as to what caused the Revolt. We turn to that next.

Why the revolt?

It should be clarified that the Revolt of 1857 is by no means a single story, rather a complex of multiple stories. Nonetheless, most important of all, it is the story of resistance by the landed aristocracy to an attempt by the colonial state to take away their traditional land rights, political power, and cultural privilege. It is a story of the then-dominant class protecting its power and privilege against the will of the colonial state.

I briefly recapitulate below the story of 1857 that is commonplace knowledge. I recount this story mostly through the writings of Marx (and Engels).

Colonial conquest: the so-called pacification

The East India Company conquered and colonised India for England piece-by-piece, in wars stretched over a long period of time. Marx pointed out that the loss of its colonial possession of America left a vacuum in the English quest for empire, which had to be filled by territorial gain elsewhere. This historic mission was carried on by the East India Company. From the 1680s onwards, the Company was engaged in making territorial gains in India, with the ultimate objective of acquiring the right to extract land revenue as a source of income. Between the 1750s and the 1840s, the Company advanced its goal of territorial gains through continuous wars against regional powers resisting its

---

10. Joshi 1957, pp. 121–3.

encroachment. The suppression of the last frontier of resistance in the Punjab in 1848 marked the end of the era of pacification. It cleared the way for the establishment of 'the one great Anglo-Indian Empire' – a result of almost two centuries of war under the name of the East India Company.[11] It is a rich tribute to colonial terminology that this period of uninterrupted wars of colonial conquest is called 'pacification', that is, a peaceful process of conflict-resolution in which war and violence is unjustifiable.

1848–56: assault on the landed gentry

'Pacification' of the Punjab in 1848 established the Company's control over what came to be British India during colonial rule, covering three fifths of the territory and three quarters of the population of the country. Two fifths of the territory *and one quarter of the population* then under the jurisdiction of the Indian princely states was still out of the direct control of Company. This was a problem for the Company. At this point, one can see an interesting connection between knowledge and power in the specific context of colonialism. Nineteenth-century England was not only the most advanced capitalist economy, with the most advanced military might. It was also the most advanced centre of development of classical political economy, as represented by the holy trinity of Adam Smith, David Ricardo, and James Mill. Colonialism as a land-grab for the extraction of rent was an economic necessity of capitalism at home. The rent of two fifths of the territory being appropriated by indigenous, precapitalist landlords of the princely states was an obstacle to colonial-capitalist accumulation – an obstacle that had to be removed.[12] Classical political economy provided a rationale for the removal of that obstacle by declaring the landed aristocracy (princes and landlords) to be parasites surviving on privileges by birth, as this was an anomaly for the emerging bourgeois-capitalist order. Acting on this basic principle of political economy, the East India Company turned its attention to the princely states, and new phase of colonial conquest, with the Doctrine of Lapse (1848–56).

The Doctrine of Lapse ruled that if a native prince died without a natural heir, his estate was annexed to the territory of the East India Company, setting aside the principle of adoption – the very cornerstone of Indian society, as Disraeli was to describe later on: 'The principle of the law of adoption is not the prerogative of the princes and principalities in India, it applies to every man in Hindustan who has landed property and who professes the Hindu religion...no one had dreamt of abolishing the law of adoption'.[13]

---

11. Marx 1978, pp. 23–4.
12. See Marx 1978, p. 45.
13. Cited by Marx 1978, p. 46.

The annexation of Oudh

Under the new rule, more than a dozen independent princely states were forcibly annexed between 1848 and 1854. Finally, in 1856, the state of Oudh was annexed, not because there was no male heir, but because the ruler of the estate was declared unfit to rule in the interest of his people.[14]

The annexation of Oudh was neither incidental nor a sudden affair. It was attempted as early as in 1831 and, again, in 1837, but reversed.[15] Then, in 1856, Lord Dalhousie invaded and took possession of Lucknow, the capital of Oudh, and took the ruler of Oudh prisoner. He was urged to cede the country to the British (which he refused). He was then taken away to Calcutta, and his estate was annexed to the territory of the East India Company.

Oudh had been an ally of the East India Company since 1798, according to a 'Treaty of Offensive and Defensive Alliance' between the Company and the then ruler of the Province. Under the Treaty, the Company collected an annual tribute of 76 lacs of rupees ($3,800,000). At the same time, according to the provision of the Treaty, the ruler was supposed to reduce taxation. As if the apparent contradiction of the above provision of the Treaty were not enough, another complicating clause was added to it in 1801, namely, that the ruler should establish a system of administration conducive to his subjects' prosperity and security. Even though the ruler of Oudh was, under the Treaty, an independent, sovereign, and free agent, the provision of 1801 gave the Company the right to break the Treaty, and annex the kingdom, if, in the estimation of the Company, the ruler was unable to ensure the security and prosperity of his subjects. This is exactly what the Company did in 1856 – 'in violation of every principle of the law of nations'.[16]

At the same time, the Company also dispossessed the landlords (*talukdars* and *zamindars*) in the province of Oudh. Not only that. It also grabbed the land-grants of temples and mosques that were free from the land-tax. In addition to seizing the lands of the landlords, mosques, and temples, the Company discontinued the pensions to the native princes – even though it was bound by treaty to pay these. It was a 'most fruitful source of public revenue ... it was confiscation by a new means, and upon a most ... shocking scale', as Disraeli later observed.[17]

The annexation of Oudh, along with the liquidation of the landed aristocracy of the province, confiscation of religious land grants, and the dispensation of pensions to princes, was the single most important factor behind the Revolt.

---

14. Marx 1978, p. 45.
15. Marx 1978, p. 134.
16. Marx 1978, p. 131.
17. Cited by Marx 1978, p. 47.

Oudh remained the main centre of the Revolt, and the final battle between the rebels and the British was fought in Lucknow, the capital of Oudh.

Pigs, cows, cartridges and the Revolt

One popular myth regarding the Revolt pertains to the introduction of the new cartridges to be used by the soldiers of the British Indian Army. Marx, among many others, noted that the alleged cause of the dissatisfaction began with the apprehension, on the part of the native soldiers, that the Government was interfering with their religion – serving out of cartridges, the paper of which was said to have been greased with the fat of cows and pigs. The compulsory biting of cartridges was an obvious infringement of the religious prescriptions of Hindus (treating cows as holy) and Muslims (detesting the unholy pig).[18]

We should not be dismissive of the role of cultural factors – creed and caste – in inciting insurgency. Rumours and fears of violation of creed and caste – conversion to Christianity by force, fraud, and/or persuasion were widespread, and a call on the soldiers of the British Indian Army 'to resist the insidious attacks on caste and religion' was in the air. There was visibly increased missionary activity on the ground. The Protestant ethic, allegedly carrying the spirit of capitalism in its womb, was, no doubt, an inspiring factor driving the colonial project. Protestantism was, after all, the religion of the 'Ruling Race'.[19]

The English were seen as usurpers of low caste, and as tyrants, who conquered India only to plunder its wealth and to subvert Indians' custom and religion.[20] There were hosts of rumours adding fuel to the smoldering fire. It was rumoured, for instance, that low-caste men would be employed to cook food for the upper-caste Brahman and Rajput soldiers, thus polluting them, defiling their caste-status, eventually destroying the caste-system altogether. Feeding the rumour was the alleged prophecy that one hundred years after the battle of Plassey (in 1757, where the British finally defeated their colonial rival, the French, thus paving the way for the British rule in India), there would be bloodshed ending the white man's rule.[21] One should not discount the force of rumour in fomenting the rebellion.[22] The greased cartridges, whatever their significance, were, however, 'only an incident . . . merely the match that exploded the mine'. As Disraeli pointed out, the same Indian soldiers in their fight against the British did

---

18. Marx 1978, p. 36; see also Wood 1908, p. 8.
19. Wood 1908, p. 6.
20. Mehta 1946, p. 10.
21. Wood 1908, pp. 6–8; Mehta 1946, p. 11.
22. For the role of rumour in rebellion, see Lefebvre 1973; see also Rudé 1973, p. xiii.

not hesitate to use freely those same cartridges 'which they declared would if used, have destroyed their caste'.

The dialectics of colonial rule[23] and resistance

Giving the multiplicity of causes its historic due, I want to turn to the principal cause of the Revolt, that is, the resistance by the dominant class, the landlords, to the attempt by the East India Company to encroach on their monopoly of economic-political power and cultural privilege.

The story of two 'Indias'

The map of India during British colonial rule was shown in two colours – red and yellow. The red, covering three fifths of the territory (and about three quarters of the population) was British India. The remaining two fifths of the territory (with about a quarter of the population) was the territory of 'Indian India'. Indian India was outside the direct jurisdiction of the colonial state. It was the domain of the Indian princes. Under the Treaties of Friendship and Subordinate Alliance, the princely rulers accepted the suzerainty of the East India Company (later on the Crown), but retained sovereignty over their respective territories. They administered their lands and people according to their customary laws, without interference from the colonial state, excepting under special circumstances; even then, their interference was limited.

Why two Indias? The standard answer of the conventional historiography of colonialism is 'indirect rule'. The idea of 'indirect rule' is misleading, insofar as it implies that the princely states were 'preserved' by the colonial state to serve its own interests. The main problem with the idea of indirect rule is that it eschews the element of resistance by the landed aristocracy (princes and landlords). It makes the colonial state all powerful and the traditional landed aristocracy totally powerless, passive tools of the colonial state. It is a conceptual tool of what I have characterised as the colonial mode of historiography.[24]

To the contrary, I have argued that the colonial state was too vulnerable to rule over the whole country on its own. It needed a local ally. The landed aristocracy was that local ally. The treaties between the East India Company (subsequently the Crown) and the princely states were not a one-way road dictated by the interests of the colonial state, or metropolitan capital. Rather, they were a result of accommodation and compromise between the colonial capitalist state

23. Cited by Joshi 1957, p. 154.
24. Singh 1998.

and precolonial, indeed, feudal landed interests. This compromise was forced on the colonial state, as a result of the resistance by the indigenous landed aristocracy, the then – dominant class in India. The Revolt of 1857 has to be situated in this wider context of colonial rule and resistance.

Between 1848 and 1856, equipped with the Doctrine of Lapse, the East India Company moved unilaterally to devour the landed aristocracy. The expropriation of the ruler of Oudh and liquidation of the landlords of the province in 1856 was a continuation of that policy. Rebellion by the landlords of Oudh *united the latter* with the soldiers of the British Indian Army in rebellion against the Company's rule. Only a fraction of the landed aristocracy of the other states, those who had fallen prey to the Doctrine of Lapse, joined the *rebellious* aristocracy of Oudh, while the majority of the aristocracy, bound by the treaties of alliance, remained loyal to the Company, and some others sat on the fence 'waiting for more fitting time'.[25]

However, the Revolt involving a fraction of the landlords, the majority of them from a single province, Oudh, drove home the point that the colonial power was too weak to break the collective power of the then-dominant class, the landlords. More importantly, it was too weak and vulnerable to rule the entire country on its own. As noted by Engels, even before the Revolt was subdued, a secret correspondence was carried on between the majority of chiefs and the British government, 'who [had] after all found it rather impracticable to pocket the whole of soil of Oudh, and [were] quite willing to let the former owners have it again on reasonable terms'.[26]

Class, caste, and the Revolt of 1857

Whether the Revolt of 1857 was a class war is still a controversial issue for Marxist scholars in India. The Revolt was led by the feudal landlords under a predominantly feudal ideology in order to protect their traditional economic, political rights and, equally importantly, to assert their legitimacy to rule. Similarly, the peasants and artisans joining in – by and large, under the leadership of the landlords – were fighting to protect their class interests. While the landlords and peasants were united against the alien, colonial power and its new-found ally, the merchant-moneylender, at no point was there a serious challenge to the authority of the traditional landlords. P.C. Joshi rightly points out that the peasantry participating in the Revolt did not challenge the economic-political power of the traditional landlords. Nor did it challenge the dominant ideology

---

25. Marx 1978, p. 40.
26. Engels 1978, p. 161.

that legitimised the landlords' right to rule. It was, therefore, not a class war, he concludes.[27] Eric Stokes has similarly argued that the peasants were acquiescing in the old order, or looking to the *taluqdars* (landlords of Oudh) for protection. He argues that 'the rebellion of 1857 was in a significant sense a peasant revolt', but it was not 'a class revolt in any simple sense', because the peasants did not rise to protect their interests against the landlords. They did not rise as a 'class for itself'.[28]

One can fully sympathise with the argument presented above, insisting that the two principal, and antagonistic, classes in the countryside – landlords and peasants – rather than fighting against each other to defend their class interests, were united together. Notwithstanding this, it was a class war insofar as the landlords and the peasants fought together to protect their class interests against the colonial power and its new ally, the class of merchants-moneylenders.

It is well-known that the East India Company, with its main interest in the regular payment of agricultural rent, allowed the merchants-moneylenders to take over the lands of the defaulting landlords and peasants in return for guaranteed payment of rents. In taking over the lands of the landlords and peasants for non-payment of rents, the merchants were supported by the new courts established by the Company. Hence, the burning of the Banias' (merchants'-moneylenders') *bahis* (account books), *katchehris* (courts), and *bungalows* (residences of the Europeans) by the rebels was invariably recorded in all the narratives of the Revolt. The *bungalows, bahis* and *kachehries* were the new symbols of common oppression of the landlords and peasants alike. Faced with a new class enemy, which was oppressing them both, the landlords and peasants overcame their class antagonism to unite against the East India Company and the merchants-moneylenders. This was a class war.

The caste factor

Before closing this discussion, it is important to note that the alliance between the landlords and peasants against the merchant-moneylender and the Company was driven not by class interests alone, in a simplistic, economistic sense. It was also driven by cultural considerations. Class and culture are not disconnected, except in the mainstream sociological theory wedded to Max Weber's distinction between class and status.[29] The cultural factor referred to, here, pertains to caste identity.

---

27. See Joshi 1957, pp. 195–206.
28. Stokes 1985, p. 224.
29. Gerth and Mills 1958, pp. 180–94.

In the social-cultural milieu of mid-nineteenth-century India, the money-lender-merchant lacked the legitimacy to replace the traditional ruling class – the landlords – whose legitimacy to rule was not yet challenged. The landlords, belonging mostly to the Rajput caste, were the traditional ruling caste, while the merchants-moneylenders belonging to the Bania caste had no legitimacy to rule. On the contrary, the Bania was perceived as unscrupulous exploiter living off interest for which he did not labour. He was also perceived as weak, needing protection of the Rajput warrior-landlord. The Rajput landlord, on the other hand, was perceived as the legitimate owner of land, leader, and the protector of lands and people. The Rajput took pride in distinguishing himself from the Bania, boasting of his chivalry, courage, commitment and loyalty, and, last but not least, his indifference to calculations of gain and loss in economic enterprise, which, in popular perception, was the main concern of the Bania.[30]

The Rajput landlords were the Ksatriyas of the *varna* system. The Bania merchants-moneylenders were the Vaisyas of the *varna* system, lower than the Ksatriyas in the *varna* hierarchy. Rule by the Ksatriya was normal; displacement of the Ksatriya by the Vaisya was a violation of the norm, and the peasants rejected that.

The social-cultural distance between the peasants and the East India Company was even greater compared to the landlords. For the peasant, the Company was a remote authority, while the landlord was ever present in their daily lives. The peasants could not identify with the Company as their ruler. They were separated from it by creed and colour, even apart from their economic interests. In the moral economy of the peasant, the Company had no place, while the landlords were its very core. As the ruling class and caste, they had the moral obligation to protect the property and person of the peasant. They were the upholders of justice. The Company, its courts, and its bureaucracy were all alien to peasants' world view. The Company's alliance with the Bania merchant-moneylender further contributed to peasants' alienation from their new rulers.

The aftermath of the Revolt: change in class- and caste-dynamics

Christopher Bayly writes that 1857 should not be seen as a thing in itself. Rather, it should be seen as part of an ongoing resistance and struggle against colonial rule throughout. The point is well made. What is problematic is, rather, his statement that the rebellion of 1857 was unique in scale but not in content, because there was almost always a revolt somewhere.[31] It is true that there were intermittent

---

30. See Joshi 1957, pp. 201–3.
31. Bayly 1990, p. 178.

uprisings against the East India Company in one part of India or the other prior to 1857. But the Revolt of 1857 was different not only in scale, but in content. The Company had used its alliance with the landlords prior to 1857 to establish its control over three fifths of the territory, and then turned on them[32] in order to devour the remaining two fifths of territory still under landlord-control. The revolt by a fraction of the landlords of a single province (Oudh) exposed the vulnerability of the colonial power, that it could not rule on its own. It needed an ally, and that ally was the landed aristocracy, the dominant class with legitimacy to rule, which could not be replaced by the class of moneylenders-merchants on account of the latter's vulnerability in terms of both class and caste *vis à vis* the landlords. That makes the Revolt of 1857 'unique' in content.[33]

Since its suppression in 1859, historians have been writing about the outcome of the Revolt of 1857. One outcome of the Revolt, about which there is no dispute, was that the East India Company was liquidated. India became a colony of England. Queen Victoria, the Queen of England, became the Empress of India. The earlier alliance between the East India Company and the landed aristocracy (princes and landlords) was replaced by a new alliance between the British Crown and the Indian landed aristocracy. Under the renewed alliance, the colonial state agreed to honor the landlords' traditional economic rights and political-juridical privileges. By accepting the renewed alliance with the Crown and the colonial state, the landlords betrayed the Revolt and their allies during the Revolt, the *peasants*. The colonial state, on the other hand, betrayed the merchants-moneylenders, allies of the Company during the Revolt, by restoring the land rights of the landlords and dissolving the legal provision through which the moneylenders were allowed to dispossess the landlords and the peasants in the case that the latter failed to pay their dues to the Company.

Whether the Revolt was restorative or revolutionary in its objective is another controversial issue among the Left in India. It has been argued that the majority of the rank-and-file of the rebels, including the rebel soldiers of the British Indian Army, were peasants, and they were also the ones who suffered and sacrificed most, hence, the Revolt was not restorative.[34] I disagree. The landlords, the leaders of the Revolt, were fighting for their traditional rights and privileges, and the peasants were similarly fighting against the erosion of their rights and securities in the traditional system. Neither the landlords nor the peasants at any stage demanded a change in the traditional agrarian relations of production, and that is exactly what happened in the aftermath of the Revolt – the traditional agrarian relations

---

32. See Marx 1978, pp. 130–1.
33. See also Joshi 1957, pp. 176–7.
34. Joshi 1957, pp. 195–203.

of production, characterised by the landlords' monopoly of economic, political, and juridical powers, were 'restored'. These traditional, albeit feudal, relations of production became the main targets of the peasant movements of the twentieth century. In order to understand this, we have to understand the fundamental shift in the class-caste dynamics in the aftermath of the Revolt. I briefly turn to this below.

The betrayal of the peasants by the landlords and of the merchants-money-lenders by the colonial state created space for an alliance between the peasants and the merchants-moneylenders against their respective allies during the Revolt, the landlords and the colonial state (which replaced the Company). The renewed alliance between the landlords and the colonial state, on the one hand, and the merchants-moneylenders and the peasants, on the other, had serious consequences for what followed in the aftermath of the Revolt. It also fundamentally changed the caste-class dynamics between the landlords and the peasants and moneylenders-merchants in India. In spite of the vast amount of writings on the Revolt of 1857, this particular aspect has not received the attention it deserves. I want to deal with this briefly.

The alliance between the Crown and the landlords (guaranteed by the colonial state) was supposed to strengthen the landlords and protect the colonial state. It did the opposite. It weakened the landlords. Most importantly, it eroded their legitimacy as the ruling class in the countryside, affecting their relations with the peasants. On the other hand, it changed the peasants' perception of the merchant-moneylender, giving the latter legitimacy to lead. The cultural shift in the peasants' class-caste perceptions affecting their relations with the landlords and merchants-moneylenders in the aftermath of the Revolt was revolutionary. In the 1920s, Gandhi, a Vaishya, became *Mahatma* (great soul) and then *Bapu* (the Father) of the Nation. A Vaishya becoming *Bapu* of the nation was simply inconceivable in India in 1857.

But was the Revolt of 1857 a success or a failure? In writing on social movements, one has to be wary of providing an assessment in terms of 'success' or 'failure'. In the short run, the merchants and peasants lost, *in the sense that colonial rule survived, and the landlords remained the dominant class in the countryside.* In the long run, however, the landlords and the colonial state were the losers. In less than half-a-century following the suppression of the Revolt, the landlords' legitimacy as rulers was eroded. The loss of the landlords' legitimacy to rule – a legitimacy they had enjoyed for centuries, even millennia – was a critical factor in the widespread peasant movements against the landlords that broke out all over India, including the princely states, in the 1910s, continuing until the 1940s.

Why did the landlords lose the legitimacy to rule? It is not possible to deal with this question in any detail. In short, in the aftermath of the Revolt the landlords enforced all their traditional rights, without being accountable to their traditional obligations. The main problem, however, was not that of landlords being negligent of their traditional obligations. It was systemic. I deal with it briefly below.

The alliance between the colonial state and the landlords, particularly in the princely states, put to an end the incessant wars between warring princes. The landlords were warriors by profession, which was a basis of the justification of their right to land and to rule. The end of wars and the establishment of peace rendered their traditional vocation (war) unnecessary. As a result, the landlords were transformed from a necessary to a superfluous class.[35] The colonial state made the argument that, freed from war, the landlords would turn to progressive farming, exchanging the sword for the ploughshare. Both class and caste played a role in preventing the landlords from taking to the ploughshare. Indeed, the distinction between the sword and the ploughshare, distinguishing the lord from the peasant, is the hallmark of feudal culture. In India, the separation of the sword and the plough was enforced not only by class, but also by caste. A Rajput with a plough in the field was as unthinkable in caste-terms as an untouchable with sword on the horseback. That was the cultural universe in the aftermath of 1857, as defined by caste.

Freed from war, disengaged from agricultural production, the landlords were preoccupied with the remaining aspect of feudal culture – conspicuous consumption – fuelled by imports of luxury goods from the metropolitan market and encouraged by the colonial state. Frightened and demoralised by the Revolt of 1857, the colonial state not only accepted a continuation of feudal culture, particularly in the princely states, but itself became a perpetuator of and participant in that culture, in the form of the Royal Durbars – the colonial *tamasha*. Landlords' increased demand for revenue to meet their consumption needs led to the further squeezing of the peasantry.

Increased demand for revenue, combined with the superfluousness of their traditional function, hastened the erosion of the landlords' legitimacy to rule, igniting peasant movements. Peasant movements were a primary factor in the decline of the landlords and the end of colonial rule. The failing of subaltern studies – 'happy narrators of tragedy'[36] – is that, restricted by their ideological commitment to ignore class, they ignore this most significant aspect of peasant insurgency in colonial India.

The decline of the landlords as the ruling class was also the decline of their caste-status. The landlords were the Rajputs, and the Rajputs were the dominant caste. This applies particularly to the landlords of Oudh, the rebels of 1857, and to the landlords of the princely states of Rajasthan (the site of my research). The decline of the status of the Rajputs in relation to that of the Banias (former

---

35. For this distinction between necessary and superfluous classes, see Engels 1972.
36. Habib 2003, p. 8.

moneylenders-merchants, now industrialists and financiers) and the Jats (former peasants) in Rajasthan (the area of my study) underlines the connection between class and caste status.

Marx, nineteenth-century India, and Marxism: an assessment

Central to Marx's understanding of nineteenth-century Indian society and history, and the future results of the British colonial rule, was his understanding of India as a case of the Asiatic mode of production. The Asiatic mode of production is a much debated issue. It cannot, however, be bypassed while considering Marx's view of the consequences of British colonial rule in India. Since it is not possible to deal with this debate in detail, one may follow Perry Anderson's suggestion that the tenability of the Asiatic mode depends, in the last analysis, on whether the empirical evidence from Oriental societies confirms its existence.[37] On this basis, Indian Marxist historians have unequivocally rejected the thesis of the Asiatic mode of production at any stage in Indian history.[38] Kevin Anderson, on the other hand, supports Marx's view of nineteenth-century India as a case of the Asiatic mode, without providing alternative evidence to counter the evidence used by the Indian historians whose views on this question are contrary to his.[39]

Irfan Habib has further argued that there are many references in Marx's miscellaneous writings where he recognises the existence of other modes of production, with intermediary classes, in India.[40] On the contrary, Kevin Anderson argues, Marx never gave up on characterising India as having an Asiatic mode of production.[41]

Habib's point that Marx recognised the possibility of other modes of production in India is well made, but the question remains as to whether, based on Marx's miscellaneous writings, it is possible to characterise precolonial India as a class society. Habib seems to be answering in the affirmative,[42] whereas I disagree. In Marx's writings, the answer to this question is ambiguous, at best. On the other hand, if one applies Marx's method to identify classes and class contradictions (for instance, Marx's writings on ground rent), one can unambiguously characterise nineteenth-century agrarian structures in many parts of India as class society. The precolonial class structure made its imprint on the colonial social formation and social movements during colonial rule.

---

37. Anderson 1974, p. 475.
38. Sharma 2009, p. 137; Thaper 2000, pp. 6–7; Habib 2003, pp. 5–7, 15–25; see also Singh 1986.
39. Anderson 2010, pp. 1–7, 162–9.
40. Habib 2003, pp. 15–25.
41. Anderson 2010, pp. 163–9.
42. Habib 2003, p. 25.

Yet Marx's assessment of the revolutionary role of British colonial rule remains problematic, irrespective of the validity or otherwise of the Asiatic mode thesis. A serious misconception in his anticipation of the outcome of colonial rule was, in fact, the absence of resistance by precolonial, precapitalist structures and interests to colonial capitalism. As argued above, rather than sweeping away precapitalist production and property relations, colonialism was forced to make a compromise and accommodation with the former. The alliance between the East India Company and the landed aristocracy before 1857, reaffirmed in the alliance between the Crown and the landlords in the aftermath of 1857, is a confirmation of this basic fact. Precapitalist production and property relations were eventually challenged in colonial India, but this challenge did not come from colonialism. Rather, it evolved in the process of opposition to colonialism and its indigenous ally, landlordism.

According to Marx, British colonial rule, apart from its revolutionary role in sweeping away the economic base of the peculiar village community, was also to liberate the Indians from their worship of monkeys and cows. But not only did the Indians keep to their faith in the monkey-god and the holy cow in India during British colonial rule, they are, in fact, worshipping them *even now, not only in India but in England itself*,[43] while at the same time, competing with the 'rational' bourgeoisie globally. Long before the inception of British colonial rule, the Indian merchants-moneylenders (forerunners of the Indian capitalist class) had learned to combine the worship of Lakshmi, the pursuit of acquisition (the spirit of capitalism, according to Max Weber), along with the worship of the monkey and the cow, going back for millennia. British colonial rule made no difference to that.

Marx also wrote that the railroad, as the 'forerunner of modern industry', would tear apart the hereditary division of labour, the basis of the traditional caste system.[44] That did not happen, mainly because the railways in India did not become the 'forerunner of modern industry'.

The impact of colonialism on caste is a topic of much interest and significance, but I cannot deal with it here in any detail. What must be underlined, however, is that the basis of the hereditary division of labour in the traditional caste system lay in the dominant form of agrarian relations. The landlords' monopoly of land ownership, political power, and cultural resources, on which the survival of all other castes depended, was key to the division of labour in the caste system. As shown above, rather than dissolving the existing agrarian relations, that is, the landlords' monopoly of economic-political power and cultural resources, the colonial state

---

43. The reference is to the resistance by the priests of a Hindu temple in Bradford, England, to surrender the bull that was diagnosed with mad-cow disease on the ground that it was a sacred animal, dedicated to the deity of the temple, and should not be subjected to the profanity of modern medical procedures. Instead, the priest and the temple-staff will take care of the bull as part of the family of the deity.

44. Marx 1978, p. 32.

was forced to allow them to continue unchanged. This does not, however, mean that caste or the caste system was a creation of colonialism – a view advanced by Nicholas Dirks, who writes that colonial rule 'invented caste as cultural technology of rule', an inspiration, he says, he received from subaltern studies.[45] We may be reminded that caste and the caste system developed in India roughly over a thousand years before the inception of colonial rule.

In challenging the landlords' monopoly of economic-political rights and their style of life, the post-1857 peasant movements (1910s–40s) also challenged the basis of the traditional caste system. The abolition of landlordism following the end of colonial rule abolished the basis of the traditional caste system (which is not to be confused with the abolition of caste as such).

There is an ambiguity in Marx's writings on the Revolt of 1857, if one reads them along with his article on the future results of the British rule. If British colonial rule was historically necessary for social revolution in Asia (India in particular), as he wrote, then the Revolt as a movement against colonial rule was obviously an impediment to the realisation of its historic outcome. In his writings on the Revolt, however, we do not find anything negative about it, notwithstanding his critique of its organisation, leadership, military tactics and strategy. There is no ambiguity whatsoever in his writings about the class character of the Revolt and its limits.

Marx's extensive coverage of the Revolt of 1857 contrasts sharply with that of the conservative historians and the officials of the East India Company and their allies at home in Britain. Marx did not accept the view that the Revolt was a 'sepoy mutiny'. Nor did he ever accept the myth that it was a reactionary, religious convulsion fomented primarily by the priestly caste or 'class'. Instead, to him, it was a mass insurrection in response to the action of the English bourgeoisie and its agent in India – the East India Company – which had violated all that was sacred to the bourgeoisie at home – 'Property, Order, Family, and Religion'.[46] As Irfan Habib and Aijaz Ahmad have shown, one can appreciate the value of Marx's insights if one compares them to those of the idealists, conservative and liberal historians and political economists, and postmodernists.[47]

Conclusion

To conclude, Marx's writings on nineteenth-century India are insightful. It is, however, the Marxist method of class analysis that is indispensable to an understanding of the colonial social formation and social movements during colonial rule in India. Class and class contradictions were central to the colonial social

---

45. Dirks 2001, p. 9.
46. Marx and Engels 1978, pp. 33–4.
47. See Habib 2003, pp. 5–7, 16–18; Ahmad 1994, pp. 221–42.

formation and its dissolution, in which class-based social movements played a key role.

To end, I must add that class and caste are the great conundrum of Indian society. Mainstream sociology happily sees caste as a unique institution that makes class and Marxism irrelevant to the study of Indian society and history. On the contrary, a Marxist perspective on 1857 and its aftermath shows the centrality of class – not to the exclusion of caste, but inclusive of it. Therein lies the relevance of Marxism.

The Black International as Social Movement Wave: C.L.R. James's *History of Pan-African Revolt*
Christian Høgsbjerg

Introduction

> The Negro's history is rich, inspiring, and unknown. Negroes revolted against the slave raiders in Africa; they revolted against the slave traders on the Atlantic passage. They revolted on the plantations...the only place where Negroes did not revolt is in the pages of capitalist historians.

So wrote the late Trinidadian Marxist historian and writer Cyril Lionel Robert James (1901–89), one of the towering figures of twentieth-century pan-Africanism, in an article on 'Revolution and the Negro' for the December 1939 issue of the Trotskyist journal *New International*.[1] James's article itself, which discussed 'the Negro and the French Revolution', 'the Haitian Revolution and World History', 'the Negro and the [American] Civil War' and 'the Negro and World Revolution', was, in a sense, a summation of the main points James had detailed at greater length the previous year in two outstanding works: his magisterial classic account of the 1791–1804 Haitian Revolution, *The Black Jacobins*, and also in a smaller volume, *A History of Negro Revolt*.[2] As Michael O. West and William G. Martin have noted, 'C.L.R. James's little gem of 1938, *A History of Negro Revolt*, which began with the Haitian Revolution and used it as a yardstick for

---

1. James 1994a, p. 77.
2. In 1969, the work was republished with a new epilogue by James as *A History of Pan-African Revolt* by Drum and Spear Press, a new Pan-Africanist collective of former Civil-Rights activists based around a bookstore in Washington, DC. See James 1995.

judging a number of subsequent pan-African struggles' was a 'pioneering and exceptional work' outlining the history of what they call the 'black international'.[3] West and Martin insist that black internationalism has 'a single defining characteristic: struggle'.

> Yet struggle, resistance to oppression by black folk, did not mechanically produce black internationalism. Rather, black internationalism is a product of consciousness, that is, the conscious interconnection and interlocution of black struggles across man-made and natural boundaries – including the boundaries of nations, empires, continents, oceans, and seas. From the outset, black internationalism envisioned a circle of universal emancipation, unbroken in space and time.[4]

Though only eighty pages long, and destined to remain forever overshadowed by the sheer majesty of *The Black Jacobins*, *A History of Negro Revolt* nonetheless establishes James as one of the path-breaking historians of revolutionary black internationalism.[5] James demonstrated how the inspirational collective memory of the Haitian Revolution, which established the first independent black republic outside of Africa, cascaded down the years and fired the imagination of many future rebels and revolutionaries across the Americas:

> The San Domingo revolution and its success dominated the minds of Negroes in the West Indies for the next generation. In America, where the slaves had periodically revolted from the very beginnings of slavery, San Domingo inspired a series of fresh revolts during the succeeding years... even as late as 1822 in Virginia, one Denmark Vesey, a free Negro, attempted to lead a revolt which was partially inspired by San Domingo.[6]

Moreover, the work – alongside *The Black Jacobins* – was an attempt by James to invoke the spirit of the Haitian Revolution in order to help ideologically arm and inspire those involved in anti-colonial movements across Africa and the Caribbean for what he saw as an emerging new wave of revolutionary struggle. The panoramic and prophetic vision that lay behind James's grand narrative of black internationalism owed much to his anti-colonial activism. As the Guyanese revolutionary historian Walter Rodney once stressed, 'C.L.R. James was a

---

3. West and Martin 2009b, p. 87; see also Edwards 2003.
4. West and Martin 2009a, p. 1.
5. West and Martin stress the existence of another, avowedly non-violent 'revivalist' tradition of black internationalism, 'evolving alongside the revolutionary tradition, and serving as its counterpart and counterpoint... with its center in the Anglo-American world and its origins in the Evangelical Revival' (West and Martin 2009b, p. 91).
6. James 1938a, pp. 22–4. Subsequent scholarship has also demonstrated the inspiring effect of the Haitian Revolution on at least a section of the black soldiers fighting for freedom in the American Civil War (Clavin 2010).

participant in some of the earliest pressure groups in the metropoles urging freedom from colonial rule in the 1930s. That is why he was capable of writing *A History of Negro Revolt* in 1938'.[7]

Black internationalism and Marxist theory

It remains remarkable that over seventy years after James's outstanding elucidation of black internationalism in the 1930s, and despite the contemporary intellectual fashion among scholars for the transnational and the diasporic – shaped not least by Paul Gilroy's highly suggestive concept of 'the black Atlantic' – that West and Martin can still note its relative marginalisation within scholarship. As they write, contemporary scholarship is still largely dominated by 'two hegemons – the Eurocentric metanarrative and the exclusivist national narrative', the second of which has long been the established frame for thinking about 'black history' in academia, with African studies, African-American studies, Caribbean studies and so on. Accordingly, West and Martin insist that the recuperation and recovery of the rich 'counter-narrative' of black internationalism remains very much a work in progress.

> Contrary to the existing literature on social movements and revolutions, we argue that black movements have been a leading force in the search for emancipation since at least the second half of the eighteenth century . . . Against the master narrative, we posit that successive waves of black international struggles have countered, shaped, and at times destroyed central pillars of capital and empire, racial and political. In short, the story of the black international requires nothing less than a rethinking of received wisdom about life under capitalism over the long *durée* – and the possibility of alternative social worlds in the past and the future.[8]

This chapter will also aim to examine and explore the question of Marxism's possible contribution to such a 'rethinking of received wisdom' through the lens of the 'black international'. Though often dismissed as 'Eurocentric', Kevin B. Anderson's recent seminal work *Marx at the Margins* offers perhaps the clearest account of Karl Marx's own thinking 'on nationalism, ethnicity, and non-Western societies' to date, stressing the way in which Marx's perspectives evolved over time. From the 1850s, when Marx made, for example, his famous critique of 'the inherent barbarism of bourgeois civilisation' amidst a discussion on 'The Future Results of British Rule in India' (dating from 1853), he begins to emerge –

---

7. Rodney 1986, p. 34.
8. West and Martin 2009a, pp. 2, 36.

according to Anderson – as 'a global theorist whose social critique included notions of capital and class that were open and broad enough to encompass the particularities of nationalism, race, and ethnicity, as well as the varieties of human social and historical development, from Europe to Asia and from the Americas to Africa'. Moreover, 'Marx's proletariat was not only white and European, but also encompassed Black labour in America, as well as the Irish, not considered "white" at the time either by the dominant cultures of Britain and North America'.[9]

James's discussion of the 1861–5 American Civil War in *A History of Negro Revolt* was one of the very first studies to take seriously what Marx himself had to say. As James noted, 'Karl Marx hailed the Civil War as the greatest event of the age...what he could see so early was the grandeur of the civilisation which lay before the States with the victory of the North'.[10] According to Anderson, James's writings should be considered alongside those of the great black American historian W.E.B. Du Bois and his monumental 1935 work *Black Reconstruction in America; An Essay Toward a History of the Part Which Black Folk Played in the Attempt to Reconstruct Democracy in America, 1860–1880*, as pioneering efforts in finding in Marx's writings on the American Civil War 'a new dialectic of race and class'.[11]

James's neglected work, certainly, then, did not dismiss Marxism as part of any kind of 'Eurocentric' master narrative, as, for instance, the likes of Cedric Robinson have done.[12] Rather, in a fast-paced and sweeping grand narrative, James portrayed and analysed from a Marxist perspective an incredibly rich and diverse range of social movements and black liberation struggles, past and present, across the African diaspora. In his discussion of these movements, James never lost sight of the concrete historical contexts of each struggle, whether discussing the Haitian Revolution of the 1790s, the movement around Marcus Garvey after the Great War or the Caribbean labour rebellions of the 1930s, and, indeed, explored how the structures set by the contemporary political economy of capital-accumulation and the power of imperialist states conditioned and constrained how each of these particular struggles played out. Yet he was ever alive to the possibilities and opportunities created by economic crises and inter-imperialist rivalries and tensions, and thus his critical stress in *A History of Negro Revolt* was on human agency rather than social structure. Indeed, James might be seen to have envisioned the revolutionary black international as a 'social movement wave', where the ideas driving black liberation struggles not only flowed into one another down the ages, but were also always intimately

---

9. Anderson 2010, pp. 3, 6, 23; see also Nimtz 2002.
10. James 1938a, pp. 28–9.
11. Anderson 2010, p. 82.
12. Robinson 1991; for a critique of Robinson, see Callinicos 1993.

intertwined with a wider struggles and movements for emancipation from exploitation and oppression.

Such a grand vision of a 'social movement wave' was, for James, fundamentally shaped by his reading of Lenin 'on national liberation and social emancipation', together with his understanding of the Marxist theories of uneven and combined development and permanent revolution, both of which had been critically developed and elucidated by Leon Trotsky in works such as *The History of the Russian Revolution*.[13] As Trotsky had noted, the peculiarities resulting from the 'backwardness' of Russian historical development had explained the 'enigma' that 'a backward country was the *first* to place the proletariat in power':

> Moreover, in Russia the proletariat did not arise gradually through the ages, carrying with itself the burden of the past as in England, but in leaps involving sharp changes of environment, ties, relations, and a sharp break with the past. It is just this fact – combined with the concentrated oppressions of czarism – that made the Russian workers hospitable to the boldest conclusions of revolutionary thought – just as the backward industries were hospitable to the last word in capitalist organization.[14]

One of James's most striking achievements in *The Black Jacobins* had been his demonstration that, just as 'the law of uneven but combined development' meant the enslaved black labourers of Saint Domingue, suffering under the 'concentrated oppressions' of slavery, were soon to be 'hospitable to the boldest conclusions of revolutionary thought' radiating from the Jacobins in revolutionary Paris, so the Marxist theory of permanent revolution illuminated not just anti-colonial struggles in the age of socialist revolution, but also the anti-slavery liberation struggle in the age of 'bourgeois-democratic' revolution.[15] *A History of Negro Revolt* saw James expand on his analysis in *The Black Jacobins* to make a path-breaking application of the Marxist theory of permanent revolution to subsequent anti-colonial and black liberation struggles across the African diaspora.

James's overriding concern with collective political agency and revolutionary leadership is, therefore, rather different to Gilroy's concern with migratory networks and cultural creation in *The Black Atlantic*. Rather, as Walter Rodney once noted, one of the 'most significant features' of *A History of Negro Revolt* was 'its emphasis on the continuity of resistance',[16] and James's determined recovery of a submerged revolutionary tradition meant that his work was rather closer in spirit to, for example, E.P. Thompson's classic *The Making of the English Working Class*[17] or Peter Linebaugh and Marcus Rediker's panoramic account of

---

13. Trotsky 1977.
14. Trotsky 1977, pp. 19–20, 33.
15. See Høgsbjerg 2010.
16. Rodney 1986, p. 35.
17. Thompson 1963.

'the revolutionary Atlantic', *The Many-Headed Hydra*. This chapter will aim to evoke a sense of how James's creative fusion of Marxist scholarship and political activism ensured that *A History of Negro Revolt* represented, in the words of Rodney, 'a mine of ideas advancing far ahead of its time'.[18]

C.L.R. James discovers 'class-struggle pan-Africanism'

It seems unlikely that many of those close to the young C.L.R. James as he grew to intellectual maturity as a black colonial subject in Trinidad would have seriously imagined that one day he should have written such a work. During the 1920s, he was a young aspiring novelist and a respected teacher of History and English at the élite school to which he had won a scholarship as a boy, Queen's Royal College, an institution modelled on the English public school. Nonetheless, it would not have come as a complete surprise that James, a modern – or, perhaps, 'Afro-modern' – young liberal-humanist West-Indian intellectual and a writer of implicitly anti-colonial 'barrack-yard stories', would, indeed, come to the fore in vindicating the intelligence and achievements of black people, including Africans, in opposition to the white supremacy that underpinned European colonialism. James's cultural activism throughout the 1920s was increasingly accompanied by a growth of political consciousness, expressed in support for the growing nationalist movement around the social-democratic Trinidad Workingmen's Association (TWA) led by the charismatic self-declared 'champion of the barefoot man', Captain Arthur Andrew Cipriani. 'My hitherto vague ideas of freedom crystallised around a political commitment: we should be free to govern ourselves', he later wrote of this period.[19]

James was, then, in the eloquent words of George Lamming, 'a spirit that came to life in the rich and humble soil of a British colony in the Caribbean'.[20] While teaching at QRC, and perhaps influenced by the wider backdrop of the Harlem Renaissance and the power of the black nationalist movement around the Jamaican pan-Africanist Marcus Garvey during the 1920s, James began to research the hidden history of black resistance to slavery and colonialism in the West Indies. 'I was tired of hearing that the West Indians were oppressed, that we were black and miserable, that we had been brought from Africa, and that we were living there and that we were being exploited'.[21] No doubt mindful of the plight of Haiti itself – under US military occupation since 1915 – James was soon reading what limited material he could find in colonial Trinidad on the Haitian Revolution. James's researches were evident in James's writings as early as 1931,

---

18. Rodney 1986, p. 31.
19. James 1969, p. 119.
20. Lamming 1960, p. 150.
21. Hall 1996, p. 21.

when, in a polemical article countering a racist English scientist, he praised the great Haitian revolutionary leader Toussaint Louverture.[22]

In Trinidad, James had begun work researching and writing a 'political biography' of TWA leader Captain Cipriani, and, indeed, in his 1932 book *The Life of Captain Cipriani*, James tore into the British Government's line of 'self-government when fit for it', demonstrating that the recent growth of the TWA was proof, if proof were needed, that the black-majority societies of the Caribbean had always been manifestly 'fit' to govern themselves. Robert Hill has noted James's biography of Captain Cipriani, a former commanding officer in the British West Indies Regiment (BWIR), 'bases its perspective on the vindication of the West Indian soldier and his achievement in the Great War of 1914–18'. The return of the BWIR from Italy – where they had revolted against racism and the War – to unemployment, poor housing and poverty in colonial Trinidad, helped spark a general strike led by dockworkers in 1919 and the rise of political nationalism. James's portrayal of the war-experience of the black soldiers of the BWIR reveal, according to Hill, how 'James by 1932 had discovered more than political nationalism ... he had discovered the socially revolutionising force of the "inarticulate" ' in a colonial society.[23]

However, while the source of works such as *The Black Jacobins* and *A History of Negro Revolt* lies, therefore, in the Caribbean, it was only after his move to England in 1932 that James's developing 'black internationalism' began to really emerge and replace his early identification with imperial 'Britishness'. This is not the place to detail his growing commitment to more radical transnational identifications with African people and people of African descent, and their culture, while in Britain. Suffice it to say that his evolution towards what Kent Worcester has usefully termed 'class-struggle pan-Africanism' in the midst of the Great Depression and the rising threat of fascism in Europe went side by side with his political radicalisation towards revolutionary Marxism.[24] By 1934, when he joined the tiny international Trotskyist movement, James had not only arrived at an explicitly anti-imperialist vision of 'West Indian self-government' but was also openly declaring in public lectures that 'there was going to be a tremendous revolt in Africa someday'.[25]

Class-struggle pan-Africanism in 1930s Britain

If Paul Robeson, the great black American star of stage and screen, could in 1953 declare that he had 'discovered Africa' and come to consider himself 'an African'

22. Scott 2004, pp. 80–1.
23. Hill 1986, pp. 64–5.
24. Worcester 1996, p. 42; see also Hill 1986; Worcester 1993; and Høgsbjerg 2006.
25. 'Racial Prejudice in England', *Nelson Leader*, 16 March 1934.

in London, his home from 1927 to 1938, in part through studying African languages and folksongs at what is now the School of Oriental and African Studies in London, the same was true for James, though he, of course, undertook no formal academic study.[26] Critical, instead, for James, was his continuing historical research into the Haitian Revolution – in March 1936, this led to the production on London's West End of his anti-imperialist play about that revolution's great leader: *Toussaint Louverture: the story of the only successful slave revolt in history*, starring Robeson himself in the title role – and also his pan-Africanist agitation and activism. James had continued his campaigning for 'West-Indian self-government' after arriving in Britain, despite securing a prestigious post as a cricket-reporter for the *Manchester Guardian*; in 1935, he became chair of the newly formed International African Friends of Abyssinia (IAFA) organised in London to rally solidarity with the people of Ethiopia in the face of Italian Fascist dictator Mussolini's barbaric war.

To justify such nineteenth-century style empire building, in time-honoured fashion, the criminal invasion and occupation of a sovereign nation was declared by Mussolini to be 'a war of civilization and liberation'.[27] Outraged Africans from across the diaspora felt Ethiopia was, in the words of IAFA member Ras Makonnen, 'the black man's last citadel' and 'letters simply poured into our office from blacks on three continents asking where they could register'.[28] Most strikingly, the IAFA considered organising an 'International Brigade' from Britain to go and fight Fascism in this 'last citadel' of pan-African pride. In a letter to his comrades inside the socialist Independent Labour Party, James explained that he hoped to join the Ethiopian army to make contact with 'the masses of the Abyssinians and other Africans': 'I did not intend to spend the rest of my life in Abyssinia, but, all things considered, I thought, and I still think, that two or three years there, given the fact that I am a Negro and am especially interested in the African revolution, was well worth the attempt'.[29]

James's pan-Africanist agitation was not just carried out alongside his work as the driving intellectual force of the tiny British Trotskyist movement, but also alongside African intellectuals in Britain such as the Kenyan nationalist leader Jomo Kenyatta. One critical relationship for James on the political scene of interwar London was with his boyhood friend, the Trinidadian George Padmore (1902–59). Unlike James, Padmore had clearly identified with pan-Africanism from his early days, reading the likes of W.E.B. Du Bois and Marcus Garvey in 1920s colonial Trinidad. Though the two had lost touch since Padmore moved to

---

26. Foner 1978, pp. 351–3.
27. Quoted in Padmore 1972, p. 153.
28. Makonnen 1973, pp. 116–17.
29. James 1974, pp. 158–9.

America in 1924, more by accident than design, they enjoyed a brief reunion in London in the summer of 1933. Padmore had risen to become one of the leading black activists in the Communist International – indeed, chair of the 'Negro Bureau' of the Red International of Labour Unions (the Profintern) and editor of the Communist publication, the *Negro Worker*, a 'seditious publication' banned across the British colonial world. However, not long after Hitler's Nazis had come to power in Germany, Stalin had moved to try and make diplomatic approaches with Britain and France for reasons of national security, and the theorists of the Communist International accordingly now drew a distinction between the 'democratic-imperialist' countries of Britain, America and France, on the one hand and the 'fascist-imperialist' powers of Germany, Italy and Japan, on the other. In August 1933, after meeting James, Padmore made what he retrospectively justified as a principled resignation from the Communist International in protest at their sidelining of support for anti-colonialist struggle against the now supposedly 'democratic' and 'peace-loving' British and French colonial dictatorships in Africa. After surviving a vicious Stalinist witch hunt, Padmore had worked in Paris with Francophone pan-Africanists, while also writing a four-hundred-page work – which would appear in 1936 as *How Britain Rules Africa* – before turning up at the door of James's flat in August 1935, and quickly throwing himself into activity.[30]

Though the agitation over Ethiopia began to fall away in Britain after Mussolini declared 'mission accomplished' in 1936, the questions that the IAFA had raised about Africa and imperialist domination in general were more relevant than ever as Europe once again headed towards war. Accordingly, Padmore, with the help of others including James, Kenyatta and also I.T.A. Wallace-Johnson – a towering giant of African trade unionism, originally from Sierra Leone – launched the International African Service Bureau for the Defence of Africans and People of African Descent (IASB) in May 1937. The IASB raised the case for, built solidarity with and helped ideologically arm colonial liberation struggles across the African diaspora.[31] As James, who edited the IASB paper *Africa and the World* and the journal *International African Opinion*, remembered:

> We carried on agitation and propaganda in England whenever we got the opportunity, speaking in Hyde Park regularly and addressing meetings of the Independent Labour Party, the Labour Party, attending all the front organisations that the communists organised ... the basis of that work and the development of ideas was Padmore's encyclopaedic knowledge of Africa, or African politics and African personalities, his tireless correspondence with Africans in all parts

30. On Padmore see James 1984; James 1992; Hooker 1967; Baptiste and Lewis 2009; and Polsgrove 2009. On the Comintern, see Adi 2009; James 1994b.
31. Derrick 2008; Edwards 2003; Polsgrove 2009.

of the continent, the unceasing stream of Africans who made the Bureau and its chairman their political headquarters when in London.[32]

The making of *A History of Negro Revolt*

Testimony to the growing profile of the IASB was the fact that in 1937, the British socialist historian Raymond Postgate, founder and editor of a new left-wing monthly review *F.A.C.T.*, asked Padmore for a piece on 'Negro revolt'. However, Padmore, whose new work *Africa and World Peace* had recently been published, claiming pressures of IASB activity, instead referred Postgate onto James, who was then busy putting the finishing touches to *The Black Jacobins*.[33] James – by this time 'within Padmore's circle of associates, the most articulate theoretician of Pan-Africanism', according to Manning Marable – wrote what became *A History of Negro Revolt* rapidly, finishing it by April 1938.[34]

Just as James's 1937 anti-Stalinist history of 'the rise and fall of the Communist International', *World Revolution, 1917–1936* was, in essence, a synthesis based on a compilation of Trotskyist literature, now James put his growing repertoire of knowledge of the history of past and present pan-African struggles to good use. There was one important precedent to James's work – Padmore's classic 1931 Communist pamphlet entitled *The Life and Struggles of Negro Toilers*.[35] Padmore was to be a critical influence on James in the writing of *A History of Negro Revolt*. James recalled how Padmore 'brought his great knowledge of Africa to bear', and how 'we had a marvelous time putting in a number of provocative statements which we knew Postgate would object to. But by putting in those and then agreeing to take them out, much really good stuff was sure to get in'.[36] James paid tribute to Padmore in the text, noting 'the files of the *Negro Worker* give many accounts of these revolts, and *The Life and Struggles of Negro Toilers*, by George Padmore, contains a great deal of coordinated information which is not easily available elsewhere'.[37]

---

32. James 1977, p. 65.
33. Hooker 1967, p. 54; Postgate and Postgate 1994, pp. 198–9.
34. Marable 1999, p. 91.
35. In 1936, Padmore had enjoyed a remarkable piece of good luck concerning this pamphlet, discovering a large stock that had long been withdrawn from sale and was languishing in the basement of the Communist Party of Great Britain's 'Workers' Bookshop', hidden away from the public. During that bookshop's move from King Street to Farringdon Road, Padmore had been able to persuade a student left in charge one lunchtime to part company with the entire stock of this now rare and valuable work for a reduced rate, enabling him to sell them on to his growing contacts. As Padmore's biographer notes, 'precisely what the store managers thought when they learned of this transaction may be surmised'. See Hooker 1967, p. 23.
36. James 1960, p. 37.
37. James 1938a, p. 53.

Recalling the writing of *The Black Jacobins*, James noted that 'historical in form, it drew its contemporaneousness, as all such books must, from the living struggle around us, and particularly from the daily activity that centred around Padmore and the African Bureau'.[38] The same and more could be applied to the writing of *A History of Negro Revolt*, which in its discussion of contemporary struggles across colonial Africa and the Caribbean, relied directly for information on the political relationships that the IASB was able to establish with activists in and from the colonial world itself. Particularly critical, here, was the rather overlooked role played by the organising secretary of the IASB, Chris Braithwaite (c. 1885–1944), a Barbadian agitator and seamen's organiser better-known under his adopted pseudonym 'Chris Jones'. Braithwaite, as leader of the Colonial Seamen's Association (CSA) formed in 1935 and an important 'class-struggle pan-Africanist' in his own right, was, perhaps, the critical lynchpin of an anti-colonial maritime subaltern network in and around the imperial metropolis of interwar London. Braithwaite wrote a monthly column for the IASB journal, *International African Opinion*, entitled 'Seamen's Notes', and through his contacts as chair of the CSA, Braithwaite was also key to the distribution of IASB literature in colonial Africa and the Caribbean.[39] As James recalled, 'we tried all ways' to get *International African Opinion* into the colonies, where such subversive literature was prohibited. 'We had one or two people who worked on the waterfront. They gave the pamphlets to seamen and people in boats... we got it around, to my astonishment and delight'.[40] The contacts Braithwaite and others made, in turn, fed information and reports back to the organisers in London. One very clear example of this can be seen in James's discussion of the heroic arc of labour-rebellions that swept the British Caribbean during the 1930s, when the Caribbean background of leading members of the IASB such as Padmore, James, Braithwaite and Makonnen, as well as their contacts with activists in places such as Trinidad and Jamaica, enabled the IASB to be at the forefront of building solidarity in Britain itself.[41]

'Revolts in Africa'

Perhaps the most important and original sections of *A History of Negro Revolt* for the future development of a Marxist optic for thinking about social movements emerge where James focused his attention on colonial Africa and the 'series of revolts, which have never ceased' since the European 'scramble' for the continent in the 1880s, up to and including the general strike in the Gold Coast (now Ghana)

---

38. James 1977, p. 66.
39. Høgsbjerg 2011b.
40. Socialist Platform 1987, p. 6.
41. Høgsbjerg 2011a.

in 1937.[42] James's stress on agency, here, made the work very different from say, Padmore's 1936 *How Britain Rules Africa*, which provided relentless detail of the exploitation of African workers through charting the precise structural differences in terms of capital formation and imperial rule that marked each individual colony. As James noted, 'the difference between the native under Belgian imperialism plain and simple, and Belgian imperialism carrying out the mandate of the League of Nations, is that the Belgian Government presents a report at Geneva on the working of the mandate. The native, however, is not likely to know this'.[43]

Despite the problems of censorship about uprisings in the colonial world, through the IASB's contacts, James, for example, managed to piece together a brief portrayal of 'the extraordinary women's revolt' against the implementation of an unfair new tax in the British colony of Nigeria in 1929. Though what is now known as the 'Women's War' was bloodily repressed, James noted this was a spontaneous rebellion, 'the strength and vigour' of which were 'a shock to the Europeans'.

> Thousands of women organised protest demonstrations against the Government and its chiefs and at Aba, the capital of the Eastern Province, the women who sold in the market, faced with the possibility of a tax which would destroy their small profits, organized a revolt. The writer is informed by Africans from Nigeria that the actual happenings in Aba have been suppressed in all official reports. The women seized public buildings and held them for days. The servants refused to cook for their white masters and mistresses and some of them made the attempt to bring the European women by force into the markets to give them some experience of what work was like ... a detachment of soldiers suppressed the revolt, shooting at the black women as they tried to escape across the river. Martial law was proclaimed and the Governor called a meeting of the African editors of Lagos threatening them with imprisonment if they published news of what was happening at Aba.[44]

Religious movements in colonial Africa

Rodney thought it particularly noteworthy that James discussed 'a series of African social movements' of the interwar years in Eastern and Central Africa, 'commonly designated as the African Independent Church movement. James unerringly identified three of the most important of these – centred on John

---

42. James 1938a, p. 37.
43. James 1938a, pp. 55–6.
44. James 1938a, pp. 45–6; see also Van Allen 1976.

Chilembwe (Malawi), Simon Kimbangu (Congo) and Harry Thuku (Kenya)'.[45] James noted that 'in the thirty years before the [First World War], the tribes simply threw themselves at the government troops and suffered the inevitable defeat. Such risings could not go on. They were too obviously suicidal'. However, beginning with the Chilembwe rising in Nyasaland in 1915, 'we have a new type – a rising led not by a tribal chief' but by an African preacher or 'prophet' who has had some religious education and so 'often translated the insurrection into religious terms'. Of 'the greatest of the religious type of revolt' which began in 1921 around Simon Kimbangu in the Belgian Congo, James noted that 'he appealed to the natives to leave the mission churches, controlled by their European masters, and to set up their own independent church organisation under his guidance. To every African such a movement is an instinctive step towards independence'.[46] As Rodney noted, James stood against the tendency in European scholarship to portray such movements 'as being exclusively related to religion or superstition' but 'distinguished between form and content, noting that the language of religion in which the protests were couched should not obscure the fact that they sprung from such things as forced labour, land alienation and colonial taxation'.[47]

An analysis of racial formation

One other critical stress that Rodney picked up on in James's chapter on 'Revolts in Africa' was the 'analysis of workers' organizations and their militancy', including 'the powerful Black trade-union activity' of the Industrial and Commercial Workers' Union (ICU) of South Africa under the leadership of Clements Kadalie.[48] Of James's careful tracing of the rise and fall of the Kadalie movement during the 1920s, Rodney notes, 'in a most economical manner, he probed the quality of the leadership, examined the relationship of leadership to the mass from which it sprang, reflected on the international context of the strikes and other protests by the African workers of South Africa at that time, and quietly indicated that within a racist situation the category of "class" must be seriously re-examined'.[49]

As James had noted of Kadalie, 'the white South African workers refused his offer of unity, for these, petty-bourgeois in outlook owing to their high wages and the social degradation of the Negro, are among the bitterest enemies of the native workers'.[50] This discussion, made long before the rise of academic 'whiteness' studies, implicitly noted the importance of what Du Bois called 'the

---

45. Rodney 1986, p. 31.
46. James 1938a, pp. 47, 49.
47. Rodney 1986, p. 32.
48. Rodney 1986, p. 32.
49. Rodney 1986, pp. 32–3.
50. James 1938a, p. 62.

public and psychological wage' gained by white workers in societies based on fixed hierarchies related to upholding ideas of white supremacy, and built on Marx's ideas of how racism could fatally undermine class unity.[51]

In *A History of Negro Revolt*, James had a fascinating analysis of what scholars now call 'racial formation' in the context of the Haitian Revolution, and James briefly recounted the process by which 'race' was socially constructed, deconstructed and then reconstructed according to shifts in wider relations of classpower on the French colony of Saint Domingue throughout the Revolution.

> The attitude of the whites towards changes in the San Domingo regime throws a valuable light on race prejudice. Before the revolution Negroes were so despised that white women undressed before them as one undresses today before a dog or a cat. Ten years after, when former slaves were now ruling the country, most of the whites accepted the new regime, fraternized with the ex-slave generals and dined at their tables; while the white women, members of some of the proudest families of the French aristocracy, threw themselves recklessly at the black dictator [Toussaint], sent him locks of hair, keepsakes, passionate letters, etc. To the labouring Negroes, however, they showed as much of their old hostility as they dared. When the [imperial French] Leclerc expedition came [in 1802], the whites rushed to join it, and took a leading part in the gladiatorial shows where dogs ate living Negroes, etc. But when they saw that Leclerc's expedition was doomed to defeat, they disentangled themselves from it and turned again to the blacks.[52]

Indeed, for James, to contextualise the Kadalie movement in its full historical perspective, one had to understand 'the real parallel to this movement is the mass uprising in San Domingo. There is the same instinctive capacity for organisation, the same throwing up of gifted leaders from the masses'. James accordingly stressed the critical importance of the relationship between resistance in the colony and in the metropolis. 'Whereas [with Haiti] there was a French Revolution in 1794 rooting out the old order in France, needing the black revolution, and sending out encouragement, organisers and arms, there was nothing like that in Britain'. While the absence of a revolutionary situation in postwar Britain ultimately ensured the movement in South Africa 'could not maintain itself... seen in that historical perspective, the Kadalie movement can be seen for the profoundly important thing that it was'.[53]

---

51. See Callinicos 1993, pp. 36–9.
52. James 1938a, p. 15.
53. James 1938a, p. 62.

The Copperbelt mineworkers' strike of 1935

James concluded his discussion of revolutionary black internationalism in *A History of Negro Revolt* with a discussion of the spontaneous mass strike of copper-miners in Northern Rhodesia (what is now Zambia) in May 1935, which he considered to be of immense historical portent and significance. The Copperbelt miners had struck in protest at an increase in the poll tax at a time of rising economic insecurity, a strike that was bloodily repressed with six miners left dead and 22 wounded. Frederick Cooper has drawn attention to the creativity of the miners and their supporters during this strike: 'The Northern Rhodesian mineworkers strike of 1935 was organised without benefit of trade unions, and it spread from mine to mine, from mine town to mine town, by personal networks, dance societies, religious organisations, and eventually mass meetings. The movement embraced non-miners in the towns, women as well as men'.[54]

One can imagine the growing excitement for a 'class-struggle pan-Africanist' and a Marxist with such understanding of the contradictions of religious belief like James, as he gradually learnt more and more about what had actually taken place. The movement was centred around the 'native proletariat' – Copperbelt miners – and, for James, the parallels between the glorious self-activity and capacity for improvisation displayed by supporters of the striking miners and the enslaved Africans who had made the Haitian Revolution were compelling: 'Should world events give these people a chance, they will destroy what has them by the throat as surely as the San Domingo blacks destroyed the French plantations'.[55] James made such a statement after noting that the official 1935 *Report of the Commission appointed to enquire into the Disturbances in the Copperbelt, Northern Rhodesia*, a Commission chaired by Sir Alison Russell, had found that 'the Watch Tower Movement has some influence among the Rhodesian natives'.[56] In his 1936 *How Britain Rules Africa*, Padmore had described how the 'Watch Tower Movement' – related to the Jehovah's Witnesses – was 'one of the most formidable organisations of tribal-"religious" character' in Africa: 'The *Watch Tower Movement*, although originating in Nyasaland, has widespread ramifications into the Belgian Congo, Northern Rhodesia and Tanganyika. Much of its activities is so interwoven in the tribal life of the people that it is difficult for Europeans to keep track of its underground activities'.[57]

For James, the 'Watch Tower Movement' was a symbol of the coming African Revolution. 'It is difficult to say exactly the true influence of the Watch Tower. The writer has been informed by Negro sailors that its influence is widely spread

---

54. Cooper 1996, p. 58; see also Perrings 1977, pp. 207–17.
55. James 1938a, p. 81.
56. James 1938a, p. 82.
57. Padmore 1936, p. 365.

throughout Africa, and that it is the most powerful revolutionary force in Africa today'. Using such sources, as well as the detail in the Russell Commission, James went on to spell out a pioneering Marxist analysis of the appeal of this millenarian movement – based on the biblical *Revelations of St. John* – to Africans suffering under European colonial domination:

> The Watch Tower bases its teaching on the second coming of Christ... [and declares] all the governments which are ruling the world, especially Great Britain and the United States of America, are organisations of Satan, and that all churches, especially the Protestant and Roman Catholic churches, are emissaries of Satan. Religion thus becomes a weapon in the class struggle.[58]

Indeed, James described how 'Watch Tower' preached 'a transparent doctrine' in colonial Africa, 'a fierce resentment against all the imperialist Powers'. 'It does not seek to distinguish between the Fascist and the democratic imperialisms. To the vast body of Africans in Africa such a distinction is meaningless'. 'Watch Tower' saw Great Britain as the 'blasphemous name' of the seventh head of 'the Beast', which represented the ruling powers of the world under the control of the Devil, 'given authority over every tribe, people, language and nation'. The League of Nations was a 'false prophet' born of the Devil and the British Empire, another beast that 'exercised all the authority of the first beast on his behalf, and made the earth and its inhabitants worship the first beast... he deceived the inhabitants of the earth'. As James commented, 'the gentle Jesus, meek and mild, of the missionaries cannot compete with the Watch Tower God':[59]

> Such are the ideas moving in the minds of these African copper miners. They are absurd only on the surface. They represent political realities and express political aspirations far more closely than programmes and policies of parties with millions of members, numerous journals and half a century of history behind them.

Just as James saw voodoo as 'the medium of the conspiracy' for the illiterate enslaved Africans on Saint Domingue in *The Black Jacobins*, he declared 'Watch Tower says what the thinking native thinks and what he is prepared to die for'.[60] It was surely the possibilities that 'the African Revolution' could begin with a series of spontaneous uprisings – some possibly waged by those inspired by the 'Watch Tower Movement' – that helped strengthen James in his decision to end both *The Black Jacobins* and *A History of Negro Revolt* with these Copperbelt miners in colonial Africa as opposed to, say, the more explicitly political labour-rebellions of the colonial Caribbean.

58. James 1938a, p. 83.
59. James 1938a, pp. 82–4.
60. James 1938a, p. 83; James 2001, p. 69.

Though often retarded and sometimes diverted, the current of history, observed from an eminence, can be seen to unite strange and diverse tributaries in its own embracing logic. The San Domingo revolutionaries, the black army in the Civil War, were unconscious but potent levers in two great propulsions forward of modern civilisation. Today the Rhodesian copper miner, living the life of three shillings a week, is but another cog in the wheels of a creaking world economy . . . but Negro emancipation has expanded with the centuries; what was local and national in San Domingo and America is today an international urgency, entangling the future of a hundred million Africans with all the hopes and fears of Western Europe. Though dimly, the political consciousness immanent in the historical process emerges in groping and neglected Africa. If Toussaint wrote in the language of '89, the grotesquerie of Watch Tower primitively approximates to the dialectic of Marx and Lenin. This it is which lifts out of bleakness and invests with meaning a record of failure almost unrelieved.[61]

The Publication of *A History of Negro Revolt*

In September 1938, *A History of Negro Revolt* was published, and James remembered it 'could be seen on all bookshops and railway stalls'.[62] Nonetheless, he recalled that 'the book has a peculiar history'.

> Postgate's name got the book sold in book-stores all over the country. When they found out what was in it some of them carefully hid it. There were places we went to where we found they had hidden it – they put it under a lot of other books, but when you asked for it they would say, yes, we have it.[63]

Such self-censorship in the 'dark heart' of imperial Britain was, perhaps, not so surprising. At the end of *The Black Jacobins*, James had described colonial Africa as a 'vast prison', and in *A History of Negro Revolt*, James concluded by noting 'the African bruises and breaks himself against his bars in the interests of freedoms wider than his own'.[64] But James also stressed that a mass prison breakout was not just necessary but, in certain conditions, possible, as there were so few white people around who could act as guards. Indeed, given 'the real basis of imperialist control in Africa is the cruisers and aeroplanes of Europe', the looming inter-imperialist war provided immense possibilities and potentialities for African revolutionaries. 'If, for instance a revolt began in the Congo and spread to South Africa, East Africa, West Africa, the Africans could easily overwhelm the whites

---

61. James 1938a, p. 85.
62. James 1974, p. 160.
63. James 1980, p. 70.
64. James 2001, p. 303; James 1938a, p. 85.

334 • Christian Høgsbjerg

if these could no longer receive assistance from abroad'.[65] Many other black writers naturally dreamt of a postcolonial Africa during the 1930s, and the black American 'literary pan-Africanist' George S. Schuyler even went so far as to imagine 'a tale of black insurrection against Italian Imperialism', a 'revolt in Ethiopia', the rise of a new 'black Internationale' and the emergence of a 'great new civilization in modern Africa', a 'black Empire', in a set of Afrocentrist stories written during the 1930s.[66] However, few others aside from 'organic intellectuals' of the pan-African movement such as James put such effort into not only working for the coming 'African Revolution', but also excavating and recovering its actual historical foundations. It was an effort appreciated by the few who took the time to read *A History of Negro Revolt*.[67] After all, for all its limitations and stylistic weaknesses, resulting from the fact it was written at great speed amidst a host of other commitments, James's 'class-struggle Pan-Africanism' gave the book a rare prophetic power and urgency. *A History of Negro Revolt* stands, just as Seymour Drescher once noted of *The Black Jacobins*, as 'one of the historiographical manifestoes of anti-imperialist scholarship on the eve of decolonization'.[68]

Conclusion

'One of the great experiences of my life'. That was how James remembered the historic transformations that have come to be known as 'decolonisation,' the decline and fall of the European empires after the Second World War. 'I want to emphasise, I hadn't the faintest idea that would happen and when that happened I was astonished'.[69] It was not, of course, the case that the author of *A History of Negro Revolt* had not believed colonial liberation to be possible. On the contrary, as we have noted, James had stressed that emancipation was inevitable. 'The imperialists envisage an eternity of African exploitation', he noted in *The Black Jacobins*, but 'they dream dreams'.[70] Yet in 1938, James, a leading member of Trotsky's Fourth International, 'world party of socialist revolution', had predicted that revolution in the colonial periphery would, as before in Haiti, be sparked by upheaval in the metropolitan countries. 'Let the blacks but hear from Europe

---

65. James 1938a, pp. 84–5.
66. Schuyler 1991; 1994.
67. The American Trotskyist George Novack, for example, welcomed the work noting 'this useful and inexpensive parcel of information ought to be in the hands of all revolutionary internationalists' See Novack 1939. Testimony to the fact that those lucky few who did acquire a copy found it tremendously valuable emerges from the correspondence I had in 2005 with the late Len Edmondson, a member of the Independent Labour Party during the 1930s.
68. Quoted in James 2001, p. viii.
69. Socialist Platform 1987.
70. James 2001, p. 303.

the slogans of Revolution, and the *Internationale*, in the same concrete manner that the slaves of San Domingo heard Liberty and Equality and the *Marseillaise*, and from the mass uprising will emerge the Toussaints, the Christophes, and the Dessalines. They will hear'.[71] Yet expectations that the Second World War would end with the turning of 'imperialist war' into 'civil war' as had happened in the First World War in Russia, were to be dashed. When the 'mass uprising' against colonialism proceeded to erupt regardless, without hearing the necessary 'slogans of Revolution' from Europe, veteran anti-colonialists like James were as astonished as colonial officials.

Yet the failure of the European working-class movements – overwhelmingly politically dominated by the politics of either social democracy or Stalinism during this period – to stir alongside 'the African Revolution' was ultimately, as James noted, one part of the explanation for the ultimate failure of victorious colonial liberation struggles to fulfil the hopes and expectations of their supporters, and the degeneration of the dream of 'pan-African socialism' into the reality of autocratic rule and bureaucratic corruption. In 1957, James insisted that 'the revolt in Kenya' would have been comparable to the inspirational Haitian Revolution had it had 'socialist allies' in power in Britain, just as the French Jacobins had been vital to the ultimate success of the revolt on Saint Domingue.[72] Nonetheless, the eruption of 'the African Revolution' – with the working class playing a central role in the struggle for independence in many places, including Nigeria and Zambi – represented a vindication of James's vision in works such as *A History of Negro Revolt*.[73] As Rodney could comment in 1972, speaking of James's discussions of African working-class militancy in *A History of Negro Revolt*, 'in each instance, he pinpointed phenomena of the greatest relevance to the creation of Africa as it is today, and he was doing so a comfortable twenty years before writings on these subjects generally acknowledged these facts'.[74]

James's vision of universal emancipation in *A History of Negro Revolt* thus went beyond even the boundaries of the submerged revolutionary tradition of black internationalism. As James insisted in 1939, 'it is not strange that the Negroes revolted. It would have been strange if they had not': 'What we as Marxists have to see is the tremendous role played by Negroes in the transformation of Western civilization from feudalism to capitalism. It is only from this vantage-ground that we shall be able to appreciate (and prepare for) the still greater role they must of necessity play in the transition from capitalism to socialism'.[75]

71. James 1938b, p. 315.
72. James 1977, p. 69.
73. See Zeilig 2009.
74. Rodney 1986, p. 32.
75. James 1994a, p. 77.

Social Movements Against Neoliberalism

Language, Marxism and the Grasping of Policy Agendas: Neoliberalism and Political Voice in Scotland's Poorest Communities
Chik Collins

Introduction: The Community Voices Network

On 5–6 March 2006, the city of Glasgow hosted the founding conference of a newly emerging organisation – one which it was hoped would duly be seen to speak for the poorest communities across the whole of Scotland. It was to be called the Community Voices Network (CVN).

But this was no 'grassroots' event. The venue was a nice hotel in the city centre – the Menzies. Welcome to attend, and to join the CVN, were residents of the 15 percent of poorest areas in Scotland, as identified by the devolved Scottish Executive's recently devised Scottish Index of Multiple Deprivation.[1] Participants were to stay overnight in the hotel – or in an 'overspill'-hotel nearby. Lunches, room and a conference dinner, including pre-dinner drinks, were to be provided. Funding was being supplied by Communities Scotland – at that time, an agency of the Scottish Executive dealing with housing and the 'regeneration' of places affected by industrial decline and its attendant effects.

---

1. Devolved government was established in Scotland following a referendum which had been promised by New Labour prior to the 1997 UK General Election. The referendum was conducted in 1997 and the first elections in 1999. The resulting Labour and Liberal-Democrat coalitions (1999–2007), fearful of nationalist sentiment, used the term 'Scottish Executive' rather than 'Scottish Government'. The latter term was used by the minority Scottish National Party administration established in 2007, and returned again in 2011 with a parliamentary majority.

Around a week previously, the Scottish Executive had launched a new 'regeneration statement'.[2] For many, the statement represented little more than a 'refreshing' of a long-familiar approach. This was the 'partnership' approach to 'regeneration' – one created in an attempt to diffuse the conflicts surrounding 'regeneration' in the later years of Margaret Thatcher's spell as UK prime minister.[3] It did so by seeking to build an apparently consensual framework of working relationships amongst the various parties involved in implementing the Conservative Party's vision of 'regeneration'. Among these various parties were the local communities affected. They, too, had been constructed as 'partners'.

This model of 'regeneration' had remained hegemonic in the intervening years. This meant that the conference taking place was not entirely unprecedented. Over the years of 'partnership', there had been ongoing attempts to co-opt and manage Scotland's local communities for the purposes of 'regeneration partnerships', at times involving conferences, trips and stays in hotels. This particular event seemed to be on a larger scale than previously, and it looked like an attempt was being made to attract new people to the task of 'representing' local communities in 'regeneration' areas across Scotland. But beyond that, there seemed little to suggest anything particularly novel was going on.

A linguistic curiosity

Little, that is, apart from the language. The opening contribution to the conference invoked a language of grassroots campaigning and political struggle.[4] CVN member Cathie Arbuckle spoke of 'unity and common purpose' and of communities speaking 'with one voice'. She summoned the name of Emmeline Pankhurst: 'With one powerful and very, very loud voice we *will* be heard'. This was a familiar language, of course, but it was one that had been *specifically delegitimated* within the framework of 'partnership' almost twenty years earlier. Partners, it had been said, are seen to 'work in harmony' – and certainly don't raise their voices against each other in public.

As indicated, this 'partnership' approach had become hegemonic from the later 1980s, steadily extending its scope beyond the field of 'regeneration' to encompass a much broader swathe of Scottish institutional life. The advent of New Labour in 1997, after 18 years of Conservative rule, and of Scottish

2. Scottish Executive 2006.
3. Scottish Office 1988.
4. The linguistic data reported here was collected in less than ideal conditions. I was initially excluded from the conference, and when I did manage to gain access, I was not in a position to make a sound recording or use a camera. The reporting is thus based on handwritten notes made from the floor of the conference and written up further in the immediate aftermath of the event.

devolution from 1999, had not altered this – indeed, these developments had seen 'partnership' embraced even more fulsomely. The Scottish Executive had, as we have also mentioned, just published a 'regeneration statement' that seemed to make its ongoing commitment to the 'partnership' principle very clear. So why were the Executive's representatives, both political and from the bureaucracy, smiling and applauding as Arbuckle invoked a language that seemed to be so at odds with that principle?

That this was not simply politeness on the part of the Executive's representatives seemed to be confirmed by the subsequent contributions. Johann Lamont, Deputy Minister for Communities in the Scottish Executive, actively endorsed the frustration of local communities with the failures of 'community participation' in the past and, indeed, the failure to address the substantive problems of poverty in 'regeneration' areas. She responded to quite pointed interventions from the floor and expressed backing for an active, energetic and enthusiastic network of community organisations, which would help to bring about change where it was needed.

But there was, perhaps, little to get excited about. Things like this had been said before, but had betokened little in terms of substantive planning for real change. Or maybe there *was* something significant happening – something of relevance to those at that time interested in the future of Scotland's poorest communities, not with a view to their subordination to external agendas, but with a view to resisting and transforming that? How would one begin to sort out this apparently confusing situation, in order to figure out what might be done to address it? What tools and resources for thinking and understanding might prove useful?

Marxism and the philosophy of language

My argument is that tools and resources to be found within Marxism are of vital relevance. This claim may seem tendentious to a good number of social-movement activists and to those who, as students over the past twenty-five to thirty years, have been provided with a 'straw man' version of Marxism in colleges and universities. Marxism, according to this kind of view, is a crude doctrine, both determinist and reductionist, inherently limited in its capacity to grapple with language and subjectivity, and the complex and unpredictable interplay of politics, identity and emotion in today's rapidly shifting and changing globalised world.

Now, Marxism in some hands may, indeed, have approximated – or even conformed – to this assessment; but the same could be said for just about any set of theoretical tools placed in the 'wrong' hands. Placed in other hands, Marxism assumes a quite different complexion. Such were the hands of Valentin

Vološinov, author of the now famous and often celebrated – though, in practice, still much too little applied – *Marxism and the Philosophy of Language*.[5]

Writing in the Soviet Union in the later 1920s, Vološinov set out to delineate the basic directions for a Marxist approach to language. He approached this task in three stages – the first two of which are of primary relevance, here. Firstly, he set out the salience of language for a series of problems and questions vital for Marxism: questions of meaning, ideology and social consciousness; the problem of accounting for relationships between 'basis' and 'superstructures' without resorting to mechanicism; the dynamics of class struggle and the task of developing an 'objective' (or 'socio-ideological') psychology, as opposed to a physiological, biological or an introspectionist one.

Secondly, Vološinov set out to identify 'the actual mode of existence of linguistic phenomena', which, he concluded, was 'the social event of verbal interaction implemented in an utterance or utterances'.[6] In opposition to both the Saussureans, and the Croceans and Vosslerites, Vološinov found the 'actual reality' of language in the real flow of speech exchange in concrete contexts of social life: 'Language acquires life and historically evolves precisely here, in concrete verbal communication, and not in the abstract system of language forms, nor in the individual psyche of speakers'.[7]

The life that language is found to acquire in this context is, for Vološinov, replete with ideology. It both reflects the divisions and struggles of the society to which it belongs, and is also an 'objective fact' and a 'real force' – at times a 'tremendous social force' – in shaping that society.[8] It is absolutely crucial to the study of human consciousness and its development – for 'the logic of consciousness is the logic of ideological communication'.[9] And the historical evolution of such communication is, at the same time, a vital *index* of the broader historical evolution of the society which has produced that language:

> Countless ideological threads running through all areas of social intercourse register effect in the word. It stands to reason then, that the word is the most sensitive *index of social changes*, and what is more, of changes still in the process of growth, still without definitive shape and not as yet accommodated into already regularized and fully defined ideological systems... The word has the capacity to register all the transitory, delicate, momentary phases of social change.[10]

---

5. Vološinov 1973.
6. Vološinov 1973, pp. xv, 94.
7. Vološinov 1973, p. 95.
8. Vološinov 1973, p. 90.
9. Vološinov 1973, p. 13.
10. Vološinov 1973, p. 19.

A sensitive index

The implications of this latter observation merit amplification. Vološinov is indicating how valuable it would be to have an analytical awareness of language, one that can detect shifts and changes in familiar forms and patterns of communication as possible indicators of significant socio-political realignment and reconstitution.

Of course, not all language is likely to provide the raw material for such analysis. Much of speech communication is bound up with 'momentary and accidental states of affairs', but it is also an inherent aspect of processes of greater significance.[11] Here, its manifestations are 'more vital, more serious'; they 'bear a creative character', prove 'mobile and sensitive' in times of change, and reflect and refract significant underlying developments 'more quickly and more vividly' than do prevailing, and typically rather more ossified, ideological systems.[12]

There is, perhaps, a particular interest, here, for those concerned not just with past experience, but also with the problems that confront collectivities in the here and now. Amongst these problems is the often difficult one of establishing what is, in fact, *happening* in the world – where the challenges are coming from, what the threats are, how they might be countered, what opportunities might be identified to exploit offensively rather than just defensively, and so on. Perhaps the kind of awareness of language Vološinov directs us towards could help with some of this?

It would not be that language could, *in and of itself*, attest to very much at all. Vološinov himself is clear that linguistic analysis can never be any kind of 'discovery-procedure'.[13]

> *Any utterance*, no matter how weighty and complete in itself, *is only a moment in the continuous process of verbal communication*. But that continuous verbal communication is, in turn, itself only a moment in the continuous, all-inclusive, generative process of a given social collective... *Verbal communication can never be understood and explained outside of this connection with a concrete situation*.[14]

Indeed, it is precisely these manifest connections that mean that linguistic analysis *can actually have* a significant role to play in a much broader process of discovery. The *internal connections* between language and everything else

---

11. Vološinov 1973, p. 92.
12. Vološinov 1973, p. 92.
13. This stands as a forceful corrective to a four-decade lineage of Critical Linguistics and Critical Discourse Analysis, which has continuously failed, even under the frustrated exhortation of its founding figure (Roger Fowler), to come to terms with the matter highlighted; see Jones and Collins 2010; Collins 2008a.
14. Vološinov 1973, p. 95.

in a given situation are what mean language has the potential to tell us about *something rather more than language itself.* The perception of linguistic change can function as a trigger for a broader investigation of emergent change and of its likely significance and implications. Moreover, given the indexical sensitivity of language, its changing can alert us to yet broader changes in the *process* of emergence and, therefore, subject to contestation, influence, harnessing, and so on. And with this thought, we return to the Menzies Hotel, Glasgow, on Saturday 5 March 2006.

Curiosity piqued

I was there. I had to work very hard indeed to get in and only just managed to get 'observer' status. What I 'observed' brought into sharp relief a 'hunch' I had already. The hunch was that the new 'regeneration statement' was, in fact, indicating not the pretty straightforward continuity with the pre-existing 'partnership' model many perceived, but a significant departure in the conception and purpose of that model. The sharp change in what was treated as 'acceptable' language now crystallised the matter.

But there were other indicators. One was the absence of some of the organisations that one might previously have expected to attend such an event. The aforementioned Communities Scotland was the affiliation of most of those other than local community members who were attending the conference. A smaller number were listed as employees of the CVN itself. Other organisations involved in 'regeneration-partnerships' over the years – most notably, local government, but also the health service and government agencies – went unrepresented. Perhaps they were being repositioned?

In perceiving the potential significance of these indicators, I was drawing on prior experience. I was able to recall the period, almost twenty years previously, in which the language of grassroots campaigning and political struggle had been delegitimated and the language of 'partnership' had come to dominate. Then, too, local government had found itself repositioned in 'regeneration'. At that point, local community organisations had struggled to come to terms – intellectually and practically – with both the shift in language and the broader changes in policy and practice to which it was linked. They had been suspicious of 'partnership', but unable to deliver an effective critique. They were duly 'sucked in' by promises of being 'empowered' in shaping a new and better future for their communities. They were then systematically *disempowered* and, by the time they were able effectively to articulate the reality – which was that they were being used to grant a spurious legitimacy to the imposition of a neoliberal agenda, not just in their own communities, but across Scotland as a whole – they had lost much of the capacity to challenge what was being done.[15] Learning came too late for it to be basis for effective action. I was conscious that something similar might happen again.

The challenge, in such a situation, would seem to be to establish how far something substantively new might *actually be* emerging. Drawing on Vološinov, this challenge might be approached by seeking to trace the key contours of the 'continuous process of verbal communication' that had first legitimated, and then delegitimated, the exercise of political voice by Scotland's poorest communities, prior to this newly apparent relegitimisation. This, of course, would mean seeing the key moments of change in more than simply linguistic terms – as moments 'in the continuous, all-inclusive, generative process' of the life and relationships of these communities. It would mean grasping situations, both immediate and broader, and the connections between these situations and the real evolution of language, *concretely*.

In what follows, I present a reconstruction of this process and of its key moments, focusing in particular on policy development, and on its linguistic framing and ramifications.

Grasping the concrete

The exercise of political voice by working-class communities has a long history in Scotland – as in many other places. The Clydeside rent strikes during WWI and the organisation of the unemployed during the 1920s and 1930s are well-known examples. After WWII, many of the demands of these movements were at least partially delivered by the Keynesian welfare state – full employment, council housing at affordable rents, the National Health Service, and more. For a time, these developments provided the basis for the myth that poverty had been abolished, but from the later 1950s, this myth was challenged by 'the rediscovery of poverty'.

The mid-1960s saw the emergence, drawing on the experience of the US, of various UK-level government 'experiments' focused on what were seen as problematic inner-city concentrations of poverty. These initiatives were given further impetus by the emergence of race as a factor in some of these areas and in national politics more generally. By the later 1960s, these developments had led to the creation of a national Urban Programme and a series of experiments across Britain in the form of the Community Development Project. The approach, here,

---

15. See Collins 2008a.

was a pathologistic one; poor communities were seen as reproducing their own poverty through cultural tendencies that made them 'hard to help'.[16]

The legitimation of political voice

However, this was also a time when local communities were rediscovering some of their prior traditions of organisation and political voice. The 'community-action' movement emerging in this period sought to democratise and decentralise the agencies of government and welfare provision, so as to render them meaningfully responsive to local needs. The influence of this movement, linked to the advent of various forms of Marxism and neo-Marxism in academia, impacted first on the *implementation* of urban policy, and later, particularly from the mid-1970s, on its *conception*. Pathologistic thinking gave way to thinking that located the primary causes of urban poverty *outside* of communities – in industrial restructuring, political decision making and economic change.

In this context, the active encouragement of community activism – or 'community development' – came to be seen as a key part of the solution to problems. There were both radical and neopluralist variants of this thinking. Radicals saw themselves working 'in and against the state'.[17] Neopluralists sought the exercise of community voice in order to secure more efficient allocation of resources to meet needs.[18] The latter thinking was progressively institutionalised across many urban areas – typically Labour-controlled – including those in the Scottish central belt. The result was that the exercise of a certain limited kind of political voice was actively encouraged by both the local and national state.

The election of Margaret Thatcher in 1979, and the ensuing neoliberal 'shock-treatment' across the UK, seems initially to have bolstered this trend, but then to have rendered it increasingly problematic. Initially, there were many more things for communities to be organising and campaigning against – mass unemployment, attacks on council housing, on local government finances, on benefit claimants, and so on. But local government was the primary employer of community development workers. It was also often the primary target for the campaigns that they helped to promote – due to the deterioration of the services that local government found itself presiding over. But what, those in local government increasingly asked, could they realistically do? 'Amplification' of the demands of the poor is one thing in a time of social democracy, and quite another in a time of neoliberal 'shock treatment'. And, in this context, there was some significant realignment. Communities were invited to seek collaboration, rather than conflict, with local government – working together to defend the poorest from the

16. Cochrane 2007.
17. London-Edinburgh Weekend Return Group 1980.
18. Cockburn 1977.

worst effects of Thatcherism, while everyone waited for an electoral triumph for the Labour Party. Here, the exercise of political voice remained legitimate, but its practice was partially – at times, substantially – suspended.

The moment of delegitimation

The attempt specifically to delegitimate the exercise of political voice came, as already indicated, in the wake of Labour's third consecutive electoral failure at the UK level. In 1987, Margaret Thatcher entered her 'triumphalist period' – with a massive parliamentary majority. But in Scotland, her party suffered what was, by the standards of the day, a humiliating defeat. The scenario – described at the time as 'the doomsday scenario' – was of a government imposing radical neoliberal policies on a nation that had resolutely rejected them. It was a discordant and volatile situation.

This moment might be seen as nodal in the transition from the 'roll back' to the 'roll out' of neoliberalism in Scotland – indeed, in the UK, and perhaps even more widely.[19] The Conservatives in Scotland attributed their electoral failure to the prevalence of a 'culture of dependency' and set out to remake the character of the nation – to create a 'culture of enterprise'. Here, the brute force of 'rollback' neoliberalism gave way to something more 'engineered' and, in its own way, developmental.

Revealing its profoundly materialist perspective on culture, the Thatcher government deduced that a rebalancing of the roles of the public and private sectors in producing the nation's life was key to a change of culture. The private sector should increasingly take the lead; the public sector should be repositioned in an 'enabling role'. But this could not *merely* be enforced; it had to be legitimated, too – and this was the problem to which the language and practice of 'partnership' was conceived as the solution. The profoundly dissensual nature of the context required the elaboration of a framework that – on the surface, at least – looked, and could actually be *experienced*, by some, as consensual. People would be encouraged to believe that they could work *together*, towards a better future for Scotland's poorest communities.

The challenge for the Government was to ensure that this new vision was institutionalised in real neoliberalising practices. Not for the first, or last, time, 'regeneration' was seen as a key policy area in this regard – an area in which experimentation was an established and familiar fact.[20] Its focus on poor communities would serve a dual purpose. Firstly, it would allow the Conservatives to re-present themselves as reflecting – albeit in their own way – Scottish society's concern about poverty. Sceptics could be encouraged to leave aside their own

---

19. Peck and Tickell 2002.
20. Cochrane 2007.

'ideological' concerns and to 'just do what was needed'. Secondly, poor communities also provided an ideal 'proving ground' for the Government's overarching project. These communities were, after all, the 'extreme case' of Scotland's alleged 'dependency culture' – owned and managed almost entirely by Labour-dominated local government and with very high levels of benefit 'dependency'. If the Government's policies could be presented as working in these areas, then this would provide a basis for the broader dissemination of neoliberalising 'partnerships' as the new 'best practice'.

Initially, in 1988, four urban areas around Scotland were identified for a high-profile and long-term 'regeneration' experiment – under the slogan *New Life for Urban Scotland*.[21] But how would these initial ventures themselves be legitimated? The government hardly possessed the credentials to justify the kind of sustained interventions in local communities being outlined. Local and regional government was dominated by 'Old Labour' (social-democratic rather than 'third-way'), and central government would not entrust the latter with the implementation of such a vital initiative. So, central government had itself to lead. In this context, the remaining source of legitimacy *could only be the local communities themselves*; their direct involvement in the *New Life* 'Partnerships' would provide *participatory* – in place of representative – legitimacy. They, too, would be 'partners'.

The broader language of 'partnership' was itself an indication of the Government's desire to depoliticise matters, and this had clear implications for the delegitimation of communities' political voice. But it was the need to legitimate 'partnership' in the poorest communities, *through the direct participation of the local communities themselves*, that provided the key *imperative* for that delegitimation. Previously, communities had collaborated with local government in opposition to central government's neoliberal policies, but now they were being invited to collaborate with a central government to *allow their implementation*. Communities might, instead, decide that such was a very bad idea, and then give expression to this in ways that would have serious implications – not just for 'regeneration' policy, but also for the broader project of neoliberalising Scotland. The whole thing was inherently risky. It might well 'blow up'. Local communities would need to be made to feel just as bound by the 'ethics' of 'partnership' as all the other agencies involved. And lest there be any doubt, this was asserted as the first implementation principle of 'partnership': 'The partners should work in harmony and be seen to be doing so'.[22]

21. Scottish Office 1988.
22. See Cambridge Policy Consultants 1999.

The hegemony of 'partnership'

The early years of the *New Life* programme were by no means unproblematic. There were moments of crisis.[23] But key aims were in significant ways achieved. Local and regional government either played the game or – beholden as it was to central government for resources – paid the price. New agencies were created to carry forward the Government's agenda – Scottish Enterprise in the area of economic development; Scottish Homes to drive privatisation of public sector housing. Local communities in the four 'partnership areas' were carefully managed: key individuals were co-opted, and where that failed, both individuals and organisations could be dispensed with and new people could be brought forward to 'front it up' in public. Through this process, 'partnership' was increasingly *normalised* and *generalised*.[24] Who could be opposed to everyone working together to try to do something for the poorest communities?

This is not to say, however, that the more *overtly professed* aims of the *New Life* programme were being met. Quite the opposite: notwithstanding substantial investment, the already severe social and economic crises of these communities intensified.[25] But such facts could be – and were – largely managed out of the discussion and the awareness, not just of the public at large, but also of many of those directly involved in 'partnership' working.[26]

When Labour failed to win the 1992 UK General Election – the Conservatives were returned under John Major – the 'roll-out' phase of neoliberalism was stepped up. In Scotland, local and regional government was subjected to a wholesale, and massively damaging, reorganisation. The regional tier was abolished and generally smaller and weaker authorities were created – within new and nakedly gerrymandered boundaries. To obtain 'regeneration' funds, the new authorities were expected to compete against each other by demonstrating their willingness to adopt, and to innovate with, the Government's 'partnership' model. Those authorities with the most intense and problematic concentrations of poverty were the biggest losers. Thus was created a new raft of Priority Partnership Areas around Scotland – now led by the rather more 'domesticated' Labour local authorities, along lines laid down by central government.[27]

In opposition, the Labour Party in Scotland had railed against all of this. But by 1997 – in which year the Party won the UK General Election – its critique

---

23. Collins 2008a.
24. Collins 2004.
25. Cambridge Policy Consultants 1999; Collins 2003.
26. From the mid-1990s, academic researchers were coming under concerted pressure to present their findings accordingly (see Hambleton and Thomas, 1995). More generally, a combination of public relations work and 'training and information' for 'best practice' with those working in the field were used to maintain the illusory belief in the efficacy of 'partnership' (see Collins 2003; 2004; and 2008b).
27. Collins 2008b.

of 'partnership', and of much else in the neoliberal lexicon, had become rather muted. Labour was now Tony Blair and Gordon Brown's 'New Labour' – a vehicle freshly prepared for the extension of 'roll-out' neoliberalism as the Conservative Party imploded after 1992. The Party's criticisms of the failures of 'partnership' in 'regeneration' gave way to enthusiastic endorsement of its achievements – even before the final and, on examination, quite damning, evaluation of the *New Life* programme had actually been conducted.[28] The Priority Partnership Areas now became Social Inclusion Partnerships (SIPs) – and a whole new raft of such 'partnerships' was designated.

'Partnership' became more hegemonic than ever. Yet, despite the ongoing repositioning of the local authorities within the 'partnership' agenda through the 1990s, the implementation of that agenda remained reliant on the claim that local communities themselves were active participants in 'partnerships' and proponents of the policies being implemented. This was no coincidence, for these partnerships were pursuing the kind of neoliberal agenda that community organisations – with a tradition of campaigning and popular mobilisation – might just be expected to challenge. It remained vital that they should feel 'bound in', and specifically discouraged – forcefully if need be – from exercising political voice.[29]

Signs of change

As the millennium approached, New Labour delivered on its promise of devolution. The Scottish Parliament, with responsibility over a range of policy areas, was reconvened after almost three hundred years. It was controlled for the next eight years (1999–2007) by a Labour and Liberal-Democrat coalition, which took charge of the new 'Scottish Executive'.

In the field of regeneration, there were already moves towards yet another generation of partnerships. These would be Community Planning Partnerships (CPPs), dealing with 'regeneration', but now within a broader framework encompassing all aspects of service delivery across local government areas. In a further stage in the normalisation of 'partnership', every local authority would soon be obliged to convene a CPP. They would then seek resources from the Executive for their 'regeneration' activities, focused on the poorest 15 percent of communi-

---

28. Collins 2003.

29. Around the millennium, there was a concerted effort to manage and control the process of 'community participation' in 'partnership' projects, to avoid some of the problems encountered in the *New Life* project, in particular by seeking to bind community representatives into primary relations of accountability to other 'partners'. The emphasis was, then, to be placed on adapting the broader community to the needs of the 'partnerships', rather than vice versa (see Collins 2003, pp. 82–3).

ties as identified by the Scottish Index of Multiple Deprivation. The SIPs were to be assimilated into these now much broader CPPs.[30]

However, around the time of the 2003 legislation that would enact this, there was a significant faltering in the confidence hitherto attached to the 'partnership' model – and, indeed, in the prevailing vision of Scotland's progress. The coalition's agenda had, to that stage, been a curious hybrid of neoliberal economics and the limited pursuit of 'social justice'. Economically, the vision was of entrepreneurialism – focused on small and medium-sized businesses.[31] Socially, the policy was one of 'inclusion' and 'closing the gap' between the most 'disadvantaged' and the mainstream.[32] But from 2003, all of this began to change. In the words of the civil servant who was later to lead on the 2006 'regeneration statement', ministers came to 'feel the need to say something about regeneration'.[33] The curious thing was, they had only very recently 'said something' about it.[34] Why so soon?

It would take three years for the new statement to be made, and when it was finally issued, it was heralded with a bold new slogan. This was *not* about the plight of local communities or the pursuit of social justice. 'The Scottish Executive', it declared, 'is open for business'.[35] This, when linked to the apparent relegitimation of the political voice of poor communities, was seemingly an indication that something quite significant was afoot – that a shift was underway. Why might that be?

Shifts in Scotland's 'economic basis'

The key trigger seems to have been the substantial collapse in Scotland's important, but largely externally owned, microelectronics industry – in 'Silicon Glen'. Between 2000 and 2003, 'substantial plant closures and contractions' saw the output of the sector fall by around a half. These were 'partly attributable to a global recession in electronics, but also to a significant shift in production towards lower cost locations in Asia and Eastern Europe'.[36] With Scotland's oil and gas sector also in sharp decline, the Edinburgh-based financial services sector was now the unassailably dominant force in the Scottish economy – and inclined to flex its muscle in relation to the newly devolved institutions. The behemoth within the sector was a certain Royal Bank of Scotland (RBS) – by

---

30. Collins 2004.
31. Scottish Executive 2001.
32. Scottish Executive 2002.
33. Collins 2006a.
34. Scottish Executive 2002.
35. Scottish Executive 2006.
36. Turok and Bailey 2004, p. 40.

2005 the fifth biggest bank in the world.[37] It was at that point, led by a certain Sir George Mathewson, assisted by his now infamous deputy and heir, Sir Fred ('the shred') Goodwin.

Within government, as Turok puts it, there was now a recognition 'of the reality of diminishing opportunities to attract inward investment in manufacturing ... and stronger pressures to support indigenous enterprises'.[38] The particular enterprises to be supported were, however, no longer primarily to be small and medium-sized. In 2004, RBS published an analysis of *Wealth Creation in Scotland*.[39] Baird, Foster and Leonard summarise it admirably.[40] Small nations, it argued, require businesses of scale – capable of competing in global markets. Scotland, it continued, compared well with other small nations by this standard, but had in the preceding years stopped generating firms of the scale required. This was largely to do with the relative decline in policies of liberalisation and privatisation, which had previously provided opportunities for indigenous firms to grow domestically and then to project themselves internationally – in the manner, for instance, of Stagecoach or First Group. The solution was to renew liberalisation and privatisation. Health and education, together with water, were specifically indicated as areas in which public expenditure could be harnessed to the task of growing globally competitive 'service providers'.[41]

'Right', said Fred; 'Yes, Sir', said the Scottish Executive

As Baird and colleagues indicated, within six months of the RBS report, the Scottish Executive had issued a 'refreshed' version of its pre-existing economic policy.[42] It carried two key changes of emphasis. Firstly, there was a new emphasis on growing companies *of scale*; secondly, on *cities* as 'vital to driving the overall economic health of Scotland'.[43]

The latter emphasis reflected the somewhat belated embrace in Scotland of what was then being called 'the new conventional wisdom' in urban policy. It was at that time described as 'a set of widely shared ideas about the emergence of a new urban era in advanced economies' related to 'a set of pervasive forces in a globalized economy'.[44] Within this view, cities were seen to have competitive advantages as business locations in a service-oriented 'knowledge-economy',

---

37. Baird, Foster, and Leonard 2005.
38. Turok 2007, p. 152.
39. Royal Bank of Scotland 2004.
40. Baird, Foster and Leonard 2005.
41. Royal Bank of Scotland 2004, p. 11.
42. Baird, Foster and Leonard 2005.
43. Scottish Executive 2001, p. 25; 2004, p. 25.
44. Buck, Gordon, Harding and Turok 2005, p. 5.

and those cities which strived for and achieved 'competitiveness', it was suggested, could become key 'drivers' of broader regional and national growth. The challenge, from this perspective, was for cities to maximise their openness to global markets and to compete as attractive business locations. The NCW was, in other words, a resolutely neoliberal approach to economic and urban policy – one based on doctrinal faith rather than on any actual evidence.[45] It had been promoted for some time by the World Bank, the OECD and the European Union.[46] It had not found favour in Scotland in the early years of devolution, but by 2003–4, in the wake of the collapse in microelectronics, it was being embraced wholesale.[47] For Cochrane, it entailed a 'redefinition of urban policy in economic terms', but the reverse formulation would seem more accurate.[48]

Yet, as Turok notes, in Scotland this far-reaching policy shift had – even by 2007 – 'received little attention among commentators in the media and academia' and it had 'generated surprisingly little public debate'.[49] Moreover, this was of significant strategic value for those driving the policy development. Scotland's urban spaces were, after all, the key locations for the delivery of those services which RBS wanted liberalised and privatised. Urban policy could be used as a way of developing the practical framework for achieving that on the ground. In the absence of much awareness of what was happening – let alone critical public scrutiny – all of this could be legitimated as 'working in partnership' to 'help the poor'.

In this light, the 2006 'regeneration statement' – *People and Place* – can be seen as a key part of the implementation strategy for the new 'firm-growing' agenda. It sought to promote the idea that businesses willing to engage early in the process would reap substantial rewards. 'Regeneration' was to be 'a crucial part of growing the economy', a matter of 'creating value', and henceforth would require 'clarity and certainty about the sustained commitment of the public sector . . . to private sector involvement'.[50] 'Regeneration' was to be about ensuring that Scotland's *poor communities* – with their many 'development opportunities', but also with their health, social and education services – would be 'open for business', and that their potential to fuel the growth of large 'service provider' companies would be realised.

People and Place outlined a quite coherent framework for the implementation of this strategy. The aforementioned CPPs were now reconceived as dissemination grounds for the more path-breaking work to be carried out in a range of

---

45. Buck, Gordon, Harding and Turok 2005.
46. Cochrane 2007, pp. 128–35.
47. Turok 2007.
48. Cochrane 2007, p. 97.
49. Turok 2007, p. 149.
50. Scottish Executive 2006, pp. 4–5, 15.

Urban Regeneration Companies.[51] In these areas, the already existing parapher-
nalia of privatisation – Public Private Partnerships, Joint Venture Companies,
Property Investment Limited Liability Partnerships – together with other new
and emerging 'forms of financial instrument', were to be deployed in new and
experimental ways.[52] It was recognised that this posed 'technical, financial, economic and legal complexities', which might 'prove insurmountable'. But 'clear
political commitment from key players' was promised.[53] Finally, *People and Place*
gave a clear indication that all of this was strongly relevant to the future of the
public services: 'The relationship between regeneration, renewal and public sector reform is a complex but critical one: we will bear it firmly in mind in the context of the forthcoming debate on the future of public services in Scotland'.[54]

'The forces of conservatism' and the Community Voices Network

There was, indeed, then, a significant new departure in urban policy in Scotland
in the early part of 2006. This was linked to a broader shift in economic policy
in the wake of a key rebalancing of the Scottish economy and the relative power
of its different lobbies. Overall, a step change in the application of neoliberalism to Scotland as a whole was being attempted. The previous 'social justice'
agenda had, to all intents and purposes, been replaced by 'trickle down'; and
the Executive was now intent on opening up public services to much greater
penetration by private interests – similar to Blair's 'modernisation' agenda in
England.

But why would the pursuit of this agenda be aided by the relegitimation of the
political voice of the poor communities who were to be the first – and almost
certainly worst – affected by all of this? Surely this would be a time to keep
the genie of community political voice firmly contained within the hegemonic
'partnership' bottle.

But perhaps not: the key reference point, here, is what Tony Blair referred to
in his 1999 Labour Party Annual Conference speech as 'the forces of conservatism' – those in the public sector and the trade unions opposed to New Labour's
'modernisation agenda'. The Executive understood that the intensified application of neoliberalism in Scotland would quickly challenge the interests of those
charged with implementing it much more pointedly than previously. The latter
were not expected always to cooperate. One of the few journalists who did pick
up on these developments recorded the fact clearly: 'each layer of government

51. Scottish Executive 2006.
52. Scottish Executive 2006, p. 23.
53. Scottish Executive 2006, p. 14.
54. Scottish Executive 2006, p. 54.

and quangocracy is currently digging its defences'.[55] How would such defences be breached?

It is in this light that one can grasp the conception of the CVN – as the leading element of a 'community engagement strategy' designed to support the new 'firm-growing' agenda. Whereas in the past 'community participation' had been a way of co-opting and managing local communities as to *allow* the implementation of neoliberal policies, now 'community engagement' aimed to recruit their *active involvement* in facing down opposition to the implementation of a new and intensified version of neoliberalism.[56]

Here, one encounters what can only be seen as breathtaking cynicism on the part of the policy makers. It was understood that after almost twenty years of 'partnership', during which time the situation of the poorest communities had greatly worsened, there was a well of frustration and resentment in these communities waiting to express itself. The idea was to gather that frustration and resentment, and to encourage its expression. However, its expression was to be legitimate only when directed at *particular targets* – those amongst the 'forces of conservatism'.[57] Symptomatically, as noted previously, all other public agencies – whether in local government, the health service, or the quangos – were actively excluded from the CVN conference. The ostensible reason was to allow communities to speak without undue inhibition. Only the Scottish Executive and Communities Scotland were present. And they presented themselves to the local communities as the friends and allies of the poor, expressing solidarity with them in their justified battle against elements in the public sector that had, over the years, benefited personally from 'regeneration' while refusing to act upon the concerns of the poor communities who had benefited so little.[58] On this basis, the Executive seemed to believe, the CVN would be at the Executive's side, with its new-found, if limited, political voice, to ensure that

---

55. Fraser 2006.

56. A useful reminder suggested by a reviewer of this chapter is that the actual language deployed in particular cases is likely to vary. The key issue is the potential significance of shifts and changes at particular moments, and the need to be alert both to their occurrence and to what may underlie them.

57. This is clearly an example of a more general phenomenon. Another contemporaneous example was the attempt to recruit the people of Rosia Montana, Romania to counter the opposition to the plans of Gabriel Resources, the Canadian-based resource-mining company, for their area – and, in particular, the company's advertisement in the *Guardian* newspaper (23 June 2006, p. 15) in response to the intervention of the actress Vanessa Redgrave.

58. An intriguing approach to eliciting the expression of such views from the attendees involved the use of a 'corporate artist' who spoke to people individually and in pairs and then depicted their experience and feelings in the form of a cartoon using a flipchart. The cartoons were then placed on the walls to construct a 'gallery' around the conference room and other attendees were invited to use 'post-it' notes to add comments to them.

'producer interests' would not block the necessary 'radical measures' in the period ahead.

Thus, in the language of *People and Place*, the CVN was part of the process of 'lifting barriers to private sector involvement'.[59] And, in order to be seen to be practicing what it was preaching, the Scottish Executive had already contracted the CVN's operation to a private firm – the 'social and economic development consultancy' Paul Zealey Associates.[60]

From grasping the concrete to grasping the moment

Along the pattern outlined above, it proved possible, in the early spring of 2006, to establish that something significant was, indeed, afoot in the world of 'regeneration' – and, indeed, much more widely – in Scotland. It was possible, moreover, to identify the intended role and purpose of the CVN within the unfolding scenario – while its role was as yet not established and its purpose not yet fulfilled. On that basis, it was possible to try to project an analysis of the situation in relevant fora – to open up to critical scrutiny the underlying processes and to undermine the ongoing attempt to portray the new 'regeneration' agenda and the creation of the CVN as well-intentioned attempts by reasonable people to help the poorest communities.[61]

More generally, it was possible to conceive and, in some ways, to act upon, an agenda of interventionist research focusing upon the emotional vulnerability of Scotland's poor communities to exploitation by purveyors of neoliberalism.[62] The aim was to work with particular communities in reconstructing the concrete process through which they had come to *feel* as they did – to be potentially vulnerable to the exploitation for external purposes of their negative emotional states – and to identify the roles of different agencies at various levels within that process.

The point, here, is not that the ultimate fate of the CVN – which was disbanded within three years, having failed to achieve anything substantive – was decided by this intervention. The intervention undoubtedly had some impact, but other factors ultimately had more. Within a few months of CVN's launch, the approach of the 2007 Scottish Parliament elections, and the Scottish National Party's adoption of the mantle of defender of public services (particularly health), had

---

59. Scottish Executive 2006, p. 15.
60. Again this outsourcing of 'public engagement' reflects a more general development (see Lee 2009 and also the same author's current project on 'Disciplining Democracy', http://sites.lafayette.edu/leecw/research/disciplining-democracy/).
61. See, for example, Collins 2006a; 2006b; 2006c; 2007.
62. See, for example, Collins 2008b.

forced what was intended to be a temporary shelving of the Labour and Liberal-Democrat coalition's 'modernisation' agenda. In the event, and in part because that agenda had been pursued too vigorously and shelved too late, a minority SNP government was returned in 2007.

Even then, there remained powerful lobbies who might well have turned the SNP to embrace a similar 'modernisation' agenda. Sir George Mathewson, then recently retired from RBS, was appointed, and remains today in 2011, the Chairman of the Scottish Government's Council of Economic Advisors. But within a few months of the 2007 elections, the unfolding 'credit crunch' was already massively undermining the prospects for 'regeneration'. A year later, with the international banking collapse, the RBS, together with the Halifax Bank of Scotland, had effectively been nationalised, and Fred 'the shred' Goodwin was pensioned off and in hiding.

In this context, the vision of 'regeneration' that had emerged in 2006 was radically undermined – politically, economically and practically. The CVN seemed no longer relevant and was vulnerable to accusations of manipulation and 'astroturfing'.[63] Moreover, its organisers had struggled to find enough in the way of actual or potential local community organisation willing to 'engage' with the CVN. Twenty years of 'partnerships' had worn out an ageing and increasingly demoralised generation of activists, and had helped to discourage a younger generation, often deprived of the trade-union experience of the older generation, from taking its place. The organisation was increasingly seen to lack even a 'surface' credibility.

The point is, rather, that an awareness of linguistic change, informed by Vološinov's *Marxism and the Philosophy of Language*, was the trigger for a broader investigation of ongoing processes of change and development in Scottish economy, politics and society. This investigation made it possible to grasp – in a way that would probably not otherwise have been possible – what was going on in a key moment of policy change and in the associated implementation frameworks. On this basis, it was possible to respond, and to help to enable others to respond, *timeously*. And within this quite specific experience lies a more general way of thinking, inspired by the kind of insight that David Bakhurst has described as 'characteristic of (good) Soviet Marxist writing in the 1920s', about language as an *index of social change*.[64] This thinking, I suggest, has a broader relevance and value to those concerned not just with understanding social change, but in engaging with it while it is still in the process of emergence, and, therefore, still susceptible to struggle and to the realisation of alternative potentialities.

---

63. Lee 2009.
64. Bakhurst 1994, p. 210.

Conclusion

Vološinov introduces his thinking about language as an index of social change in relation to Marx's metaphor of basis and superstructure. Not infrequently, this metaphor has been seen as typifying Marxism's alleged tendency towards a reductionist and mechanistic determinism. However, 'characteristic of (good) Soviet Marxist writing of the 1920s', Vološinov lays out the problem in the kind of dialectical way which immediately obviates this. The category of 'mechanical causality' is simply 'inadmissible' and instead the problem of the relationship between basis and superstructure must be approached through the rather more subtle 'material of the word'.

> The problem of the interrelationship of the basis and superstructure – a problem of exceptional complexity, requiring enormous amounts of preliminary data for its productive treatment – can be elucidated to a significant degree through the material of the word... [I]t is here, in the inner workings of this verbally materialized social psychology, that the barely noticeable shifts and changes that will later find expression in fully fledged ideological products accumulate.[65]

The observation has simplicity about it. To some, the task it describes may appear *too* simple, even in the absence of the 'enormous amounts of preliminary data' required for its 'productive treatment'. But perhaps one might better say that the task will appear simplistic *especially* in the absence of that data. For it is precisely the requirement to master the 'preliminary data' that renders the task *far* from simple. In the case laid out here, it required the critical assimilation of an historical process spanning four decades, ranging across economic, social and urban policy and engaging the complex interplay of Scottish and UK politics in a time of constitutional turmoil. On the basis of this critical assimilation, it proved possible, through narrative reconstruction, to connect major economic changes with key policy shifts and implementation strategies, and, ultimately, with the quite novel form of utterances of individual speakers in a very specific moment of the generative process of contemporary Scottish existence. The manner of the connection narrated is determinist, for sure, but, being premised on a thorough critical assimilation of an historical process, it is neither reductionist nor mechanistic. Indeed, it is likely that something at least approaching this kind of critical assimilation is a virtual prerequisite for the meaningful *perception* of the kind of linguistic shift that has been highlighted. And this returns us to what remains a vital and still under-utilised aspect of the legacy of the (good) Soviet Marxist writers of the 1920s. Linguistic analysis is, in and of itself, no discovery-procedure; but when conducted by engaged analysts, on the basis of appropriate theoretical comprehension, it can serve some very useful purposes indeed.

---

65. Vološinov 1973, pp. 17–20.

Organic Intellectuals in the Australian Global Justice Movement: The Weight of 9/11[1]
Elizabeth Humphrys

Just before the WEF [World Economic Forum] happened, we had a meeting here in this room, like the day before it started and it was literally...there were 100 people in this room, believe it or not. It was hard to believe they fitted in – and they were people from everywhere: from The Greens, from socialist groups, from the Left, from local conservation councils. And it was this incredible feeling of – oh my god – like I have never seen this many people representing this many constituencies in the one place, focused on one issue ever before. [2]

Oh, it was terrible, terrible – and I think it had quite a significant impact on the movement. I remember clearly two thoughts that I had when I saw the news footage of the 9/11 attacks. The first one was like one of awe really...and then almost instantly my thought was like you bastards, you fucked it up for us because very quickly from Seattle things went in Australia from zero to 100...The impact that Seattle had as a catalyst for a new confidence and optimism about change, which was taken up across the West in a

1. This chapter draws heavily from research conducted using semi-structured interviews with 15 Australian GJM participants who were involved between 1999 and 2002, identified here pseudonymously.
2. Interview with Paul.

pretty dramatic kind of way, Australia included, that momentum was really sort of knocked out of us by those attacks.[3]

The Global Justice Movement (GJM) that emerged at the beginning of last decade, while lasting only a few years, represented a break from patterns of social movement activism of recent decades. It went beyond single issue campaigning to take an anti-systemic orientation, and brought together previously disparate networks of participants around a shared set of causes. It was also resolutely transnational in focus; it transcended 'postmaterialist' new social movement claims around identity and rights with an explicitly political-economy framework and, most importantly, it fostered the rapid political development of a wide layer of activists while providing a strategic space in which divergent views could be debated without immediately threatening the movement's unity. It was such characteristics that led Gramscian international relations scholar Stephen Gill[4] to suggest that the GJM represented a 'postmodern prince', a contemporary solution to the Italian Marxist's stress on the need for a new type of organisational form to cohere and lead a united subaltern struggle for hegemony.

Gill's contribution both directly and indirectly raises the relevance of Gramsci's conceptions. In this chapter, I wish to examine, through Gramsci's theoretical framework, the trajectory of the Australian arm of the GJM, and, in particular, how it rapidly demobilised in the wake of the 9/11 terrorist attacks. After a brief description of key movement developments, I will examine the factors that led to its decline, linking them to movement participants' own views on these questions. By looking at these views, there emerges an unanticipated finding, that participants' mode of explanation tends towards one of two activist types, which I term movement 'campaigners' and movement 'networkers'.

By reviewing Gramsci's proposals about how subaltern resistance is built, it becomes possible to reflect on the relevance of Gill's thesis to the GJM as well as its limitations. In particular, Gill's silence on the role of 'organic intellectuals' in cohering struggle misses how such participants strive to overcome the problems created by heterogeneity within a movement. The examination of those activists in the Australian GJM closest to Gramsci's conception of organic intellectuals – the movement networkers – provides a basis for understanding how such a layer develops in a living movement. It also shows how, depending on their level of clarity, such participants may or may not adequately theorise a moment of movement impasse and resolve it through practical intervention.

---

3. Interview with Mark.
4. Gill 2000.

From Seattle to the Twin Towers

In the wake of the 30 November 1999 (N30) Seattle demonstrations against the World Trade Organisation, activists in Australia organised to blockade the Asia-Pacific Summit of World Economic Forum (WEF). They looked to harness growing disaffection with neoliberalism[5] and the hope that a different world was possible.[6] Twenty thousand protesters descended on the riverside conference venue at Crown Casino in Melbourne from 11–13 September 2000 (s11). The protest was extremely successful: the blockade tactic was effective, and two hundred delegates were unable to attend the first day of the conference; the key dinner was cancelled, as many other delegates could not get out of the venue (where they were accommodated); an address by Bill Gates to five hundred school children could not proceed; Australia's then Prime Minister John Howard was only able to get around the blockade by police boat, and there was saturation media coverage across the country.[7]

The protest was a flow on from previous global events – such as Seattle, the campaign against the Multilateral Agreement on Investment, and the 'j18' 1999 Reclaim the Streets mobilisation – congealed by a growing anti-systemic critique[8] and the wider involvement of transnational NGOs such as Jubilee 2000 in actions against the WEF.[9] Impinging on this global context were local issues, especially around labour rights, environmental questions and the rights of indigenous people. A general enemy had been located in corporate globalisation, and an accessible target identified in the WEF.

Success did not seem guaranteed in the early hours of the first morning of the protest. A sudden downpour of cold rain left many soaked to the bone and temporarily deflated. That was until the venue's entrances were overwhelmed with demonstrators, and calls for people to cover a particular location became superfluous. The large numbers of police deployed to prevent a blockade were rapidly overwhelmed by its size. While the first day was solely a mobilisation of the blockade, on 12 September trade unions organised a mass rally that marched to an adjacent location. Although the unions did not officially join the blockade, many workers and officials did and the protest peaked. The final day,

---

5. Neoliberalism is more commonly know in Australia as 'economic rationalism' (Pusey 1991), a term deployed by its critics to refer to a range of economic priorities and decisions such as privatisation, deregulation and free trade.
6. Bramble and Minns 2005; Burgmann 2003, Chapter 5.
7. Mier 2001; Rundle 2000; Sparrow 2000.
8. Callinicos 2003, p. 15.
9. Hunt 2002.

13 September, saw a march from the blockade around the streets of Melbourne, stopping at various key corporate and government targets.[10]

Like at Seattle before it, and Prague and Genoa after, there was a vicious and deliberate police response. Some two thousand police were on duty to deal with protesters throughout the three days,[11] and while day one saw the police seemingly confused as to how to deal with the effectiveness of the blockade, 12 September was different. Police charged blockade lines at dawn and dusk, both to force buses of delegates through the crowds and more generally to impress upon protesters their ability to exact a physical consequence.[12] As complaints and witness statements taken during and after the demonstration by the legal support teams detail, officers trampled on sitting protesters with horses, beat activists with batons, struck them with their fists (including on their heads), performed headlocks and chokeholds,[13] and removed their name-tags so as not to be identified.[14]

S11 was a successful demonstration, but its wider significance was threefold. Firstly, as discussed below, S11 led to clear self-awareness for the movement of a collective identity and a common project. Secondly, there was an immediate impact on public debate as a result of the success and spectacle of the blockades (in turn, giving the movement confidence). And thirdly, the movement came to view itself as one on the offensive for a better world, as opposed to defence around particular issues or attacks by élites.

Movement identity has always been a major area of interest for social movement scholars because it is key to movement formation and sustainability over time.[15] The GJM already had a number of common aims; it was opposed to corporate globalisation and saw this as a problem created by multinational corporations and neoliberalism. What was yet to emerge was a well-developed internal collective identity as a movement. As Flesher Fominaya points out, the best understanding of collective identity is not simply in regard to the ultimate 'product' of a social movement, but as an internal process (or dialogue) that is common to members. She states quite aptly, with regard to the GJM in Australia, that this conceptualisation is 'particularly useful for the study of groups who are in the early stages of developing an emerging collective identity' and for studying the GJM in particular 'because of the movement's heterogeneity, its emphasis

10. In the days prior to the blockade there was a festival and series of counter-summit events organised by the trade unions, Jubilee 2000, the Australian Fair Trade and Investment Network and various other NGOs. While not officially participating in the blockade, members of these organisations participated as individuals.

11. Grenfell 2001; McCulloch 2000, pp. 10–11.

12. Lawson 2000, pp. 14–16; Lynch 2001, p. 3.

13. Lynch 2001, p. 3.

14. The author of the present piece was herself injured in the course of a dawn police action on day two. See also Victorian Ombudsman 2001, p. 194.

15. Melucci 1995.

on diversity being the basis for unity ("the movement of movements")'.[16] GJM activist Timothy argued:

> I think a large amount of what that movement was, was about the construction of identity as well. So there's a whole bunch of elements going on and construction of identity was a really significant part of it ... and it was about creating subjectivity.

Following S11, the movement took various forms. 'M1' protests occurred in various Australian capital cities on May Day 2001 and 2002, with demonstrations at major corporations and blockades of stock exchanges, at times in collaboration with the labour movement through joint central rallies. The movement was diverse, with events like weekly blockades of the Nike superstore in downtown Melbourne,[17] an active queer segment of the movement that played a leading role,[18] and significant independent media activity including around the Indymedia network.[19] The environmental movement played a important role, and was of the key networks involved in major protests.[20] There was a significant focus on the mandatory detention of asylum seekers, with one protest at Easter 2002 at the Woomera Detention Centre in the Australian desert helping detainees to break out.[21] Protests were also organised for the Commonwealth Heads of Government Meeting (CHOGM) in 2001, and took place as a protest against the impending invasion of Afghanistan when the summit was cancelled in the wake of 9/11.[22]

9/11: the weight of the event

> If you think back to when Afghanistan was being attacked, demonstrations were actually quite small and the [one] we had in Melbourne would have been

---

16. Flesher Fominaya 2010, p. 380.
17. Whyte 2001, p. 11.
18. Humphrys 2007; Pendleton 2007, pp. 51–71.
19. Montagner 2002.
20. Arvanitakis and Healy 2001.
21. Maksimovic and Barnes 2002, pp. 28–9.
22. However, one notable feature of the Australian GJM was the uneven involvement of the mainstream workers' movement (in particular when compared with Europe). For example, while the union movement did not formally support the S11 blockade, the construction industry union in New South Wales funded buses to transport people to it and the Victorian branch coordinated and funded the first aid for the demonstration. The union movement also worked with churches and fair-trade organisations around public forums and a counter conference. On September 10, the day prior to the blockade, they helped organise the 'Other Values, Other Voices' festival in a park near the WEF venue. After s11, but prior to 9/11, it was clear that the union-movement was grappling with the implications of the wider GJM and how it could relate to it (as argued by the trade union leaders interviewed).

no more than about 1,000 people. I do think that some of that was characterised by fear, and I think it was also sort of shrouded with incomprehension
about what actually was going on. I think it bewildered a lot of people. I think
it was quite hard to make the argument to people that it was just pure war-
drive and that we had to be against it.[23]

Utilising the 9/11 attacks in New York and Washington as a critical event in the
trajectory of the GJM in Australia, my research with activists in the movement
explored the movement's formation, growth and changing dynamics. It sought
to draw out areas of agreement and divergence by listening to activists' experiences, opinions and points of view so as to illuminate what had happened
and why.

Similar to the starting point of Hadden and Tarrow regarding the United States,
my research focused on a 'seemingly paradoxical sequel' to S11, in the weakening
of the GJM in Australia.[24] Such decline was not universal, as the movement
thrived in Europe in the same period. Australia's movement rose and fell more
quickly than many activists imagined was possible. The euphoria of the mass
protest action and networking was, overnight, replaced by disorientation, retreat
and fragmentation.

It is understandable that analysis of the GJM in Australia has been preoccupied
with the events on S11,[25] often with a particular focus on the police violence at
the demonstrations[26] and the role of mainstream and alternative media.[27] Most
significantly, given the movement's collapse in the wake of 9/11, analysis has been
almost silent on the impact that the terrorist attacks had upon it. Observations
have been made about their presumed influence,[28] but there has been limited
exploration with activists themselves of what impact the attacks had and how
they interacted with other tensions and developments.

In speaking with the activists, it became clear that any simplistic notion that
the events on 9/11 caused the decline of the movement was inexact. While a
number of activists agreed that 9/11 had been the key factor in the demise of the
movement, a significant proportion argued that its trajectory was also shaped
by pre-existing political weaknesses within the Australian movement. It was not
the case that 9/11 was responsible either for everything or for nothing, but that

23. Interview with Amanda.
24. Hadden and Tarrow 2007, p. 359.
25. Bila-Gunther 2001; Bramble and Minns 2005; Burgmann 2003; Carlyon 2000; Iveson
and Scamler 2000; Mier 2001.
26. Grenfell 2001; Griffiths 2000; Heath 2000; Powell 2000.
27. Cahill 2001; Meikle 2003; Montagner 2002.
28. Couch 2003; Couch and Sullivan 2006.

the GJM's deterioration was the result of a combination of internal and external factors contingent on 9/11 but not created by it.

External factors

The external factors can be usefully delineated as material and ideological influences. Material pressures included manoeuvres by élites to wrongfoot activists, such as by moving summit venues to remote locations or incorporating dissenting voices into bodies like the World Trade Organisation. Those I interviewed also said that the space for debate in mainstream media and civil society was squeezed out. For example, Claudia argued:

> [I]t created a new environment with which those who want to challenge how society is organised, [are directed] away from certain things that we were talking about, around economics primarily and global justice, into a frame where we have to debate war and conflict and state power... [I]t directed us away from [where we wanted to be]

Activists also highlighted the impact of the decline of the movement overseas, in particular in the United States, alongside the drive to war.

Additionally, they saw ideological shifts in wider society as having an important influence on the movement, in particular that global élites had been emboldened by the War on Terror and had made a confident assertion that we were 'back to the real world'. As the *Wall Street Journal* editorialised in the immediate aftermath of 9/11:

> Remember the antitrade demonstrations? They were the top item in the news before terrorists attacked the World Trade Centre. Now they have receded to the netherworld where we have tucked all the things that seemed important then.[29]

Moreover, participants argued that an environment of fear was consciously developed. This was highlighted by many activists, often quoting George Bush's words that 'Either you are with us or you are with the terrorists'.

Finally, in this context, they argued that the drive to war led to an ideological environment emphasising race and nationalism, with a new, post-Cold War ideological binary emerging around the 'clash of civilisations':

> I think that is the most significant thing, that and that's what I was trying to say before about state legitimisation, you have the Cold War ideology which dominated for fifty years gone, and this space opened up where global powers

---

29. *Wall Street Journal* editorial, 'Adieu Seattle?', printed on 24 September 2001 and quoted in Dan Hind 2007, p. 17.

didn't have an ideological mechanism if you like, to control people, what people thought and they were flailing around for one for about a decade. I think that opened a lot of opportunities and you know, we were flailing around for quite a while too, it took us a while to get our shit together and you had those few years at the end of that decade and then 9/11 happened. Then the 'War on Terror' replaces the Cold War.

Internal factors

Issues internal to the GJM created organisational and ideological complexities with which the movement found it difficult to deal. Importantly, those interviewed argued that it was largely the internal factors, as opposed to external factors, that were most significant in the collapse of the movement in Australia. Organisational issues largely related to its lack of cohesiveness and infrastructure to assist networking across coalitions, the inability to adapt to new circumstances, the lack of 'space' or 'structures' within which to strategise, and participants taking increasingly intractable positions on key tactical questions. Arguing that when agreement could not be reached, certain sections of the movement simply walked away so they could pursue their desired activities, Paul stated:

> [I]f you remember that the movement is very broad and there is always the radical end who will firmly believe its tactics are right no matter what. There are elements of our movement that are very poor at self-reflection, but there is a big chunk of that movement which is much more nuanced and much more [thinks] the appropriateness of tactics changes according to the external circumstances. So I think people just [thought] the times are different and the tactics are different. And in many ways, that's a big chunk of what this movement is, those people, and so they went off and did other things and then at the more radical end, I think a lot of them focused very strongly on the resulting anti-war movement. So people kind of walked away for a variety of reasons.

This question of intractable positions (on tactics, in the above example) was further hampered by the lack of space for the movement to collectively strategise and come to agreement on positions. Mike argues:

> I think there was a crisis of tactics as a result of the police violence around the world at anti-globalisation protests, and I think there was a crisis of confidence arising out the September 11 2001 New York attacks. But I think a third factor was that people, perhaps myself included, got protest fatigue and there was an incapacity to sustain diverse coalitions that had real internal contradictions...

This issue of spaces within social movements to strategise, more generally, emerged from the interviews as a key concern and is returned to in discussing Gill's proposed 'postmodern prince'.

The ideological weaknesses hampering the movement included a confused and/or changing view regarding the world (who is 'with' us, and who is 'against' us), the lack of a clear alternative vision and an inability to meld anti-systemic struggles with critiques of Western imperialism and the US-led invasions. A number of activists argued that it was either easy, or necessary, to reduce the anti-systemic concerns driving the GJM into a more narrowly focused campaign against the invasion of Afghanistan, and later Iraq. Henry noted:

> So in that period the whole movement basically was an anti-war movement, peace movement, and it kind of shifted totally. I suppose in that sense it not only changed global politics, but it changed the shape of the movements as it were. So it went from being an anti-globalisation movement to being this defensive stop-the-war kind of movement.

Movement 'campaigners' and 'networkers'

As interviews progressed, and transcripts were reviewed and analysed, a distinction emerged amongst the activists, relating to how they understood the trajectory of the movement.[30] Despite all activists being heavily involved in the movement, with it occupying a significant amount of their lives, two poles of narrative and analytical approach became clear. Some activists described the movement's trajectory very much in terms of their sectional experience of it, focusing on the needs and concerns of their own campaign, party or affiliations and often unable to articulate a broader view of its components and dynamics. Other activists were better able to articulate the breadth and diversity of the movement as well as how it operated as a differentiated unity, accounting for points of friction as well as agreement.

I termed the tendencies observed amongst Australian activists movement 'campaigners' and movement 'networkers', in order to highlight the distinction in framing and practice between them.

This distinction did not arise from the formal politics of the interviewees, or whether they were engaged in more or less radical actions and tactics, but

---

30. While these characteristics were emerging during interviews, it became particularly clear as NVIVO analysis was undertaken. The use of coding nodes for a range of factors, confirmed the distinction and highlighted the connection between activists' activity in the movement and their wider conception of it.

rather was connected to *how* activists went about their activity and how they conceived of and networked within the GJM. For example, some who espoused a revolutionary political position and were, at a formal level, more committed to enhancing the anti-systemic character of the movement, were definitely 'campaigners'. Meanwhile, some apparently conservative activists were clear 'networkers', seeking to unite with more 'radical' movement elements and willing to set aside specific disagreements in order to build the largest and most diverse movement.

In their work with Canadian social movements, prior to the GJM, Carroll and Ratner identified the presence of political economy master-frames,[31] which was associated with cross-campaign collaboration. Within the Australian GJM, post-Seattle, all activists interviewed held such an outlook (which was unsurprising, as they were consciously involved in an anti-systemic movement). Carroll and Ratner's distinction is not enough to explain why there was significant differentiation among activists in Australia.

There was, instead, a correlation between three factors: 1) the more clearly an activist described seeking to deal with overcoming barriers to unity and developing the widest possible collection of campaigns and groupings; 2) the more they were able to describe a far-reaching conception and map of the movement; and 3) the more clearly they were able to provide a nuanced description of the trajectory of the movement and how that fitted into wider social developments. The 'campaigners' were at one end of this spectrum – tending to have more limited interest in negotiating across divisions, seeing the movement much more from their corner, and describing the GJM's trajectory in less nuanced and socially integrated terms. The 'networkers', on the other hand, tended to have been very concerned with the 'how' of building broad-based alliances and spoke of the movement very much as a (differentiated) whole, holding nuanced views of movement dynamics and how they integrated with wider social developments.

Notably, the research appears to indicate not two distinct 'types', but rather a continuum whose extremes help define its spread. This suggests that internal differentiation is not a clean break, but a crystallisation that occurs in the process of struggle. The relevance of a Gramscian framework to this distinction, as well as the overall trajectory of the Australian GJM, is considered in further detail below. In particular, these findings help to provide an alternative line of analysis to that proposed by Stephen Gill's invocation of the Global Justice Movement as a contemporary solution to Gramsci's search for a Modern Prince.

---

31. A 'political economy' view in terms of Carroll and Ratner's research asserts an injustice frame, where power is 'viewed as systemic, institutional, structural, and materially grounded' as well as 'concentrated, not dispersed, and this concentration is fundamental to injustice'. See Carroll and Ratner 1996, pp. 415–16.

Looking forwards, backwards to Gramsci

Since the 1960s, debates about social movements in the academy have in general terms followed parallel paths on either side of the Atlantic. Resource Mobilisation Theory and Political Process Theory have been dominant in the United States, with New Social Movement Theory dominant in France and, later, elsewhere in Western Europe.[32] However, in the period after Seattle, those debates took something of a back-seat to engagement with the emergence of the GJM, as researchers attempted to grapple with the new environment.[33]

This new movement possessed two characteristics that stood in sharp contrast to the dominant pattern of social movement activity in the preceding two decades. Firstly, the GJM brought together numerous campaigns and struggles – old Left, new movements, human rights bodies and others not falling easily into the established academic categories – and raised claims against a perceived common global corporate and financial enemy. Secondly, it went beyond any of the individual issues it fought over by making totalising anti-systemic claims.[34]

In this vein, the GJM appears to be a tailor-made example of a rising movement seeking to establish a new hegemony (from below), as understood in Gramscian-Marxist terms. It is such a reality that seems to have led Stephen Gill, writing in the aftermath of Seattle, to propose that the GJM was itself a solution to Gramsci's problem of the Modern Prince.[35] However, Gill's assertion is contested, and the relevance of this key conception of Gramsci's to the GJM needs to be closely examined.

The work of Antonio Gramsci represents, if only superficially, the closest thing to an academically acceptable version of Marxist theory formulated by a revolutionary socialist in the wake of the mass working-class struggles that followed the First World War. His *Prison Notebooks*[36] have been appropriated for a seemingly incommensurate range of projects and it seems that everyone from revolutionaries to Eurocommunists, and from radical pluralists to progressive educationalists, can locate a Gramsci that suits their particular needs. It should not be surprising then, as anti-systemic struggle returned to the world stage, that theorists would look to Gramsci.[37]

Despite the varied interpretations of Gramsci, it is difficult to ignore the unifying concern in Gramsci's theorising: to develop a sophisticated, historically informed appreciation of how social struggles and social movements develop

---

32. Della Porta and Diani 1999; Hosseini 2010; Maddison and Scalmer 2006, p. 20.
33. Cox and Nilsen 2007; Smith 2001; Wieviorka 2005.
34. Wallerstein 2002, pp. 36–7.
35. Gill 2000.
36. Gramsci 1971.
37. Ford 2003; Rupert 2003.

inside advanced capitalist societies. Gramsci analyses the use, by the capitalist class, of complex and inter-related mechanisms of consent to support its coercive rule in 'the West'. In so doing, he contrasts this with the more naked use of state coercion against the Russian masses (in 'the East'), and terms this winning of consent 'hegemony' and the coercive aspect of rule 'domination'. Large sections of the *Notebooks* examine how these distinctions require the development of novel strategies for the working class to win over a broad coalition of all 'subaltern' groups to effect social transformation. Contrary to popular focus on Gramsci's conception of hegemony, he equally emphasised the question of resistance and possibilities of transformation.[38]

It is because Gramsci's *Prison Notebooks* represent such a rich, non-reductionist vein of social study that they have attracted theorists seeking to explain modern social movements and have been posed as an alternative to the perceived limitations of both radical pluralist and orthodox Marxist explanations.[39] This is, in particular, because Gramsci's ideas convey a deep understanding of the role of cultural processes without abandoning the issues of economic and political power. However, it has been argued that to successfully elevate Gramsci to the theorist *par excellence* of social movements characterised by cross-class alliances, the Marxist core of his politics must be removed. As perhaps the most celebrated post-class appropriators of Gramsci's ideas, Laclau and Mouffe state their 'principal conclusion is that behind the concept of "hegemony" lies something more than a type of political relation complementary to the categories of Marxist theory...[and that Gramsci] introduces a logic of the social which is incompatible with those theories'.[40] Effectively, they seek to privilege a cultural interpretation of hegemony over Gramsci's integration of the concept into a broader theory of social structure and agency.

It is difficult to square their argument with Gramsci's painstaking critique of reformist strategy, in which he emphasises the need for subaltern struggles for hegemony to understand capitalism as a totality where the divisions between economic and political aspects of society are 'merely methodological' and not organic.[41]

Gramsci's theory of social change, as set out in the *Notebooks*, represents a thoroughgoing and systematic attempt to link Marxist conceptions of historical development – and hence class struggle – with the nature of strategic questions raised by, and within, actually existing social movements in the advanced

---

38. Morton 2007b, p. 171.
39. Carroll and Ratner 1994.
40. Laclau and Mouffe 2001, p. 3.
41. Gramsci 1971, p. 160.

capitalist world. At one level, he highlights the differing relative importance of the state and civil society in different countries:

> In the East the State was everything, civil society was primordial and gelatinous; in the West, there was a proper relation between State and civil society, and when the State trembled a sturdy structure of civil society was at once revealed. The state was only an outer ditch, behind which there stood a powerful system of fortresses and earthworks: more or less numerous from one State to the next, it goes without saying – but this precisely necessitated an accurate reconnaissance of each individual country.[42]

With such an array of defences at its disposal, involving mechanisms of coercion and consent, the capitalist class will not be defeated through simple full-frontal attack. Using a military analogy, Gramsci argues that such a 'war of manoeuvre' is an exception to the normal pattern of struggle. Instead, the contending forces will be forced into a prolonged siege-like situation that he calls a 'war of position', which is concentrated and difficult, and requires exceptional qualities of patience and inventiveness. In politics, the siege is a reciprocal one, despite all appearances, and the mere fact that the ruler has to muster all his resources demonstrates how seriously he takes his enemy.[43]

Gramsci's strategy for dealing with this reality is the development of a Modern Prince, or a single party of the working class. Gramsci sees this party as both emerging from subaltern movements and playing a 'directive'[44] role within them. Indeed, he foregrounds the necessary development of what he calls 'the philosophy of praxis' – a theoretical summing up of the lessons of the movement that can then serve as a guide to action. As Peter Thomas has pointed out, this terminology is consciously used: Gramsci is not merely talking about a historically frozen set of Marxist principles, but a theory that can only develop in living connection with the movement.[45] Gramsci effectively contrasts the ideas that come from close connection to the struggle with those abstractions applied from outside. The idea of the Modern Prince ties in directly with Gramsci's view that to become hegemonic, the working class must make alliances with other groupings in whose interests it is to oppose the existing order.[46] The key

---

42. Gramsci 1971, p. 238.
43. Gramsci 1971, p. 239.
44. The Italian word Gramsci uses is *'dirigente'*, which can also be taken to mean 'leading'.
45. Thomas 2008, pp. 101–2.
46. Showstack Sassoon 1980, p. 152.

question is how to forge a 'national popular collective will' to be rid of the ruling class, for only then can the struggle go over into a war of manoeuvre.[47]

Again, the Modern Prince is not born whole, but is bound up with a living process of social contestation: 'it can only be an organism, a complex element of society in which the collective will, which has already been recognised and has to some extent asserted itself in action, begins to take concrete form'.[48] Contrary to caricatures of rigid forms of party organisation, Gramsci sees the creation of the Modern Prince in terms of the coming together of partial struggles and sectional organisations: 'the theoretical truth that every class has a single party is demonstrated, at the decisive turning points, by the fact that various groupings, each of which had up till then presented itself as an "independent" party, come together to form a united bloc. The multiplicity that previously existed was purely "reformist" in character, that is to say it was concerned with partial questions'.[49]

In parallel with these organisational developments, Gramsci sees mass consciousness needing to come to a 'global' or totalising view of the world: 'One may say that no real movement becomes aware of its global character all at once, but only gradually through experience...'[50]

A '(post-)modern prince'

By arguing that the GJM was a 'postmodern prince', Gill was not adopting postmodern theoretical perspectives, instead arguing that this was an organisational form for the postmodern age – meaning the age ushered in after the dissipation of 'old' class-based struggles as well as the orthodox Marxist views of organisation that related to them. He notes that 'as such, the multiple and diverse forces that form the postmodern prince combine both defensive and forward-looking strategies. Rather than engaging in deconstruction, they seek to develop a global and universal politics of radical (re)construction'.[51] He sees the movement as 'plural and differentiated, although linked to universalism', arising in the 'strategic context...of disciplinary neoliberalism and globalisation'.[52]

Yet, as Matthew D. Stephen has argued, there are limitations to Gill's imposition of Gramsci's concepts on the GJM.[53] When the post-Seattle trajectory of the movement is considered, Gill's optimistic picture of a plural space for resolving debates and taking the struggle forward does not stand the test of reality. Even

47. Gramsci 1971, pp. 129–30.
48. Gramsci 1971, p. 129.
49. Gramsci 1971, p. 157.
50. Gramsci 1971, p. 158.
51. Gill 2000, p. 131.
52. Gill 2000, p. 137.
53. Stephen 2009.

before 9/11, there was 'growing evidence of ongoing ruptures and difficulties in negotiating differences in subjectivity'.[54] This was clearly argued by the activists involved in my research, and in particular the Bush Administration's plan to invade Iraq forced the movement to switch its master frame from one of socio-economic polarities to one of 'no war'.[55] As Luke reflected:

> I think we made some mistakes, those of us who were involved in trying to get an anti-war movement going and did so successfully actually you know. Like in Melbourne where we basically adopted the line that we should say 'no war', basically our line was 'no war'. And we didn't, we quite deliberately [did that]... [T]he main focus of the protest movement against the war, we deliberately excluded any questions of global economic power, you know, and that was probably a mistake.

The rapid collapse of mass protest after the Iraq invasion speaks to the inability of the once-confident GJM to continue to channel its aspirations on a global scale.

Conversely, the World Social Forum (WSF) project is often seen as expressing the potential for raising political consciousness and collective organisation transnationally, working as it did on an 'open-space' model. Yet in the post-Iraq period, the WSF seemed to drift, its constitutionally enshrined refusal to take political positions leading to significant doubts about its effectiveness, perhaps best exemplified by infighting over 2005 attempts by prominent activists to forge a Porto Alegre Manifesto.[56] In shoehorning a partial account of Gramsci's theoretical system into his descriptions of the GJM, Gill misses that, for Gramsci, the purpose of the Modern Prince is to forge not just 'unity', but a 'collective will'. Furthermore, the absence of any integrated consideration of the role of organic intellectuals in building unity and sustaining a collective will is a significant gap in Gill's vision. Rather than simply celebrating unity in diversity – or 'one no, many yeses'[57] – Stephen argues that this state of affairs represents only the first moment in the progress towards a new hegemonic force. This initial step is about the subaltern group coming to awareness of its own existence in relation to the existing dominant group. As Stephen puts it, 'a counter-hegemonic challenge depends not only on this moment of mutual exchange and expression of diversity, but also on a positive programme of contestation'.[58] The point is not to counterpose some idealised 'party' form with the movement, but to recognise

---

54. Stephen 2009, p. 487.
55. Stephen 2009, p. 488.
56. Stephen 2009, pp. 489–91.
57. Kingsnorth 2003.
58. Stephen 2009, p. 493.

that movement unevenness demands a conscious strategy by at least a minority to overcome the problems associated with this.

Intellectuals: traditional and organic

It is not so much in Gramsci's notion of the Modern Prince that the movement in Australia found an echo, but rather in the related conception of 'organic intellectuals'. Gramsci's analysis of how a collective will can develop rejects the notion that collaboration between sectional subaltern groupings automatically leads to the development of a united movement as a challenge to élite hegemony and as represented by a single party. A trenchant critic of teleological and fatalist conceptions, who described the philosophy of praxis as 'absolute historicism', he introduces the conscious development of a layer of 'organic intellectuals' as essential to a rising class winning hegemony.[59] He argues for the construction of certain types of organisation, and notes 'a human mass does not 'distinguish' itself, does not become independent in its own right without, in its widest sense, organising itself; and there is no organisation without intellectuals, that is, without organisers and leaders'.[60]

Gramsci's analysis of intellectuals shows that, despite their apparent location as a separate social group, their formation and function cannot be separated from the class structure of society and their role is not just in the arena of culture, but at all levels.[61] For Gramsci, everyone is a philosopher; that is, everyone thinks about ideas, but only some play a specific role in working with and disseminating them. Put another way, 'all men are intellectuals ... but not all men have in society the function of intellectuals.[62] The layer of 'traditional intellectuals' includes persons of letters, philosophers, clerics or abstract thinkers, who appear, at first glance, to transcend the conflicts of any historical period and thus stand above society. These layers indirectly represent the interests of the ruling élites because they propose a transhistorical view of human activity that does not permit serious disruption of existing social relations – instead assigning eternal characteristics to what are transient arrangements.

In contrast, organic intellectuals form a very different type of social layer. Their practice consists in 'active participation in practical life, as constructor, as organiser, "permanent persuader" and not just a simple orator (but superior at the same time to the abstract mathematical spirit)'.[63] Rather than only having

---

59. Gramsci 1971, pp. 342–3.
60. Gramsci 1971, p. 334.
61. Showstack Sassoon 1980, pp. 134–6.
62. Gramsci 1971, p. 9.
63. Gramsci 1971, p. 10.

specialised knowledge, organic intellectuals become directive – they have both particular comprehension and actively engage in politics. When Gramsci applies this category to his analysis of the struggle for hegemony, he argues: 'One of the most important characteristics of any group that is developing towards dominance is its struggle to assimilate and to conquer "ideologically" the traditional intellectuals, but this assimilation and conquest is made quicker and more efficacious the more the group in question succeeds in simultaneously elaborating its own organic intellectuals'.[64]

While this appears to be portrayed as a spontaneous elaboration, the entire purpose of Gramsci's analysis is to make the process conscious or, indeed, self-conscious. He argues that any movement that aims to be hegemonic – to replace common sense and old conceptions of the world in general – must complete two tasks:

1. Never to tire of repeating its own arguments (though offering literary variation of form): repetition is the best didactic means for working on the popular mentality.

2. To work incessantly to raise the intellectual level of ever-growing strata of the populace, in other words, to give a personality to the amorphous mass element. This means working to produce elites of intellectuals of the new type which arise directly out of the masses, but remain in contact with them to become, as it were, the whalebone in the corset.[65]

The Modern Prince represents the organisational product of this effort, in effect a 'collective intellectual' drawn from the movement but also taking on a directive/leading function. Gramsci asks 'what is the character of the political party in relation to the problem of the intellectuals?'. In response to his own question, he states that the 'political party for some social groups is nothing other than their specific way of elaborating their own category of organic intellectuals directly in the political and philosophical field'.[66]

Australian GJM participants caught in moments of transition

My research on the acute crisis of the Australian movement post-9/11 not only posed questions about why it had collapsed so quickly, but also provided a snapshot of the transformation and differentiation that was taking place at the 'micro'-level. The ability to define two poles of activist type (campaigners and networkers) suggested that the process of united struggle was not just a passive

64. Ibid.
65. Gramsci 1971, p. 340.
66. Gramsci 1971, p. 15.

process of acceptance of diversity, but also one of the formation of networkers, who were already looking beyond such a situation.

Rather than the Australian GJM being in some way an updating of Gramsci's *Modern Prince*, it was a rather more amorphous beast, in which there were the early manifestations of a process of crystallisation of a layer of activists analogous to the organic intellectuals of the *Prison Notebooks*. Such a process lies at the heart of Gramsci's theoretical project, in which there are moments of transition that can be captured and appreciated, but which are part of a ceaselessly moving course of contestation – the so-called war of position. That struggle is not to be conceptualised as the simple clash of two unchanging social forces, but a much more complex route whereby subaltern groupings develop strata who can express an embryonic collective will and consciously try to overcome the 'partial' character of the various sections of the movement.

The failure of the Australian GJM to survive the War on Terror, despite an identifiable layer of activists who could be considered organic intellectuals, does, however, beg the question of the missing Modern Prince and returns us to Gill's proposal. Despite the networkers' individual efforts to hold the movement together and their relative clarity about the problems faced when sudden developments in wider society left the movement as a whole unable to respond effectively, they had not arrived at a point where they could (or wanted to) propose a political party (or minority current), with whatever relevant form that might take. As Claudia suggested, the movement in Australia was unable to both collectively think through 9/11 and retain its broader anti-systemic critique:

> I think that...that we should've had the courage...should've stopped and reflected for a little bit longer than we did. I think that the Left in Australia has a pretty amazing problem of not valuing some kind of deeper discussion and that clearly, these events had actually just changed the world as we knew it and we're going to continue to shape the world for a long time

Many other activists, including Giulietta, echoed this:

> I think sections the anti-globalisation movement [thought] this is all too hard, and it morphed into the anti-war movement. A lot of the arguments and ideas around the impact of global capital on poverty and everything else was lost to a large degree. It got subsumed in quite a moralistic argument, so I think what happened was the conservatising effect turned into this kind of outraged moralism and lost a lot of the kind of finesse of the analysis around the movement of money and the relationship of that to war.

The movement networkers certainly did continue to have an appreciation of where the various sections of the movement had 'gone' (into electoral politics, the anti-war movement and the campaign against the mandatory detention of asylum seekers, in particular), but they did not have a clear agenda for overcoming increasing atomisation. In one sense, they did recognise that the fragile and provisional state of the movement in Australia before 9/11 meant that centrifugal forces threatened the break-up of tenuous alliances, but the process of crystallisation had not progressed far enough for a minority within the movement to come together to develop a collective intellectual. This parallels Gramsci's own description of the limitations of the most basic moment of movement formation: for want of a party to carry out the 'active and constructive' phase of the political struggle, there is the danger that collective will is left in a 'primitive and elementary phase' that can be 'scattered into an infinity of individual wills' when faced with a 'sudden confrontation'.[67]

The inability of a dynamic anti-systemic movement to surmount these difficulties highlights the issue of how movements strategise on a collective basis. Gramsci's conception of organic intellectuals – emerging from subaltern groupings but playing a directive (leadership) role within them, having both knowledge and political skills, working among fragments but seeking to transcend the partial to develop the collective will – is a powerful theoretical solution to this problem. This is especially so when it draws on the imagery of a Modern Prince, able to bring together those organic intellectuals who want to lead a wider movement towards a collective understanding and struggle for hegemony. In the struggles against neoliberal globalisation conducted by the GJM, however, the form and character of the Modern Prince failed to emerge clearly. That is a task for another day.

---

67. Gramsci 1971, pp. 128–9.

'Disorganisation' as Social Movement Tactic: Reappropriating Politics during the Crisis of Neoliberal Capitalism
Heike Schaumberg[1]

Introduction

The first national uprising to challenge the doctrine of neoliberalism erupted at the turn of the twenty-first century in Argentina, a country which the IMF had celebrated as its star pupil in 1996. Four presidents and two governments fell in the space of two weeks. The state unpegged the *peso* from the dollar, resulting in the largest debt default of any country in history. On 19 December 2001, thousands of people marched into the city centre from the barricades they had erected in their neighbourhoods across the town. Banging pots and pans, they protested at the President's declaration of martial law earlier that evening, itself a response to looting that had been spreading for several days across different provinces.

Unprecedented levels of unemployment since the early 1990s had developed, in the second half of the decade, into movements of unemployed, the *piqueteros*, who blocked the highways until their demands were met. From 1999 onwards, workers threatened with the same fate occupied factories facing bankruptcy and seized the means of production to restart work without the bosses. Neighbourhood-assemblies sprung up across Buenos Aires hoping to replace corrupt and inept politicians with collective self-government.

1. Thanks for the helpful suggestions by the editors of this volume, especially Laurence Cox.

These events responded to the economic crisis brought about by unfettered neoliberalism and the state's suicidal 1991 commitment to dollar-*peso* parity, a quick fix for brutal hyperinflation. The combination of traumatic experiences inflicted by past military régimes and these kinds of draconian economic measures – with full IMF approval – all but destroyed the local manufacturing sector and employment market, as the country opened its floodgates to unregulated foreign capital, leading to a financial and institutional breakdown in 2001. The wealthy, forewarned, moved their money out of the country in police-escorted vanloads. Workers and the middle classes were denied access to their savings and had their daily cash withdrawals from banks severely restricted in this '*Corralito*' measure.

The 2001 uprising ended the hopelessness of three decades of working-class defeats. It is a historic example of the ability of the working class to spontaneously self-mobilise. This assertion, however, differs from the autonomist celebration of anti-power and spontaneity as a strategy for building an alternative society. Such efforts to make historical events fit with particular political frameworks miss the fierce internal debates, the search for viable strategy and tactics, and the complexities of what has happened *since* the peak of the uprising. They fail to see that social movements in Argentina developed the notion of 'disorganisation' as an organisational tactic to confront the power of highly organised repressive state institutions. Critical in-depth analyses are essential, if movements elsewhere are to learn from the real challenges of the Argentinian experience.

This paper explores some social movement experiments during the '*Argentinazo*', so that contemporary working-class struggles can learn from them. It is informed by my doctoral fieldwork, conducted between 2003 and 2005 in Buenos Aires and in Mosconi, in the northern province of Salta. My research focused on social movements such as the local neighbourhood assembly and the high profile workers' cooperative Chilavert in Pompeya, one of the oldest working class neighbourhoods in the capital Buenos Aires; and on the UTD (*Unión de Trabajadores Desocupados*), an important and combative movement of the unemployed in General E. Mosconi, a working-class town created by the former state-owned oil company YPF. The comparison enabled an exploration of the uneven and heterogeneous nature of popular responses to the unfolding crisis.

Social and political science reaffirms that human beings cannot help but organise, both for resistance and the social reproduction of life. My own experiences during the collapse of the East German régime in 1989 showed me how quickly the political tide of popular outcry against repression can turn into favourable conditions for organised right-wing resurgence. This convinced me of the necessity of organised resistance in the battle for ideas and interpretation of history. Social movement claims about 'disorganisation' in Argentina made me revisit these assumptions, in order to refine the concept of the centrality of organisation and help bridge the interactions between revolutionary parties and social movements on the Left today.[2]

In this chapter, I discuss the notion of 'disorganisation' as a social movement tactic, as it was used among some of the Argentinian social movement activists of this period. I suggest that it helped them to make sense of their experience of spontaneous collective self-mobilisation in the mass uprisings at local and national level. This experience was furthered by a widespread rejection of politics 'from above', and by the limitations of practicable organisational alternatives on offer from the parties of a fragmented revolutionary Left, visibly plagued by sectarianism.

At the same time, as I will show, the notion is an ambiguous one. In a sense, the military junta (1976–82) and neoliberal adjustment had actively 'disorganised' working-class institutions. In a related sense, military and political élites (Peronist and non-Peronist alike) saw the working class as passively 'disorganised' and in need of top-down 'organisation' into a national development project. A second phase of neoliberal 'disorganising' of the rank-and-file labour movement meant that despite far-reaching aspirations, the uprising of 2001 had no capacity to capture state power.

Out of this problematic situation, social movements appropriated the notion of 'disorganisation' as a survival tactic with which to counter the inflexibility of well-organised state institutions. Such creative leadership practices highlight the complexities of social movement *practice*, as well as the organisational challenges the working class faces as a key political consequence of neoliberal restructuring.

In this sense, 'disorganisation' was a sort of 'weapon of the weak',[3] which made a virtue out of misfortune and functioned, paradoxically, as a tactic for organising movements while they confronted the reorganisation of the capitalist state after the uprising. The UTD, for example, was one of the better-organised social movements in terms of methods, scope, and impact.

---

2. It is important to clarify that the use of 'disorganisation' by these movements after 2001 was limited to an organisational tactic to contest the capitalist state's offensives, never a long term, comprehensive movement strategy.

3. Scott 1985.

Historicising 'disorganisation'

In the period in question, the Spanish term *'desorganización'* – meaning both 'disorganisation' and 'unorganisation' – was increasingly employed by diverse social movements. I will go on to explore its practical implications, but first, I want to discuss its origins.

It is significant that 'disorganisation' as a social movement tactic emerged during the crisis of neoliberal capitalism. The Argentinian uprising generated widespread rejections of politics, including its organisational embodiments, political parties and trade unions. Harman stressed that the role and nature of organisation is a political, not a technical question:[4] so what were the identifiable political trends during the uprising?

Politics and organisation were conflated in a politics of rejection. The uprising's slogan, *'que se vayan todos, que no quede ni uno solo'* ('all of them must go, not a single one is to remain'), was a demand to cleanse society of all the elements that had allowed the economic and social disaster to happen: the Government, the banks, transnational capital, the IMF, local and global political agendas, bosses, and the loss of 'community' to generalised corruption, immense greed, and individualism. Participants mostly ascribed responsibility to local politicians, the Government, political parties and trade unions precisely because their task was allegedly to defend the interests of the working- and middle-class electorate. Instead, those voters felt betrayed by the politics of representative democracy and became insurgents. However, many social movement activists subsequently criticised this slogan for its lack of concrete content to fill the political void created by the uprising.

Some scholars[5] have argued that contemporary social movement demands directly oppose key features of neoliberal domination. A corrupt establishment is countered by movements for transparency and honesty; an ideology of individualism by direct democracy; the privatisation of public spaces and national productive assets by movements aimed at reappropriating them; market-driven authoritarianism by the celebration of spontaneity and 'disorganisation'.

However, the Buenos Aires uprising on 19 and 20 December 2001 (henceforth: 19/20) did not come out of the blue: it was a reaction to the neoliberal dismantling of the traditional organisations of the working-class, which, from the second half of the 1990s, unleashed diverse historical, cultural and political processes of reorganising resistance.

---

4. Harman 1978, p. 88.
5. Harvey 2005; Thwaites Rey 2004.

The neoliberal political offensive against workers

'Disorganising' the working-class and popular resistance

The 1980s and early 1990s saw fierce political offensives against working-class opposition to wholesale privatisation and structural adjustment. The political establishment[6] succeeded in forcing the subordination of all social concerns to market diktats. Even the state became a target for the market fundamentalism enshrined in the Washington Consensus. Politicians, judges, and governments, with the complicity of union bureaucracies, designed and implemented policies that favoured banks, corrupt élites and big business over the workers and poor, but also over the interests of local small businesses and the professional middle-classes, many of whom were bankrupted. Within a short period, thousands of workers and their families were banished into long-term unemployment. By the late 1990s, this created fertile conditions for temporary solidarity stretching across a wide range social strata. First, however, the ruling-class offensive had led to the dismantling and deactivation of all sorts of traditional organisations.

The 'dirty war' waged by the military junta between 1976 and 1982 had killed and 'disappeared' some thirty thousand people (according to the estimates of various human rights organisations) most of them students and young trade-union activists. Largely understood in Argentina to have paved the way for the subsequent neoliberal offensive, the dirty war's objective was the defeat of the student and working-class militancy that had challenged the capitalist establishment since the late 1960s and early 1970s. It was the covert and mainly defensive resistance offered by workers, slowing and sabotaging production, that initiated the régime's downfall. This defensive resistance culminated in workers' mobilisations and a strike wave between 1978 and 1980, despite the ready collaboration of most of the trade-union bureaucracy with the régime.[7] An effort to rally support for the régime by stirring national sentiment led to a disastrous war with Britain over the Malvinas Islands in 1982. Argentina's defeat sealed the fate of the military régime.

---

6. The 'political establishment', here, is irrespective of the political party in power, whether the Radical Party (UCR), from 1983–9, or the *Partido Justicialista* (PJ), from 1989 to 1999. The only significant aspect is that rank-and-file anti-privatisation activism in the 1980s was tolerated by the trade-union bureaucracy, but was then actively purged and sold out as soon as the Peronist party's leader Menem took office in 1989, leading to the first CGT split in 1991, thus fragmenting the labour movement.

7. Pozzi 1988.

The neoliberal advance and trade-union disorganisation

With the return to electoral democracy came a 'war of promises',[8] where reform-ist factions struggled for hegemony over what was still a strong labour move-ment. According to my interviews with oil workers,[9] this involved persecution and workplace exclusions of workers who organised even mildly to the left of the dominant Peronist trade-union bureaucracy. This was a fierce political struggle, fought out primarily within the ranks of the labour movement, over the nature of democracy. During the so-called transition to democracy (1983–9) under the Radical Party's Alfonsín government, parties of the centre-Left and the revolu-tionary Left had mushroomed. To give just one example, MAS (*Movimiento Al Socialismo*), one of many revolutionary and socialist parties, claimed a ten-thou-sand-strong membership, thus becoming the world's largest Trotskyist party at the time.

Echegaray describes the era as one of discontent with the limitations of repre-sentative democracy, because the brutality of the military régime had nourished a desire for total democracy.[10] But this period also saw the Alfonsín government attempting to implement neoliberal adjustment policies. *Plan Houston* in 1985 envisaged a program of wholesale privatisation of the national oil company, YPF, while the *Plan Austral* the same year reoriented the Argentinian economy towards exports and attracting foreign investments. This slowed the economy, wrecked local manufacturing, and, after a very fleeting depression of prices, led to painful hyperinflation in the late 1980s.[11]

Workers responded to these attacks on their livelihoods with strikes, wild-cat action, occupations of airports, trade-union offices, and factories, not least the famous occupation by Ford car workers in the province of Buenos Aires. For one day of the strike, the workers decided to turn on their machines and pro-duce without the bosses. This sent such a powerful message that Ford workers in the UK and the US took solidarity action.[12] This widespread rank-and-file resis-tance significantly complicated the initial implementation of neoliberal adjust-ment and explains the thriving of the parties of the Left at the time. But these struggles were rapidly smothered and demoralised by the increasingly desperate

---

8. Echegaray and Raimondo 1987, p. 16.
9. I employed diverse fieldwork methods and approaches, including a hundred in-depth recorded life histories (evenly split between Mosconi and Buenos Aires), which included explorations of participants' political understandings and hopes for a better future. Because of the nature of the town, a majority of the interviewees in Mosconi were former (or current but highly flexibilised) oil workers and their families, but my inter-viewees in both locations stretched across the social, political, and cultural spectrum.
10. Echegaray and Raimondo 1987.
11. Basualdo 2001; Echegaray and Raimondo 1987.
12. Herold 2005, p. 7.

situation created by hyperinflation and food shortages, and the accompanying looting and deaths, bringing an early end to Alfonsín's second term in office.

The Peronist presidential candidate Carlos Saúl Menem captured workers' hopes with anti-privatisation promises. But soon after taking up office in 1989, he did a U-turn, imposing a comprehensive program of wholesale privatisation and structural adjustment. The Peronist party and the CGT trade-union federation were plagued by infighting and splintered, while the mass parties of the revolutionary and centre-Left almost completely disappeared from the map of political parties. The creation of the CTA ('Argentine Workers' Central Union') in 1992 as a more democratic union federation than the CGT arguably helped to weaken union militancy by splitting unions, instead of fighting internally to defend and recover rank-and-file democracy.

However, the CTA, mainly organising teachers and other public sector workers, was the only union federation to resist the neoliberal agenda with open mobilisations throughout the 1990s. In most of the labour movement, workers who mobilised against privatisation faced the frustrations and disbelief of their fellow workers, while union delegate leaders distant from the shopfloor were easily bought off by incoming foreign companies, abandoning the workers to their fate.[13] In this way, entire productive and service sectors were completely de-unionised during the first half of the 1990s, while national productive assets were sold at bargain prices to foreign bidders. Union federations became complicit in privatisation through a governmental 'politics of compensation'.[14] For example, as part of the privatisation of YPF, oil workers became company shareholders, managed by the SUPE trade union, which thus capitalised on some of the workers' share profits.[15]

In addition, IMF prescriptions for the decentralisation of public services and decision-making powers – under the guise of deepening federalism[16] – favoured élites in resource-rich provinces. There, the entry and exit of foreign capital could now circumvent national-government constraints on private sector economic activities.

Reorganisational trends

In the 1990s, the 'post-Washington Consensus' recognised that the state's ability to repress discontent needed to be safeguarded.[17] By contrast, the main organs

---

13. Arecco, Cabaña and Vega 2009.
14. Etchemendy 2001.
15. Etchemendy 2001, p. 15. By the time of my fieldwork, unemployed oil workers were still fighting to get those shares paid out.
16. Benton 2002; Mansilla 2004.
17. Fine, Lapavitsas and Pincus 2001.

384 • Heike Schaumberg

for generating consent – the political parties, social community institutions, and trade-union organisations – were seen as obstacles to the free movement of capital, to be replaced with more market-friendly and flexible NGOs.

But the historically high unemployment rate (18.6 percent in 1995) threatened not just families, but entire towns built up around particular industries, such as the oil towns Plaza Huincul and Cutral Co in Neuquén province, or Mosconi in Salta, where unemployment reached well over sixty percent.[18] Given YPF's strategic importance, these were also the sites of the first *puebladas* (uprisings) in 1996 and 1997. These *puebladas* specifically addressed the social deterioration of their towns after privatisation.

In Mosconi, former oil workers who had previously organised against privatisation now created the UTD ('Union of Unemployed Workers'). They organised in support of municipal workers fighting redundancies, occupied part of the municipal offices and began to develop the first serious and lasting organisation of unemployed workers in the country. In 1997, together with the CTA federation in neighbouring Tartagal, they co-organised a roadblock lasting over several weeks, making national headlines. This was the foundation and model of the evolving *piquetero* movement nationally:[19] the media dubbed the unemployed movements *'piqueteros'* ('pickets') on account of this tactic. Mosconi is so far from Buenos Aires (some 1,800 kilometres) that this was the first time that many Argentinians had heard of its existence.

Meanwhile, in Buenos Aires, teachers mounted the *'Carpa Blanca'* ('White Tent') outside Congress between 1997 and 1999, protesting against educational reforms and the worsening of working conditions, and receiving widespread popular support. The airline workers' strike against the privatisation of *Aerolineas Argentinas* in 2000, the last beacon of national industrial pride, legitimated popular anger at the continuation of neoliberalism.

After all, the centre-Left Alliance government led by De la Rua had displaced Menem from power in 1999, promising change. This electoral alliance had emerged out of the *Frente Grande* founded in the mid-1990s by, among others, disgruntled Peronists and other individuals, progressive parties like the PI (*Partido Intransigente*), and the Communist Party. The electorate made its general disgust spectacularly visible. In the October 2001 legislative elections, forty percent spoiled their vote or abstained, despite the legal obligation to vote. Approximately twenty percent voted for various far left parties standing on different platforms in the metropolitan areas, especially in Buenos Aires.[20]

---

18. Svampa 2003.
19. Benclowicz 2006; Svampa 2003.
20. Some working-class voters I asked about their reasons for breaking with their mainstream voting habits told me they wanted to give a chance to parties which had not previously had one.

The CTA's *Consulta contra la Pobreza* ('petition against poverty') collected millions of signatures in December 2001, but the union federation refrained from coordinating direct action. For many people, this simply highlighted the limitations of traditional forms of organisation and slow-moving bureaucracies. Nevertheless, it helped to articulate generalised dissent. The De La Rua government was not brought down by élite manoeuvres, but by its own electoral support base that felt ignored, politically alienated and cheated in its struggle for survival.

Conceptual transformations of 'disorganisation'

'Disorganisation' is not necessarily a radical concept. As this section shows, historically 'organising disorganisation', was a method of domination employed by the country's political élites to quell the revolutionary potential of the working-class. Thus, for example, trade unions had been subjected to informal patronage during the Yrigoyen presidency (1916–22, 1928–30). This strategy was later developed into an art form in Perón's concept of the 'organised community' in the late 1940s, which envisaged peaceful cooperation between the industrial capitalists and the workers for industrial development and social justice; together, they were to defeat the power of the backward-looking landed oligarchy.

In 2001, the authorities' response to widespread looting inspired then-president De La Rua's most important error of judgement, declaring martial law on 19 December. Contrary to the prevalent perception that the lootings were organised to favour political intrigue, I suggest that the élite interventions in the lootings conclude with the declaration of martial law, and reflect the political élites' desire to control the presumed 'disorganised plebeian masses'.

Commenting on Peronism, the historically most successful form of Argentinian populism, Levitsky rightly criticises Eurocentric scholarship for reducing the concept of organisation to formal institutional structures, and hence mistakenly concluding that the Peronist Justicialist Party (PJ) had effectively ceased to exist during the 1990s.[21] This is analytically misleading, as it fails to explore its informal organisation, or 'disorganised organisation', in the words of Levitsky's interviewee, a Peronist neighbourhood activist. This trend, according to Levitsky, barely changed during the 1990s. Informal Peronist base networks tended to constrain the neoliberal impositions of Menem's Peronist government.[22] But while Levitsky is right to criticise sweeping assertions about the non-existence of the Peronist party, he ignores some important changes in Peronist activities resulting from neoliberal adjustment.

First, Levitsky only discusses neighbourhood-based activism, although until neoliberal adjustment in the 1990s, the Peronist party's historical focus and key

---

21. Levitsky 2001.
22. Ibid.

recruitment source was organised labour. I have already described the devastation of rank-and-file militancy during the 1990s. The trade-union bureaucracy sold out workers' struggles against privatisation faster than Menem could sell industry. As a consequence, leftist Peronist grassroots activities in the 1990s were increasingly reduced to 'social work' activities in neighbourhood contexts (which had always existed, but were previously marginal to corporatist negotiations). When, in 1997, the economy slumped into recession, state resources became harder to access[23] even for Peronist neighbourhood organisers. By the late 1990s, many Peronist grassroots activists began to see Peronism as a political project of the past.

Second, Levitsky also misses the conceptual flaw in élitist ideology, which views the masses as unorganised. This came back to haunt the élites when these 'disorganised' masses suddenly won victories against the state and capital and, in some instances, such as in Mosconi, even proclaimed 'dual power'.[24] In June 2001, two *piqueteros* were killed during the brutal repression of a highway blockade,[25] sparking nationwide protests coordinated together with trade unions, shutting down over 300 highways and leading Juan Pablo Cafiero, Minister for Social Action, to proclaim that 'in Mosconi there is no state'.[26]

Lack of unity between movements at the first national *piquetero* congress – called by the UTD shortly after the 2001 repression, and while a six months' occupation of the town's main square protected the UTD protagonists from arrest – meant that the state began to re-emerge in Mosconi. Nevertheless, social movements had been able to appropriate and reconceptualise politics and organisation during these events. As we will see, this had subtle but lasting political consequences.

A further élite notion of 'disorganisation' appeared around the lootings that spread across several provinces for several days. The national media homed in on the looting of a small Korean neighbourhood shop in Buenos Aires and conflated this with the 19/20 uprising. The media asserted that the lootings (and, by implication, the uprising) were a ploy by particular political élites to oust the De La Rua government. Sceptical views on the Left that echoed this cynicism implicitly negated popular self-mobilisation.[27] Yet, with the exception of a small minority of manufactured incidents, looting focused entirely on commercial enterprises. Police presence, mainly at large supermarket and hypermarket

---

23. Quiroga 2002.
24. Barbetta and Bidaseca 2004; Svampa 2003.
25. The UTD in Mosconi suffered five fatalities, one member permanently hospitalised with total paralysis, and many others injured by the bullets used by the forces of repression against the *piquetes* between 2000 and 2001.
26. Schneider Mansilla 2003, p. 136.
27. See, for example, Carrera 2006.

chains, was not linked to the composition of the looting crowd, but to the type of target selected for looting.[28] The clientelist machine of Duhalde (a former provincial governor, now a senator), the media, *punteros* (brokers), and police were keen to re-impose *their* order over mass looting, which they did not control.[29] To safeguard the uprising's legitimacy from these attacks, the insurgents responded by condemning the lootings, with the exception of the hungry looting food.

'Disorganisation' and movement practices

The metropolitan uprising of 19–20 December 2001

The mobilisation of 19 and 20 December 2001, mainly in Buenos Aires, produced the resignation of Minister of the Economy Cavallo, the architect of *peso*-dollar parity, and then of President De La Rua. The uprising saw such powerful mobilisation, with such wide-ranging content, that it ousted four presidents and two governments within two weeks. It also cost 38 lives.

The uprising was spontaneous, in the sense that no particular person or organisation had planned it. Rather, people in different parts of the city responded to De La Rua's martial law by banging pots and pans. Meanwhile a small group of people began to drive their cars around the Casa Rosada in protest. Catching the eye of *Crónica* news journalists, they called on people to join them in the Plaza de Mayo, shouting '*Que se vayan todos!*'. This slogan strongly resonated with the vast majority of the population, and the square began to fill by the thousands within the hour. As protesters' barricades at street corners multiplied across the city, many decided to march into the city centre. The city was alight.

19/20 was widely celebrated as an exemplary manifestation of the people's spontaneous self-mobilisation. When I began my fieldwork in early 2003, most insurgents I spoke to reflected that 19 December was genuinely spontaneous, while the following day was 'already something else, more organised'. Those who took part in direct battles with riot police defending the square were mainly young people organised in political and trade-union groups, and some of the already radicalised movements of the unemployed, along with a spectacular display by part of a highly flexibilised workforce created by neoliberalism: the motorbike couriers, who forced the police to beat a retreat.

That these individuals were acting as part of established organisations, although they did not coordinate their actions in advance, was visible even without their waving party flags. To safeguard the *pueblada* from political co-option

---

28. Auyero and Moran 2007, p. 1357.
29. Schaumberg 2008.

as a genuine people's rising, and in the spirit of the 'politics of rejection', as soon as any union or party attempted to raise its banner amongst the crowds during 19/20, they were told by those around them to take them down. On 20 December, these more organised sectors defending the square were actively supported by the rest of the insurgents.

The uprising appeared to be driven by what Gramsci had called 'collective will'.[30] There was little need for coordination, because the objective was clear and basic; to claim the square for the people and defeat the repression. Far from being a confusing moment of history,[31] genuine revolutions and uprisings sharpen and focus collective consciousness in extraordinary ways. Most people who participate in them have never so clearly understood the world as they do then: a case of the emperor's new clothes.

The Plaza de Mayo, seat of national power, is historic for many reasons, but it is also synonymous with the unceasing human rights struggles of *Las Madres de Plaza de Mayo*, the mothers of those who were 'disappeared' during the last military régime. The running battles with police were accompanied with street-barricades and the sounds of *cacerolazos*, the banging of pots and pans, right across the city. Large mobilisations were a daily occurrence for the last two weeks of December, including a couple of unsuccessful attempts by some tendencies to storm the Casa Rosada presidential palace and Congress.

The leftist press labelled the uprising the *'Argentinazo'* on account of its national ramifications and historical resonances. However, the crisis in Argentina at the turn of the twenty-first century is just one episode of an unfolding global systemic crisis: as such, the uprising cannot be understood as a logical evolution from earlier uprisings in Argentina. I employ this term only in a restricted sense, to include in our concept of the uprising the *puebladas* and social movements that developed from the mid-1990s as part of the evolving political processes in Argentina's interior provinces, before reaching the capital and the seat of national power on the eve of 19 December 2001. The events of 19/20 represented ordinary people's ability spontaneously to self-mobilise against neoliberal oppression, while they also carried the seeds of the collective re-organisation of society 'from below'.

The unemployed workers' movement in northern Argentina

'Disorganisation' as a tactic was most clearly articulated where it seemed most dissonant with practice. José 'Pepino' Fernández (henceforth Pepino) was the leader of the UTD, the unemployed movement in Mosconi, northern Argentina.

---

30. Gramsci 1971, p. 130.
31. Lachmann 1997.

Towards the end of my fieldwork, Pepino pressed me to define the UTD. It had become well known for its militancy and a reference point for movements across the country on account of its advanced development of alternative comprehensive productive strategies. When I confirmed that I thought it was definitely an organisation, even if I struggled to define what kind, he rejected the idea. For the UTD to reject the notion of organisation seemed absurd.

According to Pepino, however, they had managed to force the retreat of the National Guard during lethal repression in 2000 and 2001 and evicted the police from the town for the subsequent two-and-a-half years, because they had surprised these highly organised institutions by their own complete 'disorganisation'. How else could their victory be explained, given that – only armed with their bodies and stones – they confronted the National Guard, its guns and gases and parachute snipers,[32] the manipulative efforts of the Church, and the media controlled by the provincial governor?

Schneider Mansilla rightly points to the uncompromising class politics of the UTD's leadership and its aspiration to represent the interests of all the exploited in northern Argentina.[33] 'Disorganisation' as a movement tactic became an integral part of this class politics, backed by the implicit threat of direct action, at least as a way of understanding their ability to manoeuvre in unfavourable conditions during their negotiations with powerful state and capital interests. Arguably, 'disorganisation' in this sense might be more usefully understood as organising within a logic that prioritises collective need over greed and thus contrasts with the capitalist norm.

The need for adequate theory

One by-product of neoliberalism was a global scarcity of public intellectuals who might offer insightful ideas, analysis and ideological orientation. Some found correlations with the power of the spontaneous multitude in Hardt and Negri's *Empire*. The book was both interesting and contradictory: Saccarelli rightly criticised it for advocating spontaneism as a revolutionary strategy.[34] *Empire* was widely read and cited amongst the educated middle classes in Argentina at the time of the uprising, but only had a brief influence on the insurgents' discussions. The uprisings' protagonists quickly realised that the spontaneously mobilised multitude had rapidly compartmentalised into popular assemblies and other movement organisations.

---

32. Witnessed and filmed by the journalist Marco Díaz Muñoz from Salta.
33. Schneider Mansilla 2003.
34. Saccarelli 2004.

While the various trends of reformist politics continued to be present, and it would be wrong to ignore political and organisational continuities,[35] these were thoroughly discredited not just as a failure, but as a betrayal. Consequently, the search was on for something new. People now wanted to run the show themselves, the self-interest and corruption of political and economic élites, bosses and union bureaucrats having driven the economy to the brink of collapse and threatened the survival of many of the country's citizens. Yet the disorganisation of the labour movement's rank-and-file inhibited the longer-term implementation and development of many of the ideas and practices related to collective self-organisation. It left social movement participants little alternative but to now fight the terms and conditions of the restoration of the reformist capitalist state. In so doing, they also resuscitated reformist objectives, tactics and strategies. However, the more revolutionary ideas, practices and hopes that had emerged with the uprising, such as direct democracy through collective decision making by assembly, did not easily give way; they thus helped produce an embattled reformist state.

Individuals, whether they knew each other personally or not, recognised each other from their joint trajectories in previous political struggles.[36] Those who had been active in the late 1960s and early 1970s, when revolutionary fervour captured the energy and imagination of an entire generation, tended to have some relationship with the Peronist Left, which had then fused diverse revolutionary currents. Nearly thirty years later, these individuals could not openly declare their ideological allegiance, many having abandoned Peronism in previous decades and hidden the origins of their political identities in 2003, as was the case with Julio, who had become the main leader of the *Asamblea de Pompeya*. Left-wing Peronists faced attacks not only from far-right opportunists, but also a generalised disgust with mainstream political traditions, Peronism in particular, for having so devastatingly betrayed its historical claims to 'social justice' – a disgust especially concentrated within the social movements.

There was a desperate need for political education: the weakness of movement politics and the lack of feasible answers during the '*Argentinazo*' led leaders like Julio to re-evaluate historically dominant political traditions. As the uprising gave way to fierce political struggles for state power, Julio had pulled some people around him in an effort to revive Peronist revolutionary ideals and political identity, but not before September 2004 did he feel confident to organise a first clearly ideologically political meeting within the *Asamblea* (as against general movement politics).

---

35. Manzano 2004.
36. Colmegna 2003; Manzano 2004.

The popular assembly movement in Buenos Aires was largely composed of the professional and educated middle classes, though it was the minority of popular assemblies in poorer working-class *barrios* such as Pompeya that survived longest. This is partly because of the nature of longer lasting and more immediate need, and partly because of differences in organisational developments and leadership. The longer these movements resisted the encroaching political reconstruction of the status quo, the more significant any issues related to organisation became, and it was at this juncture that the notion of 'disorganisation' began to be articulated, also with hindsight.

Movement protagonists relied heavily on their personal experiences to take their aspirations forward. Their touchstone was the *pueblada*, the spontaneous mobilisation of masses of people seeking to collectively run their own affairs, determined to confront the repressive state by doing things differently and in opposition to political and economic élites. Such spontaneous collective mobilisation gave birth to the notion of 'disorganisation' as a movement tactic. By turning a weakness into advantage, it subtly shaped self-organisation and the struggle for political autonomy, and it simultaneously conditioned the negotiations with the embattled political establishment and its efforts at resuscitating the legitimacy of the capitalist state.

The horizontality debate

The initial rejection of politics was increasingly challenged from within the social movements. Movements emerging from a general uprising that are, consequentially, of socially and culturally diverse composition, have to constantly adapt to rapidly changing circumstances, innovate practices and tactics, and adjust strategies.[37] In 1969, Cliff succinctly reminded revolutionaries of their 'inclination to make a virtue out of necessity, and concentrate on theories to the exclusion of practice, forgetting that above all the duty of a revolutionary is to raise theory to the level of practice'.[38] By contrast with the predominantly student-led movements of the 1960s, the uprisings against neoliberalism are much more general and multifaceted. This is reflected in the diversity of political experiences, practices and needs arising from them. To some extent, especially as regards the revolutionary Left including the autonomists, Cliff's comments were also true for Argentina in 2001.

But there were additional complexities, so much so that many ideas and efforts at putting them into practice were, indeed, ahead of their material base. The neighbourhood assemblies' initial striving for local self-government, the

---

37. Colmegna 2003; Schneider Mansilla 2003.
38. Cliff 1969.

workers' recovered factories, the unemployed movements' struggle for alternative productive strategies and their fight against labour reduction, informalisa-
tion and flexibilisation, could not be sustained, while workers, afraid of losing
their jobs, continued to produce profit for their bosses for low or no pay in the
main arteries of the economy. The Argentine experience is a strong reminder
that the challenge to state power has to be backed by a similar challenge to
economic power. But this recognition is a far cry from the autonomist argument
that the state is merely another social relation of no particular significance, one
that can be circumvented. [39]

With some hesitations,[40] Argentinian social movements came to accept
that they, too, were doing politics, but in a different way: their focus was on
self-organisation and self-management, direct democracy through horizontal
and transversal organisation amongst *el pueblo autoconvocado* ('self-mobilised
people').[41] The latter two concepts were promoted vociferously by autonomists
and anarchists, who thus helped shape early efforts at theorisation.

'Horizontality' and 'transversality' intertwined in the '*Argentinazo*', conceptu-
alising movement organisation and coordination in territorial rather than hierarchical terms.[42] In the Argentinian context, horizontality meant an effort to
generate deep and direct democracy, as opposed to top-down or representative
models, while transversality sought democratic coordination around common
goals between movements and organisations in different situations. Initially,
these concepts were adopted across movements and by sympathetic scholars.

Argentine scholars were engulfed by the very events that accorded them a
responsibility to study without the privilege of detachment, and thus in-depth
scholarly critiques took longer to emerge.[43] In mid-2004, in the *Asamblea de
Pompeya*, I was passed a photocopy of the Argentinian sociologist Thwaites Rey's
critique of Negri and Holloway's influences on the '*Argentinazo*'. This was generating interest among movement literati: the author observed that 'the revitalised
emancipatory struggle's endorsement of autonomy of the popular classes from
the political system (state institutions and its political parties) echoed with neoliberalism's anti – statist/anti-political sermon'.[44]

This perspective challenged not just Negri and Holloway, but Argentinian
movements themselves. However, it articulated criticisms that increasingly coin-
cided with activists' reflections. The concept of horizontality appeared to ham-

---

39. Holloway 2002b.
40. My PhD research explores these reservations in detail.
41. Bielsa et al. 2002; Bonzi et al. 2006.
42. Greco and Fontecoba 2005.
43. From the outset, social movements benefited from solidarity by unfunded
university collectives, which often formed in response to this need.
44. Thwaites Rey 2004.

per equal access to direct democracy, as it ignored differences in skill, confidence at public speaking and prior training.[45] It was frequently blamed for the disintegration of the early *Interbarriales*, the massive weekly open joint meetings of different neighbourhood assemblies, in the early part of 2002. Some argued that the *Asambleas* had ended up being externally directed by middle-class interests.[46] A year later, I heard similar complaints about the *Interbarriales* by working-class women in the *Asamblea de Pompeya*.

For the Uruguayan theorist Raul Zibechi, however, horizontality was only an obstacle to constructing a political party, not to democracy.[47] He was right in that there was a shift towards political parties, but because of the failures of horizontality and the *Interbarriales* to safeguard direct democracy, as described above. These were initially replaced, not by political parties, as Zibechi[48] supposed, but by regional network coordinating committees attended by assembly delegates, and by informal 'subterranean networks', by-products of the reorganisation of the assembly movement.[49]

Julio of the *Asamblea de Pompeya* reflected that ' "horizontality" might work across the movements, to coordinate between them through the regional assemblies and coordinating committees, but not within the [local] *asamblea*', or for that matter, the workers' cooperative or *piqueteros* confronting military-style repression. Skills were needed in all movements and learning was crucial, but the pressure to act meant that what was learnt had to be useful and relevant. Pragmatists criticised idealist movements who, in Pepino's words, 'talked too much and did too little'. There were, indeed, movements who exhausted their bases in large, marathon assembly meetings that lasted for days, and, in practice, mainly focused on securing subsistence from the state. The workers' cooperatives struggled to balance their commitments to solidarity and protest with the demands of production, especially where the notion of work and workplace began to intrinsically include the social and political aspects of workers' lives, but where the necessary resources were lacking. Balancing pragmatism and idealism posed a constant challenge to the movements, and usually one dominated at the expense of the other within any given movement organisation.

---

45. Barker, Johnson and Lavalette 2001.
46. Bonzi et al. 2006.
47. Zibechi 2003
48. Ibid.
49. Grado Cero 2003.

The challenges of self-organisation

'There are no leaders!' and 'We are all leaders!'

Assertions such as these bemused journalists in December 2001, when they tried to interview the leaders of the neighbourhood barricades. This rejection of leadership echoes similar experiences from earlier *puebladas* in Mosconi, where 'the whole town turned out' to fight repression and took decisions according to the need of the moment. 'Nobody commanded anybody'; in the early days, this led to mass assemblies in the middle of highway blockades. Leadership was minimised and checked, but never fully discarded.

More generally, this rejection of leadership in the *pueblada* stems from a number of sources. Firstly, it reflects the disillusionment with leaders corrupted by élites, especially during the prior decade of deep neoliberalisation. Secondly, leadership concentrated among individuals tends to facilitate state repression, as it serves to identify *'las cabecillas'* (troublemakers; literally, 'the heads'). Collective rather than individual visibility makes the task of decapitating the movements more difficult.

Finally, the rejection of leaders also reflects the ways in which the actual historical conditions of the struggle had raised collective consciousness, such that collective self-organisation and collective leadership became key aspirations of the uprising. But without the material base that only workers capable of challenging economic power can provide, these aspirations could not be turned into reality and sustained over time.

Practices of movement leadership

As scholars and activists noted, there were as many variations of leadership as there were movement organisations and networks. To the casual observer, for example, the ways in which leadership developed in the UTD of Mosconi seemed at odds with its aspiration for equality.

The only legitimate leader was Pepino, who had the final word on all decisions, even trivial ones. The UTD had earlier organised in commissions, but abandoned them when they became factionalised. They only organised general assembly meetings sporadically and when necessary. The personal adoration of the leaders and *referentes* (spokespersons) by sections of the UTD ranks, most vociferously women but also men, bemused and horrified liberal-minded revolutionary visitors and tends to be omitted from scholarly accounts. A superficial examination might use typologies of leadership such as the Weberian model of charismatic authority. However, the danger with such strict typologies is that the leaders of working-class movements might just be trying to make the best of a given situation, in what Barker reasoned were 'fields of argument as much as of unity, in which tendencies to combativity and to subordination are in constant tension'.[50]

Pepino replaced the former leader, an activist in the Maoist-leaning CCC (*Corriente Clasista y Combativa*, a party which created its own trade-union platforms and unemployed organisations, most successfully in some northern provinces), after rejecting watered-down political offers that the previous leader had been ready to accept, raising suspicions over the latter. Instead, Pepino led the blockades by heroic example. Since then, 'Pepino was the only leader, and all others were equal'. While there were other *referentes*, they did not have the final say and were subject to being questioned by the rank-and-file.

During its most stable, even if highly contentious, phase between 2001 and 2004, a permanent three-tier leadership divided up the major tasks. Pepino oversaw the UTD's overall activities and strategies and focused on negotiating with the oil companies and fighting for jobs and conditions. His brother, Hipi, negotiated on large projects with the national government and fought politically through the local and provincial state structures. Thus, he was the most exposed to élite tactics of corruption and cooptation, and his position in the movement was, at times, compromised by the political élites. However, the UTD's militancy revealed on several occasions that the leaders' safety from persecution was better secured by the UTD's support base than by the political élites, meaning that the latter's vociferous critiques also kept the UTD leaders in check.

Rodolfo 'Chiqui' Peralta administered the UTD's alternative projects through the *planes sociales* (social-workfare schemes). Social workfare was a neoliberal invention to still the hunger of a fast growing and rebellious reserve army of labour, expelled from the job market by neoliberal restructuring. Uniquely in Argentina, the early social movements of the unemployed, including the UTD in Mosconi, had in 1997 forced the Argentine state to spread these schemes, in order to answer desperate needs. But the UTD in Mosconi, for example, went further: they insisted upon managing these schemes themselves in their struggle for 'dignified work'. They hoped the *planes* would serve as initial investment in labour power to generate a comprehensive alternative economy, producing hundreds of collective productive projects geared towards generating much-needed infrastructure, and a wide range of social gain. The UTD's leaders and *referentes* had rejected these *planes* for themselves, often relying on family, friends and sympathisers' solidarity for their own survival.[51] If any of them failed to lead by example, they would be subject to immediate challenges.

---

50. Barker in Barker, Johnson and Lavalette 2001, p. 41.
51. Pepino insisted on doing everything in reverse from élite practices. Élites prioritise first themselves, then family and friends, and then others, so in the UTD everyone else's needs had to be prioritised before those of the leadership.

There was also a fourth main leader. Doña Ika, a small and frail looking woman with health problems, led the UTD in Cornejo, which is part of Mosconi but fifteen kilometres away from the centre. She complained about the lack of guidance from the other UTD *referentes*, as she was left to lead on her own. With incomplete primary school level education, and barely literate, her political training had been life itself. It may well be that other *referentes* felt as humbled by her sharp articulation of ideas and political understanding as I was. 'Pepino' generally refrained from interfering with the other *referentes'* decisions, except in moments of conflict.

There were hundreds of alternative productive projects through which the UTD sought to engender a sustainable integral alternative economy. Here, too, leadership was based on dedication, skill or experience – or availability. There were also temporary experience-based leadership roles during the roadblocks and repressions, where individuals took the initiative to organise security, maintain order, or organise cooking rotas. This is an important element of 'decision-making by consensus', the dominant form in Argentinian movements of the period. In practice, the UTD had a multiple, skill – and experience-based leadership that evolved naturally.

Edelman has persuasively argued that research on social movements should focus less on organisations, 'which tends to privilege their claims and obscure less formal processes of political and cultural change, but on the broader "social fields" in which organizations operate'.[52] The Mosconi UTD's search for democratic form and justice is thoroughly shaped by its wider geopolitical and historical context. Many inhabitants in this oil town remembered YPF workers' special benefits and status-related treatment due to YPF's national strategic importance. The UTD leaders, themselves former YPF workers, had been the first to criticise YPF's social injustice, but feelings of resentment underpinned politically tense moments and internal conflicts. YPF's social and geopolitical hierarchisation in the provincial department, San Martín, was unwittingly reproduced in the UTD. The most marginalised strata dominated amongst the beneficiaries of the workfare schemes and made up the UTD's most militant base in confrontations. But they would not, despite encouragement, speak in large meetings, and, out of lack of confidence, preferred to refer decision-making tasks back to the *referentes*.

In a province steeped in oligarchic politics, in a socially and ethnically diverse and highly conflictual border region, facing widespread social misery, with minds powerfully shaped by both official and popular religion, the UTD's educational task was huge. Their insistence on dignity through genuine and decent work underpinned their class-based struggle for an alternative future, but also

---

52. Edelman 2005, p. 41.

weakened their ideological struggle. They never hesitated to take up grievances or petitions for assistance by oppressed groups across northern Argentina, and they did so relatively successfully. To be inclusive, they needed to be open to political diversity. Pepino rejected political-party allegiances for himself, but in the UTD more generally, political-party allegiance was seen to be a personal choice. This lack of clarity left the doors open to political infiltration by élites, at times leading to physical threats and attacks on leaders and their families.

The creation of hundreds of productive projects and efforts at generating a comprehensive alternative economy was the most important place for political education, UTD-style. While individuals might feel unable to contribute to public debates, they would discuss many of the issues, either naturally or led by some of the more conscientious participants during projects focused on specific tasks. The projects acted as a form of collectivisation, and at difficult political moments kept the UTD from losing sight of its main aims. Thus the UTD saw work as the main battleground. Hundreds of structurally unemployed youths were trained and educated both in job-related skills and on their human and labour rights, and have re-entered the Argentine workforce within the oil sector and related areas.

This explains why the UTD has managed to continue, in reduced form, as a nationally important reference-point. It has shown extraordinary resilience in political downturns. Just when the local élites thought that they had sufficiently criminalised, isolated and stigmatised the UTD (through systematic media-defamation of individuals, methodically followed up by police and judicial persecution), if they went on the offensive, they found that they had misjudged the situation. Despite some (not always unreasonable) local misgivings about the UTD, the town's population perceived such attempts at disbanding the UTD as being threats against the town, just as with the violent repression of earlier massive roadblocks. While unfavourable conditions make it increasingly difficult for the UTD, its ability to continue and innovate reflects its success as an organic working-class movement – but also its limitations, as a local organisation of the unemployed, in terms of wider potential national and revolutionary projections.

Diverse forms of collective leadership and decision-making have appeared almost everywhere. While Argentinian scholars often highlight surface-appearances (positive or negative, ideology, and so on), the main contours of working-class organisation are surprisingly similar, even in different social-movement contexts. Despite many new inventions, organisational and political traditions have continued, in one way or another,[53] in all the social movements. 'Leading by example', the constant possibility of challenges to leadership, and

---

53. Manzano 2004.

'disorganisation' due to lack of formal structures, leave the UTD more responsive to political change.

The *Asamblea* in Pompeya also had a clear leader who, after the failures of horizontalism, resuscitated verticalism. While this was not reflected in the *Asemblea*'s discourse, and he did not benefit from the personal adoration of Pepino, decision making was concentrated in the hands of Julio, despite regular weekly assembly meetings where his decisions were mostly approved. Julio was accorded leadership because of his skills from prior political training and experience. The *Asamblea*'s base was politically multifaceted. This was a genuine neighbourhood assembly born in the heat of struggle, and one of the few assemblies that whole-heartedly supported the workers' occupations. Other activists took on occasional or limited leadership roles. In both fieldwork-locations, many people refused leadership positions outright, because of the level of commitment required, or the individual visibility that made them potential targets for attacks by opponents.

Dialectics

Polletta suggests that social movements might not have the time to invent new forms of democratic decision making;[54] however, for movements emerging from uprisings rather than issue based movements, this is irrelevant. Uprisings liber-ate so much creative energy[55] that an intense search for new and better prac-tices is inherent to self-organisation. The historical convulsions generated by uprisings change the balance of forces in society and provide emerging move-ments with more generalisable goals. This is why the social movement litera-ture, mostly concerned with issue-based movements, is limited in its capacity to understand these broader collective responses to the crises of neoliberal capital-ism. Sociological writings on revolution should be more enlightening, here, but tend to be centred on the revolutionary moment, as opposed to the movements that precede it or arise from it.

Recognising the centrality of the state to revolution, as the Argentinian move-ments did, is, of course, crucial. Goodwin writes that 'those who would radi-cally transform modern societies must obviously concern themselves with the state. (If they do not, the state will certainly concern itself with them!)'.[56] Yet the Weberian approach to power as top-down is one-sided and ignores the

---

54. Polletta 2002.
55. Luxemburg 2005.
56. Goodwin 1997, p. 15.

dialectical relationship between the state and social – including revolutionary – movements, without which the Argentinian experience cannot be understood.

The lack of dialectical thinking also leads to overestimating the importance of the state, one of the main anchors of Holloway's critique. If revolutionary movements attempted to take power over the state without simultaneously securing control over the key sectors of national production, they would probably be slaughtered. The conditions in the Argentina of 2001 were favourable to the uprising, but not to a revolutionary takeover of the state, because of the weaknesses of the labour movement. The idea, however, was present in movements' aspirations for self-organisation in all spheres of public life and work, even though the protagonists came to realise that they had started a long-term struggle, since revolution was not yet around the corner. Their struggle was to re-arm the working-class with its ability to self-organise, and prepare it for the struggles ahead.

Conclusion

'Disorganisation' as a movement tactic emerged not as a theory, but as a practical response to the historical 'disorganisation' of the working-class by neoliberal élites. 'Disorganisation' had both positive and negative meanings. Positively, it was seen as a successful tactic to counter repression and to get things done where bureaucratic institutions failed. Negatively, it functioned as a self-critical explanation for the movement's shortcomings: 'we are doing everything only half-way', was one complaint that I heard frequently. These complaints partly reflected the historical restrictions on turning movement aspirations into reality. The resulting power imbalance accorded the movements the difficult task of negotiating the aspirations of the uprising, while simultaneously attempting to influence the reconstruction of the capitalist state in ways favourable to continued struggle. In this process, the importance of leaders and organisation is rapidly recognised.

The danger of sociological movement leadership typologies is that they focus on identifying a stable characteristic and fail to take into account the particular historical formations and processes from which movements emerge and constantly mutate. Similarly, former allies can come to criticise a movement's practices for not fitting with particular ideas, not being sufficiently coherent, and not producing a social revolution. In Argentina in 2001, this might have been a desire for many individuals, but it could not have been a movement aim, given the objective historical conditions of the working-class. 'Chiqui' confronted such critiques by saying 'what people forget is that we are only workers'. It would not only be unfair, but politically wrong, to treat the UTD and similar groups as if they were a political party.

Paul Mattick[57] observed that the lack of prior working-class organisations does not prevent organised revolution – as in Russia in 1905 and 1917 – and that existing reformist labour organisations can be challenged by new working-class organisations – as in Germany in 1918. The key to the working-class struggle for self-emancipation is self-organisation: not how quickly, but how *best* to achieve its goals.[58]

The Argentinian working and middle-classes gave birth to these organisational experiments to confront the neoliberal crisis. It has since inspired and informed emerging movements in mass popular uprisings elsewhere. For example, activists involved in the recent 15-M movement in Spain participated in a debate in the Hotel Bauen, a workers' cooperative in Buenos Aires, to learn from the new 'social economy' developed by Argentinian movements since the uprising. The main question is no longer whether an alternative 'social economy' can exist within capitalism. It is, rather, that these experiments have continued to exist in permanent conflict with the capitalist world, but largely because neoliberal capitalism has not been able to fully absorb or defeat these challenges.

Placido, of the workers' printing cooperative Chilavert Artes Gráficas in Pompeya, Buenos Aires, was recorded as saying in the debate that 'utopia and participation is what moves us forward, because we are tired that it is always the workers who are the currency for adjustment in all crises and we want to have the opportunity to make our own mistakes'.[59] These productive alternatives, now some ten years old, are part of a strategy of collective survival. They are struggling, with all the limitations imposed by their condition, to keep experimenting with new forms of organisation (politically, socially, economically and culturally), and to make their mark on the global processes of the working-classes' reorganisation and revolutionary maturation.

57. See Mattick 1967.
58. Harman 2010.
59. Camino 2011.

'Unity of the Diverse': Working-Class Formations and Popular Uprisings from Cochabamba to Cairo
David McNally

> The concrete is concrete because it is the concentration
> of many determinations, hence unity of the diverse.[1]

We inhabit an historical moment in which class is both
everywhere and nowhere. It is everywhere, of course,
because for three decades, neoliberalism has brazenly
assisted the reconstitution and extension of capitalist
power. More recently – and more hopefully – the omni-
presence of class has burst out in resurgent working-
class protest on a scale that compels attention. At the
same time, however, class is nowhere. Largely purged
from the corporate media, the concept has simultaneously fallen into disrepute in intellectual circles, supplanted by linguistically driven theories of identity
and grand gestures to multitudes. As just one case in
point, consider a widely-used text in Middle-East studies, *A Political Economy of the Middle East*.[2] Whereas
the first edition of this text included the subtitle 'State,
Class, and Economic Development', this was dropped
in the next edition, the concept 'class' being replaced
by that of 'social actors'.[3] Ironically, this theoretical
retreat markedly reduced the text's explanatory power
in the face of recent workers' upsurges in Tunisia and
Egypt.

---

1. Marx 1973, p. 101. I would here like to thank Sue Ferguson. who, once again, provided incredibly helpful comments on an earlier draft of this chapter.
2. Richards and Waterbury 1990; 1996.
3. Beinin 2001, p. 148.

It would be instructive to explore this paradox as a point of entry into the contradictions of our age. But I intend something different, here. For this paradox
also poses important challenges to historical materialism and class-based social
movements: to renew the language of class in ways that speak compellingly to
its current forms. Instead of a doctrinaire assertion of class analyses developed
in earlier historical periods, the task confronting historical materialism is both
more onerous and more important: to meaningfully theorise the emergent class-
formations and modes of struggle that define our age. Rather than 'confront
the world with new doctrinaire principles', as the young Marx put it, our task
is the more challenging one of developing 'for the world new principles from
the existing principles of the world'.[4] Among other things, this dictum describes
the intellectual and political task of renewing the concept of class *immanently*,
by reworking it in and through the struggles of our age. Certainly, we have
the living materials with which to develop such an immanent and dialectical
account of class formation today. From Cochabamba to Cairo, new working-class
movements and mass insurgencies are at work, remaking the terrain of political
life and throwing down challenges to both radical theory and practice.

For a critical historical materialism, the living salience of class resides either
in such struggles, or nowhere. To be sure, the memory of past movements is
an indispensable resource for struggles in the present. But the reserves of the
past must be translated and *reactivated* as living social forces in the context of
today's movements. Otherwise, they remain merely objects of reflection and
contemplation, thoroughly susceptible to reification. What we seek in memories
of past struggles, therefore, are those theoretical and political resources latent
with sparks of the future, those elements of the not-yet that carry a transformative charge.[5]

To that end, this article investigates key sites of mass social struggle in recent
years – Cochabamba, Bolivia; Oaxaca, Mexico; Tunisia; and Egypt – in order to
develop a *preliminary* analysis of key movements of mass resistance and class
formation in our age. The object is not to reduce these movements to class, but
rather to demonstrate the ways in which class-dynamics decisively shape their
direction, modes of struggle, cultures of resistance and forms of organisation.
More than this, the analysis does not presume that there is an entity called
'class' that persists in a singular form across historical time. For this reason,
my analysis disavows the building of theoretical models that are then 'tested' in
relation to the facts. In contrast, it cleaves to the dialectical approach in which
theory and practice (like mind and body) refer to different aspects of a unity,
and thus treats these categories as merely different registers of a singular flow of

---

4. Marx 1975b, p. 208.
5. Bloch 1995, pp. 114–78.

experience.[6] Experiential 'evidence' is always already part of theoretical reflection – it is inside, not external to theory itself. It follows that, for dialectical theory, 'the story being told is thought to be somehow part of the very concepts with which it is told'.[7] As such, in what follows, I will endeavour to tell a 'theoretical' story of class in and through its living manifestations at specific sites and moments. I start with Bolivia's second largest city in the year 2000.

Posing the problem: workers, multitudes and classes in Bolivia

One of the first great blows against neoliberalism fell in Cochabamba, Bolivia, when popular insurgency forced the reversal of a water privatisation contract. The 'Water War' in Cochabamba rightly became an internationally celebrated example of successful anti-neoliberal struggle. Yet for many commentators, including some in Bolivia, this uprising was less about class struggle than it was a movement of the 'people' or the 'multitude'. Let us start by briefly reviewing the broad contours of the upheaval.

We begin with an oft-forgotten point: the tumultuous defeats and decomposition of the Bolivian working class under the neoliberal offensive. For more than thirty years (1952–85), the tin miners' union had been the backbone of a militant labour movement, the Bolivian Workers' Central (COB), which nurtured a combative class culture based on radical trade unionism inflected with revolutionary Marxism.[8] Then came the privatisation law of 1985 (DS 21060), under which twenty thousand out of twenty-seven thousand workers in state-owned mines lost their jobs, alongside half of all workers in the private mines. The tin miners fought back, but in September 1986 their 'March for Life' was halted by the army. 'Without a single shot being fired … The miners gave in to the state and that is when a new era began in Bolivia'.[9]

The results of this defeat were calamitous. The mines were privatised, a majority of them shut down, and the mining workforce plunged from thirty thousand to seven thousand, destroying the social base of the labour movement. In the course of the first two years of neoliberal restructuring (1985–7), more than thirty thousand public sector workers were laid off, and over a hundred factories closed their doors. The proportion of Bolivian workers with a permanent job plummeted from 71 percent in 1989 to 29 percent by 1996. As public sector employment and full-time jobs contracted, casual and part-time work grew, as did the numbers trying to make ends meet in so-called 'informal' work. By the

---

6. McNally 2001a.
7. Ollman 1971, p. 12.
8. For useful studies, see John 2009; Nash 1989; 1993; and Tapia 2008.
9. Olivera and Lewis 2004, p. 13.

1990s, half of manufacturing was being done in tiny shops of four workers or less. As the economy underwent this intense restructuring, unions fell into dramatic decline.[10]

Rather than the end of the working class, however, these processes actually signalled its tumultuous recomposition under neoliberal conditions. While full-time jobs and union strength were being destroyed, rural displacement and a low-wage economy produced both accelerated urbanisation and sustained growth of sweatshop, precarious and 'informal' employment.[11] As much as older working-class organisations and identities were eroded, 'a new urban working class' emerged, increasingly composed of women and young workers.[12] The working class had, in fact, grown considerably under twenty years of Bolivian neoliberal-ism: to a total of 3.5 million wage-workers out of a population of eight million.[13] Alongside fragmentation and disarray, therefore, a recomposition of working-class struggles occurred. This made it possible, fifteen years after the onset of neoliberalism, for this new working class to launch a titanic struggle against water privatisation. Of course, such transformations do not happen automati-cally. They require political analysis, strategy and dedicated organising.

That organising work was undertaken by the Confederation of Factory Workers (*Fabriles*). Recognising that the world of work and class experience had changed, in the late 1990s the union set up an office near the main square in Cochabamba to connect with and assist workers. In so doing, its activists discovered 'an invis-ible world of work'[14] – the new, young and largely female urban working class. To organise this new working class required novel methods of labour activism, based more on community outreach than workplace-based resistance. At the centre of this new workers' movement was Oscar Olivera, grandson of a miner, the son of a carpenter, himself a shoe factory worker, leader of the *Fabriles*, and eventually the most popular organiser of the uprising against water privatisation. As Olivera and his comrades interacted with the new 'world of work' they began to articulate a working-class politics appropriate to the neoliberal era. Speak-ing to the Eighteenth Congress of the COB union-federation, he summarised the new perspective: 'The only effective way to defend ourselves and launch a real campaign of resistance is to build organizational links to "irregular" workers (and this includes temporaries, sub-contracted workers, piecework laborers, and

---

10. This paragraph draws on Spronk 2007, pp. 9–10; Webber 2011, Chapter 4; Olivera and Lewis 2004, pp. 111, 113.

11. Spronk 2007, pp. 12–14.

12. Olivera and Lewis 2004, p. 107; Spronk 2007, pp. 13–14.

13. Olivera and Lewis 2004, p. 105. Similar trends characterised Latin America as a whole. See Barrett, Chavez and Rodríguez-Garavillo 2008, p. 7.

14. Olivera and Lewis 2004, p. 25.

seasonal employees)...we are all workers who produce wealth that ends up in the hands of the same bosses'.[15]

In November 1999, this perspective was put to a truly historic test, when, in response to the water privatisation law, the COB came together with others, particularly the coca growers' movement, to form the Coalition in Defence of Water and Life (the *Coordinadora*), which organised out of the union's offices. Within a few weeks, with Olivera as its elected president, the *Coordinadora* mobilised ten thousand rural and urban workers, and gave the Government just over a month to repeal the privatisation law and to lower water rates. When the Government failed to meet their deadline, the *Coordinadora* launched 'The Takeover of Cochabamba' (4–6 February 2000). The people seized the city centre, erected barricades, and engaged in militant street fighting.[16] In an effort to pacify the movement, the Government froze water rates. Surging forward on this wave of resistance, the *Coordinadora* gave the régime two months to repeal the privatisation law. Once more, the Government failed to heed the popular movement, and in April the protesters again seized the city. As many as fifty to seventy thousand people attended regular mass assemblies to democratically chart the direction of the uprising. Barricades returned; roadblocks were erected; mass street fighting ensued. After a week, the Government relented, the water contract was torn up, and a major multinational firm was expelled.

It is clear that specifically working-class modes of resistance and organisation were decisive to the victory of this broad-based popular upheaval. A core group of radical trade unionists drew upon rich traditions of working-class struggle in order to play crucial roles in the upsurge. But, at the same time, this movement observed different forms and cadences than had earlier proletarian movements in Bolivia. Trade-unions, while crucial, were not the governing organisational form, and earlier class combatants, like the tin miners, were not driving forces. Plebeian as the movement was, given the smaller sizes of workplaces and the large numbers of 'informal' workers, it was much more neighbourhood-based than the movements of the earlier period. Moreover, the *Coordinadora* had open membership and worked by means of an assembly-style democracy rooted in both indigenous and trade-union traditions.[17] In short, new forms of working-class insurgency, linked to novel modes of union and indigenous organising, shaped new practices of popular resistance. As Oscar Olivera explained, 'Rather than the traditional labor movement, it was the new world of work that came out

15. Olivera and Lewis 2004, pp. 124–5.
16. My account here is heavily indebted to Webber 2011; Petras and Veltmeyer 2005; McNally 2006; and Olivera and Lewis 2004.
17. Tapia 2008, p. 227.

into the streets: the unemployed, the self-employed, the young and the women. Nevertheless, the *Fabriles . . .* acted as a moral reference point'.[18]

Moreover, reminiscent of insurrectionary workers' struggles across the twentieth-century – from Russia in 1905 and 1917, to Italy in 1920, Barcelona in 1936, Budapest in 1956, or Chile in the early 1970s – the movement threw up new forms of plebeian self-government, or modes of dual power. One participant accurately wrote of Cochabamba in April 2000 that a 'dense web of assemblies and plebeian democratic practices . . . replaced the state as the mechanism of government'. Or, in the more radical idiom of Olivera, 'For one week the state had been demolished. In its place stood the self-government of the poor based on their local and regional organizational structures'.[19]

'Combined oppositional consciousness'

The uprising in Cochabamba soon inspired wave after wave of popular insurgencies, several of which brought down presidents and led to the electoral victories of the Movement Towards Socialism (MAS) in 2005, comprising what Jeffery Webber has described as 'a left-indigenous cycle of revolt'.[20] Indeed, as Webber has shown, the Water War of 2000 stimulated the emergence of a 'new Left' in Bolivia that has created a radical socialism out of 'a fruitful exchange between Marxist and indigenist ideologies'.[21] Weaving together Marxist traditions of working-class radicalism with indigenous communalism, a 'combined oppositional consciousness' emerged, a radical-left synthesis distinct from past traditions but still decidedly socialist. Building upon the analysis and practice of key union activists, Webber and other commentators trace out the ways in which class-based grievances and struggles generate rich forms of oppositional consciousness, which include powerful notions of belonging to the labouring people.

The oppositional consciousness at work has by no means developed exclusively in urban settings. Among the diverse strands of popular experience that have shaped this consciousness are those of hundreds of thousands of rural workers, among them coca growers, organised in *campesino* trade unions. Since 2000, the mobilisations of Bolivia's Landless Workers' Movement (MST) have also given a unique political inflection to the struggles of rural workers. While the MST and its Brazilian counterpart are sometimes described as movements of

18. Olivera and Lewis 2004, p. 47.
19. García Linera 2004, p. 81; Olivera and Lewis 2004, pp. 81, 125.
20. Webber 2011, Chapter 5.
21. Webber 2005, pp. 37–8. Tapia 2008, p. 216 notes the significance of similar intersections in the 1920s in Bolivia.

'peasants', this category does not fully capture the realities of capitalist transformations in global agriculture, which have driven hundreds of millions from the land in massive waves of 'primitive capitalist accumulation', thus 'depeasantising' many who remain in the countryside. As a result, millions engage in hybrid forms of household-reproduction, mixing farming and wage labour, while others have become completely dispossessed and fully reliant on waged work.[22]

For sure, working classes have always been composed of people engaged in different sectors and a wide variety of forms of employment – industrial, agricultural, domestic, commercial, retail, part-time, full-time, casual – as well as semi-employment and unemployment. This is why, rather than rigidly defining workers as those who work for a wage, we need to retain the notion of the working class as a distinctive *social relation*, in this case a relation to capital (itself a class relation to workers). Groups of people may start to recognise themselves as belonging to the same class relation not because they have identical conditions of labour or employment, but because they experience distinctively similar social circumstances. As Marcel van der Linden puts it, what defines people as workers in the modern world is not that they work entirely for wages, but that they experience 'coerced commodification of their labour power' – or, I would add, of the labour power of members of their households.[23] Grasping this commonality is difficult, however, if rural labourers are axiomatically defined as peasants, a description that greatly obscures their actual conditions and identities.[24] After all, as one analyst of land struggles in Bolivia observes, MST members 'do not exclusively identify themselves as campesinos'. Most movement members have hybrid rural-urban histories, which include 'substantial amounts of time spent living and working in urban settings doing non-agricultural work'.[25]

The same real-life complexity applies to the self-understanding of the activists of the new popular movements. As Webber persuasively shows, indigenous and class identities are co-constituted rather than mutually exclusive alternatives. Not only are the majority of Bolivian workers of indigenous descent, and the majority of indigenous peoples workers; they have also developed, as we have seen, a 'combined oppositional consciousness'[26] that draws upon Marxist-inflected union-traditions and distinctive elements of indigenous communalism. We see a similar dialectic in play with the MST, 'a *reshaping of class*', in and through struggles that simultaneously articulate racial, gender, class, urban and rural experiences, 'producing a complex, multidimensional kind of resistance'.[27]

22. McNally 2011, pp. 50–7, 134–40.
23. Van der Linden 2008, p. 34.
24. Bernstein 2010, pp. 84–7, 104–11.
25. Enzinna 2007, p. 223.
26. Webber 2011.
27. Cecena 2007, p. 245.

None of this has prevented the emergence of class identities, as we shall see. But we can appreciate this only if we vacate the analytical world of either/or, where a social formation is allowed only a narrowly reductive identity, rather than a dialectically robust one. I shall return to this question – which is really that of dialectics and method – in a moment.

Certainly, these movements are full of contradictions. They are encountering numerous difficulties – including, in Bolivia, the demobilising trap of electoralism, as many social movements bow before the requests of the Evo Morales government to curb the demands of 2000–5.[28] But they nonetheless embody important moves towards a new politics of working-class resistance appropriate to the neoliberal era – politics that connect with 'non-traditional' forms of work and with the experiences of women and young workers, and that situate anti-racist demands, like indigenous self-determination, at the heart of their struggles. And more than just aspirations in these directions, they have also made important strides in building new organisational capacities capable of spearheading mass insurgencies from below.

Nevertheless, largely because of their differences with past forms of labour and left-wing organising, a number of commentators have been disinclined to see the working-class dimension of these popular movements in Bolivia. Sociologist (and now Vice President) Alvaro García Linera, for instance, prefers the concept of *multitude* in discussing the movements. He concedes that central to the Bolivian movement is 'a reconstitution of working-class identities'. But he insists that these identities pivot not on the idea of being a 'worker', but rather on the sense of belonging to a collectivity comprised of 'ordinary working people'. But what could it mean to be part of the 'ordinary working people' without being a 'worker'? Such a distinction is possible only if a reified stereotype of 'the worker' is extracted from one historical period and used as an ostensibly timeless measure. The puzzle grows when García Linera further acknowledges that a 'plebeian and laboring identity' is characteristic of the popular movement in Bolivia, and that the movement features a 'strong presence of labor leaders'.[29] In short, a movement in which trade unionists play a central role has reconstituted 'working-class identities' based on an ethos of belonging to the 'ordinary working people'. This would seem to be an example of the very unity of the diverse that constitutes any real, living working-class movement. And just such a sense emerges from Oscar Olivera's description of the social agents and actors that have created the new movement in Bolivia: 'In Cochabamba and the Aymaran *altiplano*, working men and women, young temporary workers, impoverished neighbors, peasants and townspeople, and unemployed and employed

28. Webber 2011a.
29. García Linera 2004, pp. 70, 78, 79.

workers have reclaimed the language of the barricades, of community solidarity, and of the assembly and town meeting'.[30]

This description speaks to the complex, overlapping and intersecting struggles of indigenous peoples, factory workers, women, youth, coca growers, toilers in the informal sector, and the unemployed – the ensemble of working people in society who share conditions of 'coerced commodification' of their labour power and who are forming common goals and identifications. Here, one might suggest that we encounter that 'rich totality of many determinations and relations' that comprise real social collectivities, actual social groups whose movement and formation comprises a class. But, of course, we have a very specific sense of class in mind, here, so we would be advised to return briefly to our earlier theoretical deliberations.

Time, dialectics, class formation and class struggle

We begin with an important concession to the critics – one that must be made in the interest of critical knowledge production: there have indeed been traditions of research within historical materialism that have so flattened out the complexity of class experience, and so evaded the inherent diversity of working-class formations, that they presented us with historical episodes populated by cartoonish social groups, each united around an undifferentiated class identity, and actively engaged in mortal combat with the other. Once fully formed, these class antagonists then stride through the pages of history, never losing their identity or their sense of historical mission. Of course, a wide range of work in historical materialism never engaged such blatant reductionism. But there have been enough examples of the latter that it is far from eccentric when social scientists feel compelled to instruct us that class is not 'a singular, exclusive, all-or-nothing identity' and that 'proletarian identity does not come included as a standard accessory in the crates that bring machine technology to the factory floor'.[31]

Such strictures ought to be truisms. Historical-materialist concepts, after all, are immersed in their own time. Genuinely materialist dialectics do not aspire to a transcendent theoretical space outside the flow and flux of history; for such a place is an illusion, an evasion of the reality that all being is becoming, that our very existence is saturated with time. And if thought is part of existence, then it follows that our concepts, too, are historical formations – and thus necessarily subject to change and transformation. As the objects and relations of life change, so then must the concepts designed to illuminate them. Addressing

---

30. Olivera and Lewis 2004, p. 125.
31. Shehata 2009, p. 7; Hanagan 1994, p. 78.

readers of Marx's *Capital* on this point, Engels cautioned them against searching 'in Marx for fixed and finished definitions, applicable once and for all'. After all, he insisted, 'where things and their mutual relations are conceived not as fixed but changing, their thought images, the concepts are likewise subject to change and transformation'.[32]

This, of course, is really a rendering of Hegel's dialectical insistence that truth is a movement, not a 'minted coin'. Every attempt to arrest the historical process, to create timeless definitions, merely produces, says Hegel, a 'monotonous formalism', a 'labelling' and 'pigeon holing' in which 'the living essence of the matter has been stripped away or boxed up dead'.[33] So, when a materialist informs us, for instance, that 'class is a relation to the means of production', we need to be on high alert. Treated as a provisional and preliminary abstraction meant to be superseded in the course of ever more concrete analysis, the statement can be helpful – though much rests on what we take *relation* to mean. As Ollman points out, Marx frequently deploys the term to indicate the *internal* relations among things. What entities are, therefore, is intrinsically and essentially determined by their relations to other entities; these 'others' are thus constitutive of them, rather than merely external objects that affect fully formed and self-contained atomic parts.[34] It follows that, abstracted from such relations, and the conflicts and processes through which classes interact, 'class analysis' becomes another case of empty labelling and pigeon holing. E.P. Thompson was, perhaps, Marxism's most vigorous critic of the latter, regularly taking issue with sociological conceptions of class, including those of ostensibly historical-materialist provenance:

> Sociologists who have stopped the time machine and, with a good deal of conceptual huffing and puffing, have gone down to the engine-room to look, tell us that nowhere at all have they been able to locate and classify a class... Of course they are right, since class is not this or that part of the machine, but *the way the machine works* once it is set in motion – not this interest or that interest, but the *friction* of interests – the movement itself, the heat, the thundering noise. Class is a social and cultural formation (often finding institutional expression) which cannot be defined abstractly, or in isolation, but only in terms of relationship with other classes; and, ultimately, the definition can only be made in the medium of *time*...[35]

---

32. Engels 1981, p. 103.
33. Hegel 1977, pp. 22, 30–1.
34. Ollman 1971, Chapters 2–3.
35. Thompson 1978b, p. 85.

Let us pause, here, to look at some of the key terms Thompson employs to illuminate class: 'the way the machine works', 'heat', 'noise', 'friction', 'formation', 'relationship', 'time'. There is a dynamism at work, here, nicely captured in the insistence that class is a social and cultural *formation*. Certainly, Thompson's pioneering work did not fully grapple with the complexities of the making of the working class in England. Peter Linebaugh has shown how the absence of an attentiveness to race, in particular to the crucial role of African workers in eighteenth – and nineteenth-century London, and of Irish workers throughout England, mars Thompson's account and troubles his too-simple notion of an *English* working class.[36] Moreover, feminist historians of the working class in Britain have, similarly, rendered Thompson's tale more intricate and multi-dimensional.[37] These interventions have added greater depth and complexity to accounts of working-class formation, and have underlined that class identities pivot on the extent to which radicals organise people 'in new ways' in order 'to create a unified class consciousness out of divided communities'.[38] Demonstrating that gender and race are inherent in class formations in capitalist societies, recent historians of workers' movements have equally highlighted the ways in which class identities are always fluid and contested – and historical outcomes contingent, therefore, upon actual practices of political organising.

Grappling with these complexities of social life, a growing number of critical theorists, notably socialist feminists and anti-racists, have moved towards *intersectional* modes of analysis.[39] Much work of real importance is being done in this framework, but it remains susceptible to the criticism that it sees the various axes of social life it identifies – gender, sexuality, race, class – as constituted in advance of their intersection, rather than as internally related. It is the great merit of Himani Bannerji's anti-racist and feminist Marxism to have developed a dialectical and materialist account of the reciprocal co-constitution of these multiple relations of social life. Starting, as does Thompson, with the notion of experience, Bannerji argues for a 'relational and an integrative analysis' that can 'represent conceptually a meditational and formational view of social practice'.[40] For Bannerji, there is no category of social experience that is not inflected, refracted and constituted in and through others. The social whole is, therefore, always a (frequently antagonistic) unity of differences. A genuinely

36. Linebaugh 1981; 2003, pp. 28–326, 348–56, 414–15. Among other things, these texts are meant to problematise key parts of the narrative in Thompson 1963.
37. See especially Clark 1995.
38. Clark 1995, p. 4.
39. One recent annotated bibliography on the topic, Merich 2008, runs to 45 pages. For one sensitive example, see Brenner 2000, 'Conclusion'.
40. Bannerji 1995, p. 67. Bannerji's concept of experience is deeply indebted to Smith 1987. For an interesting effort to build on Bannerji's work, see Ferguson 2008.

dialectical theory must thus attend to the differentiated mediations of social life and their complex unity.

In turning to a number of crucial social movements of our time, and inquiring into their class dynamics, the object is thus not to prioritise class as a universal category that overrides all its differentiated moments and mediations. This would be to seek what Hegel would call an *abstract* universal, one that invariably produces a 'monochromatic formalism' capable simply of 'shapeless repetition of one and the same formula'.[41] Rather, we are endeavouring to decipher the *concrete* processes of class formation that operate in and through a continually developing and complexly organised set of social relations and differences.[42] We are seeking to decipher the ways in which social struggles that bridge racial, gender, class, urban and rural experiences, produce 'a complex, multidimensional kind of resistance'.[43]

From Cochabamba to Oaxaca: unions, class, and indigeneity

An equally compelling case of a union-inspired struggle sparking an upheaval grounded in class and indigenous demands can be found in the Oaxaca rebellion of 2006, when for five months a million people waged one of the great popular uprisings in recent history. This alone makes the Oaxacan struggle of immense importance. So does the overall context in which it arose.[44] One of the poorest states in Mexico, a majority of whose inhabitants are of indigenous descent, Oaxaca is an economic microcosm of neoliberal globalisation. With multinational corporations swooping down on communal lands rich in natural resources, displacing indigenous peoples in the process, over seventy percent of the population lives in extreme poverty.

In May 2006, the teachers of Local 22 of the National Education Workers' Union organised their annual *plantón*, or sit-in, at the city square in the state capital, Oaxaca City. In tune with their radical traditions, they went far beyond raising demands for better wages and conditions, and called on the Government to provide school children with free books, pencils and school uniforms, as well as one free pair of shoes every year. The teachers also demanded doctors' visits to the schools, and supplies for medical clinics. In all these ways, they positioned

---

41. Hegel 1977, pp. 9, 8. However, as Adorno 1994 observes, Hegel's idealism results in systematic violations of his own dialectical protocol.
42. In Camfield's 2004 formulation (pp. 421–2), we are examining classes as 'multidimensional formations constituted in time'.
43. Cecena 2007, p. 245.
44. My account draws on Denham and CASA 2008; Roman and Arregui 2007; and González and Baeza 2007.

their battle not on the terrain of narrow trade-unionism, but as a class-wide campaign against poverty.

The teachers' demands resonated widely with poor Oaxacans. On 7 June, a crowd of a hundred and twenty thousand people swept through the streets, chanting slogans of solidarity. A week later, as the teachers, their children and supporters slept, the Governor sent in battalions of state police to roust the sit-in. Deploying helicopters, tear gas and automatic weapons, the police drove the twenty-thousand-strong crowd from their encampment. But the shocked teachers regrouped, growing stronger as thousands of Oaxacans poured out of their homes to join them, and reclaimed the city centre.

The battle for the square transformed the struggle, as the insurgent population threw up hundreds of neighbourhood barricades across the city to curtail police and death squads. Local unions and their allies launched general strikes and mass marches of up to eight hundred thousand people. People's power was soon incarnated in the Popular Assembly of the Peoples of Oaxaca (APPO), formed in a three-day-long mass democratic congress involving representatives of 365 groups, including unions and indigenous peoples' organisations, alongside feminist, human rights, and student groups. Mass organising around indigenous demands also surged forward, not only with the formation of the State Forum of Indigenous Peoples of Oaxaca, but also with the reclaiming of key indigenous festivals and their repositioning as anti-racist celebrations rather than tourist-oriented commercial displays.[45] The popular uprising in Oaxaca had thus given rise to a 'combined oppositional consciousness' of the sort that Webber has identified within the Bolivian cycle of revolt of 2000–5.

Not only did APPO comprise a space of insurgent assembly-style democracy; it also emerged as a site of *dual power* – a vibrant democratic forum through which the oppressed of Oaxaca began to manage large parts of everyday social life. Indeed, for five months this popular assembly displaced the state. This dual-power situation has aptly been referred to as 'the Oaxaca Commune', in part because, as in Paris in 1871, it represented workers' power in one city. Established by neighbourhood-committees, the barricades became spaces of resistance, democratic discussion and self-organisation. The rebellious people also seized key government buildings, paralysing the traditional institutions of power. Meanwhile, mass marches brought people together in their hundreds of thousands, allowing them to claim social space and build their sense of collective power. In the process, the city landscape was remade. People awoke each morning to new stencilled art, woodblock prints, and spray-painted images and slogans. Equally crucial to the Oaxaca Commune was citizens' radio, driven

---

45. Denham and CASA 2008, pp. 109–18.

forward by the electrifying women's action of 1 August, known as the March of Pots and Pans,[46] where the voices of the oppressed burst forth from the darkness to reclaim the airwaves and coordinate resistance.

To defend their control of many government buildings, parts of the media, and their neighbourhoods, the insurgents also developed a peoples' police force, the *topiles*, based on indigenous traditions of self-defence. Organised by neighbourhood committees, these groups of young men, basically unarmed except for firecrackers and the odd machete, defended occupied government-offices and radio stations, as well as union offices, patrolled the streets, and apprehended police and members of death squads. In all these ways, in the words of two analysts, 'The APPO ran the city'.[47]

Regrettably, the working masses of Oaxaca encountered the same dilemma as had their counterparts in Paris in 1871: the precariousness of a working-class government confined to one city. In the face of the endurance of the repressive forces of the national state, popular power in one city is always tenuous. And, after disarming parts of the movement with false promises, the state mobilised massive military power to crush the Oaxaca Commune.[48] But for five months, the union-inspired insurgency in Oaxaca had served notice that new forms of working-class struggle, inflected through and through by indigenous anti-racism, could produce popular mobilisations and self-organisation on a radical scale – demonstrating, in the process, the very 'unity of the diverse' that is at the heart of real class and social movements.

Workers' struggles and the 'Arab Spring' in Tunisia and Egypt

If any recent mass social movements deserve close attention, it is the extraordinary popular uprisings throughout North Africa and the Middle East in early 2011. Here, we witness the move from intersecting 'cycles of contention' to full-fledged political insurgencies that toppled dictators. Needless to say, these have been complex social processes. But commentators have been largely agreed that these upheavals represent 'the return of the people' to political life.[49] We must add, however, that these popular uprisings cannot be grasped outside the dynamics of class struggle. This is not to reduce these momentous events to class dynamics – an absurd reductionism, if ever there was one. It is to insist, rather, that specifically working-class forms of resistance, mobilisation and organisation have been

---

46. See the personal account by one young activist in Denham and CASA 2008, pp. 85–96.
47. Roman and Velasco Arregui 2009, p. 257.
48. I tell this story in McNally 2011, pp. 167–8.
49. Corm 2011.

both central and *decisive* to these struggles. These insurgent movements simply would not have taken the forms they did without the classic weapon of working-class resistance – the strike – and, in the case of Tunisia, without the intervention of that most basic of workers' organisations, the unions.

The 2011 upsurges across North Africa and the Middle-East actually began two weeks before the start of the new year with a wave of protest in Tunisia. The riots and demonstrations originated in an outburst of anger over unemployment and rising food prices, sparked by a 17 December 2010 police attack on a street-vendor, Mohammed Bouazizi, in the central town of Sidi Bouzid. In a dramatic protest, Bouazizi bought gasoline, marched to city hall, doused his clothing and set himself ablaze. He died in hospital less than three weeks later.[50] Daily protests erupted immediately after Bouazizi's desperate act, spreading to cities and towns across the country. Unemployed teachers, bus drivers, high-school students and street-vendors joined the mobilisations, which had a distinctly working-class character. Police resorted to mass arrests to quell the upheaval, but this merely provoked larger demonstrations in solidarity with the detained. As the movement gained momentum, demonstrators became increasingly confident, torching police cars and trashing businesses linked to President Zine al-Abidine Ben Ali and his family. A week later, the protest wave toppled the President, sending him into exile.

While the Tunisian uprising caught the attention of many, few analysts seriously probed how a protest movement that emerged from a single town could have developed into a nationwide upheaval capable of overthrowing a dictator. Those who have attended to this question, however, often note the key political and organisational role played by the trade-union federation, the General Union of Tunisian Workers (UGTT, by its French initials), or, more precisely, by a layer of militant grassroots activists of the union. Despite the compromised history of the UGTT's national leaders in recent decades, and notwithstanding the latter's hesitancy about joining the struggle, local activists of the UGTT galvanised the movement at crucial junctures, turning union offices into key hubs of resistance. These rank-and-file trade unionists organised rallies and general strikes, transforming the UGTT into 'a serious political force with currently unmatched organizing capacity and national reach'.[51]

At a key juncture in the struggle, as one analyst records, 'Thirty militants got into a stormy exchange at the regional headquarters of the UGTT in Gafsa on 10 January. They had been trying for days to force the local section of the union

---

50. While Bouazizi's action was far from ordinary, it was not unprecedented. See Piot 2011.
51. Democracy Digest 2011. See also Lee and Weinthal 2011.

to organize support for the movement. But the national leadership refused'.[52] Finally, the militants prevailed. A hugely successful general strike rocked the city of Sfax on 12 January. Organised workers were now on the move, rallying and deepening the insurgency. From this point on, as one astute blogger observed, 'The trade union (UGTT) played the role of momentum regulator and political indicator. It was clear that as long as the trade union kept on declaring strikes the battle was on, and that was the signal to the people to stick to the streets'.[53] This insurgent labour activism in several cities was critical in escalating the Tunisian upheaval, raising it to a level that forced large sections of the army and bureaucracy to abandon Ben Ali's 23-year long dictatorship.

Many of the rank-and-file union militants who broke through the passivity of the UGTT central leadership and initiated strike action had been organising working-class protest since the onset of the global recession of 2008.[54] So, when the upheaval arrived, they had years of experience and established networks on which they could readily draw. Moreover, their efforts have continued since the overthrow of Ben Ali. In addition to strikes, activists of the UGTT have organised sit-ins and a 'Caravan of Liberation' that marched on the capital from several cities, in an effort to sweep away all political officials linked to the former dictator. Nevertheless, there remain conservative as well as radical forces contending over the direction of both the union movement and the Revolution, and the outcomes of these struggles will have a huge impact on how far the liberation movement in Tunisia can go.

Another critical factor will be the growth of popular power. A hugely important development has been the formation, in scores of cities and towns, of popular councils to administer local affairs. Elected at mass meetings of thousands, these councils operate as laboratories of radical democracy.[55] One mainstream journalist provides a good sense of the dynamic and democratising process in the town of Zarzis:

... it is the youth who have forced out the regime-appointed mayor and set up a committee that now controls the town.

They are organizing nascent institutions of local democracy – a concept that has never existed in their countries.

Two days after the national revolution, the Zarzis protesters held an election among their ranks to form a 20-person revolutionary committee. Then they held a town-hall meeting, with almost everyone in Zarzis attending, to decide how to create a non-authoritarian municipality.

52. Piot 2011.
53. Jahjah 2011.
54. Alexander 2011; Arieff 2011, p. 10.
55. Swagler 2011.

Virtually all of Tunisia's old regime-appointed mayors have disappeared. So have most policemen. The local bureaucracies continue to function only because officials have faith in the citizens, garbage is collected by voluntary agreement, and in a great many towns, people have had the chance to reinvent the way they are managed.[56]

There is no way of knowing how these experiments in popular democracy will be resolved; indeed, it is clear that the forces of reaction are trying to regroup in order to undermine such initiatives. What is also clear, however, is that a mass democratic upheaval in Tunisia has opened the space for such experiments – and that none of this would have been possible without the decisive role played by working-class struggle, in the concrete forms of mass strikes and a radicalised labour movement. And while there were unique dynamics at work in the next great popular uprising in the Arab World, that which rocked Egypt in January–February 2011, once again, workers' struggles figured decisively.

Insightful analysts of Egyptian politics had been tracking a growing wave of political activism and opposition to the Mubarak régime since about 2002. Movements in solidarity with the Palestinian *Intifada* and in opposition to the invasion of Iraq took to the streets in 2002–3. Shortly after this, the Egyptian Movement for Change, known as *Kifaya* ('Enough!'), organised for democratic reform, as did judges, and feminist groups began marching against sexual abuse and in defence of women's rights.[57] All of these campaigns were initiated and led by intellectuals, professionals and students, though they had much support from ordinary workers. But after 2006, as these movements ran out of steam, oppositional energies throughout Egyptian society were largely sustained by workers' mobilisations.

The rising tide of working-class protest can be traced directly to the neoliberal programme of 2004, which was based on accelerated privatisation and the establishment of low-wage export zones. As jobs were lost and wages compressed, Egyptian workers engaged in ever more confrontational forms of resistance – strikes, sit-ins and mass rallies and demonstrations – all illegal under the emergency edicts and laws that were in place. In 2006–7, this wave of workers' activism rose dramatically when mass protest erupted in the Nile Delta, spearheaded by the militancy of fifty thousand workers in textiles and the cement and poultry industries. This was followed by strikes of train drivers, journalists, truckers, miners and engineers. 2007–8 saw another explosion of labour, with riots at the state-owned weaving factory in Al-Mahla Al-Kobra and widespread strike action elsewhere. The youth-based 6 April Movement emerged at this

---

56. Saunders 2011.
57. For a good overview of these movements, see El-Mahdi 2009.

point, in support of workers' strikes. At the same time, the demands of strikers began to address the general interests of all working people, particularly the poorest, by pressing for a substantial increase in the minimum wage.[58]

Workers' protest was also becoming overtly political, linking economic and social issues to demands for democratisation, as crowds burned banners of the ruling National Democratic Party and defaced posters of President Mubarak. Upon release from jail for his role in leading the Mahalla strike action, Muhammad al-Attar told a September 2007 workers' rally, 'I want the whole government to resign – I want the Mubarak regime to come to an end. Politics and workers rights are inseparable'.[59] Statements such as these reinforce the argument classically made by Rosa Luxemburg, that mass working-class struggle tends to break down the wall between economic and political issues and opens up fundamental questions about the state and society. Analysing the mass strikes of 2007–8, historian Joel Beinin noted, 'The workers' movement – even more than the demonstrations of the intelligentsia organized by Kifaya – has popularised a culture of protest and is contributing to consciousness of citizenship and rights far more successfully than the moribund secular opposition parties or the most active NGOs'.[60] And as workers won significant concessions, their confidence grew.

Over the course of 2004–10, more than two million Egyptian workers engaged in thousands of direct actions, prompting one commentator to note in 2009 that, while other movements had retreated, 'one constituency, the workers' movement, has proved more difficult to control. Successful strikes in both state and private sectors have encouraged the largest and broadest labour movement for more than fifty years'.[61] And this wave of working-class resistance continued through 2010, with 17 different groups of workers occupying an area outside the Parliament and setting up a 'Cairo Hyde Park', in anticipation of the insurgent occupation of public space that would occur in Tahrir Square some months later.[62] When the Tunisian Revolution broke through in January 2011, therefore, years of combative working-class protest had laid the groundwork for a movement that would sweep Egypt's President Mubarak from office.

But Mubarak would not leave until workers rose – as workers – once more. To be sure, the vast majority of the millions in Egypt's streets after 25 January 2011 were working-class people. But for much of the initial period of the uprising, many workplaces were closed and the action was in the streets. As factories and offices reopened, however, and as activists of the Left called for strikes to

---

58. For background, see El-Ghobaashy 2005; Beinin 2005; Beinin and El-Hamalawy 2007; Beinin 2009.
59. Stack and Mazen 2007.
60. Beinin 2008.
61. Marfleet 2009, p. 2.
62. Topol 2010 and El-Hamalawy 2011.

topple Mubarak, the democratic demands of the movement in the streets were powerfully fused with workers' workplace-based demands for an end to poverty-wages, for the dismissal of brutal managers, and for the right to form independent democratic unions. During the week beginning 7 February, tens of thousands of workers launched powerful workplace-based actions. Thousands of rail workers walked off the job, blockading railway lines in the process. Six thousand workers at the Suez Canal Authority struck, staging sit-ins at Suez and two other cities. In Mahalla, fifteen hundred workers at Abul Sebae Textiles blockaded the highway. At the Kafr al-Zayyat hospital, hundreds of nurses staged a sit-in, and they were joined by hundreds of other hospital employees. Across Egypt, thousands of others – Cairo bus drivers, workers at Telecom Egypt, journalists, workers at pharmaceutical-plants and steel mills, faculty members at Cairo University – joined the strike wave. Everywhere they called for improved wages, the firing of ruthless managers, back pay, better working conditions and independent unions. In many cases, they also called for the resignation of President Mubarak.[63] By this point, Mubarak's days were numbered.[64] Having delayed his departure in the face of calls by millions for his resignation, Mubarak provoked a cascading wave of strikes and workers' protests that dislodged any lingering belief that he could ride out the storm without inciting serious threats to Egyptian and foreign capital. And in the months immediately following his overthrow, this stream of working-class activism continued to flow on, albeit not without difficulties, in mass strikes, demonstrations, and the formation of independent unions as well as workers' parties and coalitions.[65]

Popular insurgency and class struggle

The events of the week starting 7 February 2011 in Egypt constituted a dialectical process, in which the popular insurgency in the streets against authoritarian rule, itself made possible by years of labour struggle, in turn stimulated ever more militant workplace resistance, combativity and self-organisation. The social dynamics thus demonstrated the continuing relevance of the analysis developed by the great Polish-German socialist, Rosa Luxemburg. In her book *The Mass Strike*, based on the experience of the insurrectionary cycle of strikes against the Tsarist dictatorship in Russia in 1905, Luxemburg argued that truly revolutionary movements develop by way of interacting waves of political and economic

---

63. My sources on workers' protests include reports from 7–12 February 2011 from Al Jazeera, *Al-Masry Al-Youm*, the Center for Trade Union and Workers Services, newsocialist.org, and socialistworker.org.
64. As I argued at the time, in McNally 2011a.
65. Omar 2011; Kempf 2011; Marfleet 2011.

struggle, each enriching the other. In a passage that could have been inspired by the upheaval in Egypt, she explains,

> Every new onset and every fresh victory of the political struggle is transformed into a powerful impetus for the economic struggle ... After every foaming wave of political action a fructifying deposit remains behind from which a thousand stalks of economic struggle burst forth. And conversely. The workers condition of ceaseless economic struggle with the capitalists keeps their fighting spirit alive in every political interval...[66]

Not only does Luxemburg's text capture some of the distinctive dynamics of the mass movement in Egypt; it also returns us to some of our opening themes by demonstrating the dialectical sensitivity of a great Marxist theorist to the living pulse of class – and social struggle. Not only does *The Mass Strike* underline the central role of mass strikes – as opposed to parliamentary politics – in the class-struggle for socialism; it equally sparkles with its subtle analysis of the dialectics of class action and popular insurgency.[67]

Although the January and February 1905 general strikes in Russia began as part of a centralised political action organised by parties of the Left, the movement 'soon fell into an unending series of local, partial economic strikes in separate districts, towns and factories'. Rather than a weakness, however, Luxemburg recognised in this development the deepening of the movement, as it drew in ever more diverse sections of the working people, from domestic servants and commercial employees to artists, actors and rural workers, along with sections of the intermediate strata – many of who had been passive in the early days of the upheaval. The mass strike movement thus displayed 'a gigantic, many-colored picture ... which reflects all the complexity of social organization and of political consciousness of every section and of every district'. Rather than a cartoon-picture, in which the revolutionary workers, chomping at the bit, launch their collective struggle, Luxemburg understood that mass action transforms consciousness – that the struggle itself is a site for the self-transformation of workers who have no prior history of trade-union or political activism. In all these ways, she was deeply attentive to the dynamism of identity and consciousness, noting that for many participants the strike movement 'awoke class feeling and class consciousness in millions upon millions as if by electric shock'.[68]

---

66. Luxemburg 1970, p. 185.
67. For the historical and political context, see Nettl 1966, Vol. 1, Chapter 8 and Vol. 2, pp. 496–611. Note that Luxemburg did not oppose Marxist parties participating in parliamentary politics; she simply insisted that mass working-class action was the fundamental basis for revolutionary change.
68. Luxemburg 1970, pp. 170, 171.

Luxemburg is also at pains to underscore that the mass strike obeys no mechanical formulas. It continually shifts from political to economic demands and back again, just as it converges in great centralised actions only to fracture into hundreds of smaller, local struggles, each capable of feeding back into giant collective mobilisations, once more. Throughout, 'the living pulse beat of revolution' repeatedly changes form as new layers of the oppressed enter the struggle and new demands come to the fore. Indeed, this is what it means for the mass strike to be 'a living, powerful movement of the people'.[69] And this idea – of the genuine mass strike as 'a real *people's movement*' – is at the heart of her analysis. For Luxemburg, the working-class struggle awakens and mobilises all the oppressed layers of society, including semi-proletarianised labourers and discontented members of intermediate social groups, from actors and artists to 'professional' workers. In all of these ways, specifically working-class forms of action and organisation – strikes, unions and mass councils (or soviets) based in the workplaces and the working-class neighbourhoods – give an unrelenting impetus to a 'people's movement' and provide it with an indispensable framework. Without the collective action of workers against exploitation, abuse and authoritarian management, these insurgent movements would frequently lack the driving energy that makes determined and heroic resistance – demonstrations, street fighting, arresting the police, confronting the army – possible. And without workers' collective forms of organisation and action – unions, workers' councils, strikes and mass assemblies – these people's movements would all too often lack the popular institutions and means of struggle necessary for profound social mobilisations that can topple heads of state. Where this does happen, where working-class protest and self-organisation assist a popular upheaval throughout society, we observe that dialectical process anticipated by Marx, and set in motion in recent upsurges in Cochabamba, Oaxaca, Tunisia and Egypt, in which the movement of a particular class takes on the character of a generalising struggle for emancipation.[70]

Conclusion: class struggle and its changing forms

The four sites of mass social protest that we have analysed are all characterised by the decisive role played by organised working-class movements. In three cases, radical trade unions have been politically, culturally and organisationally indispensable to the broader social mobilisation. In Cochabamba, the manufacturing workers' union, the *Fabriles*, initiated and led the coalition responsible for

69. Luxemburg 1970, pp. 182, 187.
70. To take on such a character does not mean, it should go without saying, that such movements necessarily succeed in this project of universal emancipation.

triggering the popular upheaval that defeated water privatisation, kick-started the five-year 'cycle of revolt', and brought down three presidents. In Oaxaca, the struggle of Local 22 of the teachers' union was the rallying point for the uprising that created the 'Oaxaca Commune'. It was the teachers' union that defined the basic demands of the popular movement and whose initiative and organisation underpinned the struggle. In Tunisia, general-strike action and organising activity by militant local sections of the General Union of Tunisian Workers galvanised the popular movement such that it could topple a dictator. And while, in our fourth case, Egyptian workers lacked an independent union movement that could provide the organisational framework for a popular uprising, years of workplace-based labour action contributed decisively to the development of a robust and combative culture of resistance that seized the streets in January 2011. Moreover, the wave of strikes that broke out in early February of that year brought Mubarak's presidency to the tipping point, opening up a whole new era in Egyptian politics.

To say this, as I have been at pains to argue, is not to claim that working-class struggles are the whole story of these movements. These are complex social processes in real historical time. Yet, the story of these movements is unimaginable outside the working-class formations that are at their very core. To return to E.P. Thompson's salient argument, in modern society, class processes are intrinsic to the modes of conflict, resistance, opposition, and struggle that define the terrain on which popular movements operate. Class manifests itself in and through key dynamics of modern society; it describes *the way the machine works* once it is set in motion – not this interest or that interest, but the *friction* of interests – the movement itself, the heat, the thundering noise'.[71] It is this noise we hear roaring from the streets of Cochabamba, the teachers' encampment in Oaxaca, the general-strike movements in Sfax, Kairouan, Tozeur and Tunis, and the uprisings of textile-workers, bus drivers, steel workers, nurses, railway workers, government employees and more in Cairo, Suez, Mahalla, Alexandria and other cities and towns across Egypt.

Many commentators miss this, not only because they have capitulated to intellectual fashion and abandoned the coordinates of social class, but also because they all too frequently look in today's movements for that reified archetype, 'the worker', ostensibly characteristic of some earlier phase of working-class formation. In so doing, they forget the historical-materialist injunction that the definition of any social phenomenon 'can only be made in the medium of *time*', to again cite Thompson. Of course, rooted working-class organisers and activists know this very well. Indeed, Oscar Olivera intends precisely this when he

71. Thompson 1978b, p. 85.

reminds us that 'the conditions of class struggle have changed... the material conditions of work are different, and the ways of struggle are also different'.[72] But changing forms and conditions of class struggle are something very different from its disappearance.

Equally, we have seen that the absence of a 'pure' class consciousness, whatever that would mean, does not mean the non-existence of class identities. The 'combined oppositional consciousness' informed by indigenous radicalism, Marxism and radical trade unionism that Jeffery Webber delineates for us in Bolivia should be seen as typical of the complexity of social experience. Indeed, we encounter something very similar in Oaxaca in 2006, just as in Tunisia and Egypt we find powerful evidence of a strong 'plebeian and laboring identity' based on an ethos of belonging to the 'ordinary working people'. What radical working-class movements do is create worldviews, forms of struggle, and popular institutions that tend 'to create a unified class consciousness out of divided communities'.[73] In so doing, they cut against the grain of the many tendencies toward fragmentation, competition and atomism that run through the lives of oppressed peoples, forging bonds of solidarity, an appreciation of shared interests, and common social objectives that fit with the experiences of people whose conditions of work and life are broadly similar. In short, they struggle to create a 'unity of the diverse'. And in the four cases we have analysed above, the results have often been profound.

It is a key task of critical theory to delineate the new patterns of class formation and resistance unique to our era, to be equal to the challenges they pose. Indeed, we should ask nothing less of a genuinely *historical* materialism. And this, as we have seen, requires that critical concepts be dialectically renewed and renovated so as to be in tune with the living pulse of class formation today. More than simply a theoretical cause, this is, equally, a practical one. For we owe concrete and robust theorisations in this spirit to the activists and organisers operating on the changing terrain of class relations, as they seek to chart a path toward the liberation of the exploited and the oppressed.

---

72. Olivera and Lewis 2004, p. 125.
73. Clark 1995, p. 4.

References

Abrams, Philip 1988, 'Notes on the Difficulty of Studying the State', *Journal of Historical Sociology*, 1, 1: 58–89.

Adam, Barry 1987, *The Rise of a Gay and Lesbian Movement*, Boston: Twayne.

Adi, Hakim 2009, 'The Negro Question: The Communist International and Black Liberation in the Interwar Years', in *From Toussaint to Tupac: The Black International since the Age of Revolution*, edited by Michael O. West, William G. Martin and Fanon C. Wilkins, Chapel Hill, NC: University of North Carolina Press.

Adonis, Andrew and Stephen Pollard 1998, *A Class Act: the Myth of Britain's Classless Society*, Harmondsworth: Penguin.

Adorno, Theodor 1994, *Hegel: Three Studies*, Cambridge, MA: MIT Press.

Ahmad, Aijaz 1994, *In Theory*, London: Verso.

Alexander, Christopher 2011, 'Tunisia's Protest Wave: Where it Comes from and what it Means', *Mideast Foreign Policy*, January 3, available at <http://mideast.foreignpolicy.com/posts/2011/01/02/tunisia_s_protest_wave_where_it_comes_from_and_what_it_means_for_ben_ali>.

Alexander, Peter 2010, 'Rebellion of the Poor: South Africa's Service Delivery Protests – A Preliminary Analysis', *Review of African Political Economy*, 37, 123: 25–40.

Allen, Robert 2004, *No Global: the People of Ireland Versus the Multinationals*, London: Pluto Press.

Allen, Theodore 1997, *The Invention of the White Race*, Vol. 2, *The Origin of Racial Oppression in Anglo-America*, London: Verso.

Allen, Victor Leonard 1954, *Power in Trade Unions: A Study of the Organisation in Great Britain*, London: Longmans, Green and Co.

Althusser, Louis 1976, *Essays on Ideology*, London: Verso.

Amin, Samir 2011, *Eurocentrism: Modernity Religion and Democracy: A Critique of Eurocentrism and Culturalism*, Oxford: Pambazuka Press.

Aminzade, Ronald R. et al. 2001, *Silence and Voice in the Study of Contentious Politics*, Cambridge: Cambridge University Press.

ANC 1994, *The reconstruction and development programme: a policy framework*, Johannesburg: Umanyano Publications.

Anderson, Kevin 2010, *Marx at the Margins: On Nationalism, Ethnicity, and Non-Western Societies*, Chicago: University of Chicago Press.

Anderson, Perry 1967, 'The Limits and Possibilities of Trade Union Action', in *The Incompatibles: Trade Union Militancy and the Consensus*, edited by Robin Blackburn and Alexander Cockburn, Harmondsworth: Penguin.

—— 1974, *Lineages of the Absolutist State*, London: Verso.

—— 1980, *Arguments Within English Marxism*, London: Verso.

Anderson-Sherman, Arnold and Doug McAdam 1982, 'American Black Insurgency and the World-Economy: A Political Process Model', in *Ascent and Decline in the World-System*, edited by Edward Friedman. Beverly Hills, CA: Sage Publications.

Andors, Stephen 1977, *China's Industrial Revolution*, New York: Pantheon.

Arecco, Maxi, Alfredo Cabaña and José Vega 2009, *Nuestra Comisión Interna: La Organización De Los Trabajadores De Praxair*, Buenos Aires: Taller de Estudios Laborales.

Arieff, Alexis 2011, 'Political Transition in Tunisia', Washington: Congressional Research Service, February 2.

Armstrong, Elizabeth A. 2002, *Forging Gay Identities: Organizing Sexuality in San Francisco, 1950–1994*, Chicago: University of Chicago Press.

Armstrong, Elizabeth A. and Mary Bernstein 2008, 'Culture, Power, and Institutions: A Multi-Institutional Politics Approach to Social Movements', *Sociological Theory*, 26, 1: 74–99.

Armstrong, Elizabeth A. and Suzanna M. Crage 2006, 'Movements and Memory: The Making of the Stonewall Myth', *American Sociological Review*, 71, 5: 724–51.

Aronowitz, Stanley 2003, *How Class Works: Power and Social Movements*, New Haven, CT: Yale University Press.

Arrighi, Giovanni, Terence K. Hopkins and Immanuel Wallerstein 1989, *Anti-Systemic Movements*, London: Verso.

Arvanitakis, James and Stephen Healy 2001, 'The Third Wave of Environmentalism', *Ecopolitics*, 1, 1: 24–9.

Auyero, Javier, and Débora Alejandra Swistun 2009, *Flammable: Environmental Suffering in an Argentine Shantytown*, Oxford: Oxford University Press.

Auyero, Javier, and Timothy Patrick Moran 2007, 'The Dynamics of Collective Violence: Dissecting Food Riots in Contemporary Argentina', *Social Forces*, 85, 3: 1341–67.

Bageant, Joe 2007, *Deer Hunting with Jesus: Dispatches from America's Class War*, New York: Three Rivers Press.

Bagguley, Paul 1995, 'Middle-class Radicalism Revisited', in *Social Change and the Middle Classes*, edited by Tom Butler and Mike Savage, London: University College.

Bahro, Rudolf 1978, *The Alternative in Eastern Europe*, London: NLB.

—— 1985, *From Red to Green*, London: Verso.

Baird, Sandy, John Foster and Richard Leonard 2005, 'Ownership and Control in the Scottish Economy', in *The Red Paper on Scotland*, edited by Vince Mills, Glasgow: Research Collections @ Glasgow Caledonian University.

Bakhtin, Mikhail 1981, *The Dialogic Imagination: Four Essays*, edited by Michael Holquist, translated by Caryl Emerson and Michael Holquist, Austin, TX: University of Texas Press.

—— 1985, *The Formal Method in Literary Scholarship*, Cambridge, MA: Harvard University Press.

—— 1986, *Speech Genres and Other Late Essays*, Austin, TX: University of Texas Press.

Bakhurst, David. 1994, 'Social Memory in Soviet Thought', in *An Introduction to Vygotsky*, edited by Harry Daniels, London: Routledge.

Ball, Charles C. 1858–9, *The History of Indian Mutiny*, 2 Volumes, London: The London Publishing House.

Ballard, Richard, Adam Habib and Imraan Valodia 2006, *Voices of Protest*, Pietermaritzburg: University of KwaZulu-Natal Press.

Bannerji, Himani 1995, *Thinking Through: Essays on Feminism, Marxism and Anti-Racism*, Toronto: Women's Press.

Baptiste, Fitzroy and Rupert Lewis (eds.) 2009, *George Padmore: Pan-African Revolutionary*, Kingston, Jamaica: Ian Randle Press.

Barbetta, Pablo, and Karina Bidaseca 2004, 'Reflexiones sobre el 19 y 20 de diciembre de 2001 "Piquete y cacerola, la lucha es una sola": ¿Emergencia discursiva o nueva subjetividad?', *Revista Argentina de Sociología*, 2, 2: 67–88.

Bardhan, Pranab 1998, *The Political Economy of Development in India: Expanded Edition*, Oxford: Oxford University Press.

Barker, Colin (ed.) 1987, *Revolutionary Rehearsals*, London: Bookmarks.

—— 2001, 'Robert Michels and the "Cruel Game"', in *Leadership and Social Movements*, edited by Colin Barker, Alan Johnson and Michael Lavalette, Manchester: Manchester University Press.

—— 2006a, 'Ideology, Discourse and Moral Economy: Consulting the People of North Manchester', *Atlantic Journal of Communication*, 14, 1/2: 7–27.

—— 2006b, 'Extending Combined and Uneven Development,' in *100 years of Permanent Revolution*, edited by Bill Dunn and Hugo Radice, London: Pluto Press.

Barker, *Cont.*
—— 2009, 'Looking in the Wrong Direction? Reflections on Revolutionary Possibility in the 21st century' in *Fourteenth International Conference on Alternative Futures and Popular Protest*, edited by Colin Barker and Mike Tyldesley, Manchester Metropolitan University, April 2009.

Barker, Colin and Laurence Cox 2002, 'What Have the Romans Ever Done for Us? Academic and Activist Forms of Movement Theorizing', in *Eighth International Conference on Alternative Futures and Popular Protest*, edited by Colin Barker and Mike Tyldesley, Manchester Metropolitan University, available at <http://eprints.nuim.ie/428>

Barker, Colin and Gareth Dale 1998, 'Protest Waves in Western Europe; A Critique of "New Social Movement Theory'"', *Critical Sociology*, 24, 1/2: 65–104.

Barker, Colin, Alan Johnson and Michael Lavalette (eds.) 2001, *Leadership and Social Movements*, Manchester: Manchester University Press.

Barmeyer, Neils 2009, *Developing Zapatista Autonomy: Conflict and NGO Involvement in Rebel Chiapas*, Albuquerque: University of New Mexico Press.

Barrett, Patrick, Daniel Chavez, and César Rodríguez-Garavito 2008, 'Utopia Reborn?' in *The New Left in Latin America: Utopia Reborn*, edited by Patrick Barrett, Daniel Chavez and César Rodríguez-Garavito, London: Pluto Press.

Basualdo, Eduardo M. 2001, *Modelo de acumulación y sistema político en la Argentina. Notas sobre el transformismo argentino durante la valorización financiera (1976–2001)*, Buenos Aires: Universidad Nacional de Quilmes.

Batstone, Eric 1986, 'Bureaucracy, Oligarchy and Incorporation in Shop Steward Organisations in the 1980s', in *Technological Change, Rationalisation and Industrial Relations*, edited by Otto Jacobi, Bob Jessop, Hans Kastendiek and Marino Regini, London: Croom Helm.

—— 1988, *The Reform of Workplace Industrial Relations: Theory, Myth and Evidence*, Oxford: Clarendon Press.

Batstone, Eric, Ian Boraston and Stephen Frenkel 1977, *Shop Stewards in Action:*

The Organization of Workplace Conflict and Accommodation, Oxford: Blackwell.

—— 1978, *The Social Organisation of Strikes*, Oxford: Blackwell.

Baviskar, Amita 1995, *In the Belly of the River: Tribal Conflicts over Water in the Narmada Valley*, Oxford: Oxford University Press.

Bayly, Christopher Alan 1990, *Indian Society and the Making of the British Empire*, Cambridge: Cambridge University Press.

Beecham, Dave 1984, 'How Far Has the Rank-and-File Been Weakened and Incorporated?', *International Socialism*, 2, 23: 99–112.

Beinin, Joel 2001, *Workers and Peasants in the Modern Middle East*, Cambridge: Cambridge University Press.

—— 2005, 'Popular Social Movements and the Future of Egyptian Politics', *Middle East Report Online*, March 10, available at <http://www.mafhoum.com/press7/231S24.htm>.

—— 2008, 'Egypt: Bread Riots and Mill Strikes', *Le Monde Diplomatique*, 8 May.

—— 2009, 'Workers' Struggles under "Socialism" and Neoliberalism', in *Egypt: The Moment of Change*, edited by Rabab El-Mahdi and Philip Marfleet, London: Zed Books.

Beinin, Joel and Hossam El-Hamalawy 2007, 'Egyptian Textile Workers Confront the New Economic Order', *Middle East Report Online*, 25 March, available at <http://www.arabawy.org/2007/03/26/egyptian-textile-workers-confront-the-new-economic-order>.

Benclowicz, José 2006, 'La izquierda y la emergencia del movimiento piquetero en la Argentina: análisis de Un caso testigo', *Espiral*, 13, 37: 123–43.

Benjamin, Medea 1995, 'Interview: Subcomandante Marcos', in *First World Ha Ha Ha! The Zapatista Challenge*, edited by Elaine Katzenberger, San Francisco: City Lights.

Bennett, Tony 1979, *Formalism and Marxism*, London: Routledge.

Benton, Allyson Lucinda 2002, 'Presidentes fuertes, provincias poderosas: la economía política de la construcción de partidos en el sistema federal argentino', *Politica y Gobierno*, 10, 1: 103–37.

Berger, Mark T. 2004, 'After the Third World? History, Destiny and the Fate of

Third Worldism', *Third World Quarterly*, 25, 1: 9–39.

Berlet, Chip 1995, 'The Violence of Rightwing Populism', *Peace Review*, 7, 3/4: 283–8.

Berlet, Chip and Matthew N. Lyons 2000, *Right-Wing Populism in America: Too Close for Comfort*, New York: The Guilford Press.

Bernard, Tara Siegel, and Ron Lieber 2009, 'The High Price of Being a Gay Couple', *The New York Times*, 3 October, online edition.

Bernstein, Eduard, 1961, *Evolutionary Socialism*, New York: Schocken Books.

Bernstein, Henry 2010, *Class Dynamics of Agrarian Change*, Winnipeg: Fernwood Publishing.

BERR 2009, *Reps in Action: How Workplaces Can Gain From Modern Union Representation*, Department for Business, Enterprise and Regulatory Reform.

Bevington, Douglas and Chris Dixon 2005, 'Movement-Relevant Theory: Rethinking Social Movement Scholarship and Activism', *Social Movement Studies*, 4, 3: 185–208.

Beynon, Huw 1973, *Working for Ford*, Harmondsworth: Penguin.

—— 1984, *Working for Ford*, Second edition, Harmondsworth: Pelican.

Bielsa, Rafael Antonio et al. 2002, *Qué son las asambleas populares*, Buenos Aires: Ediciones Continente.

Bila-Gunther, Gaby 2001, 'Tram Ride from S11', *Overland*, 162: 85– 6.

Billig, Michael 1996, *Arguing and Thinking: A Rhetorical Approach to Social Psychology*, Cambridge: Cambridge University Press.

Blackledge, Paul 2006, *Reflections on the Marxist Theory of History*, Manchester: Manchester University Press.

—— 2008, 'British Marxist History', in *Critical Companion to Contemporary Marxism*, edited by Jacques Bidet and Stathis Kouvelakis, Leiden: Brill.

—— 2012, *Marxism and Ethics*, New York: SUNY Press.

Bloch, Ernst 1995, *The Principle of Hope*, Vol. 1, Cambridge, MA: MIT Press.

Bobrow-Strain, Aaron 2005, 'Articulations of Rule: Landowners, Revolution and Territory in Chiapas, Mexico, 1920–1962', *Historical Geography*, 31: 744–62.

—— Aaron 2007, *Intimate Enemies: Landowners, Power and Violence in Chiapas*, London: Duke University Press.

Boggs, Carl 1985, *Social Movements and Political Power: Emerging Forms of Radicalism in the West*, Philadelphia, Temple University Press.

Bohmke, Heinrich 2009a, 'The White Revolutionary as a Missionary?', *New Frank Talk*, 5, available at <http://www.scribd.com/doc/31891005/The-White-Revolutionary-as-a-Missionary-Contemporary-travels-and-researches-in-Caffraria>.

—— 2009b, 'The Branding of Social Movements in South Africa', available at <http://www.librarything.com/work/11812265>.

—— 2010a, 'Between the Halo and the Panga', *Dispositions*, 2, available at <http://dispositionsjournal.blogspot.com>.

—— 2010b, 'Don't Talk About Us Talking About the Poor', *PoliticsWeb*, available at <http://www.politicsweb.co.za/politicsweb/view/politicsweb/en/page71619?oid=206254&sn=Detail&pid=71616>.

Bond, Patrick 2000, *Cities of Gold, Townships of Coal*, Trenton: Africa World Press.

—— 2002, *Unsustainable South Africa*, Pietermaritzburg: University of KwaZulu-Natal Press.

—— 2005, *Elite Transition*, Pietermaritzburg: University of KwaZulu-Natal Press.

—— 2011a, 'The Right to the City and the Eco-Social Commoning of Water', in *The Right to Water*, edited by Sultana Farhana and Alex Loftus, London: Earthscan.

—— 2011b, 'Durban's Water Wars, Sewage Spills, Fish Kills and Blue Flag Beaches', in *Durban's Climate Gamble*, edited by Patrick Bond, Pretoria: University of South Africa Press.

—— 2011c, *Politics of Climate Justice*, Pietermaritzburg: University of KwaZulu-Natal Press.

Bond, Patrick and Ashwin Desai 2006, 'Explaining Uneven and Combined Development in South Africa', in *Permanent Revolution*, edited by Bill Dunn London: Pluto.

Bonzi, Leandro, Ariel Fontecoba, Santiago González, Florencia Greco, Mariela Peller, and Ignacio Sabbatella 2006,

Asambleas barriales: Indagando en el legado subjetivo del 19 y 20 de diciembre (2002–2004), available at <http://www.centrocultural.coop/uploads/texto.asambleas.barriales.pdf>.

Bookchin, Murray 1989, 'New Social Movements: the anarchist dimension', in *For Anarchism*, edited by David Goodway, London: Routledge.

—— 1996–2003, *The Third Revolution: Popular Movements in the Revolutionary Era*, 4 Vols., London: Continuum Books.

Boraston, Ian, Hugh Armstrong Clegg and Michael Rimmer 1975, *Workplace and Union*, London: Heinemann.

Boyle, Mark 2005, 'Sartre's Circular Dialectic and the Empires of Abstract Space: A History of Space and Place in Ballymun, Dublin', *Annals of the Association of American Geographers*, 95, 1: 181–201.

Bradsher, Keith 2010, 'Workers at Chinese Honda Plant March in Protest', in the *New York Times*, 10 June.

Bramble, Tom 1993, *The Contingent Conservatism of Full-time Trade Union Officials: A Case Study of the Vehicle Builders Employees' Federation of Australia, 1963 to 1991*, PhD dissertation, La Trobe University, Australia.

Bramble, Tom and John Minns 2005, 'Whose Streets? Our Streets! Activist Perspectives on the Australian Anti-Capitalist Movement', *Social Movement Studies*, 4, 2: 106–21.

Brandist, Craig 1996, 'Gramsci, Bakhtin, and the Semiotics of Hegemony', *New Left Review*, I/216: 94–109.

—— 2002, *The Bakhtin Circle*, London: Pluto.

Braverman, Harry 1974, *Labor and Monopoly Capital: The Degradation of Work in the Twentieth Century*, New York: Monthly Review Press.

Breman, Jan 1996, *Footloose Labour: Working in India's Informal Sector*, Cambridge: Cambridge University Press.

Brenner, Johanna 2000, *Women and the Politics of Class*, New York: Monthly Review Press.

Brenner, Neil 1997, 'State Territorial Restructuring and the Production of Spatial Scale', *Political Geography*, 16, 4: 273–306.

—— 1998, 'Between Fixity and Motion: Accumulation, Territorial Organization and the Historical Geography of Spatial Scales', *Environment and Planning D: Space and Society*, 16, 4: 459–81.

Bridgeman, Jean 2010, 'A Matter of Trust: The Politics of Working-Class Self-Education', *Interface*, 2, 1: 154–67.

Broad, Robin and Zahara Heckscher 2003, 'Before Seattle: The Historical Roots of the Current Movement Against Corporate-Led Globalisation', *Third World Quarterly*, 24, 4: 713–28.

Buck, Nick, Ian Gordon, Alan Harding and Ivan Turok (eds.) 2005, *Changing Cities: Rethinking Urban Competitiveness, Cohesion and Governance*, Basingstoke: Palgrave.

Buechler, Steven M. 1995, 'New Social Movement Theories', *Sociological Quarterly*, 36: 441–64.

—— 2000, *Social Movements in Advanced Capitalism: The Political Economy and Cultural Construction of Social Activism*, Oxford: Oxford University Press.

Burawoy, Michael 1982, *Manufacturing Consent: Changes in the Labor Process Under Monopoly Capitalism*, Chicago: University of Chicago Press.

Burgmann, Verity 2003, *Power, Profit and Protest: Australian Social Movements and Globalisation*, Crows Nest: Allen & Unwin.

Burris, Val 1980, 'Capital Accumulation and the Rise of the New Middle Class', *Review of Radical Political Economics*, 12, 1: 17–34.

Burstein, Paul 1998, 'Interest Organizations, Political Parties, and the Study of Democratic Politics', in *Social Movements and American Political Institutions*, edited by Anne N. Costain and Andrew S. McFarland, Lanham, MD: Rowman and Littlefield.

Byres, Terence J. 1981, 'The New Technology, Class Formation and Class Action in the Indian Countryside', *Journal of Peasant Studies*, 8, 4: 405–54.

Byrne, Paul 1997, *Social Movements in Britain*, London: Routledge.

Cahill, Damien 2001, 'The Anti-WEF Protests and the Media', *Social Alternatives*, 20, 1: 63–7.

Calhoun, Craig 1993, ' "New Social Movements" of the Early Nineteenth Century', *Social Science History*, 17, 3: 385–487.

—— 1995, ' "New Social Movements" of the Early Nineteenth Century', in Mark

Traugott (ed.), *Repertoires and Cycles of Collective Action*, London: Duke University Press.

Callinicos, Alex 1982, 'The Rank-and-File Movement Today', *International Socialism*, 2, 17: 1–38.

—— 1988, *Making History: Agency, Structure and Change in Social Theory*, Cambridge, Polity Press.

—— 1993, *Race and Class*, London: Bookmarks.

—— 1995, *Socialists in the Trade Unions*, London: Bookmarks.

—— 2001, 'Plumbing the Depths: Marxism and the Holocaust', *Yale Journal of Criticism*, 14, 2: 385–414.

—— 2003, *An Anti-Capitalist Manifesto*, Cambridge: Polity.

—— 2004, *Making History*, Leiden: Brill.

—— 2006, *The Resources of Critique*, Cambridge: Polity

—— 2010, 'The Limits of Passive Revolution', *Capital & Class*, 34, 3: 491–507.

Callinicos, Alex and Mike Simons 1985, *The Great Strike: The Miners' Strike and Its Lessons*, London: Socialist Worker.

Cambridge Policy Consultants 1999, *An Evaluation of the New Life for Urban Scotland Initiative*, Edinburgh: Scottish Office, Central Research Unit.

Camfield, David 2004, 'Reorienting Class Analysis', *Science and Society*, 68, 4: 421–46.

Camino, A. 2011, 'El 15-M Aprende Del "Corralito"', in *Canariasahora.es*, Canarias, available at <http://www.canariasahora.es/noticia/189507>.

Carlson, Laura 2008, 'Armouring NAFTA: the Battleground for Mexico's future', *NACLA Report on the Americas*, 41, 5: 17–22.

Carlyon, Patrick 2000, 'Revolution Number S11', *Bulletin*, 8 (August): 32–4.

Carrera, Iñigo Juan 2006, 'Argentina: The Reproduction of Capital Accumulation through Political Crisis', *Historical Materialism*, 14, 1: 185–219.

Carroll, William K. and Robert S. Ratner 1994, 'Between Leninism and Radical Pluralism: Gramscian Reflections on Counter-Hegemony and the New Social Movements', *Critical Sociology*, 20, 2: 1–24.

—— 'Master Framing and Cross-Movement Networking in Contemporary Social Movements', *The Sociological Quarterly*, 37, 4: 601–25.

Castells, Manuel 1983, *The City and the Grassroots: A Cross-cultural Theory of Urban Social Movements*, Berkeley, CA: University of California Press.

Castillo, Rosalva A.H. 2003, 'Between Civil Disobedience and Silent Rejection: Differing Responses by Mam Peasants to the Zapatista Rebellion', in *Mayan Lives, Mayan Utopias: The Indigenous Peoples of Chiapas and the Zapatista Rebellion*, edited by Jan Rus, Rosalva A.H. Castillo and Shannan Mattiace, Oxford: Rowman and Littlefields.

Castree, Noel 2004, 'Differential Geographies: Place, Indigenous Rights and 'Local' Resources', *Political Geography*, 23, 2: 133–67.

Cecena, Ana Esther 2007, 'On the Forms of Resistance in Latin America: Its "Native" Moment', in *Socialist Register 2008: Global Flashpoints*, edited by Leo Panitch and Colin Leys, London: Merlin Press.

Charlwood, Andy and John Forth 2008, 'Workplace Employee Representation: 1980–2004', National Institute of Economic and Social Research discussion-paper, available at: <www.niesr.ac.uk/pdf/240708_152852.pdf>.

Chatterjee, Partha 1993, *The Nation and its Fragments*, Princeton, NJ: Princeton University Press.

—— 2008, 'Democracy and Economic Transformation in India', *Economic and Political Weekly*, 43, 16: 53–62.

Chesneaux, Jean 1968, *The Chinese Labor Movement, 1919–1927*, Stanford, CA: Stanford University Press.

Chibber, Vivek 2003, *Locked in Place: State-Building and Late Industrialization in India*, Princeton, NJ: Princeton University Press.

Clack, Garfield 1965, 'How Unofficial Strikes Help Industry', *Business*, July.

Clark, Anna 1995, *The Struggle for the Breeches: Gender and the Making of the British Working Class*, Berkeley, CA: University of California Press.

Claudín, Fernando 1975, *The Communist Movement From Comintern to Cominform*, London: Peregrine.

Clavin, Matthew, J. 2010, *Toussaint Louverture and the American Civil War: The*

Promise and Peril of a Second Haitian Revolution, Philadelphia: University of Pennsylvania Press.

Clawson, Dan 2003, *The Next Upsurge: Labor and the New Social Movements*, Ithaca, NY: Cornell University Press.

Clemens, Elisabeth 1997, *The People's Lobby: Organizational Innovation and the Rise of Interest Groups in the United States, 1890–1925*, Chicago: University of Chicago Press.

Cliff, Tony 1969, 'On Perspectives', *International Socialism*, 36: 15–21.

—— 1970, *The Employers' Offensive: Productivity Deals and How to Fight Them*, London: Pluto Press.

—— 1971, 'The Bureaucracy Today', *International Socialism*, 48: 31–3.

—— 1974, *State Capitalism in Russia*, London: Bookmarks.

—— 1979, 'The Balance of Class Forces in Recent Years', *International Socialism*, 2, 6: 1–50.

—— 2003, 'Economic Roots of Reformism', in *Selected Writings*, Vol. 3, *Marxist Theory After Trotsky*, Tony Cliff, London: Bookmarks.

Cliff, Tony and Colin Barker 1966, *Incomes Policy, Legislation and Shop Stewards*, London Industrial Shop Stewards' Defence Committee.

Cliff, Tony and Donny Gluckstein 1986, *Marxism and Trade Union Struggle: The General Strike of 1926*, London: Bookmarks.

Coates, David 1975, *The Labour Party and the Struggle for Socialism*, Cambridge: Cambridge University Press.

—— 1980, *Labour in Power?*, London: Longman.

—— 1989, *The Crisis of Labour: Industrial Relations and the State in Contemporary Britain*, Oxford: Phillip Allan.

Cochrane, Alan 2007, *Understanding Urban Policy: A Critical Introduction*, Oxford: Blackwell.

Cockburn, Cynthia 1977, *The Local State*, London: Pluto Press.

Cohen, Jean 1985, 'Strategy or Identity: New Theoretical Paradigms and Contemporary Social Movements', *Social Research*, 52: 663–716.

Cohen, Sheila 2006, *Ramparts of Resistance: Why Workers Lost Their Power and How to Get it Back*, London: Pluto Press.

Coirm, George 2011, 'Is this an Arab Spring?', *Le Monde Diplomatique*, 2 April.

Colletti, Lucio 1976, *From Rousseau to Lenin: Studies in Ideology and Society*, New York: Monthly Review Press.

Collier, George A. and Jane F. Collier 2005, 'The Zapatista Rebellion in the Context of Globalization', *The Journal of Peasant Studies*, 32, 3/4: 450–60.

Collins, Chik 2003, 'Urban Policy, 'Modesty' and 'Misunderstanding': On the Mythology of 'Partnership' in Urban Scotland', in *Restructuring Local Economies: Towards a Comparative Study of Scotland and Upper Silesia*, edited by George Blazyca, Aldershot: Ashgate.

—— 2004, 'After Partnership: Looking Beyond Better Communities', *Concept*, 14, 3: 18–24.

—— 2006a, ' "The Scottish Executive is Open for Business": The New Regeneration Statement, The Royal Bank of Scotland and the Community Voices Network', *Variant* 26: 10–13.

—— 2006b, 'Where Does Community Engagement Come From?', *Scotregen*, 34: 15.

—— 2006c, 'Community Regeneration: What Lies Behind the Cloak?', *Linking Communities Conference: For a People's Clydebank, or 'Sold Doon the Watter'?*, Clydebank Unemployed Community Resource Centre, 3 November.

—— 2007, 'And They Call It "Regeneration"! *People and Place* and the Intensification of the Neo-Liberal Agenda in Scotland', *Scottish Left Review*, 42: 6–7.

—— 2008a, 'Discourse in Cultural-Historical Perspective: Critical Discourse Analysis, CHAT and the Study of Social Change', in *The Transformation of Learning: Advances in Cultural-Historical Activity Theory*, edited by Bert Van Oers, Ed Elbers, Wim Wardekker, and Rene Van der Veer, Cambridge: Cambridge University Press.

—— 2008b, *The Right to Exist: The Story of the Clydebank Independent Resource Centre*, Glasgow: Oxfam.

Colmegna, Paula 2003, 'The Unemployed Piqueteros of Argentina: Active Rejection of an Exclusionary Form of Democracy', *Theomai*, 7.

Cooper, Frederick 1996, *Decolonization and African Society: The Labor Question in French and British Africa*, Cambridge: Cambridge University Press.

Cooper, Frederick and Randall Packard 1997, 'Introduction', in *International Development and the Social Sciences: Essays on the History and Politics of Knowledge*, Berkeley, CA: University of California Press.

Corbridge, Stuart and John Harriss 2000, *Reinventing India: Liberalization, Hindu Nationalism and Popular Democracy*, Cambridge: Polity Press

Corbridge, Stuart, Glyn Williams, Manoj Srivastava and René Véron 2005, *Seeing the State: Governance and Governmentality in India*, Cambridge: Cambridge University Press.

Coronado, Jaime P. and Aarón V. Mora 2006, 'México y Centroamérica: hegemonía, resistencias y visibilidad social' in *Geoeconómiá y geopolítica en el área del Plan Puebla-Panamá*, edited by David Villafuerte Solís and Xochitl Leyva Solano, Mexico City: CIESAS.

Couch, Jen 2003, *This Is What Democracy Looks Like: The Genesis, Culture and Possibilities of Anti-Corporate Activism*, PhD dissertation, Victoria University.

Couch, Jen and Damian Sullivan 2006, 'All Over Red Rover', *Arena Magazine*, 86: 7–8.

Coulter, Carol 1993, *The Hidden Tradition: Feminism, Women and Nationalism in Ireland*, Cork: Cork University Press.

Cox, Laurence 1995, 'Six Movements in Search of a Social Basis', paper presented to Sociological Association of Ireland Conference, 1995, available at <http://eprints.nuim.ie/430>

—— 1998, 'Gramsci, Movements and Method: The Politics of Activist Research', in *Fourth International Conference on Alternative Futures and Popular Protest*, edited by Colin Barker and Mike Tyldesley, Manchester Metropolitan University, available at <http://eprints.nuim.ie/442>.

—— 1999a, *Building Counter Culture: The Radical Praxis of Social Movement Milieux*, PhD dissertation, Dublin: Trinity College.

—— 1999b, 'Power, Politics and Everyday Life: The Local Rationalities of Social Movement Milieux', in *Transforming Politics: Power and Resistance*, edited by Paul Bagguley, P. and Jeff Hearn, Basingstoke: Macmillan.

—— 2001a, 'Barbarian Resistance and Rebel Alliances: Social Movements and *Empire*', *Rethinking Marxism*, 13, 3/4: 155–67.

—— 2001b, 'Globalisation from Below? "Ordinary People", Movements and Intellectuals from Seattle to Genova', paper to William Thompson summerschool, Cork, available at <http://eprints.nuim.ie/1530>.

—— 2003, 'Eppur si Muove: Thinking "the Social Movement"', paper available at <http://eprints.nuim.ie/427>

—— 2005, 'What Should the Movement of Movements Do If We Want To Win?' in online proceedings of *Making Global Civil Society*, Lancaster University, November 2005, available at <http://knowledgelab.pbwiki.com/f/Chapter+5+Lancaster+draft.doc>

—— 2006, 'News from Nowhere: The Movement of Movements in Ireland', in *Social Movements and Ireland*, edited by Hourigan, Niamh and Linda Connolly, Manchester: Manchester University Press.

—— 2007a, 'The Grassroots Gatherings: Networking a Movement of Movements', in *Red and Black Revolution*, 12, available at <http://www.wsm.ie/c/grassroots-gatherings-ireland-history>

—— 2007b, 'Building Utopia Here and Now? Left and Working-Class Utopias in Ireland', *Ecopolitics online*, 1, 1: 123–32.

—— 2010a, 'Another World is Under Construction? Social Movement Responses to Inequality and Crisis', *Irish Left Review*, 17 May, available at <http://www.irishleftreview.org/2010/05/17/world-construction-social-movement-responses-inequality-crisis>

—— 2010b, '"The Interests of the Movement as a Whole": Response to David Harvey', *Interface: A Journal For and About Social Movements*, 2, 1: 298–308.

—— 2011, 'Popular Responses to the Irish Crisis and the Hope for Radical Change: Organic Crisis and the Different Meanings of Counter-Hegemony', paper to *Alternative Futures and Popular Protest 16*, Manchester Metropolitan University, April.

Cox, Laurence and Liz Curry, 2010, 'Revolution in the Air: Images of Winning in the Irish Anti-Capitalist Movement', *Irish Journal of Sociology*, 18, 2: 86–105.

Cox, Laurence and Cristina Flesher Fominaya 2009, 'Movement Knowledge: What Do We Know, How Do We Create Knowledge and What Do We Do With It?', *Interface: A Journal For and About Social Movements*, 1, 1: 1–20.

Cox, Laurence and Alf Gunvald Nilsen 2005a, 'Why do Activists Need Theory?', *Euromovements* newsletter, available at <http://www.euromovements.info/html/index.htm>

—— 2005b, ' "At the Heart of Society Burns the Fire of Social Movements": What Would a Marxist Theory of Social Movements Look Like?', in *Tenth International Conference on Alternative Futures and Popular Protest*, edited by Colin Barker and Mike Tyldesley, Manchester Metropolitan University, available at <http://eprints.nuim.ie/460>

—— 2007, 'Social Movements Research and the "Movement of Movements": Studying Resistance to Neo-Liberal Globalisation', *Sociological Compass*, 1, 2: 424–42.

Cox, Laurence and Ealáir Ní Dhorchaigh 2011, 'When is An Assembly Riotous, and Who Decides? The Success and Failure of Police Attempts to Criminalise Protest', in *Riotous Assemblies*, edited by William Sheehan and Maura Cronin, Cork: Mercier.

Cox, Robert W. 1987, *Production Power and World Order: Social Forces in the Making of History*, New York: Columbia University Press.

Cronin, James E. 1989, 'The "Rank-and-File" and the Social History of the Working Class', *International Review of Social History*, XXXIV: 78–88.

D'Emilio, John 1983a, *Sexual Politics, Sexual Communities: The Making of a Homosexuality Minority in the United States, 1940–1970*, Chicago: University of Chicago Press.

—— 1983b, 'Capitalism and Gay Identity', *Powers of Desire: The Politics of Sexuality*, edited by Ann Snitow, Christine Stansell, and Sharon Thompson. New York: Monthly Review Press.

Daniels, Gary and John McIlroy (eds.) 2009, *Trade Unions in a Neoliberal World: British Trade Unions Under New Labour*, London: Routledge.

Darlington, Ralph 1994, *The Dynamics of Workplace Unionism*, London: Mansell.

—— 1998, *The Political Trajectory of J. T. Murphy*, Liverpool University Press.

—— 2002, 'Shop Stewards' Leadership, Left-Wing Activism and Collective Workplace Union Organisation', *Capital & Class*, 76: 95–126.

—— 2005, ' "There is No Alternative": Exploring the Options in the 1984–5 Miners' Strike', *Capital & Class*, 87: 71–95.

—— 2008a, *Syndicalism and the Transition to Communism: An International Comparative Analysis*, Aldershot: Ashgate.

—— 2008b, 'British Syndicalism and the Critique of Trade Union Officialdom', *Historical Studies in Industrial Relations*, 25/6: 103–40.

—— 2009a, 'Organising, Militancy and Revitalisation: The Case of the RMT', in *Union Revitalisation in Advanced Economies: Assessing the Contribution of Union Organising*, edited by Gregor Gall, London: Palgrave Macmillan.

—— 2009b, 'Leadership and Union Militancy: The Case of the RMT', *Capital & Class*, 99: 3–32.

—— 2009c, 'RMT Strike Activity on London Underground: Incidence, Dynamics and Causes', International Industrial Relations Association Conference, 24–7 August 2009, Sydney Convention and Exhibition Centre, Australia.

—— 2010, 'The State of Workplace Reps' Organisation in Britain Today', *Capital & Class*, 100: 126–35.

Darlington, Ralph and Dave Lyddon 2001, *Glorious Summer: Class Struggle in Britain 1972*, London: Bookmarks.

Davidson, Neil 2005, 'The Scottish Enlightenment Considered as a Social Movement', in *10th International Conference on Alternative Futures and Popular Protest*, edited by Colin Barker and Mike Tyldesley, Manchester Metropolitan University.

Dávila, Enrique, Georgina Kessel and Santiago Levy 2002, 'El Sur También Existe: Un Ensayo Sobre el Desarrollo Regional de México', *Economía Mexicana*, 11, 2: 205–60.

Davis, Mike 1986, 'The Political Economy of Late Imperial America', in *Prisoners of the American Dream: Politics and Economy in the History of the American Working Class*, London: Verso.

—— 1990, *City of Quartz: Excavating the Future in Los Angeles*, London: Verso.

—— 2007, 'What's the Matter with America? A Debate with Thomas Frank', in *In Praise of Barbarians: Essays against Empire*, Chicago: Haymarket Books.

Day, Richard J.F. 2005, *Gramsci is Dead: Anarchist Currents in the Newest Social Movements*, London: Pluto Press.

De Ste. Croix, Geoffrey 1981, *The Class Struggle in the Ancient Greek World*, London: Duckworth.

DeFilippis, James, Robert Fisher and Eric Schragge 2010, *Contesting Community*, New Brunswick, NJ: Rutgers University Press.

Deleuze, Gilles and Félix Guattari 1988, *A Thousand Plateaus: Capitalism and Schizophrenia*, London: Athlone Press.

Della Porta, Donatella and Mario Diani 1999, *Social Movements: An Introduction*, Oxford: Blackwell.

—— 2006, *Social Movements: An Introduction*, Second edition, Oxford: Blackwell.

Democracy Digest 2011, 'Tunisian Unions Eclipsing Parties as Democratizing Force?', 24 January.

Denham, Diana and CASA Collective (eds.) 2008, *Teaching Rebellion: Stories from the Grassroots Resistance in Oaxaca*, Oakland, CA: PM Press.

Derrick, Jonathan 2008, *Africa's 'Agitators': Militant Anti-Colonialism in Africa and the West, 1918–1939*, London: Hurst & Company.

Desai, Ashwin 2002, *We are the Poors*, New York: Monthly Review.

—— 2006, 'Vans, Autos, and Kombis and and the Drivers of Social Movements,' paper presented at Harold Wolpe Memorial Lecture, University of KwaZulu-Natal Centre for Civil Society, Durban, 28 July, available at <ccs.ukzn.ac.za/default .asp?11,22,5,2258>.

Dewey, John 1938, *Logic: The Theory of Inquiry*, New York: Hold, Rinehart, and Winston.

Diamond, Sara 1995, *Roads to Dominion: Right-Wing Movements and Political Power in the United States*, New York: The Guilford Press.

Diani, Mario 1992, 'The Concept of Social Movement', *Sociological Review*, 40, 1: 1–25.

Dirks, Nicholas 2001, *Castes of Mind: Colonialism and the Making of Modern India*, Princeton, NJ: Princeton University Press.

Doyle, Arthur Conan 1981, *The Penguin Complete Sherlock Holmes*, Harmondsworth: Penguin.

Draper, Hal 1966, 'The Two Souls of Socialism', *New Politics*, 5, 1: 57–84.

—— 1970, 'Marxism and the Trade Unions (Part 3)', available at <http://www.marx ists.org/archive/draper/1970/tus/3-rand forg.htm>.

—— 1977, *Karl Marx's Theory of Revolution*, Vol. 1, *State and Bureaucracy*, New York: Monthly Review Press.

—— 1978, *Karl Marx's Theory of Revolution*, Vol. 2, *The Politics of Social Classes*, New York: Monthly Review Press.

—— 1986, *Karl Marx's Theory of Revolution*, Vol. 3, *The 'Dictatorship of the Proletariat'*, New York: Monthly Review Press.

—— 1987, *The 'Dictatorship of the Proletariat' from Marx to Lenin*, New York: Monthly Review Press.

—— 1990, *Karl Marx's Theory of Revolution*, Vol. 4, *Critique of Other Socialisms*, New York: Monthly Review Press.

Draper, Hal and Ernie Haberkern 2010, *Karl Marx's Theory of Revolution*, Vol. 5, *War and Revolution*, New York: Monthly Review Press.

Du Bois, William Edward Burghardt 1969 [1935], *Black Reconstruction in America, 1860–1880: an Essay Towards a History of the Part which Black Folk Played in that Attempt to Reconstruct Democracy in America, 1860–1880*, New York: Athenaeum.

Duggan, Christopher 2007. *The Force of Destiny: a History of Italy since 1796*, London: Allen Lane.

Dunayevskaya, Raya 2000 [1958], *Marxism and Freedom: From 1776 Until Today*, Amherst, NY: Humanity Books.

Duncan, Jane and Natasha Valley 2008, 'National Trends Around Protest Action', PowerPoint presentation, Centre for Sociological Research, University of Johannesburg.

Dwivedi, Ranjit 2006, *Conflict and Collective Action: The Sardar Sarovar Project in India*, London: Routledge.

Dworkin, Dennis 2007, *Class Struggles*, London: Longman.

Eagleton, Terry 1989, 'Base and Superstructure in Raymond Williams', in *Raymond Williams: Critical Perspectives*, Cambridge: Polity.

Echegaray, Fabián and Ezequiel Raimondo 1987, *Desencanto Político, Transición y Democracia*, Buenos Aires: Centro Editor de América Latina.

Edelman, Marc 2005, 'When Networks Don't Work: The Rise and Fall and Rise of Civil Society Initiatives in Central America', in *Social Movements: An Anthropological Reader*, edited by June Nash, Oxford: Blackwell.

Edwards, Brent Hayes 2003, *The Practice of Diaspora: Literature, Translation, and the Rise of Black Internationalism*, Cambridge, MA: Harvard University Press.

Eley, Geoff and Keith Nield 2007, *The Future of Class in History*, Ann Arbor: University of Michigan.

El-Ghobashy, Mona 2003, 'Egypt Looks Ahead to Portentous Year', in *Middle East Report Online*, 2 February, available at <http://www.merip.org/author/mona-el-ghobashy>.

El-Hamalawy, Hossam 2011, 'Egypt's Revolution has been 10 Years in the Making', *The Guardian*, 2 March.

El-Mahdi, Rabab 2009, 'The Democracy Movement: Cycles of Protest', in *Egypt: The Moment of Change*, edited by Rabab El-Mahdi and Philip Marfleet, London: Zed Books.

El-Mahdi, Rabab and Philip Marfleet 2009, 'Introduction', in *Egypt: The Moment of Change*, edited by Rabab El-Mahdi and Philip Marfleet, London: Zed Books.

Emirbayer, Mustafa and Ann Mische 1998, 'What is Agency?', *American Journal of Sociology*, 103: 962–1023.

Engels, Friedrich 1971 [1891], '"Introduction" to The Civil War in France', in *Karl Marx and Friedrich Engels. Writings*

on the Paris Commune, edited by Hal Draper, New York: Monthly Review.

—— 1972 [1881], 'Social Classes – Necessary and Superfluous', in Karl Marx, Friedrich Engels and Vladimir Lenin, *On Historical Materialism*, Moscow: Progress Publishers.

—— 1977 [1850], *The Peasant War in Germany*, Moscow: Progress Publishers.

—— 1978 [1858], 'The Revolt in India', in Marx and Engels 1978.

—— 1981 [1894], 'Introduction', in Marx 1981.

Enzinna, Wes 2007, 'All We Want is the Earth: Agrarian Reform in Bolivia', in *Socialist Register 2008: Global Flashpoints*, edited by Leo Panitch and Colin Leys, London: Merlin Press.

Epstein, Barbara 1993, *Political Protest and Cultural Revolution: Non-Violent Direct Action in the 1970s and 1980s*, Berkeley, CA: University of California Press.

Escobar, Arturo 1995, *Encountering Development: The Making and Unmaking of the Third World*, Princeton, NJ: Princeton University Press.

Esping-Andersen, Gøsta 1990, *The Three Worlds of Welfare Capitalism*, Princeton, NJ: Princeton University Press.

Esteva, Gustavo 2001, 'The Meaning and Scope of the Struggle for Autonomy', *Latin American Perspectives*, 28, 2: 120–48.

—— 2007, 'Oaxaca: The Path of Radical Democracy', *Socialism and Democracy*, 21, 2: 74–96.

Etchemendy, Sebastian 2001, 'Constructing Reform Coalitions: The Politics of Compensations in Argentina's Economic Liberalization', *Latin American Politics and Society*, 43, 3: 1–35.

Evans, Richard 2003, *The Coming of the Third Reich*, London: Allen Lane.

Fantasia, Rick 1988, *Cultures of Solidarity: Consciousness, Action, and Contemporary American Workers*, Berkeley, CA: University of California Press.

Fantasia, Rick and Kim Voss 2004, *Hard Work: Remaking the American Labor Movement*, Berkeley, CA: University of California Press.

Fantasia, Rick and Judith Stepan-Norris 2004, 'The labour movement in motion', in *The Blackwell Companion to Social Movements*, edited by David A Snow,

Sarah A Soule, and Hanspeter Kriesi, Oxford: Blackwell.

Ferguson, Sue 2008, 'Canadian Contributions to Social Reproduction Feminism: Race and Embodied Labor', *Race, Gender and Class*, 15, 1/2: 42–57.

Fine, Ben, Costas Lapavitsas and Jonathan Pincus (eds.) 2001, *Development Policy in the Twenty-First Century: Beyond the Post-Washington Consensus*, London: Routledge.

Flacks, Richard 2004, "Knowledge for What? Thoughts on the State of Social Movement Studies', in *Rethinking Social Movements: Structure, Meaning, and Emotion*, edited by Jeff Goodwin and James M. Jasper, Lanham, MD: Rowman and Littlefield.

Flanders, Allan 1970, *Management and Unions*, London: Faber.

Flesher Fominaya, Cristina, 2010, 'Creating Cohesion from Diversity: The Challenge of Collective Identity Formation in the Global Justice Movement', *Sociological Inquiry*, 80, 3: 377–404.

Flett, Keith 2006, *Chartism After 1848: The Working Class and the Politics of Radical Education*, London: Merlin Press.

Foner, Eric 1990, *A Short History of Reconstruction*. New York: Harper and Row.

Foner, Philip, S. (ed.) 1978, *Paul Robeson Speaks: Writings, Speeches, Interviews, 1918–1974*, London: Quartet Books.

Ford, Lucy H. 2003, 'Challenging Global Environmental Governance: Social Movement Agency and Civil Society', *Global Environmental Politics*, 3, 4: 120–34.

Foster, John 1985, 'The Declassing of Language', *New Left Review*, I/150: 29–45.

Fox-Genovese, Elizabeth and Eugene Genovese 1983, *Fruits of Merchant Capital: Slavery and Bourgeois Property in the Rise and Expansion of Capitalism*, Oxford: Oxford University Press.

Fracchia, Joseph 1991, 'Marx's Aufhebung of History and the Foundations of Historical-Materialistic Science', *History and Theory*, 30, 2: 153–79.

—— 2005, 'Beyond the Human-Nature Debate: Human Corporeal Constitution as the "First Fact" of Historical Materialism', *Historical Materialism*, 13, 1: 33–62.

Frank, Thomas 2004, *What's the Matter with America? The Resistible Rise of the American Right*, London: Secker and Warburg.

—— 2008, *The Wrecking Crew: The American Right and the Lust for Power*, London: Harvill Secker.

Frankel, Francine 2005, *India's Political Economy: The Gradual Revolution 1947–2004*, Oxford: Oxford University Press.

Fraser, Douglas 2006, 'The Quest for Joined-Up Government', *The Herald*, 10 March.

Fraser, Nancy 1997, *Justice Interruptus: Critical Reflections on the "Postsocialist" Condition*, New York: Routledge.

Fraser, Ronald 1988, *1968: A Student Generation in Revolt*, London: Chatto and Windus.

—— 2008, *Napoleon's Cursed War: Popular Resistance in the Spanish Peninsular War, 1808–1814*. London: Verso.

Freeman, Jo 1975, *The Politics of Women's Liberation*, London: Longman.

Friedman, Samuel R. 1984–5, 'Mass Organizations and Sects in the American Student Movement and its Aftermath', *Humboldt Journal of Social Relations*, 12, 1: 1–23.

Frölich, Paul 2010 [1928], *Rosa Luxemburg*, Chicago: Haymarket Books.

Galbraith, John Kenneth 1992, *The Culture of Contentment*, Harmondsworth: Penguin.

Gall, Gregor 2003, *The Meaning of Militancy? Post Workers and Industrial Relations*, Aldershot: Ashgate.

Gallaher, Carolyn 2004, 'Mainstreaming the Militia', in *Spaces of Hate: Geographies of Discrimination and Intolerance in the USA*, edited by Colin Flint, New York: Routledge.

Gamson, Joshua 1995, 'Must Identity Movements Self-Destruct? A *Queer Dilemma*', *Social Problems*, 42: 390–407.

Gamson, William A. and David S. Meyer 1996, 'Framing Political Opportunity', in *Comparative Perspectives on Social Movements: Political Opportunities, Mobilizing Structures, and Cultural Framings*, edited by Doug McAdam, John D. McCarthy, and Mayer N. Zald, Cambridge: Cambridge University Press.

García Linera, Alvaro 2004, 'The "Multitude"', in *Cochabamba! Water War in Bolivia*, Oscar Olivera and Tom Lewis, Cambridge: South End Press.

Geffen, Nathan 2010, *Debunking Delusions*, Johannesburg: Jacana.

Geoghegan, Martin 2000, *Meaning, Action and Activism: Community Development as a Social Movement*, MA thesis, Waterford Institute of Technology.

Geoghegan, Martin and Laurence Cox 2001, 'Outside the Whale: (Re)thinking Social Movements and the Voluntary Sector', in *Seventh International Conference on Alternative Futures and Popular Protest*, Colin Barker and Mike Tyldesley, Manchester Metropolitan University, available at <http://eprints.nuim.ie/434>.

Gerlach, Luther P., and Virginia H. Hine 1970, *People, Power, Change: Movements of Social Transformation*, Indianapolis: Bobbs-Merrill.

Gibler, John 2009, *Mexico Unconquered: Chronicles of Power and Revolt*, San Francisco: City Lights.

Gibson, Edward 2005, 'Boundary Control: Subnational Authoritarianism in Democratic Countries', *World Politics*, 58: 101–32.

Gibson-Graham, J.K 2006, *The End of Capitalism (As We Knew It): A Feminist Critique of Political Economy*, London: University of Minnesota Press.

Gill, Stephen 2000, 'Towards a Postmodern Prince? The Battle in Seattle as a Moment in the New Politics of Globalisation', *Millennium*, 29, 1: 131–40.

Gillan, Margaret 2010a, *Class, Voice and State: Knowledge Production in Self-Organised Working-Class Activity and the Politics of Developing Community Television in Ireland*, PhD dissertation, Department of Sociology, NUI Maynooth, available at <http://eprints.nuim.ie/2293>.

—— 2010b, 'Class and Voice: Challenges for Grassroots Community Activists Using Media in 21st Century Ireland', *Interface*, 2, 2: 126–48.

Goldmann, Lucien 1964, *The Hidden God: A Study of the Tragic Vision in the Pensees of Pascal and the Tragedies of Racine*, London: Routledge & Kegan Paul.

Goldstein, Joseph 1952, *The Government of British Trade Unions: A Study in the Apathy and the Democratic Process in the Transport and General Workers Union*, London: Allen and Unwin.

González Cassanova, Pablo 2005, 'The Zapatista "Caracoles": Networks of Resistance and Autonomy', *Socialism and Democracy*, 19, 3: 79–92.

González, B. Gloria Martínez and Alejandro Valle Baeza 2007, 'Oaxaca: Rebellion against Marginalization, Extreme Poverty, and Abuse of Power', *Monthly Review*, 59, 3: 26–37.

Goodwin, Jeff 1997, 'State-Centred Approaches to Social Revolutions', in *Theorizing Revolutions*, edited by John Foran, London: Routledge.

Goodwin, Jeff and James M. Jasper 2002, *The Social Movements Reader: Cases and Concepts*, Oxford: Wiley-Blackwell.

Gore, Van 1982, 'Rank-and-File Dissent', in *A History of British Industrial Relations: 1875–1914*, edited by Chris Wrigley, Brighton: Harvester Press.

Gorz, André 1967, *A Atrategy for Labor*, Boston: Beacon Press.

Gould, Deborah B. 2009, *Moving Politics: Emotion and ACT UP's Fight Against AIDS*, Chicago: University of Chicago Press.

Gowan, Peter 1997, 'British Euro-Solipsism', in *The Question of Europe*, edited by Peter Gowan and Perry Anderson, London: Verso.

Grado Cero 2003, 'Pensamiento Asambleario En Argentina', *Athenea digital*, 3.

Gramsci, Antonio 1969, *Soviets in Italy*, Nottingham: Institute for Workers' Control.

—— 1971, *Selections from the Prison Notebooks*, translated and edited by Quintin Hoare and Geoffrey Nowell Smith, New York: International Publishers.

—— 1977a [1917], 'The revolution against *Capital*', in *Selections from Political Writings (1910–1920)*, translated and edited by Quintin Hoare, London: Lawrence & Wishart.

—— 1977b [1919], 'Unions and Councils', in *Selections from Political Writings (1910–1920)*, edited by Quintin Hoare, London: Lawrence & Wishart.

—— 1998, *Selections from the Prison Notebooks*, London: Lawrence & Wishart.

—— 2001, *Selections from the Prison Notebooks*, London: Electric Book Company.

Greco, Florencia and Ariel Fontecoba 2005, 'Incertidumbre neoliberal y asambleas barriales: ¿Hacia un nuevo activismo político?', *III Jornadas de Jóvenes Investigadores*, Instituto de Investigaciones Gino Germani, Facultad de Ciencias Sociales Universidad de Buenos Aires.

Green, Marcus 2002, 'Gramsci Cannot Speak: Presentations and Interpretations of Gramsci's Concept of the Subaltern', *Rethinking Marxism*, 3, 14: 1–24.

Grenfell, Damian 2001 *The State and Protest in Australia: From Vietnam to S11*, PhD dissertation, Monash University.

Griffiths, Tom 2000, 'S11, School Students, and the End of Liberalism', in the proceedings for the Australian Association for Research in Education (AARE) Conference, University of Sydney.

Guha, Ranajit 1997, *Dominance Without Hegemony: History and Power in Colonial India*, Cambridge, MA: Harvard University Press.

Habib, Irfan 2003, *Essays in Indian History: Towards a Marxist Perspective*, London: Anthem Press.

Hadden, Jennifer and Sidney Tarrow 2007, 'Spillover or Spillout? The Global Justice Movement in the United States after 9/11', *Mobilization: An International Quarterly*, 12, 4: 359–76.

Hall, Gillette and Christopher Humphrey 2003, 'Mexico: Southern States Development Strategy, Volume 1: Synthesis Report', available at <http://documents.worldbank.org/curated/en/2003/10/5531347/mexico-southern-states-development-strategy>.

Hall, Peter A., and David Soskice (eds.) 2001, *Varieties of Capitalism: The Institutional Foundations of Comparative Advantage*. Oxford: Oxford University Press.

Hall, Stuart 1983, 'The Great Moving Right Show', in *The Politics of Thatcherism*, edited by Stuart Hall and Martin Jacques, London: Lawrence & Wishart.

—— 1996, 'A Conversation with C.L.R. James', in *Rethinking C.L.R. James*, edited by Grant Farred, Oxford: Blackwell.

Hallas, Duncan 1985, *The Comintern*, London: Bookmarks.

Halperin, Sandra 2003, *War and Social change in Modern Europe:* The Great Transformation *Revisited*, Cambridge: Cambridge University Press.

Hambleton, Robin and Huw Thomas (eds.) 1995, *Urban Policy Evaluation: Challenge and Change*, London: Paul Chapman.

Hanieh, Adam 2011, 'Egypt's Uprising: Not Just a Question of "Transition"', *The Bullet: Social Project E-Bulletin*, 462 available at <http://www.socialistproject.ca/bullet/462.php>.

Hankiss, Elemér 1989, "Demobilisation, Self-mobilisation and Quasi-Mobilisation in Hungary, 1948–1987', *East European Politics and Society*, 3, 1: 105–51.

Hanley, Brian and Scott Millar 2009, *The Lost Revolution: The Story of the Official IRA and the Workers Party*, Harmondsworth: Penguin.

Hansen, Roger D. 1971, *The Politics of Mexican Development*, Baltimore: John Hopkins University Press.

Hardt, Michael and Antonio Negri 2000, *Empire*, Cambridge, MA: Harvard University Press.

Harman, Chris 1978, 'Crisis of the European Revolutionary Left', *International Socialism*, 2, 4: 49–107.

—— 1998a, *The Fire Last Time: 1968 and After*, London: Bookmarks.

—— 1998b, *Marxism and History*, London: Bookmarks.

—— 2010, 'Party and Class', in *Selected Writings*, London: Bookmarks Publications.

Harris, Nigel 1971 [1968], *Beliefs in Society: the Problem of Ideology*, Harmondsworth: Penguin.

Hart, Gillian 2002, 'Development/s Beyond Neoliberalism? Power, Culture, Political Economy', *Progress in Human Geography*, 26, 6: 812–22.

Harvey, David 1990, *The Condition of Postmodernity: An Enquiry Into the Origins of Cultural Change*, Oxford: Blackwell.

—— 1993, 'From Space to Place and Back Again', in *Mapping the Futures: Local Cultures, Global Change*, edited by Jon Bird, Barry Curtis, Tim Putnam and Lisa Tickner, London: Routledge.

—— 1996, *Justice, Nature and the Geography of Difference*, Oxford: Blackwell.

—— 2000, *Spaces of Hope*, Edinburgh: Edinburgh University Press.

—— 2001, *Spaces of Capital: Towards a Critical Geography*, Edinburgh: Edinburgh University Press.

Harvey, *Cont.*
—— 2003, *The New Imperialism*, Oxford: Oxford University Press.
—— 2005, *A Brief History of Neoliberalism*, Oxford: Oxford University Press.
—— 2006, *The Limits to Capital*, New and fully updated version, London: Verso.
—— 2008, 'The Right to the City', *New Left Review*, II/53, available at <http://newleft review.org/?view=2740>.
—— 2010, *A Companion to Marx's Capital*, London: Verso.
Harvey, Neil 1999, 'Resisting Neoliberalism, Constructing Citizenship: Indigenous Movements in Chiapas', in *Subnational Politics and Democratization in Mexico*, edited by Wayne Cornelius, Todd Eisenstadt and Jane Hindley, San Diego: Centre for US-Mexican Studies.
—— 2001, 'Globalisation and Resistance in Post-Cold War Mexico: Difference, Citizenship and Biodiversity Conflicts in Chiapas', *Third World Quarterly*, 22, 6: 1045–61.
—— 2006, 'La Disputa Por Los Recursos Naturales en el Area del Plan Puebla-Panamá', in *Geoeconómiá y geopolítica en el área del Plan Puebla-Panamá*, edited by David Villafuerte Solís and Xochitl Leyva Solano, Mexico City: CIE-SAS.
Heath, Anthony and Mike Savage 1995, 'Political Alignments within the Middle Classes, 1972–89', in *Social Change and the Middle Classes*, edited by Tom Butler and Mike Savage, London: University College.
Heath, Mary 2000, 'Police and Protest: Alice's Adventures at S11', *Alternative Law Journal*, 25, 6: 299–301.
Heery, Edmund and John Kelly 1988, 'Do Female Representatives Make a Difference? Women Full-time Officials and Trade Union Work', *Work, Employment and Society*, 2, 4: 487–505.
—— 1990, 'Full-Time Officers and the Shop Steward Network: Patterns of Co-Operation and Interdependence', in *Trade Unions and the Their Members: Studies in Union Democracy and Organisation*, edited by Patricia Fosh and Edmund Heery, Basingstoke: Macmillan.
Heery, Edmund and Patricia Fosh 1990, 'Introduction: Whose Union? Power and

Bureaucracy in the Labour Movement', in *Trade Unions and the Their Members: Studies in Union Democracy and Organisation*, Basingstoke: Macmillan.
Heller, Patrick 2000, *The Labour of Development: Workers and the Transformation of Capitalism in Kerala*, Ithaca, NY: Cornell University Press.
Hemson, David 2005, 'Can Participation Make a Difference?', Durban: Human Sciences Research Council.
Herold, Conrad M. 2005, 'Class Struggle and Structural Reform: An Exploratory Outline of the Case of the Capital Account in Argentina', paper presented at the Department of Economics, University of Massachusetts Amherst.
Hershatter, Gail 1986, *The Workers of Tianjin, 1900–1949*, Stanford, CA: Stanford University Press.
Hesketh, Chris 2010, 'From Passive Revolution to Silent Revolution: Class Forces and the Production of State, Space and Scale in Modern Mexico', *Capital & Class*, 34, 3: 383–407.
Hill, Christopher 1975, *The World Turned Upside Down*, Harmondsworth: Penguin.
—— 1990, *A Nation of Change and Novelty*, London: Routledge.
—— 1996, *Liberty Against the Law*, Harmondsworth: Penguin.
Hill, Robert, A. 1986, 'In England, 1932–1938', in *C.L.R. James: His Life and Work*, edited by Paul Buhle, London: Allison & Busby.
Hilton, Rodney (ed.) 1976, *Peasants, Heretics and Knights*, Cambridge: Cambridge University Press.
Hilton, Rodney 1973, *Bond Men Made Free: Medieval Peasant Movements and the English Rising of 1381*, London: Methuen.
—— 1990, *Class Conflict and the Crisis of Feudalism*, London: Verso.
—— 2003, *Bond Men Made Free: Medieval Peasant Movements and the English Rising of 1381*, London: Routledge.
Hind, Dan 2007, *The Threat to Reason: How the Enlightenment was Hijacked and How We Can Reclaim It*, London: Verso.
Hinely, Rebecca 2009, 'Poors of Chatsworth Take Charge', *The Mercury*, 16 September.
Hinton, James 1973, *The First Shop Stewards' Movement*, London: Allen and Unwin.

Hinton, James and Richard Hyman 1975, *Trade Unions and Revolution: The Industrial Policies of the Early British Communist Party*, London: Pluto Press.

Hobsbawm, Eric J. 1965, *Primitive Rebels: Studies in Archaic Forms of Social Movement in the 19th Century*, New York: W. W. Norton and Co.

—— 1971, *Primitive Rebels*, Manchester: Mancheser University Press.

—— 1973, *Revolutionaries*, London: Phoenix.

—— 1988a, *The Age of Revolution: 1789–1848*, London: Abacus.

—— 1988b, *The Age of Capital: 1848–1875*, London: Abacus.

—— 1989, *The Age of Empire: 1875–1914*, London: Abacus.

—— 1997, *On History*, Harmondsworth: Penguin.

—— 1998, 'Introduction' in Marx and Engels 1998.

—— 2001, *Bandits*, London: Abacus.

—— 2011, *How to Change the World*, London: Little Brown.

Hobsbawm, Eric and George Rudé 1969, *Captain Swing*, London: Pimlico.

Høgsbjerg, Christian 2006, 'C.L.R. James: The Revolutionary as Artist', *International Socialism*, 112: 163–82.

—— 2010, 'C.L.R. James and the Black Jacobins', *International Socialism*, 126: 95–120.

—— 2011a, ' "A Thorn in the Side of Great Britain": C.L.R. James and the Caribbean Labour Rebellions of the 1930s', *Small Axe*, 15, 2: 24–42.

—— 2011b, 'Mariner, Renegade, Castaway: Chris Braithwaite, Seamen's Organizer and Pan-Africanist', *Race and Class* 53, 2: 36–57.

Hollibaugh, Amber, and Nikhil Pal Singh 2001, 'Sexuality, Labor, and the New Trade Unionism', in *Out at Work: Building a Gay-Labor Alliance*, edited by Kitty Krupat and Patrick McCreery, Minneapolis: University of Minnesota Press.

Holloway, John 2002a, *Change the World Without Taking Power: The Meaning of Revolution Today*, London: Pluto Press.

—— 2002b, *Cambiar el Mundo Sin Tomar el Poder*, Buenos Aires: Colección Herramienta.

Holstun, James 2000, *Ehud's Dagger: Class Struggle in the English Revolution*, London: Verso.

Holton, Bob 1976, *British Syndicalism 1900–1914*, London: Pluto Press.

Honig, Emily 1986, *Sisters and Strangers: Women in the Shanghai Cotton Mills, 1919–1949*, Stanford, CA: Stanford University Press.

Hoogvelt, Ankie 2001, *Globalisation and the Postcolonial World: The New Political Economy of Development* Second Edition, London: Macmillan Press.

Hooker, James, R. 1967, *Black Revolutionary: George Padmore's path from Communism to Pan-Africanism*, London: Pall Mall Press.

Hosseini, S.A. Hamed 2010, *Alternative Globalisations*, Oxford: Routledge.

Howard, Joshua 1998, *Workers at War: Labor in the Nationalist Arsenals of Chongqing, 1937–1949*, PhD dissertation, University of California at Berkeley.

Huchzermeyer, Marie 2009, 'Does Recent Litigation Bring Us Any Closer to a Right to the City?', paper presented at the University of Johannesburg Workshop on Intellectuals, Ideology, Protests, and Civil Society, 3 October.

Hughley, Michael 1995 [1982], 'The New Conservatism: Political Ideology and Class Structure in America', in *The New Middle Classes: Life-styles, Status Claims and Political Orientations*, edited by Arthur J. Vidich, London: Macmillan.

Humphrys, Elizabeth 2007, ' "With their bodies on the line": Activist Space and Sexuality in the Australian Alter-Globalisation Movement', in the proceedings for *Queer Space Conference*, University of Technology Sydney.

Hunt, Alan and Gary Wickham 1994, *Foucault and Law*, London: Pluto Press.

Hunt, Gerald (ed.) 1999a, *Laboring For Rights: Unions and Sexual Diversity Across Nations*, Philadelphia: Temple University Press.

—— 1999b, 'Introduction', in Hunt (ed.) 1999a.

Hunt, Janet 2002, 'The Jubilee 2000 Campaign in Australia: An Evaluation', Report of Jubilee Australia.

Hutton, Ronald 1999, *The Triumph of the Moon: A History of Modern Pagan Witchcraft*, Oxford: Oxford University Press.

Hyman, Richard 1971, *Marxism and the Sociology of Trade Unionism*, London: Pluto Press.

Hyman, *Cont.*
—— 1973, 'Industrial Conflict and the Political Economy', *Socialist Register*, 10: 101–53.
—— 1975a, *Industrial Relations: A Marxist Introduction*, Basingstoke: Macmillan.
—— 1975b, 'Foreword to the 1975 Edition', in *The Frontier of Control: A Study in British Workshop Politics*, edited by Carter L. Goodrich, London: Pluto Press.
—— 1979a, 'British Trade Unionism in the '70s', *Studies in Political Economy*, 1: 93–112.
—— 1979b, 'The Politics of Workplace Trade Unionism: Recent Tendencies and Some Problems in Theory', *Capital & Class*, 8: 54–67.
—— 1980, 'British Trade Unionism: Post-War Trends and Future Prospects', *International Socialism*, 2, 8: 64–79.
—— 1984, *Strikes*, London: Macmillan.
—— 2003, Book Review: Ralph Darlington and Dave Lyddon, *Glorious Summer: Class Struggle in Britain, 1972*, London: Bookmarks, 2001, *International Labor and Working Class History*, 64: 187–9.
Hyman, Richard and R.H. Fryer 1975, 'Trade Unions: Sociology and Political Economy', in *Processing People: Studies in Organisational Behaviour*, edited by John McKinley, Austin, TX: Holt, Rinehart and Winston.
Ilyenkov, Evald Vasilyevich 1982, *Dialectics of the Abstract and Concrete in Marx's Capital*, Moscow: Progress Publishers.
Inglehart, Ronald 1990, *Culture Shift in Advanced Industrial Society*, Princeton, NJ: Princeton University Press.
Ita, Ana 2006, 'Land Concentration in Mexico after PROCEDE', in *Promised Land: Competing Visions of Agrarian Reform*, edited by Peter Rosset, Raj Patel and M. Corville, Oakland, CA: Food First Books.
Ives, Peter 2003, *Gramsci's Politics of Language: Engaging the Bakhtin Circle and the Frankfurt School*, Toronto: University of Toronto Press, 2003.
Iveson, Kurt and Sean Scamler 2000, 'Contesting the "Inevitable": Notes on S11', *Overland*, 161: 4–13.
Jahjah, Dyab Abou 2011, 'Notes on the Tunisian Revolution', available at <http://www.aboujahjah.com/?p=237>.

James, Cyril Lionel Robert 1938a, *A History of Negro Revolt*, London: F.A.C.T.
—— 1938b, *The Black Jacobins: Toussaint Louverture and the San Domingo Revolution*, London: Secker & Warburg.
—— 1960, 'Notes on the Life of George Padmore', Unpublished manuscript, copy available at the Institute of Commonwealth Studies, London.
—— 1969, *Beyond a Boundary*, London: Hutchinson.
—— 1974, 'Black Intellectuals in Britain', in *Colour, Culture and Consciousness: immigrant intellectuals in Britain*, edited by Bhikhu Parekh, London: Allen & Unwin.
—— 1977, *Nkrumah and the Ghana Revolution*, London: Allison & Busby.
—— 1980, *The Future in the Present: Selected Writings*, Vol. 1, London: Allison & Busby.
—— 1984, *At the Rendezvous of Victory: Selected Writings*, Vol. 3, London: Allison & Busby.
—— 1992, 'Writings from *The Nation*', in *The C.L.R. James Reader*, edited by Anna Grimshaw, Oxford: Blackwell.
—— 1994a, 'Revolution and the Negro', in *C.L.R. James and Revolutionary Marxism: Selected Writings of C.L.R. James, 1939–49*, edited by Scott McLemee and Paul Le Blanc, New Jersey: Humanities Press.
—— 1994b, *World Revolution 1917–1936: The Rise and Fall of the Communist International*, New Jersey: Humanities Press.
—— 1995, *A History of Pan-African Revolt*, Chicago: Charles H. Kerr.
—— 2001 [1938], *The Black Jacobins: Toussaint L'Ouverture and the San Domingo Revolution*, Harmondsworth: Penguin.
Jarvis, Simon 1998, *Adorno*, Cambridge: Polity.
Jasper, James M. 1997, *The Art of Moral Protest: Culture, Biography and Creativity in Social Movements*, Chicago: University of Chicago Press.
—— 2004, 'A Strategic Approach to Collective Action: Looking for Agency in Social Movement Choices,' *Mobilization*, 9: 1–16.
—— 2007, 'Cultural Approaches to the Study of Social Movements', in *Handbook of Social Movements Across Disciplines*, edited by Bert Klandermans and Conne Roggeband, New York: Springer.

Jessop, Bob 1982, *The Capitalist State: Marxist Theories and Methods*, Oxford: Martin Robertson.

—— 1990, *State Theory: Putting the Capitalist State in its Place*, Cambridge: Polity Press.

John, S. Sándor 2009, *Bolivia's Radical Tradition: Permanent Revolution in the Andes*, Tucson: University of Arizona Press.

Johnson, Carol 1980, 'The problem of reformism and Marx's theory of fetishism', *New Left Review*, I/119: 70–96.

Johnston, Hank and Bert Klandermans 1995, *Social Movements and Culture*, London: Routledge.

Jones, Peter and Chik Collins 2010, 'State Ideology and Oppositional Discourses: Conceptual and Methodological Issues', in *Oppositional Discourses and Democracies*, edited by Michael Huspek, London: Routledge.

Joshi, Puran Chand 1957, '1857 in Our History', in *Rebellion of 1857: A Symposium*, Delhi: Peoples Publishing House.

Joyce, Patrick 1993, *Visions of the People: Industrial England and the Question of Class, 1848–1914*, Cambridge: Cambridge University Press.

Kala, Pablo 2001, 'In the Spaces of Erasure: Globalisation, Resistance and Narmada River', *Economic and Political Weekly*, 36, 22: 1991–2002.

Katsiaficas, George 1987, *The Imagination of the New Left: A Global Analysis of 1968*, Boston: South End Press.

Katznelson, Ira 1981, *City Trenches*, Chicago: University of Chicago Press.

—— 1986, 'Working-Class Formation: Constructing Cases and Comparisons', in *Working-Class Formation: Nineteenth-Century Patterns in Western Europe and the United States*, edited by Ira Katznelson and Aristede Zolberg, Princeton, NJ: Princeton University Press.

Kaufman, Herbert 1956, 'Emerging Conflicts in the Doctrine of Public Administration', *American Political Science Review*, 50: 1057–73.

Kaviraj, Sudipta 1997, 'A Critique of the Passive Revolution', in *State and Politics in India*, edited by Partha Chatterjee, Oxford: Oxford University Press.

Kaye, Harvey 1984, *The British Marxist Historians*, Cambridge: Polity Press.

—— 1988, 'George Rudé, Social Historian', in Harvey Kaye ed. *The Face of the Crowd*, Atlantic Highlands, NJ: Humanities Press.

—— 1995, *The British Marxist Historians*, London: Palgrave.

Kaye, Harvey and McClelland, Keith (eds.) 1990, *E.P. Thompson: Critical Perspectives*, London: Polity Press.

Kaye, John 1984, 'Why The Bureaucrats Betray', *Socialist Review*, 61: 10–13.

—— 1988, *Trade Unions and Socialist Politics*, London: Verso.

Kelly, John and Edmund Heery 1994, *Working for the Union: British Trade Union Officers*, Cambridge: Cambridge University Press.

Kempf, Raphael 2011, 'Egypt: First Democracy, then a Pay Rise', *Le Monde diplomatique*, March.

Kershaw, Ian 2000, *Hitler, 1936–1945: Nemesis*, London: Allen Lane.

—— 2007. *Fateful Choices: Ten Decisions that Changed the World, 1940–1941*, London: Allen Lane.

Khaldun, Talmiz 1957, 'The Great Rebellion', in *The Rebellion of 1857: A Symposium*, edited by P.C. Joshi, Delhi: Peoples Publishing House.

Kiely, Ray 2009, *The New Political Economy of Development: Globalization, Imperialism, Hegemony*, London: Palgrave.

Kiernan, Victor 1989, *Poets, Politics and the People*, London: Verso.

—— 1993, *Shakespeare: Poet and Citizen*, London: Verso.

—— 1996, *Eight Tragedies of Shakespeare*, London: Verso.

Kilgore, Deborah W. 1999, 'Understanding Learning in Social Movements: A Theory of Collective Learning', *International Journal of Lifelong Education*, 18, 3: 191–202.

Kimber, Charlie 2009, 'In the Balance', *International Socialism*, 122: 33–64.

Kingsnorth, Paul 2003, *One No, Many Yeses*, London: The Free Press.

Kirk, Neville 1996, 'Class and the "Linguistic Turn" in Chartist and Post-Chartist Historiography' in *Social Class and Marxism*, edited by Neville Kirk, Aldershot: Ashgate.

—— 1997, 'History, Language, Ideas and Postmodernism: A Materialist View' in

The Postmodern History Reader, edited by Keith Jenkins, London: Routledge.

Klandermans, Bert 1992, 'The Social Construction of Protest and Multiorganizational Fields', in *Frontiers in Social Movement Theory*, edited by Aldon Morris and Carol McClurg Mueller, New Haven, CT: Yale University Press.

Klein, Ethel 1984, *Gender Politics: From Consciousness to Mass Politics*, Cambridge, MA: Harvard University Press.

Klein, Naomi 2007, *The Shock Doctrine: The Rise of Disaster Capitalism*, London: Allen Lane.

Klingensmith, Daniel 2007, *One Valley and a Thousand: Dams, Nationalism, and Development*, Oxford: Oxford University Press.

Kohli, Atul 2004, *State-Directed Development: Political Power and Industrialization in the Global Periphery*, Cambridge: Cambridge University Press.

Kotz, David M., Terence McDonough and Michael Reich 1994, *Social Structures of Accumulation: The Political Economy of Growth and Crisis*, Cambridge: Cambridge University Press.

Krinsky, John 2007, *Free Labor: Workfare and the Contested Language of Neoliberalism*, Chicago: University of Chicago Press.

Krinsky, John and Colin Barker 2009, 'Movement Strategizing as Developmental Learning: Perspectives from Cultural Historical Activity Theory', in *Culture, Protest, and Social Movements*, edited by Hank Johnston, Aldershot: Ashgate.

Krupat, Kitty 2001, 'Out of Labor's Dark Age', in Krupat and McCreery (eds.) 2001a.

Krupat, Kitty and Patrick McCreery (eds.) 2001a, *Out at Work: Building a Gay-Labor Alliance*, Minneapolis: University of Minnesota Press.

—— 2001b, 'Introduction', in Krupat and McCreery (eds.) 2001a.

Lachmann, Richard 1997, 'Agents of Revolution: Elite Conflicts and Mass Mobilization Fom the Medici to Yeltsin', in *Theorizing Revolutions*, edited by John Foran, London: Routledge.

Laclau, Ernesto and Chantal Mouffe 1985, *Hegemony and Socialist Strategy* London: Verso.

—— 2001, *Hegemony And Socialist Strategy: Towards A Radical Democratic Politics*, Second edition, London: Verso.

Lamming, George 1960, *The Pleasures of Exile*, London: Michael Joseph.

Lane, Tony 1974, *The Union Makes Us Strong*, London: Arrow.

Lash, Scott and John Urry 1987, *The End of Organized Capitalism*, Madison, WI: University of Wisconsin Press.

Lawson, Damien 2000, 'Copping it at S11', *Overland*, 161: 14–16.

Lecercle, Jean Jacques 2006, *A Marxist Philosophy of Language*, Leiden: Brill.

Lee, Caroline 2009, 'The Roots of Astroturfing', *Contexts*, 9, 1: 75–7.

Lee, Ching-Kwan 2007, *Against the Law: Labor Protests in China's Rustbelt and Sunbelt*, Berkeley, CA: University of California Press.

Lee, Eric and Benjamin Weinthal 2011, 'Trade Unions: The Revolutionary Social Network at Play in Egypt and Tunisia', *The Guardian*, 10 February.

Lefebvre, Georges 1973, *The Great Fear of 1789: Rural Panic in Revolutionary France*, New York: Schoken Books.

Lefebvre, Henri 1976, *The Survival of Capitalism: Reproduction of the Relations of Production*, London: Allison and Busby.

—— 1991, *The Production of Space*, Oxford: Blackwell.

—— 1996, 'The Right to the City', in *Writings on Cities*, Oxford: Blackwell.

—— 2003, 'Space and State', in *State/Space: A Reader*, edited by Neil Brenner, Bob Jessop, Martin Jones and Gordon Macloed, Oxford: Blackwell.

Lenin, Vladimir I. 1916, *Imperialism: The Highest Phase of Capitalism*, available at <http://marxists.org/archive/lenin/works/1916/imp-hsc/ch09.htm>.

—— 1920, *Left-wing Communism: an Infantile Disorder*, available at <http://www.marxists.org/archive/lenin/works/1920/lwc>.

—— 1961 [1902], 'What Is To Be Done? Burning Questions of our Movement', in *Collected Works*, Vol. 5, London: Lawrence & Wishart.

—— 1964 [1916], 'The Discussion on Self-determination Summed Up', in *Collected Works*, Vol. 22, London: Lawrence & Wishart.

Lenin, *Cont.*
—— 1999 [1920], *'Left-Wing Communism'
– An Infantile Disorder*, Chippendale,
NSW: Resistance Books.

Levitsky, Steven 2001, 'An "Organised Disorganisation": Informal Organisation
and the Persistence of Local Party Structures in Argentine Peronism', *Journal of
Latin American Studies*, 33, 1: 29–66.

Leys, Colin 2009, *The Rise and Fall of Development Theory*, Bloomington: Indiana
University Press.

Leyva Solano, Xochitl 2001, 'Communal,
and Organizational Transformations in
Las Cañadas', *Latin American Perspectives*, 28, 2: 20–44.

Lilla, Mark 2010, 'The Tea Party Jacobins',
New York Review of Books, 27 May.

Linebaugh, Peter 1981, 'What if C.L.R.
James had met E.P. Thompson in London in 1792?', available at <http://
www.sojournertruth.net/epthompson
.html>.

—— 1991, *The London Hanged*, Harmondsworth: Penguin.

—— 2003, *The London Hanged*, Second
edition, London: Verso.

Linebaugh, Peter and Marcus Rediker
2000, *The Many-Headed Hydra*, London:
Verso.

Lipset, Seymour M., Martin Trow and
James Coleman 1962, *Union Democracy:
What Makes Democracy Work in Labour
Unions and Other Organisations*, New
York: Anchor Books.

Lockwood, David 1992, *Solidarity and
Schism: 'The Problem of Disorder' in Dur-
kheimian and Marxist Sociology*, Oxford:
Clarendon Press.

London-Edinburgh Weekend Return
Group 1980, *In and Against the State*,
London: Pluto Press.

Lorde, Audre 1984, *Sister Outsider: Essays
and Speeches*, Berkeley, CA: The Crossing
Press.

Lorenzano, Luis 1998, 'Zapatismo: Recomposition of Labour, Radical Democracy
and Revolutionary Project', in *Zapatista!
Reinventing Revolution in Mexico*, edited
by John Holloway and Eloina Peláez,
London: Pluto Press.

Lukács, Georg 1970 [1924], *Lenin: a Study in
the Unity of his Thought*, London: New
Left Books.

—— 1971 [1923], *History and Class Consciousness: Studies in Marxist Dialectics*,
Cambridge, MA: The MIT Press.

Luna, Juan Pablo and Filgueira, Fernando
2009, 'The Left Turns Are Multiple Paradigmatic Crises', *Third World Quarterly*,
30, 2: 371–95.

Luxemburg, Rosa 1970, *Rosa Luxemburg
Speaks*, edited by Mary-Alice Waters,
New York: Pathfinder.

—— 1986 [1906], *The Mass Strike, the Political Party and the Trade Unions*, London:
Bookmarks.

—— 2005 [1906], *The Mass Strike, the Political Party and the Trade Unions*, New
edition, London: Bookmarks.

Lyddon, Dave 1977, 'British Leyland: The
Shop Stewards and Participation', *International Socialism*, 1, 102: 20–6.

Lyder, André 2005, *Pushers Out: The Inside
Story of Dublin's Anti-Drugs Movement*,
Bloomington, IN: Trafford Publishing.

Lynch, Jackie 2001, 'Ombudsman clears
police of S11 violence', *Green Left Weekly*,
452: 3.

MacIntyre, Alasdair 1967, *A Short History of
Ethics*, London: Duckworth.

—— 2008, 'Notes from the Moral Wilderness', in *Alasdair MacIntyre's Engagement with Marxism*, edited by Paul
Blackledge and Neil Davidson, Leiden:
Brill.

Maddison, Sarah and Sean Scalmer 2006,
Activist Wisdom, Sydney: University of
New South Wales Press.

Magnusson, Warren 1996, *The Search for
Political Space: Globalization, Social
Movements and the Urban Political Expe-
rience*, Toronto: University of Toronto
Press.

Magri, Lucio 2011, *The Tailor of Ulm: A History of Communism*, London: Verso.

Makonnen, Ras 1973, *Pan-Africanism
From Within*, Oxford: Oxford University
Press.

Maksimovic, Andrea and Tom Barnes
2002, 'Woomera 2002', *CounterAction*, 1,
2: 28–9.

Mansilla, Diego, and Lucía Tumini 2004.
*Un análisis del acuerdo con el Fmi: ¿Un
nuevo rumbo o el mismo camino?*, Buenos Aires: Centro Cultural de la Coop-
eración, Departamento de Economía
Política.

Manzano, Virginia 2004, 'Tradiciones Políticas, Acciones Colectivas E Intervenciones Estatales: Una Apoximación Antopológica a La Formación Del Movimiento Piquetero De La Matanza', in *Segundas Jornadas de Investigación en Antropología Social*, Filosofía y Letras, Instituto de Ciencias Antropológicas, Universidad de Buenos Aires.

Marable, Manning 1999, *Black Leadership*, Harmondsworth: Penguin.

Marcos, Subcomandante 2001, *Our Word is our Weapon*, London: Serpent's Tail.

—— 2004, 'Two Flaws', available at <http://flag.blackened.net/revolt/mexico/ezln/2004/marcos/flawsAUG.html>.

Marfleet, Phil 2011, 'Act One of the Egyptian Revolution', *International Socialism*, 130, available at <http://www.isj.org.uk/index.php4?id=721&issue=130>.

MARHO, (Mid-Atlantic Radical Historians' Organisation) 1983, *Visions of History*, Manchester: Manchester University Press.

Marston, Sallie 2000, 'The social construction of scale', *Progress in Human Geography* 24, 2: 219–42.

Martínez Vásquez, Victor Raúl 2007, *Autoritarismo, Movimiento Popular y Crisis Política: Oaxaca 2006*, Oaxaca: Universidad Autónoma 'Benito Juárez' de Oaxaca.

Marwell, Gerald, and Pamela Oliver 1984, 'Collective Action Theory and Social Movements Research', in *Research in Social Movements, Conflict and Change*, edited by Louis Kriesberg, Greenwich, CT: Jai Press.

Marx, Karl 1904 [1859], 'Author's Preface', in *A Contribution to the Critique of Political Economy*, Chicago: Charles H. Kerr.

—— 1963a [1852], *The Eighteenth Brumaire of Louis Bonaparte*, New York: International Publishers.

—— 1963b, *Selected Writings in Sociology and Social Philosophy*, Harmondsworth: Penguin.

—— 1964, *Pre-Capitalist Economic Formations*, London: Verso.

—— 1965a [1852], 'Letter to J Weydemeyer, March 5, 1852', in Marx and Engels 1965a.

—— 1965b [1871], 'Letter to F. Bolte, November 23, 1871', in Marx and Engels 1965a.

—— 1965c [1869], 'Letter from Marx to Engels In Manchester December 10, 1869', in Marx and Engels 1965a.

—— 1973 [1857–8], *Grundrisse*, Harmondsworth: Penguin

—— 1974a, *The First International and After*, edited by David Fernbach, Harmondsworth: Penguin.

—— 1974b [1871], 'The Civil War in France', in Marx 1974a.

—— 1975a [1845], 'Theses on Feuerbach', in Karl Marx and Friedrich Engels, *Collected Works*, Vol. 5, London: Lawrence & Wishart.

—— 1975b, *Early Writings*, Harmondsworth: Penguin.

—— 1976a [1867] *Capital*, Vol. I, Translated by Ben Fowkes, Harmondsworth: Penguin.

—— 1976b [1873], 'Preface to the Second Edition', in Marx 1976a.

—— 1978 [1853], 'British Rule in India', in Marx and Engels 1978.

—— 1981 [1894], *Capital: A Critique of Political Economy*, Vol. III, Harmondsworth: Penguin.

—— 1984 [1852], *The Eighteenth Brumaire of Louis Napoleon*, London: Lawrence & Wishart.

Marx, Karl and Friedrich Engels 1965a, *Selected Correspondence*, Moscow: Progress Publishers.

—— 1965b [1845], *The German Ideology*, London: Lawrence & Wishart.

—— 1973 [1848], 'Manifesto of the Communist Party', in *Marx: The Revolutions of 1848*, edited by David Fernbach, Harmondsworth: Penguin.

—— 1975a, *Selected Correspondence*, Third edition, Moscow: Progress Publishers.

—— 1975b [1845], *The German Ideology*, in *Collected Works*, Vol. 5, London: Lawrence & Wishart.

—— 1978, *The First Indian War of Independence, 1857–59*, Progress Publishers: Moscow.

—— 1998 [1848], *The Communist Manifesto: A Modern Edition*, London: Verso.

Mason, Tim 1995 [1975], 'The Primacy of Politics: Politics and Economics in National Socialist Germany', in *Nazism, Fascism and the Working Class*, edited by Jane Caplan, Cambridge: Cambridge University Press.

Matellart, Armand 2010, *The Globalization of Surveillance: The Origin of the Securitarian Order*, Cambridge: Polity Press.

McAdam, Doug 1982, *Political Process and the Development of Black Insurgency 1930–1970*, Chicago: University of Chicago Press.

—— 1999, *Political Process and the Development of Black Insurgency, 1930–1970*, Second edition, Chicago: University of Chicago Press.

McAdam, Doug, John D. McCarthy, and Mayer Zald (eds.) 1996, *Comparative Perspectives on Social Movements: Political Opportunities, Mobilizing Structures, and Cultural Framings*, Cambridge: Cambridge University Press.

McAdam, Doug, Sidney Tarrow, and Charles Tilly 2001, *Dynamics of Contention*, Cambridge: Cambridge University Press.

McCann, Eamonn 1972, 'After 5 October 1968', *International Socialism*, 1, 51: 9–12.

McCarthy, John D. and Mayer Zald 1977, 'Resource Mobilization and Social Movements: A Partial Theory', *American Journal of Sociology*, 82: 1212–41.

McCarthy, William Edward 1967, *The Role of Shop Stewards in British Industrial Relations*, Research Paper 1: Royal Commission on Trade Unions and Employers' Associations, London: HMSO.

McCarthy, William Edward and Stanley Robert Parker 1968, *Shop Stewards and Workplace Relations*, Research Paper 10, Royal Commission on Trade Unions and Employers' Associations, London: HMSO.

McCaughan, Edward J. 1993, 'Mexico's Long Crisis: Towards New Regimes of Accumulation and Domination', *Latin American Perspectives*, 20, 3: 6–31.

McCulloch, Jude 2000, 'Globalising Violence: Civil Protest is being used as a Pretext for Paramilitary Policing', *Arena Magazine*, 50: 10–11.

McKay, George 1996, *Senseless Acts of Beauty: Cultures of Resistance since the Sixties*, London: Verso.

McIlroy, John 1988, *Trade Unions in Britain Today*, Manchester: Manchester University Press.

McIlroy, John and Alan Campbell 1999, 'Organising the Militants: The Liaison Committee for the Defence of Trade Unions, 1966–1979', *British Journal of Industrial Relations*, 37, 1: 1–31.

McMichael, Philip 2009, *Contesting Development: Critical Struggles for Social Change*, London: Routledge.

McNally, David 1993, 'EP Thompson: Class Struggle and Historical Materialism', *International Socialism Journal*, 61, available at <http://pubs.socialistreviewindex.org.uk/isj61/mcnally.htm>.

—— 2001, *Bodies of Meaning: Studies in Language, Labour and Liberation*, New York: SUNY Press.

—— 2006, *Another World is Possible: Globalization and Anti-Capitalism* Second Edition, Winnipeg: Arbeiter Ring Publishing.

—— 2011a, *Global Slump: The Economics and Politics of Crisis and Resistance*, Oakland, CA: PM Press.

—— 2011b, 'Mubarak's Folly: The Rising of Egypt's Workers', available at <http://davidmcnally.org/?p=354>.

Mehta, Asoka 1946, *1857: The Great Rebellion*, Bombay: Hind Kitabs Ltd.

Meikle, Graham 2003 'Indymedia and the New Net News', in *M/C Journal*, 6, 2, available at <www.media-culture.org.au>.

Meikle, Scott 1983, 'Marxism and the Necessity of Essentialism', *Critique*, 16: 149–66.

Meiksins Wood, Ellen 1995, *Democracy Against Capitalism: Renewing Historical Materialism*, Cambridge: Cambridge University Press.

—— 1998, *The Retreat from Class: The New 'True' Socialism*, London: Verso.

Melucci, Alberto 1989, *Nomads of the Present: Social Movements and Individual Needs in Contemporary Society*, London: Hutchinson.

—— 1992, 'Frontier Land: Collective Action Between Actors and Systems', in *Studying Collective Action*, edited by Mario Diani and Ron Eyerman, Newbury Park: Sage Publications.

—— 1995, 'The Process of Collective Identity', in *Social Movements and Culture*, edited by Hank Johnston and Bert Klandermans, Minneapolis: University of Minnesota.

—— 1996a, *Challenging Codes: Collective Action in the Information Age*, Cambridge: Cambridge University Press.

Melucci, *Cont.*
—— 1996b, *The Playing Self,* Cambridge: Cambridge University Press.

Merich, Diego de 2008 'Intersectionality from Theory to Practice', available at <http://www.whrn.ca/documents/Anno tatedBibliographyINTERSECTIONAL ITY.pdf.>

Mertes, Tom (ed.) 2004, *A Movement of Movements: is Another World Really Possible?,* London: Verso.

Metcalf, Thomas. 1964, *The Aftermath of Revolt: India, 1857–1870,* Princeton, NJ: Princeton University Press.

Meyer, David 2007, *The Politics of Protest: Social Movements in America,* Oxford: Oxford University Press.

Meyer, David and Sidney Tarrow 1998: *The Social Movement Society: Contentious Politics for a New Millennium,* Lanham, MD: Rowman and Littlefield.

Michels, Robert 1962 [1915], *Political Parties: A Sociological Study of the Oligarchical Tendencies of Modern Democracy,* New York: Collier Books.

Mier, Tracey 2001, 'The Impact of the Anti-Corporate Globalisation Movement S11', unpublished Honours-thesis, University of Melbourne.

Miliband, Ralph 1972, *Parliamentary Socialism: The Politics of Labour,* London: Merlin Press.

Miller, Richard 1984, *Analyzing Marx,* Princeton, NJ: Princeton University Press.

Mills, C. Wright 1948, *The New Men of Power: America's Labor Leaders,* New York: Harcourt Brace.

Miraftab, Faranak 2004, 'Invited and Invented Spaces of Participation', *Wagadu,* 1, 1.

Mitchell, David 1970, *1919: Red Mirage,* New York: Macmillan.

Monbiot, George 2010, 'The Tea Party Movement: Deluded and Inspired by Billionaires', *The Guardian,* 25 October.

Montagner, Kate 2002, 'The Whole World is Watching: S11, Global Communications and Cyber-Democracy', *Australian Screen Education Online,* 25: 4–12.

Moore Jr., Barrington 1991, *Social Origins of Dictatorship and Democracy: Lord and Peasant in the Making of the Modern World,* Harmondsworth: Penguin.

Moore, Donald S. 1998, 'Subaltern Struggles and the Politics of Place: Remapping Resistance in Zimbabwe's Eastern Highlands', *Cultural Anthropology,* 13, 3: 1–38.

—— 2000, 'The Crucible of Cultural Politics: Reworking "Development" in Zimbabwe's Eastern Highlands', *American Ethnologist,* 26, 3: 654–89.

Mora, Mariana 2007, 'Zapatista Anticapitalist Politics and the "Other Campaign": Learning from the Struggle for Indigenous Rights and Autonomy', *Latin American Perspectives,* 34, 2: 64–77.

Moran, Michael 1974, *The Union of Post Office Workers: A Study in Political Sociology,* London: Macmillan.

Morris, Morris D. 1969, 'The Reinterpretation of the Nineteenth Century Indian Economic History', *Indian Economic and Social History Review,* 6, 1: 606–18.

Morris, William 2001 [1888], *A Dream of John Ball,* Virginia: Electric Book Company.

Morton, Adam D. 2007a, 'Waiting for Gramsci: State Formation, Passive Revolution and the International', *Millennium,* 35, 3: 597–621.

—— 2007b, *Unravelling Gramsci: Hegemony and Passive Revolution in the Global Political Economy,* London: Pluto Press.

—— 2010, 'Reflections on Uneven Development: Mexican Revolution, Primitive Accumulation, Passive Revolution', *Latin American Perspectives,* 37, 1: 7–34.

—— 2011, *Revolution and State in Modern Mexico: The Political Economy of Uneven Development,* Plymouth: Roman and Littlefield.

Moschonas, Gerrassimos and Gregory Elliott 2002, *In the Name of Social Democracy: The Great Transformation: 1945 to the Present,* London: Merlin.

Motta, Sara C. 2008, 'The Chilean Socialist Party (PSCh): Constructing Consent and Disarticulating Dissent to Neo-Liberal Hegemony in Chile', *British Journal of Politics and International Relations,* 10, 2: 303–27.

Motta, Sara C. and Alf Gunvald Nilsen 2011, 'Social Movements and/in the Postcolonial: Dispossession, Development and Resistance in the Global South', in

Social Movements in the Global South: Dispossession, Development and Resistance, edited by Sara C. Motta and Alf Gunvald Nilsen: London: Palgrave.

Mottiar, Shauna and Patrick Bond 2011, 'Social Protest in South Africa', paper presented to the International Society for Third Sector Research, Stellenbosch Unviersity, 24 August.

Mueller, Carol McClurg 1992, 'Building Social Movement Theory', in *Frontiers in Social Movement Theory*, edited by Aldon Morris and Carol McClurg Mueller, New Haven, CT: Yale University Press.

Mullan, Caitriona and Laurence Cox 2000, 'Social Movements Never Died: Community Politics and the Social Economy in the Irish Republic', paper to ISA/BSA social-movements conference, November 2000, available at <http://eprints.nuim.ie/1529>.

Murphy, Arthur and Alex Stepick 1991, *Social Inequality in Oaxaca: A History of Resistance and Change*, Philadelphia: Temple University Press.

Murphy, John Thomas 1941, *New Horizons*, London: The Bodley Head.

—— 1972 [1917], *The Workers' Committee: An Outline of its Principles and Structure*, London: Pluto Press.

Nash, Andrew 1999, 'The Moment of Western Marxism, in South Africa', *Comparative Studies of South Asia, Africa and the Middle East*, 19, 1: 61–72.

Nash, June 1989, 'Cultural Resistance and Class Consciousness in Bolivian Tin-Mining Communities', in *Power and Popular Protest: Latin America Social Movements*, edited by Susan Eckstein, Berkeley, CA: University of California Press.

—— 1993, *We Eat the Mines and the Mines Eat Us*, Second edition, New York: Columbia University Press.

—— 1994, 'Global Integration and Subsistence Insecurity', *American Anthropologist*, 96, 1: 7–30.

Nash, Kate 2000, *Contemporary Political Sociology*, Oxford: Blackwell.

NBA 2000, 'September 17, Conclusion of Narmada Satyagraha, Jalsindhi and Domkhedi', press-note 16 September 2000, received from medhapatkar@vsnl.com.

Neale, Jonathan 2001, *The American War: Vietnam 1960–1975*, London: Bookmarks.

Nettl, John Peter 1966, *Rosa Luxemburg*, 2 Vols., Oxford: Oxford University Press.

Nicholson, Linda and Steven Seidman 1995, *Social Postmodernism: Beyond Identity Politics*, Cambridge: Cambridge University Press.

Nilsen, Alf Gunvald 2006, *The Valley and the Nation – The River and the Rage: A Study of Dispossession and Resistance in the Narmada Valley, India*, PhD dissertation, Bergen: University of Bergen.

—— 2007a, ' "History Does Nothing": Notes Towards a Marxist Theory of Social Movements', *Sosiologisk Årbok*, 1/2: 1–30.

—— 2007b: 'On New Social Movements and "the Reinvention of India" ', *Forum for Development Studies*, 34, 2: 271–93.

—— 2008, 'Political Economy, Social Movements and State Power: A Marxian Perspective on Two Decades of Resistance to the Narmada Dam Projects', *Journal of Historical Sociology*, 21, 2/3: 303–30.

—— 2009a, 'The Authors and the Actors of their own Drama': Towards a Marxist Theory of Social Movements', *Capital & Class*, 33, 3: 109–39.

—— 2009b, 'Autonome Domener eller Relasjonelle Praksiser: Makt og Motstand i Indisk Historie og Samtid', *Agora*, 27, 1: 126–65.

—— 2010, *Dispossession and Resistance in India: The River and the Rage*, London: Routledge.

—— 2011, ' "Not Suspended in Mid-Air": Critical Reflections on Subaltern Encounters with the Indian State', in *Social Movements in the Global South: Dispossession, Development and Resistance*, edited by Sara Catherine Motta and Alf Gunvald Nilsen, London: Palgrave.

Nilsen, Alf Gunvald and Laurence Cox 2006, ' "The Bourgeoisie, Historically, Has Played a Most Revolutionary Part": Understanding Social Movements from Above', in *Eleventh international conference on alternative futures and popular protest*, edited by Colin Barker and Mike

Tyldesley, Manchester Metropolitan University, available at <http://eprints.nuim.ie/458>.

Nimtz, August 2002, 'The Eurocentric Marx and Engels and Other Related Myths', in *Marxism, Modernity, and Postcolonial Studies*, edited by Crystal Bartolovich and Neil Lazarus, Cambridge: Cambridge University Press.

Noticias 2009, 'Paran en Zaachila el trazo del presunto "Libramiento Sur"', 2 April.

—— 2010a, '¿Libramiento Sur en Villa de Zaachila?', 24 January.

—— 2010b, 'Rechazan al Libramiento Sur', 24 January.

Novack, George E. 1939, 'Revolution, Black and White', *New International*, 5, 5, available at <http://www.marxists.org/archive/novack/1939/05/james.htm>.

Nowak, Paul 2009, 'Building Stronger Unions: A Review of Organising in Britain', in *Union Revitalisation in Advanced Economies: Assessing the Contribution of Union Organising*, edited by Gregor Gall London: Palgrave Macmillan.

O'Connor, Alan 1989, *Raymond Williams: Writing, Culture, Politics*, Oxford: Blackwell.

Oestreicher, Richard Jules 1986, *Solidarity and Fragmentation: Working People and Class Consciousness in Detroit, 1875–1900*, Chicago: University of Illinois Press.

Offe, Claus 1985a, *Disorganized Capitalism: Contemporary Transformations of Work and Politics*, Cambridge, MA: MIT Press.

—— 1985b, 'New Social Movements: Challenging the Boundaries of Institutional Politics', *Social Research*, 52: 817–68.

Olivera, Oscar and Tom Lewis 2004, *Cochabamba! Water War in Bolivia*, Cambridge: South End Press.

Ollman, Bertell 1971, *Alienation: Marx's Concept of Man in Capitalist Society*, Cambridge: Cambridge University Press.

—— 2003, *Dance of the Dialectic: Steps in Marx's Method*, Chicago: University of Illinois Press.

Omar, Mostafa 2011, 'The Spring of the Egyptian Revolution', in *Socialist Worker Online*, available at <http://socialistworker.org/2011/03/30/spring-of-the-revolution>.

Omvedt, Gail 1993, *Reinventing Revolution: New Social Movements and the Socialist Tradition in India*, New York: East Gate.

Otero, Gerardo 1999, *Farewell to the Peasantry? Political Class Formation in Rural Mexico*, Oxford: Westview Press.

Overbeek, Henk 1990, *Global Capitalism and National Decline: The Thatcher Decade in Perspective*, London: Routledge.

Oxhorn, Phillip 1995, 'From Controlled Inclusion to Coerced Marginalization', in *Civil Society: Theory, History, Comparison*, edited by John A. Hall, Cambridge: Polity Press.

Padmore, George 1936, *How Britain Rules Africa*. London: Wishart Books.

—— 1972, *Africa and World Peace*. London: Frank Cass.

Paige, Jeffery M. 1975, *Agrarian Revolution: Social Movements and Export Agriculture in the Underdeveloped World*, New York: Free Press.

Palmer, Bryan 1990, *Descent into Discourse*, Philadelphia: Temple University Press.

—— 1994, *E. P. Thompson: Objections and Oppositions*, London: Verso.

Pannekoek, Anton 1936, 'Trade Unionism', *International Council Correspondence*, available at <http://marxists.org/archive/pannekoe/1936/union.htm>.

Parajuli, Pramod 1996, 'Ecological Ethnicity in the Making: Developmentalist Hegemonies and Emergent Identities in India', *Identities*, 3, 1–2: 15–59.

Parasuraman, Saroj 1999, *The Development Dilemma: Displacement in India*, London: Macmillan Press.

Passmore, Kevin 2003, 'Poststructuralism and History' in *Writing History*, edited by Stefan Berger et al, New York: Arnold.

Peck, Jamie and Adam Tickell 2002, 'Neoliberalizing Space', *Antipode*, 34, 3: 380–404.

Peluso, Nancy L. 1992, *Rich Forests, Poor People: Resource Control and Resistance in Java*, Berkeley, CA: University of California Press.

Pendleton, Mark 2007, 'Looking Back to Look Forward: The Past in Australia Queer Anti-Capitalism 1999–2002', *Melbourne Historical Journal*, 35: 51–71.

Perelman, Michael 2000, *The Invention of Capitalism: Classical Political Economy and the Secret History of Primitive Accumulation*, Durham: Duke University Press.

Perrings, Charles 1979, *Black Mineworkers in Central Africa: Industrial Strategies and the Evolution of an African Proletariat in the Copperbelt 1911–1941*, London: Heinemann.

Perrow, Charles 1979, 'The Sixties Observed', in *The Dynamics of Social Movements*, edited by Mayer N. Zald and John D. McCarthy, Cambridge: Winthrop.

Perry, Elizabeth 1993, *Shanghai on Strike: The Politics of Chinese Labor*, Stanford, CA: Stanford University Press.

—— 1994, 'Shanghai's Strike Wave of 1957', *China Quarterly*, 137: 1–27.

—— 2006, *Patrolling the Revolution: Worker Militias, Citizenship and the Modern Chinese State*, Lanham, MD: Rowman and Littlefield.

Perry, Elizabeth and Li Xun 1997, *Proletarian Power: Shanghai in the Cultural Revolution*, Boulder, CO: Westview.

Petras, James and Morris Morley 1990, *US Hegemony Under Siege*, London: Verso.

Petras, James and Henry Veltmeyer 2005, *Social Movements and State Power: Argentina, Brazil, Bolivia, Ecuador*, London: Pluto Press.

Phillips, Kevin 2006, *American Theocracy: the Peril and Politics of Radical Religion, Oil, and Borrowed Money in the 21st Century*, New York: Viking Penguin.

Pilger, John 2003, *The New Rulers of the World*, London: Verso.

Piot, Olivier 2011, 'Tunisia: Diary of a Revolution', *Le Monde Diplomatique*, February.

Pisa, Rosaria A. 1994, 'Popular Responses To The Reform of Article 27: State Intervention and Community Resistance in Oaxaca', *Urban Anthropology*, 23, 2/3: 267–306.

Piven, Frances Fox and Richard A. Cloward 1977, *Poor People's Movements: Why They Succeed, How They Fail*, New York: Vintage Books.

PNUD 2009, *Indicadores de Desarrollo Humano y Género en México 2005–2009*, Mexico City: Programa de las Naciones Unidas para el Desarrollo.

Polletta, Francesca 2002, *Freedom Is an Endless Meeting*, Chicago: University of Chicago Press.

—— 2005, 'How Participatory Democracy Became White', *Mobilizations*, 10, 1: 271–88.

—— 2006, *It Was Like A Fever: Storytelling in Protest and Politics*, Chicago: University of Chicago Press.

Polsgrove, Carol 2009, *Ending British Rule in Africa: Writers in a Common Cause*, Manchester: Manchester University Press.

Poole, Deborah 2007a, 'Political Autonomy and Cultural Diversity in the Oaxaca Rebellion', *Anthropology News*, 48, 3: 10–11.

—— 2007b, 'The Right to be Heard', *Socialism and Democracy*, 21, 2: 113–16.

—— 2009, 'Affective Distinctions: Race and Place in Oaxaca', in *Contested Histories in Public Space: Memory, Race, and Nation*, edited by Daniel Walkowitz and Lisa Maya Knauer, London: Duke University Press.

Portes, Alejandro 1985, 'Latin American Class Structures: Their Composition and Change during the Last Decades', *Latin American Research Review*, 20, 3: 7–39.

Post, Charles 2010, 'Exploring Working-Class Consciousness: A Critique of the Theory of the "Labour-Aristocracy"', *Historical Materialism* 18, 4: 3–38.

Postgate, John and Mary Postgate 1994, *A Stomach for Dissent: The Life of Raymond Postgate*, Keele: Keele University Press.

Poulantzas, Nicos 1978, *State, Power, Socialism*, London: New Left Books.

Powell, Fred and Martin Geoghegan 2004, *The Politics of Community Development: Reclaiming Civil Society or Reinventing Governance?*, Dublin: A&A Farmar.

Powell, Sian 2000, 'Fights, Cameras … Activists', *The Australian*, 8–9 July: 4–6.

Pozzi, Pablo 1988, *Oposición Obrera a La Dictadura*, Buenos Aires: Editorial Contrapunto.

Prashad, Vijay 2008, *The Darker Nations: A People's History of the Third World*, New York: The New Press.

Pribicevic, Branko 1959, *The Shop Stewards' Movement and Workers' Control*, Oxford: Blackwell.

Price, Richard 1989, '"What's in a Name?": Workplace History and "Rank-and-Filism"', *International Review of Social History*, XXXIV: 62–77.

Punch, Michael 2009, 'Contested Urban Environments: Perspectives on the Place and Meaning of Community Action in

Central Dublin, Ireland', *Interface* 1, 2: 83–107.

Pusey, Michael 1992, *Economic Rationalism in Canberra: A Nation Building State Changes its Mind*, Cambridge: University of Cambridge.

Quiroga, Annabella 2002, 'El Impacto De La Crisis: $42.000 Millones Menos En 12 Meses', *Clarín*, Buenos Aires.

Raban, Jonathan 2010, 'Say What?' *The Guardian*, 16 October.

Raeburn, Nicole C. 2004, *Changing Corporate America from Inside Out: Lesbian and Gay Workplace Rights*, Minneapolis: University of Minnesota Press.

Rangachari, R., Nirmal Sengupta, Ramaswamy R. Iyer, P. Banerji, and S. Singh, 2000, *Large Dams: India's Experience*, available at <www.dams.org>.

Rangan, Hariapriya 2000, *Of Myths and Movements: Rewriting Chipko into Himalayan History*, Oxford: Oxford University Press

Raschke, Joachim 1988, *Soziale Bewegungen: Ein Historisch-Systematisches Grundriss*, Frankfurt: Campus.

Rayside, David 1999, 'On the Fringes of the New Europe: Sexual Diversity Activism and the Labor Movement', in Hunt (ed.) 1999a.

Rediker, Marcus 2007, *The Slave Ship*, London: John Murray.

Republic of South Africa 1994, *A new housing policy and strategy for South Africa*, South African Government Information Service, available at <http://www.info.gov.za/whitepapers/1994/housing.htm>.

Richards, Alan and John Waterbury 1990, *A Political Economy of the Middle East*, Boulder, CO: Westview Press.

—— 1996, *A Political Economy of the Middle East*, Second edition, Boulder, CO: Westview Press.

Riddell, John (ed.) 1986, *The German Revolution and the Debate on Soviet Power: Documents, 1918–19* (*The Communist International in Lenin's Time*), New York: Monad.

—— 1993, *To See the Dawn: Baku, 1920– First Congress of the Peoples of the East*, New York: Pathfinder.

—— 2002, *Lenin's Struggle for a Revolutionary International: Documents: 1907– 1916, The Preparatory Years*, New York: Pathfinder.

—— 2003, *Founding the Communist International: First Congress Proceedings and Documents, 1919*, New York: Pathfinder.

—— 2004, *Workers of the World and Oppressed Peoples, Unite!: Proceedings and Documents of the Second Congress, 1920*, 2 Vols., New York: Pathfinder.

—— 2011a, 'The Origins of the United Front Policy', *International Socialism*, 130:113–40.

—— 2011b, *Toward the United Front: Proceedings of the Fourth Congress of the Communist International, 1922*, Leiden: Brill.

—— forthcoming, *Proceedings of the Third Congress of the Communist International, 1921*, Leiden: Brill.

Rimmerman, Craig A. 2008, *The Lesbian and Gay Movements: Assimilation or Liberation?*, Boulder, CO: Westview Press.

Ríos, Patricia M. 2009, 'Unos 600 campesinos denuncian despojo para beneficiar a mineras de Canadá', *La Jornada*, 6 April.

Roberts, Geoff 1976, 'The Strategy of Rank-and-Filism', *Marxism Today*, December: 375–83.

Robinson, Cedric J. 1991, *Black Marxism: The Making of the Black Radical Tradition*, New Jersey: Biblio Distribution Center.

Robinson, William I. 2004, *A Theory of Global Capitalism: Production, Class and State in a Transnational World*, Baltimore: John Hopkins University Press.

—— 2008, *Latin America and Global Capitalism: A Critical Globalization Perspective*, Baltimore: John Hopkins University Press.

Rodney, Walter 1986, 'The African Revolution', in *C.L.R. James: His Life and Work*, edited by Paul Buhle, London: Allison & Busby.

Roman, Richard and Edur Velasco Arregui 2007, 'Mexico's Oaxaca Commune', *Socialist Register 2008: Global Flashpoints*, edited by Leo Panitch and Colin Leys, London: Merlin Press.

Roseberry, William 1994, 'Hegemony and the Languages of Contention', in *Everyday Forms of State Formation: Revolution and the Negotiation of Rule in Mexico*, edited by Gilbert M. Joseph and Daniel Nugent, Durham: Duke University Press.

Roseberry, *Cont.*
—— 1995, 'Hegemony, Power, and Languages of Contention', in *The Politics of Difference: Ethnic Premises in a World of Power*, edited by Edwin N. Wilmsen and Patrick McAllister, Chicago, University of Chicago Press.

Rosen, Nir 2011, 'Thugs on the Payroll', *New Statesman*, 21 March: 34–5.

Rosenberg, Gerald 1993, *The Hollow Hope*, Chicago: University of Chicago Press, 1993.

Ross, Andrew 1989, *Universal Abandon? Politics of Postmodernism*, Minneapolis: University of Minnesota Press.

Rowbotham, Sheila, Lynne Segal and Hilary Wainwright 1981, *Beyond the Fragments: Feminism and the Making of Socialism*, London: Merlin.

Roy, Arundhati 2002, *The Algebra of Infinite Justice*, Harmondsworth: Penguin.

Royal Bank of Scotland 2004, *Wealth Creation in Scotland: A Study of Scotland's Top 100 Companies*, Edinburgh: Royal Bank of Scotland.

Royal Commission on Trade Unions and Employers' Associations 1968, *Report*, Cmnd 3624. London: HMSO.

Rudé, George 1973, 'Introduction', in Lefebvre 1973.

—— 1980, *Ideology and Popular Protest*, London: Lawrence & Wishart.

—— 1983, 'Marxism and History', in *Marx: 100 Years On*, edited by Bette Matthews, London: Lawrence & Wishart.

Runciman, Carin 2011, 'Questioning Resistance in Post-Apartheid South Africa', *Review of African Political Economy*, 38, 130: 607–14.

Rundle, Guy 2000, 'Now, 511 (Editorial)', *Arena Magazine*, 49: 2–3.

Rupert, Mark 2003, 'Globalizing Common Sense: A Marxian-Gramscian (re)Vision of the Politics of Governance/Resistance', *Review of International Studies*, 29: 181–98.

Saccarelli, Emanuele 2004, '*Empire*, Rifondazione Comunista, and the Politics of Spontaneity', *New Political Science*, 26, 4: 569–91.

Samuel, Raphael 1992, 'Reading the Signs: II. Fact-Grubbers and Mind-Readers', *History Workshop Journal*, 33, 1: 220–51.

Sandbrook, Richard, Marc Edelman, Patrick Heller, and Judith Teichman 2007, *Social Democracy in the Global Periphery: Origins, Challenges, Prospects*, Cambridge: Cambridge University Press.

Sarkar, Sumit 1983, *Modern India, 1885–1947*, London: Macmillan.

Saul, John 1975, 'The "Labor Aristocracy" Thesis Reconsidered' in *The Development of an African Working Class*, edited by Richard Sandbrook and Robin Cohen, Toronto: University of Toronto Press.

Saunders, Doug 2011, 'A Self-Taught Democracy Emerges from Tunisia's Classrooms', *Globe and Mail*, February 28.

Savage, Mike, James Barlow, Peter Dickens and Tony Fielding 1995, *Property, Bureaucracy and Culture: Middle-Class Formation in Contemporary Britain*, London: Routledge.

Saville, John 1987, *1848: The British State and The Chartist Movement*, Cambridge: Cambridge University Press.

Sayers, Andrew 2000, *Realism and Social Science*, London: Sage.

Schaumberg, Heike 2008, 'In Search of Alternatives: The Making of Grassroots Politics and Power in Argentina', *Bulletin of Latin American Research*, 27, 3: 368–87.

Schneider Mansilla, Iván and Rodrigo Adrián Conti 2003, *Piqueteros. Una Mirada Histórica*, Buenos Aires: Cooperativa editora Astralib.

Schurman, Rachel and William Munro 2009, 'Targeting Capital: A Cultural Economy Approach to Understanding the Efficacy of Two Anti–Genetic Engineering Movements', *American Journal of Sociology* 115, 1: 155–202.

Schuyler, George S. 1991, *Black Empire*. Boston: Northeastern University Press.

—— 1994, *Ethiopian Stories*, Boston: Northeastern University Press.

Schwartz, Michael 1988, *Radical Protest and Social Structure: The Southern Farmers' Alliance and Cotton Tenancy, 1880–1890*, Chicago: University of Chicago Press.

Scott, David 2004, *Conscripts of Modernity: The Tragedy of Colonial Enlightenment*, London: Duke University Press.

Scott, James C. 1985, *Weapons of the Weak: Everyday Forms of Peasant Resistance*, New Haven, CT: Yale University Press.

Scott, *Cont.*
—— 1990, *Domination and the Arts of Resistance: Hidden Transcripts*, New Haven, CT: Yale University Press.

Scottish Executive 2001, *A Smart Successful Scotland*, Edinburgh: Scottish Executive.

—— 2002, *Better Communities in Scotland: Closing the Gap*, Edinburgh: Scottish Executive.

—— 2004, *A Smart Successful Scotland*, Revised edition, Edinburgh: Scottish Executive.

—— 2006, *People and Place: Regeneration Policy Statement*, Edinburgh: Scottish Executive.

Scottish Office 1988, *New Life for Urban Scotland*, Edinburgh: HMSO.

Seddon, David 2012, *Theories of Development: In Comparative and Historical Perspective*, London: Routledge.

Sewell, William H. 1992, 'A Theory of Structure: Duality, Agency, and Transformation', *American Journal of Sociology*, 98, 1: 1–29.

Shaffer, Linda 1982, *Mao and the Workers*, Armonk, NY: M.E. Sharpe.

Shandro, Alan 1995, ' "Consciousness from Without": Marxism, Lenin and the Proletariat', *Science and Society* 59: 268–97.

Shanin, Teodor 1986, *Russia 1905–07: Revolution As a Moment of Truth*, London: Macmillan.

Sharma, Ram Sharan 2009, *Rethinking India's Past*, Oxford: Oxford University Press.

Showstack Sassoon, Anne 1980, *Gramsci's Politics*, London: Croom Helm.

Silver, Beverly and David Slater 1999, 'The Social Origins of World Hegemonies', in *Chaos and Governance in the Modern World System*, edited by Giovanni Arrighi and Beverly Silver, Minneapolis: University of Minnesota Press.

Singh, Hira 1986, 'The Asiatic Mode of Production: A Critical Analysis', *Social Science Probings*, 3, 2: 167–81.

—— 1993, 'Classifying Non-European, Pre-Colonial Social Formations: More Than a Quarrel Over a Name', *Journal of Peasant Studies*, 20, 2: 317–47.

—— 1998, *Colonial Hegemony and Popular Resistance: Princes, Peasants, and Paramount Power*, London: Sage.

Singh, M.M.P. and R. Awasthi, 2010, *1857 ki Kranti*, Delhi: Shilp Granthi.

Singh, Satyajit 1997, *Taming the Waters: The Political Economy of Large Dams in India*, Oxford: Oxford University Press.

Sinha, Subir 2003, 'Development Counter-Narratives: Taking Social Movements Seriously', in *Regional Modernities: The Cultural Politics of Development in India*, edited by K. Sivaramakrishnan and Arun Agrawal, Stanford, CA: Stanford University Press.

Sinwell, Luke 2009, *Participation as Popular Agency*, PhD dissertation, Johannesburg: University of the Witwatersrand.

—— 2011, 'Is "Another World" Really Possible?', *Review of African Political Economy*, 38, 127: 61–76.

Sklair, Leslie 1995, 'Social Movements and Global Capitalism', *Sociology*, 29, 3: 495–512.

Skocpol, Theda 1979, *States and Social Revolutions*, Cambridge: Cambridge University Press.

Skocpol, Theda and Ellen Kay Trimberger 1994, 'Revolutions and the World-Historical Development of Capitalism', in *Social Revolutions in the Modern World*, edited by Theda Skocpol, Cambridge: Cambridge University Press.

Smelser, Neil J. 1962, *Theory of Collective Behavior*, New York: Free Press.

Smith, Dorothy 1987, *The Everyday World as Problematic: A Feminist Sociology*, Toronto: University of Toronto Press.

Smith, Jackie 2001, 'Globalizing Resistance: The Battle of Seattle and the Future of Social Movements', *Mobilization* 6, 1: 1–19.

Smith, Martin 2002, 'The Return of the Rank and File?', *International Socialism*, 94: 49–74.

—— 2003, *The Awkward Squad: New Labour and the Rank and File*, London: Socialist Workers Party.

Smith, Neil 1991, *Uneven Development: Nature, Capital and the Production of Space*, Oxford: Blackwell.

—— 1993, 'Homeless/Global: Scaling Places', in *Mapping the Futures: Local Cultures, Global Change*, edited by John Bird, Barry Curtis, Tim Putnam and Lisa Tickner, London: Routledge.

Smith, *Cont.*

—— 2008, *Uneven Development: Nature, Capital and the Production of Space*, London: University of Georgia Press.

Smith, Stephen Anthony 2002, *Like Cattle and Horses: Nationalism and Labor in Shanghai, 1895–1927*, Durham: Duke University Press.

Smith, Tony 1990, *The Logic of Marx's Capital: Replies to Hegelian Criticisms*, New York: SUNY Press.

Snow, David A., Sarah A. Soule and Hanspeter Kriesi (eds.) 2004, *The Blackwell Companion to Social Movements*, Malden, MA: Blackwell.

Socialist Platform 1987, *C.L.R. James and British Trotskyism: An Interview*, London: Socialist Platform.

Soule, Sarah A. 2009, *Contention and Corporate Social Responsibility*, Cambridge: Cambridge University Press.

Sparrow, Jeff 2000, 'The Victory at S11', *Overland*, 161: 19–20.

Spronk, Susan 2007, 'Roots of Resistance to Urban Water Privatization in Bolivia: The "New Working Class", the Crisis of Neoliberalism, and Public Services', *International Labor and Working-Class History*, 71: 8–28.

Stauber, John, and Sheldon Rampton 1995, *Toxic Sludge is Good for You! Lies, Damn Lies and the Public Relations Industry*, Monroe, ME: Common Courage Press.

Stedman Jones, Gareth 1983, *Languages of Class*, Cambridge: Cambridge University Press.

Steinberg, Marc W. 1994, 'The Dialogue of Struggle: The Contest over Ideological Boundaries in the Case of the London Silk Weavers in the Early Nineteenth Century', *Social Science History*, 18: 505–41.

—— 1996, 'Culturally speaking: finding a commons between post-structuralism and the Thompsonian Perspective', *Social History*, 21, 2: 193–214.

—— 1999a, 'The Talk and Back Talk of Collective Action: A Dialogic Analysis of Repertoires of Discourse Among Nineteenth-Century English Cotton Spinners', *American Journal of Sociology*, 105, 3: 736–80.

—— 1999b, *Fighting Words: Working-Class Formation, Collective Action, and Discourse in Early Nineteenth Century England*, Ithaca, NY: Cornell University Press.

Steinmetz, George 1994, 'Regulation Theory, Post-Marxism, and the New Social Movements', *Comparative Studies in Society and History* 36, 1: 176–212.

Stephen, Lynn 1998, 'The Cultural and Political Dynamics of Agrarian Reform in Oaxaca and Chiapas', in *The Future Role of the Ejido in Rural Mexico*, edited by Richard Snyder and Gabriel Torres, San Diego: Center for US-Mexican Studies.

Stephen, Matthew D. 2009, 'Alter-Globalisation as Counter-Hegemony: Evaluating the "postmodern prince"', *Globalizations*, 6, 4: 483–98.

Stout, Robert J. 2010, 'Awakening in Oaxaca: Stirrings of the People's Giant', *Monthly Review*, June 2010: 29–39.

Svampa, Maristella and Sebastián Pereyra 2003, *Entre la ruta y el barrio. La experiencia de las organizaciones piqueteras*, Buenos Aires: Editorial Biblos.

Swagler, Matt 2011, 'Tunisia's Ongoing Revolution', *Socialist Worker Online*, 22 March, available at <http://news-www.socialistworker.org/2011/03/22/tunisias-ongoing-revolution>.

Sweeney, John 2001, 'The Growing Alliance Between Gay and Union Activists', in *Out at Work: Building a Gay-Labor Alliance*, edited by Kitty Krupat and Patrick McCreery. Minneapolis: University of Minnesota Press.

Szymanski, Albert 1976, 'Racial Discrimination and White Gain', *American Sociological Review*, 41, 3: 403–14.

Tapia, Luis 2008, 'Bolivia: The Left and the Popular Movements', in *The New Left in Latin America: Utopia Reborn*, edited by Patrick Barrett, Daniel Chavez and César Rodríguez-Garavito, London: Pluto Press.

Tarrow, Sidney 1989a, *Democracy and Disorder: Protest and Politics in Italy 1965–1975*, Oxford: Oxford University Press.

—— 1989b, *Struggle, Politics and Reform: Collective Action, Social Movements, and Cycles of Protest*, Ithaca, NY: Cornell University Press.

—— 1994, *Power in Movement: Social Movements, Collective Action and Politics*, Cambridge: Cambridge University Press.

Tarrow, *Cont.*
—— 1998, *Power in Movement: Social Movements and Contentious Politics*, Second edition, Cambridge: Cambridge University Press.

Taylor, Andrew J. 1989, *Trade Unions and Politics: A Comparative Introduction*, Houndmills: Macmillan.

Taylor, Robert 1993, *The Trade Union Question in British Politics: Government and Unions Since 1945*, Oxford: Blackwell.

Taylor, Verta and Nella Van Dyke 2004, ' "Get Up, Stand Up": Tactical Repertoires of Social Movements', in *The Blackwell Companion to Social Movements*, edited by David A. Snow, Sarah A. Soule and Hanspeter Kriesi, Malden, MA: Blackwell.

Taylor, Verta, Katrina Kimport, Nella Van Dyke and Ellen Ann Andersen 2009, 'Culture and Mobilization: Tactical Repertoires, Same-Sex Weddings, and the Impact on Gay Activism', *American Sociological Review* 74, 6: 86–90.

Taylor, William 1972, *Landlord and Peasant in Colonial Oaxaca*, Stanford, CA: Stanford University Press.

Terry, Michael 1978, 'The Emergence of a Lay Elite? Some Recent Changes in Shop Steward Organisation', SSRC Industrial Relations Research Unit Discussion Paper, 14, University of Warwick.

—— 1983, 'Shop Stewards Through Expansion and Recession', *Industrial Relations Journal*, 14, 3: 49–58.

Thapar, Romila 2000, *Cultural Pasts: Essays in Early Indian History*, Oxford: Oxford University Press.

Therborn, Goran 1992, 'Swedish Social Democracy and the Transition from Industrial to Postindustrial Politics', in *Labor Parties in Postindustrial Societies*, edited by Frances Fox Piven, Oxford: Oxford University Press.

—— 2004, *Between Sex and Power: Family in the World, 1900–2000*, New York: Routledge.

Thomas, Donald 1998, *The Victorian Underworld*, London: John Murray.

Thomas, Peter 2008, *The Gramscian Moment*, PhD dissertation, University of Queensland.

Thompson, Dorothy 1993, *Outsiders: Class, Gender and Nation*, London: Verso.

Thompson, Edward Palmer 1957, 'Socialist Humanism', *The New Reasoner*, 1: 105–43.

—— 1963, *The Making of the English Working Class*, Harmondsworth: Penguin.

—— 1965, 'The Peculiarities of the English', in *The Socialist Register 1965*, edited by Ralph Miliband and John Saville, London: Merlin.

—— 1966 [1963], *The Making of the English Working Class*, New York: Vintage Books.

—— 1976, *William Morris: Romantic to Revolutionary*, New York: Pantheon.

—— 1978a, 'Eighteenth Century English Society: Class Struggle Without Class', in *Social History*, 3, 2: 133–65.

—— 1978b, *The Poverty of Theory and Other Essays*, London: Merlin.

—— 1980 [1963], *The Making of the English Working Class*, New edition, Harmondsworth: Penguin.

—— 1990, *Whigs and Hunters: Origins of the Black Act*, Harmondsworth: Penguin.

—— 1991, *Customs in Common*, Harmondsworth: Penguin.

—— 1993, *Witness Against the Beast: William Blake and the Moral Law*, Cambridge: Cambridge University Press.

Thwaites Rey, Mabel 2004, *La Autonomia Como Busqueda, El Estado Como Contradicción*. Buenos Aires: Editorial Prometeo.

Tilly, Charles 1978, *From Mobilization to Revolution*, New York: Random House.

—— 1982, 'Proletarianization and Rural Collective Action in East Anglia and Elsewhere, 1500–1900', *Peasant Studies* 10: 5–34.

—— 1986, *The Contentious French: Four Centuries of Popular Struggle*, Cambridge, MA: Harvard University Press.

—— 1993, 'Contentious repertoires in Great Britain, 1758–1834', *Social Science History* 17, 2: 253–80.

—— 1995, *Popular Contention in Great Britain, 1758–1834*, Cambridge, MA: Harvard University Press.

—— 2004, *Social Movements, 1768–2004*, Boulder, CO: Paradigm Publishers.

Tilly, Charles and Sidney Tarrow 2007, *Contentious Politics*, Boulder, CO: Paradigm Publishers.

Tilly, Charles, Louise Tilly and Richard Tilly 1975, *The Rebellious Century,*

1830–1930, Cambridge, MA: Harvard University Press.

Tilly, Charles and Lesley Wood 2009, *Social Movements*, London: Paradigm.

Tolnay, Stephen E. and E.M. Beck 1992, *A Festival of Violence: an Analysis of Southern Lynching, 1882–1830*, Chicago: University of Illinois Press.

Topol, Sarah A. 2010, 'Mubarak's Reign Unsettled by Strikes and Protests', *aolnews.com*, 6 May, available at <http://www.aolnews.com/2010/05/06/mubaraks-reign-unsettled-by-strikes-and-protests>.

Torras, Jaume 1977, 'Peasant Counter-Revolution?' *Journal of Peasant Studies*, 5, 1: 66–78.

Touraine, Alain 1981, *The Voice and the Eye: an Analysis of Social Movements*, Cambridge: Cambridge University Press.

—— 1985, 'An Introduction to the Study of Social Movements', *Social Research*, 52: 749–87.

—— 2007, *A New Paradigm for Understanding Today's World*, Cambridge: Polity.

Trotsky, Leon 1962, *The Permanent Revolution and Results and Prospects*, London: New Park Publications.

—— 1975 [1932], 'The Only Road', in *The Struggle against Fascism in Germany*, Harmondsworth: Penguin.

—— 1977 [1930], *The History of the Russian Revolution*, London: Pluto Press.

Tsin, Michael 1999, *Nation, Governance and Modernity in China: Canton, 1900–1927*, Stanford, CA: Stanford University Press.

Turner, H.A., Garfield Clack and Geoffrey Roberts 1967, *Labour Relations in the Motor Industry*, London: Allen and Unwin.

Turok, Ivan 2007, 'Urban Policy in Scotland: New Conventional Wisdom, Old Problems?', in *Scottish Social Democracy: Progressive Ideas for Public Policy*, edited by Michael Keating, Brussels: PIE Peter Lang.

Turok, Ivan and Nick Bailey 2004, 'Glasgow's Recent Trajectory: Partial Recovery and its Consequences', in *Divided Scotland? The Nature, Causes and Consequences of Economic Disparities within Scotland*, edited by David Newlands, Mike Danson, and John McCarthy, Aldershot: Ashgate.

Undy, Roger and Roderick Martin 1984, *Ballots and Trade Union Democracy*, Oxford: Blackwell.

Upchurch, Martin, Matt Flynn and Richard Croucher 2008, 'The Activist as Subject: Political Congruence and the PCS Activist', British Universities Industrial Relations Association Conference, University of the West of England, Bristol, 25–7 July.

Upchurch, Martin, Graham Taylor and Andrew Mathers 2009, *The Crisis of Social Democratic Trade Unionism in Western Europe: The Search for Alternatives*, Aldershot: Ashgate.

Valocchi, Steve 1999, 'The Class-Inflected Nature of Gay Identity', *Social Problems*, 46, 2: 207–24.

Van Allen, Judith 1976, ' "Aba Riots" or Igbo "Women's War"? Ideology, Stratification, and the Invisibility of Women', in *Women in Africa: Studies in Social and Economic Change*, edited by Nancy J. Haflin and Edna G. Gray, Stanford: Stanford University Press.

Van der Haar, Gemma 2005, 'Land Reform, the State, and the Zapatista Uprising in Chiapas', *The Journal of Peasant Studies*, 32, 3/4: 484–507.

Van der Linden, Marcel 2008, *Workers of the World: Essays toward a Global Labor History*, Leiden: Brill.

Van der Pijl, Kees 1995, 'The Second Glorious Revolution: Globalizing Elites and Historical Change', in *International Political Economy: Understanding Global Disorder*, edited by Björn Hettne, London: Zed Books.

Vanaik, Achin 1990, *The Painful Transition: Bourgeois Democracy in India*, London: Verso.

Vavi, Zwelinzima 2011, 'Address by COSATU General Secretary at the Anti-Corruption Summit', Johannesburg, 8 December.

Vester, Michael 1975, *Die Entstehung des Proletariats als Lernprozess: die Entstehung antikapitalistischer Theorie und Praxis in England 1792–1848*, Frankfurt: Europäischer Verlagsanstalt.

Victorian Ombudsman 2001, 'Investigation of Police Action at the World Economic Forum Demonstrations September 2000', Melbourne: Victorian Ombudsman.

Villafuerte Solis, David 2005, 'Rural Chiapas Ten Years after the Armed Uprising of

1994: An Economic Overview', *The Journal of Peasant Studies*, 32, 3/4: 461–83.

Virdée, Satnam 2000, 'A Marxist Critique of Black Radical Theories of Trade-Union Racism', *Sociology*, 34, 3: 545–65.

—— 2010, 'Racism, Class and the Dialectics of Social Transformation', in *Handbook of Race and Ethnic Studies*, edited by Patricia Hill-Collins and John Solomos, London: Sage Publications.

Vološinov, Valentin Nikolaevich 1973, *Marxism and the Philosophy of Language*, translated by Ladislav Matejka and I.R. Titunik, Cambridge, MA: Harvard University Press.

Von Stein, Lorentz 1850–5, *Die Sociale Bewegung in Frankreich: Von 1789 bis auf unsere Tage*, 3 Vols., Leipzig: O. Wigand.

Vygotsky, Lev Semyonovich 1978, *Mind in Society: The Development of Higher Psychological Processes*. Edited by Michael Cole, Vera John-Steiner, Sylvia Scribner, and Ellen Souberman, Cambridge, MA: Harvard University Press.

—— 1986, *Thought and Language – Revised Edition*, Cambridge, MA: MIT Press.

Wacquant, Loïc 2009, *Punishing the Poor: the Neoliberal Government of Social Insecurity*, Durham: Duke University Press.

Waddington, Jeremy and Allan Kerr 2009, 'Transforming a Trade Union? An Assessment of the Introduction of an Organising Initiative', *British Journal of Industrial Relations*, 47, 1: 27–54.

Wainwright, Hilary 1979, 'Introduction', in Rowbotham, Segal and Wainwright 1979: 1–20.

—— 1994, *Arguments for a New Left: Answering the Free-Market Right*, Oxford, Blackwell.

—— 2009, *Reclaim the State: Experiments in Popular Democracy*, London: Seagull.

Wainwright, Joel 2008, *Decolonising Development: Colonial Power and the Maya*, Oxford: Blackwell.

Walder, Andrew G. 2009, 'Political Sociology and Social Movements', *Annual Review of Sociology*, 35: 393–412.

Walecki, Andrzej 1997, *Marxism and the Leap to the Kingdom of Freedom: The Rise and Fall of the Communist Utopia*, Stanford: Stanford University Press.

Wallerstein, Immanuel 2002, 'New Revolts Against the System', *New Left Review*, II/18: 29–39.

—— 2006, 'The Curve of American Power', *New Left Review*, II/40: 77–94.

Walsh, Shannon 2008, 'Uncomfortable Collaborations', *Review of African Political Economy*, 35, 116: 255–79.

Walton, John and David Seddon 1994, *Free Markets and Food Riots: The Politics of Global Adjustment*, Oxford: Blackwell.

Waterbury, Ronald 2007, 'The Rise and Fracture of the Popular Assembly of the Peoples of Oaxaca', *Anthropology News*, 48, 3: 8–10.

Watts, Michael 2000, '1968 and all that...', *Progress in Human Geography*, 25, 2: 157–88.

Webb, Sidney and Beatrice Webb 1920, *History of Trade Unionism 1666–1920*, London: Longmans, Green and Co.

Webber, Jeffrey 2005, 'Left-Indigenous Struggles in Bolivia: Searching for Revolutionary Democracy', *Monthly Review*, 57, 4: 34–48.

—— 2011a, *Red October: Left-Indigenous Struggles in Modern Bolivia*, Leiden: Brill.

—— 2011b, *From Rebellion to Reform: Class Struggle, Indigenous Liberation and the Politics of Evo Morales*, Chicago: Haymarket Books.

Weber, Max 1949, 'Objective Possibility and Adequate Causation in Historical Explanation', in *The Methodology of the Social Sciences*, Max Weber, New York: Free Press.

—— 1958a, 'Class, Status, Party', in *From Max Weber: Essays in Sociology*, edited by Hans Heinrich Gerth and C. Wright Mills, Oxford: Oxford University Press.

—— 1958b, *The Protestant Ethic and the Spirit of Capitalism*, Charles Scribner's Sons.

WERS 2004, *Workplace Employment Relations Survey*, available at <www.wers2004. info>.

West, Michael, O. and William, G. Martin 2009a, 'Contours of the Black International', in *From Toussaint to Tupac: The Black International since the Age of Revolution*, edited by Michael O. West, William G. Martin and Fanon C. Wilkins, Chapel Hill, NC: University of North Carolina Press.

—— 2009b, 'Haiti, I'm Sorry: The Haitian Revolution and the Forging of the Black International', in *From Toussaint to*

Tupac: The Black International since the Age of Revolution, edited by Michael O. West, William G. Martin and Fanon C. Wilkins, Chapel Hill, NC: University of North Carolina Press.

Whitehead, Judith 2003, 'Space, Place and Primitive Accumulation in Narmada Valley and Beyond', *Economic and Political Weekly*, 38, 40: 4224–30.

—— 2010, *Development and Dispossession in the Narmada Valley*, London: Pearson.

Whyte, Nick 2001, 'Nike Protests Defy Police Intimidation', *Socialist Worker*, 22 June.

Wieviorka, Michel 2005, 'After New Social Movements', *Social Movement Studies*, 4, 1: 1–19.

Wilkin, Peter 2000, 'Solidarity in a Global Age: Seattle and Beyond', *Journal of World-Systems Research*, 6, 1: 20–65.

Williams, John 2006, 'Community Participation', *Policy Studies*, 27, 3.

Williams, Raymond 1977, *Marxism and Literature*, Oxford: Oxford University Press.

—— 1983, *Keywords: A Vocabulary of Culture and Society*, London: Fontana.

—— 1989, *Resources of Hope: Culture, Democracy, Socialism:* London, Verso.

Willis, Paul 1977, *Learning to Labor: How Working Class Kids Get Working Class Jobs*, Farnham: Ashgate Publishing.

Wolf, Eric 1999 [1969], *Peasant Wars of the Twentieth Century*, Norman, OK: University of Oklahoma Press.

Wolf, Sherry 2009, 'LGBT Liberation: Build a Broad Movement: Interview with John D'Emilio', *International Socialist Review*, 65, available at <http://www.isreview.org/issues/65/feat-demilio.shtml>.

Wolpe, Harold (ed.) 1980, *The Articulation of Modes of Production*, London: Routledge.

Wood, Evelyn 1908, *The Revolt in Hindustan: 1857–59*, London: Methuen & Co.

Woolf, Virginia 2005, *A Room of One's Own*, Orlando, FL: Harcourt.

Worcester, Kent 1993, 'C.L.R. James and the Development of a Pan-African Problematic', *Journal of Caribbean History*, 27, 1: 54–80.

—— 1996, *C.L.R. James: A Political Biography*, New York: SUNY Press.

Wright, Erik Olin 1979 [1976], 'The Class Structure of Advanced Capitalist Societies', in *Class, Crisis and the State*, London: Verso.

Yashar, Deborah 2005, *Contesting Citizenship in Latin America: the Rise of Indigenous Movements and the Postliberal Challenge*, Cambridge: Cambridge University Press.

Young, Iris Marion 1990, *Justice and the Politics of Difference*, Princeton, NJ: Princeton University Press.

Zeilig, Leo (ed.) 2009, *Class Struggle and Resistance in Africa*, Chicago: Haymarket.

Zeitlin, Jonathan 1987, 'From Labour History to the History of Industrial Relations', *Economic History Review*, XL: 159–84.

—— 1989a, '"Rank and Filism" in British Labour History: A Critique: *International Review of Social History*, XXXIV: 42–61.

—— 1989b, '"Rank and Filism" and Labour History: A Rejoinder to Price and Cronin', *International Review of Social History*, XXXIV: 89–102.

Zibechi, Raúl 2003, *Genealogía De La Revuelta. Argentina: La Sociedad En Movimiento*, Montevideo: Nordan-Comunidad.

Zirakzadeh, Cyrus Ernesto 2006, *Social Movements in Politics: A Comparative Study*, London: Longman.

Index

CPSIA information can be obtained
at www.ICGtesting.com
Printed in the USA
LVOW01s1059020216

473314LV00003B/17/P